FOURTH EDITION

OPERATING SYSTEM CONCEPTS

Abraham Silberschatz
University of Texas

Peter B. Galvin
Brown University

♣ **Addison-Wesley Publishing Company**

Reading, Massachusetts · Menlo Park, California · New York
Don Mills, Ontario · Wokingham, England · Amsterdam · Bonn
Sydney · Singapore · Tokyo · Madrid · San Juan · Milan · Paris

Sponsoring Editor: *Deborah Lafferty*
Senior Editor: *Tom Stone*
Senior Production Supervisor: *Helen Wythe*
Marketing Manager: *Phyllis Cerys*
Technical Art Coordinator: *Susan London-Payne*
Cover and Endpaper Designer: *Howard S. Friedman*
Manufacturing Manager: *Roy Logan*

Many of the designations used by manufacturers and sellers to distinguish their products are claimed as trademarks. Where those designations appear in this book, and Addison-Wesley was aware of a trademark claim, the designations have been printed in initial caps or all caps.

The procedures and applications presented in this book have been included for their instructional value. They have been tested with care but are not guaranteed for any particular purpose. The publisher does not offer any warranties or representations, nor does it accept any liabilities with respect to the programs or applications.

Library of Congress Cataloging-in-Publication Data

Silberschatz, Abraham.
    Operating system concepts / Abraham Silberschatz, Peter B. Galvin.
       p.   cm.
    Includes bibliographical references and index.
    ISBN 0-201-50480-4
    1. Operating systems (Computers)   I. Galvin, Peter B.   II. Title.
QA76.76.063S5583 1994
005.4'3--dc20   93-24415
                                                          CIP

Reproduced by Addison-Wesley from camera-ready copy supplied by the authors.

ISBN 0-201-50480-4
1 2 3 4 5 6 7 8 9 10-MA-959493

To my parents, Wira and Mietek,
my wife, Haya,
and my children, Lemor, Sivan and Aaron.

Avi Silberschatz

To Carla and Gwendolyn.

Peter Galvin

PREFACE

Operating systems are an essential part of a computer system. Similarly, a course on operating systems is an essential part of a computer-science education. This book is intended as a text for an introductory course in operating systems at the junior or senior undergraduate level, or first-year graduate level. It provides a clear description of the *concepts* that underlie operating systems.

This book does not concentrate on any particular operating system or hardware. Instead, it discusses fundamental concepts that are applicable to a variety of systems. We do, however, present a large number of examples that pertain to UNIX and other popular operating systems. In particular, we use Sun Microsystem's Solaris 2 operating system, a version of UNIX, which recently has been transformed into a modern operating system with support for threads at the kernel and user levels, symmetric multiprocessing, and real-time scheduling. Other examples used include Microsoft MS-DOS, Windows, and Windows/NT, IBM OS/2, the Apple Macintosh Operating System, and DEC VMS and TOPS-20, among others.

Prerequisites

As prerequisites, we assume that the reader is familiar with general computer organization and a high-level language, such as PASCAL. The hardware topics required for an understanding of operating systems are included in Chapter 2. We use pseudo-PASCAL notation for code examples, but the algorithms can be understood without a thorough knowledge of PASCAL.

v

Content of this Book

The text is organized in six major parts:

- **Overview** (Chapters 1 to 3). These chapters explain what operating systems *are*, what they *do*, and how they are *designed* and *constructed*. They explain how the concept of an operating system has developed, what the common features of an operating system are, what an operating system does for the user, and what it does for the computer-system operator. The presentation is motivational, historical, and explanatory in nature. We have avoided a discussion of how things are done internally in these chapters. Therefore, they are suitable for individuals or lower-level classes who want to learn what an operating system is, without getting into the details of the internal algorithms. Additionally, Chapter 2 covers the hardware topics which are important to an understanding of operating systems. Readers well-versed in hardware topics, including I/O, DMA, and hard disk operation, may chose to skim or skip this chapter.

- **Process management** (Chapters 4 to 7). The process concept and concurrency are at the very heart of modern operating systems. A *process* is the unit of work in a system. Such a system consists of a collection of *concurrently* executing processes, some of which are operating-system processes (those that execute system code), and the rest of which are user processes (those that execute user code). These chapters cover various methods for process scheduling, interprocess communication, process synchronization, and deadlock handling. Also included under this topic is a discussion of threads.

- **Storage management** (Chapters 8 to 12). A process must be in main memory (at least partially) during execution. To improve both the utilization of CPU and the speed of its response to its users, the computer must keep several processes in memory. There are many different memory-management schemes. These schemes reflect various approaches to memory management, and the effectiveness of the different algorithms depends on the particular situation. Since main memory is usually too small to accommodate all data and programs and cannot store data permanently, the computer system must provide secondary storage to back up main memory. Most modern computer systems use disks as the primary on-line storage medium for information (both programs and data). The file system provides the mechanism for on-line storage of and access to both data and programs residing on the disks. These chapters deal with the classic internal algorithms and structures of storage management. They provide a firm practical understanding of the algorithms used — the properties, advantages, and disadvantages.

- **Protection and security** (Chapters 13 and 14). The various processes in an operating system must be protected from one another's activities. For that purpose, mechanisms exist that can be used to ensure that the files, memory segments, CPU, and other resources can be operated on by only those processes that have gained proper authorization from the operating system. Protection is a mechanism for controlling the access of programs, processes, or users to the resources defined by a computer system. This mechanism must provide a means for specification of the controls to be imposed, together with some means of enforcement. Security protects the information stored in the system (both data and code), as well as the physical resources of the computer system, from unauthorized access, malicious destruction or alteration, and accidental introduction of inconsistency.

- **Distributed systems** (Chapters 15 to 18). A *distributed system* is a collection of processors that do not share memory or a clock. Such a system provides the user with access to the various resources the system maintains. Access to a shared resource allows computation speedup and improved data availability and reliability. Such a system also provides the user with a distributed file system, which is a file-service system whose users, servers, and storage devices are dispersed among the various sites of a distributed system. A distributed system must provide various mechanisms for process synchronization and communication, for dealing with the deadlock problem and the variety of failures that are not encountered in a centralized system.

- **Case studies** (Chapters 19 to 21). The various concepts described in this book can be drawn together by describing real operating systems. Two UNIX-based operating systems are covered in detail — Berkeley 4.3BSD and Mach. These operating systems were chosen in part because UNIX at one time was almost small enough to understand and yet was not a toy operating system. Most of its internal algorithms were selected for *simplicity*, not for speed or sophistication. UNIX is readily available to computer-science departments, so many students have access to it. Mach provides an opportunity for us to study a modern operating system that provides compatibility with 4.3BSD but has a drastically different design and implementation. Chapter 21 briefly describes some of the most influential operating systems.

- **The Nachos System** (Appendix). A good way to gain a deeper understanding of modern operating systems concepts is for the students to get their hands dirty — to take apart the code for an operating system, to see how it works at a low level, to build significant pieces of the operating system themselves, and to observe the impact of those changes. The Nachos instructional operating system, which is briefly described in the Appendix, provides the opportunity to see how the basic concepts introduced in this text can be used to solve real-world problems. The Nachos system was developed by Professor Thomas Anderson from the University of California at Berkeley, to complement the third edition of this text, and it is freely available in the public domain via the Internet. Reviewers, who have used the Nachos project at other universities, call it a practical and positive supplement.

The Fourth Edition

Many comments and suggestions were forwarded to us concerning our previous editions. These, together with our own observations, have prodded us to produce this fourth edition. Our basic procedure was to reorganize and rewrite the material in each chapter, adding new information, examples, and diagrams where appropriate. We also brought older material up to date and removed material that was no longer of interest. Finally, we improved the exercises and updated the references.

Substantive revisions were made in the following chapters:

- **Chapter 1.** We have condensed some of the material related to older systems and have expanded our discussion of parallel, distributed, and real-time systems.

- **Chapter 2.** We collected coverage of strictly-hardware topics from the other chapters and reorganized them here, making this material easier to skip if it is already understood, and easier to use as a reference. We also expanded discussion of I/O topics, caching, and protection.

- **Chapter 4.** This chapter introduces the process concept. The material in this chapter appeared in parts of old Chapters 4 and 5. We moved the IPC material from old Chapter 5 to Chapter 4, since we believe that the material should be covered as part of the discussion on the process concept rather that as part of the process coordination chapter. We also expanded our discussion on threads considerably, and included Solaris 2 threads as an example.

- **Chapter 5.** This chapter is a reorganized old Chapter 4. It now deals primarily with CPU scheduling issues.

- **Chapter 6.** This chapter is a reorganized old Chapter 5. We removed Eisenberg and McGuire's solution to the critical-section problem for n processes from the main text (it is now an exercise). We also condensed the discussions concerning the critical region concept. We added new material on atomic transactions, including write-ahead logging and concurrency control schemes. Synchronization in Solaris 2 is included as an example.

- **Chapters 8 and 9.** We have added new material on up-to-date computer architectures that support paging and segmentation for large address spaces. Segmentation and paging are illuminated by an OS/2 example.

- **Chapters 10, 11, and 12.** We have expanded the material and completely reorganized the presentation of the file-system concept and implementation. We now present the logical aspect of the file system in Chapter 10, the implementation issues in Chapter 11, and the underlying secondary storage system in Chapter 12. We also have added new material on swap space, stable storage, recovery, reliability and performance.

- **Chapters 13 and 14.** We have separated old Chapter 11 into two chapters — one dealing with protection issues (Chapter 13), the other dealing with security issues (Chapter 14). In each of these chapters, we have reorganized the material, and have added new information. Major expansions include coverage of the Internet Worm and viruses.

- **Chapters 15 and 16.** We have separated old Chapter 12 into two chapters — one dealing with network structures (Chapter 15), the other dealing with distributed system structure (Chapter 16). In each of these chapters, we have reorganized the material, and have added new information. Major expansions include coverage of network protocols and functionality, remote services, thread-management, and the Open Software Foundation's Distributed Computing Environment (DCE) thread package.

- **Chapter 17.** This is old Chapter 14 on distributed file systems. We have brought the material up-to-date in this rapidly changing area.

- **Chapter 18.** This is old Chapter 13 on distributed coordination. We have brought the material up-to-date and added new sections on the two-phase commit protocol and concurrency control schemes.

- **Chapter 19.** This chapter on UNIX has been updated to reflect the current state of BSD UNIX and its current implementation.

- **Chapter 20.** This is old Chapter 16 on the Mach operating system. It has been updated to describe components of Mach version 3.

- **Appendix.** This is a new Appendix, which was was authored by Professor Thomas Anderson from UC Berkeley. This Appendix provides a brief tutorial introduction to the Nachos system. The Appendix presents the philosophy governing the Nachos environment as well as providing a general introduction to the Nachos operating system and the five project activities which accompany the software. The Appendix concludes with instructions for retrieving Nachos from the Internet via ftp.

Mailing List and Supplements

We now provide an environment where users can communicate among themselves and with us. We have created a mailing list consisting of users of our book with the e-mail address — os-book@cs.utexas.edu. If you wish to be on the list, please send a message to avi@cs.utexas.edu indicating your name, affiliation, and e-mail address.

For information about the teaching supplements, which complement this book, mail may be sent to OS4E@aw.com.

Errata

We have attempted to clean up every error in this new edition, but — as happens with operating systems — there will undoubtedly still be some obscure bugs. We would appreciate it if you, the reader, would notify us of any errors or omissions in the book. Also, if you would like to suggest improvements or to contribute exercises, we would be glad to hear from you. Any correspondence should be sent to A. Silberschatz, Department of Computer Sciences, The University of Texas, Austin, TX 78712 (e-mail — avi@cs.utexas.edu).

Acknowledgments

This book is derived from the previous editions, and so has been helped by many people, including Randy Bentson, Jeff Brumfield, Gael Buckley, Thomas Casavant, Ajoy Kumar Datta, Joe Deck, Tom Doeppner, Robert Fowler, G. Scott Graham, Rebecca Hartman, Wayne Hathaway, Christopher Haynes, Richard Kieburtz, Carol Kroll, Thomas LeBlanc, John Leggett, Ted Leung, Michael Molloy, Ed Posnak, Boris Putanec, John Quarterman, Charles Oualline, John Stankovic, Adam Stauffer, Steven Stepanek, Louis Stevens, and John Werth.

Lyn Dupré copyedited the book; Sara Strandtman edited our text into troff format. Debbie Lafferty, Tom Stone, and Helen Wythe were very helpful with the book production.

Chapter 17 was derived from a paper by Levy and Silberschatz [1990]. Chapter 19 was derived from a paper by Quarterman et al. [1985]. John Quarterman helped us to convert the material on UNIX 4.2BSD to UNIX 4.3BSD. David Black worked extensively with us to update Chapter 20.

We thank the following people, who reviewed this edition of the book: Joseph Boykin, P. C. Capon, John Carpenter, Thomas Doeppner, Caleb Drake, Hans Flack, Mark Holliday, Jerrold Leichter, Gary Lippman, Carolyn Miller, Yoichi Muraoka, Jim M. Ng, Hal Stern, David Umbaugh, Steve Vinoski, and J. S. Weston.

A.S.
P.B.G.

CONTENTS

PART ONE ■ OVERVIEW

Chapter 1   Introduction

1.1 What Is an Operating System?   3
1.2 Early Systems   6
1.3 Simple Batch Systems   7
1.4 Multiprogrammed Batched Systems   13
1.5 Time-Sharing Systems   15
1.6 Personal-Computer Systems   17
1.7 Parallel Systems   20
1.8 Distributed Systems   22
1.9 Real-Time Systems   23
1.10 Summary   25
Exercises   26
Bibliographic Notes   27

Chapter 2   Computer-System Structures

2.1 Computer-System Operation   29
2.2 I/O Structure   32
2.3 Storage Structure   37
2.4 Storage Hierarchy   42
2.5 Hardware Protection   45
2.6 General-System Architecture   51
2.7 Summary   52
Exercises   53
Bibliographic Notes   55

Chapter 3   Operating-System Structures

3.1 System Components   57
3.2 Operating-System Services   63
3.3 System Calls   65
3.4 System Programs   74
3.5 System Structure   76
3.6 Virtual Machines   82

3.7 System Design and
     Implementation 86
3.8 System Generation 89

3.9 Summary 90
     Exercises 91
     Bibliographic Notes 92

PART TWO ■ PROCESS MANAGEMENT

Chapter 4   Processes

4.1 Process Concept 97
4.2 Process Scheduling 100
4.3 Operation on Processes 105
4.4 Cooperating Processes 108
4.5 Threads 111

4.6 Interprocess Communication 116
4.7 Summary 126
     Exercises 127
     Bibliographic Notes 129

Chapter 5   CPU Processing

5.1 Basic Concepts 131
5.2 Scheduling Criteria 135
5.3 Scheduling Algorithms 137
5.4 Multiple-Processor Scheduling 149
5.5 Real-Time Scheduling 150

5.6 Algorithm Evaluation 152
5.7 Summary 158
     Exercises 159
     Bibliographic Notes 161

Chapter 6   Process Synchronization

6.1 Background 163
6.2 The Critical-Section Problem 165
6.3 Synchronization Hardware 172
6.4 Semaphores 175
6.5 Classical Problems of
     Synchronization 181
6.6 Critical Regions 186

6.7   Monitors 190
6.8   Synchronization in Solaris 2 198
6.9   Atomic Transactions 199
6.10 Summary 208
      Exercises 210
      Bibliographic Notes 214

Chapter 7   Deadlocks

7.1 System Model 217
7.2 Deadlock Characterization 219
7.3 Methods for Handling
     Deadlocks 223

7.4 Deadlock Prevention 224
7.5 Deadlock Avoidance 227
7.6 Deadlock Detection 234
7.7 Recovery from Deadlock 238

7.8 Combined Approach to
    Deadlock Handling 240
7.9 Summary 241

Bibliographic Notes 245
Exercises 242

PART THREE ■ STORAGE MANAGEMENT

Chapter 8   Memory Management

8.1 Background 249
8.2 Logical versus Physical
    Address Space 255
8.3 Swapping 256
8.4 Contiguous Allocation 259
8.5 Paging 267

8.6 Segmentation 283
8.7 Segmentation with Paging 290
8.8 Summary 294
    Exercises 296
    Bibliographic Notes 299

Chapter 9   Virtual Memory

9.1 Background 301
9.2 Demand Paging 303
9.3 Performance of Demand Paging 309
9.4 Page Replacement 312
9.5 Page-Replacement Algorithms 315
9.6 Allocation of Frames 326

9.7 Thrashing 329
9.8 Other Considerations 334
9.9 Demand Segmentation 341
9.10 Summary 342
     Exercises 343
     Bibliographic Notes 348

✓Chapter 10   File-System Interface

10.1 File Concept 349
10.2 Access Methods 358
10.3 Directory Structure 361
10.4 Protection 373

10.5 Consistency Semantics 378
10.6 Summary 379
     Exercises 380
     Bibliographic Notes 381

Chapter 11   File-System Implementation

11.1 File-System Structure 383
11.2 Allocation Methods 387
11.3 Free-Space Management 397
11.4 Directory Implementation 399
11.5 Efficiency and Performance 401

11.6 Recovery 403
11.7 Summary 405
     Exercises 406
     Bibliographic Notes 408

Chapter 12   Secondary-Storage Structure

12.1 Disk Structure   409
12.2 Disk Scheduling   410
12.3 Disk Management   417
12.4 Swap-Space Management   419
12.5 Disk Reliability   422

12.6 Stable-Storage
      Implementation   424
12.7 Summary   425
      Exercises   426
      Bibliographic Notes   427

PART FOUR ■ PROTECTION AND SECURITY

Chapter 13   Protection

13.1 Goals of Protection   431
13.2 Domain of Protection   432
13.3 Access Matrix   438
13.4 Implementation of Access
      Matrix   443
13.5 Revocation of Access Rights   446

13.6 Capability-Based Systems   448
13.7 Language-Based Protection   451
13.8 Summary   455
      Exercises   455
      Bibliographic Notes   457

Chapter 14   Security

14.1 The Security Problem   459
14.2 Authentication   461
14.3 Program Threats   464
14.4 System Threats   465
14.5 Threat Monitoring   469

14.6 Encryption   471
14.7 Summary   473
      Exercises   473
      Bibliographic Notes   474

PART FIVE ■ DISTRIBUTED SYSTEMS

√ # Chapter 15   Network Structures

15.1 Background   479
15.2 Motivation   481
15.3 Topology   482
15.4 Network Types   488
15.5 Communication   491

15.6 Design Strategies   498
15.7 Networking Example   501
15.8 Summary   504
      Exercises   504
      Bibliographic Notes   505

Chapter 16   Distributed-System Structures

16.1 Network-Operating Systems   507
16.2 Distributed-Operating Systems   509
16.3 Remote Services   512
16.4 Robustness   517
16.5 Design Issues   519
16.6 Summary   521
Exercises   522
Bibliographic Notes   523

Chapter 17   Distributed-File Systems

17.1 Background   525
17.2 Naming and Transparency   527
17.3 Remote File Access   531
17.4 Stateful versus Stateless Service   536
17.5 File Replication   538
17.6 Example Systems   539
17.7 Summary   567
Exercises   568
Bibliographic Notes   569

Chapter 18   Distributed Coordination

18.1 Event Ordering   571
18.2 Mutual Exclusion   574
18.3 Atomicity   577
18.4 Concurrency Control   581
18.5 Deadlock Handling   586
18.6 Election Algorithms   595
18.7 Reaching Agreement   598
18.8 Summary   600
Exercises   601
Bibliographic Notes   602

PART SIX ■ CASE STUDIES

Chapter 19   The UNIX System

19.1 History   607
19.2 Design Principles   613
19.3 Programmer Interface   615
19.4 User Interface   623
19.5 Process Management   627
19.6 Memory Management   632
19.7 File System   636
19.8 I/O System   645
19.9 Interprocess Communication   649
19.10 Summary   655
Exercises   655
Bibliographic Notes   657

Chapter 20   The Mach System

20.1 History   659
20.2 Design Principles   661
20.3 System Components   662
20.4 Process Management   666
20.5 Interprocess Communication   673
20.6 Memory Management   679
20.7 Programmer Interface   685
20.8 Summary   686
Exercises   687
Bibliographic Notes   688

Chapter 21   Historical Perspective

21.1 Atlas   691
21.2 XDS-940   692
21.3 THE   693
21.4 RC 4000   694

21.5 CTSS   695
21.6 MULTICS   696
21.7 OS/360   696
21.8 Other Systems   698

Appendix   The Nachos System

A.1 Overview   700
A.2 Nachos Software Structure   702
A.3 Sample Assignments   705
A.4 Information on Obtaining a
       Copy of Nachos   711

A.5 Conclusions   713
       Bibliographic Notes   713

Bibliography   715

Credits   745

Index   747

PART ONE

OVERVIEW

An *operating system* is a program that acts as an intermediary between a user of a computer and the computer hardware. The purpose of an operating system is to provide an environment in which a user can execute programs in a *convenient* and *efficient* manner.

We trace the development of operating systems from the first hands-on systems to current multiprogrammed and time-shared systems. Understanding the reasons behind the development of operating systems gives us an appreciation for what an operating system does and how it does it.

The operating system must ensure the correct operation of the computer system. To prevent user programs from interfering with the proper operation of the system, the hardware must provide appropriate mechanisms to ensure such proper behavior. We describe the basic computer architecture that makes it possible to write a correct operating system.

The operating system provides certain services to programs and to the users of those programs in order to make the programming task easier. The specific services provided will, of course, differ from one operating system to another, but there are some common classes of services that we identify and explore.

CHAPTER 1

INTRODUCTION

An *operating system* is a program that acts as an intermediary between a user of a computer and the computer hardware. The purpose of an operating system is to provide an environment in which a user can execute programs. The primary goal of an operating system is thus to make the computer system *convenient* to use. A secondary goal is to use the computer hardware in an *efficient* manner.

To understand what operating systems are, we must first understand how they have developed. In this chapter, we trace the development of operating systems from the first hands-on systems to current multiprogrammed and time-shared systems. As we move through the various stages, we see how the components of operating systems evolved as natural solutions to problems in early computer systems. Understanding the reasons behind the development of operating systems gives us an appreciation for what tasks an operating system does and how it does them.

1.1 ■ What Is an Operating System?

An operating system is an important part of almost every computer system. A computer system can be divided roughly into four components: the *hardware,* the *operating system,* the *applications programs,* and the *users* (Figure 1.1).

The hardware — the central processing unit (CPU), memory, and input/output (I/O) devices — provides the basic computing resources. The applications programs — such as compilers, database systems, games, and

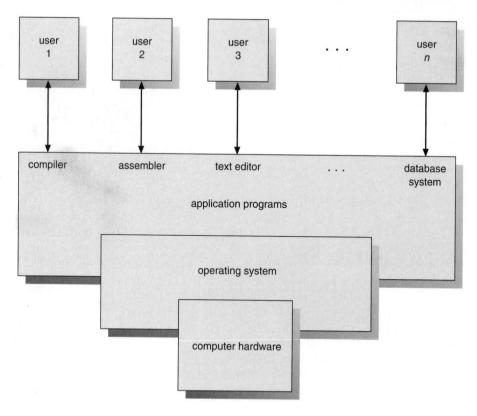

Figure 1.1   Abstract view of the components of a computer system.

business programs — define the ways in which these resources are used to solve the computing problems of the users. There may be many different users (people, machines, other computers) trying to solve different problems. Accordingly, there may be many different applications programs. The operating system controls and coordinates the use of the hardware among the various applications programs for the various users.

An operating system is similar to a *government*. The components of a computer system are its hardware, software, and data. The operating system provides the means for the proper use of these resources in the operation of the computer system. Like a government, the operating system performs no useful function by itself. It simply provides an *environment* within which other programs can do useful work.

We can view an operating system as a *resource allocator*. A computer system has many resources (hardware and software) that may be required to solve a problem: CPU time, memory space, file storage space, I/O devices, and so on. The operating system acts as the manager of these resources and allocates them to specific programs and users as necessary for their tasks. Since there may be many, possibly conflicting, requests for resources, the operating system must decide which requests are allocated resources to operate the computer system efficiently and fairly.

A slightly different view of an operating system focuses on the need to control the various I/O devices and user programs. An operating system is a *control program*. A control program controls the execution of user programs to prevent errors and improper use of the computer. It is especially concerned with the operation and control of I/O devices.

In general, however, there is no completely adequate definition of an operating system. Operating systems exist because they are a reasonable way to solve the problem of creating a usable computing system. The fundamental goal of computer systems is to execute user programs and to make solving user problems easier. Toward this goal, computer hardware is constructed. Since bare hardware alone is not particularly easy to use, applications programs are developed. These various programs require certain common operations, such as those controlling the I/O devices. The common functions of controlling and allocating resources are then brought together into one piece of software: the operating system.

There is also no universally accepted definition of what is part of the operating system and what is not. A simple viewpoint is that everything a vendor ships when you order "the operating system" should be considered. The memory requirements and features included, however, vary greatly across systems. Some take up less than 1 megabyte of space (a megabyte is one million bytes) and lack even a full-screen editor, while others require hundreds of megabytes of space and include spelling checkers and entire "window systems." A more common definition is that the operating system is the one program running at all times on the computer (usually called the *kernel*), with all else being applications programs. The latter is more common and is the one we generally follow.

It is easier to define operating systems by what they *do*, rather than by what they *are*. The primary goal of an operating system is *convenience for the user*. Operating systems exist because they are supposed to make it easier to compute with one than without one. This view is particularly clear when you look at operating systems for small personal computers.

A secondary goal is *efficient* operation of the computer system. This goal is particularly important for large, shared multiuser systems. These systems are typically expensive, so it is desirable to make them as efficient as possible. These two goals, convenience and efficiency, are sometimes contradictory. In the past, efficiency considerations were often more important than convenience. Thus, much of operating-system theory concentrates on optimal use of computing resources.

To see what operating systems are and what operating systems do, let us consider how they have developed over the last 30 years. By tracing that evolution, we can identify the common elements of operating systems and see how and why these systems have developed as they have.

Operating systems and computer architecture have had a great deal of influence on each other. To facilitate the use of the hardware, operating systems were developed. As operating systems were designed and used, it became obvious that changes in the design of the hardware could simplify them. In this short historical review, notice how operating-system problems lead to the introduction of new hardware features.

1.2 ■ Early Systems

Early computers were (physically) enormously large machines run from a console. The programmer, who was also the operator of the computer system, would write a program, and then would operate the program directly from the operator's console. First, the program would be loaded manually into memory, from the front panel switches (one instruction at a time), from paper tape, or from punched cards. Then, the appropriate buttons would be pushed to set the starting address and to start the execution of the program. As the program ran, the programmer/operator could monitor its execution by the display lights on the console. If errors were discovered, the programmer could halt the program, examine the contents of memory and registers, and debug the program directly from the console. Output was printed, or was punched onto paper tape or cards for later printing.

As time went on, additional software and hardware were developed. Card readers, line printers, and magnetic tape became commonplace. Assemblers, loaders, and linkers were designed to ease the programming task. Libraries of common functions were created. Common functions could then be copied into a new program without having to be written again, providing software reusability.

The routines that performed I/O were especially important. Each new I/O device had its own characteristics, requiring careful programming. A special subroutine was written for each I/O device. Such a subroutine is called a *device driver*. A device driver knows how the buffers, flags, registers, control bits, and status bits for a particular device should be used. Each different type of device has its own driver. A simple task, such as reading a character from a paper-tape reader, might involve complex sequences of device-specific operations. Rather than writing the necessary code every time, the device driver was simply used from the library.

Later, compilers for FORTRAN, COBOL, and other languages appeared, making the programming task much easier, but the operation of the computer more complex. To prepare a FORTRAN program for execution, for example, the programmer would first need to load the FORTRAN compiler into the computer. The compiler was normally kept on magnetic tape, so the proper tape would need to be mounted on a tape drive. The program would be read through the card reader and written onto another tape. The

FORTRAN compiler produced assembly-language output, which then needed to be assembled. This procedure required mounting another tape with the assembler. The output of the assembler would need to be linked to supporting library routines. Finally, the binary object form of the program would be ready to execute. It could be loaded into memory and debugged from the console, as before.

Notice that there could be a significant amount of *set-up time* involved in the running of a job. Each job consisted of many separate steps: loading the FORTRAN compiler tape, running the compiler, unloading the compiler tape, loading the assembler tape, running the assembler, unloading the assembler tape, loading the object program, and running the object program. If an error occurred during any step, you might have to start over at the beginning. Each job step might involve the loading and unloading of magnetic tapes, paper tapes, and punch cards.

1.3 ■ Simple Batch Systems

The job set-up time was a real problem. While tapes were being mounted or the programmer was operating the console, the CPU sat idle. Remember that, in the early days, few computers were available, and they were expensive (they cost millions of dollars). In addition, there were the operational costs of power, cooling, programmers, and so on. Thus, computer time was extremely valuable, and owners wanted their computers to be used as much as possible. They needed high *utilization* to get as much as they could from their investments.

1.3.1 Resident Monitor

The solution was two-fold. First, a professional computer operator was hired. The programmer no longer operated the machine. As soon as one job was finished, the operator could start the next. Since the operator had more experience with mounting tapes than a programmer, set-up time was reduced. The user provided whatever cards or tapes were needed, as well as a short description of how the job was to be run. Of course, the operator could not debug an incorrect program at the console, since the operator would not understand the program. Therefore, in the case of program error, a dump of memory and registers was taken, and the programmer had to debug from the dump. Dumping the memory and registers allowed the operator to continue immediately with the next job, but left the programmer with a much more difficult debugging problem.

The second major time savings involved reducing set-up time. Jobs with similar needs were *batched* together and run through the computer as a group. For instance, suppose the operator received one FORTRAN job, one COBOL job, and another FORTRAN job. If she ran them in that order, she would have to set up for FORTRAN (load the compiler tapes, and so on), then set up for COBOL, and then set up for FORTRAN again. If she ran the two FORTRAN programs as a batch, however, she could set up only once for FORTRAN, saving operator time.

These changes, making the operator distinct from the user and batching similar jobs, improved utilization quite a bit. Programmers would leave their programs with the operator. The operator would sort them into batches with similar requirements and, as the computer became available, would run each batch. The output from each job would be sent back to the appropriate programmer.

But there were still problems. For example, when a job stopped, the operator would have to notice that fact by observing the console, determine why the program stopped (normal or abnormal termination), take a dump if necessary, and then load the appropriate device with the next job and restart the computer. During this transition from one job to the next, the CPU sat idle.

To overcome this idle time, people developed *automatic job sequencing;* with this technique, the first rudimentary operating systems were created. What was desired was a procedure for automatically transferring control from one job to the next. A small program, called a *resident monitor,* was created for this purpose (Figure 1.2). The resident monitor is always (resident) in memory.

When the computer was turned on, the resident monitor was invoked, and it would transfer control to a program. When the program terminated,

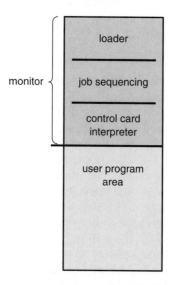

Figure 1.2 Memory layout for a resident monitor.

it would return control to the resident monitor, which would then go on to the next program. Thus, the resident monitor would automatically sequence from one program to another and from one job to another.

But how would the resident monitor know which program to execute? Previously, the operator had been given a short description of what programs were to be run on what data. So that this information could be provided directly to the monitor, *control cards* were introduced. The idea is quite simple. In addition to the program or data for a job, the programmer included special cards (control cards) containing directives to the resident monitor indicating the program to run. For example, a normal user program might require one of three programs to run: the FORTRAN compiler (FTN), the assembler (ASM), or the user's program (RUN). We could use a separate control card for each of these:

> $FTN — Execute the FORTRAN compiler.
> $ASM — Execute the assembler.
> $RUN — Execute the user program.

These cards tell the resident monitor which programs to run.

We can use two additional control cards to define the boundaries of each job:

> $JOB — First card of a job.
> $END — Last card of a job.

These two cards might be useful for accounting for the machine resources used by the programmer. Parameters can be used to define the job name, account number to be charged, and so on. Other control cards can be defined for other functions, such as asking the operator to load or unload a tape.

One problem with control cards is how to distinguish them from data or program cards. The usual solution is to identify them by a special character or pattern on the card. Several systems used the dollar-sign character ($) in the first column to identify a control card. Others used a different code. IBM's Job Control Language (JCL) used slash marks (//) in the first two columns. Figure 1.3 shows a sample card-deck setup for a simple batch system.

A resident monitor thus has several identifiable parts. One is the *control-card interpreter* that is responsible for reading and carrying out the instructions on the cards at the point of execution. The control-card interpreter at intervals invokes a loader to load systems programs and applications programs into memory. Thus, a loader is a part of the resident monitor. Both the control-card interpreter and the loader need to perform I/O, so the resident monitor has a set of device drivers for the system's I/O devices. Often, the system and applications programs are linked to these

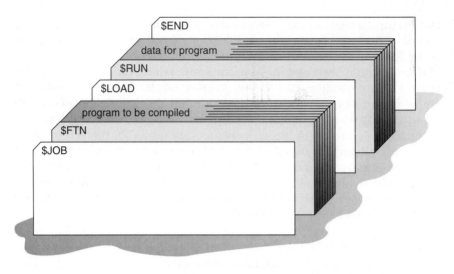

Figure 1.3 Card deck for a simple batch system.

same device drivers, providing continuity in their operation, as well as saving memory space and programming time.

These batch systems work fairly well. The resident monitor provides automatic job sequencing as indicated by the control cards. When a control card indicates that a program is to be run, the monitor loads the program into memory and transfers control to it. When the program completes, it transfers control back to the monitor, which reads the next control card, loads the appropriate program, and so on. This cycle is repeated until all control cards are interpreted for the job. Then, the monitor automatically continues with the next job.

A batch operating system, thus, normally reads a stream of separate jobs (from a card reader, for example), each with its own control cards that predefine what the job does. When the job is complete, its output is usually printed (on a line printer, for example). The definitive feature of a batch system is the *lack* of interaction between the user and the job while that job is executing. The job is prepared and submitted. At some later time (perhaps minutes, hours, or days), the output appears. The delay between job submission and job completion (called *turnaround* time) may result from the amount of computing needed, or from delays before the operating system starts to process the job.

1.3.2 Overlapped CPU and I/O Operations

The switch to batch systems with automatic job sequencing was made to improve performance. The problem, quite simply, is that humans are extremely slow (relative to the computer, of course). Consequently, it is desirable to replace human operation by operating-system software. Automatic job sequencing eliminates the need for human set-up time and job sequencing.

Even with automatic job sequencing, however, the CPU is often idle. The problem is the speed of the mechanical I/O devices, which are intrinsically slower than electronic devices. Even a slow CPU works in the microsecond range, with millions of instructions executed per second. A fast card reader, on the other hand, might read 1200 cards per minute (17 cards per second). Thus, the difference in speed between the CPU and its I/O devices may be three orders of magnitude or more. Over time, of course, improvements in technology resulted in faster I/O devices. Unfortunately, CPU speeds increased even faster, so that the problem was not only unresolved, but also exacerbated.

1.3.2.1 Off-line processing

One common solution was to replace the very slow card readers (input devices) and line printers (output devices) with magnetic-tape units. The majority of computer systems in the late 1950s and early 1960s were batch systems reading from card readers and writing to line printers or card punches. Rather than have the CPU read directly from cards, however, the cards were first copied onto a magnetic tape via a separate device. When the tape was sufficiently full, it was taken down and carried over to the computer. When a card was needed for input to a program, the equivalent record was read from the tape. Similarly, output was written to the tape and the contents of the tape would be printed later. The card readers and line printers were operated *off-line*, rather than by the main computer (Figure 1.4).

The main advantage of off-line operation was that the main computer was no longer constrained by the speed of the card readers and line printers, but was limited by only the speed of the much faster magnetic

Figure 1.4 Operation of I/O devices. (a) On-line. (b) Off-line.

tape units. This technique of using magnetic tape for all I/O could be applied with any similar equipment (card readers, card punches, plotters, paper tape, printers).

The real gain in off-line operation comes from the possibility of using multiple reader-to-tape and tape-to-printer systems for one CPU. If the CPU can process input twice as fast as the reader can read cards, then two readers working simultaneously can produce enough tape to keep the CPU busy. On the other hand, there is now a longer delay in getting a particular job run. It must first be read onto tape. Then, there is a delay until enough other jobs are read onto the tape to "fill" it. The tape must then be rewound, unloaded, hand-carried to the CPU, and mounted on a free tape drive. This process is not unreasonable for batch systems, of course. Many similar jobs can be batched onto a tape before it is taken to the computer.

1.3.2.2 Spooling

Although off-line preparation of jobs continued for some time, it was quickly replaced in most systems. Disk systems became widely available and greatly improved on off-line operation. The problem with tape systems was that the card reader could not write onto one end of the tape while the CPU read from the other. The entire tape had to be written before it was rewound and read, because tapes are by nature *sequential-access devices.* Disk systems eliminated this problem by being *random-access devices.* Because the head is moved from one area of the disk to another, a disk can switch rapidly from the area on the disk being used by the card reader to store new cards, to the position needed by the CPU to read the "next" card.

In a disk system, cards are read directly from the card reader onto the disk. The location of card images is recorded in a table kept by the operating system. When a job is executed, the operating system satisfies its requests for card-reader input by reading from the disk. Similarly, when the job requests the printer to output a line, that line is copied into a system buffer and is written to the disk. When the job is completed, the output is actually printed.

This form of processing is called *spooling* (Figure 1.5). The name is an acronym for simultaneous peripheral operation on-line. Spooling, in essence, uses the disk as a very large buffer, for reading as far ahead as possible on input devices and for storing output files until the output devices are able to accept them.

Spooling is also used for processing data at remote sites. The CPU sends the data via communications paths to a remote printer (or accepts an entire input job from a remote card reader). The remote processing is done at its own speed with no CPU intervention. The CPU just needs to be notified when the processing is completed, so that it can spool the next batch of data.

Figure 1.5 Spooling.

Spooling overlaps the I/O of one job with the computation of other jobs. Even in a simple system, the spooler may be reading the input of one job while printing the output of a different job. During this time, still another job (or jobs) may be executed, reading their "cards" from disk and "printing" their output lines onto the disk.

Spooling has a direct beneficial effect on the performance of the system. For the cost of some disk space and a few tables, the computation of one job can overlap with the I/O of other jobs. Thus, spooling can keep both the CPU and the I/O devices working at much higher rates.

1.4 ■ Multiprogrammed Batched Systems

Spooling provides an important data structure: a *job pool*. Spooling will generally result in several jobs that have already been read waiting on disk, ready to run. A pool of jobs on disk allows the operating system to select which job to run next, in order to increase CPU utilization. When jobs come in directly on cards or even on magnetic tape, it is not possible to run jobs in a different order. Jobs must be run sequentially, on a first-come, first-served basis. However, when several jobs are on a direct-access device, such as a disk, *job scheduling* becomes possible. We discuss job and CPU scheduling in greater detail in Chapter 5; a few important aspects are covered here.

The most important aspect of job scheduling is the ability to *multiprogram*. Off-line operation and spooling for overlapped I/O have their limitations. A single user cannot, in general, keep either the CPU or the I/O devices busy at all times. Multiprogramming increases CPU utilization by organizing jobs so that the CPU always has something to execute.

The idea is as follows. The operating system keeps several jobs in memory at a time (Figure 1.6). This set of jobs is a subset of the jobs kept in the job pool (since the number of jobs that can be kept simultaneously in memory is usually much smaller than the number of jobs that can be in the job pool.) The operating system picks and begins to execute one of the jobs in the memory. Eventually, the job may have to wait for some task, such as a tape to be mounted, a command to be typed on a keyboard, or an I/O operation to complete. In a nonmultiprogrammed system, the CPU would sit idle. In a multiprogramming system, the operating system simply switches to and executes another job. When *that* job needs to wait, the CPU is switched to another job, and so on. Eventually, the first job finishes waiting and gets the CPU back. As long as there is always some job to execute, the CPU will never be idle.

This idea is quite common in other life situations. A lawyer does not have only one client at a time. Rather, several clients may be in the process of being served at the same time. While one case is waiting to go to trial or to have papers typed, the lawyer can work on another case. With enough clients, a lawyer need never be idle. (Idle lawyers tend to become politicians, so there is a certain social value in keeping lawyers busy.)

Multiprogramming is the first instance where the operating system must make decisions for the users. Multiprogrammed operating systems are therefore fairly sophisticated. All the jobs that enter the system are kept in the job pool. This pool consists of all processes residing on mass storage awaiting allocation of main memory. If several jobs are ready to be brought into memory, and there is not enough room for all of them, then the system must choose among them. This decision is *job scheduling*, which

Figure 1.6 Memory layout for a multiprogramming system.

is discussed in Chapter 5. When the operating system selects a job from the job pool, it loads it into memory for execution. Having several programs in memory at the same time requires some form of memory management, which is covered in Chapters 8 and 9. In addition, if several jobs are ready to run at the same time, the system must choose among them. This decision is CPU *scheduling*, which is discussed in Chapter 5. Finally, multiple jobs running concurrently require that their ability to affect one another be limited in all phases of the operating system, including process scheduling, disk storage, and memory management. These considerations are discussed throughout the text.

1.5 ■ Time-Sharing Systems

Multiprogrammed batched systems provide an environment where the various system resources (for example, CPU, memory, peripheral devices) are utilized effectively. There are some difficulties with a batch system from the point of view of the programmer or user, however. Since the user cannot interact with the job when it is executing, the user must set up the control cards to handle all possible outcomes. In a multistep job, subsequent steps may depend on the result of earlier ones. The running of a program, for example, may depend on successful compilation. It can be difficult to define completely what to do in all cases.

Another difficulty is that programs must be debugged statically, from snapshot dumps. A programmer cannot modify a program as it executes to study its behavior. A long turnaround time inhibits experimentation with a program. (Conversely, this situation may instill a certain amount of discipline into the writing and testing of programs.)

Time sharing (or *multitasking*) is a logical extension of multiprogramming. Multiple jobs are executed by the CPU switching between them, but the switches occur so frequently that the users may interact with each program while it is running.

An *interactive*, or *hands-on*, computer system provides on-line communication between the user and the system. The user gives instructions to the operating system or to a program directly, and receives an immediate response. Usually, a keyboard is used to provide input, and a display screen (such as a cathode-ray tube (CRT), or monitor) is used to provide output. When the operating system finishes the execution of one command, it seeks the next "control statement" not from a card reader, but rather from the user's keyboard. The user gives a command, waits for the response, and decides on the next command, based on the result of the previous one. The user can easily experiment, and can see results immediately. Most systems have an interactive text editor for entering programs, and an interactive debugger for assisting in debugging programs.

If users are to be able to access both data and code conveniently, an *on-line file system* must be available. A *file* is a collection of related information defined by its creator. Commonly, files represent programs (both source and object forms) and data. Data files may be numeric, alphabetic, or alphanumeric. Files may be free-form, such as text files, or may be rigidly formatted. In general, a file is a sequence of bits, bytes, lines, or records whose meaning is defined by its creator and user. The operating system implements the abstract concept of a file by managing mass-storage devices, such as tapes and disks. Files are normally organized into logical clusters, or *directories*, which makes them easier to use. Since multiple users have access to files, it is desirable to control by whom and in what ways files may be accessed.

Batch systems are quite appropriate for executing large jobs that need little interaction. The user can submit jobs and return later for the results; it is not necessary to wait while the job is processed. Interactive jobs tend to be composed of many short actions, where the results of the next command may be unpredictable. The user submits the command and then waits for the results. Accordingly, the *response* time should be quite short — on the order of seconds at most. An interactive system is used when a short response time is required.

Early computers were interactive systems. That is, the entire system was at the immediate disposal of the programmer/operator. This situation allowed the programmer great flexibility and freedom in program testing and development. But, as we saw, this arrangement resulted in substantial idle time while the CPU waited for some action to be taken by the programmer/operator. Because of the high cost of these early computers, idle CPU time was undesirable. Batch operating systems were developed to avoid this problem. Batch systems improved system utilization for the owners of the computer systems.

Time-sharing systems were developed to provide interactive use of a computer system at a reasonable cost. A time-shared operating system uses CPU scheduling and multiprogramming to provide each user with a small portion of a time-shared computer. Each user has at least one separate program in memory. A program that is loaded into memory and is executing is commonly referred to as a *process*. When a process executes, it typically executes for only a short time before it either finishes or needs to perform I/O. I/O may be interactive; that is, output is to a display for the user and input is from a user keyboard. Since interactive I/O typically runs at people speeds, it may take a long time to complete. Input, for example, may be bounded by the user's typing speed; five characters per second is fairly fast for people, but is very slow for computers. Rather than let the CPU sit idle when this interactive input takes place, the operating system will rapidly switch the CPU to the program of some other user.

A time-shared operating system allows the many users to *share* the computer simultaneously. Since each action or command in a time-shared system tends to be short, only a little CPU time is needed for each user. As the system switches rapidly from one user to the next, each user is given the impression that she has her own computer, whereas actually one computer is being shared among many users.

The idea of time sharing was demonstrated as early as 1960, but since time-shared systems are more difficult and expensive to build (due to the numerous I/O devices needed), they did not become common until the early 1970s. As the popularity of time sharing has grown, researchers have attempted to merge batch and time-shared systems. Many computer systems that were designed as primarily batch systems have been modified to create a time-sharing subsystem. For example, IBM's OS/360, a batch system, was modified to support the Time-Sharing Option (TSO). At the same time, time-sharing systems have often added a batch subsystem. Today, most systems provide both batch processing and time sharing, although their basic design and use tends to be one or the other type.

Time-sharing operating systems are even more complex than are multiprogrammed operating systems. As in multiprogramming, several jobs must be kept simultaneously in memory, which requires some form of memory management and protection (Chapter 8). So that a reasonable response time can be obtained, jobs may have to be swapped in and out of main memory to the disk that now serves as a backing store for main memory. A common method for achieving this goal is *virtual memory*, which is a technique that allows the execution of a job that may not be completely in memory (Chapter 9). The main visible advantage of this scheme is that programs can be larger than physical memory. Further, it abstracts main memory into a large, uniform array of storage, separating logical memory as viewed by the user from physical memory. This frees programmers from concern over memory storage limitations. Time-sharing systems must also provide an on-line file system (Chapters 10 and 11). The file system resides on a collection of disks; hence, disk management must also be provided (Chapter 12). Also, time-sharing systems provide a mechanism for concurrent execution, which requires sophisticated CPU scheduling schemes (Chapter 5). To ensure orderly execution, the system must provide mechanisms for job synchronization and communication (Chapter 6), and must ensure that jobs do not get stuck in a deadlock, forever waiting for each other (Chapter 7).

Multiprogramming and time sharing are the central themes of modern operating systems, and are the central themes of this book.

1.6 ■ Personal-Computer Systems

As hardware costs have decreased, it has once again become feasible to have a computer system dedicated to a single user. These types of computer systems are usually referred to as *personal computers*, or just *PCs*.

The I/O devices have certainly changed, with panels of switches and card readers replaced with typewriter-like keyboards and mice. Line printers and card punches have succumbed to display screens and small, fast printers.

Personal computers appeared in the 1970s. They are microcomputers that are considerably smaller and less expensive than mainframe systems. Until recently, the CPUs of these types of computer systems have been lacking the features needed to protect an operating system from user programs. Their operating systems therefore have been neither multiuser nor multitasking. However, the goals of these operating systems have changed with time; instead of trying to maximize CPU and peripheral utilization, the systems opt for user convenience and responsiveness. These systems include both the IBM PC family of computers running the MS-DOS operating system, and the Apple Macintosh and its software. MS-DOS has been extended by Microsoft to include a window system, and IBM has upgraded MS-DOS with the OS/2 multitasking system. The Apple Macintosh operating system has been ported to more advanced hardware, and now includes new features such as virtual memory.

Operating systems for these computers have benefited from the development of operating systems for mainframes in several ways. Microcomputers were immediately able to adopt the technology developed for larger operating systems. On the other hand, the hardware costs for microcomputers are sufficiently low that individuals have sole use of the computer, and CPU utilization is no longer a prime concern. Thus, some of the design decisions that are made in operating systems for mainframes may not be appropriate for smaller systems. For example, file protection may not seem necessary on a personal machine. MS-DOS, the world's most common operating system, provides no such protection.

Some people have argued that the development of cheap microprocessors and cheap memory will make operating systems (and courses that teach them) obsolete. We do not believe that this prediction is true. Rather, the decrease in hardware costs will allow relatively sophisticated operating-system concepts (such as time sharing and virtual memory) to be implemented on an even greater number of systems. Thus, the decrease in the cost of computer hardware, such as microprocessors, will increase our need to understand the concepts of operating systems.

For example, although file protection may not seem necessary for isolated personal computers, these computers are often tied into other computers over telephone lines or local-area networks. When other computers and other users can access the files on a personal computer, file protection again becomes a necessary feature of an operating system. The lack of such protection enables malicious programs to destroy data on systems such as MS-DOS and the Macintosh operating system. These programs may be self-replicating, and may spread rapidly via *worm* or *virus* mechanisms to disrupt entire companies or even worldwide networks. Protection and security are considered further in Chapters 13 and 14.

In fact, an examination of operating systems for mainframes and microcomputers shows that features that were at one time available only on mainframes have been adopted by microcomputers. The same concepts are appropriate for the various different classes of computers: mainframes, minicomputers, and microcomputers (Figure 1.7).

A good example of this movement occurred with the MULTICS operating system. MULTICS was developed from 1965 to 1970 at the Massachusetts Institute of Technology (MIT) as a computing *utility*. It ran on a large and complex mainframe computer (the GE 645). Many of the ideas that were developed for MULTICS were subsequently used at Bell Labs (one of the original partners in the development of MULTICS) in the design of UNIX. The UNIX operating system was designed circa 1970 for a PDP-11 minicomputer. Around 1980, the features of UNIX became the basis for UNIX-like operating systems on microcomputer systems, and are being included in more mainstream operating systems such as Microsoft Windows, IBM OS/2, Macintosh Operating System version 7, and the recently released Microsoft Windows/NT. Thus, the features developed for a large mainframe system have moved to microcomputers, over time.

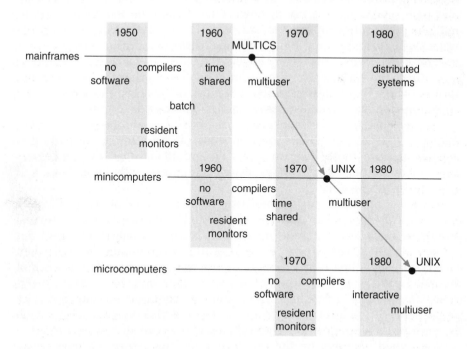

Figure 1.7 Migration of operating-system concepts and features.

At the same time that features of large operating systems were being scaled down to fit personal computers, more powerful, faster, and more sophisticated hardware systems were being developed. The *personal workstation* is a large personal computer, such as the Sun, HP/Apollo, or IBM RS/6000 computer. Many universities and businesses have large numbers of workstations tied together with local-area networks. As the PC systems gain more sophisticated hardware and software, and workstations become less expensive, the line dividing the two breeds is becoming blurry. In the future, the two may merge into one category.

1.7 ■ Parallel Systems

Most systems to date are single-processor systems; that is, they have only one main CPU. However, there is a trend toward multiprocessor systems. Such systems have more than one processor in close communication, sharing the computer bus, the clock, and sometimes memory and peripheral devices. These systems are referred to as *tightly coupled* systems.

There are several reasons for building such systems. One advantage is increased *throughput*. By increasing the number of processors, we would hope to get more work done in a shorter period of time. The speed-up ratio with *n* processors is not *n*, however, but rather is less than *n*. When multiple processors cooperate on a task, a certain amount of overhead is incurred in keeping everything working correctly. This overhead, plus contention for shared resources, lowers the expected gain from additional processors. Similarly, a group of *n* programmers working closely together does not result in *n* times the amount of work being accomplished.

Multiprocessors can also save money compared to multiple single systems because the processors can share peripherals, cabinets, and power supplies. If several programs are to operate on the same set of data, it is cheaper to store those data on one disk and to have all the processors share them, rather than to have many computers with local disks and many copies of the data.

Another reason for multiprocessor systems is that they increase reliability. If functions can be distributed properly among several processors, then the failure of one processor will not halt the system, but rather will only slow it down. If we have 10 processors and one fails, then each of the remaining nine processors must pick up a share of the work of the failed processor. Thus, the entire system runs only 10 percent slower, rather than failing altogether. This ability to continue providing service proportional to the level of nonfailed hardware is called *graceful degradation.* Systems that are designed for graceful degradation are also called *fail-soft.*

Continued operation in the presence of failures requires a mechanism to allow the failure to be detected, diagnosed, and corrected (if possible). The Tandem system uses both hardware and software duplication to ensure continued operation despite faults. The system consists of two identical processors, each with its own local memory. The processors are connected by a bus. One processor is the primary, and the other is the backup. Two copies are kept of each process; one on the primary machine and the other on the backup. At fixed checkpoints in the execution of the system, the state information of each job (including a copy of the memory image) is copied from the primary machine to the backup. If a failure is detected, the backup copy is activated, and is restarted from the most recent checkpoint. This solution is obviously an expensive one, since there is considerable hardware duplication.

The most common multiple-processor systems now use the *symmetric multiprocessing* model, in which each processor runs an identical copy of the operating system, and these copies communicate with one another as needed. Some systems use *asymmetric multiprocessing*, in which each processor is assigned a specific task. A master processor controls the system; the other processors either look to the master for instruction or have predefined tasks. This scheme defines a master–slave relationship. The master processor schedules and allocates work to the slave processors.

An example of the symmetric multiprocessing system is Encore's version of UNIX for the Multimax computer. This computer can be configured to employ dozens of processors, all running a copy of UNIX. The benefit of this model is that many processes can run at once (N processes if there are N CPUs) without causing a deterioration of performance. However, we must carefully control I/O to ensure that data reach the appropriate processor. Also, since the CPUs are separate, one may be sitting idle while another is overloaded, resulting in inefficiencies. To avoid these inefficiencies, the processors can share certain data structures. A multiprocessor system of this form will allow jobs and resources to be shared dynamically among the various processors, and can lower the variance among the systems. However, such a system must be written carefully, as we shall see in Chapter 6.

Asymmetric multiprocessing is more common in extremely large systems, where one of the most time-consuming activities is simply processing I/O. In older batch systems, small processors, located at some distance from the main CPU, were used to run card readers and line printers and to transfer these jobs to and from the main computer. These locations are called *remote job entry (RJE)* sites. In a time-sharing system, a main I/O activity is processing the I/O of characters between the terminals and the computer. If the main CPU must be interrupted for every character for every terminal, it may spend all its time simply processing characters. So that this situation is avoided, most systems have a separate front-end processor that handles all the terminal I/O. For example, a large IBM system might use an IBM Series/1 minicomputer as a front-end. The front-end acts as a buffer between the terminals and the main CPU, allowing the main CPU to handle lines and blocks of characters, instead of individual characters.

Such systems suffer from decreased reliability through increased specialization.

It is important to recognize that the difference between symmetric and asymmetric multiprocessing may be the result of either hardware or software. Special hardware may exist to differentiate the multiple processors, or the software may be written to allow only one master and multiple slaves. For instance, Sun's operating system SunOS Version 4 provides asymmetric multiprocessing, whereas Version 5 (Solaris 2) is symmetric.

As microprocessors become less expensive and more powerful, additional operating-system functions are off-loaded to slave processors (or back-ends). For example, it is fairly easy to add a microprocessor with its own memory to manage a disk system. The microprocessor could receive a sequence of requests from the main CPU and implement its own disk queue and scheduling algorithm. This arrangement relieves the main CPU of the overhead of disk scheduling. The IBM PC contains a microprocessor in its keyboard to convert the key strokes into codes to be sent to the CPU. In fact, this use of microprocessors has become so common that it is no longer considered multiprocessing.

1.8 ■ Distributed Systems

A recent trend in computer systems is to distribute computation among several processors. In contrast to the tightly coupled systems discussed in Section 1.7, the processors do not share memory or a clock. Instead, each processor has its own local memory. The processors communicate with one another through various communication lines, such as high-speed buses or telephone lines. These systems are usually referred to as *loosely coupled* systems, or *distributed* systems.

The processors in a distributed system may vary in size and function. They may include small microprocessors, workstations, minicomputers, and large general-purpose computer systems. These processors are referred to by a number of different names, such as *sites, nodes, computers,* and so on, depending on the context in which they are mentioned.

There are a variety of reasons for building distributed systems, the major ones being these:

- **Resource sharing.** If a number of different sites (with different capabilities) are connected to one another, then a user at one site may be able to use the resources available at another. For example, a user at site A may be using a laser printer available only at site B. Meanwhile, a user at B may access a file that resides at A. In general, resource sharing in a distributed system provides mechanisms for sharing files at remote sites, processing information in a distributed database, printing files at remote sites, using remote specialized hardware devices (such as a high-speed array processor), and performing other operations.

- **Computation speedup.** If a particular computation can be partitioned into a number of subcomputations that can run concurrently, then a distributed system may allow us to distribute the computation among the various sites — to run that computation concurrently. In addition, if a particular site is currently overloaded with jobs, some of them may be moved to other, lightly loaded, sites. This movement of jobs is called *load sharing*.

- **Reliability.** If one site fails in a distributed system, the remaining sites can potentially continue operating. If the system is composed of a number of large autonomous installations (that is, general-purpose computers), the failure of one of them should not affect the rest. If, on the other hand, the system is composed of a number of small machines, each of which is responsible for some crucial system function (such as terminal character I/O or the file system), then a single failure may effectively halt the operation of the whole system. In general, if enough redundancy exists in the system (in both hardware and data), the system can continue with its operation, even if some of its sites have failed.

- **Communication.** There are many instances in which programs need to exchange data with one another on one system. Window systems are one example, since they frequently share data or transfer data between displays. When a number of sites are connected to one another by a communication network, the processes at different sites have the opportunity to exchange information. Users may initiate file transfers or communicate with one another via *electronic mail*. A user can send mail to another user at the same site or at a different site.

Distributed systems are discussed in great detail in Chapter 15 through Chapter 18.

1.9 ■ Real-Time Systems

Another form of a special-purpose operating system is the *real-time* system. A real-time system is used when there are rigid time requirements on the operation of a processor or the flow of data, and thus is often used as a control device in a dedicated application. Sensors bring data to the computer. The computer must analyze the data and possibly adjust controls to modify the sensor inputs. Systems that control scientific experiments, medical imaging systems, industrial control systems, and some display systems are real-time systems. Also included are some automobile-engine fuel-injection systems, home-appliance controllers, and weapon systems. A real-time operating system has well-defined, fixed time constraints. Processing *must* be done within the defined constraints, or the system will fail. For instance, it would not do for a robot arm to be instructed to halt *after* it had smashed into the car it was building. A real-time system is considered to function correctly only if it returns the correct result within any time constraints. Contrast this requirement to a time-sharing system, where it is desirable (but not mandatory) to respond quickly, or to a batch system, where there may be no time constraints at all.

There are two flavors of real-time systems. A *hard real-time* system guarantees that critical tasks complete on time. This goal requires that all delays in the system be bounded, from the retrieval of stored data to the time it takes the operating system to finish any request made of it. Such time constraints dictate the facilities that are available in hard real-time systems. Secondary storage of any sort is usually limited or missing, with data instead being stored in short-term memory, or in read-only memory (ROM). ROM is a nonvolatile storage device that retains its content even in the case of electric outage; most other types of memory are volatile. Most advanced operating-system features are absent too, since they tend to separate the user further from the hardware, and that separation results in uncertainty as to the amount of time an operation will take. For instance, virtual memory (discussed in Chapter 9) is almost never found on real-time systems. Therefore, hard real-time systems conflict with the operation of time-sharing systems, and the two cannot be mixed. Since none of the existing general-purpose operating systems support hard real-time functionality, we do not concern ourselves with this type of system in this text.

A less restrictive type of real-time system is a *soft real-time* system, where a critical real-time task gets priority over other tasks, and retains that priority until it completes. As in hard real-time systems, kernel delays still need to be bound. A real-time task cannot be kept waiting indefinitely for the kernel to run it. Soft real-time is an achievable goal that is amenable to mixing with other types of systems. Soft real-time systems, however, have more limited utility than do hard real-time systems. Given their lack of deadline support, they cannot be used for industrial control and robotics. There are several areas in which they are useful, however, including multimedia, virtual reality, and advanced scientific projects such as undersea exploration and planetary rovers. These systems need advanced operating-system features that cannot be supported by hard real-time systems. Because of the expanded uses for soft real-time functionality, it is finding its way into most current operating systems, including the two major versions of UNIX.

In Chapter 5, we consider the scheduling facility needed to implement soft real-time functionality in an operating system. In Chapter 9, we describe the design of memory management for real-time computing. Finally, in Chapter 20, we describe the real-time components of the Mach operating system.

1.10 ■ Summary

Operating systems have developed over the past 40 years for two main purposes. First, operating systems attempt to schedule computational activities to ensure good performance of the computing system. Second, they provide a convenient environment for the development and execution of programs.

Initially, computer systems were used from the front console. Software such as assemblers, loaders, linkers, and compilers improved the convenience of programming the system, but also required substantial set-up time. To reduce the set-up time, facilities hired operators and batched similar jobs.

Batch systems allowed automatic job sequencing by a resident monitor and greatly improved the overall utilization of the computer. The computer no longer had to wait for human operation. CPU utilization was still low, however, because of the slow speed of the I/O devices relative to that of the CPU. Off-line operation of slow devices provides a means to use multiple reader-to-tape and tape-to-printer systems for one CPU. Spooling allows the CPU to overlap the input of one job with the computation and output of other jobs.

To improve the overall performance of the system, developers introduced the concept of multiprogramming. With multiprogramming, several jobs are kept in memory at one time; the CPU is switched back and forth among them to increase CPU utilization and to decrease the total time needed to execute the jobs.

Multiprogramming, which was developed to improve performance, also allows time sharing. Time-shared operating systems allow many users (from one to several hundred) to use a computer system interactively at the same time.

Personal computer systems are microcomputers that are considerably smaller and less expensive than are mainframe systems. Operating systems for these computers have benefited from the development of operating systems for mainframes in several ways. However, since individuals have sole use of the computer, CPU utilization is no longer a prime concern. Hence, some of the design decisions that are made in operating systems for mainframes may not be appropriate for smaller systems.

Parallel systems have more than one CPU in close communication; the CPUs share the computer bus, and sometimes memory and peripheral devices. Such systems provide increased throughput and enhanced reliability.

A distributed system is a collection of processors that do not share memory or a clock. Instead, each processor has its own local memory, and the processors communicate with each other through various communication lines, such as high-speed buses or telephone lines. A distributed system provides the user with access to the various resources located at remote sites.

A hard real-time system is often used as a control device in a dedicated application. A hard real-time operating system has well-defined, fixed time constraints. Processing *must* be done within the defined constraints, or the system will fail. Soft real-time systems have less stringent timing constraints, and do not support deadline scheduling.

We have shown the logical progression of operating-system development, driven by inclusion of features in the CPU hardware that are needed for advanced operating-system functionality. This trend can be seen today in the evolution of personal computers, with inexpensive hardware being improved enough to allow, in turn, improved characteristics.

■ Exercises

1.1 What are the three main purposes of an operating system?

1.2 List the four steps that are necessary to run a program on a completely dedicated machine.

1.3 An extreme method of spooling, known as *staging* a tape, is to read the entire contents of a magnetic tape onto disk before using it. Discuss the main advantage of such a scheme.

1.4 In a multiprogramming and time-sharing environment, several users share the system simultaneously. This situation can result in various security problems.

  a. What are two such problems?

  b. Can we ensure the same degree of security in a time-shared machine as we have in a dedicated machine? Explain your answer.

1.5 What is the main advantage of multiprogramming?

1.6 What are the main differences between operating systems for mainframe computers and personal computers?

1.7 Define the essential properties of the following types of operating systems:

    a. Batch

    b. Interactive

    c. Time-sharing

    d. Real-time

    e. Distributed

1.8 We have stressed the need for an operating system to make efficient use of the computing hardware. When is it appropriate for the operating system to forsake this principle and *waste* resources? Why is such a system not really wasteful?

1.9 Under what circumstances would a user be better off using a time-sharing system rather than a personal computer or single-user workstation?

1.10 Describe the differences between symmetric and asymmetric multiprocessing. What are the advantages and disadvantages of multiprocessor systems?

1.11 Why are distributed systems desirable?

1.12 What is the main difficulty a person must overcome in writing an operating system for a real-time environment?

Bibliographic Notes

Discussions concerning the historical evolution of computer hardware and software systems were presented by Rosen [1969], Denning [1971], and Weizer [1981].

Off-line systems (satellite processing) were used by the IBM FORTRAN Monitor system from the late 1950s to the middle of 1960. Spooling was pioneered on the Atlas computer system at Manchester University [Kilburn et al. 1961]. Spooling was also used on the Univac EXEC II system [Lynch 1972]. Spooling is now a standard feature of most systems, but it was not an integral part of IBM's OS/360 operating system for the 360 family of computers when OS/360 was introduced in the early sixties. Instead, spooling was a special feature added by the Houston computation center of the National Aeronautics and Space Administration (NASA). Hence, it is known as the Houston Automatic Spooling Priority (HASP) system.

Time-sharing systems were proposed first by Strachey [1959]. The earliest time-sharing systems were the Compatible Time-Sharing System

(CTSS) developed at MIT [Corbato et al. 1962] and the SDC Q-32 system built by the System Development Corporation [Schwartz et al. 1964, Schwartz and Weissman 1967]. Other early, but more sophisticated, systems include the MULTIplexed Information and Computing Services (MULTICS) system developed at MIT [Corbato and Vyssotsky 1965], the XDS-940 system developed at the University of California at Berkeley [Lichtenberger and Pirtle 1965], and the IBM TSS/360 system [Lett and Konigsford 1968].

Tabak [1990] discussed operating systems for multiprocessor hardware. Forsdick et al. [1978] and Donnelley [1979] discussed operating systems for computer networks. A survey of distributed operating systems was offered by Tanenbaum and Van Renesse [1985]. Real time operating systems are discussed by Stankovic and Ramamrithan [1989]. A special issue on real-time operating systems was edited by Zhao [1989].

The MS-DOS and the IBM-PC family were described by Norton [1986], and Norton and Wilton [1988]. Apple provides an overview of the Apple Macintosh hardware and software [Apple 1987]. Microsoft covers the OS/2 operating system [Microsoft 1989]. More OS/2 information can be found in Letwin [1988] and Deitel and Kogan [1992]. Custer [1993] discussed the structure of Microsoft Windows/NT.

There are numerous up-to-date general textbooks on operating systems. These include Comer [1984], Maekawa et al. [1987], Milenkovic [1987], Bic and Shaw [1988], Finkel [1988], Krakowiak [1988], Pinkert and Wear [1989], Deitel [1990], Stallings [1992], and Tanenbaum [1992]. Useful bibliographies were presented by Metzner [1982] and Brumfield [1986].

CHAPTER 2

COMPUTER-SYSTEM STRUCTURES

We need to have a general knowledge of the structure of a computer system before we can explore the details of system operation. In this chapter, several disparate parts of this structure are presented to round out our background knowledge. This chapter is mostly concerned with computer-system architecture, so you can skim or skip it if you already understand the concepts. Because an operating system is intimately tied to the I/O mechanisms of a computer, I/O is discussed first. The following sections discuss the data-storage structure.

The operating system must also ensure the correct operation of the computer system. So that user programs will not interfere with the proper operation of the system, the hardware must provide appropriate mechanisms to ensure correct behavior. Later in this chapter, we describe the basic computer architecture that makes it possible to write a functional operating system.

2.1 ■ Computer-System Operation

A modern, general-purpose computer system consists of a CPU and a number of device controllers that are connected through a common bus that provides access to shared memory (Figure 2.1). Each device controller is in charge of a specific type of device (for example, disk drives, audio devices, and video displays). The CPU and the device controllers can execute concurrently, competing for memory cycles. To ensure orderly access to the shared memory, a memory controller is provided whose function is to synchronize access to the memory.

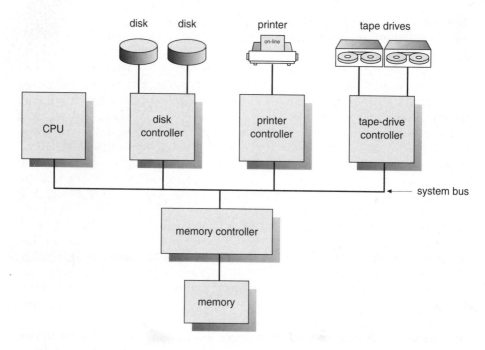

Figure 2.1   A modern computer system.

For a computer to start running — for instance, when it is powered up or rebooted — it needs to have an initial program to run. This initial program, or *bootstrap program*, tends to be simple. It initializes all aspects of the system, from CPU registers to device controllers to memory contents. The bootstrap program must know how to load the operating system and to start it executing. To accomplish this goal, the bootstrap program must locate the operating system kernel and load it into memory. The operating system then starts executing the first process, such as "init", and waits for some event to occur. The occurrence of an event is usually signaled by an *interrupt* from either the hardware or software. Hardware may trigger an interrupt at any time by sending a signal to the CPU, usually by way of the system bus. Software may trigger an interrupt by executing a special operation called a *system call* (also called a *monitor call*).

There are many different types of events that may trigger an interrupt, for example, the completion of an I/O operation, division by zero, invalid memory access, and a request for some operating system service. For each such interrupt, a service routine is provided that is responsible for dealing with the interrupt.

When the CPU is interrupted, it stops what it is doing and immediately transfers execution to a fixed location. The fixed location usually contains the starting address where the service routine for the interrupt is located.

The interrupt service routine executes, and upon completion, the CPU resumes the interrupted computation. A time line of this operation is shown in Figure 2.2.

Interrupts are an important part of a computer architecture. Each computer design has its own interrupt mechanism, but several functions are common. The interrupt must transfer control to the appropriate interrupt service routine. The straightforward method for handling this transfer would be to invoke a generic routine to examine the interrupt information, and it, in turn, would call the interrupt-specific handler. However, interrupts must be handled very quickly, and given that there are a predefined number of possible interrupts, a table of pointers to interrupt routines may be used instead. The interrupt routine is then called indirectly through the table, with no intermediate routine needed. Generally, the table of pointers is stored in low memory (the first 100 or so locations). These locations hold the addresses of the interrupt service routines for the various devices. This array, or *interrupt vector*, of addresses is then indexed by a unique device number, given with the interrupt request, to provide the address of the interrupt service routine for the interrupting device. Operating systems as different as MS-DOS and UNIX dispatch interrupts in this manner.

The interrupt architecture must also save the address of the interrupted instruction. Many old designs simply stored the interrupt address in a fixed location or in a location indexed by the device number. More recent architectures store the return address on the system stack. If the interrupt routine needs to modify the processor state, for instance, by modifying register values, it must explicitly save the current state and then restore it before returning. After the interrupt is serviced, the saved return address is loaded into the program counter, and the interrupted computation will resume as though the interrupt had not occurred.

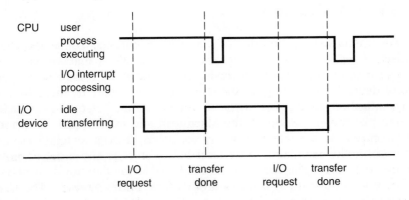

Figure 2.2 Interrupt time line.

Usually, interrupts are *disabled* while an interrupt is being processed, delaying any incoming interrupts until the operating system is done with the current one, after which interrupts are *enabled*. If they were not thus disabled, the processing of the second interrupt while the first was being serviced would overwrite the first's data, and the first would be a *lost interrupt*. Sophisticated interrupt architectures allow for one interrupt to be processed during another. They often use a priority scheme in which request types are assigned priorities according to their relative importance, and interrupt processing information is stored separately for each priority. A higher-priority interrupt will be taken even if a lower-priority interrupt is active, but interrupts at the same or lower levels are *masked*, or selectively disabled, to prevent lost interrupts or unnecessary ones.

Modern operating systems are *interrupt driven*. If there are no processes to execute, no I/O devices to service, and no users to whom to respond, an operating system will sit quietly, waiting for something to happen. Events are almost always signaled by the occurrence of an interrupt, or a trap. A *trap* (or an exception) is a software-generated interrupt caused either by an error (for example, division by zero or invalid memory access), or by a specific request from a user program that an operating-system service be performed.

The interrupt-driven nature of an operating system defines that system's general structure. When an interrupt (or trap) occurs, the hardware transfers control to the operating system. First, the operating system preserves the state of the CPU by storing registers and the program counter. Then, it determines which type of interrupt has occurred. This determination may require *polling*, the querying of all I/O devices to detect which requested service, or it may be a natural result of a vectored interrupt system. For each type of interrupt, separate segments of code in the operating system determine what action should be taken.

2.2 ■ I/O Structure

As was discussed in Section 2.1, a general-purpose computer system consists of a CPU and a number of device controllers that are connected through a common bus. Each device controller is in charge of a specific type of device. Depending on the controller, there may be more than one device attached to it. For instance the SCSI (Small Computer Systems Interface) controller, found on the Macintosh and many small- to medium-sized computers, can have as many as seven devices attached to it. A device controller maintains some local buffer storage and a set of special-purpose registers. The controller is responsible for moving data between the peripheral device(s) it controls and its local buffer storage. The size of the local buffer within a device controller varies from one controller to another, depending on the particular device being controlled. For example, the size of the buffer of a disk controller is the same as or a multiple of the size of the smallest addressable portion of a disk (a *sector*), which is usually 512 bytes.

2.2.1 I/O Interrupts

To start an I/O operation, the CPU loads the appropriate registers within the device controller. The device controller, in turn, examines the contents of these registers to determine what action to take. For example, if it finds a read request, the controller will start the transfer of data from the device to its local buffer. Once the transfer of data is complete, the device controller informs the CPU that it has finished its operation. It accomplishes this communication by causing an interrupt.

This situation will occur, in general, as the result of a user process requesting I/O. Once the I/O is started, two courses of action are possible. In the simplest case, the I/O is started; then, at I/O completion, control is returned to the user process. This is known as *synchronous* I/O. The other possibility (*asynchronous* I/O) is to return control to the user program without waiting for the I/O to complete. The I/O then can continue while other system operations occur.

Waiting for I/O completion may be accomplished in one of two ways. Some computers have a special **wait** instruction that idles the CPU until the next interrupt. Machines that do not have such an instruction may have a wait loop:

Loop: jmp Loop

This very tight loop simply continues until an interrupt occurs, transferring control to another part of the operating system. Such a loop might also need to poll any I/O devices which do not support the interrupt structure; instead they simply set a flag in one of their registers and expect the operating system to notice it. The **wait** instruction is probably better than a loop, since a wait loop generates a series of instruction fetches, which may cause significant contention for memory access. The contention is caused by the I/O device transferring information and the CPU transferring instructions.

One major advantage of always waiting for I/O completion is that at most one I/O request is outstanding at a time. Thus, whenever an I/O interrupt occurs, the operating system knows exactly which device is interrupting. On the other hand, this approach excludes simultaneous I/O processing.

An alternative is to start the I/O and immediately to return control to the user program. A *system call* (a request to the operating system) is then needed to allow the user to wait for I/O completion, if desired. Hence, we still require the wait code that we needed before. We also need to be able

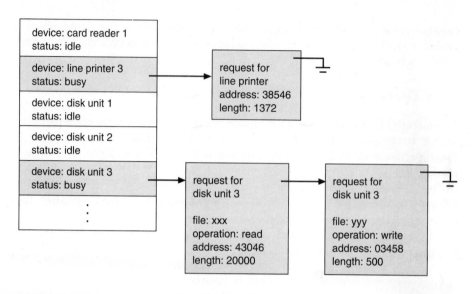

Figure 2.3   Device-status table.

to keep track of many I/O requests at the same time. For this purpose, the operating system uses a table containing an entry for each I/O device: the *device-status table* (Figure 2.3). Each table entry indicates the device's type, its address, and its state (not functioning, idle, or busy). If the device is busy with a request, the type of request and other parameters will be stored in the table entry for that device. Since it is possible for other processes to issue requests to the same device, we may have a list or chain of waiting requests. Thus, in addition to the I/O device table, an operating system may have a request list for each device.

An I/O device interrupts when it needs service. When an interrupt occurs, the operating system first determines which I/O device caused the interrupt. It then indexes into the I/O device table to determine the status of that device, and modifies the table entry to reflect the occurrence of the interrupt. For most devices, an interrupt signals completion of an I/O request. If there is an additional request waiting for this device, the operating system starts processing that request.

Finally, control is returned from the I/O interrupt. If a process was waiting for this request to complete (as recorded in the device-status table), we may now return control to it. Otherwise, we return to whatever we were doing before the I/O interrupt: to the execution of the user program (the program started an I/O operation and that operation has now finished, but the program has not yet waited for the operation to complete) or to the wait loop (the program started two or more I/O operations and is waiting for a particular one to finish, but this interrupt was from one of the others).   In a time-sharing system, the operating system could switch to another ready-to-run process.

The schemes used by some input devices may vary from this one. Many interactive systems allow users to type ahead, or to enter data before the data are requested, on their terminal. In this case, interrupts may occur, signaling the arrival of characters from the terminal, while the device-status block indicates that no program has requested input from this device. If typeahead is to be allowed, then a buffer must be provided to store the typeahead characters until some program wants them. In general, we may need a buffer for each input terminal.

The main advantage of asynchronous I/O is the increased system efficiency. While I/O is taking place, the system CPU can be used for processing, or even scheduling other I/O. Because I/O can be quite slow compared to processor speed, the system makes much better use of its facilities.   In the next section, we shall see another mechanism for improving system performance.

2.2.2 DMA Structure

Consider a simple terminal input driver. When a line is to be read from the terminal, the first character typed is sent to the computer. When that character is received, the asynchronous communication (or serial port) device to which the terminal line is connected will interrupt the CPU. When the interrupt request from the terminal arrives, the CPU will be about to execute some instruction. (If the CPU is in the middle of executing an instruction, the interrupt is normally held pending until the instruction execution is complete.) The address of this interrupted instruction is saved, and control is transferred to the interrupt service routine for the device.

The interrupt service routine saves the contents of any CPU registers it will need to use. It checks for any error conditions that might have resulted from the last input operation. It then takes the character from the device, and stores that character in a buffer.   The interrupt routine must also adjust pointer and counter variables, to be sure that the next input character will be stored at the next location in the buffer. The interrupt routine next sets a flag in memory indicating to the other parts of the operating system that new input has been received.   The other parts are responsible for processing the data in the buffer, and for transferring the characters to the program requesting input (see Section 2.5). Then, the interrupt service routine restores the contents of any saved registers, and transfers control back to the interrupted instruction.

If characters are being typed to a 9600-baud terminal, the terminal can accept and transfer one character approximately every 1 millisecond, or 1000 microseconds. A well-written interrupt service routine to input characters into a buffer may require 2 microseconds per character, leaving 998 microseconds out of every 1000 for CPU computation (and servicing of other interrupts). Given this disparity, asynchronous I/O is usually assigned a low interrupt priority, allowing other, more important interrupts to be processed first, or even to preempt the current interrupt for another. A high-speed device, however, such as a tape, disk, or communications network, may be able to transmit information at close to memory speeds; the CPU would need 2 microseconds to respond to each interrupt, with interrupts arriving every 4 microseconds (for example). This would not leave much time for process execution.

To solve this problem, direct memory access (DMA) is used for high-speed I/O devices. After setting up buffers, pointers, and counters for the I/O device, the device controller transfers an entire block of data to or from its own buffer storage to memory directly, with no intervention by the CPU. Only one interrupt is generated per block, rather than the one interrupt per byte (or word) generated for low-speed devices.

The basic operation of the CPU is the same. A user program, or the operating system itself, may request data transfer. The operating system finds a buffer (an empty buffer for input, or a full buffer for output) from a queue of buffers for the transfer. (A buffer is typically 128 to 4096 bytes, depending on the device type.) The DMA controller then has its registers set to the appropriate source and destination addresses, and transfer length. This register setting is usually done by a *device driver*, which knows exactly how this information is to be provided to the controller. The DMA controller is then instructed (via control bits in a control register) to start the I/O operation. Meanwhile, the CPU has been free to perform other tasks since it gave the transfer information to the controller. The DMA controller interrupts the CPU when the transfer has been completed. A comparison of standard interrupt-driven I/O and DMA I/O is shown in Figure 2.4.

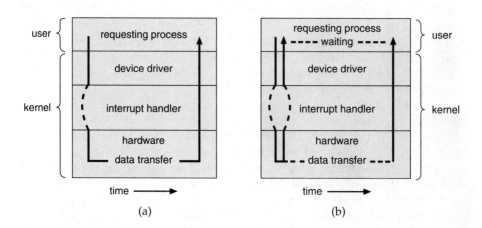

Figure 2.4   Two I/O methods. (a) Interrupt-driven. (b) DMA.

As an example of the utility of DMA, consider a typical IBM PC. The PC supports interrupt-based I/O, as well as DMA channels. The backup program, which is included with the MS-DOS PC operating system, uses only interrupt-based I/O to copy data between a hard disk and a floppy disk. Several companies have written similar programs that take advantage of DMA data transfer, and the result is a several-fold increase in backup speed.

2.3 ■ Storage Structure

For a computer to do its job of executing programs, the programs must be in main memory. Main memory is the only large storage area that the processor can access directly. It is an array of words or bytes, ranging in size from hundreds of thousands to hundreds of millions. Each word has its own address. Interaction is achieved through a sequence of **load** or **store** instructions to specific memory addresses. The load instruction moves a word from main memory to an internal register within the CPU, while the store instruction moves the content of a register to main memory. Aside from explicit loads and stores, the CPU automatically loads instructions from main memory for execution.

A typical instruction-execution cycle, as executed on a *von Neumann* architecture system, will first fetch an instruction from memory and store it in the *instruction register*. The instruction is then decoded and may cause operands to be fetched from memory and stored in some internal register. After the instruction on the operands has been executed, the result may be stored back in memory. Notice that the memory unit sees only a stream of memory addresses; it does not know how they are generated (the instruction counter, indexing, indirection, literal addresses, and so on) or what they are for (instructions or data). Accordingly, we can ignore *how* a memory address is generated by a program. We are interested in only the sequence of memory addresses generated by the running program.

Ideally, we would want the programs and data to reside in main memory permanently. This arrangement is not possible for the following two reasons:

1. Main memory is usually too small to store all needed programs and data permanently.

2. Main memory is a *volatile* storage device that loses its contents when power is turned off or lost.

Thus, most computer systems provide *secondary storage* as an extension of main memory. The main requirement of secondary storage is thus to be able to hold extremely large numbers of data permanently.

The most common secondary-storage device is a magnetic disk, which provides storage of both programs and data. Most programs (compilers, assemblers, sort routines, editors, formatters, and so on) are stored on a disk until loaded into memory. They then use the disk as both the source and destination of the information for their processing. Hence, the proper management of disk storage is of central importance to a computer system, as will be discussed in Chapter 12.

In a larger sense, however, the storage structure that we have described — consisting of registers, main memory, and magnetic disks — is only one of many possible storage systems. There are also cache memory, optical disks, magnetic tapes, and so on. Each storage system provides the basic functions of storing a datum, and holding that datum until it is retrieved at a later time. The main differences among the various storage systems lie in speed, cost, size, and volatility. In Sections 2.3.1 to 2.3.4, we describe the important storage systems.

2.3.1 Main Memory

Main memory and the registers built into the processor itself are the only storage that the CPU can access directly. (Consider that there are machine instructions which take memory addresses as arguments, but none that take disk addresses.) Therefore, any instructions in execution, and any data being used by the instructions, must be in one of these direct-access storage devices. If the data are not in memory, they must be moved there before the CPU can operate on them.

In the case of I/O, as mentioned in Section 2.1, each I/O controller includes registers to hold commands and the data being transferred. Usually, special I/O instructions allow data transfers between these registers and system memory. To allow more convenient access to I/O devices, some systems, including the IBM PC and Apple Macintosh, provide *memory-mapped I/O*. In this case, ranges of memory addresses are set aside, and are physically mapped to the device registers. Reads and writes to these memory addresses cause the data to be transferred to and from the device registers. This method is appropriate for devices with fast response times, such as video controllers. In the IBM PC, each location on the screen is mapped to a memory location. Displaying text on the screen is almost as easy as writing the text into the appropriate memory-mapped locations.

Memory-mapped I/O is also convenient for frequently used devices, such as a serial port. So that a system can communicate with another computer over a modem and telephone line, characters are read and written to a one-byte location in memory. Note that polling is again needed in this circumstance, with the computer looping, constantly checking to see whether a character is available for reading. Interrupts for signaling the availability of new input could be used instead, depending on the hardware configuration.

Given that registers are built into the CPU, they are accessible within one cycle of the CPU clock. The CPU can decode an instruction and perform the given operation on a register's contents all in the same clock tick. The same cannot be said for main memory, which may be located on a system bus and take several cycles to access. In this case, the processor normally needs to *stall* while waiting for the access to complete. This situation is intolerable because of the frequency of memory accesses. The remedy is to add fast memory between the CPU and main memory. A memory buffer used to accommodate a speed differential is called a *cache*, as described in Section 2.4.1.

2.3.2 Magnetic Disks

Magnetic disks provide the bulk of secondary storage for modern computer systems. Physically, disks are relatively simple (Figure 2.5). Each disk *platter* has a flat circular shape, like a phonograph record. Its two surfaces are covered with a magnetic material, similar to magnetic tape. Information is recorded on the surfaces.

When the disk is in use, a drive motor spins it at high speed (usually 60 revolutions per second). There is a read–write head positioned just above the surface of the platter. The disk surface is logically divided into *tracks*, which are subdivided into *sectors*. We store information by

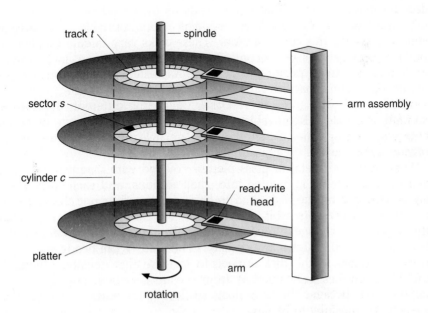

Figure 2.5   Moving-head disk mechanism.

recording it magnetically on the sector under the read—write head. There may be hundreds of concentric tracks on a disk surface, containing thousands of sectors. The platter itself may be between 1.8 inches and 14 inches wide. The larger sizes are common on large systems because of their higher storage capacities and transfer rates. The smaller sizes are found on PCs, since they have lower cost.

A *fixed-head disk* has a separate head for each track. This arrangement allows the computer to switch from track to track quickly, but it requires a large number of heads, making the device extremely expensive. Much more common, is only one head, which moves across the disk to access different tracks. This *moving-head disk*, or simply *hard disk*, requires hardware to move the head, but only a single head is needed, resulting in a much less expensive system. The disk platters, mounted on a spindle and surrounded by heads driven by a motor, are known as *head—disk assemblies* and come in a complete package.

Disks were originally designed for file storage, so the primary design criteria were cost, size, and speed. To provide additional storage capacity, developers took several approaches. They made the primary gain by improving the recording density, allowing more bits to be put on a surface. The density is reflected by the number of tracks per inch, sectors per track, and bits per sector. In addition, with separate heads on each side of the platter, disk capacity can be doubled at minimal cost. We can extend this approach by stacking several disks, each with two recording surfaces, on one spindle. Since all the disks rotate together, only one drive motor is needed, although each surface still needs its own read—write head. The most common disks, used in systems from portable PCs through mainframes, have this configuration. These disks vary in data transfer rate from 1 to 5 megabytes per second. The average access time, including the time for a head to be positioned over the requested data, is from 10 to 40 milliseconds. The capacities range from 10 to 7500 megabytes.

Finally, the disk can be *removable*, allowing different disks to be mounted as needed. Removable disk packs may consist of one or several platters on one spindle. Generally, they are held in hard plastic cases to prevent damage while they are not in the disk drive.

Disks are rigid metal or glass platters covered with magnetic recording material. Each platter is divided into small sections, and each such section may be changed by the disk head to be in a charged or not charged state. Each section represents a bit and is 0 or 1 depending on its charge state. The smaller the changeable sections are, the more bits can be put on a platter and thus the higher the density. The read—write heads are kept as close as possible to the disk surface to increase this density. Often, the head floats or flies only microns from the disk surface, supported by a cushion of air. Because the head floats so close to the surface, platters must be machined carefully to be flat.

Head crashes can be a problem. If the head contacts the disk surface (due to a power failure, for example), the head will scrape the recording medium off the disk, destroying the data that had been there. Usually, the head touching the surface causes the removed medium to become airborne and to come between the other heads and their platters, causing more crashes. Under normal circumstances, a head crash results in the entire disk failing and needing to be replaced.

Floppy disks take a different approach. The disks are coated with a hard surface, so the read–write head can sit directly on the disk surface without destroying the data. Thus, the disk itself is much less expensive to produce and use. The floppy disk must rotate much more slowly than a hard disk, due to the resulting friction. Also, the coating (and the read–write head) will wear with use, and need to be replaced eventually. Because they are more rugged, floppy disks are removable. The disks are not permanently mounted in a head–disk assembly. Instead, the disk is slipped manually into a slot which contains a spindle to rotate it, and a head and motor to access it. This arrangement keeps the cost of floppy disks low because one drive can be used to access hundreds or thousands of disks.

Floppy disks usually have a much lower capacity than do hard disks because they have much lower storage densities, have only one platter, and spin slower. They hold from 100 kilobytes (a kilobyte is 1024 bytes) to a few megabytes per disk. They come in many variations (single-sided, double-sided, single-density, and double-density) and sizes (5 1/4 inch, 3 1/2 inch, and so on). Generally, they are formatted and used in the same way as are hard disks, except that all floppy disks are removable and may therefore be used conveniently to transfer data between computers.

A disk drive has a *disk controller* that determines the logical interaction between the device and the computer. The controller takes instructions from the CPU and orders the disk drive to carry out the instruction. Some disk controllers have a built-in cache, which holds data recently read from or written to the disk. If data are currently in the cache, the need for a disk transfer is obviated.

2.3.3 Other Disk Types

There are many variations on magnetic disks among which we do not distinguish, from an operating-system point of view. Generally, they are treated as normal hard disks except at the device-driver level. There is the *drum*, which has a head over each track. Previously, these fast devices were used for *backing store* (see Chapters 8 and 9), but they are now used rarely due to the improved speed and price–performance ratio of standard hard disks. An up-and-coming device is the *optical disk*, which uses lasers to melt and fill holes on a plastic medium. These drives have been slower but less costly and more rugged than magnetic hard disks in the past, but their performance is increasing. Because they are more rugged, they, like floppy disks, have the added advantage of removability.

2.3.4 Magnetic Tapes

Magnetic tape was used as an early secondary-storage media. Although it is relatively permanent, and can hold large numbers of data, magnetic tape is quite slow in comparison to the access time of main memory. Even more important, magnetic tape is limited to sequential access. Thus, it is unsuitable for providing the random access needed for most secondary-storage requirements. Tapes are used mainly for backup, for storage of infrequently used information, and as a medium for transferring information from one system to another.

A tape is kept in a spool, and is wound or rewound past a read–write head. Moving to the correct spot on a tape can take minutes rather than milliseconds; once positioned, however, tape drives can write data at densities and speeds approaching those of disk drives. Capacities vary depending on the length and width of the tape, and on the density at which the head can read and write. A tape drive is usually named by its width. Thus, there are 8-millimeter, 1/4-inch, and 1/2-inch (also known as 9-track) tape drives. The 8-millimeter tape drives have the highest density, due to the technology they use; they currently store 5 gigabytes of data (a gigabyte is one billion bytes) on a 350-foot tape.

2.4 ■ Storage Hierarchy

The wide variety of storage systems in a computer system can be organized in a hierarchy (Figure 2.6) according to their speed and their cost. The higher levels are expensive, but are fast. As we move down the hierarchy, the cost per bit decreases, whereas the access time increases. This tradeoff is reasonable; if a given storage system were both faster and less expensive than another — other properties being the same — then there would be no reason to use the slower, more expensive memory. In fact, many early storage devices, including paper tape and core memories, are relegated to museums now that magnetic tape and semiconductor memory have become faster and cheaper.

In addition to the speed and cost of the various storage systems, there is also the issue of storage volatility. Volatile storage loses its contents when the power to the device is removed. In the absence of expensive battery and generator backup systems, data must be written to nonvolatile storage for safekeeping. In the hierarchy shown in Figure 2.6, the storage system above disks is volatile, whereas the storage system below main memory is nonvolatile. The design of a complete memory system attempts to balance all these factors: It uses only as much expensive memory as

Figure 2.6 Storage-device hierarchy.

necessary, while providing as much inexpensive, nonvolatile, memory as possible. Caches can be installed to ameliorate performance differences where there is a large access-time or transfer-rate disparity between two components.

2.4.1 Caching

Caching is an important principle of computer systems, in both hardware and software. Information is normally kept in some storage system (such as main memory). As it is used, it is copied into a faster storage system, the cache, on a temporary basis. When we need a particular piece of information, we first check whether it is in the cache. If it is, we use the information directly from the cache; if it is not, we use the information from the main storage system, putting a copy in the cache under the assumption that there is a high probability that it will be needed again.

Extending this view, internal programmable registers, such as index registers and accumulators, are a high-speed cache for main memory. The programmer (or compiler) implements the register-allocation and register-replacement algorithms to decide which information to keep in registers and which to keep in main memory. There are also caches that are implemented totally in hardware. For instance, most systems have an instruction cache to hold the next instructions expected to be executed. Without this cache, the CPU would have to wait several cycles while an instruction was fetched from main memory. We are not concerned with these hardware-only caches in this text, since they are outside of the control of the operating system.

Since caches have limited size, *cache management* is an important design problem. Careful selection of the cache size and of a replacement policy can result in 80 to 99 percent of all accesses being in the cache, resulting in extremely high performance. Various replacement algorithms for software-controlled caches are discussed in Chapter 9.

Main memory can be viewed as a fast *cache* for secondary memory, since data on secondary storage must be copied into main memory for use, and data must be in main memory before being moved to secondary storage for safekeeping. The file system itself, which must reside on nonvolatile storage, may have several levels of storage. At the highest level, we have the electronic (or RAM) disk storage, which is backed up by the larger, but slower, magnetic-disk storage. The magnetic-disk storage, in turn, is backed up by the larger, but slower, tape storage. Optical disks are also efficient high-capacity but low-cost storage media. When compared to magnetic tape, they have the drawback of higher cost, but offer much greater speed and convenience. Transfers between these two storage levels are generally requested explicitly, but some systems now automatically archive a file that has not been used for a long time (for example, 1 month), and then automatically fetch back the file to disk when it is next referenced.

The movement of information between levels of a storage hierarchy may be either explicit or implicit, depending on the hardware design and the controlling operating-system software. For instance, data transfer from cache to CPU and registers is usually a hardware function, with no operating-system intervention. On the other hand, transfer of data from disk to memory is usually controlled by the operating system.

2.4.2 Coherency and Consistency

In a hierarchical storage structure, the same datum may appear in different storage systems. For example, consider an integer A located in file B that is to be incremented by 1. Suppose that file B resides on magnetic disk. The increment operation proceeds by first issuing an I/O operation to copy the disk block on which A resides to main memory. This operation is followed by a possible copying of A to the cache, and by copying A to an internal register. Thus, the copy of A appears in several places. Once the increment takes place in the internal register, the value of A differs in the various storage systems. The value of A becomes the same only after the new value of A is written back to the magnetic disk.

In an environment where there is only one single process executing at a time, this arrangement poses no difficulties, since an access to the integer A will always be to the copy at the highest level of the hierarchy. However, in a multitasking environment, where the CPU is switched back and forth among various processes, extreme care must be taken to ensure that if several processes wish to access A, then each of these processes will obtain the most recently updated value of A.

The situation becomes more complicated in a multiprocessor environment where, in addition to internal registers, the CPU also contains a local cache. In such an environment, a copy of A may exist simultaneously in several caches. Since the various CPUs can all execute concurrently, we must make sure that an update to the value of A in one cache is immediately reflected in all other caches where A resides. This problem is called *cache coherency*, and is usually a hardware issue (handled below the operating system level).

In a distributed environment, the situation becomes even more complex. In such an environment, several copies (replicas) of the same file can be kept on different computers that are distributed in space. Since the various replicas may be accessed and updated concurrently, we must ensure that when a replica is updated in one place, then all other replicas are brought up to date as soon as possible. There is a variety of ways for achieving this guarantee, as will be discussed in Chapter 17.

2.5 ■ Hardware Protection

Early computer systems were single-user programmer-operated systems. When the programmers operated the computer from the console, they had complete control over the system. As operating systems developed, however, this control was given to the operating system. Starting with the resident monitor, the operating system began performing many of the functions, especially I/O, for which the programmer had been responsible previously.

In addition, to improve system utilization, the operating system began to *share* system resources among several programs simultaneously. With spooling, one program might have been executing while I/O occurred for other processes; the disk simultaneously held data for many processes. Multiprogramming put several programs in memory at the same time.

This sharing created both improved utilization and increased problems. When the system was run without sharing, an error in a program could cause problems for only the one program that was running. With sharing, many processes could be adversely affected by a bug in one program.

For example, consider the earliest resident monitor, providing nothing more than automatic job sequencing (Section 1.3). Suppose a program gets stuck in a loop reading input cards. The program will read through all its data and, unless something stops it, will continue reading the cards of the next job, and the next, and so on. This loop could prevent the correct operation of many jobs.

Even more subtle errors could occur in a multiprogramming system, where one erroneous program might modify the program or data of another program, or even the resident monitor itself. MS-DOS and Macintosh OS both allow this kind of error.

Without protection against these sorts of errors, either the computer must execute only one process at a time, or all output must be suspect. A properly designed operating system must ensure that an incorrect (or malicious) program cannot cause other programs to execute incorrectly.

Many programming errors are detected by the hardware. These errors are normally handled by the operating system. If a user program fails in some way — such as an attempt either to execute an illegal instruction, or to access memory that is not in the user's address space — then the hardware will trap to the operating system. The trap transfers control through the interrupt vector to the operating system just like an interrupt. Whenever a program error occurs, the operating system must abnormally terminate the program. This situation is handled by the same code as is a user-requested abnormal termination. An appropriate error message is given, and the memory of the program is dumped. In a batch system, the memory dump may be printed, allowing the user to try to find the cause of the error by examining the printed dump. In an interactive system, the memory dump may be written to a file. The user may then examine it on-line, and perhaps correct and restart the program.

2.5.1 Dual-Mode Operation

To ensure proper operation, we must protect the operating system and all other programs and their data from any malfunctioning program. Protection is needed for any shared resource. The approach taken is to provide hardware support to allow us to differentiate among various modes of executions. At the very least, we need two separate *modes* of operation: *user mode* and *monitor mode* (also called *supervisor mode*, *system mode*, or *privileged mode*). A bit, called the *mode bit*, is added to the hardware of the computer to indicate the current mode: monitor (0) or user (1). With the mode bit, we are able to distinguish between an execution that is done on behalf of the operating system, and one that is done on behalf of the user. As we shall see, this architectural enhancement is useful for many other aspects of system operation.

At system boot time, the hardware starts in monitor mode. The operating system is then loaded, and starts user processes in user mode.

Whenever a trap or interrupt occurs, the hardware switches from user mode to monitor mode (that is, changes the state of the mode bit to be 0). Thus, whenever the operating system gains control of the computer, it is in monitor mode. The system always switches to user mode (by setting the mode bit to 1) before passing control to a user program.

The dual mode of operation provides us with the means for protecting the operating system from errant users, and errant users from one another. We accomplish this protection by designating some of the machine instructions that may cause harm as *privileged instructions*. The hardware allows privileged instructions to be executed only in monitor mode. If an attempt is made to execute a privileged instruction in user mode, the hardware does not execute the instruction, but rather treats the instruction as illegal and traps to the operating system.

The lack of a hardware-supported dual mode can cause serious shortcomings in an operating system. For instance, MS-DOS was written for the Intel 8088 architecture, which has no mode bit, and therefore no dual mode. A user program running awry can wipe out the operating system by writing over it with data, and multiple programs are able to write to a device at the same time, with possibly disastrous results. More recent and advanced versions of the Intel CPU, such as the 80486, do provide dual-mode operation. As a result, more recent operating systems, such as Microsoft Windows/NT, and IBM OS/2, take advantage of this feature and provide greater protection for the operating system.

2.5.2 I/O Protection

A user program may disrupt the normal operation of the system by issuing illegal I/O instructions, by accessing memory locations within the operating system itself, or by refusing to relinquish the CPU. Various mechanisms are used to ensure that such disruptions cannot take place in the system.

To prevent a user from performing illegal I/O, we define all I/O instructions to be privileged instructions. Thus, users cannot issue I/O instructions directly; they must do it through the operating system. For I/O protection to be complete, we must be sure that a user program can never gain control of the computer in monitor mode. If it could, I/O protection could be compromised.

Consider the computer executing in user mode. It will switch to monitor mode whenever an interrupt or trap occurs, jumping to the address determined from the interrupt vector. Suppose a user program, as part of its execution, stores a new address in the interrupt vector. This new address could overwrite the previous address with an address in the user program. Then, when a corresponding trap or interrupt occurred, the hardware would switch to monitor mode, and would transfer control through the (modified) interrupt vector to the user program! The user program could gain control of the computer in monitor mode.

2.5.3 Memory Protection

To ensure correct operation, we must protect the interrupt vector from modification by a user program. In addition, we must also protect the interrupt service routines in the operating system from modification. Otherwise, a user program might overwrite instructions in the interrupt service routine with jumps to the user program, thus gaining control from the interrupt service routine that was executing in monitor mode. Even if the user did not gain unauthorized control of the computer, modifying the interrupt service routines would probably disrupt the proper operation of the computer system and of its spooling and buffering.

We see then that we must provide memory protection at least for the interrupt vector and the interrupt service routines of the operating system. In general, however, we want to protect the operating system from access by user programs, and, in addition, to protect user programs from one another. This protection must be provided by the hardware. It can be implemented in several ways, as we shall see in Chapter 8. Here, we outline one such possible implementation.

What is needed to separate each program's memory space is an ability to determine the range of legal addresses that the program may access, and to protect the memory outside that space. We can provide this protection by using two registers, usually a *base* and a *limit*, as illustrated in Figure 2.7. The base register holds the smallest legal physical memory address, and the limit register contains the size of the range. For example, if the base register holds 300040 and limit register is 120900, then the

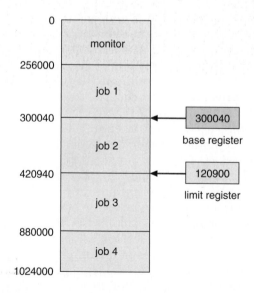

Figure 2.7 A base and a limit register define a logical address space.

program can legally access all addresses from 300040 through 420940 inclusive.

This protection is accomplished by the CPU hardware comparing *every* address generated in user mode with the registers. Any attempt by a program executing in user mode to access monitor memory or other users' memory results in a trap to the monitor, which treats the attempt as a fatal error (Figure 2.8). This scheme prevents the user program from (accidentally or deliberately) modifying the code or data structures of either the operating system or other users.

The base and limit registers can be loaded by only the operating system, which uses a special privileged instruction. Since privileged instructions can be executed only in monitor mode, and since only the operating system executes in monitor mode, only the operating system can load the base and limit registers. This scheme allows the monitor to change the value of the registers, but prevents user programs from changing the registers' contents.

The operating system, executing in monitor mode, is given unrestricted access to both monitor and users' memory. This provision allows the operating system to load users' programs into users' memory, to dump them out in case of errors, to access and modify parameters of system calls, and so on.

2.5.4 CPU Protection

The third piece of the protection puzzle is ensuring that the operating system maintains control. We must prevent a user program from getting stuck in an infinite loop, and never returning control to the operating system. To accomplish this goal, we can use a *timer*. A timer can be set to

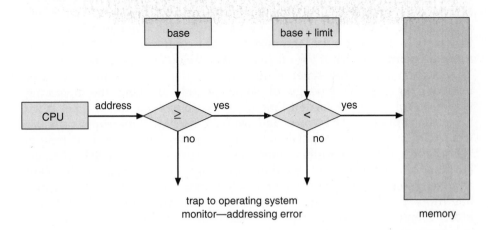

Figure 2.8   Hardware address protection with base and limit registers.

interrupt the computer after a specified period. The period may be fixed (for example, 1/60 second) or variable (for example, from 1 millisecond to 1 second, in increments of 1 millisecond). A variable timer is generally implemented by a fixed-rate clock and a counter. The operating system sets the counter. Every time the clock ticks, the counter is decremented. When the counter reaches zero, an interrupt occurs. For instance, a 10-bit counter with a 1-millisecond clock would allow interrupts at intervals from 1 millisecond to 1024 milliseconds, in steps of 1 millisecond.

Before turning over control to the user, the operating system ensures that the timer is set to interrupt. If the timer interrupts, control transfers automatically to the operating system, which may treat the interrupt as a fatal error or give the program more time. Instructions that modify the operation of the timer are clearly privileged.

Thus, the timer can be used to prevent a user program from running too long. A simple technique is to initialize a counter with the amount of time that a program is allowed to run. A program with a 7-minute time limit, for example, would have its counter initialized to 420. Every second, the timer interrupts and the counter is decremented by 1. As long as the counter is positive, control is returned to the user program. When the counter becomes negative, the operating system terminates the program for exceeding its time limit.

A more common use of a timer is to implement time sharing. In the most straightforward case, the timer could be set to interrupt every N milliseconds where N is the *time-slice* each user is allowed to execute before the next user gets control of the CPU. The operating system is invoked at the end of each time-slice to perform various housekeeping tasks, such as adding the value N to the record that specifies (for accounting purposes) the amount of time the user program has executed thus far. The operating system also resets registers, internal variables, and buffers, and changes several other parameters to prepare for the next program to run. (This procedure is known as a *context switch*, and is explored in Chapter 4.) Following a context switch, the next program continues with its execution from the point at which it left off (when its previous time-slice ran out).

Another use of the timer is to compute the current time. A timer interrupt signals the passage of some period, allowing the operating system to compute the current time in reference to some initial time. If we have interrupts every 1 second, and we have had 1427 interrupts since we were told it was 1:00 P.M., then we can compute that the current time is 1:23:47 P.M. Some computers determine the current time in this manner, but the calculations must be done carefully for the time to be kept accurately, since the interrupt-processing time (and other times when interrupts are disabled) tends to cause the software clock to slow down. Most computers have a separate hardware time-of-day clock that is independent of the operating system.

2.6 ■ General-System Architecture

The desire to improve the utilization of the computer system led to the development of multiprogramming and time sharing, where the resources of the computer system are shared among many different programs and processes. Sharing led directly to modifications of the basic computer architecture, to allow the operating system to maintain control over the computer system, and especially over I/O. Control must be maintained if we are to provide continuous, consistent, and correct operation.

To maintain control, developers introduced a dual mode of execution (user mode and monitor mode). This scheme supports the concept of privileged instructions, which can be executed only in monitor mode. I/O instructions and instructions to modify the memory-management registers or the timer are privileged instructions.

As you can imagine, several other instructions are also classified as privileged. For instance, the **halt** instruction is privileged; a user program should never be able to halt the computer. The instructions to turn the interrupt system on and off are also privileged, since proper operation of the timer and I/O depends on the ability to respond to interrupts correctly. The instruction to change from user mode to monitor mode is privileged, and on many machines any change to the mode bit is privileged.

Because I/O instructions are privileged, they can be executed by only the operating system. Then how does the user program perform I/O? By making I/O instructions privileged, we have prevented user programs from doing any I/O, either valid or invalid. The solution to this problem is that, because only the monitor can do I/O, the user must *ask* the monitor to do I/O on the user's behalf.

Such a request is known as a *system call* (also called a *monitor call* or *operating system function call*). A system call is invoked in a variety of ways, depending on the functionality provided by the underlying processor. In all forms, it is the method used by a process to request action by the operating system. A system call usually takes the form of a trap to a specific location in the interrupt vector. This trap can be executed by a generic **trap** instruction, although some systems (like the Mips R2000 family) have a specific **syscall** instruction.

When a system call is executed, it is treated by the hardware as a software interrupt. Control passes through the interrupt vector to a service routine in the operating system, and the mode bit is set to monitor mode. The system-call service routine is a part of the operating system. The monitor examines the interrupting instruction to determine what system call has occurred; a parameter indicates what type of service the user program is requesting. Additional information needed for the request may be passed in registers, on the stack, or in memory (with pointers to the memory locations passed in registers). The monitor verifies that the parameters are correct and legal, executes the request, and returns control to the instruction following the system call.

Thus, to do I/O, a user program executes a system call to request that the operating system perform I/O on its behalf (Figure 2.9). The operating system, executing in monitor mode, checks that the request is valid, and (if the request is valid) does the I/O requested. The operating system then returns to the user.

2.7 ■ Summary

Multiprogramming and time-sharing systems require the overlap of CPU and I/O operations on a single machine. Such an overlap requires that data transfer between the CPU and the I/O devices be handled by one or both of the following methods: (1) interrupt-initialized data transfer, (2) DMA data transfer.

For a computer to do its job of executing programs, the programs must be in main memory. Main memory is the only large storage area that the processor can access directly. It is an array of words or bytes, ranging in

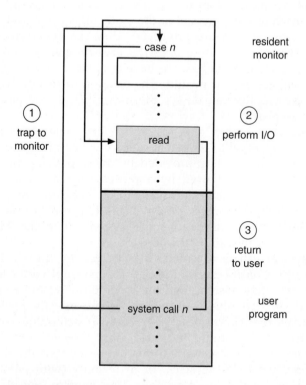

Figure 2.9 Use of a system call to perform I/O.

size from hundreds of thousands to hundreds of millions. Each word has its own address. The main memory is a *volatile* storage device that loses its contents when power is turned off or lost. Most computer systems provide *secondary storage* as an extension of main memory. The main requirement of secondary storage is to be able to hold extremely large numbers of data permanently. The most common secondary-storage device is a magnetic disk, which provides storage of both programs and data. A magnetic disk is a *nonvolatile* storage device that also provides random access. Magnetic tapes are used mainly for backup, for storage of infrequently used information, and as a medium for transferring information from one system to another.

The wide variety of storage systems in a computer system can be organized in a hierarchy according to their speed and their cost. The higher levels are expensive, but are fast. As we move down the hierarchy, the cost per bit decreases, whereas the access time increases.

The operating system must ensure correct operation of the computer system. To prevent user programs from interfering with the proper operation of the system, developers modified the hardware to create two modes: user mode and monitor mode. Various instructions (such as I/O instructions and halt instructions) are privileged, and can be executed in only monitor mode. The memory in which the operating system resides must also be protected from modification by the user. A timer prevents infinite loops. Once these changes (dual mode, privileged instructions, memory protection, timer interrupt) have been made to the basic computer architecture, it is possible to ensure the correct operation of the system. Chapter 3 continues this discussion with details of the facilities that operating systems provide.

■ Exercises

2.1 Buffering is a method of overlapping the I/O of a job with that job's own computation. The idea is quite simple. After data have been read and the CPU is about to start operating on them, the input device is instructed to begin the next input immediately. The CPU and input device are then both busy. With luck, by the time that the CPU is ready for the next data item, the input device will have finished reading it. The CPU can then begin processing the newly read data, while the input device starts to read the following data. Similarly, the same process can be used for output. In this case, the CPU creates data that are put into a buffer until an output device can accept them.

Compare the buffering scheme with the spooling scheme where the CPU overlaps the input of one job with the computation and output of other jobs.

2.2 Show how a desire for control cards leads naturally to the creation of separate user and monitor modes of operation.

2.3 How does the distinction between monitor mode and user mode function as a rudimentary form of protection (security) system?

2.4 What are the differences between a trap and an interrupt? What is the use of each function?

2.5 For what types of operations is DMA useful? Why?

2.6 Which of the following instructions should be privileged?

    a. Set value of timer.

    b. Read the clock.

    c. Clear memory.

    d. Turn off interrupts.

    e. Switch from user to monitor mode.

2.7 Many computer systems do not provide dual-mode operation in hardware. Consider whether it is possible to construct a secure operating system for these computers. Give arguments both that it is and that it is not possible.

2.8 Some early computers protected the operating system by placing it in a memory partition that could not be modified by either the user job or the operating system itself. Describe two difficulties that you think could arise with such a scheme.

2.9 Protecting the operating system is crucial to ensuring that the computer system operates correctly. Provision of this protection is the reason behind dual-mode operation, memory protection, and the timer. To allow maximum flexibility, however, we would also like to place minimal constraints on the user. The following is a list of operations that are normally protected. What is the *minimal* set of instructions that must be protected?

    a. Change to user mode.

    b. Change to monitor mode.

    c. Read from monitor memory.

    d. Write into monitor memory.

    e. Fetch an instruction from monitor memory.

    f. Turn on timer interrupt.

    g. Turn off timer interrupt.

2.10 When are caches useful? What problems do they solve? What problems do they cause? If a cache can be made as large as the device it is caching for (for instance, a cache as large as a disk) why not do so and eliminate the device?

2.11 Writing an operating system that can operate without interference from malicious or undebugged user programs requires some hardware assistance. Name three hardware aids for writing an operating system, and describe how they may be used together to protect the operating system.

Bibliographic Notes

A detailed description of I/O architectures such as channels and DMA on large systems appears in Baer [1980]. Hennessy and Patterson [1990] provide modern coverage of I/O systems and buses, and of system architecture in general. Tanenbaum [1990] describes the architecture of microcomputers, starting at a detailed hardware level.

General discussions concerning multiprocessing are given by Jones and Schwarz [1980]. Multiprocessor hardware is discussed by Satyanarayanan [1980]. Performance of multiprocessor systems is presented by Maples [1985], Sanguinetti [1986], Agrawal et al. [1986], and Bhuyan et al. [1989]. A survey of parallel computer architectures is presented by Duncan [1990].

Discussions concerning magnetic-disk technology are presented by Freedman [1983], and Harker et al. [1981]. Optical disks are covered by Kenville [1982], Fujitani [1984], O'Leary and Kitts [1985], Gait [1988], and Olsen and Kenly [1989]. Discussions of floppy disks are offered by Pechura and Schoeffler [1983] and Sarisky [1983].

Cache memories, including associative memory, are described and analyzed by Smith [1982]. This paper also includes an extensive bibliography on the subject. Hennessy and Patterson [1990] discuss the hardware aspects of TLBs, caches, and MMUs.

General discussions concerning mass-storage technology are offered by Chi [1982] and Hoagland [1985].

CHAPTER 3

OPERATING-SYSTEM STRUCTURES

An operating system provides the environment within which programs are executed. Internally, operating systems vary greatly in their makeup, being organized along many different lines. The design of a new operating system is a major task. It is important that the goals of the system be well defined before the design begins. The type of system desired is the foundation for choices among various algorithms and strategies that will be necessary.

There are several vantage points from which to view an operating system. One is by examining the services it provides. Another is by looking at the interface it makes available to users and programmers. A third is by disassembling the system into its components and their interconnections. In this chapter, we explore all three aspects of operating systems, to show them from the viewpoints of users, programmers, and operating-system designers. We consider what services an operating system provides, how they are provided, and what the various methodologies are for designing such systems.

3.1 ■ System Components

We can create a system as large and complex as an operating system only by partitioning it into smaller pieces. Each of these pieces should be a well-delineated portion of the system, with carefully defined inputs, outputs, and function. Obviously, not all systems have the same structure. However, many modern systems share the goal of supporting the types of system components outlined in Sections 3.1.1 through 3.1.8.

3.1.1 Process Management

A program does nothing unless its instructions are executed by a CPU. A *process* can be thought of as a program in execution, but its definition will broaden as we explore it further. Typically, a batch job is a process. A time-shared user program is a process. A system task, such as spooling output to a printer, also is a process. For now, you can consider a process to be a job or a time-shared program, but the concept is actually more general. As we shall see in Chapter 4, it is possible to provide system calls that allow processes to create subprocesses to execute concurrently.

A process needs certain resources, including CPU time, memory, files, and I/O devices, to accomplish its task. These resources are either given to the process when it is created, or allocated to it while it is running. In addition to the various physical and logical resources that a process obtains when it is created, some initialization data (input) may be passed along. For example, consider a process whose function is to display the status of a file on the screen of a terminal. The process will be given as an input the name of the file, and will execute the appropriate instructions and system calls to obtain the desired information and display it on the terminal. When the process terminates, the operating system will reclaim any reusable resources.

We emphasize that a program by itself is not a process; a program is a *passive* entity, such as the contents of a file stored on disk, whereas a process is an *active* entity, with a *program counter* specifying the next instruction to execute. The execution of a process must progress in a sequential fashion. The CPU executes one instruction of the process after another, until the process completes. Further, at any point in time, at most one instruction is executed on behalf of the process. Thus, although two processes may be associated with the same program, they are nevertheless considered two separate execution sequences. It is common to have a program that spawns many processes as it runs.

A process is the unit of work in a system. Such a system consists of a collection of processes, some of which are operating-system processes (those that execute system code) and the rest of which are user processes (those that execute user code). All these processes can potentially execute concurrently, by multiplexing the CPU among them.

The operating system is responsible for the following activities in connection with process management:

- The creation and deletion of both user and system processes
- The suspension and resumption of processes
- The provision of mechanisms for process synchronization
- The provision of mechanisms for process communication
- The provision of mechanisms for deadlock handling

Process-management techniques will be discussed in great detail in Chapters 4 to 7.

3.1.2 Main-Memory Management

As discussed in Chapter 1, memory is central to the operation of a modern computer system. Memory is a large array of words or bytes, each with its own address. It is a repository of quickly accessible data shared by the CPU and I/O devices. The central processor reads instructions from main memory during the instruction-fetch cycle, and both reads and writes data from main memory during the data-fetch cycle. I/O implemented via DMA also reads and writes data in main memory. Main memory is generally the only storage device that the CPU is able to address directly. For example, for the CPU to process data from disk, those data must first be transferred to main memory by CPU-generated I/O calls. Equivalently, instructions must be in memory for the CPU to execute them.

For a program to be executed, it must be mapped to absolute addresses and loaded into memory. As the program executes, it accesses program instructions and data from memory by generating these absolute addresses. Eventually, the program terminates, its memory space is declared available, and the next program can be loaded and executed.

To improve both the utilization of CPU and the speed of the computer's response to its users, we must keep several programs in memory. There are many different memory-management schemes. These schemes reflect various approaches to memory management, and the effectiveness of the different algorithms depends on the particular situation. Selection of a memory-management scheme for a specific system depends on many factors — especially on the *hardware* design of the system. Each algorithm requires its own hardware support.

The operating system is responsible for the following activities in connection with memory management:

- Keep track of which parts of memory are currently being used and by whom

- Decide which processes are to be loaded into memory when memory space becomes available

- Allocate and deallocate memory space as needed

Memory-management techniques will be discussed in great detail in Chapters 8 and 9.

3.1.3 Secondary-Storage Management

The main purpose of a computer system is to execute programs. These programs, with the data they access, must be in main memory (*primary storage*) during execution.   Because main memory is too small to accommodate all data and programs, and its data are lost when power is lost, the computer system must provide *secondary storage* to back up main memory. Most modern computer systems use disks as the principle on-line storage medium, for both programs and data. Most programs — including compilers, assemblers, sort routines, editors, and formatters — are stored on a disk until loaded into memory, and then use the disk as both the source and destination of their processing. Hence, the proper management of disk storage is of central importance to a computer system.

The operating system is responsible for the following activities in connection with disk management:

- Free-space management

- Storage allocation

- Disk scheduling

Because secondary storage is used frequently, it must be used efficiently. The entire speed of operation of a computer may hinge on the disk subsystem and the algorithms which manipulate it.   Techniques for secondary-storage management will be discussed in detail in Chapter 12.

3.1.4 I/O System Management

One of the purposes of an operating system is to hide the peculiarities of specific hardware devices from the user.   For example, in UNIX, the peculiarities of I/O devices are hidden from the bulk of the operating system itself by the *I/O system*. The I/O system consists of

- A buffer-caching system

- A general device-driver interface

- Drivers for specific hardware devices

Only the device driver knows the peculiarities of the specific device to which it is assigned.

We have already discussed in Chapter 2 how interrupt handlers and device drivers are used in the construction of efficient I/O systems.   In Chapter 12, we shall discuss at great length how a particular device (the disk) is managed effectively.

3.1.5 File Management

File management is one of the most visible components of an operating system. Computers can store information on several different types of physical media. Magnetic tape, magnetic disk, and optical disk are the most common media. Each of these media has its own characteristics and physical organization. Each medium is controlled by a device, such as a disk drive or tape drive, with its own unique characteristics. These properties include speed, capacity, data transfer rate, and access method (sequential or random access method).

For convenient use of the computer system, the operating system provides a uniform logical view of information storage. The operating system abstracts from the physical properties of its storage devices to define a logical storage unit, the *file*. The operating system maps files onto physical media, and accesses these files via the storage devices.

A file is a collection of related information defined by its creator. Commonly, files represent programs (both source and object forms) and data. Data files may be numeric, alphabetic, or alphanumeric. Files may be free-form, such as text files, or may be formatted rigidly. A file consists of a sequence of bits, bytes, lines, or records whose meanings are defined by their creators. The concept of a file is an extremely general one.

The operating system implements the abstract concept of a file by managing mass storage media, such as tapes and disks, and the devices which control them. Also, files are normally organized into directories to ease their use. Finally, when multiple users have access to files, it may be desirable to control by whom and in what ways files may be accessed.

The operating system is responsible for the following activities in connection with file management:

- The creation and deletion of files

- The creation and deletion of directories

- The support of primitives for manipulating files and directories

- The mapping of files onto secondary storage

- The backup of files on stable (nonvolatile) storage media

File-management techniques will be discussed in Chapters 10 and 11.

3.1.6 Protection System

If a system has multiple users and allows multiple concurrent processes, the various processes must be protected from one another's activities. For that purpose, mechanisms are provided to ensure that the files, memory segments, CPU, and other resources can be operated on by only those processes that have gained proper authorization from the operating system.

For example, memory-addressing hardware ensures that a process can execute only within its own address space. The timer ensures that no process can gain control of the CPU without eventually relinquishing control. Finally, users are not allowed to do their own I/O, so that the integrity of the various peripheral devices is protected.

Protection refers to a mechanism for controlling the access of programs, processes, or users to the resources defined by a computer system. This mechanism must provide a means for specification of the controls to be imposed, together with a means of enforcement.

Protection can improve reliability by detecting latent errors at the interfaces between component subsystems. Early detection of interface errors can often prevent contamination of a healthy subsystem by a subsystem that is malfunctioning. An unprotected resource cannot defend against use (or misuse) by an unauthorized or incompetent user. A protection-oriented system provides a means to distinguish between authorized and unauthorized usage, as will be discussed in Chapter 13.

3.1.7 Networking

A *distributed* system is a collection of processors that do not share memory or a clock. Instead, each processor has its own local memory, and the processors communicate with one another through various communication lines, such as high-speed buses or telephone lines. The processors in a distributed system vary in size and function. They may include small microprocessors, workstations, minicomputers, and large general-purpose computer systems.

The processors in the system are connected through a *communication network*, which can be configured in a number of different ways. The network may be fully or partially connected. The communication-network design must consider routing and connection strategies, and the problems of contention and security.

A distributed system collects physically separate, possibly heterogeneous systems into a single coherent system, providing the user with access to the various resources that the system maintains. Access to a shared resource allows computation speedup, increased data availability, and enhanced reliability. Operating systems usually generalize network access as a form of file access, with the details of networking being contained in the network interface's device driver.

Discussions concerning network and distributed systems are presented in Chapters 15 to 18.

3.1.8 Command-Interpreter System

One of the most important system programs for an operating system is the *command interpreter*, which is the interface between the user and the operating system. Some operating systems include the command interpreter in the kernel. Other operating systems, such as MS-DOS and UNIX, treat the command interpreter as a special program that is running when a job is initiated, or when a user first logs on (on time-sharing systems).

Many commands are given to the operating system by *control statements*. When a new job is started in a batch system, or when a user logs on to a time-shared system, a program that reads and interprets control statements is executed automatically. This program is variously called the *control-card interpreter*, the *command-line interpreter*, the *shell* (in UNIX), and so on. Its function is quite simple: Get the next command statement and execute it.

Operating systems are frequently differentiated in the area of command interpretation, with a user-friendly interpreter making the system more agreeable to some users. An example of a user-friendly interface is the Macintosh interpreter, a window and menu system that is almost exclusively mouse-based. The user uses the mouse to point with the cursor to images (or *icons*) on the screen that represent programs, files, and system functions. Depending on the cursor location, clicking the mouse's button can invoke a program, select a file or directory (known as a *folder*), or pull down a menu containing commands. More powerful, complex, and difficult-to-learn interpreters are appreciated by other, more sophisticated users. On these interpreters, commands are typed on a keyboard and displayed on a screen or printing terminal, with the enter (or return) key signaling that a command is complete and is ready to be executed. The UNIX shells run in this mode.

The command statements themselves deal with process creation and management, I/O handling, secondary-storage management, main memory management, file-system access, protection, and networking.

3.2 ■ Operating-System Services

An operating system provides an environment for the execution of programs. The operating system provides certain services to programs and to the users of those programs. The specific services provided will, of course, differ from one operating system to another, but there are some common classes that we can identify. These operating-system services are provided for the convenience of the programmer, to make the programming task easier.

- **Program execution:** The system must be able to load a program into memory and to run it. The program must be able to end its execution, either normally or abnormally (indicating error).

- **I/O operations:** A running program may require I/O. This I/O may involve a file or an I/O device. For specific devices, special functions may be desired (such as rewind a tape drive, or blank the screen on a CRT). For efficiency and protection, users cannot control I/O devices directly. Therefore, the operating system must provide some means to do I/O.

- **File-system manipulation:** The file system is of particular interest. It should be obvious that programs need to read and write files. They also need to create and delete files by name.

- **Communications:** There are many circumstances in which one process needs to exchange information with another process. There are two major ways in which such communication can occur. The first takes place between processes executing on the same computer; the second takes place between processes executing on different computer systems that are tied together by a computer network. Communications may be implemented via *shared memory*, or by the technique of *message passing*, in which packets of information are moved between processes by the operating system.

- **Error detection:** The operating system constantly needs to be aware of possible errors. Errors may occur in the CPU and memory hardware (such as a memory error or a power failure), in I/O devices (such as a parity error on tape, a connection failure on a network, or lack of paper in the printer), or in the user program (such as an arithmetic overflow, an attempt to access an illegal memory location, or a too great use of CPU time). For each type of error, the operating system should take the appropriate action to ensure correct and consistent computing.

In addition, another set of operating-system functions exists not for helping the user, but rather for ensuring the efficient operation of the system itself. Systems with multiple users can gain efficiency by sharing the computer resources among the users.

- **Resource allocation:** When there are multiple users or multiple jobs running at the same time, resources must be allocated to each of them. Many different types of resources are managed by the operating system. Some (such as CPU cycles, main memory, and file storage) may have special allocation code, whereas others (such as I/O devices) may have much more general request and release code. For instance, in determining how best to use the CPU, operating systems have CPU-scheduling routines that take into account the speed of the CPU, the jobs that must be executed, the number of registers available, and other factors. There might also be routines to allocate a tape drive for use by a job. One such routine locates an unused tape drive and marks an internal table to record the drive's new user. Another routine is used to clear that table. These routines may also be used to allocate plotters, modems, and other peripheral devices.

- **Accounting:** We want to keep track of which users use how much and what kinds of computer resources. This record keeping may be for accounting (so that users can be billed) or simply for accumulating usage statistics. Usage statistics may be a valuable tool for researchers who wish to reconfigure the system to improve computing services.

- **Protection:** The owners of information stored in a multiuser computer system may want to control its use. When several disjoint processes execute concurrently, it should not be possible for one process to interfere with the others, or with the operating system itself. Protection involves ensuring that all access to system resources is controlled. *Security* of the system from outsiders is also important. Such security starts with each user having to authenticate himself or herself to the system, usually by means of a password, to be allowed access to the resources. It extends to defending external I/O devices, including modems and network adapters, from invalid access attempts, and to recording all such connections for detection of breakins. If a system is to be protected and secure, precautions must be instituted throughout it. A chain is only as strong as its weakest link.

3.3 ∎ System Calls

System calls provide the interface between a process and the operating system. These calls are generally available as assembly-language instructions, and are usually listed in the manuals used by assembly-language programmers.

Some systems may allow system calls to be made directly from a higher-level language program, in which case the calls normally resemble predefined function or subroutine calls. They may generate a call to a special run-time routine that makes the system call, or the system call may be generated directly in-line.

Several languages — such as C, Bliss, BCPL, and PL/360 — have been defined to replace assembly language for systems programming. These languages allow system calls to be made directly. Some Pascal systems also provide an ability to make system calls directly from a Pascal program to the operating system. Most FORTRAN systems provide similar capabilities, often by a set of library routines.

As an example of how system calls are used, consider writing a simple program to read data from one file and to copy them to another file. The first input that the program will need is the names of the two files: the input file and the output file. These names can be specified in many ways, depending on the operating-system design. One approach is for the program to ask the user for the names of the two files. In an interactive system, this approach will require a sequence of system calls, first to write a prompting message on the screen, and then to read from the keyboard the characters that define the two files. Another approach, frequently used for batch systems, is to specify the names of the files with control cards. In this case, there must be a mechanism for passing these parameters from the control cards to the executing program. On mouse-based and icon-based systems, a menu of file names is usually displayed in a window. The user can then use the mouse to select the source name, and a window can be opened for the destination name to be specified.

Once the two file names are obtained, the program must open the input file and create the output file. Each of these operations requires another system call. There are also possible error conditions for each operation. When the program tries to open the input file, it may find that there is no file of that name or that the file is protected against access. In these cases, the program should print a message on the console (another sequence of system calls) and then terminate abnormally (another system call). If the input file exists, then we must create a new output file. We may find that there is already an output file with the same name. This situation may cause the program to abort (a system call), or we may delete the existing file (another system call) and create a new one (another system call). Another option, in an interactive system, is to ask the user (a sequence of system calls to output the prompting message and to read the response from the terminal) whether to replace the existing file or to abort.

Now that both files are set up, we enter a loop that reads from the input file (a system call) and writes to the output file (another system call). Each read and write must return status information regarding various possible error conditions. On input, the program may find that the end of the file has been reached, or that there was a hardware failure in the read (such as a parity error). The write operation may encounter various errors, depending on the output device (no more disk space, physical end of tape, printer out of paper, and so on).

Finally, after the entire file is copied, the program may close both files (another system call), write a message to the console (more system calls), and finally terminate normally (the last system call). As we can see, programs may make heavy use of the operating system.

Most users never see this level of detail, however. The run-time support system for most programming languages provides a much simpler interface. For example, a *write* statement in Pascal or FORTRAN probably is compiled into a call to a run-time support routine that issues the necessary system calls, checks for errors, and finally returns to the user program. Thus, most of the details of the operating-system interface are hidden from the programmer by the compiler and by the run-time support package.

System calls occur in different ways, depending on the computer in use. Often, more information is required than simply the identity of the desired system call. The exact type and amount of information vary according to the particular operating system and call. For example, to get input, we may need to specify the file or device to use as the source, and the address and length of the memory buffer into which the input should be read. Of course, the device or file and length may be implicit in the call.

Three general methods are used to pass parameters to the operating system. The simplest approach is to pass the parameters in *registers*. In some cases, however, there may be more parameters than registers. In these cases, the parameters are generally stored in a *block* or table in memory, and the address of the block is passed as a parameter in a register (Figure 3.1). Parameters also can be placed, or *pushed*, onto the *stack* by the program, and *popped* off the stack by the operating system. Some operating systems prefer the block or stack methods, because they do not limit the number or length of parameters being passed.

System calls can be roughly grouped into five major categories: *process control, file manipulation, device manipulation, information maintenance,* and *communications*. In Sections 3.3.1 to 3.3.5, we discuss briefly the types of system calls that may be provided by an operating system. Unfortunately, our description may seem somewhat shallow, as most of these system calls support, or are supported by, concepts and functions that are discussed in later chapters. Figure 3.2 summarizes the types of system calls normally provided by an operating system.

3.3.1 Process and Job Control

A running program needs to be able to halt its execution either normally (**end**) or abnormally (**abort**). If a system call is made to terminate the currently running program abnormally, or if the program runs into a problem and causes an error trap, a dump of memory is sometimes taken and an error message generated. The dump is written to disk and may be examined by a *debugger* to determine the cause of the problem. Under either normal or abnormal circumstances, the operating system must

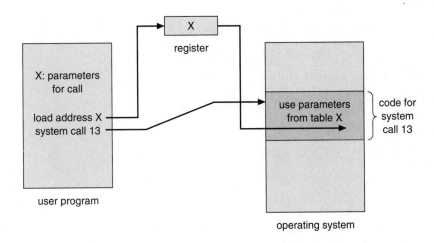

Figure 3.1 Passing of parameters as a table.

- Process control
  - ○ end, abort
  - ○ load, execute
  - ○ create process, terminate process
  - ○ get process attributes, set process attributes
  - ○ wait for time
  - ○ wait event, signal event
  - ○ allocate and free memory
- File manipulation
  - ○ create file, delete file
  - ○ open, close
  - ○ read, write, reposition
  - ○ get file attributes, set file attributes
- Device manipulation
  - ○ request device, release device
  - ○ read, write, reposition
  - ○ get device attributes, set device attributes
  - ○ logically attach or detach devices
- Information maintenance
  - ○ get time or date, set time or date
  - ○ get system data, set system data
  - ○ get process, file, or device attributes
  - ○ set process, file, or device attributes
- Communications
  - ○ create, delete communication connection
  - ○ send, receive messages
  - ○ transfer status information
  - ○ attach or detach remote devices

Figure 3.2 Types of system calls.

transfer control to the command interpreter. The command interpreter then reads the next command. In an interactive system, the command interpreter simply continues with the next command; it is assumed that the user will issue an appropriate command to respond to any error. In a batch system, the command interpreter usually terminates the entire job and continues with the next job. Some systems allow control cards to indicate special recovery actions in case an error occurs. If the program discovers an error in its input and wants to terminate abnormally, it may also want to define an error level. More severe errors can be indicated by a higher-level error parameter. It is then possible to combine normal and abnormal termination by defining a normal termination as error at level 0. The command interpreter or a following program can use this error level to determine the next action automatically.

A process or job executing one program may want to **load** and **execute** another program. This feature allows the command interpreter to execute a program as directed by, for example, a user command, the click of a mouse, or a batch command. An interesting question is where to return control when the loaded program terminates. This question is related to the problem of whether the existing program is lost, saved, or allowed to continue execution concurrently with the new program.

If control returns to the existing program when the new program terminates, we must save the memory image of the existing program; thus, we have effectively created a mechanism for one program to call another program. If both programs continue concurrently, we have created a new job or process to be multiprogrammed. Often, there is a system call specifically for this purpose (**create process** or **submit job**).

If we create a new job or process, or perhaps even a set of jobs or processes, we should be able to control its execution. This control requires the ability to determine and reset the attributes of a job or process, including the job's priority, its maximum allowable execution time, and so on (**get process attributes** and **set process attributes**). We may also want to terminate a job or process that we created (**terminate process**) if we find that it is incorrect or is no longer needed.

Having created new jobs or processes, we may need to wait for them to finish their execution. We may want to wait for a certain amount of time (**wait time**); more probably, we may want to wait for a specific event to occur (**wait event**). The jobs or processes should then signal when that event has occurred (**signal event**). System calls of this type, dealing with the coordination of concurrent processes, are discussed in great detail in Chapter 6.

Another set of system calls is helpful in debugging a program. Many systems provide system calls to **dump** memory. This provision is useful for debugging. A program **trace** lists each instruction as it is executed; it is provided by fewer systems. Even microprocessors provide a CPU mode known as *single step*, in which a trap is executed by the CPU after every instruction. The trap is usually caught by a debugger, which is a system program designed to aid the programmer in finding and correcting bugs.

A time profile of a program is provided by many systems. It indicates the amount of time that the program executes at a particular location or set of locations. A time profile requires either a tracing facility or regular timer interrupts. At every occurrence of the timer interrupt, the value of the program counter is recorded. With sufficiently frequent timer interrupts, a statistical picture of the time spent on various parts of the program can be obtained.

There are so many facets of and variations in process and job control that we shall use examples to clarify these concepts. The MS-DOS operating system is an example of a single-tasking system, which has a command interpreter that is invoked when the computer is started (Figure 3.3(a)). Because MS-DOS is single-tasking, it uses a simple method to run a program, and does not create a new process. It loads the program into memory, writing over most of itself to give the program as much memory as possible (Figure 3.3(b)). It then sets the instruction pointer to the first instruction of the program. The program then runs and either an error causes a trap, or the program executes a system call to terminate. In either case, the error code is saved in the system memory for later use. Following this action, the small portion of the command interpreter that was not overwritten resumes execution. Its first task is to reload the rest of the command interpreter from disk. Once this task is accomplished, the command interpreter makes the previous error code available to the user or to the next program.

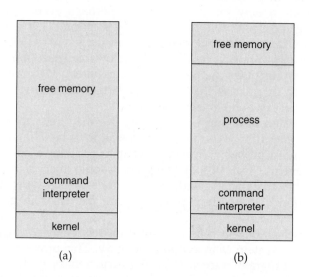

Figure 3.3 MS-DOS execution. (a) At system startup. (b) Running a program.

Berkeley UNIX, on the other hand, is an example of a multitasking system. When a user logs on to the system, a command interpreter (called a *shell*) of the user's choice is run. This shell is similar to the MS-DOS command interpreter (in fact, MS-DOS is modeled after UNIX) in that it accepts commands and executes programs that the user requests. However, since UNIX is a multitasking system, the command interpreter may continue running while another program is executed (Figure 3.4). To start a new process, the shell executes a **fork** system call. Then, the selected program is loaded into memory via an **exec** system call, and the program is then executed. Depending on the way the command was issued, the shell then either waits for the process to finish, or runs the process "in the background". In the latter case, the shell immediately requests another command. When a process is running in the background, it cannot receive input directly from the user, because the shell is expecting input also. I/O is therefore done through files. Meanwhile, the user is free to ask the shell to run other programs, to monitor the progress of the running process, to change that program's priority, and so on. When the process is done, it executes an **exit** system call to terminate, returning to the invoking process a status code of 0, or a nonzero error code. This status or error code is then available to the shell or other programs. Processes are discussed in Chapter 4.

3.3.2 File Manipulation

The file system will be discussed in more detail in Chapters 10 and 11. We can identify several common system calls dealing with files, however.

Figure 3.4 UNIX running multiple programs.

We first need to be able to **create** and **delete** files. Either system call requires the name of the file and perhaps some of the file's attributes. Once the file is created, we need to **open** it and to use it. We may also **read, write,** or **reposition** (rewinding or skipping to the end of the file, for example). Finally, we need to **close** the file, indicating that we are no longer using it.

We may need these same sets of operations for directories if we have a directory structure for organizing files in the file system. In addition, for either files or directories, we need to be able to determine the values of various attributes, and perhaps to reset them if necessary. File attributes include the file name, a file type, protection codes, accounting information, and so on. At least two system calls, **get file attribute** and **set file attribute,** are required for this function. Some operating systems provide many more calls.

3.3.3 Device Management

A program, as it is running, may need additional resources to proceed. Additional resources may be more memory, tape drives, access to files, and so on. If the resources are available, they can be granted, and control can be returned to the user program; otherwise, the program will have to wait until sufficient resources are available.

Files can be thought of as abstract or virtual devices. Thus, many of the system calls for files are also needed for devices. If there are multiple users of the system, however, we must first **request** the device, to ensure exclusive use of it. After we are finished with the device, we must **release** it. These functions are similar to the **open** and **close** system calls for files.

Once the device has been requested (and allocated to us), we can **read, write,** and (possibly) **reposition** the device, just as we can with files. In fact, the similarity between I/O devices and files is so great that many operating systems, including UNIX and MS-DOS, merge the two into a combined file−device structure. In this case, I/O devices are identified by special file names.

3.3.4 Information Maintenance

Many system calls exist simply for the purpose of transferring information between the user program and the operating system. For example, most systems have a system call to return the current **time** and **date.** Other system calls may return information about the system, such as the number of current users, the version number of the operating system, the amount of free memory or disk space, and so on.

In addition, the operating system keeps information about all its processes, and there are system calls to access this information. Generally, there are also calls to reset the process information (**get process attributes** and **set process attributes**). In Section 4.1.3, we discuss what information is normally kept.

3.3.5 Communication

There are two common models of communication. In the *message-passing model*, information is exchanged through an interprocess-communication facility provided by the operating system. Before communication can take place, a connection must be opened. The name of the other communicator must be known, be it another process on the same CPU, or a process on another computer connected by a communications network. Each computer in a network has a *host name* by which it is commonly known. Similarly, each process has a *process name*, which is translated into an equivalent identifier by which the operating system can refer to it. The **get hostid,** and **get processid** system calls do this translation. These identifiers are then passed to the general-purpose **open** and **close** calls provided by the file system, or to specific **open connection** and **close connection** system calls, depending on the system's model of communications. The recipient process usually must give its permission for communication to take place with an **accept connection** call. Most processes that will be receiving connections are special-purpose *daemons*, which are system programs provided for that purpose. They execute a **wait for connection** call and are awakened when a connection is made. The source of the communication, known as the *client*, and the receiving daemon, known as a *server*, then exchange messages by **read message** and **write message** system calls. The **close connection** call terminates the communication.

In the *shared-memory model*, processes use **map memory** system calls to gain access to regions of memory owned by other processes. Recall that, normally, the operating system tries to prevent one process from accessing another process' memory. Shared memory requires that two or more processes agree to remove this restriction. They may then exchange information by reading and writing data in these shared areas. The form of the data and the location are determined by these processes and are not under the operating system's control. The processes are also responsible for ensuring that they are not writing to the same location simultaneously. Such mechanisms are discussed in Chapter 6.

Both of these methods are common in operating systems, and some systems even implement both. Message passing is useful when smaller numbers of data need to be exchanged, because no conflicts need to be avoided. It is also easier to implement than is shared memory for intercomputer communication. Shared memory allows maximum speed and convenience of communication, as it can be done at memory speeds when within a computer. Problems exist, however, in the areas of protection and synchronization. The two communications models are contrasted in Figure 3.5.

3.4 ■ System Programs

Another aspect of a modern system is the collection of system programs. Recall Figure 1.1, which depicted the logical computer hierarchy. At the lowest level is hardware, of course. Next is the operating system, then the systems programs, and finally the application programs. System programs provide a more convenient environment for program development and execution. Some of them are simply user interfaces to system calls, whereas others are considerably more complex. They can be divided into several categories:

- **File manipulation:** These programs create, delete, copy, rename, print, dump, list, and generally manipulate files and directories.

- **Status information:** Some programs simply ask the system for the date, time, amount of available memory or disk space, number of users, or similar status information. That information is then formatted, and is printed to the terminal or other output device or file.

- **File modification:** Several text editors may be available to create and modify the content of files stored on disk or tape.

- **Programming-language support:** Compilers, assemblers, and interpreters for common programming languages (such as FORTRAN, COBOL, Pascal, BASIC, C, and LISP) are often provided to the user with

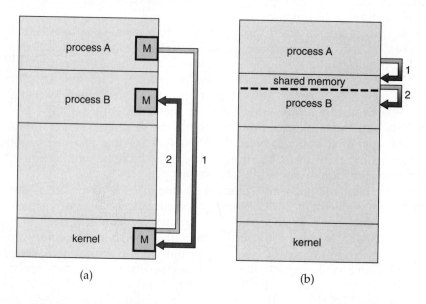

Figure 3.5 Communications models. (a) Message passing. (b) Shared memory.

the operating system. Many of these programs are now priced and provided separately.

- **Program loading and execution:** Once a program is assembled or compiled, it must be loaded into memory to be executed. The system may provide absolute loaders, relocatable loaders, linkage editors, and overlay loaders. Debugging systems for either higher-level languages or machine language are needed also.

- **Communications:** These programs provide the mechanism for creating virtual connections among processes, users, and different computer systems. They allow users to send messages to each other's screens, to send larger messages as electronic mail, or to transfer files from one machine to another, and even to use other computers remotely as though these machines were local (known as *remote login*).

- **Application programs:** Most operating systems are supplied with programs that are useful to solve common problems, or to perform common operations. Such programs include compiler compilers, text formatters, plotting packages, database systems, spreadsheets, statistical-analysis packages, and games.

Perhaps the most important system program for an operating system is the *command interpreter*, the main function of which is to get and execute the next user-specified command.

Many of the commands given at this level manipulate files: create, delete, list, print, copy, execute, and so on. There are two general ways in which these commands can be implemented. In one approach, the command interpreter itself contains the code to execute the command. For example, a command to delete a file may cause the command interpreter to jump to a section of its code that sets up the parameters and makes the appropriate system call. In this case, the number of commands that can be given determines the size of the command interpreter, since each command requires its own implementing code.

An alternative approach used by UNIX, among other operating systems, implements most commands by special systems programs. In this case, the command interpreter does not "understand" the command in any way; it merely uses the command to identify a file to be loaded into memory and executed. Thus, a command

delete G

would search for a file called *delete*, load the file into memory, and execute it with the parameter G. The function associated with the **delete** command would be defined completely by the code in the file *delete*. In this way, programmers can add new commands to the system easily by creating new files of the proper name. The command-interpreter program, which can now be quite small, does not have to be changed for new commands to be added.

There are problems with this approach to the design of a command interpreter. Notice first that, because the code to execute a command is a separate system program, the operating system must provide a mechanism for passing parameters from the command interpreter to the system program. This task can often be clumsy, because the command interpreter and the system program may not both be in memory at the same time, and the parameter list can be extensive. Also, it is slower to load a program and to execute it than simply to jump to another section of code within the current program.

Another problem is that the interpretation of the parameters is left up to the programmer of the system program. Thus, parameters may be provided inconsistently across programs that appear similar to the user, but that were written at different times by different programmers.

The view of the operating system seen by most users is thus defined by the systems programs, rather than by the actual system calls. Consider IBM PC compatibles. Running the same MS-DOS operating system, the user could see a command-line−based command interpreter, or, could run the Windows program to invoke a graphical, Apple Macintosh−like interface. Both use the same set of system calls, but they appear and act dissimilar. Consequently, this user view may be substantially removed from the actual system structure. The design of a useful and friendly user interface is therefore not a direct function of the operating system. In this book, we shall concentrate on the fundamental problems of providing adequate service to user programs. From the point of view of the operating system, we do not distinguish between user programs and systems programs.

3.5 ■ System Structure

A system as large and complex as a modern operating system must be engineered carefully if it is to function properly and to be modified easily. A common approach is to partition the task into small components, rather than have one monolithic system. Each of these modules should be a well-defined portion of the system, with carefully defined inputs, outputs, and function. We have already discussed briefly the common components of operating systems (Section 3.1). In this section, we discuss the way that these components are interconnected and melded into a kernel.

3.5.1 Simple Structure

There are numerous commercial systems that do not have a well-defined structure. Frequently, such operating systems started as small, simple, and limited systems, and then grew beyond their original scope. An example of such a system is MS-DOS, the best-selling microcomputer operating system. MS-DOS was originally designed and implemented by a few people who had no idea that it would become so popular. It was written to provide the most functionality in the least space, because of the limited hardware on which it ran, so it was not divided into modules carefully. Figure 3.6 shows its current structure.

Although MS-DOS does have some structure, its interfaces and levels of functionality are not well separated. For instance, applications programs are able to access the basic I/O routines to write directly to the display and disk drives. Such freedom leaves MS-DOS vulnerable to errant (or malicious) programs, causing entire system crashes or disk erasures when user programs fail. Of course, MS-DOS is also limited by the hardware on which it runs. Because the Intel 8088 for which it was written provides no dual mode and no hardware protection, the designers of MS-DOS had no choice but to leave the base hardware accessible.

Another example of limited structuring is the original UNIX operating system. UNIX is another system that initially was limited by hardware functionality. It consists of two separable parts: the kernel and the systems programs. The kernel is further separated into a series of interfaces and device drivers, which have been added and expanded over the years as UNIX has evolved. We can view the UNIX operating system as being layered as shown in Figure 3.7. Everything below the system-call interface and above the physical hardware is the kernel. The kernel provides the file system, CPU scheduling, memory management, and other operating-system functions through system calls. Taken in sum, that is an enormous amount

Figure 3.6 MS-DOS layer structure.

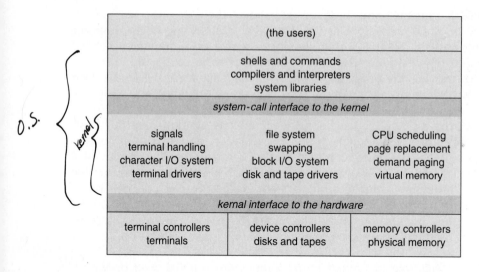

O.S. { kernel {

(the users)		
shells and commands compilers and interpreters system libraries		
system-call interface to the kernel		
signals terminal handling character I/O system terminal drivers	file system swapping block I/O system disk and tape drivers	CPU scheduling page replacement demand paging virtual memory
kernal interface to the hardware		
terminal controllers terminals	device controllers disks and tapes	memory controllers physical memory

Figure 3.7 UNIX system structure.

of functionality to be combined into one level. Systems programs use the kernel-supported system calls to provide useful functions, such as compilation and file manipulation.

System calls define the *programmer interface* to UNIX; the set of systems programs commonly available defines the *user interface*. The programmer and user interfaces define the context that the kernel must support. Several versions of UNIX have been developed in which the kernel is partitioned further along functional boundaries. The AIX operating system, IBM's version of UNIX, separates the kernel into two parts. Mach, from Carnegie Mellon University, reduces the kernel to a small set of core functions by moving all nonessentials into systems and even into user-level programs. What remains is a *microkernel* operating system implementing only a small set of necessary primitives.

3.5.2 Layered Approach

These new UNIX versions are designed to use more advanced hardware. Given proper hardware support, operating systems may be broken into smaller, more appropriate pieces than those allowed by the original MS-DOS or UNIX. The operating system can then retain much greater control over the computer and the applications that make use of that computer. Implementors have more freedom to make changes to the inner workings of the system. Familiar techniques are used to aid in the creation of modular operating systems. Under the top-down approach, the overall functionality and features can be determined and separated into components. Information hiding is also important, leaving programmers free to implement the low-level routines as they see fit, provided that the external interface of the routine stays unchanged and the routine itself performs the advertised task.

The modularization of a system can be done in many ways; the most appealing is the layered approach, which consists of breaking the operating system into a number of layers (levels), each built on top of lower layers. The bottom layer (layer 0) is the hardware; the highest (layer N) is the user interface.

An operating-system layer is an implementation of an abstract object that is the encapsulation of data, and operations that can manipulate those data. A typical operating-system layer — say layer M — is depicted in Figure 3.8. It consists of some data structures and a set of routines that can be invoked by higher-level layers. Layer M, in return, can invoke operations on lower-level layers.

The main advantage of the layered approach is *modularity*. The layers are selected such that each uses functions (operations) and services of only lower-level layers. This approach simplifies debugging and system verification. The first layer can be debugged without any concern for the rest of the system, because, by definition, it uses only the basic hardware (which is assumed correct) to implement its functions. Once the first layer is debugged, its correct functioning can be assumed while the second layer is worked on, and so on. If an error is found during the debugging of a particular layer, we know that the error must be on that layer, because the layers below it are already debugged. Thus, the design and implementation of the system is simplified when the system is broken down into layers.

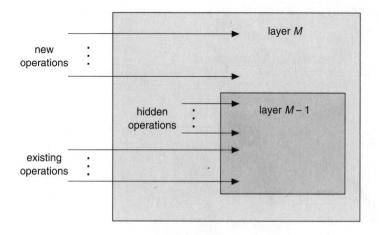

Figure 3.8 An operating-system layer.

Each layer is implemented using only those operations provided by lower-level layers. A layer does not need to know how these operations are implemented; it needs to know only what these operations do. Hence, each layer hides the existence of certain data structures, operations, and hardware from higher-level layers.

The layer approach to design was first used in the THE operating system at the Technische Hogeschool Eindhoven. The THE system was defined in six layers, as shown in Figure 3.9. The bottom layer was the hardware. The next layer implemented CPU scheduling. The next layer implemented memory management; the memory-management scheme was virtual memory (Chapter 9). Layer 3 contained the device driver for the operator's console. Because it, as well as the I/O buffering, was placed at layer 4, above memory management, the device buffers could be placed in virtual memory. The I/O buffering was also above the operator's console, so that I/O error conditions could be output to the operator's console.

This approach can be used in many ways. For example, the Venus system was also designed using a layered approach. The lower layers (0 to 4), dealing with CPU scheduling and memory management, were then put into microcode. This decision provided the advantages of additional speed of execution and a clearly defined interface between the microcoded layers and the higher layers (Figure 3.10).

The major difficulty with the layered approach involves the appropriate definition of the various layers. Because a layer can use only those layers that are at a lower level, careful planning is necessary. For example, the device driver for the backing store (disk space used by virtual-memory algorithms) must be at a level lower than that of the memory-management routines, because memory management requires the ability to use the backing store.

Other requirements may not be so obvious. The backing-store driver would normally be above the CPU scheduler, because the driver may need

layer 5:	user programs
layer 4:	buffering for input and output devices
layer 3:	operator-console device driver
layer 2:	memory management
layer 1:	CPU scheduling
layer 0:	hardware

Figure 3.9 THE layer structure.

layer 6:	user programs
layer 5:	device drivers and schedulers
layer 4:	virtual memory
layer 3:	I/O channel
layer 2:	CPU scheduling
layer 1:	instruction interpreter
layer 0:	hardware

Figure 3.10   Venus layer structure.

to wait for I/O and the CPU can be rescheduled during this time. However, on a large system, the CPU scheduler may have more information about all the active processes than can fit in memory. Therefore, this information may need to be swapped in and out of memory, requiring the backing-store driver routine to be below the CPU scheduler.

A final problem with layered implementations is that they tend to be less efficient than other types. For instance, for a user program to execute an I/O operation, it executes a system call which is trapped to the I/O layer, which calls the memory-management layer, through to the CPU scheduling layer, and finally to the hardware. At each layer, the parameters may be modified, data may need to be passed, and so on. Each layer adds *overhead* to the system call and the net result is a system call that takes longer than one does on a nonlayered system.

These limitations have caused a small backlash against layering in recent years. Fewer layers with more functionality are being designed, providing most of the advantages of modularized code while avoiding the difficult problems of layer definition and interaction. OS/2, a direct descendant of MS-DOS, was created to overcome the limitations of MS-DOS. OS/2 adds multitasking and dual-mode operation, as well as other new features. Because of this added complexity and the more powerful hardware for which OS/2 was designed, the system was implemented in a more layered fashion. Contrast the MS-DOS structure to that shown in Figure 3.11. It should be clear that, from both the system-design and implementation standpoints, OS/2 has the advantage. For instance, direct user access to low-level facilities is not allowed, providing the operating system with more control over the hardware and more knowledge of which resources each user program is using.

Figure 3.11 OS/2 layer structure.

3.6 ■ Virtual Machines

Conceptually, a computer system is made up of layers. The hardware is the lowest level in all such systems. The kernel running at the next level uses the hardware instructions to create a set of system calls for use by outer layers. The systems programs above the kernel are therefore able to use either system calls or hardware instructions, and in some ways these programs do not differentiate between these two. Thus, although they are accessed differently, they both provide functionality that the program can use to create even more advanced functions. System programs, in turn, treat the hardware and the system calls as though they both are at the same level.

Some systems carry this scheme even a step further by allowing the system programs to be called easily by the application programs. As before, although the system programs are at a level higher than that of the other routines, the application programs may view everything under them in the hierarchy as though the latter were part of the machine itself. This layered approach is taken to its logical conclusion in the concept of a *virtual machine*. The VM operating system for IBM systems is the best example of the virtual-machine concept, because IBM pioneered the work in this area.

By using CPU scheduling (Chapter 5) and virtual-memory techniques (Chapter 9), an operating system can create the illusion of multiple processes, each executing on its own processor with its own (virtual) memory. Of course, normally, the process has additional features, such as system calls and a file system, which are not provided by the bare hardware. The virtual-machine approach, on the other hand, does not provide any additional function, but rather provides an interface that is *identical* to the underlying bare hardware. Each process is provided with a (virtual) copy of the underlying computer (Figure 3.12).

The resources of the physical computer are shared to create the virtual machines. CPU scheduling can be used to share the CPU and to create the appearance that users have their own processor. Spooling and a file system can provide virtual card readers and virtual line printers. A normal user time-sharing terminal provides the function of the virtual machine operator's console.

A major difficulty with the virtual machine-approach involves disk systems. Suppose that the physical machine has three disk drives but wants to support seven virtual machines. Clearly, it cannot allocate a disk

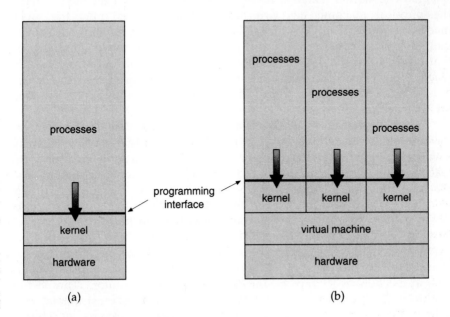

Figure 3.12   System models. (a) Nonvirtual machine. (b) Virtual machine.

drive to each virtual machine. Remember that the virtual-machine software itself will need substantial disk space to provide virtual memory and spooling. The solution is to provide virtual disks, which are identical in all respects except size. These are termed *minidisks* in IBM's VM operating system. The system implements each minidisk by allocating as many tracks as the minidisk needs on the physical disks. Obviously, the sum of the sizes of all minidisks must be less than the actual amount of physical disk space available.

Users thus are given their own virtual machine. They can then run any of the operating systems or software packages that are available on the underlying machine. For the IBM VM system, a user normally runs CMS, a single-user interactive operating system. The virtual-machine software is concerned with multiprogramming multiple virtual machines onto a physical machine, but does not need to consider any user-support software. This arrangement may provide a useful partitioning of the problem of designing a multiuser interactive system into two smaller pieces.

Although the virtual machine concept is useful, it is difficult to implement. Much effort is required to provide an *exact* duplicate of the underlying machine. Remember, for example, that the underlying machine has two modes: user mode and monitor mode. The virtual-machine software can run in monitor mode, since it is the operating system. The virtual machine itself can execute in only user mode. Just as the physical machine has two modes, however, so must the virtual machine. Consequently, we must have a virtual user mode and a virtual monitor mode, both of which run in a physical user mode. Those actions that cause a transfer from user mode to monitor mode on a real machine (such as a system call or an attempt to execute a privileged instruction) must also cause a transfer from virtual user mode to virtual monitor mode on a virtual machine.

This transfer can generally be done fairly easily. When a system call, for example, is made by a program running on a virtual machine in virtual user mode, it will cause a transfer to the virtual-machine monitor in the real machine. The virtual user mode is also a physical user mode. When the virtual-machine monitor gains control, it can change the register contents and program counter for the virtual machine to simulate the effect of the system call. It can then restart the virtual machine, noting that it is now in virtual monitor mode. If the virtual machine then tries, for example, to read from its virtual card reader, it will execute a privileged I/O instruction. Because the virtual machine is running in physical user mode, this instruction will trap to the virtual-machine monitor. The virtual-machine monitor must then simulate the effect of the I/O instruction. First, it finds the spooled file that implements the virtual card reader. Then, it translates the read of the virtual card reader into a read on the spooled disk file, and transfers the next virtual "card image" into the virtual memory of the virtual machine. Finally, it can restart the virtual machine. The state of the virtual machine has been modified exactly as though the I/O instruction had been executed with a real card reader for a real machine executing in a real monitor mode.

The major difference is, of course, time. Whereas the real I/O might have taken 100 milliseconds, the virtual I/O might take less time (because it is spooled) or more (because it is interpreted). In addition, the CPU is being multiprogrammed among many virtual machines, further slowing down the virtual machines in unpredictable ways. In the extreme case, it may be necessary to simulate all instructions to provide a true virtual machine. VM works for IBM machines because normal instructions for the virtual machines can execute directly on the hardware. Only the privileged instructions (needed mainly for I/O) must be simulated and hence execute more slowly.

The virtual-machine concept has several advantages. Notice that in this environment there is complete protection of the various system resources. Each virtual machine is completely isolated from all other virtual machines, so there are no security problems. On the other hand, there is no direct sharing of resources. To provide sharing, two approaches have been implemented. First, it is possible to share a minidisk. This scheme is modeled after a physical shared disk, but is implemented by software. With this technique, files can be shared. Second, it is possible to define a network of virtual machines, each of which can send information over the virtual communications network. Again, the network is modeled after physical communication networks, but is implemented in software.

Such a virtual-machine system is a perfect vehicle for operating-systems research and development. Normally, changing an operating system is a difficult task. Because operating systems are large and complex programs, it is difficult to be sure that a change in one point will not cause obscure bugs in some other part. This situation can be particularly dangerous because of the power of the operating system. Because the operating system executes in monitor mode, a wrong change in a pointer could cause an error that would destroy the entire file system. Thus, it is necessary to test all changes to the operating system carefully.

The operating system, however, runs on and controls the entire machine. Therefore, the current system must be stopped and taken out of use while changes are made and tested. This period is commonly called *system-development time*. Since it makes the system unavailable to users, system-development time is often scheduled late at night or on weekends, when system load is low.

A virtual-machine system can eliminate much of this problem. System programmers are given their own virtual machine, and system development is done on the virtual machine, instead of on a physical machine. Normal system operation seldom needs to be disrupted for system development.

Virtual machines are coming back into fashion as a means of solving system compatibility problems. For instance, there are thousands of programs available for MS-DOS on Intel CPU-based systems. Computer vendors like Sun Microsystems and Digital Equipment Corporation (DEC) use other, faster processors, but would like their customers to be able to run these MS-DOS programs. The solution is to create a virtual Intel machine on top of the native processor. An MS-DOS program is run in this environment, and its Intel instructions are translated into the native instruction set. MS-DOS is also run in this virtual machine, so the program can make its system calls as usual. The net result is a program which appears to be running on an Intel-based system but is really executing on a very different processor. If the processor is sufficiently fast, the MS-DOS program will run quickly even though every instruction is being translated into several native instructions for execution.

3.7 ■ System Design and Implementation

In this section, we discuss the problems of designing and implementing a system. There are, of course, no complete solutions to the design problems, but there are approaches that have been successful.

3.7.1 Design Goals

The first problem in designing a system is to define the goals and specifications of the system. At the highest level, the design of the system will be affected by the choice of hardware and type of system: batch, time-shared, single-user, multiuser, distributed, real-time, or general purpose.

Beyond this highest design level, the requirements may be much harder to specify. The requirements can be divided into two basic groups: *user* goals and *system* goals.

Users desire certain obvious properties in a system: The system should be convenient to use, easy to learn, easy to use, reliable, safe, and fast. Of course, these specifications are not particularly useful in the system design, since there is no general agreement on how to achieve these goals.

A similar set of requirements can be defined by those people who must design, create, maintain, and operate the system: The operating system should be easy to design, implement, and maintain; it should be flexible, reliable, error-free, and efficient. Again, these requirements are vague and have no general solution.

There is no unique solution to the problem of defining the requirements for an operating system. The wide range of systems shows that different requirements can result in a large variety of solutions for different environments. For example, the requirements for MS-DOS, a single-user system for microcomputers, must have been substantially different from those for MVS, the large multiuser, multiaccess operating system for IBM mainframes.

The specification and design of an operating system is a highly creative task. No mere textbook can solve that problem. There are, however, general principles that have been suggested. *Software engineering* is the general field for these principles; certain ideas from this field are especially applicable to operating systems.

3.7.2 Mechanisms and Policies

One important principle is the separation of *policy* from *mechanism*. Mechanisms determine *how* to do something. In contrast, policies decide *what* will be done. For example, a mechanism for ensuring CPU protection is the timer construct (see Section 2.5). The decision of for how long the timer is set for a particular user, on the other hand, is a policy decision.

The separation of policy and mechanism is important for flexibility. Policies are likely to change from place to place or time to time. In the worst case, each change in policy would require a change in the underlying mechanism. A general mechanism would be more desirable. A change in policy would then require redefinition of only certain parameters of the system. For instance, if, in one computer system, a policy decision is made that I/O-intensive programs should have priority over CPU-intensive ones, then the opposite policy could be instituted easily on some other computer system if the mechanism were properly separated and were policy independent.

Microkernel-based operating systems take the separation of mechanism and policy to extreme, by implementing a basic set of primitive building blocks. These blocks are almost policy-free, allowing more advanced mechanisms and policies to be added via user-created kernel modules, or user programs themselves. At the other extreme is a system such as the Apple Macintosh operating system, in which both mechanism and policy are encoded in the system to enforce a global look and feel to the system. All applications have similar interfaces, because the interface itself is built into the kernel.

Policy decisions are important for all resource allocation and scheduling problems. Whenever it is necessary to decide whether or not to allocate a resource, a policy decision must be made. Whenever the question is "how" rather than "what", it is a mechanism that must be determined.

3.7.3 Implementation

Once an operating system is designed, it must be implemented. Traditionally, operating systems have been written in assembly language. However, that is generally no longer true. Operating systems can now be written in higher-level languages.

The first system that was not written in assembly language was probably the Master Control Program (MCP) for Burroughs computers. MCP was written in a variant of ALGOL. MULTICS, developed at MIT, was written mainly in PL/1. The Primos operating system for Prime computers is written in a dialect of FORTRAN. The UNIX operating system, OS/2, and Windows/NT are mainly written in C. Only some 900 lines of code of the original UNIX were in assembly language, most of which constituted the scheduler and device drivers.

The advantages of using a higher-level language, or at least a systems-implementation language, for implementing operating systems are the same as those accrued when the language is used for application programs: The code can be written faster, is more compact, and is easier to understand and debug. The major claimed disadvantages are reduced speed and increased storage requirements. Although no compiler can produce consistently more efficient code than can an expert assembly-language programmer, a compiler often can produce code at least as good as that written by the average assembly-language programmer. In addition, replacing the compiler with a better compiler will uniformly improve the generated code for the entire operating system by simple recompilation. Finally, an operating system is far easier to *port* — to move to some other hardware — if it is written in a high-level language. For example, MS-DOS was written in Intel 8088 assembly language. Consequently, it is available on only the Intel family of CPUs. The UNIX operating system, which is written mostly in C, on the other hand, is available on a number of different CPUs, including Intel 80X86, Motorola 680X0, SPARC, and Mips RX000.

As with other systems, major performance improvements are more likely to be the result of better data structures and algorithms than of cleaner coding. In addition, although operating systems are large systems, only a small amount of the code is critical to high performance; the memory manager and the CPU scheduler are probably the most critical routines. After the system is written and is working correctly, bottleneck routines can be identified, and can be replaced with assembly-language equivalents.

To identify bottlenecks, we must be able to monitor the system performance. Code must be added to compute and display measures of system behavior. In a number of systems, the operating system does this task by producing trace listings of system behavior. All interesting events are logged with their time and important parameters, and are written to a file. Later, an analysis program can process the log file to determine system performance and to identify bottlenecks and inefficiencies. These same traces could also be run as input for a simulation of a suggested improved system. Traces also can be useful in finding errors in operating-system behavior.

An alternative possibility is to compute and display performance measures in real time. This approach may allow the system operators to become more familiar with system behavior and to modify system operation in real time.

3.8 ■ System Generation

It is possible to design, code, and implement an operating system specifically for one machine at one site. More commonly, however, operating systems are designed to run on any of a class of machines at a variety of sites with a variety of peripheral configurations. The system must then be configured or generated for each specific computer site. This process is known as *system generation (SYSGEN)*.

The operating system is normally distributed on tape or disk. To generate a system, we use a special program. The SYSGEN program reads from a file or asks the operator for information concerning the specific configuration of the hardware system:

- What CPU is to be used? What options (extended instruction sets, floating-point arithmetic, and so on) are installed? For multiple CPU systems, each CPU must be described.

- How much memory is available? Some systems will determine this value themselves by referencing memory location after memory location until an "illegal address" fault is generated. This procedure defines the final legal address and hence the amount of available memory.

- What devices are available? The system will need to know how to address each device (the device number), the device interrupt number, the device's type and model, and any special device characteristics.

- What operating-system options are desired, or what parameter values are to be used? These options or values might include how many buffers of which sizes should be used, what CPU-scheduling algorithm is desired, what the maximum number of processes to be supported is, and so on.

Once this information is defined, it can be used in several ways. At one extreme, it can be used to modify a copy of the source code of the operating system. The operating system would then be completely compiled. Data declarations, initializations, and constants, along with conditional compilation, would produce an output object version of the operating system that is tailored to the system described.

At a slightly less tailored level, the system description could cause the creation of tables and the selection of modules from a precompiled library. These modules would be linked together to form the generated operating system. Selection would allow the library to contain the device drivers for all supported I/O devices, but only those actually needed would be linked into the operating system. Because the system would not be recompiled, system generation would be faster, but might result in a system with more generality than was actually needed.

At the other extreme, it would be possible to construct a system that was completely table driven. All the code would always be a part of the system, and selection would occur at execution time, rather than at compile or link time. System generation involves simply creating the appropriate tables to describe the system.

The major differences among these approaches are the size and generality of the generated system and the ease of modification as the hardware configuration changes. Consider the cost of modifying the system to support a newly acquired graphics terminal or another disk drive. Balanced against that cost, of course, is the frequency (or infrequency) of such changes.

After an operating system is generated, it must be made available for use by the hardware. But how does the hardware know where the kernel is, or how to load it? The procedure of starting a computer by loading the kernel is known as *booting* the system. On most systems, there is a small piece of code, stored in ROM, known as the *bootstrap program* or *bootstrap loader*. This code is able to locate the kernel, load it into memory, and start its execution. Some systems, like IBM PCs running MS-DOS, turn this into a two-step process by having a very simple bootstrap loader load a more complex boot program, which in turn loads the kernel. Booting a system is further discussed in Section 12.3.2 and Chapter 19.

3.9 ■ Summary

Operating systems provide a number of services. At the lowest level, system calls allow a running program to make requests from the operating system directly. At a higher level, the command interpreter provides a mechanism for a user to issue a request without writing a program. Commands may come from cards (in a batch system) or directly from a terminal (in an interactive or time-shared system). Systems programs provide another mechanism for satisfying user requests.

The types of requests vary according to the level of the request. The system-call level must provide the basic functions, such as process control and file and device manipulation. Higher-level requests, satisfied by the command interpreter or systems programs, are translated into a sequence of system calls. System services can be classified into several categories:

program control, status requests, and I/O requests. Program errors can be considered implicit requests for service.

Once the system services are defined, the structure of the operating system can be developed. Various tables are needed to record the information that defines the state of the computer system and the status of the system's jobs.

The design of a new operating system is a major task. It is important that the goals of the system be well defined before the design begins. The type of system desired is the foundation for choices among various algorithms and strategies that will be necessary.

Since an operating system is large, modularity is important. The design of a system as a sequence of layers is considered an important design technique. The virtual-machine concept takes the layered approach to heart and treats the kernel of the operating system and the hardware as though they were all hardware. Even other operating systems may be loaded on top of this virtual machine.

Throughout the entire operating-system design cycle, we must be careful to separate policy decisions from implementation details. This separation allows maximum flexibility if policy decisions are to be changed later.

Operating systems are now almost always written in a systems-implementation language or in a higher-level language. This feature improves their implementation, maintenance, and portability. To create an operating system for a particular machine configuration, we must perform system generation.

■ Exercises

3.1 What are the five major activities of an operating system in regard to process management?

3.2 What are the three major activities of an operating system in regard to memory management?

3.3 What are the three major activities of an operating system in regard to secondary-storage management?

3.4 What are the five major activities of an operating system in regard to file management?

3.5 What is the purpose of the command interpreter? Why is it usually separate from the kernel?

3.6 List five services provided by an operating system. Explain how each provides convenience to the users. Explain also in which cases it would be impossible for user-level programs to provide these services.

3.7 What is the purpose of system calls?

3.8 What is the purpose of system programs?

3.9 What is the main advantage of the layered approach to system design?

3.10 What is the main advantage for an operating-system designer of using a virtual-machine architecture? What is the main advantage for a user?

3.11 Why is the separation of mechanism and policy a desirable property?

3.12 Consider the experimental Synthesis operating system, which has an assembler incorporated within the kernel. To optimize system-call performance, the kernel assembles routines within kernel space to minimize the path the system call must take through the kernel. This approach is the antithesis of the layered approach, in which the path through the kernel is extended so that building the operating system is made easier. Discuss the pros and cons of this approach to kernel design and to system-performance optimization.

Bibliographic Notes

Command languages can be seen as special-purpose programming languages. Brunt and Tuffs [1976] argued that a command language should provide a rich set of functions; Frank [1976] argued for a more limited, simpler command language. An excellent case study is the UNIX shell, as described by Bourne [1978].

Dijkstra [1968] advocated the layered approach to operating-system design. The THE system was described in [Dijkstra 1968]; the Venus system was described in [Liskov 1972].

Brinch Hansen [1970] was an early proponent of the construction of an operating system as a kernel (or nucleus) on which can be built more complete systems. A computer architecture for supporting level-structured operating systems was described by Bernstein and Siegel [1975].

The first operating system to provide a virtual machine was the CP/67 on an IBM 360/67 and is described by Meyer and Seawright [1970]. CP/67 provided each user with a virtual 360 Model 65, including I/O devices. The commercially available IBM VM/370 operating system was derived from CP/67 and is described by Seawright and MacKinnon [1979], Holley et al. [1979], and Creasy [1981]. Hall et al. [1980] promoted the use of virtual machines for increasing operating-system portability. Jones [1978] suggested the use of virtual machines to enforce the isolation of processes for protection purposes. General discussions concerning virtual machines have been presented by Hendricks and Hartmann [1979], MacKinnon [1979], and Schultz [1988].

MS-DOS, Version 3.1, is described in [Microsoft 1986]. Windows/NT is described by Custer [1993]. The Apple Macintosh operating system is described in [Apple 1987]. Berkeley UNIX is described in [CSRG 1986]. The standard AT&T UNIX system V is described in [AT&T 1986]. A good description of OS/2 is given in [Iacobucci 1988]. Mach is introduced in [Accetta et al. 1986], and AIX is presented in [Loucks and Sauer 1987]. The experimental Synthesis operating system is discussed in [Massalin and Pu 1989].

PART TWO

PROCESS MANAGEMENT

A *process* can be thought of as a program in execution. A process will need certain resources — such as CPU time, memory, files, and I/O devices — to accomplish its task. These resources are allocated to the process either when it is created, or while it is executing.

A process is the unit of work in most systems. Such a system consists of a collection of processes: Operating-system processes execute system code, and user processes execute user code. All these processes can potentially execute concurrently.

The operating system is responsible for the following activities in connection with process management: the creation and deletion of both user and system processes; the scheduling of processes; and the provision of mechanisms for synchronization, communication, and deadlock handling for processes.

CHAPTER 4

PROCESSES

Early computer systems allowed only one program to be executed at a time. This program had complete control of the system, and had access to all of the system's resources. Current-day computer systems allow multiple programs to be loaded into memory and to be executed concurrently. This evolution required firmer control and more compartmentalization of the various programs. These needs resulted in the notion of a *process*, which is a program in execution. A process is the unit of work in a modern time-sharing system.

The more complex the operating system, the more it is expected to do on behalf of its users. Although its main concern is the execution of user programs, it also needs to take care of various system tasks that are better left outside the kernel itself. A system therefore consists of a collection of processes: Operating-system processes executing system code, and user processes executing user code. All these processes can potentially execute concurrently, with the CPU (or CPUs) multiplexed among them. By switching the CPU between processes, the operating system can make the computer more productive.

4.1 ■ Process Concept

One hindrance to the discussion of operating systems is the question of what to call all the CPU activities. A batch system executes *jobs*, whereas a time-shared system has *user programs*, or *tasks*. Even on a single-user system, such as MS-DOS and Macintosh OS, a user may be able to run several programs at one time: one interactive and several batch programs.

Even if the user can execute only one program at a time, the operating system may need to support its own internal programmed activities, such as spooling. In many respects, all of these activities are similar, so we call all of them *processes*.

The terms *job* and *process* are used almost interchangeably in this text. Although we personally prefer the term *process*, much of operating-system theory and terminology was developed during a time when the major activity of operating systems was job processing. It would be misleading to avoid the use of commonly accepted terms that include the word *job* (such as job scheduling) simply because the term *process* has superseded it.

4.1.1 The Process

Informally, a *process* is a program in execution. The execution of a process must progress in a sequential fashion. That is, at any time, at most one instruction is executed on behalf of the process.

A process is more than the program code (sometimes known as the *text section*). It also includes the current activity, as represented by the value of the *program counter* and the contents of the processor's registers. A process generally also includes the process *stack*, containing temporary data (such as subroutine parameters, return addresses, and temporary variables), and a *data section* containing global variables.

We emphasize that a program by itself is not a process; a program is a *passive* entity, such as the contents of a file stored on disk, whereas a process is an *active* entity, with a program counter specifying the next instruction to execute and a set of associated resources.

Although two processes may be associated with the same program, they are nevertheless considered two separate execution sequences. For instance, several users may be running copies of the mail program, or the same user may invoke many copies of the editor program. Each of these is

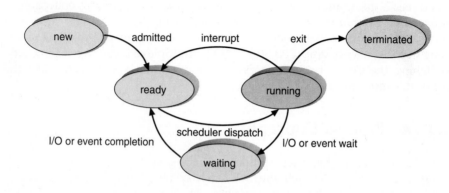

Figure 4.1 Diagram of process state.

a separate process, and, although the text sections are equivalent, the data sections will vary. It is also common to have a process that spawns many processes as it runs. This issue will be further discussed in Section 4.4.

4.1.2 Process State

As a process executes, it changes *state*. The state of a process is defined in part by the current activity of that process. Each process may be in one of the following states:

- **New:** The process is being created.

- **Running:** Instructions are being executed.

- **Waiting:** The process is waiting for some event to occur (such as an I/O completion or reception of a signal).

- **Ready:** The process is waiting to be assigned to a processor.

- **Terminated:** The process has finished execution.

These names are arbitrary, and vary between operating systems. The states that they represent are found on all systems, however. Certain operating systems also distinguish among more finely delineating process states. It is important to realize that only one process can be *running* on any processor at any instant. Many processes may be *ready* and *waiting*, however. The state diagram corresponding to these states is presented in Figure 4.1.

4.1.3 Process Control Block

Each process is represented in the operating system by a *process control block (PCB)* — also called a task control block. A PCB is shown in Figure 4.2. It contains many pieces of information associated with a specific process, including these:

- **Process state:** The state may be new, ready, running, waiting, halted, and so on.

- **Program counter:** The counter indicates the address of the next instruction to be executed for this process.

- **CPU registers:** The registers vary in number and type, depending on the computer architecture. They include accumulators, index registers, stack pointers, and general-purpose registers, plus any condition-code information. Along with the program counter, this state information must be saved when an interrupt occurs, to allow the process to be continued correctly afterward (Figure 4.3).

Figure 4.2   Process control block.

- **CPU scheduling information:** This information includes a process priority, pointers to scheduling queues, and any other scheduling parameters. (Chapter 5 describes process scheduling.)

- **Memory-management information:** This information may include the value of the base and limit registers, the page tables, or the segment tables depending on the memory system used by the operating system (Chapter 8).

- **Accounting information:** This information includes the amount of CPU and real time used, time limits, account numbers, job or process numbers, and so on.

- **I/O status information:** The information includes the list of I/O devices (such as tape drives) allocated to this process, a list of open files, and so on.

The PCB simply serves as the repository for any information that may vary from process to process.

4.2 ■ Process Scheduling

The objective of multiprogramming is to have some process running at all times, to maximize CPU utilization. The objective of time sharing is to switch the CPU among processes so frequently that users can interact with each program while it is running. For a uniprocessor system, there will never be more than one running process. If there are more processes, the rest will have to wait until the CPU is free and can be rescheduled.

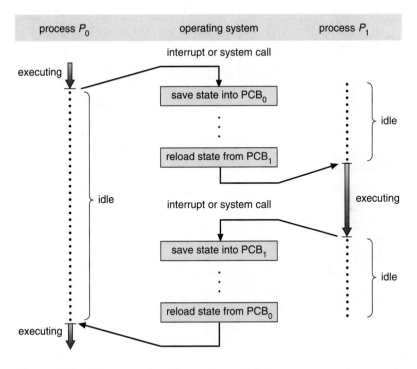

Figure 4.3   Diagram showing CPU switch from process to process.

4.2.1 Scheduling Queues

As processes enter the system, they are put into a *job queue*. This queue consists of all processes in the system. The processes that are residing in main memory and are ready and waiting to execute are kept on a list called the *ready queue*. This queue is generally stored as a linked list. A ready-queue header will contain pointers to the first and last PCBs in the list. Each PCB has a pointer field that points to the next process in the ready queue.

There are also other queues in the system. When a process is allocated the CPU, it executes for awhile and eventually quits, is interrupted, or waits for the occurrence of a particular event, such as the completion of an I/O request. In the case of an I/O request, such a request may be to a dedicated tape drive, or to a shared device, such as a disk. Since there are many processes in the system, the disk may be busy with the I/O request of some other process. The process therefore may have to wait for the disk. The list of processes waiting for a particular I/O device is called a *device queue*. Each device has its own device queue (Figure 4.4).

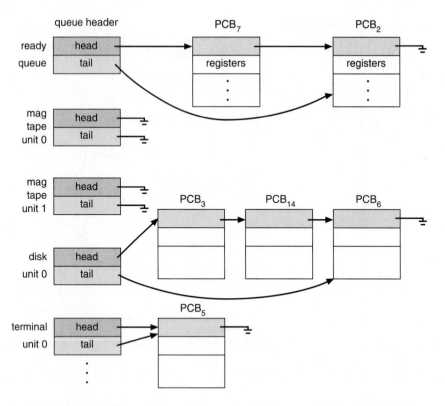

Figure 4.4   The ready queue and various I/O device queues.

A common representation for a discussion of process scheduling is a *queueing diagram,* such as that in Figure 4.5. Each rectangular box represents a queue. Two types of queues are present: the ready queue and a set of device queues. The circles represent the resources that serve the queues, and the arrows indicate the flow of processes in the system.

A new process is initially put in the ready queue. It waits in the ready queue until it is selected for execution (or *dispatched*) and is given the CPU. Once the process is allocated the CPU and is executing, one of several events could occur:

- The process could issue an I/O request, and then be placed in an I/O queue.

- The process could create a new subprocess and wait for its termination.

- The process could be removed forcibly from the CPU, as a result of an interrupt, and be put back in the ready queue.

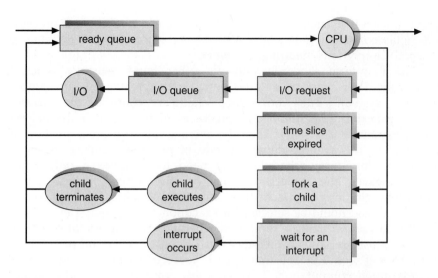

Figure 4.5 Queueing-diagram representation of process scheduling.

In the first two cases, the process eventually switches from the waiting state to the ready state, and is then put back in the ready queue. A process continues this cycle until it terminates, at which time it is removed from all queues and has its PCB and resources deallocated.

4.2.2 Schedulers

A process migrates between the various scheduling queues throughout its lifetime. The operating system must select processes from these queues in some fashion. The selection process is carried out by the appropriate *scheduler*.

In a batch system, there are often more processes submitted than can be executed immediately. These processes are spooled to a mass-storage device (typically a disk), where they are kept for later execution. The *long-term scheduler* (or *job scheduler*) selects processes from this pool and loads them into memory for execution. The *short-term scheduler* (or *CPU scheduler*) selects from among the processes that are ready to execute, and allocates the CPU to one of them.

The primary distinction between these two schedulers is the frequency of their execution. The short-term scheduler must select a new process for the CPU quite frequently. A process may execute for only a few milliseconds before waiting for an I/O request. Often, the short-term scheduler executes at least once every 100 milliseconds. Because of the short duration of time between executions, the short-term scheduler must be very fast. If it takes 10 milliseconds to decide to execute a process for 100 milliseconds, then $10/(100 + 10) = 9$ percent of the CPU is being used (wasted) simply for scheduling the work.

The long-term scheduler, on the other hand, executes much less frequently. There may be minutes between the creation of new processes in the system. The long-term scheduler controls the *degree of multiprogramming* (the number of processes in memory). If the degree of multiprogramming is stable, then the average rate of process creation must be equal to the average departure rate of processes leaving the system. Thus, the long-term scheduler may need to be invoked only when a process leaves the system. Because of the longer interval between executions, the long-term scheduler can afford to take more time to decide which process should be selected for execution.

It is important that the long-term scheduler make a careful selection. In general, most processes can be described as either I/O bound or CPU bound. An *I/O-bound process* is one that spends more of its time doing I/O than it spends doing computations. A *CPU-bound process*, on the other hand, is one that generates I/O requests infrequently, using more of its time doing computation than an I/O-bound process uses. It is important that the long-term scheduler select a good *process mix* of I/O-bound and CPU-bound processes. If all processes are I/O bound, the ready queue will almost always be empty, and the short-term scheduler will have little to do. If all processes are CPU bound, the I/O waiting queue will almost always be empty, devices will go unused, and again the system will be unbalanced. The system with the best performance will have a combination of CPU-bound and I/O-bound processes.

On some systems, the long-term scheduler may be absent or minimal. For example, time-sharing systems often have no long-term scheduler, but simply put every new process in memory for the short-term scheduler. The stability of these systems depends either on a physical limitation (such as the number of available terminals) or on the self-adjusting nature of human users. If the performance declines to unacceptable levels, some users will simply quit, and will do something else.

Some operating systems, such as time-sharing systems, may introduce an additional, intermediate level of scheduling. This *medium-term scheduler* is diagrammed in Figure 4.6. The key idea behind a medium-term scheduler is that sometimes it can be advantageous to remove processes from memory (and from active contention for the CPU), and thus to reduce the degree of multiprogramming. At some later time, the process can be reintroduced into memory and its execution can be continued where it left off. This scheme is called *swapping*. The process is swapped out and swapped in later by the medium-term scheduler. Swapping may be necessary to improve the process mix, or because a change in memory requirements has overcommitted available memory, requiring memory to be freed up. Swapping is discussed in more detail in Chapter 8.

Figure 4.6 Addition of medium-term scheduling to the queueing diagram.

4.2.3 Context Switch

Switching the CPU to another process requires saving the state of the old process and loading the saved state for the new process. This task is known as a *context switch*. Context-switch time is pure overhead, because the system does no useful work while switching. Its speed varies from machine to machine, depending on the memory speed, the number of registers which must be copied, and the existence of special instructions (such as a single instruction to load or store all registers). Typically, the speed ranges from 1 to 1000 microseconds.

Context-switch times are highly dependent on hardware support. For instance, some processors (such as the DECSYSTEM-20) provide multiple sets of registers. A context switch simply includes changing the pointer to the current register set. Of course, if there are more active processes than there are register sets, the system resorts to copying register data to and from memory, as before. Also, the more complex the operating system, the more work must be done during a context switch. As we shall see in Chapter 8, advanced memory-management techniques may require extra data to be switched with each context. For instance, the address space of the current process must be preserved as the space of the next task is prepared for use. How the address space is preserved, and the amount of work needed to do it, depend on the memory-management method of the operating system. As we shall see in Section 4.5, context switching has become such a performance bottleneck that new structures (threads) are being used to avoid it whenever possible.

4.3 ■ Operation on Processes

The processes in the system can execute concurrently, and must be created and deleted dynamically. Thus, the operating system must provide a mechanism for process creation and termination.

4.3.1. Process Creation

A process may create several new processes, via a create-process system call, during the course of execution. The creating process is called a *parent* process, whereas the new processes are called the *children* of that process. Each of these new processes may in turn create other processes, forming a *tree* of processes (Figure 4.7).

In general, a process will need certain resources (CPU time, memory, files, I/O devices) to accomplish its task. When a process creates a subprocess, the subprocess may be able to obtain its resources directly from the operating system, or it may be constrained to a subset of the resources of the parent process. The parent may have to partition its resources among its children, or it may be able to share some resources (such as memory or files) among several of its children. Restricting a child process to a subset of the parent's resources prevents any process from overloading the system by creating too many subprocesses.

In addition to the various physical and logical resources that a process obtains when it is created, initialization data (input) may be passed along by the parent process to the child process. For example, consider a process whose function is to display the status of a file, say *F1*, on the screen of a terminal. When it is created, it will get, as an input from its parent process, the name of the file *F1*, and it will execute using that datum to obtain the desired information. It may also get the name of the

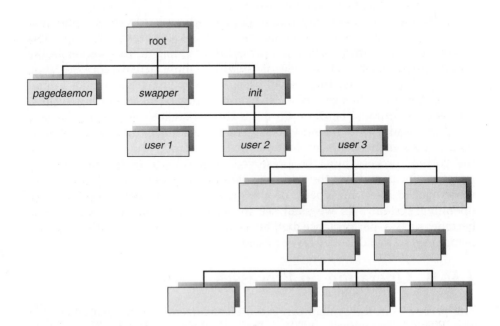

Figure 4.7   A tree of processes on a typical UNIX system.

output device. Some operating systems pass resources to child processes. On such a system, the new process may get two open files, *F1* and the terminal device, and may just need to transfer the datum between the two.

When a process creates a new process, two possibilities exist in terms of execution:

- The parent continues to execute concurrently with its children.
- The parent waits until some or all of its children have terminated.

There are also two possibilities in terms of the address space of the new process:

- The child process is a duplicate of the parent process.
- The child process has a program loaded into it.

To illustrate these different implementations, let us consider the UNIX operating system. In UNIX, each process is identified by its *process identifier*, which is a unique integer. A new process is created by the **fork** system call. The new process consists of a copy of the address space of the original process. This mechanism allows the parent process to communicate easily with its child process. Both processes (the parent and the child) continue execution at the instruction after the **fork** with one difference: The return code for the **fork** is zero for the new (child) process, whereas the (nonzero) process identifier of the child is returned to the parent.

Typically, the **execve** system call is used after a **fork** by one of the two processes to replace the process' memory space with a new program. The **execve** system call loads a binary file into memory (destroying the memory image of the program containing the **execve** system call) and starts its execution. In this manner, the two processes are able to communicate, and then to go their separate ways. The parent can then create more children, or, if it has nothing else to do while the child runs, it can issue a **wait** system call to move itself off the ready queue until the termination of the child.

The DEC VMS operating system, in contrast, creates a new process, loads a specified program into that process, and starts it running. The Microsoft Windows/NT operating system supports both models: the parent's address space may be duplicated, or the parent may specify the name of a program for the operating system to load into the address space of the new process.

4.3.2 Process Termination

A process terminates when it finishes executing its last statement and asks the operating system to delete it by using the *exit* system call. At that point, the process may return data (output) to its parent process (via the

fork system call). All of the resources of the process, including physical and virtual memory, open files, and I/O buffers, are deallocated by the operating system.

There are additional circumstances when termination occurs. A process can cause the termination of another process via an appropriate system call (for example, **abort**). Usually, such a system call can be invoked by only the parent of the process that is to be terminated. Otherwise, users could arbitrarily kill each other's jobs. Note that a parent needs to know the identities of its children. Thus, when one process creates a new process, the identity of the newly created process is passed to the parent.

A parent may terminate the execution of one of its children for a variety of reasons, such as:

- The child has exceeded its usage of some of the resources it has been allocated.

- The task assigned to the child is no longer required.

- The parent is exiting, and the operating system does not allow a child to continue if its parent terminates.

To determine the first case, the parent must have a mechanism to inspect the state of its children.

Many systems, including VMS, do not allow a child to exist if its parent has terminated. In such systems, if a process terminates (either normally or abnormally), then all its children must also be terminated. This phenomenon is referred to as *cascading termination* and is normally initiated by the operating system.

To illustrate process execution and termination, let us consider again the UNIX system. In UNIX, a process may terminate by using the **exit** system call, and its parent process may wait for that event by using the **wait** system call. The **wait** system call returns the process identifier of a terminated child, so that the parent can tell which of the possibly many children has terminated. If the parent terminates, however, all the children are terminated by the operating system. Without a parent, UNIX does not know to whom to report the activities of a child.

4.4 ■ Cooperating Processes

The concurrent processes executing in the operating system may be either independent processes or cooperating processes. A process is *independent* if it cannot affect or be affected by the other processes executing in the system. Clearly, any process that does not share any data (temporary or persistent) with any other process is independent. On the other hand, a process is *cooperating* if it can affect or be affected by the other processes executing in the system. Clearly, any process that shares data with other processes is a cooperating process.

There are several reasons for providing an environment that allows process cooperation:

- **Information sharing:** Since several users may be interested in the same piece of information (for instance, a shared file), we must provide an environment to allow concurrent access to these types of resources.

- **Computation speedup:** If we want a particular task to run faster, we must break it into subtasks, each of which will be executing in parallel with the others. Notice that such a speedup can be achieved only if the computer has multiple processing elements (such as CPUs or I/O channels).

- **Modularity:** We may want to construct the system in a modular fashion, dividing the system functions into separate processes, as was discussed in Chapter 3.

- **Convenience:** Even an individual user may have many tasks to work on at one time. For instance, a user may be editing, printing, and compiling in parallel.

Concurrent execution that requires cooperation among the processes requires mechanisms to allow processes to communicate with each other (Section 4.6), and to synchronize their actions (Chapter 6).

To illustrate the concept of cooperating processes, let us consider the producer–consumer problem, which is a common paradigm for cooperating processes. A *producer* process produces information that is consumed by a *consumer* process. For example, a print program produces characters that are consumed by the printer driver. A compiler may produce assembly code, which is consumed by an assembler. The assembler, in turn, may produce object modules, which are consumed by the loader.

To allow producer and consumer processes to run concurrently, we must have available a buffer of items that can be filled by the producer and emptied by the consumer. A producer can produce one item while the consumer is consuming another item. The producer and consumer must be synchronized, so that the consumer does not try to consume an item that has not yet been produced. In this situation, the consumer must wait until an item is produced.

The *unbounded-buffer* producer–consumer problem places no practical limit on the size of the buffer. The consumer may have to wait for new items, but the producer can always produce new items. The *bounded-buffer* producer–consumer problem assumes that there is a fixed buffer size. In this case, the consumer must wait if the buffer is empty and the producer must wait if the buffer is full.

The buffer may be either provided by the operating system through the use of IPC (Section 4.6), or explicitly coded by the application programmer with the use of shared memory. Let us illustrate a shared-memory solution to the bounded-buffer problem. The producer and consumer processes share the following variables:

```
var n;
type item = ... ;
var buffer: array [0..n−1] of item;
in, out: 0..n−1;
```

with *in, out* initialized to the value 0. The shared buffer is implemented as a circular array with two logical pointers: *in* and *out*. The variable *in* points to the next free position in the buffer; *out* points to the first full position in the buffer. The buffer is empty when *in = out;* the buffer is full when *in +* 1 **mod** *n = out.*

The code for the producer and consumer processes follows. The *no-op* is a do-nothing instruction. Thus, **while** *condition* **do** *no-op* simply tests the condition repetitively until it becomes false.

The producer process has a local variable *nextp,* in which the new item to be produced is stored:

```
repeat
      ...
   produce an item in nextp
      ...
   while in+1 mod n = out do no-op;
   buffer[in] := nextp;
   in := in+1 mod n;
until false;
```

The consumer process has a local variable *nextc,* in which the item to be consumed is stored:

```
repeat
   while in = out do no-op;
   nextc := buffer[out];
   out := out+1 mod n;
      ...
   consume the item in nextc
      ...
until false;
```

This scheme allows at most $n - 1$ items in the buffer at the same time. We leave it as an exercise for you to provide a solution where n items can be in the buffer at the same time.

In Chapter 6, we shall discuss in great detail how synchronization among cooperating processes can be implemented effectively in a shared-memory environment.

4.5 ■ Threads

Recall that a process is defined by the resources it uses and by the location at which it is executing. There are many instances, however, in which it would be useful for resources to be shared and accessed concurrently. This situation is similar to the case where a **fork** system call is invoked with a new program counter, or thread of control, executing within the same address space. This concept is so useful that several new operating systems are providing a mechanism to support it through a *thread* facility.

4.5.1 Thread Structure

A *thread*, sometimes called a *lightweight process* (LWP), is a basic unit of CPU utilization, and consists of a program counter, a register set, and a stack space. It shares with peer threads its code section, data section, and operating-system resources such as open files and signals, collectively known as a *task*. A traditional or *heavyweight* process is equal to a task with one thread. A task does nothing if no threads are in it, and a thread must be in exactly one task. The extensive sharing makes CPU switching among peer threads and the creation of threads inexpensive, compared with context switches among heavyweight processes. Although a thread context switch still requires a register set switch, no memory-management−related work need be done.

Also, some systems implement *user-level threads* in user-level libraries, rather than via system calls, so thread switching does not need to call the operating system, and to cause an interrupt to the kernel. Switching between user-level threads can be done independently of the operating system and, therefore, very quickly. Thus, blocking a thread and switching to another thread is a reasonable solution to the problem of how a server can handle many requests efficiently. User-level threads do have disadvantages, however. For instance, if the kernel is single-threaded, then any user-level thread executing a system call will cause the entire task to wait until the system call returns.

We can grasp the functionality of threads by comparing multiple-thread control with multiple-process control. With multiple processes, each process operates independently of the others; each process has its own program counter, stack register, and address space. This type of organization is useful when the jobs performed by the processes are unrelated. For instance, in single-CPU operating systems, a file server may have to block while waiting for disk access. System performance would improve if another server process could operate while the first one was blocked, yet because they would have to occupy the same address space, it is not possible to create a second, independent server process.

Threads operate, in many respects, in the same manner as processes. Threads can be in one of several states: ready, blocked, running, or terminated. Like processes, threads share the CPU, and only one thread at a time is active (running). A thread within a process executes sequentially, and each thread has its own stack and program counter. Threads can create child threads, and can block waiting for system calls to complete; if one thread is blocked, another thread can run. However, unlike processes, threads are not independent of one another. Because all threads can access every address in the task, a thread can read or write over any other thread's stacks. This structure does not provide protection between threads. Such protection, however, should not be necessary. Whereas processes may originate from different users, and may be hostile to one another, only a single user can own an individual task with multiple threads. The threads, in this case, probably would be designed to assist one another, and therefore would not require mutual protection. Figure 4.8 depicts a task with multiple threads.

Let us return to our example of the blocked file-server process in the single-process model. In this scenario, no other server process can execute until the first process is unblocked. By contrast, in the case of a task that contains multiple threads, while one server thread is blocked and waiting, a second thread in the same task could run. In this application, the cooperation of multiple threads that are part of the same job confers the advantages of higher throughput and improved performance. Other applications, such as the producer–consumer problem, require sharing a common buffer and so also benefit from this feature of thread utilization: The producer and consumer could be threads in a task. Little overhead is needed to switch between them, and, on a multiprocessor system, they could execute in parallel on two processors for maximum efficiency.

Threads provide a mechanism that allows sequential processes to make blocking system calls while also achieving parallelism. To illustrate the advantage of this mechanism, we shall consider writing a file server in a system where threads are not available. We have already seen that, in a single-threaded file server, the server process must carry a request to completion before acquiring new work. If the request involves waiting for disk access, the CPU is idle during the wait. Hence, the number of requests per second that can be processed is much less than with parallel execution. Without the option of multiple threads, a system designer seeking to minimize the performance slowdown of single-threaded

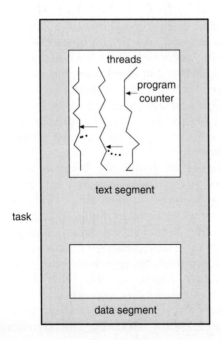

Figure 4.8   Multiple threads within a task.

processes would need to mimic the parallel structure of threads with the use of heavyweight process. She could do so, but at the cost of a complex nonsequential program structure.

The abstraction presented by a group of lightweight processes is that of multiple threads of control associated with several shared resources. There are many alternatives regarding threads; we mention a few of them briefly. Threads can be supported by the kernel (as in the Mach and OS/2 operating systems). In this case, a set of system calls similar to those for processes is provided. Alternatively, they can be supported above the kernel, via a set of library calls at the user level (as is done in Project Andrew from CMU).

Why should an operating system support one version or the other? User-level threads do not involve the kernel, and therefore are faster to switch among than kernel-supported threads. However, any calls to the operating system cause the entire process to wait, because the kernel schedules only processes (having no knowledge of threads), and a process which is waiting gets no CPU time. Scheduling can also be unfair. Consider two processes, one with 1 thread (process *a*) and the other with 100 threads (process *b*). Each process generally receives the same number of time slices, so the thread in process *a* runs 100 times as fast as a thread in process *b*. On systems with kernel-supported threads, switching among the threads is more time-consuming because the kernel (via an interrupt) must do the switch. Each thread may be scheduled independently, however, so process b could receive 100 times the CPU time that process a receives. Additionally, process b could have 100 system calls in operation concurrently, accomplishing far more than the same process would on a system with only user-level thread support.

Because of the compromises involved in each of these two approaches to threading, some systems use a hybrid approach in which both user-level and kernel-supported threads are implemented. Solaris 2 is such a system and is described below.

Threads are gaining in popularity because they have some of the characteristics of heavyweight processes but can execute more efficiently. There are many applications where this combination is useful. For instance, the UNIX kernel is usually single tasking: Only one task can be executing code in the kernel at a time. Many problems, such as synchronization of data access (locking of data structures while they are being modified) are avoided, because only one process is allowed to be doing the modification. Mach, on the other hand, is multithreaded, allowing the kernel to service many requests simultaneously. In this case, the threads themselves are synchronous: another thread in the same group may run only if the currently executing thread relinquishes control. Of course, the current thread would relinquish control only when it was not modifying shared data. On systems on which threads are asynchronous, some explicit locking mechanism must be used, just as in systems where multiple processes share data. Process synchronization is discussed in Chapter 6.

4.5.2 Example: Solaris 2

An examination of the thread system in a current operating system should help us to clarify many issues. For this purpose, we choose Solaris 2, a version of UNIX, which until 1992 supported only traditional heavyweight processes. It has been transformed into a modern operating system with support for threads at the kernel and user levels, symmetric multiprocessing, and real-time scheduling.

Solaris 2 supports user-level threads, as described in Section 4.5.1. They are supported by a library for their creation and scheduling, and the kernel knows nothing of these threads. Solaris 2 expects potentially thousands of user-level threads to be vying for CPU cycles.

Solaris 2 defines an intermediate level of threads as well. Between user-level threads and kernel-level threads are lightweight processes. Each task (still called a "process" in SunOS nomenclature) contains at least one LWP. These LWPs are manipulated by the thread library. The user-level threads are multiplexed on the LWPs of the process, and only user-level threads currently connected to LWPs accomplish work. The rest are either blocked or waiting for an LWP on which they can run.

All operations within the kernel are executed by standard kernel-level threads. There is a kernel-level thread for each LWP, and there are some kernel-level threads which run on the kernel's behalf and have no associated LWP (for instance, a thread to service disk requests). The entire thread system is depicted in Figure 4.9. Kernel-level threads are the only objects scheduled within the system (see Chapter 5). Some kernel-level threads are multiplexed on the processors in the system, whereas some are tied to a specific processor. For instance, the kernel thread associated with a device driver for a device connected to a specific processor will run only on that processor. By request, a thread can also be *pinned* to a processor. Only that thread runs on the processor, with the processor allocated to only that thread (see the rightmost thread in Figure 4.9).

Consider this system in operation. Any one task may have many user-level threads. These user-level threads may be scheduled and switched among kernel-supported lightweight processes without the intervention of the kernel. No context switch is needed for one user-level thread to block and another to start running, so user-level threads are extremely efficient.

These user-level threads are supported by lightweight processes. Each LWP is connected to exactly one kernel-level thread, whereas each user-level thread is independent of the kernel. There may be many LWPs in a task, but they are needed only when threads need to communicate with the kernel. For instance, one LWP is needed for every thread that may block concurrently in system calls. Consider five different file read requests that could be occurring simultaneously. Then, five LWPs would be needed, because they could all be waiting for I/O completion in the kernel.

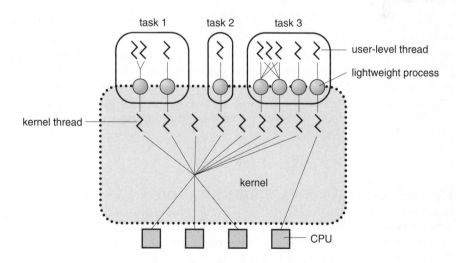

Figure 4.9 Threads in Solaris 2.

If a task had only four LWPs, then the fifth request would have to wait for one of the LWPs to return from the kernel. Adding a sixth LWP would gain us nothing if there were only enough work for five. No LWP is needed for user-level threads that do not make system calls concurrently with other threads.

The kernel threads are scheduled by the kernel's scheduler and execute on the CPU or CPUs in the system. If a kernel thread blocks (usually waiting for an I/O operation to complete), the processor is free to run another kernel thread. If the thread that blocked was running on behalf of an LWP, the LWP blocks as well. Up the chain, the user-level thread currently attached to the LWP also blocks. If the task containing that thread has only one LWP, the whole task blocks until the I/O completes. This behavior is the same as that of a process under an older version of the operating system.

With Solaris 2, a task no longer must block while waiting for I/O to complete. The task may have multiple LWPs; if one blocks, the others can continue to execute within the task. Further, even if all the task's LWPs are blocked, user-level threads may continue to run, as long as they do not need to contact the kernel (which they can do only through a lightweight process).

We conclude this example by examining the resource needs of each of these thread types.

- A kernel thread has only a small data structure and a stack. Switching between kernel threads does not require changing memory access information, and therefore is relatively fast.

- An LWP contains a process control block with register data, accounting information, and memory information. Switching between LWPs therefore requires quite a bit of work and is relatively slow.

- A user-level thread needs only a stack and a program counter: no kernel resources are required. The kernel is not involved in scheduling these user-level threads; therefore, switching among them is fast. There may be thousands of these user-level threads, but all the kernel will ever see is the LWPs in the process that support these user-level threads.

4.6 ■ Interprocess Communication

In Section 4.4, we showed how cooperating processes can communicate in a shared-memory environment. The scheme requires that these processes share a common buffer pool, and that the code for implementing the buffer be explicitly written by the application programmer. Another way to achieve the same effect is for the operating system to provide the means for cooperating processes to communicate with each other via an *interprocess-communication (IPC)* facility.

IPC provides a mechanism to allow processes to communicate and to synchronize their actions. Interprocess-communication is best provided by a message system. Message systems can be defined in many different ways. Message-passing systems also have other advantages, as will be shown in Chapter 16.

Note that the shared-memory and message-system communication schemes are not mutually exclusive, and could be used simultaneously within a single operating system or even a single process.

4.6.1 Basic Structure

The function of a message system is to allow processes to communicate with each other without the need to resort to shared variables. An IPC facility provides at least the two operations: **send***(message)* and **receive***(message)*.

Messages sent by a process can be of either fixed or variable size. If only fixed-sized messages can be sent, the physical implementation is straightforward. This restriction, however, makes the task of programming more difficult. On the other hand, variable-sized messages require a more complex physical implementation, but the programming task becomes simpler.

If processes P and Q want to communicate, they must send messages to and receive messages from each other; a *communication link* must exist between them. This link can be implemented in a variety of ways. We are concerned here not with the link's physical implementation (such as shared memory, hardware bus, or network, which are covered in Chapter 15), but rather with the issues of its logical implementation, such as its logical properties. Some basic implementation questions are these:

- How are links established?

- Can a link be associated with more than two processes?

- How many links can there be between every pair of processes?

- What is the capacity of a link? That is, does the link have some buffer space? If it does, how much?

- What is the size of messages? Can the link accommodate variable-sized or only fixed-sized messages?

- Is a link unidirectional or bidirectional? That is, if a link exists between P and Q, can messages flow in only one direction (such as only from P to Q) or in both directions?

The definition of *unidirectional* must be stated more carefully, since a link may be associated with more than two processes. Thus, we say that a link is unidirectional only if each process connected to the link can either send or receive, but not both, and each link has at least one receiver process connected to it.

In addition, there are several methods for logically implementing a link and the **send/receive** operations:

- Direct or indirect communication

- Symmetric or asymmetric communication

- Automatic or explicit buffering

- Send by copy or send by reference

- Fixed-sized or variable-sized messages

For the remainder of this section, we elaborate on these types of message systems.

4.6.2 Naming

Processes that want to communicate must have a way to refer to each other. They can use either *direct communication* or *indirect communication*, as we shall discuss in the next two subsections.

4.6.2.1 Direct Communication

In the direct-communication discipline, each process that wants to communicate must explicitly name the recipient or sender of the communication. In this scheme, the **send** and **receive** primitives are defined as follows:

> **send**(P, *message*). Send a *message* to process P.
> **receive**(Q, *message*). Receive a *message* from process Q.

A communication link in this scheme has the following properties:

- A link is established automatically between every pair of processes that want to communicate. The processes need to know only each other's identity to communicate.

- A link is associated with exactly two processes.

- Between each pair of processes, there exists exactly one link.

- The link may be unidirectional, but is usually bidirectional.

To illustrate, let us present a solution to the producer–consumer problem. To allow the producer and consumer processes to run concurrently, we allow the producer to produce one item while the consumer is consuming another item. When the producer finishes generating an item, it **sends** that item to the consumer. The consumer gets that item via the **receive** operation. If an item has not been produced yet, the consumer process must wait until an item is produced. The *producer* process is defined as

> **repeat**
> > ...
> > produce an item in *nextp*
> > ...
> > **send***(consumer,nextp);*
> **until** *false;*

The *consumer* process is defined as

> **repeat**
> > **receive***(producer,nextc);*
> > ...
> > consume the item in *nextc*
> > ...
> **until** *false;*

This scheme exhibits a symmetry in addressing; that is, both the sender and the receiver processes have to name each other to communicate. A variant of this scheme employs asymmetry in addressing. Only the sender names the recipient; the recipient is not required to name the sender. In this scheme, the **send** and **receive** primitives are defined as follows:

- **send***(P, message)*. Send a *message* to process *P*.

- **receive***(id, message)*. Receive a *message* from any process; the variable *id* is set to the name of the process with which communication has taken place.

The disadvantage in both of these schemes (symmetric and asymmetric) is the limited modularity of the resulting process definitions. Changing the name of a process may necessitate examining all other process definitions. All references to the old name must be found, so that they can be modified to the new name. This situation is not desirable from the viewpoint of separate compilation.

4.6.2.2 Indirect Communication

With indirect communication, the messages are sent to and received from *mailboxes* (also referred to as *ports*). A mailbox can be viewed abstractly as an object into which messages can be placed by processes and from which messages can be removed. Each mailbox has a unique identification. In this scheme, a process can communicate with some other process via a number of different mailboxes. Two processes can communicate only if the processes have a shared mailbox. The **send** and **receive** primitives are defined as follows:

> **send**(*A, message*). Send a *message* to mailbox *A*.
> **receive**(*A, message*). Receive a *message* from mailbox *A*.

In this scheme, a communication link has the following properties:

- A link is established between a pair of processes only if they have a shared mailbox.

- A link may be associated with more than two processes.

- Between each pair of communicating processes, there may be a number of different links, each link corresponding to one mailbox.

- A link may be either unidirectional or bidirectional.

Now suppose that processes P_1, P_2, and P_3 all share mailbox A. Process P_1 sends a message to A, while P_2 and P_3 each execute a **receive** from A. Which process will receive the message sent by P_1? This question can be resolved in a variety of ways:

- Allow a link to be associated with at most two processes.

- Allow at most one process at a time to execute a **receive** operation.

- Allow the system to select arbitrarily which process will receive the message (that is, either P_2 or P_3, but not both, will receive the message). The system may identify the receiver to the sender.

A mailbox may be owned either by a process or by the system. If the mailbox is owned by a process (that is, the mailbox is attached to or defined as part of the process), then we distinguish between the owner (who can only receive messages through this mailbox) and the user of the mailbox (who can only send messages to the mailbox). Since each mailbox has a unique owner, there can be no confusion about who should receive a message sent to this mailbox. When a process that owns a mailbox terminates, the mailbox disappears. Any process that subsequently sends a

message to this mailbox must be notified that the mailbox no longer exists
(via exception handling, described in Section 4.6.4).

There are various ways to designate the owner and users of a
particular mailbox. One possibility is to allow a process to declare variables
of type *mailbox*. The process that declares a mailbox is that mailbox's
owner. Any other process that knows the name of this mailbox can use
this mailbox.

On the other hand, a mailbox that is owned by the operating system
has an existence of its own. It is independent, and is not attached to any
particular process. The operating system provides a mechanism that allows
a process:

- To create a new mailbox

- To send and receive messages through the mailbox

- To destroy a mailbox

The process that creates a new mailbox is that mailbox's owner by default.
Initially, the owner is the only process that can receive messages through
this mailbox. However, the ownership and receive privilege may be passed
to other processes through appropriate system calls. Of course, this
provision could result in multiple receivers for each mailbox. Processes
may also share a mailbox through the process-creation facility. For
example, if process P created mailbox A, and then created a new process
Q, P and Q may share mailbox A. Since all processes with access rights to
a mailbox may ultimately terminate, after some time a mailbox may no
longer be accessible by any process. In this case, the operating system
should reclaim whatever space was used for the mailbox. This task may
require some form of *garbage collection* (see Section 10.3.5), in which a
separate operation occurs to search for and deallocate memory that is no
longer in use.

4.6.3 Buffering

A link has some capacity that determines the number of messages that can
reside in it temporarily. This property can be viewed as a queue of
messages attached to the link. Basically, there are three ways that such a
queue can be implemented:

- **Zero capacity:** The queue has maximum length 0; thus, the link cannot
  have any messages waiting in it. In this case, the sender must wait
  until the recipient receives the message. The two processes must be
  synchronized for a message transfer to take place. This
  synchronization is called a *rendezvous*.

- **Bounded capacity:** The queue has finite length n; thus, at most n messages can reside in it. If the queue is not full when a new message is sent, the latter is placed in the queue (either the message is copied or a pointer to the message is kept), and the sender can continue execution without waiting. The link has a finite capacity, however. If the link is full, the sender must be delayed until space is available in the queue.

- **Unbounded capacity:** The queue has potentially infinite length; thus, any number of messages can wait in it. The sender is never delayed.

The zero-capacity case is sometimes referred to as a message system with no buffering; the other cases provide automatic buffering.

We note that, in the nonzero-capacity cases, a process does not know whether a message has arrived at its destination after the **send** operation is completed. If this information is crucial for the computation, the sender must communicate explicitly with the receiver to find out whether the latter received the message. For example, suppose process P sends a message to process Q and can continue its execution only after the message is received. Process P executes the sequence

$$\textbf{send}(Q, message);$$
$$\textbf{receive}(Q, message);$$

Process Q executes

$$\textbf{receive}(P, message);$$
$$\textbf{send}(P, \text{``acknowledgment''});$$

Such processes are said to communicate *asynchronously*.

There are special cases that do not fit directly into any of the categories that we have discussed:

- The process sending a message is never delayed. However, if the receiver has not received the message before the sending process sends another message, the first message is lost. The advantage of this scheme is that large messages do not need to be copied more than once. The main disadvantage is that the programming task becomes more difficult. Processes need to synchronize explicitly, to ensure both that messages are not lost and that the sender and receiver do not manipulate the message buffer simultaneously.

- The process sending a message is delayed until it receives a reply. This scheme was adopted in the *Thoth* operating system. In this system, messages are of fixed size (eight words). A process P that sends a message is blocked until the receiving process has received the message and has sent back an eight-word reply by the **reply**(*P*, *message)* primitive. The reply message overwrites the original message buffer. The only difference between the **send** and **reply** primitives is that a **send** causes the sending process to be blocked, whereas the **reply** allows both the sending process and the receiving process to continue with their executions immediately.

This synchronous communication method can be expanded easily into a full-featured *remote procedure call (RPC)* system. An RPC system is based on the realization that a subroutine or procedure call in a single-processor system acts exactly like a message system in which the sender blocks until it receives a reply. The message is then like a subroutine call, and the return message contains the value of the subroutine computed. The next logical step, therefore, is for concurrent processes to be able to call each other as subroutines using RPC. In fact, we shall see in Chapter 16 that RPCs can be used between processes running on separate computers to allow multiple computers to work together in a mutually beneficial way.

4.6.4 Exception Conditions

A message system is particularly useful in a distributed environment, where processes may reside at different sites (machines). In such an environment, the probability that an error will occur during communication (and processing) is much larger than in a single-machine environment. In a single-machine environment, messages are usually implemented in shared memory. If a failure occurs, the entire system fails. In a distributed environment, however, messages are transferred by communication lines, and the failure of one site (or link) does not necessarily result in the failure of the entire system.

When a failure occurs in either a centralized or distributed system, some error recovery (exception-condition handling) must take place. Let us discuss briefly some of the exception conditions that a system must handle in the context of a message scheme.

4.6.4.1 Process Terminates

Either a sender or a receiver may terminate before a message is processed. This situation will leave messages that will never be received or processes waiting for messages that will never be sent. We consider two cases here:

1. A receiver process *P* may wait for a message from a process *Q* that has terminated. If no action is taken, *P* will be blocked forever. In this case, the system may either terminate *P* or notify *P* that *Q* has terminated.

2. Process *P* may send a message to a process *Q* that has terminated. In the automatic-buffering scheme, no harm is done; *P* simply continues

with its execution. If P needs to know that its message has been processed by Q, it must program explicitly for an acknowledgment. In the no-buffering case, P will be blocked forever. As in case 1, the system may either terminate P or notify P that Q has terminated.

4.6.4.2 Lost Messages

A message from process P to process Q may become lost somewhere in the communications network, due to a hardware or communication-line failure. There are three basic methods for dealing with this event:

1. The operating system is responsible for detecting this event and for resending the message.

2. The sending process is responsible for detecting this event and for retransmitting the message, if it so wants.

3. The operating system is responsible for detecting this event; it then notifies the sending process that the message has been lost. The sending process can proceed as it chooses.

It is not always necessary to detect lost messages. In fact, some network protocols specify that messages are unreliable, whereas some guarantee reliability (see Chapter 15). The user must specify (that is, either notify the system, or program this requirement itself) that such a detection should take place.

How do we detect that a message is lost? The most common detection method is to use *timeouts*. When a message is sent out, a reply message, acknowledging reception of the message, is always sent back. The operating system or a process may then specify a time interval during which it expects the acknowledgment message to arrive. If this time period elapses before the acknowledgment arrives, the operating system (or process) may assume that the message is lost, and the message is resent. It is possible, however, that a message did not get lost, but simply took a little longer than expected to travel through the network. In this case, we may have multiple copies of the same message flowing through the network. A mechanism must exist to distinguish between these various types of messages. This problem is discussed in more detail in Chapter 16.

4.6.4.3 Scrambled Messages

The message may be delivered to its destination, but be scrambled on the way (for example, because of noise in the communications channel). This case is similar to the case of a lost message. Usually, the operating system will retransmit the original message. Checksums (such as parity or CRC) are commonly used to detect this type of error.

4.6.5 An Example: Mach

As an example of a message-based operating system, consider the Mach operating system, developed at Carnegie Mellon University. The Mach kernel supports the creation and destruction of multiple tasks, which are similar to processes but have multiple threads of control. Most communication in Mach, including most of the system calls and all intertask information, is carried out by *messages*. Messages are sent to and received from mailboxes, called *ports* in Mach.

Even system calls are made by messages. When each task is created, two special mailboxes, the Kernel mailbox and the Notify mailbox, are also created. The Kernel mailbox is used by the kernel to communicate with the task. The kernel sends notification of event occurrences to the Notify port. Only three system calls are needed for message transfer. The *msg_send* call sends a message to a mailbox. A message is received via *msg_receive*. RPCs are executed via *msg_rpc*, which sends a message and waits for exactly one return message from the sender.

The *port_allocate* system call creates a new mailbox and allocates space for its queue of messages. The maximum size of the message queue defaults to eight messages. The task that creates the mailbox is that mailbox's owner. The owner also is given receive access to the mailbox. Only one task at a time can either own or receive from a mailbox, but these rights can be sent to other tasks if desired.

The mailbox has an initially empty queue of messages. As messages are sent to the mailbox, the messages are copied into the mailbox. All messages have the same priority. Mach guarantees that multiple messages from the same sender are queued in first-in, first-out (FIFO) order, but does not guarantee an absolute ordering. For instance, messages sent from each of two senders may be queued in any order.

The messages themselves consist of a fixed-length header, followed by a variable-length data portion. The header includes the length of the message and two mailbox names. When a message is sent, one mailbox name is the mailbox to which the message is being sent. Commonly, the sending thread expects a reply; the mailbox name of the sender is passed on to the receiving task, which may use it as a "return address" to send messages back.

The variable part of a message is a list of typed data items. Each entry in the list has a type, size, and value. The type of the objects specified in the message is important, since operating-system–defined objects — such as the ownership or receive access rights, task states, and memory segments — may be sent in messages.

The send and receive operations themselves are quite flexible. For instance, when a message is sent to a mailbox, the mailbox may be full. If the mailbox is not full, the message is copied to the mailbox and the sending thread continues. If the mailbox is full, the sending thread has four options:

1. Wait indefinitely until there is room in the mailbox.

2. Wait at most *n* milliseconds.

3. Do not wait at all, but return immediately.

4. Temporarily cache a message. One message can be given to the operating system to keep even though the mailbox to which it is being sent is full. When the message can actually be put in the mailbox, a message is sent back to the sender; only one such message to a full mailbox can be pending at any time for a given sending thread.

The last option is meant for server tasks, such as a line-printer driver. After finishing a request, these tasks may need to send a one-time reply to the task that had requested service, but must also continue with other service requests, even if the reply mailbox for a client is full.

The receive operation must specify from which mailbox or mailbox set to receive a message. A *mailbox set* is a collection of mailboxes, as declared by the task, which can be grouped together and treated as one mailbox for the purposes of the task. Threads in a task can receive from only a mailbox or mailbox set for which that task has receive access. A *port_status* system call returns the number of messages in a given mailbox. The receive operation attempts to receive from (1) any mailbox in a mailbox set, or (2) a specific (named) mailbox. If no message is waiting to be received, the receiving thread may wait, wait at most *n* milliseconds, or not wait.

The Mach system was especially designed for distributed systems, which we discuss in Chapters 15 through 18, but Mach is also suitable for single-processor systems. The major problem with message systems has generally been poor performance caused by copying the message first from the sender to the mailbox, and then from the mailer to the receiver. The Mach message system attempts to avoid double copy operations by using virtual-memory management techniques (Chapter 9). Essentially, Mach maps the address space containing the sender's message into the receiver's address space. The message itself is never actually copied. This message-management technique provides a large performance boost, but works for only intrasystem messages. The Mach operating system is discussed in detail in Chapter 20.

4.7 ■ Summary

A *process* is a program in execution. As a process executes, it changes *state*. The state of a process is defined by that process's current activity. Each process may be in one of the following states: *new, ready, running, waiting,* or *halted*. Each process is represented in the operating system by its own *process control block (PCB)*.

A process, when it is not executing, is placed in some waiting queue. There are two major classes of queues in an operating system: I/O request queues and the ready queue. The ready queue contains all the processes that are ready to execute and are waiting for the CPU. Each process is represented by a PCB, and the PCBs can be linked together to form a ready queue. Long-term (job) scheduling is the selection of processes to be allowed to contend for the CPU. Normally, long-term scheduling is heavily influenced by resource-allocation considerations, especially memory management. Short-term (CPU) scheduling is the selection of one process from the ready queue.

The processes in the system can execute concurrently. There are several reasons for allowing concurrent execution: information sharing, computation speedup, modularity, and convenience. Concurrent execution requires a mechanism for process creation and deletion.

The processes executing in the operating system may be either independent processes or cooperating processes. Cooperating processes must have the means to communicate with each other. Principally, there exist two complementary communication schemes: shared memory and message systems. The *shared-memory* method requires communicating processes to share some variables. The processes are expected to exchange information through the use of these shared variables. In a shared-memory system, the responsibility for providing communication rests with the application programmers; the operating system needs to provide only the shared memory. The *message-system* method allows the processes to exchange messages. The responsibility for providing communication then rests with the operating system itself. These two schemes are not mutually exclusive, and could be used simultaneously within a single operating system.

Cooperating processes that directly share a logical address space can be implemented as lightweight processes or threads. A *thread* is a basic unit of CPU utilization, and it shares with peer threads its code section, data section, and operating-system resources, collectively known as a *task*. A task does nothing if no threads are in it, and a thread must be in exactly one task. The extensive sharing makes CPU switching among peer threads and thread creation inexpensive, compared with context switches among heavyweight processes.

■ Exercises

4.1 Several popular microcomputer operating systems provide little or no means of concurrent processing. Discuss the major complications that concurrent processing adds to an operating system.

4.2 Describe the differences among short-term, medium-term, and long-term scheduling.

4.3 A DECSYSTEM-20 computer, has multiple register sets. Describe the actions of a context switch if the new context is already loaded into one of the register sets. What else must happen if the new context is in memory rather than a register set, and all the register sets are in use?

4.4 What two advantages do threads have over multiple processes? What major disadvantage do they have? Suggest one application that would benefit from the use of threads, and one that would not.

4.5 What resources are used when a thread is created? How do they differ from those used when a process is created?

4.6 Describe the actions taken by a kernel to context switch

a. Among threads.

b. Among processes.

4.7 What are the differences between user-level threads and kernel-supported threads? Under what circumstances is one type "better" than the other?

4.8 The correct producer–consumer algorithm presented in Section 4.6 allows only $n - 1$ buffers to be full at any time. Modify the algorithm to allow all the buffers to be utilized fully.

4.9 Consider the interprocess-communication scheme where mailboxes are used.

a. Suppose a process P wants to wait for two messages, one from mailbox A and one from mailbox B. What sequence of **send** and **receive** should it execute?

b. What sequence of **send** and **receive** should P execute if P wants to wait for one message either from mailbox A or from mailbox B (or from both)?

c. A **receive** operation makes a process wait until the mailbox is nonempty. Either devise a scheme that allows a process to wait until a mailbox is empty, or explain why such a scheme cannot exist.

4.10 Consider an operating system that supports both the IPC and RPC schemes. Give examples of problems that could be solved with each type of scheme. Explain why each problem is best solved by the method that you specify.

Bibliographic Notes

Doeppner [1987] discussed early work in implementing threads at the user level. Thread performance issues were discussed in Anderson et al. [1989]. Anderson et al. [1991] continued this work by evaluating the performance of user-level threads with kernel support. Marsh et al. [1991] discussed first-class user-level threads. Bershad et al. [1990] described combining threads with RPC. Draves et al. [1991] discussed the use of continuations to implement thread management and communication in operating systems,

The IBM OS/2 operating system is a multithreaded operating system that runs on personal computers [Kogan and Rawson 1988]. The *Synthesis* high-performance kernel uses threads as well [Massalin and Pu 1989]. The implementation of threads in Mach was described in Tevanian et al. [1987a]. Birrell [1989] discussed programming with threads. Debugging multithreaded applications continues to be a difficult problem that is under investigation. Caswell and Black [1990] implemented a debugger in Mach.

Sun Microsystem's Solaris 2 thread structure was described in Eykholt et al. [1992]. The user-level threads were detailed in Stein and Shaw [1992]. Peacock [1992] discussed the multithreading of the file system in Solaris 2.

The subject of interprocess communication was discussed by Brinch Hansen [1970] with respect to the RC 4000 system. The interprocess communication facility in the Thoth operating system was discussed by Cheriton et al. [1979]; the one for the Accent operating system was discussed by Rashid and Robertson [1981]; the one for the Mach operating system was discussed by Accetta et al. [1986]. Schlichting and Schneider [1982] discussed asynchronous message-passing primitives. The IPC facility implemented at the user level was described in Bershad et al. [1990].

Discussions concerning the implementation of RPCs were presented by Birrell and Nelson [1984]. A design of a reliable RPC mechanism was presented by Shrivastava and Panzieri [1982]. A survey of RPCs was presented by Tay and Ananda [1990]. Stankovic [1982] and Staunstrup [1982] discussed the issues of procedure calls versus message-passing communication.

CHAPTER 5

CPU SCHEDULING

CPU scheduling is the basis of multiprogrammed operating systems. By switching the CPU among processes, the operating system can make the computer more productive. In this chapter, we introduce the basic scheduling concepts and present several different CPU scheduling algorithms. We also consider the problem of selecting an algorithm for a particular system.

5.1 ■ Basic Concepts

The objective of multiprogramming is to have some process running at all times, to maximize CPU utilization. For a uniprocessor system, there will never be more than one running process. If there are more processes, the rest will have to wait until the CPU is free and can be rescheduled.

The idea of multiprogramming is relatively simple. A process is executed until it must wait, typically for the completion of some I/O request. In a simple computer system, the CPU would then just sit idle. All this waiting time is wasted; no useful work is accomplished. With multiprogramming, we try to use this time productively. Several processes are kept in memory at one time. When one process has to wait, the operating system takes the CPU away from that process and gives the CPU to another process. This pattern continues. Every time one process has to wait, another process may take over the use of the CPU.

Scheduling is a fundamental operating-system function. Almost all computer resources are scheduled before use. The CPU is, of course, one of the primary computer resources. Thus, its scheduling is central to operating-system design.

5.1.1 CPU–I/O Burst Cycle

The success of CPU scheduling depends on the following observed property of processes: Process execution consists of a *cycle* of CPU execution and I/O wait. Processes alternate back and forth between these two states. Process execution begins with a *CPU burst*. That is followed by an *I/O burst*, which is followed by another CPU burst, then another I/O burst, and so on. Eventually, the last CPU burst will end with a system request to terminate execution, rather than with another I/O burst (Figure 5.1).

The durations of these CPU bursts have been measured. Although they vary greatly from process to process and computer to computer, they tend to have a frequency curve similar to that shown in Figure 5.2. The curve is generally characterized as exponential or hyperexponential. There is a large

Figure 5.1 Alternating sequence of CPU and I/O bursts.

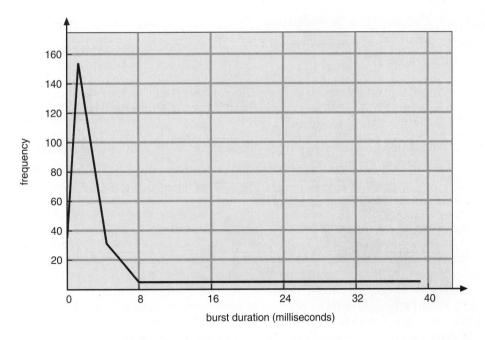

Figure 5.2 Histogram of CPU-burst times.

number of short CPU bursts, and there is a small number of long CPU bursts. An I/O-bound program would typically have many very short CPU bursts. A CPU-bound program might have a few very long CPU bursts. This distribution can be important in the selection of an appropriate CPU scheduling algorithm.

5.1.2 CPU Scheduler

Whenever the CPU becomes idle, the operating system must select one of the processes in the ready queue to be executed. The selection process is carried out by the *short-term scheduler* (or CPU scheduler). The scheduler selects from among the processes in memory that are ready to execute, and allocates the CPU to one of them.

Note that the ready queue is not necessarily a first-in, first-out (FIFO) queue. As we shall see when we consider the various scheduling algorithms, a ready queue may be implemented as a FIFO queue, a priority queue, a tree, or simply an unordered linked list. Conceptually, however, all the processes in the ready queue are lined up waiting for a chance to run on the CPU. The records in the queues are generally PCBs of the processes.

5.1.3 Preemptive Scheduling

CPU scheduling decisions may take place under the following four circumstances:

1. When a process switches from the running state to the waiting state (for example, I/O request, or invocation of wait for the termination of one of the child processes)

2. When a process switches from the running state to the ready state (for example, when an interrupt occurs)

3. When a process switches from the waiting state to the ready state (for example, completion of I/O)

4. When a process terminates

For circumstances 1 and 4, there is no choice in terms of scheduling. A new process (if one exists in the ready queue) must be selected for execution. There is a choice, however, for circumstances 2 and 3.

When scheduling takes place only under circumstances 1 and 4, we say the scheduling scheme is *nonpreemptive*; otherwise, the scheduling scheme is *preemptive*. Under nonpreemptive scheduling, once the CPU has been allocated to a process, the process keeps the CPU until it releases the CPU either by terminating or by switching to the waiting state. This scheduling method is used by the Microsoft Windows environment. It is the only method that can be used on certain hardware platforms, because it does not require the special hardware (for example, a timer) needed for preemptive scheduling.

Unfortunately, preemptive scheduling incurs a cost. Consider the case of two processes sharing data. One may be in the midst of updating the data when it is preempted and the second process is run. The second process may try to read the data, which are currently in an inconsistent state. New mechanisms thus are needed to coordinate access to shared data; this topic is discussed in Chapter 6.

Preemption also has an effect on the design of the operating-system kernel. During the processing of a system call, the kernel may be busy with an activity on behalf of a process. Such activities may involve changing important kernel data (for instance, I/O queues). What happens if the process is preempted in the middle of these changes, and the kernel (or the device driver) needs to read or modify the same structure? Chaos ensues. Some operating systems, including most versions of UNIX, deal with this problem by waiting either for a system call to complete, or for an I/O block to take place, before doing a context switch. This scheme ensures that the kernel structure is simple, since the kernel will not preempt a process while the kernel data structures are in an inconsistent state.

Unfortunately, this kernel execution model is a poor one for supporting real-time computing and multiprocessing. These problems, and their solutions, are described in Sections 5.4 and 5.5.

In the case of UNIX, there are still sections of code at risk. Because interrupts can, by definition, occur at any time, and because interrupts cannot always be ignored by the kernel, the sections of code affected by interrupts must be guarded from simultaneous use. The operating system needs to accept interrupts at almost all times, since otherwise input might be lost or output overwritten. So that these sections of code are not accessed concurrently by several processes, they disable interrupts at entry and reenable interrupts at exit.

5.1.4 Dispatcher

Another component involved in the CPU scheduling function is the *dispatcher*. The dispatcher is the module that gives control of the CPU to the process selected by the short-term scheduler. This function involves:

- Switching context

- Switching to user mode

- Jumping to the proper location in the user program to restart that program

The dispatcher should be as fast as possible, given that it is invoked during every process switch. The time it takes for the dispatcher to stop one process and start another running is known as the *dispatch latency*.

5.2 ■ Scheduling Criteria

Different CPU scheduling algorithms have different properties and may favor one class of processes over another. In choosing which algorithm to use in a particular situation, we must consider the properties of the various algorithms.

Many criteria have been suggested for comparing CPU scheduling algorithms. Which characteristics are used for comparison can make a substantial difference in the determination of the best algorithm. Criteria that are used include the following:

- **CPU utilization**. We want to keep the CPU as busy as possible. CPU utilization may range from 0 to 100 percent. In a real system, it should range from 40 percent (for a lightly loaded system) to 90 percent (for a heavily used system).

- **Throughput**. If the CPU is busy, then work is being done. One measure of work is the number of processes that are completed per time unit, called *throughput*. For long processes, this rate may be one process per hour; for short transactions, throughput might be 10 processes per second.

- **Turnaround time**. From the point of view of a particular process, the important criterion is how long it takes to execute that process. The interval from the time of submission to the time of completion is the *turnaround time*. Turnaround time is the sum of the periods spent waiting to get into memory, waiting in the ready queue, executing on the CPU, and doing I/O.

- **Waiting time**. The CPU scheduling algorithm does not affect the amount of time during which a process executes or does I/O; it affects only the amount of time that a process spends waiting in the ready queue. Waiting time is the sum of the periods spent waiting in the ready queue.

- **Response time**. In an interactive system, turnaround time may not be the best criterion. Often, a process can produce some output fairly early, and can continue computing new results while previous results are being output to the user. Thus, another measure is the time from the submission of a request until the first response is produced. This measure, called *response time*, is the amount of time it takes to start responding, but not the time that it takes to output that response. The turnaround time is generally limited by the speed of the output device.

It is desirable to maximize CPU utilization and throughput, and to minimize turnaround time, waiting time, and response time. In most cases, we optimize the average measure. However, there are circumstances when it is desirable to optimize the minimum or maximum values, rather than the average. For example, to guarantee that all users get good service, we may want to minimize the maximum response time.

It has also been suggested that, for interactive systems (such as time-sharing systems), it is more important to minimize the *variance* in the response time than it is to minimize the average response time. A system with reasonable and *predictable* response time may be considered more desirable than is a system that is faster on the average, but is highly variable. However, little work has been done on CPU scheduling algorithms to minimize variance.

As we discuss various CPU scheduling algorithms, we want to illustrate their operation. An accurate illustration should involve many processes, each being a sequence of several hundred CPU bursts and I/O bursts. For simplicity of illustration, we consider only one CPU burst (in milliseconds) per process in our examples. Our measure of comparison is the average waiting time. More elaborate evaluation mechanisms are discussed in Section 5.6.

5.3 ■ Scheduling Algorithms

CPU scheduling deals with the problem of deciding which of the processes in the ready queue is to be allocated the CPU. There are many different CPU scheduling algorithms. In this section, we describe several of these algorithms.

5.3.1 First-Come, First-Served Scheduling

By far the simplest CPU scheduling algorithm is the *first-come, first-served scheduling (FCFS)* algorithm. With this scheme, the process that requests the CPU first is allocated the CPU first. The implementation of the FCFS policy is easily managed with a FIFO queue. When a process enters the ready queue, its PCB is linked onto the tail of the queue. When the CPU is free, it is allocated to the process at the head of the queue. The running process is then removed from the queue. The code for FCFS scheduling is simple to write and understand.

The average waiting time under the FCFS policy, however, is often quite long. Consider the following set of processes that arrive at time 0, with the length of the CPU-burst time given in milliseconds:

Process	Burst Time
P_1	24
P_2	3
P_3	3

If the processes arrive in the order P_1, P_2, P_3, and are served in FCFS order, we get the result shown in the following *Gantt chart*:

P_1	P_2	P_3

0   24   27   30

The waiting time is 0 milliseconds for process P_1, 24 milliseconds for process P_2, and 27 milliseconds for process P_3. Thus, the average waiting time is $(0 + 24 + 27)/3 = 17$ milliseconds. If the processes arrive in the order P_2, P_3, P_1, however, the results will be as shown in the following Gantt chart:

P_2	P_3	P_1

```
0        3        6                                              30
```

The average waiting time is now $(6 + 0 + 3)/3 = 3$ milliseconds. This reduction is substantial.   Thus, the average waiting time under a FCFS policy is generally not minimal, and may vary substantially if the process CPU-burst times vary greatly.

In addition, consider the performance of FCFS scheduling in a dynamic situation. Assume we have one CPU-bound process and many I/O-bound processes.   As the processes flow around the system, the following scenario may result. The CPU-bound process will get the CPU and hold it. During this time, all the other processes will finish their I/O and move into the ready queue, waiting for the CPU. While the processes wait in the ready queue, the I/O devices are idle. Eventually, the CPU-bound process finishes its CPU burst and moves to an I/O device. All the I/O-bound processes, which have very short CPU bursts, execute quickly and move back to the I/O queues. At this point, the CPU sits idle. The CPU-bound process will then move back to the ready queue and be allocated the CPU. Again, all the I/O processes end up waiting in the ready queue until the CPU-bound process is done. There is a *convoy effect*, as all the other processes wait for the one big process to get off the CPU. This effect results in lower CPU and device utilization than might be possible if the shorter processes were allowed to go first.

The FCFS scheduling algorithm is nonpreemptive. Once the CPU has been allocated to a process, that process keeps the CPU until it releases the CPU, either by terminating or by requesting I/O. The FCFS algorithm is particularly troublesome for time-sharing systems, where it is important that each user get a share of the CPU at regular intervals. It would be disastrous to allow one process to keep the CPU for an extended period.

5.3.2 Shortest-Job-First Scheduling

A different approach to CPU scheduling is the *shortest-job-first* (SJF) algorithm. This algorithm associates with each process the length of the latter's next CPU burst. When the CPU is available, it is assigned to the process that has the smallest next CPU burst. If two processes have the same length next CPU burst, FCFS scheduling is used to break the tie. Note that a more appropriate term would be the *shortest next CPU burst*, because the scheduling is done by examining the length of the next CPU-burst of a process, rather than its total length. We use the term SJF because most people and textbooks refer to this type of scheduling discipline as SJF.

As an example, consider the following set of processes, with the length of the CPU burst time given in milliseconds:

Process	Burst Time
P_1	6
P_2	8
P_3	7
P_4	3

Using SJF scheduling, we would schedule these processes according to the following Gantt chart:

P_4	P_1	P_3	P_2

```
0       3           9              16                24
```

The waiting time is 3 milliseconds for process P_1, 16 milliseconds for process P_2, 9 milliseconds for process P_3, and 0 milliseconds for process P_4. Thus, the average waiting time is $(3 + 16 + 9 + 0)/4 = 7$ milliseconds. If we were using the FCFS scheduling, then the average waiting time would be 10.25 milliseconds.

The SJF scheduling algorithm is provably *optimal*, in that it gives the minimum average waiting time for a given set of processes. By moving a short process before a long one the waiting time of the short process decreases more than it increases the waiting time of the long process. Consequently, the *average* waiting time decreases.

The real difficulty with the SJF algorithm is knowing the length of the next CPU request. For long-term (job) scheduling in a batch system, we can use as the length the process time limit that a user specifies when he submits the job. Thus, users are motivated to estimate the process time limit accurately, since a lower value may mean faster response. (Too low a value will cause a time-limit-exceeded error and require resubmission.) SJF scheduling is used frequently in long-term scheduling.

Although the SJF algorithm is optimal, it cannot be implemented at the level of short-term CPU scheduling. There is no way to know the length of the next CPU burst. One approach is to try to approximate SJF scheduling. We may not *know* the length of the next CPU burst, but we may be able to *predict* its value. We expect that the next CPU burst will be similar in length to the previous ones. Thus, by computing an approximation of the length of the next CPU burst, we can pick the process with the shortest predicted CPU burst.

The next CPU burst is generally predicted as an exponential average of the measured lengths of previous CPU bursts. Let t_n be the length of the nth CPU burst, and let τ_{n+1} be our predicted value for the next CPU burst. Then, for α, $0 \leq \alpha \leq 1$, define

$$\tau_{n+1} = \alpha t_n + (1 - \alpha)\tau_n.$$

This formula defines an *exponential average*. The value of t_n contains our most recent information; τ_n stores the past history. The parameter α controls the relative weight of recent and past history in our prediction. If $\alpha = 0$, then $\tau_{n+1} = \tau_n$, and recent history has no effect (current conditions are assumed to be transient); if $\alpha = 1$, then $\tau_{n+1} = t_n$, and only the most recent CPU burst matters (history is assumed to be old and irrelevant). More commonly, $\alpha = 1/2$, so recent history and past history are equally weighted. Figure 5.3 shows an exponential average with $\alpha = 1/2$. The initial τ_0 can be defined as a constant or as an overall system average.

To understand the behavior of the exponential average, we can expand the formula for τ_{n+1} by substituting for τ_n, to find

$$\tau_{n+1} = \alpha t_n + (1-\alpha)\alpha t_{n-1} + \ldots + (1-\alpha)^j \alpha t_{n-j} + \ldots + (1-\alpha)^{n+1} \tau_0.$$

Since both α and $(1 - \alpha)$ are less than or equal to 1, each successive term has less weight than its predecessor.

The SJF algorithm may be either *preemptive* or *nonpreemptive*. The choice arises when a new process arrives at the ready queue while a previous process is executing. The new process may have a shorter next CPU burst than what is left of the currently executing process. A preemptive SJF algorithm will preempt the currently executing process, whereas a

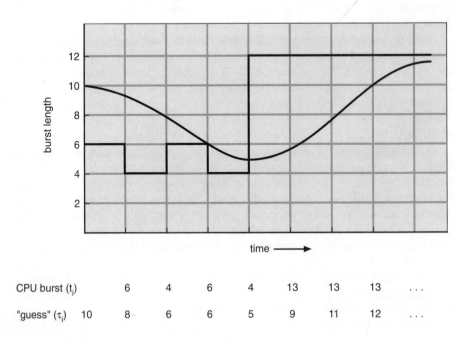

Figure 5.3 Prediction of the length of the next CPU burst.

nonpreemptive SJF algorithm will allow the currently running process to finish its CPU burst. Preemptive SJF scheduling is sometimes called *shortest-remaining-time-first* scheduling.

As an example, consider the following four processes, with the length of the CPU-burst time given in milliseconds:

Process	Arrival Time	Burst Time
P_1	0	8
P_2	1	4
P_3	2	9
P_4	3	5

If the processes arrive at the ready queue at the times shown and need the indicated burst times, then the resulting preemptive SJF schedule is as depicted in the following Gantt chart:

P_1	P_2	P_4	P_1	P_3

```
0   1       5          10          17              26
```

Process P_1 is started at time 0, since it is the only process in the queue. Process P_2 arrives at time 1. The remaining time for process P_1 (7 milliseconds) is larger than the time required by process P_2 (4 milliseconds), so process P_1 is preempted, and process P_2 is scheduled. The average waiting time for this example is $((10 - 1) + (1 - 1) + (17 - 2) + (5 - 3))/4 = 26/4 = 6.5$ milliseconds. A nonpreemptive SJF scheduling would result in an average waiting time of 5.75 milliseconds.

5.3.3 Priority Scheduling

The SJF algorithm is a special case of the general *priority* scheduling algorithm. A priority is associated with each process, and the CPU is allocated to the process with the highest priority. Equal-priority processes are scheduled in FCFS order.

An SJF algorithm is simply a priority algorithm where the priority (p) is the inverse of the (predicted) next CPU burst (τ): $p = 1/\tau$. The larger the CPU burst, the lower the priority, and vice versa.

Note that we discuss scheduling in terms of *high* priority and *low* priority. Priorities are generally some fixed range of numbers, such as 0 to 7, or 0 to 4095. However, there is no general agreement on whether 0 is the highest or lowest priority. Some systems use low numbers to represent low priority; others use low numbers for high priority. This difference can lead to confusion. In this text, we assume that low numbers represent high priority.

As an example, consider the following set of processes, assumed to have arrived at time 0, in the order P_1, P_2, ..., P_5, with the length of the CPU-burst time given in milliseconds:

Process	Burst Time	Priority
P_1	10	3
P_2	1	1
P_3	2	3
P_4	1	4
P_5	5	2

Using priority scheduling, we would schedule these processes according to the following Gantt chart:

P_2	P_5	P_1	P_3	P_4

```
0   1         6                        16    18   19
```

The average waiting time is 8.2 milliseconds.

Priorities can be defined either internally or externally. Internally defined priorities use some measurable quantity or quantities to compute the priority of a process. For example, time limits, memory requirements, the number of open files, and the ratio of average I/O burst to average CPU burst have been used in computing priorities. External priorities are set by criteria that are external to the operating system, such as the importance of the process, the type and amount of funds being paid for computer use, the department sponsoring the work, and other, often political, factors.

Priority scheduling can be either preemptive or nonpreemptive. When a process arrives at the ready queue, its priority is compared with the priority of the currently running process. A preemptive priority scheduling algorithm will preempt the CPU if the priority of the newly arrived process is higher than is the priority of the currently running process. A nonpreemptive priority scheduling algorithm will simply put the new process at the head of the ready queue.

A major problem with priority scheduling algorithms is *indefinite blocking* or *starvation*. A process that is ready to run but lacking the CPU can be considered blocked, waiting for the CPU. A priority scheduling algorithm can leave some low-priority processes waiting indefinitely for the CPU. In a heavily loaded computer system, a steady stream of higher-priority processes can prevent a low-priority process from ever getting the CPU. Generally, one of two things will happen. Either the process will eventually be run (at 2 A.M. Sunday, when the system is finally lightly loaded), or the computer system will eventually crash and lose all unfinished low-priority processes. (Rumor has it that, when they shut down the IBM 7094 at MIT in 1973, they found a low-priority process that had been submitted in 1967 and had not yet been run.)

A solution to the problem of indefinite blockage of low-priority processes is *aging*. Aging is a technique of gradually increasing the priority of processes that wait in the system for a long time. For example, if priorities range from 0 (low) to 127 (high), we could increment the priority of a waiting process by 1 every 15 minutes. Eventually, even a process with an initial priority of 0 would have the highest priority in the system and would be executed. In fact, it would take no more than 32 hours for a priority 0 process to age to a priority 127 process.

5.3.4 Round-Robin Scheduling

The *round-robin (RR)* scheduling algorithm is designed especially for time-sharing systems. It is similar to FCFS scheduling, but preemption is added to switch between processes. A small unit of time, called a *time quantum*, or time slice, is defined. A time quantum is generally from 10 to 100 milliseconds. The ready queue is treated as a circular queue. The CPU scheduler goes around the ready queue, allocating the CPU to each process for a time interval of up to 1 time quantum.

To implement RR scheduling, we keep the ready queue as a FIFO queue of processes. New processes are added to the tail of the ready queue. The CPU scheduler picks the first process from the ready queue, sets a timer to interrupt after 1 time quantum, and dispatches the process.

One of two things will then happen. The process may have a CPU burst of less than 1 time quantum. In this case, the process itself will release the CPU voluntarily. The scheduler will then proceed to the next process in the ready queue. Otherwise, if the CPU burst of the currently running process is longer than 1 time quantum, the timer will go off and will cause an interrupt to the operating system. A context switch will be executed, and the process will be put at the *tail* of the ready queue. The CPU scheduler will then select the next process in the ready queue.

The average waiting time under the RR policy, however, is often quite long. Consider the following set of processes that arrive at time 0, with the length of the CPU-burst time given in milliseconds:

Process	Burst Time
P_1	24
P_2	3
P_3	3

If we use a time quantum of 4 milliseconds, then process P_1 gets the first 4 milliseconds. Since it requires another 20 milliseconds, it is preempted after the first time quantum, and the CPU is given to the next process in the queue, process P_2. Since process P_2 does not need 4 milliseconds, it quits before its time quantum expires. The CPU is then given to the next process, process P_3. Once each process has received 1 time quantum, the CPU is returned to process P_1 for an additional time quantum. The resulting RR schedule is

P_1	P_2	P_3	P_1	P_1	P_1	P_1	P_1
0	4	7	10	14	18	22	26	30

The average waiting time is 17/3 = 5.66 milliseconds.

In the RR scheduling algorithm, no process is allocated the CPU for more than 1 time quantum in a row. If a process' CPU burst exceeds 1 time quantum, that process is *preempted* and is put back in the ready queue. The RR scheduling algorithm is preemptive.

If there are n processes in the ready queue and the time quantum is q, then each process gets $1/n$ of the CPU time in chunks of at most q time units. Each process must wait no longer than $(n - 1) \times q$ time units until its next time quantum. For example, if there are five processes, with a time quantum of 20 milliseconds, then each process will get up to 20 milliseconds every 100 milliseconds.

The performance of the RR algorithm depends heavily on the size of the time quantum. At one extreme, if the time quantum is very large (infinite), the RR policy is the same as the FCFS policy. If the time quantum is very small (say 1 microsecond), the RR approach is called *processor sharing*, and appears (in theory) to the users as though each of n processes has its own processor running at $1/n$ the speed of the real processor. This approach was used in Control Data Corporation (CDC) hardware to implement 10 peripheral processors with only one set of hardware and 10 sets of registers. The hardware executes one instruction for one set of registers, then goes on to the next. This cycle continues, resulting in 10 slow processors rather than one fast one. (Actually, since the processor was much faster than memory and each instruction referenced memory, the processors were not much slower than a single processor would have been.)

In software, however, we need also to consider the effect of context switching on the performance of RR scheduling. Let us assume that we have only one process of 10 time units. If the quantum is 12 time units, the process finishes in less than 1 time quantum, with no overhead. If the quantum is 6 time units, however, the process requires 2 quanta, resulting in a context switch. If the time quantum is 1 time unit, then nine context switches will occur, slowing the execution of the process accordingly (Figure 5.4).

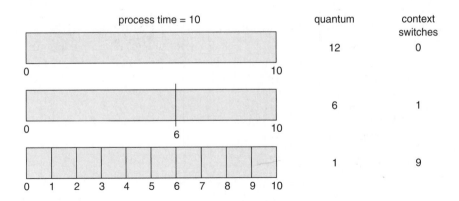

Figure 5.4 Showing how a smaller time quantum increases context switches.

Thus, we want the time quantum to be large with respect to the context-switch time. If the context-switch time is approximately 10 percent of the time quantum, then about 10 percent of the CPU time will be spent in context switch.

Turnaround time also depends on the size of the time quantum. As we can see from Figure 5.5, the average turnaround time of a set of processes does not necessarily improve as the time-quantum size increases. In general, the average turnaround time can be improved if most processes finish their next CPU burst in a single time quantum. For example, given three processes of 10 time units each and a quantum of 1 time unit, the average turnaround time is 29. If the time quantum is 10, however, the average turnaround time drops to 20. If context-switch time is added in, the average turnaround time increases for a smaller time quantum, since more context switches will be required.

On the other hand, if the time quantum is too large, RR scheduling degenerates to FCFS policy. A rule of thumb is that 80 percent of the CPU bursts should be shorter than the time quantum.

5.3.5 Multilevel Queue Scheduling

Another class of scheduling algorithms has been created for situations in which processes are easily classified into different groups. For example, a common division is made between *foreground* (interactive) processes and *background* (batch) processes. These two types of processes have different response-time requirements, and so might have different scheduling needs. In addition, foreground processes may have priority (externally defined) over background processes.

A *multilevel queue-scheduling algorithm* partitions the ready queue into several separate queues (Figure 5.6). The processes are permanently

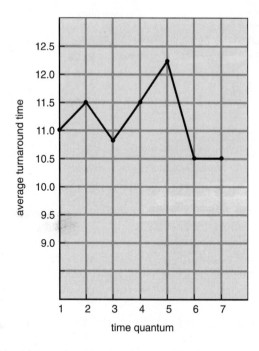

process	time
P_1	6
P_2	3
P_3	1
P_4	7

Figure 5.5 Showing how turnaround time varies with the time quantum.

assigned to one queue, generally based on some property of the process, such as memory size, process priority, or process type. Each queue has its own scheduling algorithm. For example, separate queues might be used for foreground and background processes. The foreground queue might be scheduled by an RR algorithm, while the background queue is scheduled by an FCFS algorithm.

In addition, there must be scheduling between the queues, which is commonly implemented as a fixed-priority preemptive scheduling. For example, the foreground queue may have absolute priority over the background queue.

Let us look at an example of a multilevel queue scheduling algorithm with five queues:

1. System processes

2. Interactive processes

3. Interactive editing processes

4. Batch processes

5. Student processes

highest priority

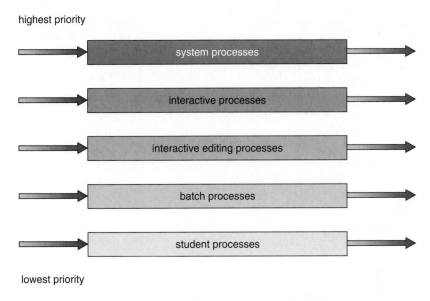

lowest priority

Figure 5.6   Multilevel queue scheduling.

Each queue has absolute priority over lower-priority queues. No process in the batch queue, for example, could run unless the queues for system processes, interactive processes, and interactive editing processes were all empty. If an interactive editing process entered the ready queue while a batch process was running, the batch process would be preempted.

Another possibility is to time slice between the queues. Each queue gets a certain portion of the CPU time, which it can then schedule among the various processes in its queue. For instance, in the foreground-background queue example, the foreground queue can be given 80 percent of the CPU time for RR scheduling among its processes, whereas the background queue receives 20 percent of the CPU to give to its processes in a FCFS manner.

5.3.6 Multilevel Feedback Queue Scheduling

Normally, in a multilevel queue-scheduling algorithm, processes are permanently assigned to a queue on entry to the system. Processes do not move between queues. If there are separate queues for foreground and background processes, for example, processes do not move from one queue to the other, since processes do not change their foreground or background nature. This setup has the advantage of low scheduling overhead, but is inflexible.

Multilevel feedback queue scheduling, however, allows a process to move between queues. The idea is to separate processes with different CPU-burst characteristics. If a process uses too much CPU time, it will be moved to a lower-priority queue. This scheme leaves I/O-bound and interactive processes in the higher-priority queues. Similarly, a process that waits too long in a lower-priority queue may be moved to a higher-priority queue. This form of aging prevents starvation.

For example, consider a multilevel feedback queue scheduler with three queues, numbered from 0 to 2 (Figure 5.7). The scheduler first executes all processes in queue 0. Only when queue 0 is empty will it execute processes in queue 1. Similarly, processes in queue 2 will only be executed if queues 0 and 1 are empty. A process that arrives for queue 1 will preempt a process in queue 2. A process in queue 1 will in turn be preempted by a process arriving for queue 0.

A process entering the ready queue is put in queue 0. A process in queue 0 is given a time quantum of 8 milliseconds. If it does not finish within this time, it is moved to the tail of queue 1. If queue 0 is empty, the process at the head of queue 1 is given a quantum of 16 milliseconds. If it does not complete, it is preempted and is put into queue 2. Processes in queue 2 are run on an FCFS basis, only when queues 0 and 1 are empty.

This scheduling algorithm gives highest priority to any process with a CPU burst of 8 milliseconds or less. Such a process will quickly get the CPU, finish its CPU burst, and go off to its next I/O burst. Processes that need more than 8, but less than 24, milliseconds are also served quickly, although with lower priority than shorter processes. Long processes automatically sink to queue 2 and are served in FCFS order with any CPU cycles left over from queues 0 and 1.

In general, a multilevel feedback queue scheduler is defined by the following parameters:

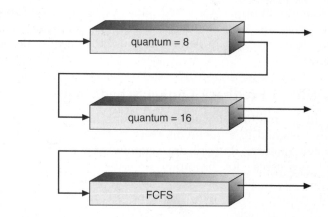

Figure 5.7 Multilevel feedback queues.

- The number of queues

- The scheduling algorithm for each queue

- The method used to determine when to upgrade a process to a higher-priority queue

- The method used to determine when to demote a process to a lower-priority queue

- The method used to determine which queue a process will enter when that process needs service

The definition of a multilevel feedback queue scheduler makes it the most general CPU scheduling algorithm. It can be configured to match a specific system under design. Unfortunately, it also requires some means of selecting values for all the parameters to define the best scheduler. Although a multilevel feedback queue is the most general scheme, it is also the most complex.

5.4 ■ Multiple-Processor Scheduling

Our discussion thus far has focused on the problems of scheduling the CPU in a system with a single processor. If multiple CPUs are available, the scheduling problem is correspondingly more complex. Many possibilities have been tried, and, as we saw with single-processor CPU scheduling, there is no one best solution. In the following, we discuss briefly some of the issues concerning multiprocessor scheduling. A complete coverage is beyond the scope of this text.

The processors within a multiprocessor are identical (*homogeneous*) in terms of their functionality. Any available processor can then be used to run any processes in the queue. If the processors were different (a *heterogeneous* system), only programs compiled for a given processor's instruction set could be run on that processor. This is sometimes the case with distributed systems, as we shall see in Chapters 15 though 18. There are sometimes limitations on scheduling even within homogeneous multiprocessors. Consider a system with an I/O device attached to a private bus of one processor. Processes wishing to use that device must be scheduled to run on that processor, otherwise the device would not be available.

If several identical processors are available, then *load sharing* can occur. It would be possible to provide a separate queue for each processor. In this case, however, one processor could be idle, with an empty queue, while another processor was very busy. To prevent this situation, we use a common ready queue. All processes go into one queue and are scheduled onto any available processor.

In such a scheme, one of two scheduling approaches may be used. In one approach, each processor is self-scheduling. Each processor examines the common ready queue and selects a process to execute. As we shall see in Chapter 6, if we have multiple processors trying to access and update a common data structure, each processor must be programmed very carefully. We must ensure that two processors do not choose the same process, and that processes are not lost from the queue. The other approach avoids this problem by appointing one processor as scheduler for the other processors, thus creating a master–slave structure.

Some systems carry this structure one step further, by having all scheduling decisions, I/O processing, and other system activities handled by one single processor — the master server. The other processors only execute user code. This *asymmetric multiprocessing* is far simpler than symmetric multiprocessing, because only one processor accesses the system data structures, alleviating the need for data sharing.

5.5 ■ Real-Time Scheduling

In Chapter 1, we gave an overview of real-time operating systems and discussed their growing importance. Here, we continue the discussion by describing the scheduling facility needed to support real-time computing within a general-purpose computer system.

Real-time computing is divided into two types. *Hard real-time* systems are required to complete a critical task within a guaranteed amount of time. Generally, a process is submitted along with a statement of the amount of time in which it needs to complete or perform I/O. The scheduler then either admits the process, guaranteeing that the process will complete on time, or rejects the request as impossible. This is known as *resource reservation*. Such a guarantee requires that the scheduler know exactly how long each type of operating-system function takes to perform, and therefore each operation must be guaranteed to take a maximum amount of time. Such a guarantee is impossible in a system with secondary storage or virtual memory, as we shall show in the next few chapters, because these subsystems cause unavoidable and unforeseeable variation in the amount of time to execute a particular process. Therefore, hard real-time systems are composed of special-purpose software running on hardware dedicated to their critical process, and lack the full functionality of modern computers and operating systems.

Soft real-time computing is less restrictive. It requires that critical processes receive priority over less fortunate ones. Although adding soft real-time functionality to a time-sharing system may cause an unfair allocation of resources and may result in longer delays, or even starvation, for some processes, it is at least possible to achieve. The result is a general-purpose system that can also support multimedia, high-speed interactive graphics, and a variety of tasks that would not function acceptably in an environment that does not support soft real-time computing.

Implementing soft real-time functionality requires careful design of the scheduler and related aspects of the operating system. First, the system must have priority scheduling, and real-time processes must have the highest priority. The priority of real-time processes must not degrade over time, even though the priority of non−real-time processes may. Second, the dispatch latency must be small. The smaller the latency, the faster a real-time process can start executing once it is runable.

It is relatively simple to ensure that the former property holds. For example, we can disallow process aging on real-time processes, thereby guaranteeing that the priority of the various processes does not change. However, ensuring the latter property is much more involved. The problem is that many operating systems, including most versions of UNIX, are forced to wait for either a system call to complete or for an I/O block to take place before doing a context switch. The dispatch latency in such systems can be long, since some system calls are complex and some I/O devices are slow.

To keep dispatch latency low, we need to allow system calls to be preemptible. There are several ways to achieve this goal. One is to insert *preemption points* in long-duration system calls, which check to see whether a high-priority process needs to be run. If so, a context switch takes place and, when the high-priority process terminates, the interrupted process continues with the system call. Preemption points can be placed at only "safe" locations in the kernel — only where kernel data structures are not being modified. Even with preemption points dispatch latency can be large, because only a few preemption points can be practically added to a kernel.

Another method for dealing with preemption is to make the entire kernel preemptible. So that correct operation is ensured, all kernel data structures must be protected through the use of various synchronization mechanisms that we discuss in Chapter 6. With this method, the kernel can always be preemptible, because any kernel data being updated are protected from modification by the high-priority process. This is the method used in Solaris 2.

But what happens if the higher-priority process needs to read or modify kernel data that are currently being accessed by another, lower-priority process? The high-priority process would be waiting for a lower-priority one to finish. This situation is known as *priority inversion*. In fact, there could be a chain of processes, all accessing resources that the high-priority process needs. This problem can be solved via the *priority-inheritance protocol*, in which all these processes (the processes that are

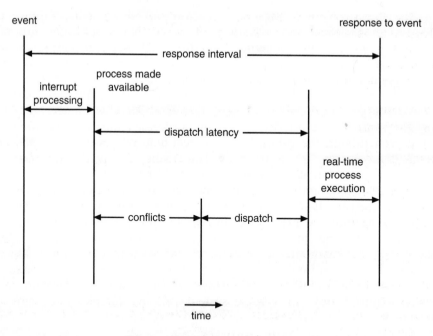

Figure 5.8 Dispatch latency.

accessing resources that the high-priority process needs) inherit the high priority until they are done with the resource in question. When they are finished, their priority reverts to its natural value.

In Figure 5.8, we show the makeup of dispatch latency. The *conflict phase* of dispatch latency has three components:

1. Preemption of any process running in the kernel

2. Low-priority processes releasing resources needed by the high-priority process

3. Context switching from the current process to the high-priority process

As an example, in Solaris 2, the dispatch latency with preemption disabled is over 100 milliseconds. However, the dispatch latency with preemption enabled is usually reduced to 2 milliseconds.

5.6 ■ Algorithm Evaluation

How do we select a CPU scheduling algorithm for a particular system? As we saw in Section 5.3, there are many scheduling algorithms, each with its own parameters. As a result, selecting an algorithm can be difficult.

The first problem is defining the criteria to be used in selecting an algorithm. As we saw in Section 5.2, criteria are often defined in terms of CPU utilization, response time, or throughput. To select an algorithm, we must first define the relative importance of these measures. Our criteria may include several measures, such as:

- Maximize CPU utilization under the constraint that the maximum response time is 1 second

- Maximize throughput such that turnaround time is (on average) linearly proportional to total execution time

Once the selection criteria have been defined, we want to evaluate the various algorithms under consideration. There are a number of different evaluation methods, which we describe in Sections 5.6.1 through 5.6.4.

5.6.1 Deterministic modeling

One major class of evaluation methods is called *analytic evaluation*. Analytic evaluation uses the algorithm and the system workload to produce a formula or number that evaluates the performance of the algorithm for that workload.

One type of analytic evaluation is *deterministic modeling*. This method takes a particular predetermined workload and defines the performance of each algorithm for that workload.

For example, assume that we have the workload shown. All five processes arrive at time 0, in the order given, with the length of the CPU-burst time given in milliseconds:

Process	Burst Time
P_1	10
P_2	29
P_3	3
P_4	7
P_5	12

Consider the FCFS, SJF, and RR (quantum = 10 milliseconds) scheduling algorithms for this set of processes. Which algorithm would give the minimum average waiting time?

For the FCFS algorithm, we would execute the processes as

P_1	P_2	P_3	P_4	P_5

0   10   39   42   49   61

The waiting time is 0 milliseconds for process P_1, 10 milliseconds for process P_2, 39 milliseconds for process P_3, 42 milliseconds for process P_4, and 49 milliseconds for process P_5. Thus, the average waiting time is (0 + 10 + 39 + 42 + 49)/5 = 28 milliseconds.

With nonpreemptive SJF scheduling, we execute the processes as

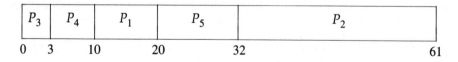

The waiting time is 10 milliseconds for process P_1, 32 milliseconds for process P_2, 0 milliseconds for process P_3, 3 milliseconds for process P_4, and 20 milliseconds for process P_5. Thus, the average waiting time is (10 + 32 + 0 + 3 + 20)/5 = 13 milliseconds.

With the RR algorithm, we start process P_2, but preempt it after 10 milliseconds, putting it in the back of the queue:

P_1	P_2	P_3	P_4	P_5	P_2	P_5	P_2
0	10	20	23	30	40	50	52	61

The waiting time is 0 milliseconds for process P_1, 32 milliseconds for process P_2, 20 milliseconds for process P_3, 23 milliseconds for process P_4, and 40 milliseconds for process P_5. Thus, the average waiting time is (0 + 32 + 20 + 23 + 40)/5 = 23 milliseconds.

We see that, *in this case*, the SJF policy results in less than one-half the average waiting time obtained with FCFS scheduling; the RR algorithm gives us an intermediate value.

Deterministic modeling is simple and fast. It gives exact numbers, allowing the algorithms to be compared. However, it requires exact numbers for input, and its answers apply to only those cases. The main uses of deterministic modeling are in describing scheduling algorithms and providing examples. In cases where we may be running the same programs over and over again and can measure the program's processing requirements exactly, we may be able to use deterministic modeling to select a scheduling algorithm. Over a set of examples, deterministic modeling may indicate trends that can then be analyzed and proved separately. For example, it can be shown that, for the environment described (all processes and their times available at time 0), the SJF policy will always result in the minimum waiting time.

In general, however, deterministic modeling is too specific, and requires too much exact knowledge, to be useful.

5.6.2 Queueing models

The processes that are run on many systems vary from day to day, so there is no static set of processes (and times) to use for deterministic modeling. What can be determined, however, is the distribution of CPU and I/O bursts. These distributions may be measured and then approximated or simply estimated. The result is a mathematical formula describing the probability of a particular CPU burst. Commonly, this distribution is exponential and is described by its mean. Similarly, the distribution of times when processes arrive in the system (the arrival-time distribution) must be given. From these two distributions, it is possible to compute the average throughput, utilization, waiting time, and so on for most algorithms.

The computer system is described as a network of servers. Each server has a queue of waiting processes. The CPU is a server with its ready queue, as is the I/O system with its device queues. Knowing arrival rates and service rates, we can compute utilization, average queue length, average wait time, and so on. This area of study is called *queueing-network analysis*.

As an example, let n be the average queue length (excluding the process being serviced), let W be the average waiting time in the queue, and let λ be the average arrival rate for new processes in the queue (such as three processes per second). Then, we expect that during the time W that a process waits, $\lambda \times W$ new processes will arrive in the queue. If the system is in a steady state, then the number of processes leaving the queue must be equal to the number of processes that arrive. Thus,

$$n = \lambda \times W.$$

This equation is known as *Little's formula*. Little's formula is particularly useful because it is valid for any scheduling algorithm and arrival distribution.

We can use Little's formula to compute one of the three variables, if we know the other two. For example, if we know that seven processes arrive every second (on average), and that there are normally 14 processes in the queue, then we can compute the average waiting time per process as 2 seconds.

Queueing analysis can be useful in comparing scheduling algorithms, but it also has limitations. At the moment, the classes of algorithms and distributions that can be handled are fairly limited. The mathematics of complicated algorithms or distributions can be difficult to work with. Thus, arrival and service distributions are often defined in unrealistic, but mathematically tractable, ways. It is also generally necessary to make a number of independent assumptions, which may not be accurate. Thus, so that they will be able to compute an answer, queueing models are often only an approximation of a real system. As a result, the accuracy of the computed results may be questionable.

5.6.3 Simulations

To get a more accurate evaluation of scheduling algorithms, we can use *simulations*. Simulations involve programming a model of the computer system. Software data structures represent the major components of the system. The simulator has a variable representing a clock; as this variable's value is increased, the simulator modifies the system state to reflect the activities of the devices, the processes, and the scheduler. As the simulation executes, statistics that indicate algorithm performance are gathered and printed.

The data to drive the simulation can be generated in several ways. The most common method uses a random-number generator, which is programmed to generate processes, CPU-burst times, arrivals, departures, and so on, according to probability distributions. The distributions may be defined mathematically (uniform, exponential, Poisson) or empirically. If the distribution is to be defined empirically, measurements of the actual system under study are taken. The results are used to define the actual distribution of events in the real system, and this distribution can then be used to drive the simulation.

A distribution-driven simulation may be inaccurate, however, due to relationships between successive events in the real system. The frequency distribution indicates only how many of each event occur; it does not indicate anything about the order of their occurrence. To correct this problem, we can use *trace tapes*. We create a trace tape by monitoring the real system, recording the sequence of actual events (Figure 5.9). This sequence is then used to drive the simulation. Trace tapes provide an excellent way to compare two algorithms on exactly the same set of real inputs. This method can produce accurate results for its inputs.

Simulations can be expensive, however, often requiring hours of computer time. A more detailed simulation provides more accurate results, but also requires more computer time. In addition, trace tapes can require large amounts of storage space. Finally, the design, coding, and debugging of the simulator can be a major task.

5.6.4 Implementation

Even a simulation is of limited accuracy. The only completely accurate way to evaluate a scheduling algorithm is to code it up, to put it in the operating system, and to see how it works. This approach puts the actual algorithm in the real system for evaluation under real operating conditions.

The major difficulty is the cost of this approach. The expense is incurred not only in coding the algorithm and modifying the operating

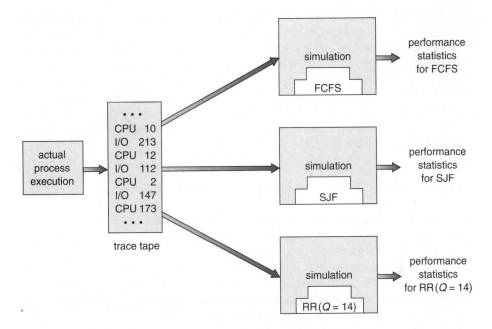

Figure 5.9   Evaluation of CPU schedulers by simulation.

system to support it as well as its required data structures, but also in the reaction of the users to a constantly changing operating system. Most users are not interested in building a better operating system; they merely want to get their processes executed and to use their results. A constantly changing operating system does not help the users to get their work done.

The other difficulty with any algorithm evaluation is that the environment in which the algorithm is used will change. The environment will change not only in the usual way, as new programs are written and the types of problems change, but also as a result of the performance of the scheduler. If short processes are given priority, then users may break larger processes into sets of smaller processes. If interactive processes are given priority over noninteractive processes, then users may switch to interactive use.

For example, researchers tried designing one system to classify interactive and noninteractive processes automatically by looking at the amount of terminal I/O. If a process did not input or output to the terminal in a 1-second interval, the process was classified as noninteractive and was moved to a lower-priority queue. This policy resulted in a situation where one programmer modified his programs to write an arbitrary character to the terminal at regular intervals of less than 1 second. The system gave his programs a high priority, even though the terminal output was completely meaningless.

The most flexible scheduling algorithms can be altered by the system managers. During operating-system build time, boot time, or run time, the variables used by the schedulers can be changed to reflect the expected future use of the system. The need for flexible scheduling is another instance where the separation of mechanism from policy is useful. For instance, if paychecks need to be processed and printed immediately, but are normally done as a low-priority batch job, the batch queue could be given a higher priority temporarily. Unfortunately, few operating systems allow this type of tunable scheduling.

5.7 ■ Summary

CPU scheduling is the task of selecting a waiting process from the ready queue and allocating the CPU to it. The CPU is allocated to the selected process by the dispatcher.

First-come, first-served (FCFS) scheduling is the simplest scheduling algorithm, but it can cause short processes to wait for very long processes. Shortest-job-first (SJF) scheduling is provably optimal, providing the shortest average waiting time. Implementing SJF scheduling is difficult because predicting the length of the next CPU burst is difficult. The SJF algorithm is a special case of the general priority scheduling algorithm, which simply allocates the CPU to the highest-priority process. Both priority and SJF scheduling may suffer from starvation. Aging is a technique to prevent starvation.

Round-robin (RR) scheduling is more appropriate for a time-shared system. RR scheduling allocates the CPU to the first process in the ready queue for q time units, where q is the time quantum. After q time units, the CPU is preempted and the process is put at the tail of the ready queue. The major problem is the selection of the time quantum. If the quantum is too large, RR scheduling degenerates to FCFS scheduling; if the quantum is too small, scheduling overhead in the form of context-switch time becomes excessive.

The FCFS algorithm is nonpreemptive; the RR algorithm is preemptive. The SJF and priority algorithms may be either preemptive or nonpreemptive.

Multilevel queue algorithms allow different algorithms to be used for various classes of processes. The most common is a foreground interactive queue, which uses RR scheduling, and a background batch queue, which uses FCFS scheduling. Multilevel feedback queues allow processes to move from one queue to another.

The wide variety of scheduling algorithms demands that we have methods to select among algorithms. Analytic methods use mathematical analysis to determine the performance of an algorithm. Simulation methods determine performance by imitating the scheduling algorithm on a "representative" sample of processes, and computing the resulting performance.

■ Exercises

5.1 A CPU scheduling algorithm determines an order for the execution of its scheduled processes. Given n processes to be scheduled on one processor, how many possible different schedules are there? Give a formula in terms of n.

5.2 Define the difference between preemptive and nonpreemptive scheduling. State why strict nonpreemptive scheduling is unlikely to be used in a computer center.

5.3 Consider the following set of processes, with the length of the CPU-burst time given in milliseconds:

Process	Burst Time	Priority
P_1	10	3
P_2	1	1
P_3	2	3
P_4	1	4
P_5	5	2

The processes are assumed to have arrived in the order P_1, P_2, P_3, P_4, P_5, all at time 0.

a. Draw four Gantt charts illustrating the execution of these processes using FCFS, SJF, a nonpreemptive priority (a smaller priority number implies a higher priority), and RR (quantum = 1) scheduling.

b. What is the turnaround time of each process for each of the scheduling algorithms in part a?

c. What is the waiting time of each process for each of the scheduling algorithms in part a?

d. Which of the schedules in part a results in the minimal average waiting time (over all processes)?

5.4 Suppose that the following processes arrive for execution at the times indicated. Each process will run the listed amount of time. In answering the questions, use nonpreemptive scheduling and base all decisions on the information you have at the time the decision must be made.

Process	Arrival Time	Burst Time
P_1	0.0	8
P_2	0.4	4
P_3	1.0	1

a. What is the average turnaround time for these processes with the FCFS scheduling algorithm?

b. What is the average turnaround time for these processes with the SJF scheduling algorithm?

c. The SJF algorithm is supposed to improve performance, but notice that we chose to run process P_1 at time 0 because we did not know that two shorter processes would arrive soon. Compute what the average turnaround time will be if the CPU is left idle for the first 1 unit and then SJF scheduling is used. Remember that processes P_1 and P_2 are waiting during this idle time, so their waiting time may increase. This algorithm could be known as future-knowledge scheduling.

5.5 Consider a variant of the RR scheduling algorithm where the entries in the ready queue are pointers to the PCBs.

a. What would be the effect of putting two pointers to the same process in the ready queue?

b. What would be the major advantages and disadvantages of this scheme?

c. How would you modify the basic RR algorithm to achieve the same effect without the duplicate pointers?

5.6 What advantage is there in having different time-quantum sizes on different levels of a multilevel queueing system?

5.7 Consider the following preemptive priority-scheduling algorithm based on dynamically changing priorities. Larger priority numbers imply higher priority. When a process is waiting for the CPU (in the ready queue, but not running), its priority changes at a rate α; when it is running, its priority changes at a rate β. All processes are given a priority of 0 when they enter the ready queue. The parameters α and β can be set to give many different scheduling algorithms.

a. What is the algorithm that results from $\beta > \alpha > 0$?

b. What is the algorithm that results from $\alpha < \beta < 0$?

5.8 Many CPU scheduling algorithms are parameterized. For example, the RR algorithm requires a parameter to indicate the time slice. Multilevel feedback queues require parameters to define the number of queues, the scheduling algorithms for each queue, the criteria used to move processes between queues, and so on.

These algorithms are thus really sets of algorithms (for example, the set of RR algorithms for all time slices, and so on). One set of algorithms may include another (for example, the FCFS algorithm is the RR algorithm with an infinite time quantum). What (if any) relation holds between the following pairs of sets of algorithms?

a. Priority and SJF

b. Multilevel feedback queues and FCFS

c. Priority and FCFS

d. RR and SJF

5.9 Suppose that a scheduling algorithm (at the level of short-term CPU scheduling) favors those processes that have used the least processor time in the recent past. Why will this algorithm favor I/O-bound programs and yet not permanently starve CPU-bound programs?

5.10 Explain the differences in the degree to which the following scheduling algorithms discriminate in favor of short processes:

a. FCFS

b. RR

c. Multilevel feedback queues

Bibliographic Notes

Lampson [1968] provided general discussions concerning scheduling. More formal treatments of scheduling theory were contained in Kleinrock [1975], Sauer and Chandy [1981], and Lazowska et al. [1984]. A unifying approach to scheduling was presented by Ruschitzka and Fabry [1977]. Haldar and Subramanian [1991] discuss fairness in processor scheduling in time-sharing systems.

Feedback queues were originally implemented on the CTSS system described in Corbato et al. [1962]. This queueing system was analyzed by Schrage [1967]; variations on multilevel feedback queues were studied by Coffman and Kleinrock [1968]. Additional studies were presented by Coffman and Denning [1973] and Svobodova [1976]. A data structure for manipulating priority queues was presented by Vuillemin [1978]. The preemptive priority-scheduling algorithm of Exercise 5.9 was suggested by Kleinrock [1975].

Anderson et al. [1989] discussed thread scheduling. Discussions concerning multiprocessor scheduling were presented by Jones and Schwarz [1980], Tucker and Gupta [1989], Zahorjan and McCann [1990], Feitelson and Rudolph [1990], and Leutenegger and Vernon [1990].

Discussions concerning scheduling in real-time systems were offered by Liu and Layland [1973], Abbot [1984], Jensen et al. [1985], Hong et al. [1989], and Khanna et al. [1992]. A special issue on real-time operating systems was edited by Zhao [1989]. Eykholt et al. [1992] described the real-time component of Solaris 2.

Fair share schedulers were covered by Henry [1984], Woodside [1986], and Kay and Lauder [1988].

Discussions concerning scheduling policies used in the MVS operating system were presented by Samson [1990]; the one for the OS/2 operating system was presented by Iacobucci [1988]; the one for the UNIX V operating system was presented by Bach [1987]; and the one for the Mach operating system was presented by Black [1990].

CHAPTER 6

PROCESS SYNCHRONIZATION

A *cooperating* process is one that can affect or be affected by the other processes executing in the system. Cooperating processes may either directly share a logical address space (that is, both code and data), or be allowed to share data only through files. The former case is achieved through the use of *lightweight* processes or *threads*, which we discussed in Section 4.5. Concurrent access to shared data may result in data inconsistency. In this chapter, we discuss various mechanisms to ensure the orderly execution of cooperating processes that share a logical address space, so that data consistency is maintained.

6.1 ■ Background

In Chapter 4, we developed a model of a system consisting of a number of cooperating sequential processes, all running asynchronously and possibly sharing data. We have illustrated this model with the bounded buffer scheme, which is representative of operating systems.

Let us return to the shared-memory solution to the bounded-buffer problem that we presented in Section 4.6. As we pointed out, our solution allows at most $n - 1$ items in the buffer at the same time. Suppose that we wanted to modify the algorithm to remedy this deficiency. One possibility is to add an integer variable *counter*, initialized to 0. *Counter* is incremented every time we add a new item to the buffer, and is decremented every time we remove one item from the buffer. The code for the producer process can be modified as follows:

> **repeat**
>> ...
>> produce an item in *nextp*
>> ...
>> **while** *counter* = *n* **do** *no-op;*
>> *buffer*[*in*] := *nextp;*
>> *in* := *in*+1 **mod** *n;*
>> *counter* := *counter* + 1;
> **until** *false;*

The code for the consumer process can be modified as follows:

> **repeat**
>> **while** *counter* = *0* **do** *no-op;*
>> *nextc* := *buffer*[*out*];
>> *out* := *out*+1 **mod** *n;*
>> *counter* := *counter* − 1;
>>
>> ...
>> consume the item in *nextc*
>> ...
> **until** *false;*

Although both the producer and consumer routines are correct separately, they may not function correctly when executed concurrently. As an illustration, suppose that the value of the variable *counter* is currently 5, and that the producer and consumer processes execute the statements "*counter* := *counter* + 1" and "*counter* := *counter* − 1" concurrently. Following the execution of these two statements, the value of the variable *counter* may be 4, 5, or 6! The only correct result is *counter* = 5, which is generated correctly if the producer and consumer execute separately.

We can show that the value of *counter* may be incorrect, as follows. Note that the statement "*counter* := *counter*+1" may be implemented in machine language (on a typical machine) as

$$register_1 := counter;$$
$$register_1 := register_1+1;$$
$$counter := register_1$$

where $register_1$ is a local CPU register. Similarly, the statement "*counter* := *counter* − 1" is implemented as follows:

$$register_2 := counter$$
$$register_2 := register_2 − 1;$$
$$counter := register_2$$

where again *register$_2$* is a local CPU register. Even though *register$_1$* and *register$_2$* may be the same physical registers (an accumulator, say), remember that the contents of this register will be saved and restored by the interrupt handler (Section 2.1).

The concurrent execution of the statements "*counter := counter + 1*" and "*counter := counter − 1*" is equivalent to a sequential execution where the lower-level statements presented previously are interleaved in some arbitrary order (but the order within each high-level statement is preserved). One such interleaving is

T_0:	*producer*	**execute**	*register$_1$* := *counter*	{*register$_1$* = 5}
T_1:	*producer*	**execute**	*register$_1$* := *register$_1$* + 1	{*register$_1$* = 6}
T_2:	*consumer*	**execute**	*register$_2$* := *counter*	{*register$_2$* = 5}
T_3:	*consumer*	**execute**	*register$_2$* := *register$_2$* − 1	{*register$_2$* = 4}
T_4:	*producer*	**execute**	*counter* := *register$_1$*	{*counter* = 6}
T_5:	*consumer*	**execute**	*counter* := *register$_2$*	{*counter* = 4}

Notice that we have arrived at the incorrect state "*counter* = 4," recording that there are four full buffers, when, in fact, there are five full buffers. If we reversed the order of the statements at T_4 and T_5, we would arrive at the incorrect state "*counter* = 6."

We would arrive at this incorrect state because we allowed both processes to manipulate the variable *counter* concurrently. A situation like this, where several processes access and manipulate the same data concurrently, and the outcome of the execution depends on the particular order in which the access takes place, is called a *race condition*. To guard against the race condition above, we need to ensure that only one process at a time can be manipulating the variable *counter*. To make such a guarantee, we require some form of synchronization of the processes. Such situations occur frequently in operating systems as different parts of the system manipulate resources and we want the changes not to interfere with one another. A major portion of this chapter is concerned with the issue of process synchronization and coordination.

6.2 ■ The Critical-Section Problem

Consider a system consisting of n processes $\{P_0, P_1, ..., P_{n-1}\}$. Each process has a segment of code, called a *critical section*, in which the process may be changing common variables, updating a table, writing a file, and so on. The important feature of the system is that, when one process is executing in its critical section, no other process is to be allowed to execute in its critical section. Thus, the execution of critical sections by the processes is *mutually exclusive* in time. The critical-section problem is to design a protocol that the processes can use to cooperate. Each process must request permission to enter its critical section. The section of code implementing this request is the *entry* section. The critical section may be followed by an *exit* section. The remaining code is the *remainder* section.

A solution to the critical-section problem must satisfy the following three requirements:

1. **Mutual Exclusion:** If process P_i is executing in its critical section, then no other processes can be executing in their critical sections.

2. **Progress:** If no process is executing in its critical section and there exist some processes that wish to enter their critical sections, then only those processes that are not executing in their remainder section can participate in the decision of which will enter its critical section next, and this selection cannot be postponed indefinitely.

3. **Bounded Waiting:** There must exist a bound on the number of times that other processes are allowed to enter their critical sections after a process has made a request to enter its critical section and before that request is granted.

We assume that each process is executing at a nonzero speed. However, we can make no assumption concerning the *relative* speed of the *n* processes.

In Sections 6.2.1 and 6.2.2, we work up to solutions to the critical-section problem that satisfy these three requirements. The solutions do not rely on any assumptions concerning the hardware instructions or the number of processors that the hardware supports. We do, however,

repeat

> entry section

critical section

> exit section

remainder section

until *false;*

Figure 6.1 General structure of a typical process P_i.

assume that the basic machine-language instructions (the primitive instructions such as load, store, and test) are executed atomically. That is, if two such instructions are executed concurrently, the result is equivalent to their sequential execution in some unknown order. Thus, if a load and a store are executed concurrently, the load will get either the old value or the new value, but not some combination of the two.

When presenting an algorithm, we define only the variables used for synchronization purposes, and describe only a typical process P_i whose general structure is shown in Figure 6.1. The *entry section* and *exit section* are enclosed in boxes to highlight these important segments of code.

6.2.1 Two-Process Solutions

In this section, we restrict our attention to algorithms that are applicable to only two processes at a time. The processes are numbered P_0 and P_1. For convenience, when presenting P_i, we use P_j to denote the other process; that is, $j = 1 - i$.

6.2.1.1 Algorithm 1

Our first approach is to let the processes share a common integer variable *turn* initialized to 0 (or 1). If *turn* $= i$, then process P_i is allowed to execute in its critical section. The structure of process P_i is shown in Figure 6.2.

This solution ensures that only one process at a time can be in its critical section. However, it does not satisfy the progress requirement, since it requires strict alternation of processes in the execution of the critical section. For example, if *turn* $= 0$ and P_1 is ready to enter its critical section, P_1 cannot do so, even though P_0 may be in its remainder section.

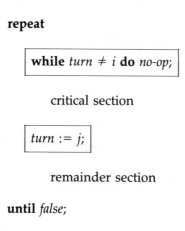

repeat

> **while** *turn* $\neq$ i **do** *no-op;*

critical section

> *turn* $:= j;$

remainder section

until *false;*

Figure 6.2   The structure of process P_i in algorithm 1.

6.2.1.2 Algorithm 2

The problem with algorithm 1 is that it does not retain sufficient information about the state of each process; it remembers only which process is allowed to enter that process' critical section. To remedy this problem, we can replace the variable *turn* with the following array:

$$\textbf{var } flag: \textbf{array } [0..1] \textbf{ of } boolean;$$

The elements of the array are initialized to *false*. If *flag[i]* is *true*, this value indicates that P_i *is ready* to enter the critical section. The structure of process P_i is shown in Figure 6.3.

In this algorithm, process P_i first sets *flag[i]* to be *true*, signaling that it is ready to enter its critical section. Then, P_i checks to verify that process P_j is not also ready to enter its critical section. If P_j were ready, then P_i would wait until P_j had indicated that it no longer needed to be in the critical section (that is, until *flag[j]* was *false*). At this point, P_i would enter the critical section. On exiting the critical section, P_i would set its *flag* to be *false*, allowing the other process (if it is waiting) to enter its critical section.

In this solution, the mutual-exclusion requirement is satisfied. Unfortunately, the progress requirement is not met. To illustrate this problem, we consider the following execution sequence:

$$T_0: \quad P_0 \text{ sets } flag[0] = true$$
$$T_1: \quad P_1 \text{ sets } flag[1] = true$$

Now P_0 and P_1 are looping forever in their respective **while** statements.

repeat

> *flag[i]* := *true*;
> **while** *flag[j]* **do** *no-op*;

critical section

> *flag[i]* := *false*;

remainder section

until *false*;

Figure 6.3 The structure of process P_i in algorithm 2.

This algorithm is crucially dependent on the exact timing of the two processes. The sequence could have been derived in an environment where there are several processors executing concurrently, or where an interrupt (such as a timer interrupt) occurs immediately after step T_0 is executed, and the CPU is switched from one process to another.

Note that switching the order of the instructions for setting $flag[i]$, and testing the value of a $flag[j]$, will not solve our problem. Rather, we will have a situation where it is possible for both processes to be in the critical section at the same time, violating the mutual-exclusion requirement.

6.2.1.3 Algorithm 3

By combining the key ideas of algorithm 1 and algorithm 2, we obtain a correct solution to the critical-section problem, where all three requirements are met. The processes share two variables:

> **var** *flag*: **array** [0..1] **of** *boolean*;
> *turn*: 0..1;

Initially $flag[0] = flag[1] = false$, and the value of *turn* is immaterial (but is either 0 or 1). The structure of process P_i is shown in Figure 6.4.

To enter the critical section, process P_i first sets $flag[i]$ to be *true*, and then asserts that it is the other process' turn to enter if appropriate (*turn* = *j*). If both processes try to enter at the same time, *turn* will be set to both *i* and *j* at roughly the same time. Only one of these assignments will last; the other will occur, but will be overwritten immediately. The eventual

repeat

```
flag[i] := true;
turn := j;
while (flag[j] and turn=j) do no-op;
```

critical section

```
flag[i] := false;
```

remainder section

until *false*;

Figure 6.4   The structure of process P_i in algorithm 3.

value of *turn* decides which of the two processes is allowed to enter its critical section first.

We now prove that this solution is correct. We need to show that:

1. Mutual exclusion is preserved,

2. The progress requirement is satisfied,

3. The bounded-waiting requirement is met.

To prove property 1, we note that each P_i enters its critical section only if either *flag[j]* = *false* or *turn* = *i*. Also note that, if both processes can be executing in their critical sections at the same time, then *flag[0]* = *flag[1]* = *true*. These two observations imply that P_0 and P_1 could not have executed successfully their **while** statements at about the same time, since the value of *turn* can be either 0 or 1, but cannot be both. Hence, one of the processes — say P_j — must have executed successfully the **while** statement, whereas P_i had to execute at least one additional statement ("*turn* = *j*"). However, since, at that time, *flag[j]* = *true*, and *turn* = *i*, and this condition will persist as long as P_j is in its critical section, the result follows: Mutual exclusion is preserved.

To prove properties 2 and 3, we note that a process P_i can be prevented from entering the critical section only if it is stuck in the **while** loop with the condition *flag[j]* = *true* and *turn* = *j*; this loop is the only one. If P_j is not ready to enter the critical section, then *flag[j]* = *false*, and P_i can enter its critical section. If P_j has set *flag[j]* = *true* and is also executing in its **while** statement, then either *turn* = *i* or *turn* = *j*. If *turn* = *i*, then P_i will enter the critical section. If *turn* = *j*, then P_j will enter the critical section. However, once P_j exits its critical section, it will reset *flag[j]* to *false*, allowing P_i to enter its critical section. If P_j resets *flag[j]* to *true*, it must also set *turn* = *i*. Thus, since P_i does not change the value of the variable *turn* while executing the **while** statement, P_i will enter the critical section (progress) after at most one entry by P_j (bounded waiting).

6.2.2 Multiple-Process Solutions

We have seen that algorithm 3 solves the critical-section problem for two processes. Now let us develop an algorithm for solving the critical-section problem for *n* processes. This algorithm is known as the *bakery algorithm*, and it is based on a scheduling algorithm commonly used in bakeries, ice-cream stores, meat markets, motor-vehicle registries, and other locations where order must be made out of chaos. This algorithm was developed for a distributed environment, but at this point we are concerned with only those aspects of the algorithm that pertain to a centralized environment.

On entering the store, each customer receives a number. The customer with the lowest number is served next. Unfortunately, the bakery algorithm cannot guarantee that two processes (customers) do not receive the same number. In the case of a tie, the process with the lowest name is served first. That is, if P_i and P_j receive the same number and if $i < j$, then P_i is served first. Since process names are unique and totally ordered, our algorithm is completely deterministic.

The common data structures are

> var *choosing*: **array** [$0..n-1$] **of** *boolean*;
> *number*: **array** [$0..n-1$] **of** *integer*;

Initially, these data structures are initialized to *false* and 0, respectively. For convenience, we define the following notation:

- $(a,b) < (c,d)$ if $a < c$ or if $a = c$ and $b < d$.

- $max(a_0, ..., a_{n-1})$ is a number, k, such that $k \geq a_i$ for $i = 0, ..., n-1$.

The structure of process P_i is shown in Figure 6.5.

To prove that the bakery algorithm is correct, we need first to show that, if P_i is in its critical section and P_k ($k \neq i$) has already chosen its

repeat

```
choosing[i] := true;
number[i] := max(number[0], number[1], ..., number[n−1]) + 1;
choosing[i] := false;
for j := 0 to n−1
    do begin
            while choosing[j] do no-op;
            while number[j] ≠ 0
                and (number[j],j) < (number[i],i) do no-op;
    end;
```

critical section

```
number[i] := 0;
```

remainder section

until *false*;

Figure 6.5   The structure of process P_i in the bakery algorithm.

number[*k*] ≠ 0, then (*number*[*i*],*i*) < (*number*[*k*],*k*). The proof of this algorithm is left to you in Exercise 6.2.

Given this result, it is now simple to show that mutual exclusion is observed. Indeed, consider P_i in its critical section and P_k trying to enter the P_k critical section. When process P_k executes the second **while** statement for $j = i$, it finds that

- *number*[*i*] ≠ 0

- (*number*[*i*],*i*) < (*number*[*k*],*k*).

Thus, it continues looping in the **while** statement until P_i leaves the P_i critical section.

If we wish to show that the progress and bounded-waiting requirements are preserved, and that the algorithm ensures fairness, it is sufficient to observe that the processes enter their critical section on a first-come, first-served basis.

6.3 ■ Synchronization Hardware

As with other aspects of software, features of the hardware can make the programming task easier and improve system efficiency. In this section, we present some simple hardware instructions that are available on many systems, and show how they can be used effectively in solving the critical-section problem.

The critical-section problem could be solved simply if we could disallow interrupts to occur while a shared variable is being modified. In this manner, we could be sure that the current sequence of instructions would be allowed to execute in order without preemption. No other instructions would be run, so no unexpected modifications could be made to the shared variable.

Unfortunately, this solution is not always feasible. Disabling interrupts on a multiprocessor can be time-consuming, as the message is passed to all the processors. This message passing delays entry into each critical section, and system efficiency decreases. Also, consider the effect on a system's clock, if the clock is kept updated by interrupts.

Many machines therefore provide special hardware instructions that allow us either to test and modify the content of a word, or to swap the contents of two words, atomically. We can use these special instructions to solve the critical-section problem in a relatively simple manner. Rather than discussing one specific instruction for one specific machine, let us abstract the main concepts behind these types of instructions. The *Test-and-Set* instruction can be defined as follows:

```
function Test-and-Set (var target: boolean): boolean;
    begin
        Test-and-Set := target;
        target := true;
    end;
```

The important characteristic is that this instruction is executed atomically — that is, as one uninterruptible unit. Thus, if two *Test-and-Set* instructions are executed simultaneously (each on a different CPU), they will be executed sequentially in some arbitrary order.

If the machine supports the *Test-and-Set* instruction, then we can implement mutual exclusion by declaring a Boolean variable *lock,* initialized to *false*. The structure of process P_i is shown in Figure 6.6.

The *Swap* instruction swaps the contents of two words, atomically, and is defined as follows:

```
procedure Swap (var a, b: boolean);
    var temp: boolean;
    begin
        temp := a;
        a := b;
        b := temp;
    end;
```

As in the case of the *Test-and-Set* instruction, the *Swap* instruction is also executed atomically.

repeat

```
while Test-and-Set(lock) do no-op;
```

critical section

```
lock := false;
```

remainder section

until *false;*

Figure 6.6 Mutual-exclusion implementation with *Test-and-Set.*

If the machine supports the *Swap* instruction, then mutual exclusion can be provided as follows. A global Boolean variable *lock* is declared and is initialized to *false*. In addition, each process also has a local Boolean variable *key*. The structure of process P_i is shown in Figure 6.7.

These algorithms do not satisfy the bounded-waiting requirement. We present an algorithm that uses the *Test-and-Set* instruction in Figure 6.8. This algorithm satisfies all the critical-section requirements. The common data structures are

> **var** *waiting*: **array** $[0..n-1]$ **of** *boolean*
> *lock*: *boolean*

These data structures are initialized to *false*.

To prove that the mutual-exclusion requirement is met, we note that process P_i can enter its critical section only if either *waiting[i]* = *false* or *key* = *false*. *Key* can become *false* only if the *Test-and-Set* is executed. The first process to execute the *Test-and-Set* will find *key* = *false*; all others must wait. The variable *waiting[i]* can become false only if another process leaves its critical section; only one *waiting[i]* is set to *false*, maintaining the mutual-exclusion requirement.

To prove the progress requirement, we note that the arguments presented for mutual exclusion also apply here, since a process exiting the critical section either sets *lock* to *false*, or sets *waiting[j]* to *false*. Both allow a process that is waiting to enter its critical section to proceed.

repeat

```
key := true;
repeat
    Swap(lock,key);
until key = false;
```

critical section

```
lock := false;
```

remainder section

until *false*;

Figure 6.7 Mutual-exclusion implementation with the *Swap* instruction.

var j: $0..n-1$;
   key: *boolean*;

lock:=true **repeat**

> $waiting[i]$:= *true*;
> key := *true*;
> **while** $waiting[i]$ **and** key **do** key := $Test\text{-}and\text{-}Set(lock)$;
> $waiting[i]$:= *false*;

    critical section

> j := $i+1$ **mod** n;
> **while** $(j \neq i)$ **and** (**not** $waiting[j]$) **do** j := $j+1$ **mod** n;
> **if** $j = i$ **then** $lock$:= *false*
>   **else** $waiting[j]$:= *false*;

    remainder section

  until *false*;

Figure 6.8 Bounded-waiting mutual exclusion with *Test-and-Set*.

To prove bounded waiting, we note that, when a process leaves its critical section, it scans the array *waiting* in the cyclic ordering ($i + 1$, $i + 2$, ..., $n - 1$, 0, ..., $i - 1$). It designates the first process in this ordering that is in the entry section ($waiting[j]$ = *true*) as the next one to enter the critical section. Any process waiting to enter its critical section will thus do so within $n - 1$ turns. Unfortunately for hardware designers, implementing atomic test-and-set instructions on multiprocessors is not a trivial task. Such implementations are discussed in books on computer architecture.

Disadv
         Cannot generalize for more processors.
         busy waiting

6.4 ■ Semaphores

The solutions to the critical-section problem presented in Section 6.3 are not easy to generalize to more complex problems. To overcome this difficulty, we can use a synchronization tool, called a *semaphore*. A semaphore S is an integer variable that, apart from initialization, is accessed only through two standard *atomic* operations: *wait* and *signal*. These operations were originally termed P (for *wait*; from the Dutch *proberen*, to test) and V (for *signal*; from *verhogen*, to increment). The classical definitions of *wait* and *signal* are

$$wait(S): \textbf{ while } S \le 0 \textbf{ do } no\text{-}op;$$
$$S := S - 1;$$

$$signal(S): \ S := S + 1;$$

Modifications to the integer value of the semaphore in the *wait* and *signal* operations must be executed indivisibly. That is, when one process modifies the semaphore value, no other process can simultaneously modify that same semaphore value. In addition, in the case of the *wait(S)*, the testing of the integer value of S ($S \le 0$), and its possible modification ($S := S - 1$), must also be executed without interruption. We shall see how these operations can be implemented in Section 6.4.2; first, let us see how semaphores can be used.

6.4.1 Usage

We can use semaphores to deal with the n-process critical-section problem. The n processes share a semaphore, *mutex* (standing for *mutual exclusion*), initialized to 1. Each process P_i is organized as shown in Figure 6.9.

We can also use semaphores to solve various synchronization problems. For example, consider two concurrently running processes: P_1 with a statement S_1, and P_2 with a statement S_2. Suppose that we require that S_2 be executed only after S_1 has completed. We can implement this scheme readily by letting P_1 and P_2 share a common semaphore *synch*, initialized to 0, and by inserting the statements

$$S_1;$$
$$signal(synch);$$

in process P_1, and the statements

$$wait(synch);$$
$$S_2;$$

in process P_2. Because *synch* is initialized to 0, P_2 will execute S_2 only after P_1 has invoked *signal(synch)*, which is after S_1.

6.4.2 Implementation

The main disadvantage of the mutual-exclusion solutions of Section 6.2, and of the semaphore definition given here, is that they all require *busy waiting*. While a process is in its critical section, any other process that tries to enter its critical section must loop continuously in the entry code. This continual looping is clearly a problem in a real multiprogramming system, where a single CPU is shared among many processes. Busy waiting wastes

repeat

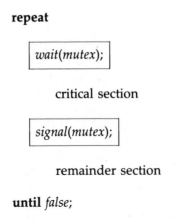

critical section

until *false*;

Figure 6.9 Mutual-exclusion implementation with semaphores.

CPU cycles that some other process might be able to use productively. This type of semaphore is also called a *spinlock* (because the process "spins" while waiting for the lock). Spinlocks are useful in multiprocessor systems, as shown in Chapter 20. The advantage of a spinlock is that no context switch is required when a process must wait on a lock, and a context switch may take considerable time. Thus, when locks are expected to be held for short times, spinlocks are useful.

To overcome the need for busy waiting, we can modify the definition of the *wait* and *signal* semaphore operations. When a process executes the *wait* operation and finds that the semaphore value is not positive, it must wait. However, rather than busy waiting, the process can *block* itself. The block operation places a process into a waiting queue associated with the semaphore, and the state of the process is switched to the waiting state. Then, control is transferred to the CPU scheduler, which selects another process to execute.

A process that is blocked, waiting on a semaphore S, should be restarted when some other process executes a *signal* operation. The process is restarted by a *wakeup* operation, which changes the process from the waiting state to the ready state. The process is then placed in the ready queue. (The CPU may or may not be switched from the running process to the newly ready process, depending on the CPU-scheduling algorithm.)

To implement semaphores under this definition, we define a semaphore as a record:

```
type semaphore = record
                    value: integer;
                    L: list of process;
                 end;
```

Each semaphore has an integer value and a list of processes. When a process must wait on a semaphore, it is added to the list of processes. A *signal* operation removes one process from the list of waiting processes, and awakens that process.

The semaphore operations can now be defined as

> *wait(S)*: *S.value* := *S.value* − 1;
>   **if** *S.value* < 0
>   **then begin**
>   add this process to *S.L*;
>   *block*;
>   **end**;

> *signal(S)*: *S.value* := *S.value* + 1;
>   **if** *S.value* ≤ 0
>   **then begin**
>   remove a process *P* from *S.L*;
>   *wakeup(P)*;
>   **end**;

The *block* operation suspends the process that invokes it. The *wakeup(P)* operation resumes the execution of a blocked process *P*. These two operations are provided by the operating system as basic system calls.

Note that, although under the classical definition of semaphores with busy waiting the semaphore value is never negative, this implementation may have negative semaphore values. If the semaphore value is negative, its magnitude is the number of processes waiting on that semaphore. This fact is a result of the switching of the order of the decrement and the test in the implementation of the *wait* operation.

The list of waiting processes can be easily implemented by a link field in each process control block (PCB). Each semaphore contains an integer value and a pointer to a list of PCBs. One way to add and remove processes from the list, which ensures bounded waiting, would be to use a first-in, first-out (FIFO) queue, where the semaphore contains both head and tail pointers to the queue. In general, however, the list may use *any* queueing strategy. Correct usage of semaphores does not depend on a particular queueing strategy for the semaphore lists.

The critical aspect of semaphores is that they are executed atomically. We must guarantee that no two processes can execute *wait* and *signal* operations on the same semaphore at the same time. This situation is a critical-section problem, and can be solved in either of two ways.

In a uniprocessor environment (that is, where only one CPU exists), we can simply inhibit interrupts during the time the *wait* and *signal* operations are executing. This scheme works in a uniprocessor environment because, once interrupts are inhibited, instructions from different processes cannot be interleaved. Only the currently running process executes, until interrupts are reenabled and the scheduler can regain control.

In a multiprocessor environment, inhibiting interrupts does not work. Instructions from different processes (running on different processors) may be interleaved in some arbitrary way. If the hardware does not provide any special instructions, we can employ any of the correct software solutions for the critical-section problem (Section 6.2), where the critical sections consist of the *wait* and *signal* procedures.

It is important to admit that we have not completely eliminated busy waiting with this definition of the *wait* and *signal* operations. Rather, we have removed busy waiting from the entry to the critical sections of applications programs. Furthermore, we have limited it to only the critical sections of the *wait* and *signal* operations, and these sections are short (if properly coded, they should be no more than about 10 instructions). Thus, the critical section is almost always empty, and busy waiting occurs rarely, and then for only a short time. An entirely different situation exists with applications programs whose critical sections may be long (hours) or may be almost always occupied. In this case, busy waiting is extremely inefficient.

6.4.3 Deadlocks and Starvation

The implementation of a semaphore with a waiting queue may result in a situation where two or more processes are waiting indefinitely for an event that can be caused by only one of the waiting processes. The event in question is the execution of a *signal* operation. When such a state is reached, these processes are said to be *deadlocked*.

To illustrate this, we consider a system consisting of two processes, P_0 and P_1, each accessing two semaphores, S and Q, set to the value 1:

P_0	P_1
wait(S);	*wait(Q);*
wait(Q);	*wait(S);*
.	.
.	.
.	.
signal(S);	*signal(Q);*
signal(Q);	*signal(S);*

Suppose that P_0 executes *wait(S)*, and then P_1 executes *wait(Q)*. When P_0 executes *wait(Q)*, it must wait until P_1 executes *signal(Q)*. Similarly, when P_1 executes *wait(S)*, it must wait until P_0 executes *signal(S)*. Since these signal operations cannot be executed, P_0 and P_1 are deadlocked.

We say that a set of processes is in a deadlock state when every process in the set is waiting for an event that can be caused only by another process in the set. The events with which we are mainly concerned here are resource acquisition and release. However, other types of events may result in deadlocks, as we shall show in Chapter 7. In that chapter, we shall describe various mechanisms for dealing with the deadlock problem.

Another problem related to deadlocks is *indefinite blocking* or *starvation*, a situation where processes wait indefinitely within the semaphore. Indefinite blocking may occur if we add and remove processes from the list associated with a semaphore in LIFO order.

6.4.4 Binary Semaphores

The semaphore construct described in the previous sections is commonly known as a *counting* semaphore, since its integer value can range over an unrestricted domain. A *binary* semaphore is a semaphore with an integer value that can range only between 0 and 1. A binary semaphore can be simpler to implement than a counting semaphore, depending on the underlying hardware architecture. We will now show how a counting semaphore can be implemented using binary semaphores.

Let S be a counting semaphore. To implement it in terms of binary semaphores we need the following data structures:

> **var** $S1$: *binary-semaphore*;
> $S2$: *binary-semaphore*;
> $S3$: *binary-semaphore*;
> C: *integer*;

Initially $S1 = S3 = 1$, $S2 = 0$, and the value of integer C is set to the initial value of the counting semaphore S.

The *wait* operation on the counting semaphore S can be implemented as follows:

> *wait*($S3$);
> *wait*($S1$);
> $C := C - 1$;
> **if** $C < 0$
> **then begin**
> > *signal*($S1$);
> > *signal*($S2$);
>
> **end**
> **else** *signal*($S1$);
> *signal*($S3$);

The *signal* operation on the counting semaphore *S* can be implemented as follows:

```
wait(S1);
C := C + 1;
if C ≤ 0 then signal(S2);
signal(S1);
```

The *S3* semaphore has no effect on *signal(S)*, it merely serializes the *wait(S)* operations.

6.5 ■ Classical Problems of Synchronization

In this section, we present a number of different synchronization problems that are important mainly because they are examples for a large class of concurrency-control problems. These problems are used for testing nearly every newly proposed synchronization scheme. Semaphores are used for synchronization in our solutions.

6.5.1 The Bounded-Buffer Problem

The bounded-buffer problem was introduced in Section 6.1; it is commonly used to illustrate the power of synchronization primitives. We present here a general structure of this scheme, without committing ourselves to any particular implementation. We assume that the pool consists of n buffers, each capable of holding one item. The *mutex* semaphore provides mutual exclusion for accesses to the buffer pool and is initialized to the value 1. The *empty* and *full* semaphores count the number of empty and full buffers, respectively. (Semaphores with initial values other than 1 are sometimes known as *counting semaphores*.) The semaphore *empty* is initialized to the value n; the semaphore *full* is initialized to the value 0.

The code for the producer process is shown in Figure 6.10; the code for the consumer process is shown in Figure 6.11. Note the symmetry between the producer and the consumer. We can interpret this code as the producer producing full buffers for the consumer, or as the consumer producing empty buffers for the producer.

6.5.2 The Readers and Writers Problem

A data object (such as a file or record) is to be shared among several concurrent processes. Some of these processes may want only to read the content of the shared object, whereas others may want to update (that is, to read and write) the shared object. We distinguish between these two types of processes by referring to those processes that are interested in

```
        repeat
                ...
            produce an item in nextp
                ...
            wait(empty);
            wait(mutex);
                ...
            add nextp to buffer
                ...
            signal(mutex);
            signal(full);
        until false;
```

Figure 6.10   The structure of the producer process.

only reading as *readers*, and to the rest as *writers*. Obviously, if two readers access the shared data object simultaneously, no adverse effects will result. However, if a writer and some other process (either a reader or a writer) access the shared object simultaneously, chaos may ensue.

To ensure that these difficulties do not arise, we require that the writers have exclusive access to the shared object. This synchronization problem is referred to as the *readers−writers* problem. Since it was originally stated, it has been used to test nearly every new synchronization primitive. The readers−writers problem has several variations, all involving priorities. The simplest one, referred to as the *first* readers−writers problem, requires that no reader will be kept waiting unless a writer has already obtained permission to use the shared object. In other words, no reader should wait for other readers to finish simply


```
        repeat
            wait(full);
            wait(mutex);
                ...
            remove an item from buffer to nextc
                ...
            signal(mutex);
            signal(empty);
                ...
            consume the item in nextc
                ...
        until false;
```

Figure 6.11   The structure of the consumer process.

wait(wrt);

...

writing is performed

...

signal(wrt);

Figure 6.12   The structure of a writer process.

because a writer is waiting. The *second* readers–writers problem requires that, once a writer is ready, that writer performs its write as soon as possible. In other words, if a writer is waiting to access the object, no new readers may start reading.

We note that a solution to either problem may result in *starvation*. In the first case, writers may starve; in the second case, readers may starve. For this reason, other variants of the problem have been proposed. In this section, we present a solution to the first readers–writers problem. Refer to the Bibliographic Notes for relevant references on starvation-free solutions to the readers–writers problem.

In the solution to the first readers–writers problem, the reader processes share the following data structures:

var *mutex, wrt*: *semaphore*;
readcount : *integer*;

The semaphores *mutex* and *wrt* are initialized to 1; *readcount* is initialized to 0. The semaphore *wrt* is common to both the reader and writer processes. The *mutex* semaphore is used to ensure mutual exclusion when the variable *readcount* is updated. *Readcount* keeps track of how many processes are currently reading the object. The semaphore *wrt* functions as a mutual exclusion semaphore for the writers. It also is used by the first or last reader that enters or exits the critical section. It is not used by readers who enter or exit while other readers are in their critical sections.

The code for a writer process is shown in Figure 6.12; the code for a reader process is shown in Figure 6.13. Note that, if a writer is in the critical section and n readers are waiting, then one reader is queued on *wrt*, and $n - 1$ readers are queued on *mutex*. Also observe that, when a writer executes *signal(wrt)*, we may resume the execution of either the waiting readers or a single waiting writer. The selection is made by the scheduler.

6.5.3   The Dining-Philosophers Problem

Consider five philosophers who spend their lives thinking and eating. The philosophers share a common circular table surrounded by five chairs, each belonging to one philosopher. In the center of the table there is a

```
wait(mutex);
    readcount := readcount + 1;
    if readcount = 1 then wait(wrt);
signal(mutex);

       ...
    reading is performed
       ...
wait(mutex);
    readcount := readcount - 1;
    if readcount = 0 then signal(wrt);
signal(mutex);
```

Figure 6.13   The structure of a reader process.

bowl of rice, and the table is laid with five single chopsticks (Figure 6.14). When a philosopher thinks, she does not interact with her colleagues. From time to time, a philosopher gets hungry and tries to pick up the two chopsticks that are closest to her (the chopsticks that are between her and her left and right neighbors). A philosopher may pick up only one chopstick at a time. Obviously, she cannot pick up a chopstick that is already in the hand of a neighbor. When a hungry philosopher has both her chopsticks at the same time, she eats without releasing her chopsticks. When she is finished eating, she puts down both of her chopsticks and starts thinking again.

The dining-philosophers problem is considered a classic synchronization problem, neither because of its practical importance, nor because computer scientists dislike philosophers, but because it is an example for a large class of concurrency-control problems. It is a simple

Figure 6.14   The situation of the dining philosophers.

representation of the need to allocate several resources among several processes in a deadlock and starvation-free manner.

One simple solution is to represent each chopstick by a semaphore. A philosopher tries to grab the chopstick by executing a *wait* operation on that semaphore; she releases her chopsticks by executing the *signal* operation on the appropriate semaphores. Thus, the shared data are

var *chopstick*: **array** [0..4] **of** *semaphore*;

where all the elements of *chopstick* are initialized to 1. The structure of philosopher *i* is shown in Figure 6.15.

Although this solution guarantees that no two neighbors are eating simultaneously, it nevertheless must be rejected because it has the possibility of creating a deadlock. Suppose that all five philosophers become hungry simultaneously, and each grabs her left chopstick. All the elements of *chopstick* will now be equal to 0. When each philosopher tries to grab her right chopstick, she will be delayed forever.

Several possible remedies to the deadlock problem are listed next. In Section 6.7, we present a solution to the dining-philosophers problem that ensures freedom from deadlocks.

- Allow at most four philosophers to be sitting simultaneously at the table.

- Allow a philosopher to pick up her chopsticks only if both chopsticks are available (note that she must pick them up in a critical section).

- Use an asymmetric solution; that is, an odd philosopher picks up first her left chopstick and then her right chopstick, whereas an even philosopher picks up her right chopstick and then her left chopstick.

```
repeat
    wait(chopstick[i]);
    wait(chopstick[i+1 mod 5]);
        ...
    eat
        ...
    signal(chopstick[i]);
    signal(chopstick[i+1 mod 5]);
        ...
    think
        ...
until false;
```

Figure 6.15   The structure of philosopher *i*.

Finally, any satisfactory solution to the dining-philosophers problem must guard against the possibility that one of the philosophers will starve to death. A deadlock-free solution does not necessarily eliminate the possibility of starvation.

6.6 ■ Critical Regions

Although semaphores provide a convenient and effective mechanism for process synchronization, their incorrect use can still result in timing errors that are difficult to detect, since these errors happen only if some particular execution sequences take place, and these sequences do not always occur.

We have seen an example of such types of errors in the use of counters in our solution to the producer–consumer problem (Section 6.1). In that example, the timing problem happened only rarely, and even then the counter value appeared to be a reasonable value — off by only 1. Nevertheless, this solution is obviously not an acceptable one. It is for this reason that semaphores were introduced in the first place.

Unfortunately, such timing errors can still occur with the use of semaphores. To illustrate how, let us review the solution to the critical-section problem using semaphores. All processes share a semaphore variable *mutex*, which is initialized to 1. Each process must execute *wait(mutex)* before entering the critical section, and *signal(mutex)* afterward. If this sequence is not observed, two processes may be in their critical sections simultaneously.

Let us examine the various difficulties that may result. Note that these difficulties will arise even if a *single* process is not well behaved. This situation may be the result of an honest programming error or of an uncooperative programmer.

- Suppose that a process interchanges the order in which the *wait* and *signal* operations on the semaphore *mutex* are executed, resulting in the following execution:

$$signal(mutex);$$
$$...$$
$$\text{critical section}$$
$$...$$
$$wait(mutex);$$

In this situation, several processes may be executing in their critical section simultaneously, violating the mutual-exclusion requirement. This error may be discovered only if several processes are simultaneously active in their critical sections. Note that this situation may not always be reproducible.

- Suppose that a process replaces *signal(mutex)* with *wait(mutex)*. That is, it executes

$$wait(mutex);$$
$$\ldots$$
$$\text{critical section}$$
$$\ldots$$
$$wait(mutex);$$

In this case, a deadlock will occur.

- Suppose that a process omits the *wait(mutex)*, or the *signal(mutex)*, or both. In this case, either mutual exclusion is violated or a deadlock will occur.

These examples illustrate that various types of errors can be generated easily when semaphores are used incorrectly to solve the critical-section problem. Similar problems may arise in the other synchronization models we discussed in Section 6.5.

To deal with the type of errors we have outlined, a number of high-level language constructs have been introduced. In this section, we describe one fundamental high-level synchronization construct — the *critical region* (sometimes referred to as *conditional critical region*). In Section 6.7, we present another fundamental synchronization construct — the *monitor*. In our presentation of these two constructs, we assume that a process consists of some local data, and a sequential program that can operate on the data. The local data can be accessed by only the sequential program that is encapsulated within the same process. That is, one process cannot directly access the local data of another process. Processes can, however, share global data.

The *critical-region* high-level synchronization construct requires that a variable v of type T, which is to be shared among many processes, be declared as

var v: **shared** T;

The variable v can be accessed only inside a *region* statement of the following form:

region v **when** B **do** S;

This construct means that, **while** statement S is being executed, no other process can access the variable v. The expression B is a Boolean expression that governs the access to the critical region. When a process tries to enter the critical-section region, the Boolean expression B is evaluated. If the expression is true, statement *S* is executed. If it is false, the process relinquishes the mutual exclusion and is delayed until *B* becomes true and no other process is in the region associated with *v*. Thus, if the two statements,

> **region** *v* **when** *true* **do** *S1;*
> **region** *v* **when** *true* **do** *S2;*

are executed concurrently in distinct sequential processes, the result will be equivalent to the sequential execution "*S1* followed by *S2*," or "*S2* followed by *S1*."

The critical-region construct guards against certain simple errors associated with the semaphore solution to the critical-section problem that may be made by a programmer. Note that it does not necessarily eliminate all synchronization errors; rather, it reduces their number. If errors occur in the logic of the program, reproducing a particular sequence of events may not be simple.

The critical-region construct can be effectively used to solve certain general synchronization problems. To illustrate, let us code the bounded-buffer scheme. The buffer space and its pointers are encapsulated in

> **var** *buffer*: **shared record**
> > *pool*: **array** $[0..n-1]$ **of** *item;*
> > *count,in,out*: *integer;*
> **end;**

The producer process inserts a new item *nextp* into the shared buffer by executing

> **region** *buffer* **when** *count < n*
> > **do begin**
> > > *pool*[*in*] := *nextp;*
> > > *in* := *in*+1 **mod** *n;*
> > > *count* := *count* + 1;
> > **end;**

The consumer process removes an item from the shared buffer and puts it in *nextc* by executing

> **region** *buffer* **when** *count > 0*
> > **do begin**
> > > *nextc* := *pool*[*out*];
> > > *out* := *out*+1 **mod** *n;*
> > > *count* := *count* − 1;
> > **end;**

Let us illustrate how the conditional critical region could be implemented by a compiler. With each shared variable, the following variables are associated:

> **var** *mutex, first-delay, second-delay: semaphore;*
> *first-count, second-count: integer;*

The semaphore *mutex* is initialized to 1; the semaphores *first-delay* and *second-delay* are initialized to 0. The integers *first-count* and *second-count* are initialized to 0.

Mutually exclusive access to the critical section is provided by *mutex*. If a process cannot enter the critical section because the Boolean condition *B* is false, it initially waits on the *first-delay* semaphore. A process waiting on the *first-delay* semaphore is eventually moved to the *second-delay* semaphore before it is allowed to reevaluate its Boolean condition *B*. We keep track of the number of processes waiting on *first-delay* and *second-delay*, with *first-count* and *second-count* respectively.

When a process leaves the critical section, it may have changed the value of some Boolean condition *B* that prevented another process from

```
wait(mutex);
while not B
    do begin
        first-count := first-count + 1;
        if second-count > 0
            then signal(second-delay)
            else signal(mutex);
        wait(first-delay);
        first-count := first-count - 1;
        second-count := second-count + 1;
        if first-count > 0
            then signal(first-delay)
            else signal(second-delay);
        wait(second-delay);
        second-count := second-count - 1;
    end;
S;
if first-count > 0
    then signal(first-delay);
    else if second-count > 0
            then signal(second-delay);
            else  signal(mutex);
```

Figure 6.16 Implementation of the conditional-region construct.

entering the critical section. Accordingly, we must trace through the queue of processes waiting on *first-delay* and *second-delay* (in that order) allowing each process to test its Boolean condition. When a process tests its Boolean condition (during this trace), it may discover that the latter now evaluates to the value *true*. In this case, the process enters its critical section. Otherwise, the process must wait again on the *first-delay* and *second-delay* semaphores, as described previously. Accordingly, for a shared variable x, the statement

region x **when** B **do** S;

can be implemented as shown in Figure 6.16. Note that this implementation requires the reevaluation of the expression B for any waiting processes every time a process leaves the critical region. If several processes are delayed, waiting for their respective Boolean expressions to become true, this reevaluation overhead may result in inefficient code. There are various optimization methods that we can use to reduce this overhead. Refer to the Bibliographic Notes for relevant references.

6.7 ■ Monitors

Another high-level synchronization construct is the *monitor* type. A monitor is characterized by a set of programmer-defined operators. The representation of a monitor type consists of declarations of variables whose values define the state of an instance of the type, as well as the bodies of procedures or functions that implement operations on the type. The syntax of a monitor is

type *monitor-name* = **monitor**
    variable declarations

    procedure entry $P1$ (...);
        begin ... **end**;

    procedure entry $P2$ (...);
        begin ... **end**;

    .

    .

    .

    procedure entry Pn (...);
        begin ... **end**;

    begin
        initialization code
    end.

The representation of a monitor type cannot be used directly by the various processes. Thus, a procedure defined within a monitor can access only those variables declared locally within the monitor and the formal parameters. Similarly, the local variables of a monitor can be accessed by only the local procedures.

The monitor construct ensures that only one process at a time can be active within the monitor. Consequently, the programmer does not need to code this synchronization constraint explicitly (Figure 6.17). Thus, the monitor, as defined so far, is similar in many respects to the critical region. As we have seen, the critical region is not sufficiently powerful for modeling some synchronization schemes, and has thus been extended to the conditional critical region. Similarly, we need additional mechanisms with monitors for synchronization. These mechanisms are provided by the *condition* construct. A programmer who needs to write her own tailor-made synchronization scheme can define one or more variables of type *condition*:

$$\textbf{var } x,y: condition;$$

The only operations that can be invoked on a condition variable are *wait* and *signal*. The operation

$$x.wait;$$

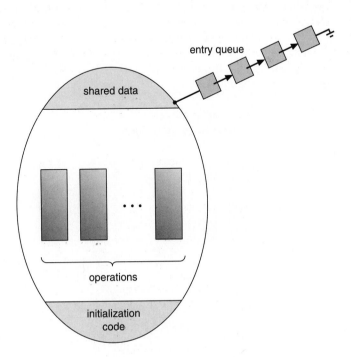

Figure 6.17 Schematic view of a monitor.

means that the process invoking this operation is suspended until another process invokes

$$x.signal;$$

The *x.signal* operation resumes exactly one suspended process. If no process is suspended, then the *signal* operation has no effect; that is, the state of *x* is as though the operation was never executed (Figure 6.18). Contrast this operation with the *signal* operation associated with semaphores, which always affects the state of the semaphore.

Now suppose that, when the *x.signal* operation is invoked by a process *P*, there is a suspended process *Q* associated with condition *x*. Clearly, if the suspended process *Q* is allowed to resume its execution, the signaling process *P* must wait. Otherwise, both *P* and *Q* will be active simultaneously within the monitor. Note, however, that both processes can conceptually continue with their execution. Two possibilities exist:

1. *P* either waits until *Q* leaves the monitor, or waits for another condition.

2. *Q* either waits until *P* leaves the monitor, or waits for another condition.

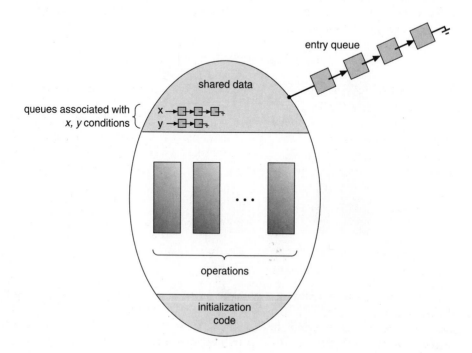

Figure 6.18 Monitor with condition variables.

There are reasonable arguments in favor of adopting either option 1 or option 2. Since P was already executing in the monitor, choice 2 seems more reasonable. However, if we allow process P to continue, the "logical" condition for which Q was waiting may no longer hold by the time Q is resumed.

Choice 1 was advocated by Hoare, mainly because the preceding argument in favor of it translates directly to simpler and more elegant proof rules. A compromise between these two choices was adopted in the language Concurrent Pascal. When process P executes the *signal* operation, it immediately leaves the monitor. Hence, Q is immediately resumed. This model is less powerful than Hoare's, because a process cannot signal more than once during a single procedure call.

Let us illustrate these concepts by presenting a deadlock-free solution to the dining-philosophers problem. Recall that a philosopher is allowed to pick up her chopsticks only if both of them are available. To code this solution, we need to distinguish between three states in which a philosopher may be. For this purpose, we introduce the following data structure:

var *state*: **array** [0..4] **of** (*thinking, hungry, eating*);

Philosopher i can set the variable *state*[i] = *eating* only if her two neighbors are not eating (*state*[i+4 **mod** 5] ≠ *eating* **and** *state*[i+1 **mod** 5] ≠ *eating*).

We also need to declare

var *self*: **array** [0..4] **of** *condition*;

where philosopher i can delay herself when she is hungry, but is unable to obtain the chopsticks she needs.

We are now in a position to describe our solution. The distribution of the chopsticks is controlled by the monitor shown in Figure 6.19. Philosopher i must invoke the operations *pickup* and *putdown* on an instance *dp* of the *dining-philosophers* monitor in the following sequence:

dp.pickup(i);

...

eat

...

dp.putdown(i);

It is easy to show that this solution ensures that no two neighbors are eating simultaneously, and that no deadlocks will occur. We note, however, that it is possible for a philosopher to starve to death. We shall not present a solution to this problem, but rather shall leave it as an exercise for you.

```
type dining-philosophers = monitor
    var state : array [0..4] of (thinking, hungry, eating);
    var self : array [0..4] of condition;

    procedure entry pickup (i: 0..4);
        begin
            state[i] := hungry;
            test (i);
            if state[i] ≠ eating then self[i].wait;
        end;

    procedure entry putdown (i: 0..4);
        begin
            state[i] := thinking;
            test (i+4 mod 5);
            test (i+1 mod 5);
        end;

    procedure test (k: 0..4);
        begin
            if state[k+4 mod 5] ≠ eating
                and state[k] = hungry
                and state[k+1 mod 5] ≠ eating
                then begin
                        state[k] := eating;
                        self[k].signal;
                    end;
        end;

    begin
        for i := 0 to 4
            do state[i] := thinking;
    end.
```

Figure 6.19 A monitor solution to the dining-philosopher problem.

We shall now consider a possible implementation of the monitor mechanism using semaphores. For each monitor, a semaphore *mutex* (initialized to 1) is provided. A process must execute *wait(mutex)* before entering the monitor, and must execute *signal(mutex)* after leaving the monitor.

Since a signaling process must wait until the resumed process either leaves or waits, an additional semaphore, *next*, is introduced, initialized to

0, on which the signaling processes may suspend themselves. An integer variable *next-count* will also be provided to count the number of processes suspended on *next*. Thus, each external procedure *F* will be replaced by

$$wait(mutex);$$
$$\dots$$
$$\text{body of } F;$$
$$\dots$$
$$\textbf{if } next\text{-}count > 0$$
$$\quad \textbf{then } signal(next)$$
$$\quad \textbf{else } signal(mutex);$$

Mutual exclusion within a monitor is ensured.

We can now describe how condition variables are implemented. For each condition *x*, we introduce a semaphore *x-sem* and an integer variable *x-count*, both initialized to 0. The operation *x.wait* can now be implemented as

$$x\text{-}count := x\text{-}count + 1;$$
$$\textbf{if } next\text{-}count > 0$$
$$\quad \textbf{then } signal(next)$$
$$\quad \textbf{else } signal(mutex);$$
$$wait(x\text{-}sem);$$
$$x\text{-}count := x\text{-}count - 1;$$

The operation *x.signal* can be implemented as

$$\textbf{if } x\text{-}count > 0$$
$$\quad \textbf{then begin}$$
$$\qquad next\text{-}count := next\text{-}count + 1;$$
$$\qquad signal(x\text{-}sem);$$
$$\qquad wait(next);$$
$$\qquad next\text{-}count := next\text{-}count - 1;$$
$$\quad \textbf{end};$$

This implementation is applicable to the definitions of monitors given by both Hoare and Brinch Hansen. In some cases, however, the generality of the implementation is unnecessary, and a significant improvement in efficiency is possible. We leave this problem to you in Exercise 6.12.

We turn now to the subject of process-resumption order within a monitor. If several processes are suspended on condition *x*, and an *x.signal* operation is executed by some process, then how do we determine which of the suspended processes should be resumed next? One simple solution is to use an FCFS ordering, so that the process waiting the longest is resumed first. There are, however, many circumstances in which such a simple scheduling scheme is not adequate. For this purpose, the *conditional-wait* construct can be used; it has the form

$$x.wait(c);$$

where *c* is an integer expression that is evaluated when the wait operation is executed. The value of *c*, which is called a *priority number,* is then stored with the name of the process that is suspended. When *x.signal* is executed, the process with the smallest associated priority number is resumed next.

To illustrate this new mechanism, we consider the monitor shown in Figure 6.20, which controls the allocation of a single resource among competing processes. Each process, when requesting an allocation of its resources, specifies the maximum time it plans to use the resource. The monitor allocates the resource to that process that has the shortest time-allocation request.

A process that needs to access the resource in question must observe the following sequence:

$$R.acquire(t);$$
$$...$$
access the resource;
$$...$$
$$R.release;$$

where *R* is an instance of type *resource-allocation.*

Unfortunately, the monitor concept cannot guarantee that the preceding access sequences will be observed. In particular,

- A process might access the resource without first gaining access permission to that resource.

- A process might never release the resource once it has been granted access to that resource.

- A process might attempt to release a resource that it never requested.

- A process might request the same resource twice (without first releasing that resource).

Note that the same difficulties are encountered with the critical section construct, and these difficulties are similar in nature to those that encouraged us to develop the critical-region and monitor constructs in the first place. Previously, we had to worry about the correct use of semaphores. Now, we have to worry about the correct use of higher-level

```
type resource-allocation = monitor
    var busy: boolean;
        x: condition;

procedure entry acquire (time: integer);
    begin
        if busy then x.wait(time);
        busy := true;
    end;

procedure entry release;
    begin
        busy := false;
        x.signal;
    end;

begin
    busy := false;
end.
```

Figure 6.20   A monitor to allocate a single resource.

programmer-defined operations, with which the compiler can no longer assist us.

One possible solution to the above problem is to include the resource-access operations within *resource-allocation* monitor. However, this solution will result in scheduling being done according to the built-in monitor-scheduling algorithm, rather than by the one we have coded.

To ensure that the processes observe the appropriate sequences, we must inspect all the programs that make use of the *resource-allocation* monitor and its managed resource. There are two conditions that we must check to establish the correctness of this system. First, user processes must always make their calls on the monitor in a correct sequence. Second, we must be sure that an uncooperative process does not simply ignore the mutual-exclusion gateway provided by the monitor, and try to access the shared resource directly, without using the access protocols. Only if these two conditions can be ensured can we guarantee that no time-dependent errors will occur, and that the scheduling algorithm will not be defeated.

Although this inspection may be possible for a small, static system, it is not reasonable for a large system or for a dynamic system. This *access-control problem* can be solved only by additional mechanisms that will be elaborated in Chapter 13.

6.8 ■ Synchronization in Solaris 2

To solidify this discussion, we now return to Solaris 2. Before the advent of Solaris 2, SunOS used critical sections to guard important data structures. The system implemented the critical sections by setting the interrupt level to as high as or higher than any interrupt that could modify the same data. Thus, no interrupt would occur that would allow a change to the same data.

In Section 5.5, we described the changes needed to support real-time computing on a time-sharing system. Solaris 2 was designed to provide real-time capabilities, be multithreaded, and support multiprocessors. Continuing to use critical sections would have caused a large performance degradation, as the kernel bottlenecked waiting for entry into critical sections. Further, critical sections could not have been implemented via interrupt elevation because interrupts could occur on other processors on a multiprocessor system. To avoid these problems, Solaris 2 uses *adaptive mutexes* to protect access to every critical data item.

On a multiprocessor system, an adaptive mutex starts as a standard semaphore implemented as a spinlock. If the data are locked, and therefore already in use, the adaptive mutex does one of two things. If the lock is held by a thread that is currently running, the thread waits for the lock to become available because the thread holding the lock is likely to be done soon. If the thread holding the lock is not currently in run state, the thread blocks, going to sleep until it is awakened by the lock being released. It is put to sleep so that it will avoid spinning when the lock will not be freed reasonably quickly. A lock held by a sleeping thread is likely to be in this category. On a uniprocessor system, the thread holding the lock is never running if the lock is being tested by another thread, because only one thread can run at a time. Therefore, on a uniprocessor system, threads always sleep rather than spin if they encounter a lock.

For more complex synchronization situations, Solaris 2 uses condition variables and readers–writers locks. The adaptive mutex method described above is used to protect only those data that are accessed by short code segments. That is, a mutex is used if a lock will be held for less than a few hundred instructions. If the code segment is longer than that, spin waiting will be exceedingly inefficient. For longer code segments, condition variables are used. If the desired lock is already held, the thread issues a wait and sleeps. When a thread frees the lock, it issues a signal to the next sleeping thread in the queue. The extra cost of putting a thread to sleep and waking it, and of the associated context switches, is less than the cost of wasting several hundred instructions waiting in a spinlock.

The readers–writers locks are used to protect data that are accessed frequently, but usually only in a read-only manner. In these circumstances, readers–writers locks are more efficient than are semaphores, because multiple threads may be reading data concurrently, whereas semaphores would always serialize access to the data. Readers–writers locks are expensive to implement, so again they are used on only long sections of code.

6.9 ■ Atomic Transactions

The mutual exclusion of critical sections ensures that the critical sections are executed atomically. That is, if two critical sections are executed concurrently, the result is equivalent to their sequential execution in some unknown order. Although this property is useful in many application domains, there are many cases where we would like to make sure that a critical section forms a single logical unit of work that either is performed in its entirety or is not performed at all. An example is funds transfer, in which one account is debited and another is credited. Clearly, it is essential for data consistency that either both the credit and debit occur, or that neither occur.

The remainder of this section is related to the field of database systems. *Databases* are concerned with the storage and retrieval of data, and with the consistency of the data. Recently, there has been an upsurge of interest in using database-systems techniques in operating systems. Operating systems can be viewed as manipulators of data; as such, they can benefit from the advanced techniques and models available from database research. For instance, many of the ad hoc techniques used in operating systems to manage files could be more flexible and powerful if more formal database methods were used in their place. In Sections 6.9.2 to 6.9.4, we describe what these database techniques are, and how they can be used by operating systems.

6.9.1 System Model

A collection of instructions (operations) that performs a single logical function is called a *transaction*. A major issue in processing transactions is the preservation of atomicity despite the possibility of failures within the computer system. In Section 6.9, we describe various mechanisms for ensuring transaction atomicity. We do so by first considering an environment where only one transaction can be executing at a time. Then, we consider the case where multiple transactions are active simultaneously.

A transaction is a program unit that accesses and possibly updates various data items that may reside on the disk within some files. From our point of view, a transaction is simply a sequence of **read** and **write** operations, terminated by either a **commit** operation or an **abort** operation.

A commit operation signifies that the transaction has terminated its execution successfully, whereas an abort operation signifies that the transaction had to seize its normal execution due to some logical error. A terminated transaction that has completed its execution successfully is *committed*; otherwise, it is *aborted*. The effect of a committed transaction cannot be undone by abortion of the transaction.

A transaction may also cease its normal execution due to a system failure. In either case, since an aborted transaction may have already modified the various data that it has accessed, the state of these data may not be the same as it would be had the transaction executed atomically. So that the atomicity property is ensured, an aborted transaction must have no effect on the state of the data that it has already modified. Thus, the state of the data accessed by an aborted transaction must be restored to what it was just before the transaction started executing. We say that such a transaction has been *rolled back*. It is part of the responsibility of the system to ensure this property.

To determine how the system should ensure atomicity, we need first to identify the properties of devices used for storing the various data accessed by the transactions. Various types of storage media are distinguished by their relative speed, capacity, and resilience to failure.

- **Volatile storage:** Information residing in volatile storage does not usually survive system crashes. Examples of such storage are main and cache memory. Access to volatile storage is extremely fast, both because of the speed of the memory access itself and because it is possible to access directly any data item in volatile storage.

- **Nonvolatile storage:** Information residing in nonvolatile storage usually survives system crashes. Examples of media for such storage are disk and magnetic tapes. Disks are more reliable than is main memory, but are less reliable than are magnetic tapes. Both disks and tapes, however, are subject to failure, which may result in loss of information. Currently, nonvolatile storage is slower than volatile storage by several orders of magnitude, because disk and tape devices are electromechanical and require physical motion to access data.

- **Stable storage:** Information residing in stable storage is *never* lost (*never* should be taken with a grain of salt, since theoretically such absolutes cannot be guaranteed). To implement an approximation of such storage, we need to replicate information in several nonvolatile storage caches (usually disk) with independent failure modes, and to update the information in a controlled manner (see Section 12.6).

Here, we are concerned only with ensuring transaction atomicity in an environment where failures result in the loss of information on volatile storage.

6.9.2 Log-Based Recovery

One way to ensure atomicity is to record, on stable storage, information describing all the modifications made by the transaction to the various data it accessed. The most widely used method for achieving this form of recording is *write-ahead logging*. The system maintains, on stable storage, a data structure called the *log*. Each log record describes a single operation of a transaction write, and has the following fields:

- **Transaction name:** The unique name of the transaction that performed the **write** operation

- **Data item name:** The unique name of the data item written

- **Old value:** The value of the data item prior to the write

- **New value:** The value that the data item will have after the write

Other special log records exist to record significant events during transaction processing, such as the start of a transaction and the commit or abort of a transaction.

Before a transaction T_i starts its execution, the record $<T_i$ **starts**$>$ is written to the log. During its execution, any **write** operation by T_i is *preceded* by the writing of the appropriate new record to the log. When T_i commits, the record $<T_i$ **commits**$>$ is written to the log.

Because the information in the log is used in reconstructing the state of the data items accessed by the various transactions, we cannot allow the actual update to a data item to take place before the corresponding log record is written out to stable storage. We therefore require that, prior to a **write**(X) operation being executed, the log records corresponding to X be written onto stable storage.

Note the performance penalty inherent in this system. Two physical writes are required for every logical write requested. Also, more storage is needed: for the data themselves and for the log of the changes. In cases where the data are extremely important, and fast failure recovery is necessary, the price is worth the functionality.

Using the log, the system can handle any failure that does not result in the loss of information on nonvolatile storage. The recovery algorithm uses two procedures:

- **undo**(T_i), which restores the value of all data updated by transaction T_i to the old values

- **redo**(T_i), which sets the value of all data updated by transaction T_i to the new values

The set of data updated by T_i and their respective old and new values can be found in the log.

The **undo** and **redo** operations must be idempotent (that is, multiple executions of an operation have the same result as does one execution) to guarantee correct behavior, even if a failure occurs during the recovery process.

If a transaction T_i aborts, then we can restore the state of the data that it has updated by simply executing **undo**(T_i). If a system failure occurs, we restore the state of all updated data by consulting the log to determine which transactions need to be redone and which need to be undone. This classification of transactions is accomplished as follows:

- Transaction T_i needs to be undone if the log contains the record <T_i **starts**>, but does not contain the record <T_i **commits**>.

- Transaction T_i needs to be redone if the log contains both the record <T_i **starts**> and the record <T_i **commits**>.

6.9.3 Checkpoints

When a system failure occurs, we must consult the log to determine those transactions that need to be redone and those that need to be undone. In principle, we need to search the entire log to make these determinations. There are two major drawbacks to this approach:

1. The searching process is time-consuming.

2. Most of the transactions that, according to our algorithm, need to be redone, have already actually updated the data that the log says they need to modify. Although redoing the data modifications will cause no harm (due to idempotency), it will nevertheless cause recovery to take longer.

To reduce these types of overhead, we introduce the concept of *checkpoints*. During execution, the system maintains the write-ahead log. In addition, the system periodically performs checkpoints, which require the following sequence of actions to take place:

1. Output all log records currently residing in volatile storage (usually main memory) onto stable storage.

2. Output all modified data residing in volatile storage to the stable storage.

3. Output a log record <**checkpoint**> onto stable storage.

The presence of a <**checkpoint**> record in the log allows the system to streamline its recovery procedure. Consider a transaction T_i that

committed prior to the checkpoint.   The $<T_i$ **commits**$>$ record appears in
the log before the $<$**checkpoint**$>$ record.   Any modifications made by T_i
must have been written to stable storage either prior to the checkpoint, or
as part of the checkpoint itself.   Thus, at recovery time, there is no need to
perform a redo operation on T_i.

This observation allows us to refine our previous recovery algorithm.
After a failure has occurred, the recovery routine examines the log to
determine the most recent transaction T_i that started executing before the
most recent checkpoint took place.   It finds such a transaction by searching
the log backward to find the first $<$**checkpoint**$>$ record, and then finding
the subsequent $<T_i$ **start**$>$ record.

Once transaction T_i has been identified, the **redo** and **undo** operations
need to be applied to only transaction T_i and all transactions T_j that started
executing after transaction T_i.   Let us denote these transactions by the set
T.   The remainder of the log can thus be ignored.   The recovery operations
that are required are as follows:

- For all transactions T_k in T such that the record $<T_k$ **commits**$>$ appears
  in the log, execute **redo**(T_k).

- For all transactions T_k in T that have no $<T_k$ **commits**$>$ record in the
  log, execute **undo**(T_k).

6.9.4   Concurrent Atomic Transactions

Because each transaction is atomic, the concurrent execution of transactions
must be equivalent to the case where these transactions executed serially in
some arbitrary order.   This property, called *serializability*, can be maintained
by simply executing each transaction within a critical section.   That is, all
transactions share a common semaphore *mutex*, which is initialized to 1.
When a transaction starts executing, its first action is to execute
wait(mutex).   After the transaction either commits or aborts, it executes
signal(mutex).

Although this scheme ensures the atomicity of all concurrently
executing transactions, it nevertheless is too restrictive.   As we shall see,
there are many cases where we can allow transactions to overlap their
execution, while maintaining serializability.   There are a number of different
concurrency-control algorithms to ensure serializability.   These are described
below.

6.9.4.1   Serializability

Consider a system with two data items A and B, that are both read and
written by two transactions T_0 and T_1.   Suppose that these transactions are
executed atomically in the order T_0 followed by T_1.   This execution

T_0	T_1
read(A)	
write(A)	
read(B)	
write(B)	
	read(A)
	write(A)
	read(B)
	write(B)

Figure 6.21 Schedule 1: A serial schedule in which T_0 is followed by T_1.

sequence, which is called a *schedule,* is represented in Figure 6.21. In schedule 1 of Figure 6.21, the sequence of instruction steps is in chronological order from top to bottom, with instructions of T_0 appearing in the left column and instructions of T_1 appearing in the right column.

A schedule where each transaction is executed atomically is called a *serial schedule.* Each serial schedule consists of a sequence of instructions from various transactions where the instructions belonging to one single transaction appear together in that schedule. Thus, for a set of n transactions, there exist $n!$ different valid serial schedules. Each serial schedule is correct, because it is equivalent to the atomic execution of the various participating transactions, in some arbitrary order.

If we allow the two transactions to overlap their execution, then the resulting schedule is no longer serial. A nonserial schedule does not necessarily imply that the resulting execution is incorrect (that is, is not equivalent to a serial schedule). To see that this is the case, we need to define the notion of *conflicting operations.* Consider a schedule S in which there are two consecutive operations O_i and O_j of transactions T_i and T_j, respectively. We say that O_i and O_j *conflict* if they access the same data item, and at least one of these operations is a **write** operation. To illustrate the concept of conflicting operations, we consider the nonserial schedule 2 of Figure 6.22. The **write**(A) operation of T_0 conflicts with the **read**(A) operation of T_1. However, the **write**(A) operation of T_1 does not conflict with the **read**(B) operation of T_0, because the two operations access different data items.

Let O_i and O_j be consecutive operations of a schedule S. If O_i and O_j are operations of different transactions and O_i and O_j do not conflict, then we can swap the order of O_i and O_j to produce a new schedule S'. We expect S to be equivalent to S', as all operations appear in the same order in both schedules, except for O_i and O_j, whose order does not matter.

Let us illustrate the swapping idea by considering again schedule 2 of Figure 6.22. As the **write**(A) operation of T_1 does not conflict with the

T_0	T_1
read(A)	
write(A)	
	read(A)
	write(A)
read(B)	
write(B)	
	read(B)
	write(B)

Figure 6.22   Schedule 2: A concurrent serializable schedule.

read(B) operation of T_0, we can swap these operations to generate an equivalent schedule. Regardless of the initial system state, both schedules produce the same final system state. Continuing with this procedure of swapping nonconflicting operations, we get:

- Swap the **read**(B) operation of T_0 with the **read**(A) operation of T_1.

- Swap the **write**(B) operation of T_0 with the **write**(A) operation of T_1.

- Swap the **write**(B) operation of T_0 with the **read**(A) operation of T_1.

The final result of these swaps, is schedule 1 in Figure 6.21, which is a serial schedule. Thus, we have shown that schedule 2 is equivalent to a serial schedule. This result implies that, regardless of the initial system state, schedule 2 will produce the same final state as will some serial schedule.

If a schedule S can be transformed into a serial schedule S' by a series of swaps of nonconflicting operations, we say that a schedule S is *conflict serializable*. Thus, schedule 2 is conflict serializable, because it can be transformed into the serial schedule 1.

6.9.4.2 Locking Protocol

One way to ensure serializability is to associate with each data item a lock, and to require that each transaction follow a *locking protocol* that governs how locks are acquired and released. There are various modes in which a data item can be locked. In this section, we restrict our attention to two modes:

- **Shared:** If a transaction T_i has obtained a shared-mode lock (denoted by S) on data item Q, then T_i can read this item, but it cannot write Q.

- **Exclusive:** If a transaction T_i has obtained an exclusive-mode lock (denoted by X) on data item Q, then T_i can both read and write Q.

We require that every transaction request a lock in an appropriate mode on data item Q, depending on the type of operations it will perform on Q.

To access a data item Q, transaction T_i must first lock Q in the appropriate mode. If Q is not currently locked, then the lock is granted, and T_i can now access it. However, if the data item Q is currently locked by some other transaction, then T_i may have to wait. More specifically, suppose that T_i requests an exclusive lock on Q. In this case, T_i must wait until the lock on Q is released. If T_i requests a shared lock on Q, then T_i must wait if Q is locked in exclusive mode. Otherwise, it can obtain the lock and access Q. Notice that this scheme is quite similar to the readers–writers algorithm discussed in Section 6.5.2.

A transaction may unlock a data item that it had locked at an earlier point. It must, however, hold a lock on a data item as long as it accesses that item. Moreover, it is not always desirable for a transaction to unlock a data item immediately after its last access of that data item, because serializability may not be ensured.

One protocol that ensures serializability is the *two-phase locking protocol*. This protocol requires that each transaction issue lock and unlock requests in two phases:

- **Growing phase:** A transaction may obtain locks, but may not release any lock.

- **Shrinking phase:** A transaction may release locks, but may not obtain any new locks.

Initially, a transaction is in the growing phase. The transaction acquires locks as needed. Once the transaction releases a lock, it enters the shrinking phase, and no more lock requests can be issued.

The two-phase locking protocol ensures conflict serializability (see Exercise 6.21). It does not, however, ensure freedom from deadlock. We note that it is possible that, for a set of transactions, there are conflict serializable schedules that cannot be obtained through the two-phase locking protocol. However, to improve performance over two-phase locking, we need either to have additional information about the transactions or to impose some structure or ordering on the set of data.

6.9.4.3 Timestamp-Based Protocols

In the locking protocols described above, the order between every pair of conflicting transactions is determined at execution time by the first lock that they both request and that involves incompatible modes. Another method for determining the serializability order is to select an ordering among transactions in advance. The most common method for doing so is to use a *timestamp-ordering* scheme.

With each transaction T_i in the system, we associate a unique fixed timestamp, denoted by TS(T_i). This timestamp is assigned by the system before the transaction T_i starts execution. If a transaction T_i has been assigned timestamp TS(T_i), and a new transaction T_j enters the system, then TS(T_i) < TS(T_j). There are two simple methods for implementing this scheme:

- Use the value of the system clock as the timestamp; that is, a transaction's timestamp is equal to the value of the clock when the transaction enters the system. This method will not work for transactions that occur on separate systems or for processors that do not share a clock.

- Use a logical counter as the timestamp; that is, a transaction's timestamp is equal to the value of the counter when the transaction enters the system. The counter is incremented after a new timestamp is assigned.

The timestamps of the transactions determine the serializability order. Thus, if TS(T_i) < TS(T_j), then the system must ensure that the produced schedule is equivalent to a serial schedule in which transaction T_i appears before transaction T_j.

To implement this scheme, we associate with each data item Q two timestamp values:

- **W-timestamp**(Q), which denotes the largest timestamp of any transaction that executed **write**(Q) successfully

- **R-timestamp**(Q), which denotes the largest timestamp of any transaction that executed **read**(Q) successfully

These timestamps are updated whenever a new **read**(Q) or **write**(Q) instruction is executed.

The timestamp-ordering protocol ensures that any conflicting **read** and **write** operations are executed in timestamp order. This protocol operates as follows:

- Suppose that transaction T_i issues **read**(Q).

  ○ If TS(T_i) < W-timestamp(Q), then this state implies that T_i needs to read a value of Q which was already overwritten. Hence, the **read** operation is rejected, and T_i is rolled back.

  ○ If TS(T_i) ≥ W-timestamp(Q), then the **read** operation is executed, and R-timestamp(Q) is set to the maximum of R-timestamp(Q) and TS(T_i).

- Suppose that transaction T_i issues **write**(Q):

  ○ If TS(T_i) < R-timestamp(Q), then this state implies that the value of Q that T_i is producing was needed previously and T_i assumed that this value would never be produced. Hence, the **write** operation is rejected, and T_i is rolled back.

  ○ If TS(T_i) < W-timestamp(Q), then this state implies that T_i is attempting to write an obsolete value of Q. Hence, this **write** operation is rejected, and T_i is rolled back.

  ○ Otherwise, the **write** operation is executed.

A transaction T_i, which is rolled back by the concurrency-control scheme as result of the issuing of either a **read** or **write** operation, is assigned a new timestamp and is restarted.

To illustrate this protocol, we consider schedule 3 of Figure 6.23 with transactions T_2 and T_3. We assume that a transaction is assigned a timestamp immediately before its first instruction. Thus, in schedule 3, TS(T_2) < TS(T_3), and the schedule is possible under the timestamp protocol.

We note that this execution can also be produced by the two-phase locking protocol. There are, however, schedules that are possible under the two-phase locking protocol but are not possible under the timestamp protocol, and vice versa (see Exercise 6.22).

The timestamp-ordering protocol ensures conflict serializability. This capability follows from the fact that conflicting operations are processed in timestamp order. The protocol ensures freedom from deadlock, because no transaction ever waits.

6.10 ■ Summary

Given a collection of cooperating sequential processes that share data, mutual exclusion must be provided. One solution is to ensure that a critical section of code is in use by only one process or thread at a time. Different algorithms exist for solving the critical-section problem, with the assumption that only storage interlock is available.

The main disadvantage of these user coded solutions is that they all require busy waiting. Semaphores overcome this difficulty. Semaphores can be used to solve various synchronization problems, and can be implemented efficiently, especially if hardware support for atomic operations is available.

Various different synchronization problems (such as the bounded-buffer problem, the readers–writers problem, and the dining-philosophers problem) are important mainly because they are examples of a large class

T_2	T_3
read(B)	
	read(B)
	write(B)
read(A)	
	read(A)
	write(A)

Figure 6.23 Schedule 3: A schedule possible under the timestamp protocol.

of concurrency-control problems. These problems are used to test nearly every newly proposed synchronization scheme.

The operating system must provide the means to guard against timing errors. Several language constructs have been proposed to deal with these problems. Critical regions can be used to implement mutual-exclusion and arbitrary-synchronization problems safely and efficiently. Monitors provide the synchronization mechanism for sharing abstract data types. A condition variable provides a method for a monitor procedure to block its execution until it is signaled to continue.

Solaris 2 is an example of a modern operating system which implements a variety of locks to support multitasking, multithreading (including real-time threads), and multiprocessing. It uses adaptive mutexes for efficiency when protecting data from short code segments. Condition variables and readers–writers locks are used when longer sections of code need access to data.

A *transaction* is a program unit that must be executed atomically; that is, either all the operations associated with it are executed to completion, or none are performed. To ensure atomicity despite system failure, we can use a *write-ahead* log. All updates are recorded on the log, which is kept in stable storage. If a system crash occurs, the information in the log is used in restoring the state of the updated data items, which is accomplished with the use of the **undo** and **redo** operations. To reduce the overhead in searching the log after a system failure has occurred, we can use a *checkpoint* scheme.

When several transactions overlap their execution, the resulting execution may no longer be equivalent to an execution where these transactions executed atomically. To ensure correct execution, we must use a *concurrency-control* scheme to guarantee *serializability*. There are various different concurrency-control schemes that ensure serializability by either delaying an operation or aborting the transaction that issued the operation. The most common ones are *locking protocols* and *timestamp-ordering* schemes.

■ Exercises

6.1 What is the meaning of the term *busy waiting*? What other kinds of waiting are there? Can busy waiting be avoided altogether? Explain your answer.

6.2 Prove that, in the bakery algorithm (Section 6.2.2), the following property holds: If P_i is in its critical section and P_k $(k \neq i)$ has already chosen its *number[k]* $\neq 0$, then $(number[i], i) < (number[k], k)$.

6.3 The first known correct software solution to the critical-section problem for two processes was developed by Dekker. The two processes, P_0 and P_1, share the following variables:

> **var** *flag*: **array** [0..1] **of** *boolean*;   (* initially false *)
> *turn*: 0..1;

The structure of process P_i (i = 0 or 1), with P_j (j = 1 or 0) being the other process, is shown in Figure 6.24.

Prove that the algorithm satisfies all three requirements for the critical-section problem.

repeat

```
flag[i] := true;
while flag[j]
    do if turn = j
            then begin
                    flag[i] := false;
                    while turn = j do no-op;
                    flag[i] := true;
                end;
```

critical section

```
turn := j;
flag[i] := false;
```

remainder section

until *false*;

Figure 6.24   The structure of process P_i in Dekker's algorithm.

var j: $0..n$;
repeat

```
repeat
    flag[i] := want-in;
    j := turn;
    while j ≠ i
        do if flag[j] ≠ idle
            then j := turn
            else j := j+1 mod n;
    flag[i] := in-cs;
    j := 0;
    while (j < n) and (j = i or flag[j] ≠ in-cs) do j := j+1;
until (j ≥ n) and (turn = i or flag[turn] = idle);
turn := i;
```

critical section

```
j := turn+1 mod n;
while (flag[j] = idle) do j := j+1 mod n;
turn := j;
flag[i] := idle;
```

remainder section

until *false*;

Figure 6.25   The structure of P_i in Eisenberg and McGuire's algorithm.

6.4 The first known correct software solution to the critical-section problem for n processes with a lower bound on waiting of $n - 1$ turns, was presented by Eisenberg and McGuire. The processes share the following variables:

$$\textbf{var } flag\text{: } \textbf{array } [0..n-1] \textbf{ of } (idle, \; wa0\text{-}in, \; in\text{-}cs);$$
$$turn\text{: } 0..n-1;$$

All the elements of *flag* are initially *idle*; the initial value of *turn* is immaterial (between 0 and $n-1$). The structure of process P_i is shown in Figure 6.25.

Prove that the algorithm satisfies all three requirements for the critical-section problem.

6.5 In Section 6.3, we mentioned that disabling interrupts frequently could affect the system's clock. Explain why it could, and how such effects could be minimized.

6.6 Show that, if the *wait* and *signal* operations are not executed atomically, then mutual exclusion may be violated.

6.7 *The Sleeping-Barber Problem.* A barbershop consists of a waiting room with n chairs, and the barber room containing the barber chair. If there are no customers to be served, the barber goes to sleep. If a customer enters the barbershop and all chairs are occupied, then the customer leaves the shop. If the barber is busy, but chairs are available, then the customer sits in one of the free chairs. If the barber is asleep, the customer wakes up the barber. Write a program to coordinate the barber and the customers.

6.8 *The Cigarette-Smokers Problem.* Consider a system with three *smoker* processes and one *agent* process. Each smoker continuously rolls a cigarette and then smokes it. But to roll and smoke a cigarette, the smoker needs three ingredients: tobacco, paper, and matches. One of the smoker processes has paper, another has tobacco, and the third has matches. The agent has an infinite supply of all three materials. The agent places two of the ingredients on the table. The smoker who has the remaining ingredient then makes and smokes a cigarette, signaling the agent on completion. The agent then puts out another two of the three ingredients, and the cycle repeats. Write a program to synchronize the agent and the smokers.

6.9 Demonstrate that monitors, conditional critical regions, and semaphores are all equivalent, insofar as the same types of synchronization problems can be implemented with them.

6.10 Write a bounded-buffer monitor in which the buffers (portions) are embedded within the monitor itself.

6.11 The strict mutual exclusion within a monitor makes the bounded-buffer monitor of Exercise 6.10 mainly suitable for small portions.

a. Explain why this assertion is true.

b. Design a new scheme that is suitable for larger portions.

6.12 Suppose that the *signal* statement can appear as only the last statement in a monitor procedure. Suggest how the implementation described in Section 6.7 can be simplified.

6.13 Consider a system consisting of processes P_1, P_2, ..., P_n, each of which has a unique priority number. Write a monitor that allocates three identical line printers to these processes, using the priority numbers for deciding the order of allocation.

6.14 A file is to be shared among different processes, each of which has a unique number. The file can be accessed simultaneously by several processes, subject to the following constraint: The sum of all unique numbers associated with all the processes currently accessing the file must be less than n. Write a monitor to coordinate access to the file.

6.15 Suppose that we replace the *wait* and *signal* operations of monitors with a single construct *await(B)*, where B is a general Boolean expression that causes the process executing it to wait until B becomes true.

a. Write a monitor using this scheme to implement the readers–writers problem.

b. Explain why, in general, this construct cannot be implemented efficiently.

c. What restrictions need to be put on the *await* statement so that it can be implemented efficiently? (Hint: Restrict the generality of B; see Kessels [1977].)

6.16 Write a monitor that implements an *alarm clock* that enables a calling program to delay itself for a specified number of time units (*ticks*). You may assume the existence of a real hardware clock, which invokes a procedure *tick* in your monitor at regular intervals.

6.17 Why does Solaris 2 implement multiple locking mechanisms? Under what circumstances does it use spinlocks, blocking semaphores, conditional variables, and readers–writers locks? Why does it use each mechanism?

6.18 Explain the differences, in terms of cost, among the three storage types: volatile, nonvolatile, and stable.

6.19 Explain the purpose of the checkpoint mechanism. How often should checkpoints be performed? How does the frequency of checkpoints affect:

● System performance when no failure occurs?

● The time it takes to recover from a system crash?

● The time it takes to recover from a disk crash?

6.20 Explain the concept of transaction atomicity.

6.21 Show that the two-phase locking protocol ensures conflict serializability.

6.22 Show that there are schedules that are possible under the two-phase locking protocol but are not possible under the timestamp protocol, and vice versa.

Bibliographic Notes

The mutual-exclusion algorithms 1 to 2 for two processes were first discussed in the classical paper by Dijkstra [1965a]. Dekker's algorithm (Exercise 6.3) — the first correct software solution to the two-process mutual-exclusion problem — was developed by the Dutch mathematician T. Dekker. This algorithm also was discussed by Dijkstra [1965a]. A simpler solution to the two-process mutual-exclusion problem has since been presented by Peterson [1981] (algorithm 3).

Dijkstra [1965b] presented the first solution to the mutual-exclusion problem for n processes. This solution, however does not have an upper bound on the amount of time a process must wait before that process is allowed to enter the critical section. Knuth [1966] presented the first algorithm with a bound; his bound was 2^n turns. A refinement of Knuth's algorithm by deBruijn [1967] reduced the waiting time to n^2 turns, after which Eisenberg and McGuire [1972] (Exercise 6.4) succeeded in reducing the time to the lower bound of $n - 1$ turns. The bakery algorithm (algorithm 5) was developed by Lamport [1974]; it also requires $n - 1$ turns, but it is easier to program and to understand. Burns [1978] developed the hardware-solution algorithm that satisfies the bounded waiting requirement.

General discussions concerning the mutual-exclusion problem were offered by Lamport [1986, 1991]. A collection of algorithms for mutual exclusion were given by Raynal [1986].

The semaphore concept was suggested by Dijkstra [1965a]. Patil [1971] examined the question of whether semaphores can solve all possible synchronization problems. Parnas [1975] discussed some of the flaws in Patil's arguments. Kosaraju [1973] followed up on Patil's work to produce a problem that cannot be solved by *wait* and *signal* operations. Lipton [1974] discussed the limitation of various synchronization primitives.

The classic process-coordination problems that we have described are paradigms for a large class of concurrency-control problems. The bounded-buffer problem, the dining-philosophers problem, and the sleeping-barber problem (Exercise 6.7) were suggested by Dijkstra [1965a, 1971]. The cigarette-smokers problem (Exercise 6.8) was developed by Patil [1971]. The readers–writers problem was suggested by Courtois et al. [1971]. The issue of concurrent reading and writing was discussed by Lamport [1977]. The problem of synchronization of independent processes was discussed Lamport [1976].

The critical-region concept was suggested by Hoare [1972] and by Brinch Hansen [1972]. The monitor concept was developed by Brinch Hansen [1973]. A complete description of the monitor was given by Hoare [1974]. Kessels [1977] proposed an extension to the monitor to allow automatic signaling. General discussions concerning concurrent programming were offered by Ben-Ari [1990].

Some details of the locking mechanisms used in Solaris 2 are presented in Khanna et al. [1992], Powell et al. [1991], and especially Eykholt et al. [1992]. Note that the locking mechanisms used by the kernel are implemented for user-level threads as well, so the same types of locks are available inside and outside of the kernel.

The write-ahead log scheme was first introduced in System R [Gray et al. 1981]. The concept of serializability was formulated by Eswaran et al. [1976] in connection with their work on concurrency control for System R. The two-phase locking protocol was introduced by Eswaran et al. [1976]. The timestamp-based concurrency-control scheme was provided by Reed [1983]. An exposition of various timestamp-based concurrency-control algorithms was presented by Bernstein and Goodman [1980].

CHAPTER 7

DEADLOCKS

In a multiprogramming environment, several processes may compete for a finite number of resources. A process requests resources; if the resources are not available at that time, the process enters a wait state. It may happen that waiting processes will never again change state, because the resources they have requested are held by other waiting processes. This situation is called a *deadlock*. We have already discussed this issue briefly in Chapter 6, in connection with semaphores.

Perhaps the best illustration of a deadlock can be drawn from a law passed by the Kansas legislature early in this century. It said, in part: "When two trains approach each other at a crossing, both shall come to a full stop and neither shall start up again until the other has gone."

In this chapter, we describe methods that an operating system can use to deal with the deadlock problem. Note, however, that most current operating systems do not provide deadlock-prevention facilities. Such features probably will be added over time, as deadlock problems become more common. Several trends will cause this situation, including larger numbers of processes, many more resources (including CPUs) within a system, and the emphasis on long-lived file and database servers rather than batch systems.

7.1 ■ System Model

A system consists of a finite number of resources to be distributed among a number of competing processes. The resources are partitioned into several types, each of which consists of some number of identical instances.

Memory space, CPU cycles, files, and I/O devices (such as printers and tape drives) are examples of resource types. If a system has two CPUs, then the resource type *CPU* has two instances. Similarly, the resource type *printer* may have five instances.

If a process requests an instance of a resource type, the allocation of *any* instance of the type will satisfy the request. If it will not, then the instances are not identical, and the resource type classes have not been defined properly. For example, a system may have two printers. These two printers may be defined to be in the same resource class if no one cares which printer prints which output. However, if one printer is on the ninth floor and the other is in the basement, then people on the ninth floor may not see both printers as equivalent, and separate resource classes may need to be defined for each printer.

A process must request a resource before using it, and must release the resource after using it. A process may request as many resources as it requires to carry out its designated task. Obviously, the number of resources requested may not exceed the total number of resources available in the system. In other words, a process cannot request three printers if the system only has two.

Under the normal mode of operation, a process may utilize a resource in only the following sequence:

1. **Request:** If the request cannot be granted immediately (for example, the resource is being used by another process), then the requesting process must wait until it can acquire the resource.

2. **Use:** The process can operate on the resource (for example, if the resource is a printer, the process can print on the printer).

3. **Release:** The process releases the resource.

The request and release of resources are system calls, as explained in Chapter 3. Examples are the **request** and **release device, open** and **close file,** and **allocate** and **free memory** system calls. Request and release of other resources can be accomplished through the *wait* and *signal* operations on semaphores. Therefore, for each use, the operating system checks to make sure that the using process has requested and been allocated the resource. A system table records whether each resource is free or allocated, and, if a resource is allocated, to which process. If a process requests a resource that is currently allocated to another process, it can be added to a queue of processes waiting for this resource.

A set of processes is in a deadlock state when every process in the set is waiting for an event that can be caused by only another process in the set. The events with which we are mainly concerned here are resource acquisition and release. The resources may be either physical resources (for example, printers, tape drives, memory space, and CPU cycles) or logical resources (for example, files, semaphores, and monitors). However, other types of events may result in deadlocks (for example, the IPC facility discussed in Chapter 4).

To illustrate a deadlock state, we consider a system with three tape drives. Suppose that there are three processes, each holding one of these tape drives. If each process now requests another tape drive, the three processes will be in a deadlock state. Each is waiting for the event "tape drive is released," which can be caused only by one of the other waiting processes. This example illustrates a deadlock involving processes competing for the same resource type.

Deadlocks may also involve different resource types. For example, consider a system with one printer and one tape drive. Suppose that process P_i is holding the tape drive and process P_j is holding the printer. If P_i requests the printer and P_j requests the tape drive, a deadlock occurs.

7.2   ■   Deadlock Characterization

It should be obvious that deadlocks are undesirable. In a deadlock, processes never finish executing and system resources are tied up, preventing other jobs from ever starting. Before we discuss the various methods for dealing with the deadlock problem, we shall describe features that characterize deadlocks.

7.2.1 Necessary Conditions

A deadlock situation can arise if the following four conditions hold simultaneously in a system:

1. **Mutual exclusion:** At least one resource must be held in a nonsharable mode; that is, only one process at a time can use the resource. If another process requests that resource, the requesting process must be delayed until the resource has been released.

2. **Hold and wait:** There must exist a process that is holding at least one resource and is waiting to acquire additional resources that are currently being held by other processes.

3. **No preemption:** Resources cannot be preempted; that is, a resource can be released only voluntarily by the process holding it, after that process has completed its task.

4. **Circular wait:** There must exist a set $\{P_0, P_1, ..., P_n\}$ of waiting processes such that P_0 is waiting for a resource that is held by P_1, P_1 is waiting for a resource that is held by P_2, ..., P_{n-1} is waiting for a resource that is held by P_n, and P_n is waiting for a resource that is held by P_0.

We emphasize that all four conditions must hold for a deadlock to occur. The circular-wait condition implies the hold-and-wait condition, so the four conditions are not completely independent. We shall see in Section 7.4, however, that it is useful to consider each condition separately.

7.2.2 Resource-Allocation Graph

Deadlocks can be described more precisely in terms of a directed graph called a *system resource-allocation graph*. This graph consists of a set of vertices V and a set of edges E. The set of vertices V is partitioned into two types $P = \{P_1, P_2, ..., P_n\}$, the set consisting of all the processes in the system, and $R = \{R_1, R_2, ..., R_m\}$, the set consisting of all resource types in the system.

A directed edge from process P_i to resource type R_j is denoted by $P_i \rightarrow R_j$; it signifies that process P_i requested an instance of resource type R_j and is currently waiting for that resource. A directed edge from resource type R_j to process P_i is denoted by $R_j \rightarrow P_i$; it signifies that an instance of resource type R_j has been allocated to process P_i. A directed edge $P_i \rightarrow R_j$ is called a *request edge*; a directed edge $R_j \rightarrow P_i$ is called an *assignment edge*.

Pictorially, we represent each process P_i as a circle, and each resource type R_j as a square. Since resource type R_j may have more than one instance, we represent each such instance as a dot within the square. Note that a request edge points to only the square R_j, whereas an assignment edge must also designate one of the dots in the square.

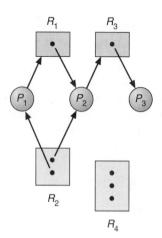

Figure 7.1   Resource-allocation graph.

When process P_i requests an instance of resource type R_j, a request edge is inserted in the resource-allocation graph. When this request can be fulfilled, the request edge is *instantaneously* transformed to an assignment edge. When the process later releases the resource, the assignment edge is deleted.

The resource-allocation graph in Figure 7.1 depicts the following situation.

- The sets P, R, and E:
  - $P = \{P_1, P_2, P_3\}$
  - $R = \{R_1, R_2, R_3, R_4\}$
  - $E = \{P_1 \rightarrow R_1, P_2 \rightarrow R_3, R_1 \rightarrow P_2, R_2 \rightarrow P_2, R_2 \rightarrow P_1, R_3 \rightarrow P_3\}$

- Resource instances:
  - One instance of resource type R_1
  - Two instances of resource type R_2
  - One instance of resource type R_3
  - Three instances of resource type R_4

- Process states:
  - Process P_1 is holding an instance of resource type R_2, and is waiting for an instance of resource type R_1.
  - Process P_2 is holding an instance of R_1 and R_2, and is waiting for an instance of resource type R_3.
  - Process P_3 is holding an instance of R_3.

Given the definition of a resource-allocation graph, it can be shown easily that, if the graph contains no cycles, then no process in the system is deadlocked. If, on the other hand, the graph contains a cycle, then a deadlock may exist.

If each resource type has exactly one instance, then a cycle implies that a deadlock has occurred. If the cycle involves only a set of resource types, each of which has only a single instance, then a deadlock has occurred. Each process involved in the cycle is deadlocked. In this case, a cycle in the graph is both a necessary and a sufficient condition for the existence of deadlock.

If each resource type has several instances, then a cycle does not necessarily imply that a deadlock occurred. In this case, a cycle in the graph is a necessary but not a sufficient condition for the existence of deadlock.

To illustrate this concept, let us return to the resource-allocation graph depicted in Figure 7.1. Suppose that process P_3 requests an instance of resource type R_2. Since no resource instance is currently available, a request edge $P_3 \rightarrow R_2$ is added to the graph (Figure 7.2). At this point, two minimal cycles exist in the system:

$$P_1 \rightarrow R_1 \rightarrow P_2 \rightarrow R_3 \rightarrow P_3 \rightarrow R_2 \rightarrow P_1$$
$$P_2 \rightarrow R_3 \rightarrow P_3 \rightarrow R_2 \rightarrow P_2$$

Processes P_1, P_2, and P_3 are deadlocked. Process P_2 is waiting for the resource R_3, which is held by process P_3. Process P_3, on the other hand, is waiting for either process P_1 or process P_2 to release resource R_2. In addition, process P_1 is waiting for process P_2 to release resource R_1.

Now consider the resource-allocation graph in Figure 7.3. In this example, we also have a cycle

$$P_1 \rightarrow R_1 \rightarrow P_3 \rightarrow R_2 \rightarrow P_1$$

However, there is no deadlock. Observe that process P_4 may release its instance of resource type R_2. That resource can then be allocated to P_3, breaking the cycle.

In summary, if a resource-allocation graph does not have a cycle, then the system is *not* in a deadlock state. On the other hand, if there is a cycle, then the system may or may not be in a deadlock state. This observation is important when we deal with the deadlock problem.

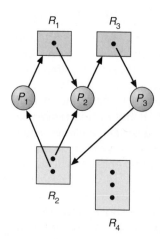

Figure 7.2 Resource-allocation graph with a deadlock.

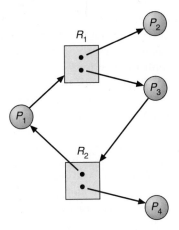

Figure 7.3 Resource-allocation graph with a cycle but no deadlock.

7.3 ■ Methods for Handling Deadlocks

Principally, there are three methods for dealing with the deadlock problem:

- We can use a protocol to ensure that the system will *never* enter a deadlock state.

- We can allow the system to enter a deadlock state and then recover.

- We can ignore the problem all together, and pretend that deadlocks never occur in the system. This solution is the one used by most operating systems, including UNIX.

We shall elaborate briefly on each method. Then, in Sections 7.4 to 7.8, we shall present detailed algorithms.

To ensure that deadlocks never occur, the system can use either a deadlock-prevention or a deadlock-avoidance scheme. *Deadlock prevention* is a set of methods for ensuring that at least one of the necessary conditions (Section 7.2.1) cannot hold. These methods prevent deadlocks by constraining how requests for resources can be made. We discuss these methods in Section 7.4. *Deadlock avoidance*, on the other hand, requires that the operating system be given in advance additional information concerning which resources a process will request and use during its lifetime. With this additional knowledge, we can decide for each request whether or not the process should wait. Each request requires that the system consider the resources currently available, the resources currently allocated to each process, and the future requests and releases of each process, to decide whether the current request can be satisfied or must be delayed. We discuss these schemes in Section 7.5.

If a system does not employ either a deadlock-prevention or a deadlock-avoidance algorithm, then a deadlock situation may occur. In this environment, the system can provide an algorithm that examines the state of the system to determine whether a deadlock has occurred, and an algorithm to recover from the deadlock (if a deadlock has indeed occurred). We discuss these issues in Section 7.6 and Section 7.7.

If a system does not ensure that a deadlock will never occur, and also does not provide a mechanism for deadlock detection and recovery, then we may arrive at a situation where the system is in a deadlock state yet has no way of recognizing what has happened. In this case, the undetected deadlock will result in the deterioration of the system performance, because resources are being held by processes that cannot run, and because more and more processes, as they make requests for resources, enter a deadlock state. Eventually, the system will stop functioning and will need to be restarted manually.

Although this method does not seem to be a viable approach to the deadlock problem, it is nevertheless used in some operating systems. In many systems, deadlocks occur infrequently (say, once per year); thus, it is cheaper to use this method instead of the costly deadlock prevention, deadlock avoidance, or deadlock detection and recovery methods that must be used constantly. Also, there are circumstances in which the system is in a frozen state without it being in a deadlock state. As an example of this situation, consider a real-time process running at the highest priority (or any process running on a non-preemptive scheduler) and never returning control to the operating system.

7.4 ■ Deadlock Prevention

As we noted in Section 7.2.1, for a deadlock to occur, each of the four necessary conditions must hold. By ensuring that at least one of these conditions cannot hold, we can *prevent* the occurrence of a deadlock. Let us elaborate on this approach by examining each of the four necessary conditions separately.

7.4.1 Mutual Exclusion

The mutual-exclusion condition must hold for nonsharable resources. For example, a printer cannot be simultaneously shared by several processes. Sharable resources, on the other hand, do not require mutually exclusive access, and thus cannot be involved in a deadlock. Read-only files are a good example of a sharable resource. If several processes attempt to open a read-only file at the same time, they can be granted simultaneous access to the file. A process never needs to wait for a sharable resource. In general, however, it is not possible to prevent deadlocks by denying the mutual-exclusion condition: Some resources are intrinsically nonsharable.

7.4.2 Hold and Wait

To ensure that the hold-and-wait condition never occurs in the system, we must guarantee that, whenever a process requests a resource, it does not hold any other resources. One protocol that can be used requires each process to request and be allocated all its resources before it begins execution. We can implement this provision by requiring that system calls requesting resources for a process precede all other system calls.

An alternative protocol allows a process to request resources only when the process has none. A process may request some resources and use them. Before it can request any additional resources, however, it must release all the resources that it is currently allocated.

To illustrate the difference between these two protocols, we consider a process that copies data from a tape drive to a disk file, sorts the disk file, and then prints the results to a printer. If all resources must be requested at the beginning of the process, then the process must initially request the tape drive, disk file, and the printer. It will hold the printer for its entire execution, even though it needs the printer only at the end.

The second method allows the process to request initially only the tape drive and disk file. It copies from the tape drive to the disk, then releases both the tape drive and the disk file. The process must then again request the disk file and the printer. After copying the disk file to the printer, it releases these two resources and terminates.

There are two main disadvantages to these protocols. First, *resource utilization* may be low, since many of the resources may be allocated but unused for a long period. In the example given, for instance, we can release the tape drive and disk file, and then again request the disk file and printer, only if we can be sure that our data will remain on the disk file. If we cannot be assured that they will, then we must request all resources at the beginning for both protocols.

Second, *starvation* is possible. A process that needs several popular resources may have to wait indefinitely, because at least one of the resources that it needs is always allocated to some other process.

7.4.3 No Preemption

The third necessary condition is that there be no preemption of resources that have already been allocated. To ensure that this condition does not hold, we can use the following protocol. If a process that is holding some resources requests another resource that cannot be immediately allocated to it (that is, the process must wait), then all resources currently being held are preempted. That is, these resources are implicitly released. The preempted resources are added to the list of resources for which the process is waiting. The process will be restarted only when it can regain its old resources, as well as the new ones that it is requesting.

Alternatively, if a process requests some resources, we first check whether they are available. If they are, we allocate them. If they are not available, we check whether they are allocated to some other process that is waiting for additional resources. If so, we preempt the desired resources from the waiting process and allocate them to the requesting process. If the resources are not either available or held by a waiting process, the requesting process must wait. While it is waiting, some of its resources may be preempted, but only if another process requests them. A process can be restarted only when it is allocated the new resources it is requesting and recovers any resources that were preempted while it was waiting.

This protocol is often applied to resources whose state can be easily saved and restored later, such as CPU registers and memory space. It cannot generally be applied to such resources as printers and tape drives.

7.4.4 Circular Wait

One way to ensure that the circular-wait condition never holds is to impose a total ordering of all resource types, and to require that each process requests resources in an increasing order of enumeration.

Let $R = \{R_1, R_2, ..., R_m\}$ be the set of resource types. We assign to each resource type a unique integer number, which allows us to compare two resources and to determine whether one precedes another in our ordering. Formally, we define a one-to-one function $F: R \rightarrow N$, where N is the set of natural numbers. For example, if the set of resource types R includes tape drives, disk drives, and printers, then the function F might be defined as follows:

$$F(\text{tape drive}) = 1,$$
$$F(\text{disk drive}) = 5,$$
$$F(\text{printer}) = 12.$$

We can now consider the following protocol to prevent deadlocks: Each process can request resources only in an increasing order of enumeration. That is, a process can initially request any number of instances of a resource type, say R_i. After that, the process can request instances of resource type R_j if and only if $F(R_j) > F(R_i)$. If several instances of the same resource type are needed, a *single* request for all of them must be issued. For example, using the function defined previously, a process that wants to use the tape drive and printer at the same time must first request the tape drive and then request the printer.

Alternatively, we can simply require that, whenever a process requests an instance of resource type R_j, it has released any resources R_i such that $F(R_i) \geq F(R_j)$.

If these two protocols are used, then the circular-wait condition cannot hold. We can demonstrate this fact by assuming that a circular wait exists (proof by contradiction). Let the set of processes involved in the circular wait be $\{P_0, P_1, ..., P_n\}$, where P_i is waiting for a resource R_i, which is held by process P_{i+1}. (Modulo arithmetic is used on the indexes, so that P_n is waiting for a resource R_n held by P_0.) Then, since process P_{i+1} is holding resource R_i while requesting resource R_{i+1}, we must have $F(R_i) < F(R_{i+1})$, for all i. But this condition means that $F(R_0) < F(R_1) < ... < F(R_n) < F(R_0)$. By transitivity, $F(R_0) < F(R_0)$, which is impossible. Therefore, there can be no circular wait.

Note that, the function F should be defined according to the normal order of usage of the resources in a system. For example, since the tape drive is usually needed before the printer, it would be reasonable to define $F(\text{tape drive}) < F(\text{printer})$.

7.5 ■ Deadlock Avoidance

Deadlock-prevention algorithms, as discussed in Section 7.4, prevent deadlocks by restraining how requests can be made. The restraints ensure that at least one of the necessary conditions for deadlock cannot occur, and, hence, that deadlocks cannot hold. Possible side effects of preventing deadlocks by this method, however, are low device utilization and reduced system throughput.

An alternative method for avoiding deadlocks is to require additional information about how resources are to be requested. For example, in a system with one tape drive and one printer, we might be told that process P will request first the tape drive, and later the printer, before releasing both resources. Process Q, on the other hand, will request first the printer, and then the tape drive. With this knowledge of the complete sequence of requests and releases for each process, we can decide for each request whether or not the process should wait. Each request requires that the system consider the resources currently available, the resources currently allocated to each process, and the future requests and releases of each process, to decide whether the current request can be satisfied or must wait to avoid a possible future deadlock.

The various algorithms differ in the amount and type of information required. The simplest and most useful model requires that each process declare the *maximum number* of resources of each type that it may need. Given a priori information, for each process, about the maximum number of resources of each type that may be requested, it is possible to construct an algorithm that ensures that the system will never enter a deadlock state. This algorithm defines the *deadlock-avoidance* approach. A deadlock-avoidance algorithm dynamically examines the resource-allocation state to ensure that there can never be a circular-wait condition. The resource-allocation *state* is defined by the number of available and allocated resources, and the maximum demands of the processes.

7.5.1 Safe State

A state is *safe* if the system can allocate resources to each process (up to its maximum) in some order and still avoid a deadlock. More formally, a system is in a safe state only if there exists a *safe sequence*. A sequence of processes $<P_1, P_2, ..., P_n>$ is a safe sequence for the current allocation state if, for each P_i, the resources that P_i can still request can be satisfied by the currently available resources plus the resources held by all the P_j, with $j <$ i. In this situation, if the resources that process P_i needs are not immediately available, then P_i can wait until all P_j have finished. When they have finished, P_i can obtain all of its needed resources, complete its designated task, return its allocated resources, and terminate. When P_i terminates, P_{i+1} can obtain its needed resources, and so on. If no such sequence exists, then the system state is said to be *unsafe*.

A safe state is not a deadlock state. Conversely, a deadlock state is an unsafe state. Not all unsafe states are deadlocks, however (Figure 7.4). An unsafe state *may* lead to a deadlock. As long as the state is safe, the operating system can avoid unsafe (and deadlock) states. In an unsafe state, the operating system cannot prevent processes from requesting resources such that a deadlock occurs: The behavior of the processes controls unsafe states.

To illustrate, we consider a system with 12 magnetic tape drives and 3 processes: P_0, P_1, and P_2. Process P_0 requires 10 tape drives, process P_1 may need as many as 4, and process P_2 may need up to 9 tape drives. Suppose that, at time t_0, process P_0 is holding 5 tape drives, process P_1 is holding 2, and process P_2 is holding 2 tape drives. (Thus, there are 3 free tape drives.)

	Maximum Needs	Current Needs
P_0	10	5
P_1	4	2
P_2	9	2

At time t_0, the system is in a safe state. The sequence $<P_1, P_0, P_2>$ satisfies the safety condition, since process P_1 can immediately be allocated all its tape drives and then return them (the system will then have 5 available tape drives), then process P_0 can get all its tape drives and return them (the system will then have 10 available tape drives), and finally process P_2 could get all its tape drives and return them (the system will then have all 12 tape drives available).

Note that it is possible to go from a safe state to an unsafe state. Suppose that, at time t_1, process P_2 requests and is allocated 1 more tape drive. The system is no longer in a safe state. At this point, only process P_1 can be allocated all its tape drives. When it returns them, the system

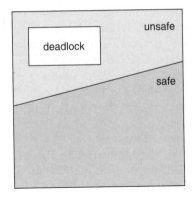

Figure 7.4 Safe, unsafe, and deadlock state spaces.

will have only 4 available tape drives. Since process P_0 is allocated 5 tape drives, but has a maximum of 10, it may then request 5 more tape drives. Since they are unavailable, process P_0 must wait. Similarly, process P_2 may request an additional 6 tape drives and have to wait, resulting in a deadlock.

Our mistake is in granting the request from process P_2 for one more tape drive. If we had made P_2 wait until either of the other processes had finished and released its resources, then we could have avoided the deadlock situation.

Given the concept of a safe state, we can define avoidance algorithms that ensure that the system will never deadlock. The idea is simply to ensure that the system will always remain in a safe state. Initially, the system is in a safe state. Whenever a process requests a resource that is currently available, the system must decide whether the resource can be allocated immediately or whether the process must wait. The request is granted only if the allocation leaves the system in a safe state.

Note that, in this scheme, if a process requests a resource that is currently available, it may still have to wait. Thus, resource utilization may be lower than it would be without a deadlock-avoidance algorithm.

7.5.2 Resource-Allocation Graph Algorithm

If we have a resource-allocation system with only one instance of each resource type, a variant of the resource-allocation graph defined in Section 7.2.2 can be used for deadlock avoidance.

In addition to the request and assignment edges, we introduce a new type of edge, called a *claim edge*. A claim edge $P_i \rightarrow R_j$ indicates that process P_i may request resource R_j at some time in the future. This edge resembles a request edge in direction, but is represented by a dashed line.

When process P_i requests resource R_j, the claim edge $P_i \rightarrow R_j$ is converted to a request edge. Similarly, when a resource R_j is released by P_i, the assignment edge $R_j \rightarrow P_i$ is reconverted to a claim edge $P_i \rightarrow R_j$. We note that the resources must be claimed a priori in the system. That is, before process P_i starts executing, all its claim edges must already appear in the resource-allocation graph. We can relax this condition by allowing a claim edge $P_i \rightarrow R_j$ to be added to the graph only if all the edges associated with process P_i are claim edges.

Suppose that process P_i requests resource R_j. The request can be granted only if converting the request edge $P_i \rightarrow R_j$ to an assignment edge $R_j \rightarrow P_i$ does not result in the formation of a cycle in the resource-allocation graph. Note that we check for safety by using a cycle-detection algorithm. An algorithm for detecting a cycle in this graph requires an order of n^2 operations, where n is the number of processes in the system.

If no cycle exists, then the allocation of the resource will leave the system in a safe state. If a cycle is found, then the allocation will put the system in an unsafe state. Therefore, process P_i will have to wait for its requests to be satisfied.

To illustrate this algorithm, we consider the resource-allocation graph of Figure 7.5. Suppose that P_2 requests R_2. Although R_2 is currently free, we cannot allocate it to P_2, since this action will create a cycle in the graph (Figure 7.6). A cycle indicates that the system is in an unsafe state. If P_1 then requests R_2, a deadlock will occur.

7.5.3 Banker's Algorithm

The resource-allocation graph algorithm is not applicable to a resource-allocation system with multiple instances of each resource type. The deadlock-avoidance algorithm that we describe next is applicable to such a system, but is less efficient than the resource-allocation graph scheme. This algorithm is commonly known as the *banker's algorithm*. The name was

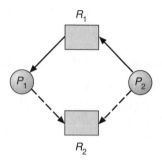

Figure 7.5 Resource-allocation graph for deadlock avoidance.

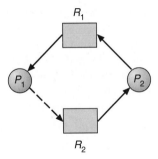

Figure 7.6 An unsafe state in a resource-allocation graph.

chosen because this algorithm could be used in a banking system to ensure that the bank never allocates its available cash such that it can no longer satisfy the needs of all its customers.

When a new process enters the system, it must declare the maximum number of instances of each resource type that it may need. This number may not exceed the total number of resources in the system. When a user requests a set of resources, the system must determine whether the allocation of these resources will leave the system in a safe state. If it will, the resources are allocated; otherwise, the process must wait until some other process releases enough resources.

Several data structures must be maintained to implement the banker's algorithm. These data structures encode the state of the resource-allocation system. Let n be the number of processes in the system and m be the number of resource types. We need the following data structures:

- *Available:* A vector of length m indicates the number of available resources of each type. If $Available[j] = k$, there are k instances of resource type R_j available.

- *Max:* An $n \times m$ matrix defines the maximum demand of each process. If $Max[i,j] = k$, then process P_i may request at most k instances of resource type R_j.

- *Allocation:* An $n \times m$ matrix defines the number of resources of each type currently allocated to each process. If $Allocation[i,j] = k$, then process P_i is currently allocated k instances of resource type R_j.

- *Need:* An $n \times m$ matrix indicates the remaining resource need of each process. If $Need[i,j] = k$, then process P_i may need k more instances of resource type R_j to complete its task. Note that $Need[i,j] = Max[i,j] - Allocation[i,j]$.

These data structures vary over time in both size and value.

To simplify the presentation of the banker's algorithm, let us establish some notation. Let X and Y be vectors of length n. We say that $X \leq Y$ if and only if $X[i] \leq Y[i]$ for all $i = 1, 2, ..., n$. For example, if $X = (1,7,3,2)$ and $Y = (0,3,2,1)$, then $Y \leq X$. $Y < X$ if $Y \leq X$ and $Y \neq X$.

We can treat each row in the matrices *Allocation* and *Need* as vectors and refer to them as *Allocation*$_i$ and *Need*$_i$, respectively. The vector *Allocation*$_i$ specifies the resources currently allocated to process P_i; the vector *Need*$_i$ specifies the additional resources that process P_i may still request to complete its task.

7.5.3.1 Safety Algorithm

The algorithm for finding out whether or not a system is in a safe state can be described as follows:

1. Let *Work* and *Finish* be vectors of length m and n, respectively. Initialize *Work* := *Available* and *Finish*[i] := *false* for $i = 1, 2, ..., n$.

2. Find an i such that both

   a. *Finish*[i] = *false*

   b. *Need*$_i$ $\leq$ *Work*

   If no such i exists, go to step 4.

3. *Work* := *Work* + *Allocation*$_i$
   Finish[i] := *true*
   go to step 2.

4. If *Finish*[i] = *true* for all i, then the system is in a safe state.

This algorithm may require an order of $m \times n^2$ operations to decide whether a state is safe.

7.5.3.2 Resource-Request Algorithm

Let *Request*$_i$ be the request vector for process P_i. If *Request*$_i$[j] = k, then process P_i wants k instances of resource type R_j. When a request for resources is made by process P_i, the following actions are taken:

1. If *Request*$_i$ $\leq$ *Need*$_i$, go to step 2. Otherwise, raise an error condition, since the process has exceeded its maximum claim.

2. If *Request*$_i$ $\leq$ *Available*, go to step 3. Otherwise, P_i must wait, since the resources are not available.

3. Have the system pretend to have allocated the requested resources to process P_i by modifying the state as follows:

$$Available := Available - Request_i;$$
$$Allocation_i := Allocation_i + Request_i;$$
$$Need_i := Need_i - Request_i;$$

If the resulting resource-allocation state is safe, the transaction is completed and process P_i is allocated its resources. However, if the new state is unsafe, then P_i must wait for $Request_i$ and the old resource-allocation state is restored.

7.5.3.3 An Illustrative Example

Consider a system with five processes P_0 through P_4 and three resource types A, B, C. Resource type A has 10 instances, resource type B has 5 instances, and resource type C has 7 instances. Suppose that, at time T_0, the following snapshot of the system has been taken:

	Allocation	Max	Available
	A B C	A B C	A B C
P_0	0 1 0	7 5 3	3 3 2
P_1	2 0 0	3 2 2	
P_2	3 0 2	9 0 2	
P_3	2 1 1	2 2 2	
P_4	0 0 2	4 3 3	

The content of the matrix $Need$ is defined to be $Max - Allocation$ and is

	Need
	A B C
P_0	7 4 3
P_1	1 2 2
P_2	6 0 0
P_3	0 1 1
P_4	4 3 1

We claim that the system is currently in a safe state. Indeed, the sequence $<P_1, P_3, P_4, P_2, P_0>$ satisfies the safety criteria.

Suppose now that process P_1 requests one additional instance of resource type A and two instances of resource type C, so $Request_1 = (1,0,2)$. To decide whether this request can be immediately granted, we first check that $Request_1 \le Available$ (that is, $(1,0,2) \le (3,3,2)$), which is true. We then pretend that this request has been fulfilled, and we arrive at the following new state:

	Allocation	Need	Available
	A B C	A B C	A B C
P_0	0 1 0	7 4 3	2 3 0
P_1	3 0 2	0 2 0	
P_2	3 0 2	6 0 0	
P_3	2 1 1	0 1 1	
P_4	0 0 2	4 3 1	

We must determine whether this new system state is safe. To do so, we execute our safety algorithm and find that the sequence $<P_1, P_3, P_4, P_0, P_2>$ satisfies our safety requirement. Hence, we can immediately grant the request of process P_1.

You should be able to see, however, that when the system is in this state, a request for (3,3,0) by P_4 cannot be granted, since the resources are not available. A request for (0,2,0) by P_0 cannot be granted, even though the resources are available, since the resulting state is unsafe.

7.6 ■ Deadlock Detection

If a system does not employ either a deadlock-prevention or a deadlock-avoidance algorithm, then a deadlock situation may occur. In this environment, the system must provide:

● An algorithm that examines the state of the system to determine whether a deadlock has occurred

● An algorithm to recover from the deadlock

In the following discussion, we elaborate on these two requirements as they pertain to systems with only a single instance of each resource type, as well as to systems with several instances of each resource type. At this point, however, let us note that a detection and recovery scheme requires overhead that includes not only the run-time costs of maintaining the necessary information and executing the detection algorithm, but also the potential losses inherent in recovering from a deadlock.

7.6.1 Single Instance of Each Resource Type

If all resources have only a single instance, then we can define a deadlock detection algorithm that uses a variant of the resource-allocation graph, called a *wait-for* graph. We obtain this graph from the resource-allocation graph by removing the nodes of type resource and collapsing the appropriate edges.

More precisely, an edge from P_i to P_j in a wait-for graph implies that process P_i is waiting for process P_j to release a resource that P_i needs. An edge $P_i \rightarrow P_j$ exists in a wait-for graph if and only if the corresponding resource-allocation graph contains two edges $P_i \rightarrow R_q$ and $R_q \rightarrow P_j$ for some resource R_q. For example, in Figure 7.7, we present a resource-allocation graph and the corresponding wait-for graph.

As before, a deadlock exists in the system if and only if the wait-for graph contains a cycle. To detect deadlocks, the system needs to *maintain* the wait-for graph and periodically to *invoke an algorithm* that searches for a cycle in the graph.

An algorithm to detect a cycle in a graph requires an order of n^2 operations, where n is the number of vertices in the graph.

7.6.2 Several Instances of a Resource Type

The wait-for graph scheme is not applicable to a resource-allocation system with multiple instances of each resource type. The deadlock-detection algorithm that we describe next is applicable to to such a system. The algorithm employs several time-varying data structures that are similar to those used in the banker's algorithm (Section 7.5.3):

- *Available:* A vector of length m indicates the number of available resources of each type.

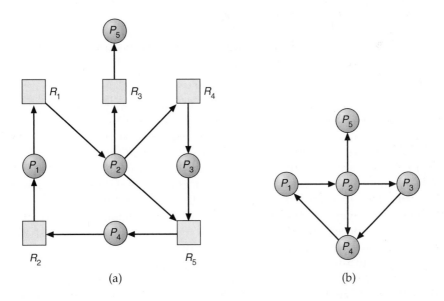

(a) (b)

Figure 7.7 (a) Resource-allocation graph. (b) Corresponding wait-for graph.

- *Allocation:* An $n \times m$ matrix defines the number of resources of each type currently allocated to each process.

- *Request:* An $n \times m$ matrix indicates the current request of each process. If $Request[i,j] = k$, then process P_i is requesting k more instances of resource type R_j.

The less-than relation ($<$) between two vectors is defined as in Section 7.5.3. To simplify notation, we shall again treat the rows in the matrices *Allocation* and *Request* as vectors, and shall refer to them as $Allocation_i$ and $Request_i$, respectively. The detection algorithm described here simply investigates every possible allocation sequence for the processes that remain to be completed. Compare this algorithm with the banker's algorithm of Section 7.5.3.

1. Let *Work* and *Finish* be vectors of length m and n, respectively. Initialize *Work* := *Available*. For $i = 1, 2, ..., n$, if $Allocation_i \neq 0$, then $Finish[i] :=$ *false*; otherwise, $Finish[i] :=$ *true*.

2. Find an index i such that both

    a. $Finish[i] =$ *false*.

    b. $Request_i \leq Work$.

    If no such i exists, go to step 4.

3. *Work* := *Work* + $Allocation_i$
   $Finish[i] :=$ *true*
   go to step 2.

4. If $Finish[i] =$ false, for some i, $1 \leq i \leq n$, then the system is in a deadlock state. Moreover, if $Finish[i] =$ *false*, then process P_i is deadlocked.

This algorithm requires an order of $m \times n^2$ operations to detect whether the system is in a deadlocked state.

You may wonder why we reclaim the resources of process P_i (in step 3) as soon as we determine that $Request_i \leq Work$ (in step 2b). We know that P_i is currently *not* involved in a deadlock (since $Request_i \leq Work$). Thus, we take an optimistic attitude, and assume that P_i will require no more resources to complete its task; it will thus soon return all currently allocated resources to the system. If our assumption is incorrect, a deadlock may occur later. That deadlock will be detected the next time that the deadlock-detection algorithm is invoked.

To illustrate this algorithm, we consider a system with five processes P_0 through P_4 and three resource types A, B, C. Resource type A has 7 instances, resource type B has 2 instances, and resource type C has 6 instances. Suppose that, at time T_0, we have the following resource-allocation state:

	Allocation	Request	Available
	A B C	A B C	A B C
P_0	0 1 0	0 0 0	0 0 0
P_1	2 0 0	2 0 2	
P_2	3 0 3	0 0 0	
P_3	2 1 1	1 0 0	
P_4	0 0 2	0 0 2	

We claim that the system is not in a deadlocked state. Indeed, if we execute our algorithm, we will find that the sequence $<P_0, P_2, P_3, P_1, P_4>$ will result in $Finish[i]$ = true for all i.

Suppose now that process P_2 makes one additional request for an instance of type C. The $Request$ matrix is modified as follows:

	Request
	A B C
P_0	0 0 0
P_1	2 0 2
P_2	0 0 1
P_3	1 0 0
P_4	0 0 2

We claim that the system is now deadlocked. Although we can reclaim the resources held by process P_0, the number of available resources is not sufficient to fulfill the requests of the other processes. Thus, a deadlock exists, consisting of processes P_1, P_2, P_3, and P_4.

7.6.3 Detection-Algorithm Usage

When should we invoke the detection algorithm? The answer depends on two factors:

1. How *often* is a deadlock likely to occur?

2. How *many* processes will be affected by deadlock when it happens?

If deadlocks occur frequently, then the detection algorithm should be invoked frequently. Resources allocated to deadlocked processes will be idle until the deadlock can be broken. In addition, the number of processes involved in the deadlock cycle may grow.

Deadlocks can come into being only when some process makes a request that cannot be granted immediately. It is possible that this request is the final request that completes a chain of waiting processes. In the extreme, we could invoke the deadlock-detection algorithm every time a request for allocation cannot be granted immediately. In this case, we can identify not only the set of processes that is deadlocked, but also the specific process that "caused" the deadlock. (In reality, each of the deadlocked processes is a link in the cycle in the resource graph, so all of them, jointly, caused the deadlock.) If there are many different resource types, one request may cause many cycles in the resource graph, each cycle completed by the most recent request, and "caused" by the one identifiable process.

Of course, invoking the deadlock-detection algorithm for every request may incur a considerable overhead in computation time. A less expensive alternative is simply to invoke the algorithm at less frequent intervals — for example, once per hour, or whenever CPU utilization drops below 40 percent. (A deadlock eventually cripples system throughput and will cause CPU utilization to drop.) If the detection algorithm is invoked at arbitrary points in time, there may be many cycles in the resource graph. We would generally not be able to tell which of the many deadlocked processes "caused" the deadlock.

7.7 ■ Recovery from Deadlock

When a detection algorithm determines that a deadlock exists, several alternatives exist. One possibility is to inform the operator that a deadlock has occurred, and to let the operator deal with the deadlock manually. The other possibility is to let the system *recover* from the deadlock automatically. There are two options for breaking a deadlock. One solution is simply to abort one or more processes to break the circular wait. The second option is to preempt some resources from one or more of the deadlocked processes.

7.7.1 Process Termination

To eliminate deadlocks by aborting a process, we use one of two methods. In both methods, the system reclaims all resources allocated to the terminated processes.

- **Abort all deadlocked processes:** This method clearly will break the deadlock cycle, but at a great expense, since these processes may have computed for a long time, and the results of these partial computations must be discarded, and probably must be recomputed later.

- **Abort one process at a time until the deadlock cycle is eliminated:** This method incurs considerable overhead, since, after each process is aborted, a deadlock-detection algorithm must be invoked to determine whether any processes are still deadlocked.

Notice that aborting a process may not be easy. If the process was in the midst of updating a file, terminating it in the middle will leave that file in an incorrect state. Similarly, if the process was in the midst of printing data on the printer, the system must reset the state of the printer to a correct state before proceeding with the printing of the next job.

If the partial termination method is used, then, given a set of deadlocked processes, we must determine which process (or processes) should be terminated in an attempt to break the deadlock. This determination is a policy decision, similar to CPU-scheduling problems. The question is basically an economic one; we should abort those processes the termination of which will incur the minimum cost. Unfortunately, the term *minimum cost* is not a precise one. Many factors may determine which process is chosen, including:

1. What the priority of the process is

2. How long the process has computed, and how much longer the process will compute before completing its designated task

3. How many and what type of resources the process has used (for example, whether the resources are simple to preempt)

4. How many more resources the process needs in order to complete

5. How many processes will need to be terminated

6. Whether the process is interactive or batch

7.7.2 Resource Preemption

To eliminate deadlocks using resource preemption, we successively preempt some resources from processes and give these resources to other processes until the deadlock cycle is broken.

If preemption is required to deal with deadlocks, then three issues need to be addressed:

1. **Selecting a victim:** Which resources and which processes are to be preempted? As in process termination, we must determine the order of preemption to minimize cost. Cost factors may include such parameters as the number of resources a deadlock process is holding, and the amount of time a deadlocked process has thus far consumed during its execution.

2. **Rollback:** If we preempt a resource from a process, what should be done with that process? Clearly, it cannot continue with its normal execution; it is missing some needed resource. We must roll back the process to some safe state, and restart it from that state.

Since, in general, it is difficult to determine what a safe state is, the simplest solution is a total rollback: Abort the process and then restart it. However, it is more effective to roll back the process only as far as necessary to break the deadlock. On the other hand, this method requires the system to keep more information about the state of all the running processes.

3. **Starvation:** How do we ensure that starvation will not occur? That is, how can we guarantee that resources will not always be preempted from the same process?

In a system where victim selection is based primarily on cost factors, it may happen that the same process is always picked as a victim. As a result, this process never completes its designated task, a *starvation* situation that needs to be dealt with in any practical system. Clearly, we must ensure that a process can be picked as a victim only a (small) finite number of times. The most common solution is to include the number of rollbacks in the cost factor.

7.8 ■ Combined Approach to Deadlock Handling

Researchers have argued that none of the basic approaches for handling deadlocks (prevention, avoidance, and detection) alone is appropriate for the entire spectrum of resource-allocation problems encountered in operating systems. One possibility is to combine the three basic approaches, allowing the use of the optimal approach for each class of resources in the system. The proposed method is based on the notion that resources can be partitioned into classes that are hierarchically ordered. A resource-ordering technique (Section 7.4.4) is applied to the classes. Within each class, the most appropriate technique for handling deadlocks can be used.

It is easy to show that a system that employs this strategy will not be subjected to deadlocks. Indeed, a deadlock cannot involve more than one class, since the resource-ordering technique is used. Within each class, one of the basic approaches is used. Consequently, the system is not subject to deadlocks.

To illustrate this technique, we consider a system that consists of the following four classes of resources:

- **Internal resources:** Resources used by the system, such as a process control block

- **Central memory:** Memory used by a user job

- **Job resources:** Assignable devices (such as a tape drive) and files

- **Swappable space:** Space for each user job on the backing store

One mixed deadlock solution for this system orders the classes as shown, and uses the following approaches to each class:

- **Internal resources:** Prevention through resource ordering can be used, since run-time choices between pending requests are unnecessary.

- **Central memory:** Prevention through preemption can be used, since a job can always be swapped out, and the central memory can be preempted.

- **Job resources:** Avoidance can be used, since the information needed about resource requirements can be obtained from the job-control cards.

- **Swappable space:** Preallocation can be used, since the maximum storage requirements are usually known.

This example shows how various basic approaches can be mixed within the framework of resource ordering, to obtain an effective solution to the deadlock problem.

7.9 ■ Summary

A deadlock state occurs when two or more processes are waiting indefinitely for an event that can be caused only by one of the waiting processes. Principally, there are three methods for dealing with deadlocks:

- Use some protocol to ensure that the system will never enter a deadlock state.

- Allow the system to enter deadlock state and then recover.

- Ignore the problem all together, and pretend that deadlocks never occur in the system. This solution is the one used by most operating systems, including UNIX.

A deadlock situation may occur if and only if four necessary conditions hold simultaneously in the system: mutual exclusion, hold and wait, no preemption, and circular wait. To prevent deadlocks, we ensure that at least one of the necessary conditions never holds.

Another method for avoiding deadlocks that is less stringent than the prevention algorithms is to have a priori information on how each process will be utilizing the resources. The banker's algorithm needs to know the maximum number of each resource class that may be requested by each process. Using this information, we can define a deadlock-avoidance algorithm.

If a system does not employ a protocol to ensure that deadlocks will never occur, then a detection and recovery scheme must be employed. A deadlock-detection algorithm must be invoked to determine whether a deadlock has occurred. If a deadlock is detected, the system must recover either by terminating some of the deadlocked processes, or by preempting resources from some of the deadlocked processes.

In a system that selects victims for rollback primarily on the basis of cost factors, starvation may occur. As a result, the selected process never completes its designated task.

Finally, researchers have argued that none of these basic approaches alone are appropriate for the entire spectrum of resource-allocation problems in operating systems. The basic approaches can be combined, allowing the separate selection of an optimal one for each class of resources in a system.

■ Exercises

7.1 List three examples of deadlocks that are not related to a computer-system environment.

7.2 Is it possible to have a deadlock involving only one single process? Explain your answer.

7.3 People have said that proper spooling would eliminate deadlocks. Certainly, it eliminates from contention card readers, plotters, printers, and so on. It is even possible to spool tapes (called *staging* them), which would leave the resources of CPU time, memory, and disk space. Is it possible to have a deadlock involving these resources? If it is, how could such a deadlock occur? If it is not, why not? What deadlock scheme would seem best to eliminate these deadlocks (if any are possible), or what condition is violated (if they are not possible)?

7.4 Consider the traffic deadlock depicted in Figure 7.8.

   a. Show that the four necessary conditions for deadlock indeed hold in this example.

   b. State a simple rule that will avoid deadlocks in this system.

7.5 Suppose that a system is in an unsafe state. Show that it is possible for the processes to complete their execution without entering a deadlock state.

Figure 7.8 Traffic deadlock for Exercise 7.4.

7.6 In a real computer system, neither the resources available nor the demands of processes for resources are consistent over long periods (months). Resources break or are replaced, new processes come and go, new resources are bought and added to the system. If deadlock is controlled by the banker's algorithm, which of the following changes can be made safely (without introducing the possibility of deadlock), and under what circumstances?

  a. Increase *Available* (new resources added)

  b. Decrease *Available* (resource permanently removed from system)

  c. Increase *Max* for one process (the process needs more resources than allowed, it may want more)

  d. Decrease *Max* for one process (the process decides it does not need that many resources)

  e. Increase the number of processes

  f. Decrease the number of processes

7.7 Prove that the safety algorithm presented in Section 7.5.3 requires an order of $m \times n^2$ operations.

7.8 Consider a system consisting of four resources of the same type that are shared by three processes, each of which needs at most two resources. Show that the system is deadlock-free.

7.9 Consider a system consisting of m resources of the same type, being shared by n processes. Resources can be requested and released by processes only one at a time. Show that the system is deadlock free if the following two conditions hold:

a. The maximum need of each process is between 1 and m resources

b. The sum of all maximum needs is less than $m + n$

7.10 Consider a computer system that runs 5000 jobs per month with no deadlock-prevention or deadlock-avoidance scheme. Deadlocks occur about twice per month, and the operator must terminate and rerun about 10 jobs per deadlock. Each job is worth about $2 (in CPU time), and the jobs terminated tend to be about half-done when they are aborted.

A systems programmer has estimated that a deadlock-avoidance algorithm (like the banker's algorithm) could be installed in the system with an increase in the average execution time per job of about 10 percent. Since the machine currently has 30-percent idle time, all 5000 jobs per month could still be run, although turnaround time would increase by about 20 percent on average.

a. What are the arguments for installing the deadlock-avoidance algorithm?

b. What are the arguments against installing the deadlock-avoidance algorithm?

7.11 Consider the following snapshot of a system:

	Allocation	Max	Available
	A B C D	A B C D	A B C D
P_0	0 0 1 2	0 0 1 2	1 5 2 0
P_1	1 0 0 0	1 7 5 0	
P_2	1 3 5 4	2 3 5 6	
P_3	0 6 3 2	0 6 5 2	
P_4	0 0 1 4	0 6 5 6	

Answer the following questions using the banker's algorithm:

a. What is the content of the matrix *Need*?

b. Is the system in a safe state?

c. If a request from process P_1 arrives for (0,4,2,0) can the request be granted immediately?

7.12 Consider the following resource-allocation policy. Requests and releases for resources are allowed at any time. If a request for resources cannot be satisfied because the resources are not available, then we check any processes that are blocked, waiting for resources. If they have the desired resources, then these resources are taken away from them and are given to the requesting process. The vector of resources for which the waiting process is waiting is increased to include the resources that were taken away.

For example, consider a system with three resource types and the vector *Available* initialized to $(4,2,2)$. If process P_0 asks for $(2,2,1)$, it gets them. If P_1 asks for $(1,0,1)$, it gets them. Then, if P_0 asks for $(0,0,1)$, it is blocked (resource not available). If P_2 now asks for $(2,0,0)$, it gets the available one $(1,0,0)$ and one that was allocated to P_0 (since P_0 is blocked). P_0's *Allocation* vector goes down to $(1,2,1)$, and its *Need* vector goes up to $(1,0,1)$.

   a. Can deadlock occur? If so, give an example. If not, which necessary condition cannot occur?

   b. Can indefinite blocking occur?

7.13 Can a system detect that some of its processes are starving? If you answer "yes," explain how it can. If you answer "no," explain how the system can deal with the starvation problem.

7.14 We can obtain the banker's algorithm for a single resource type from the general banker's algorithm simply by reducing the dimensionality of the various arrays by 1. Show through an example that the multiple-resource-type banker's scheme cannot be implemented by individual application of the single-resource-type scheme to each resource type.

7.15 Suppose that you have coded the deadlock-avoidance safety algorithm and now wish to implement the deadlock-detection algorithm. Can you do so by simply using the safety algorithm code and redefining $Max_i = Waiting_i + Allocation_i$, where $Waiting_i$ is a vector specifying the resources process i is waiting for, and $Allocation_i$ is as defined in Section 7.5? Explain your answer.

Bibliographic Notes

Dijkstra [1965a] was one of the first and most influential contributors in the deadlock area. Holt [1972] was the first person to formalize the notion of deadlocks in terms of a graph-theoretical model similar to the one presented in this chapter. The issue of starvation was covered by Holt

[1972].   Hyman [1985] provided the deadlock example from the Kansas legislature.

The various prevention algorithms were suggested by Havender [1968], who has devised the resource-ordering scheme for the IBM OS/360 system.

The banker's algorithm for avoiding deadlocks was developed for a single resource type by Dijkstra [1965a], and was extended to multiple resource types by Habermann [1969]. General discussions concerning avoiding deadlocks by stating claims have been written by Habermann [1969], Holt [1971, 1972], and Parnas and Habermann [1972]. Exercises 7.8 and 7.9 are from Holt [1971].

The deadlock-detection algorithm for multiple instances of a resource type, which was described in Section 7.6.2, was written by Coffman et al. [1971]. The combined approach to deadlocks described in Section 7.8 was originally suggested by Howard [1973].

General surveys and useful bibliographies have been offered by Isloor and Marsland [1980], Newton [1979], and Zoble [1983].

PART THREE

STORAGE MANAGEMENT

The main purpose of a computer system is to execute programs. These programs, together with the data they access, must be in main memory (at least partially) during execution.

To improve both the utilization of CPU and the speed of its response to its users, the computer must keep several processes in memory. There are many different memory-management schemes. These schemes reflect various approaches to memory management, and the effectiveness of the different algorithms depends on the particular situation. Selection of a memory-management scheme for a specific system depends on many factors, especially on the *hardware* design of the system. Each algorithm requires its own hardware support.

Since main memory is usually too small to accommodate all data and programs permanently, the computer system must provide secondary storage to back up main memory. Most modern computer systems use disks as the primary on-line storage medium for information (both programs and data). The file system provides the mechanism for on-line storage of and access to both data and programs residing on the disks. A file is a collection of related information defined by its creator. Files are mapped, by the operating system, onto physical devices. Files are normally organized into directories to ease their use.

CHAPTER 8

MEMORY MANAGEMENT

In Chapter 5, we showed how the CPU can be shared by a set of processes. As a result of CPU scheduling, we can improve both the utilization of the CPU and the speed of the computer's response to its users. To realize this increase in performance, however, we must keep several processes in memory; we must *share* memory.

In this chapter, we discuss various ways to manage memory. The memory-management algorithms vary from a primitive bare-machine approach to paging and segmentation strategies. Each approach has its own advantages and disadvantages. Selection of a memory-management scheme for a specific system depends on many factors, especially on the *hardware* design of the system. As we shall see, many algorithms require hardware support.

8.1 ■ Background

As was shown in Chapter 1, memory is central to the operation of a modern computer system. Memory is a large array of words or bytes, each with its own address. The CPU fetches instructions from memory according to the value of the program counter. These instructions may cause additional loading from and storing to specific memory addresses.

A typical instruction execution cycle, for example, will first fetch an instruction from memory. The instruction is then decoded and may cause operands to be fetched from memory. After the instruction has been executed on the operands, results may be stored back in memory. Notice that the memory unit sees only a stream of memory addresses; it does not know how they are generated (the instruction counter, indexing, indirection, literal addresses, and so on) or what they are for (instructions or data). Accordingly, we can ignore *how* a memory address is generated by a program. We are interested in only the sequence of memory addresses generated by the running program.

8.1.1 Address Binding

Usually, a program resides on a disk as a binary executable file. The program must be brought into memory and placed within a process for it to be executed. Depending on the memory management in use, the process may be moved between disk and memory during its execution. The collection of processes on the disk that are waiting to be brought into memory for execution forms the *input queue*.

The normal procedure is to select one of the processes in the input queue and to load that process into memory. As the process is executed, it accesses instructions and data from memory. Eventually, the process terminates, and its memory space is declared available.

Most systems allow a user process to reside in any part of the physical memory. Thus, although the address space of the computer starts at 00000, the first address of the user process does not need to be 00000. This arrangement affects the addresses that the user program can use. In most cases, a user program will go through several steps (some of which may be optional) before being executed (Figure 8.1). Addresses may be represented in different ways during these steps. Addresses in the source program are generally symbolic (such as *count*). A compiler will typically *bind* these symbolic addresses to relocatable addresses (such as "14 bytes from the beginning of this module"). The linkage editor or loader will in turn bind these relocatable addresses to absolute addresses (such as 74014). Each binding is a mapping from one address space to another.

Classically, the *binding* of instructions and data to memory addresses can be done at any step along the way:

- **Compile time:** If it is known at compile time where the process will reside in memory, then *absolute* code can be generated. For example, if it is known a priori that a user process resides starting at location R, then the generated compiler code will start at that location and extend up from there. If, at some later time, the starting location changes, then it will be necessary to recompile this code. The MS-DOS .COM-format programs are absolute code bound at compile time.

- **Load time:** If it is not known at compile time where the process will reside in memory, then the compiler must generate *relocatable* code. In this case, final binding is delayed until load time. If the starting address changes, we need only to reload the user code to incorporate this changed value.

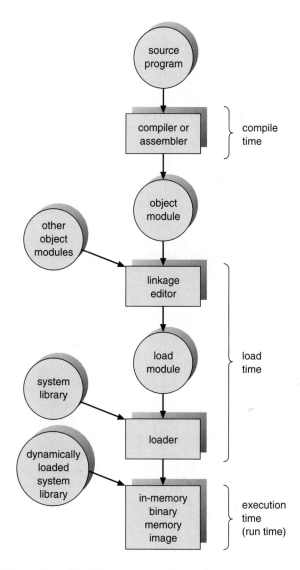

Figure 8.1 Multistep processing of a user program.

- **Execution time:** If the process can be moved during its execution from one memory segment to another, then binding must be delayed until run time. Special hardware must be available for this scheme to work, as will be discussed in Section 8.2.

A major portion of this chapter is devoted to showing how these various bindings can be implemented effectively in a computer system, and discussing appropriate hardware support.

8.1.2 Dynamic Loading

To obtain better memory-space utilization, we can use *dynamic loading*. With dynamic loading, a routine is not loaded until it is called. All routines are kept on disk in a relocatable load format. The main program is loaded into memory and is executed. When a routine needs to call another routine, the calling routine first checks to see whether the other routine has been loaded. If it has not been, the relocatable linking loader is called to load the desired routine into memory and to update the program's address tables to reflect this change. Then, control is passed to the newly loaded routine.

The advantage of dynamic loading is that an unused routine is never loaded. This scheme is particularly useful when large amounts of code are needed to handle infrequently occurring cases, such as error routines. In this case, although the total program size may be large, the portion that is actually used (and hence actually loaded) may be much smaller.

Dynamic loading does not require special support from the operating system. It is the responsibility of the users to design their programs to take advantage of such a scheme. Operating systems may help the programmer, however, by providing library routines to implement dynamic loading.

8.1.3 Dynamic Linking

Notice that Figure 8.1 also shows *dynamically linked* libraries. Most operating systems support only *static linking,* in which system language libraries are treated like any other object module and are combined by the loader into the binary program image. The concept of dynamic linking is similar to that of dynamic loading. Rather than loading being postponed until execution time, linking is postponed. This feature is usually used with system libraries, such as language subroutine libraries. Without this facility, all programs on a system need to have a copy of their language library (or at least the routines referenced by the program) included in the executable image. This requirement wastes both disk space and main memory. With dynamic linking, a *stub* is included in the image for each library-routine reference. This stub is a small piece of code that indicates how to locate the appropriate memory-resident library routine, or how to load the library if the routine is not already present.

When this stub is executed, it checks to see whether the needed routine is already in memory. If the routine is not in memory, the program loads it into memory. Either way, the stub replaces itself with the address of the routine, and executes the routine. Thus, the next time that that code segment is reached, the library routine is executed directly, incurring no cost for dynamic linking. Under this scheme, all processes that use a language library execute only one copy of the library code.

This feature can be extended to library updates (such as bug fixes). A library may be replaced by a new version, and all programs that reference the library will automatically use the new version. Without dynamic linking, all such programs would need to be relinked to gain access to the new library. So that programs will not accidentally execute new, incompatible versions of libraries, version information is included in both the program and the library. More than one version of a library may be loaded into memory, and each program uses its version information to decide which copy of the library to use. Minor changes retain the same version number, whereas major changes increment the version number. Thus, only programs that are compiled with the new library version are affected by the incompatible changes incorporated in it. Other programs linked before the new library was installed will continue using the older library. This system is also known as *shared libraries.*

Unlike dynamic loading, dynamic linking generally requires some help from the operating system. If the processes in memory are protected from one another (Section 8.4.1), then the operating system is the only entity that can check to see whether the needed routine is in another processes' memory space, and can allow multiple processes to access the same memory addresses. This concept is expanded when used in conjunction with paging, as discussed in Section 8.5.5.

8.1.4 Overlays

In our discussion so far, the entire program and data of a process must be in physical memory for the process to execute. The size of a process is limited to the size of physical memory. So that a process can be larger than the amount of memory allocated to it, a technique called *overlays* is sometimes used. The idea of overlays is to keep in memory only those instructions and data that are needed at any given time. When other instructions are needed, they are loaded into space that was occupied previously by instructions that are no longer needed.

As an example, consider a two-pass assembler. During pass 1, it constructs a symbol table; then, during pass 2, it generates machine-language code. We may be able to partition such an assembler into pass 1 code, pass 2 code, the symbol table, and common support routines used by both pass 1 and pass 2. Assume that the sizes of these components are as follows (K stands for "kilobyte," which is 1024 bytes):

Pass 1	70K
Pass 2	80K
Symbol table	20K
Common routines	30K

To load everything at once, we would require 200K of memory. If only

150K is available, we cannot run our process. However, notice that pass 1 and pass 2 do not need to be in memory at the same time. We thus define two overlays: Overlay *A* is the symbol table, common routines, and pass 1, and overlay *B* is the symbol table, common routines, and pass 2.

We add an overlay driver (10K) and start with overlay *A* in memory. When we finish pass 1, we jump to the overlay driver, which reads overlay *B* into memory, overwriting overlay *A*, and then transfers control to pass 2. Overlay *A* needs only 120K, whereas overlay *B* needs 130K (Figure 8.2). We can now run our assembler in the 150K of memory. It will load somewhat faster because fewer data need to be transferred before execution starts. However, it will run somewhat slower, due to the extra I/O to read the code for overlay *B* over the code for overlay *A*.

The code for overlay *A* and the code for overlay *B* are kept on disk as absolute memory images, and are read by the overlay driver as needed. Special relocation and linking algorithms are needed to construct the overlays.

As in dynamic loading, overlays do not require any special support from the operating system. They can be implemented completely by the user with simple file structures, reading from the files into memory and then jumping to that memory and executing the newly read instructions. The operating system notices only that there is more I/O than usual.

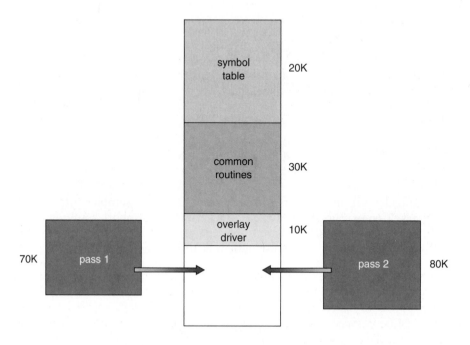

Figure 8.2   Overlays for a two-pass assembler.

The programmer, on the other hand, must design and program the overlay structure properly. This task can be a major undertaking, requiring complete knowledge of the structure of the program, its code, and its data structures. Because the program is, by definition, large (small programs do not need to be overlayed), obtaining a sufficient understanding of the program may be difficult. For these reasons, the use of overlays is currently limited to microcomputer and other systems that have limited amounts of physical memory and that lack hardware support for more advanced techniques. Some microcomputer compilers provide to the programmer support of overlays to make the task easier. Automatic techniques to run large programs in limited amounts of physical memory are certainly preferable.

8.2 ■ Logical versus Physical Address Space

An address generated by the CPU is commonly referred to as a *logical address*, whereas an address seen by the memory unit (that is, the one loaded into the *memory address register* of the memory) is commonly referred to as a *physical address*.

The compile-time and load-time address-binding schemes result in an environment where the logical and physical addresses are the same. However, the execution-time address-binding scheme results in an environment where the logical and physical addresses differ. In this case, we usually refer to the logical address as a *virtual address*. We use *logical address* and *virtual address* interchangeably in this text. The set of all logical addresses generated by a program is referred to as a *logical address space*; the set of all physical addresses corresponding to these logical addresses is referred to as a *physical address space*. Thus, in the execution-time address-binding scheme, the logical and physical address spaces differ.

The run-time mapping from virtual to physical addresses is done by the *memory-management unit (MMU)*, which is a hardware device. There are a number of different schemes for accomplishing such a mapping, as will be discussed in Sections 8.4.1, 8.5, 8.6, and 8.7. For the time being, we shall illustrate this mapping with a simple MMU scheme, which is a generalization of the base-register scheme described in Section 2.4.

As illustrated in Figure 8.3, this scheme requires hardware support slightly different from the hardware configuration discussed in Section 2.4. The base register is now called a *relocation* register. The value in the relocation register is *added* to every address generated by a user process at the time it is sent to memory. For example, if the base is at 14,000, then an attempt by the user to address location 0 is dynamically relocated to location 14,000; an access to location 346 is mapped to location 14346. The MS-DOS operating system running on the Intel 80X86 family of processors uses four relocation registers when loading and running processes.

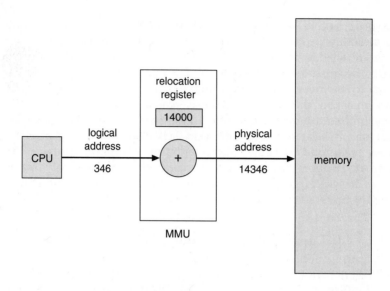

Figure 8.3   Dynamic relocation using a relocation register.

Notice that the user program never sees the real physical addresses. The program can create a pointer to location 346, store it in memory, manipulate it, compare it to other addresses — all as the number 346. Only when it is used as a memory address (in an indirect load or store, perhaps) is it relocated relative to the base register. The user program deals with *logical* addresses. The memory-mapping hardware converts logical addresses into physical addresses. This form of execution-time binding was discussed in Section 8.1.1. The final location of a referenced memory address is not determined until the reference is made.

Notice also that we now have two different types of addresses: logical addresses (in the range 0 to *max*) and physical addresses (in the range $R + 0$ to $R + max$ for a base value R). The user generates only logical addresses and thinks that the process runs in locations 0 to *max*. The user program supplies logical addresses; these logical addresses must be mapped to physical addresses before they are used.

The concept of a *logical address space* that is bound to a separate *physical address space* is central to proper memory management.

8.3 ■ Swapping

A process needs to be in memory to be executed. A process, however, can be *swapped* temporarily out of memory to a *backing store*, and then brought back into memory for continued execution. For example, assume a multiprogramming environment with a round-robin CPU-scheduling algorithm. When a quantum expires, the memory manager will start to swap out the process that just finished, and to swap in another process to the memory space that has been freed (Figure 8.4). In the meantime, the CPU scheduler will allocate a time slice to some other process in memory. When each process finishes its quantum, it will be swapped with another process. Ideally, the memory manager can swap processes fast enough that there are always processes in memory, ready to execute, when the CPU scheduler wants to reschedule the CPU. The quantum must also be sufficiently large that reasonable amounts of computing are done between swaps.

A variant of this swapping policy is used for priority-based scheduling algorithms. If a higher-priority process arrives and wants service, the memory manager can swap out the lower-priority process so that it can load and execute the higher-priority process. When the higher-priority process finishes, the lower-priority process can be swapped back in and continued. This variant of swapping is sometimes called *roll out, roll in*.

Normally a process that is swapped out will be swapped back into the same memory space that it occupied previously. This restriction is dictated by the method of address binding. If binding is done at assembly or load time, then the process cannot be moved to different locations. If execution-time binding is being used, then it is possible to swap a process into a different memory space, because the physical addresses are computed during execution time.

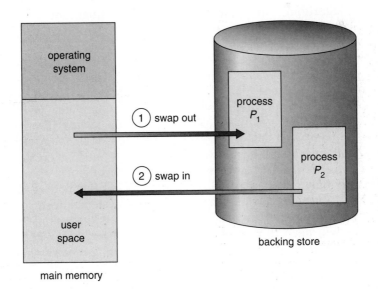

Figure 8.4 Swapping of two processes using a disk as a backing store.

Swapping requires a *backing store*. The backing store is commonly a fast disk. It must be large enough to accommodate copies of all memory images for all users, and must provide direct access to these memory images. The system maintains a *ready queue* consisting of all processes whose memory images are on the backing store or in memory and are ready to run. Whenever the CPU scheduler decides to execute a process, it calls the dispatcher. The dispatcher checks to see whether the next process in the queue is in memory. If the process is not, and there is no free memory region, the dispatcher swaps out a process currently in memory and swaps in the desired process. It then reloads registers as normal and transfers control to the selected process.

It should be clear that the context-switch time in such a swapping system is fairly high. To get an idea of the context-switch time, let us assume that the user process is of size 100K and the backing store is a standard hard disk with a transfer rate of 1 megabyte per second. The actual transfer of the 100K process to or from memory takes

$$100K \ / \ 1000K \text{ per second } = 1/10 \text{ second}$$
$$= 100 \text{ milliseconds}$$

Assuming that no head seeks are necessary and an average latency of 8 milliseconds, the swap time takes 108 milliseconds. Since we must both swap out and swap in, the total swap time is then about 216 milliseconds.

For efficient CPU utilization, we want our execution time for each process to be long relative to the swap time. Thus, in a round-robin CPU-scheduling algorithm, for example, the time quantum should be substantially larger than 0.216 seconds.

Notice that the major part of the swap time is transfer time. The total transfer time is directly proportional to the *amount* of memory swapped. If we have a computer system with 1 megabyte of main memory and a resident operating system taking 100K, the maximum size of the user process is 900K. However, many user processes may be much smaller than this size — say, 100K. A 100K process could be swapped out in 108 milliseconds, compared to the 908 milliseconds for swapping 900K. Therefore, it would be useful to know exactly how much memory a user process *is* using, not simply how much it *might be* using. Then, we would need to swap only what is actually used, reducing swap time. For this scheme to be effective, the user must keep the system informed of any changes in memory requirements. Thus, a process with dynamic memory requirements will need to issue system calls (**request memory** and **release memory**) to inform the operating system of its changing memory needs.

There are other constraints on swapping. If we want to swap a process, we must be sure that it is completely idle. Of particular concern is any pending I/O. If a process is waiting for an I/O operation, we may want to swap that process to free up its memory. However, if the I/O is asynchronously accessing the user memory for I/O buffers, then the process cannot be swapped. Assume that the I/O operation was queued because the device was busy. Then, if we were to swap out process P_1 and swap in process P_2, the I/O operation might then attempt to use memory that now belongs to process P_2. The two main solutions to this problem are (1) never to swap a process with pending I/O, or (2) to execute I/O operations only into operating-system buffers. Transfers between operating-system and process memory then occur only when the process is swapped in.

The assumption that swapping requires few if any head seeks needs further explanation. We postpone discussing this issue until Chapter 12, where secondary-storage structure is covered. Generally, swap space is allocated as a separate chunk of disk, separate from the file system, so that its use is as fast as possible.

Currently, standard swapping is used in few systems. It requires too much swapping time and provides too little execution time to be a reasonable memory-management solution. Modified versions of swapping, however, are found on many systems.

A modification of swapping is used in many versions of UNIX. Swapping was normally disabled, but would start if many processes were running and were using a threshold amount of memory. Swapping would again be halted if the load on the system was reduced. Memory management in UNIX is described fully in Section 19.6.

PCs lack sophisticated hardware (or operating systems that take advantage of the hardware) to implement more advanced memory-management methods, but they are being used to run multiple, large processes, and a modified version of swapping is the best means to allow them to run. A prime example is the Microsoft Windows operating system, which supports concurrent execution of processes in memory. If a new process is loaded and there is insufficient main memory, an old process is swapped to disk. This operating system, however, does not provide full swapping, because the user, rather than the scheduler, decides when it is time to swap one process for another. Any swapped-out process remains swapped out (and not executing) until the user selects that process to run. The follow-on Microsoft operating system, Windows/NT, takes advantage of advanced MMU features now found even on PCs. In Section 8.7.2, we describe the memory-management hardware found on the Intel 386 family of processors used in many PCs. In that section, we also describe the memory management used on this CPU by another advanced operating system for PCs: IBM OS/2.

8.4 ■ Contiguous Allocation

The main memory must accommodate both the operating system and the various user processes. The memory is usually divided into two partitions,

0

512K

Figure 8.5 Memory partition.

one for the resident operating system, and one for the user processes. It is possible to place the operating system in either low memory or high memory. The major factor affecting this decision is the location of the interrupt vector. Since the interrupt vector is often in low memory, it is more common to place the operating system in low memory. Thus, we shall discuss only the situation where the operating system resides in low memory (Figure 8.5). The development of the other situation is similar.

8.4.1 Single-Partition Allocation

If the operating system is residing in low memory and the user processes are executing in high memory, we need to protect the operating-system code and data from changes (accidental or malicious) by the user processes. We also need to protect the user processes from one another. We can provide this protection by using a relocation register, as discussed in Section 8.2, with a limit register, as discussed in Section 2.5.3. The relocation register contains the value of the smallest physical address; the limit register contains the range of logical addresses (for example, relocation = 100,040 and limit = 74,600). With relocation and limit registers, each logical address must be less than the limit register; the MMU maps the logical address *dynamically* by adding the value in the relocation register. This mapped address is sent to memory (Figure 8.6).

When the CPU scheduler selects a process for execution, the dispatcher loads the relocation and limit registers with the correct values as part of the context switch. Because every address generated by the CPU is checked

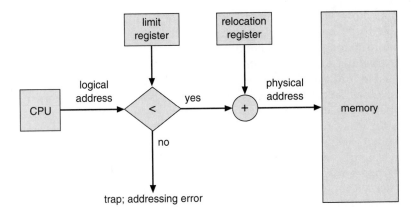

Figure 8.6 Hardware support for relocation and limit registers.

against these registers, we can protect both the operating system and the other users' programs and data from being modified by this running process.

Note that the relocation-register scheme provides an effective way to allow the operating-system size to change dynamically. This flexibility is desirable in many situations. For example, the operating system contains code and buffer space for device drivers. If a device driver (or other operating-system service) is not commonly used, it is undesirable to keep the code and data in memory, as we might be able to use that space for other purposes. Such code is sometimes called *transient* operating-system code; it comes and goes as needed. Thus, using this code changes the size of the operating system during program execution.

8.4.2 Multiple-Partition Allocation

Because it is desirable, in general, that there be several user processes residing in memory at the same time, we need to consider the problem of how to allocate available memory to the various processes that are in the input queue waiting to be brought into memory. One of the simplest schemes for memory allocation is to divide memory into a number of fixed-sized *partitions*. Each partition may contain exactly one process. Thus, the degree of multiprogramming is bound by the number of partitions. When a partition is free, a process is selected from the input queue and is loaded into the free partition. When the process terminates, the partition becomes available for another process. This scheme was originally used by the IBM OS/360 operating system (called MFT); it is no longer in use. The scheme described next is a generalization of the fixed-partition scheme (called MVT) and is used primarily in a batch environment.

We note, however, that many of the ideas presented here are also applicable to a time-sharing environment where pure segmentation is used for memory management (Section 8.6).

The operating system keeps a table indicating which parts of memory are available and which are occupied. Initially, all memory is available for user processes, and is considered as one large block of available memory, a *hole*. When a process arrives and needs memory, we search for a hole large enough for this process. If we find one, we allocate only as much memory as is needed, keeping the rest available to satisfy future requests.

For example, assume that we have 2560K of memory available and a resident operating system of 400K. This situation leaves 2160K for user processes, as shown in Figure 8.7. Given the input queue in the figure, and FCFS job scheduling, we can immediately allocate memory to processes P_1, P_2, and P_3, creating the memory map of Figure 8.8(a). We have a hole of size 260K that cannot be used by any of the remaining processes in the input queue. Using a round-robin CPU-scheduling with a quantum of 1 time unit, process P_2 will terminate at time 14, releasing its memory. This situation is illustrated in Figure 8.8(b). We then return to our job queue and schedule the next process, process P_4, to produce the memory map of Figure 8.8(c). Process P_1 will terminate at time 28 to produce Figure 8.8(d); process P_5 is then scheduled, producing Figure 8.8(e).

This example illustrates the general structure of the allocation scheme. As processes enter the system, they are put into an input queue. The operating system takes into account the memory requirements of each process and the amount of available memory space in determining which

job queue		
process	memory	time
P_1	600K	10
P_2	1000K	5
P_3	300K	20
P_4	700K	8
P_5	500K	15

Figure 8.7 Scheduling example.

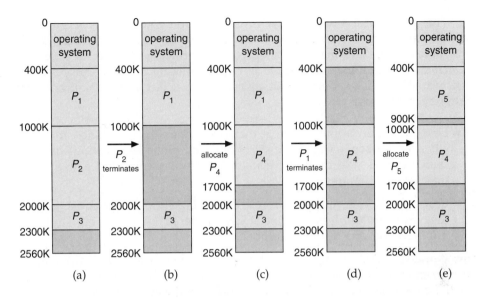

Figure 8.8 Memory allocation and long-term scheduling.

processes are allocated memory. When a process is allocated space, it is loaded into memory and it can then compete for the CPU. When a process terminates, it releases its memory, which the operating system may then fill with another process from the input queue.

At any given time, we have a list of available block sizes and the input queue. The operating system can order the input queue according to a scheduling algorithm. Memory is allocated to processes until, finally, the memory requirements of the next process cannot be satisfied; no available block of memory (hole) is large enough to hold that process. The operating system can then wait until a large enough block is available, or it can skip down the input queue to see whether the smaller memory requirements of some other process can be met.

In general, there is at any time a *set* of holes, of various sizes, scattered throughout memory. When a process arrives and needs memory, we search this set for a hole that is large enough for this process. If the hole is too large, it is split into two: One part is allocated to the arriving process; the other is returned to the set of holes. When a process terminates, it releases its block of memory, which is then placed back in the set of holes. If the new hole is adjacent to other holes, we merge these adjacent holes to form one larger hole. At this point, we may need to check whether there are processes waiting for memory and whether this newly freed and recombined memory could satisfy the demands of any of these waiting processes.

This procedure is a particular instance of the general *dynamic storage-allocation* problem, which is how to satisfy a request of size *n* from a list of free holes. There are many solutions to this problem. The set of holes is searched to determine which hole is best to allocate. *First-fit, best-fit,* and *worst-fit* are the most common strategies used to select a free hole from the set of available holes.

- **First-fit:** Allocate the *first* hole that is big enough. Searching can start either at the beginning of the set of holes or where the previous first-fit search ended. We can stop searching as soon as we find a free hole that is large enough.

- **Best-fit:** Allocate the *smallest* hole that is big enough. We must search the entire list, unless the list is kept ordered by size. This strategy produces the smallest leftover hole.

- **Worst-fit:** Allocate the *largest* hole. Again, we must search the entire list, unless it is sorted by size. This strategy produces the largest leftover hole, which may be more useful than the smaller leftover hole from a best-fit approach.

Simulations have shown that both first-fit and best-fit are better than worst-fit in terms of decreasing both time and storage utilization. Neither first-fit nor best-fit is clearly best in terms of storage utilization, but first-fit is generally faster.

8.4.3 External and Internal Fragmentation

The algorithms described in Section 8.4.2 suffer from *external fragmentation*. As processes are loaded and removed from memory, the free memory space is broken into little pieces. External fragmentation exists when enough total memory space exists to satisfy a request, but it is not contiguous; storage is fragmented into a large number of small holes. Looking back at Figure 8.8, we can see two such situations. In Figure 8.8(a), there is a total external fragmentation of 260K, a space that is too small to satisfy the requests of either of the two remaining processes, P_4 and P_5. In Figure 8.8(c), however, we have a total external fragmentation of 560K (= 300K + 260K). This space would be large enough to run process P_5 (which needs 500K), *except* that this free memory is not contiguous. The free memory space is fragmented into two pieces, neither one of which is large enough, by itself, to satisfy the memory request of process P_5.

This fragmentation problem can be severe. In the worst case, we could have a block of free (wasted) memory between every two processes. If all this memory were in one big free block, we might be able to run several more processes. The selection of first-fit versus best-fit can affect the amount of fragmentation. (First-fit is better for some systems, and best-fit is better for others.) Another factor is which end of a free block is allocated. (Which is the leftover piece — the one on the top, or the one on the bottom?) No matter which algorithms are used, however, external fragmentation will be a problem.

Depending on the total amount of memory storage and the average process size, external fragmentation may be either a minor or a major problem. Statistical analysis of first-fit, for instance, reveals that, even with some optimization, given N allocated blocks, another $0.5N$ blocks will be lost due to fragmentation. That is, one-third of memory may be unusable! This property is known as the *50-percent rule*.

Another problem that arises with the multiple partition allocation scheme is illustrated by Figure 8.9. Consider the hole of 18,464 bytes. Suppose that the next process requests 18,462 bytes. If we allocate exactly the requested block, we are left with a hole of 2 bytes. The overhead to keep track of this hole will be substantially larger than the hole itself. The general approach is to allocate very small holes as part of the larger request. Thus, the allocated memory may be slightly larger than the requested memory. The difference between these two numbers is *internal fragmentation* — memory that is internal to a partition, but is not being used.

One solution to the problem of external fragmentation is *compaction*. The goal is to shuffle the memory contents to place all free memory together in one large block. For example, the memory map of Figure 8.8(e) can be compacted, as shown in Figure 8.10. The three holes of sizes 100K, 300K, and 260K can be compacted into one hole of size 660K.

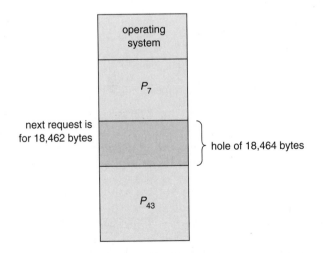

Figure 8.9 Memory allocation made in some multiple of bytes.

Compaction is not always possible. Notice that, in Figure 8.10, we moved processes P_4 and P_3. For these processes to be able to execute in their new locations, all internal addresses must be relocated. If relocation is static and is done at assembly or load time, compaction cannot be done; compaction is possible *only* if relocation is dynamic, and is done at execution time.

If addresses are relocated dynamically, relocation requires only moving the program and data, and then changing the base register to reflect the new base address.

When compaction is possible, we must determine its cost. The simplest compaction algorithm is simply to move all processes toward one end of memory; all holes move in the other direction, producing one large hole of available memory. This scheme can be quite expensive.

Consider the memory allocation shown in Figure 8.11. If we use this simple algorithm, we must move processes P_3 and P_4, for a total of 600K moved. In this situation, we could simply move process P_4 above process P_3, moving only 400K, or move process P_3 below process P_4, moving only 200K. Note that, in this last instance, our one large hole of available memory is not at the end of memory, but rather is in the middle. Also notice that, if the queue contained only one process that wanted 450K, we could satisfy that *particular* request by moving process P_2 somewhere else (such as below process P_4). Although this solution does not create a single large hole, it does create a hole big enough to satisfy the immediate request. Selecting an optimal compaction strategy is quite difficult.

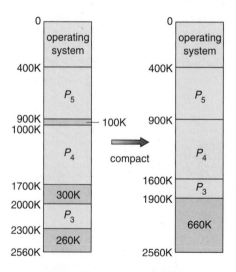

Figure 8.10 Compaction.

8.5 Paging ■ 267

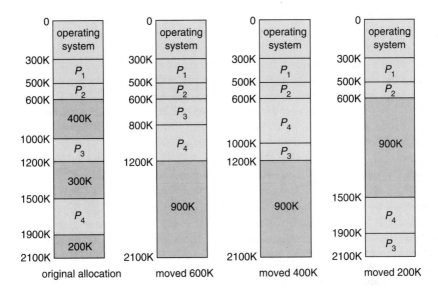

Figure 8.11 Comparison of some different ways to compact memory.

Swapping can also be combined with compaction. A process can be rolled out of main memory to a backing store and rolled in again later. When the process is rolled out, its memory is released, and perhaps is reused for another process. When the process is to be rolled back in, several problems may arise. If static relocation is used, the process must be rolled into the exact same memory locations that it occupied previously. This restriction may require that other processes be rolled out to free that memory.

If dynamic relocation (such as with base and limit registers) is used, then a process can be rolled into a different location. In this case, we find a free block, compacting if necessary, and roll in the process.

One approach to compaction is to roll out those processes to be moved, and to roll them into different memory locations. If swapping or roll-in, roll-out is already a part of the system, the additional code for compaction may be minimal.

8.5 ■ Paging

Another possible solution to the external fragmentation problem is to permit the logical address space of a process to be noncontiguous, thus allowing a process to be allocated physical memory wherever the latter is available. One way of implementing this solution is through the use of a *paging* scheme. Paging avoids the considerable problem of fitting the varying-sized memory chunks onto the backing store, from which most of the previous memory-management schemes suffered. When some code fragments or data residing in main memory need to be swapped out, space must be found on the backing store. The fragmentation problems discussed in connection with main memory are also prevalent with backing store, except that access is much slower, so compaction is impossible. Because of its advantages over the previous methods, paging in its various forms is commonly used in many operating systems.

8.5.1 Basic Method

Physical memory is broken into fixed-sized blocks called *frames*. Logical memory is also broken into blocks of the same size called *pages*. When a process is to be executed, its pages are loaded into any available memory frames from the backing store. The backing store is divided into fixed-sized blocks that are of the same size as the memory frames.

The hardware support for paging is illustrated in Figure 8.12. Every address generated by the CPU is divided into two parts: a *page number (p)* and a *page offset (d)*. The page number is used as an index into a *page table*. The page table contains the base address of each page in physical memory. This base address is combined with the page offset to define the physical

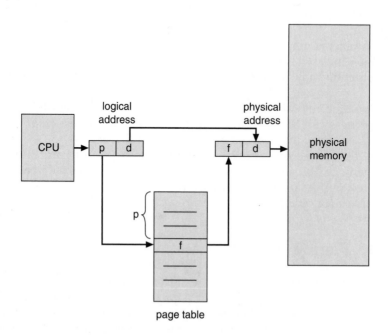

Figure 8.12 Paging hardware.

memory address that is sent to the memory unit. The paging model of memory is shown in Figure 8.13.

The page size (like the frame size) is defined by the hardware. The size of a page is typically a power of 2 varying between 512 bytes and 8192 bytes per page, depending on the computer architecture. The selection of a power of 2 as a page size makes the translation of a logical address into a page number and page offset particularly easy. If the size of logical address space is 2^m, and a page size is 2^n addressing units (bytes or words), then the high-order $m - n$ bits of a logical address designate the page number, and the n low-order bits designate the page offset. Thus, the logical address is as follows:

page number	page offset
p	d
$m - n$	m

where p is an index into the page table and d is the displacement within the page.

For a concrete, although minuscule, example, consider the memory of Figure 8.14. Using a page size of 4 bytes and a physical memory of 32 bytes (8 pages), we show an example of how the user's view of memory

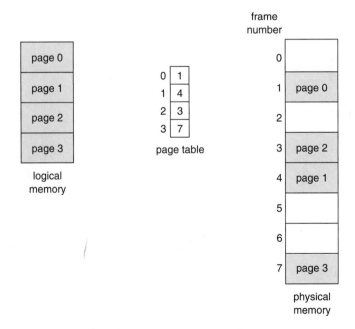

Figure 8.13 Paging model of logical and physical memory.

can be mapped into physical memory. Logical address 0 is page 0, offset 0. Indexing into the page table, we find that page 0 is in frame 5. Thus, logical address 0 maps to physical address 20 (= (5 × 4) + 0). Logical address 3 (page 0, offset 3) maps to physical address 23 (= (5 × 4) + 3). Logical address 4 is page 1, offset 0; according to the page table, page 1 is mapped to frame 6. Thus, logical address 4 maps to physical address 24 (= (6 × 4) + 0). Logical address 13 maps to physical address 9.

Notice that paging itself is a form of dynamic relocation. Every logical address is bound by the paging hardware to some physical address. The observant reader will have realized that paging is similar to using a table of base (relocation) registers, one for each frame of memory.

Figure 8.14 Paging example for a 32-byte memory with 4-byte pages.

When we use a paging scheme, we have no external fragmentation: *Any* free frame can be allocated to a process that needs it. However, we may have some internal fragmentation. Notice that frames are allocated as units. If the memory requirements of a process do not happen to fall on page boundaries, the *last* frame allocated may not be completely full. For example, if pages are 2048 bytes, a process of 72,766 bytes would need 35 pages plus 1086 bytes. It would be allocated 36 frames, resulting in an internal fragmentation of $2048 - 1086 = 962$ bytes. In the worst case, a process would need n pages plus one byte. It would be allocated $n + 1$ frames, resulting in an internal fragmentation of almost an entire frame. If process size is independent of page size, we expect internal fragmentation to average one-half page per process. This consideration suggests that small page sizes are desirable. However, there is quite a bit of overhead involved in each page-table entry, and this overhead is reduced as the size of the pages increases. Also, disk I/O is more efficient when the number of data being transferred is larger (Chapter 12). Generally, page sizes have grown over time as processes, data sets, and main memory have become larger. Today, pages typically are either 2 or 4 kilobytes.

When a process arrives to be executed, its size, expressed in pages, is examined. Each user page needs one frame. Thus, if the process requires n pages, there must be n frames available in memory. If there are n frames available, they are allocated to this process. The first page of the process is loaded into one of the allocated frames, and the frame number is put in the page table for this process. The next page is loaded into another frame, and its frame number is put into the page table, and so on (Figure 8.15).

An important aspect of paging is the clear separation between the user's view of memory and the actual physical memory. The user program views that memory as one single contiguous space, containing only this one program. In fact, the user program is scattered throughout physical memory, which also holds other programs. The difference between the user's view of memory and the actual physical memory is reconciled by the address-translation hardware. The logical addresses are translated into physical addresses. This mapping is hidden from the user and is controlled by the operating system. Notice that the user process by definition is unable to access memory it does not own. It has no way of addressing memory outside of its page table, and the table includes only those pages that the process owns.

Because the operating system is managing physical memory, it must be aware of the allocation details of physical memory: which frames are allocated, which frames are available, how many total frames there are, and so on. This information is generally kept in a data structure called a *frame table*. The frame table has one entry for each physical page frame, indicating whether the latter is free or allocated and, if it is allocated, to which page of which process or processes.

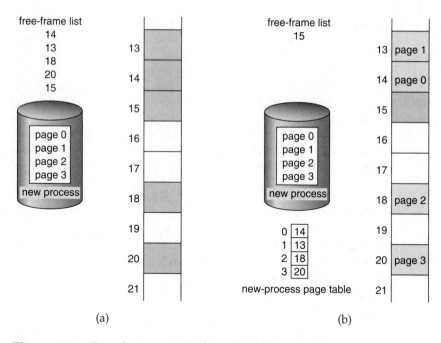

Figure 8.15 Free frames. (a) Before allocation, and (b) after allocation.

In addition, the operating system must be aware that user processes operate in user space, and all logical addresses must be mapped to produce physical addresses. If a user makes a system call (to do I/O, for example) and provides an address as a parameter (a buffer, for instance), that address must be mapped to produce the correct physical address. The operating system maintains a copy of the page table for each user, just as it maintains a copy of the instruction counter and register contents. This copy is used to translate logical addresses to physical addresses whenever the operating system must map a logical address to a physical address manually. It is also used by the CPU dispatcher to define the hardware page table when a process is to be allocated the CPU. Paging therefore increases the context-switch time.

8.5.2 Structure of the Page Table

Each operating system has its own methods for storing page tables. Most allocate a page table for each process. A pointer to the page table is stored with the other register values (like the instruction counter) in the process control block. When the dispatcher is told to start a process, it must reload the user registers and define the correct hardware page-table values from the stored user page table.

8.5.2.1 Hardware Support

The hardware implementation of the page table can be done in a number of different ways. In the simplest case, the page table is implemented as a set of dedicated *registers*. These registers should be built with very high-speed logic to make the paging address translation efficient. Every access to memory must go through the paging map, so efficiency is a major consideration. The CPU dispatcher reloads these registers, just as it reloads the other registers. Instructions to load or modify the page-table registers are, of course, privileged, so that only the operating system can change the memory map. The DEC PDP-11 is an example of such an architecture. The address consists of 16 bits, and the page size is 8K. The page table, thus, consists of eight entries that are kept in fast registers.

The use of registers for the page table is satisfactory if the page table is reasonably small (for example, 256 entries). Most contemporary computers, however, allow the page table to be very large (for example, 1 million entries). For these machines, the use of fast registers to implement the page table is not feasible. Rather, the page table is kept in main memory, and a *page-table base register (PTBR)* points to the page table. Changing page tables requires changing only this one register, substantially reducing context-switch time.

The problem with this approach is the time required to access a user memory location. If we want to access location i, we must first index into the page table, using the value in the PTBR offset by the page number for i. This task requires a memory access. It provides us with the frame number, which is combined with the page offset to produce the actual address. We can then access the desired place in memory. With this scheme, *two* memory accesses are needed to access a byte (one for the page-table entry, one for the byte). Thus, memory access is slowed by a factor of 2. This delay would be intolerable under most circumstances. We might as well resort to swapping!

The standard solution to this problem is to use a special, small, fast-lookup hardware cache, variously called *associative registers* or *translation look-aside buffers (TLBs)*. A set of associative registers is built of especially high-speed memory. Each register consists of two parts: a key and a value. When the associative registers are presented with an item, it is compared with all keys simultaneously. If the item is found, the corresponding value field is output. The search is fast; the hardware, however, is expensive. Typically, the number of entries in a TLB varies between 8 and 2048.

Associative registers are used with page tables in the following way. The associative registers contain only a few of the page-table entries. When a logical address is generated by the CPU, its page number is presented to a set of associative registers that contain page numbers and their corresponding frame numbers. If the page number is found in the associative registers, its frame number is immediately available and is used to access memory. The whole task may take less than 10 percent longer than it would were an unmapped memory reference used.

If the page number is not in the associative registers, a memory reference to the page table must be made. When the frame number is obtained, we can use it to access memory (as desired). In addition, we add the page number and frame number to the associative registers, so that they will be found quickly on the next reference (Figure 8.16). If the TLB is already full of entries, the operating system must select one for replacement. Unfortunately, every time a new page table is selected (for instance, each context switch), the TLB must be *flushed* (erased) to ensure that the next executing process does not use the wrong translation information. Otherwise, there could be old entries in the TLB that contain valid virtual addresses but have incorrect or invalid physical addresses left over from the previous process.

The percentage of times that a page number is found in the associative registers is called the *hit ratio*. An 80-percent hit ratio means that we find the desired page number in the associative registers 80 percent of the time. If it takes 20 nanoseconds to search the associative registers, and 100 nanoseconds to access memory, then a mapped memory access takes 120 nanoseconds when the page number is in the associative registers. If we

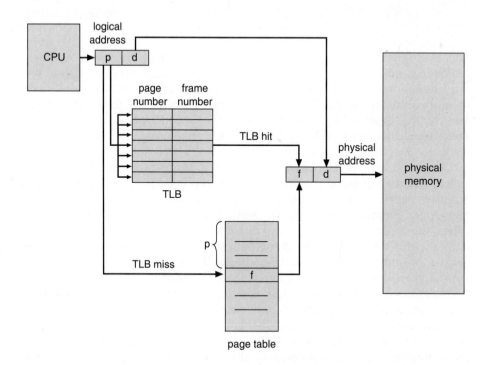

Figure 8.16 Paging hardware with TLB.

fail to find the page number in the associative registers (20 nanoseconds), then we must first access memory for the page table and frame number (100 nanoseconds), and then access the desired byte in memory (100 nanoseconds), for a total of 220 nanoseconds. To find the *effective memory-access time*, we must weigh each case by its probability:

$$\text{effective access time} = 0.80 \times 120 + 0.20 \times 220$$
$$= 140 \text{ nanoseconds.}$$

In this example, we suffer a 40-percent slowdown in memory access time (from 100 to 140 nanoseconds).

For a 98-percent hit ratio, we have

$$\text{effective access time} = 0.98 \times 120 + 0.02 \times 220$$
$$= 122 \text{ nanoseconds.}$$

This increased hit rate produces only a 22-percent slowdown in memory access time.

The hit ratio is clearly related to the number of associative registers. With the number of associative registers ranging between 16 and 512, a hit ratio of 80 to 98 percent can be obtained. The Motorola 68030 processor (used in Apple Macintosh systems) has a 22-entry TLB. The Intel 80486 CPU (found in some IBM PC compatibles) has 32 registers, and claims a 98-percent hit ratio.

8.5.2.2 Protection

Memory protection in a paged environment is accomplished by protection bits that are associated with each frame. Normally, these bits are kept in the page table. One bit can define a page to be read and write or read-only. Every reference to memory goes through the page table to find the correct frame number. At the same time that the physical address is being computed, the protection bits can be checked to verify that no writes are being made to a read-only page. An attempt to write to a read-only page causes a hardware trap to the operating system (memory-protection violation).

This approach to protection can be expanded easily to provide a finer level of protection. We can create hardware to provide read-only, read-write, or execute-only protection. Or, by providing separate protection bits for each kind of access, any combination of these accesses can be allowed, and illegal attempts will be trapped to the operating system.

One more bit is generally attached to each entry in the page table: a *valid−invalid* bit. When this bit is set to "valid," this value indicates that the associated page is in the process's logical address space, and is thus a legal (valid) page. If the bit is set to "invalid," this value indicates that the page

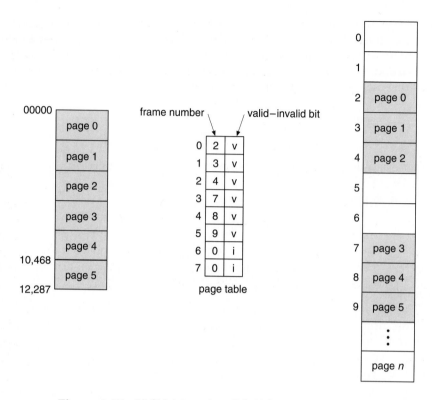

Figure 8.17   Valid (v) or invalid (i) bit in a page table.

is not in the process's logical address space. Illegal addresses are trapped by using the valid–invalid bit. The operating system sets this bit for each page to allow or disallow accesses to that page. For example, in a system with a 14-bit address space (0 to 16,383), we may have a program that should use only addresses 0 to 10,468. Given a page size of 2K, we get the situation shown in Figure 8.17. Addresses in pages 0, 1, 2, 3, 4, and 5 are mapped normally through the page table. Any attempt to generate an address in pages 6 or 7, however, finds that the valid–invalid bit is set to invalid, and the computer will trap to the operating system (invalid page reference).

Notice that as the program extends only to address 10,468, any reference beyond that address is illegal. However, references to page 5 are classified as valid, so accesses to addresses up to 12,287 are valid. Only addresses from 12,288 to 16,383 are invalid. This problem is a result of the 2K page size and reflects the internal fragmentation of paging.

Rarely does a process use all of its address range. In fact, many processes use only a small fraction of the address space available to them. It would be wasteful in these cases to create a page table with entries for every page in the address range. Most of this table would be unused, but would take up valuable memory space. Some systems provide hardware, in the form of a *page-table length register (PTLR)*, to indicate the size of the page table. This value is checked against every logical address to verify that the address is in the valid range for the process. Failure of this test causes an error trap to the operating system.

8.5.3 Multilevel Paging

Most modern computer systems support a very large logical address space (2^{32} to 2^{64}). In such an environment the page table itself becomes excessively large. For example, consider a system with a 32-bit logical address space. If the page size in such a system is 4K bytes (2^{12}), then a page table may consist of up to 1 million entries ($2^{32} / 2^{12}$). Because each entry consists of 4 bytes, each process may need up to 4 megabytes of physical address space for the page table alone. Clearly, we would not want to allocate the page table contiguously in main memory. One simple solution to this is to divide the page table into smaller pieces. There are several different ways to accomplish this.

One way is to use a two-level paging scheme, in which the page table itself is also paged (Figure 8.18). To illustrate this, let us return to our 32-bit machine example, with a page size of 4K bytes. A logical address is divided into a page number consisting of 20 bits, and a page offset consisting of 12 bits. Since we page the page table, the page number is further divided into a 10-bit page number, and a 10-bit page offset. Thus, a logical address is as follows:

page number		page offset
p_1	p_2	d
10	10	12

where p_1 is an index into the outer page table, and p_2 is the displacement within the page of the outer page table. The address-translation scheme for this architecture is shown in Figure 8.19. The VAX architecture supports two-level paging. The VAX is a 32-bit machine with page size of 512 bytes. The logical address space of a process is divided into four equal sections, each of which consists of 2^{30} bytes. Each section represents a different part of the logical address space of a process. The first 2 high-order bits of the logical address designate the appropriate section. The next 21 bits represent the logical page number of that section, and the last 9 bits represent an offset in the desired page. By partitioning the page table in this manner, we allow the operating system to leave partitions unused until a process needs them. An address on the VAX architecture is as follows:

section	page	offset
s	p	d
2	21	9

where s designates the section number, p is an index into the page table, and d is the displacement within the page.

Consider a VAX process consisting of only 100 pages of memory. A one-level page table for this process would be 4 megabytes. With two-level paging, only one of the four sections would be needed, reducing the table size to 1 megabyte.

For a system with a 64-bit logical address space, a two-level paging scheme is no longer appropriate. To illustrate this point, let us suppose that the page size in such a system is 4K bytes. In this case, the page table will consist of up to 2^{52} entries. If we use a two-level paging scheme, then the outer page table will consist of 2^{32} entries. Clearly, we would not want to allocate the outer page table contiguously in main memory. (Note that

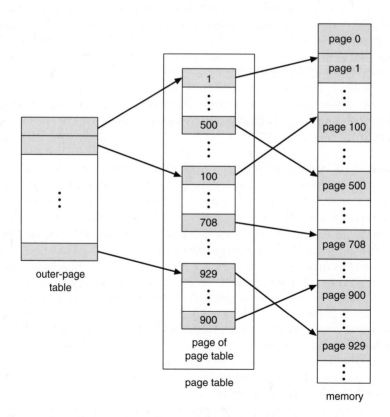

Figure 8.18 A two-level page-table scheme.

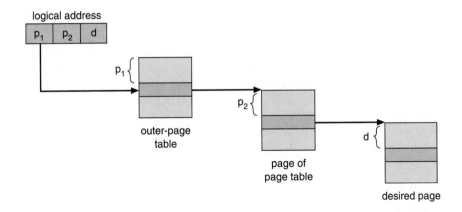

logical address

Figure 8.19 Address translation for a two-level 32-bit paging architecture.

it will require up to 16 gigabytes of physical main memory just to store the outer page table!) The obvious solution is to divide the outer page table into smaller pieces. This solution is also used on some 32-bit processors for added flexibility and efficiency.

There are a number of different ways to accomplish this. We can use a three-level paging scheme, where the outer page table itself is also paged (resulting in a second-level outer page), or a four-level paging scheme, where the second-level outer page table itself is also paged. The SPARC architecture (with 32-bit addressing) supports a three-level paging scheme, whereas the 32-bit Motorola 68030 architecture supports a four-level paging scheme.

How does multilevel paging affect system performance? Given that each level is stored as a separate table in memory, converting a logical address to a physical one may take four memory accesses. We have now quintupled the amount of time needed for one memory access! Caching again pays dividends, however, and performance remains reasonable. Given a cache hit rate of 98 percent, we have

$$\text{effective access time} = 0.98 \times 120 + 0.02 \times 520$$
$$= 128 \text{ nanoseconds.}$$

Thus, even with the extra levels of table lookup, we have only a 28-percent slowdown in memory access time.

8.5.4 Inverted Page Table

Usually, each process has a page table associated with it. The page table has one entry for each page that the process is using (or one slot for each virtual address, regardless of the latter's validity). This table representation is a natural one, since processes reference pages through the pages' virtual addresses. The operating system must then translate this reference into a physical memory address. Since the table is sorted by virtual address, the operating system is able to calculate where in the table the associated physical-address entry is, and to use that value directly. One of the drawbacks of this scheme is that each page table may consist of millions of entries. These tables may consume large amounts of physical memory, which is required just to keep track of how the other physical memory is being used.

To solve this problem, we can use an *inverted page table*. An inverted page table has one entry for each real page (frame) of memory. Each entry consists of the virtual address of the page stored in that real memory location, with information about the process that owns that page. Thus, there is only one page table in the system, and it has only one entry for each page of physical memory. Figure 8.20 shows the operation of an inverted page table. Compare it to Figure 8.12, which depicts a standard page table in operation. Examples of systems using such a scheme are the IBM System/38 computer, the IBM RISC System 6000, IBM RT, and Hewlett-Packard Spectrum workstations.

To illustrate this scheme, we shall describe a simplified version of the implementation of the inverted page table used in the IBM RT. Each virtual address in the system consists of a triple

<process-id, page-number, offset>.

Each inverted page-table entry is a pair <process-id, page-number>. When a memory reference occurs, part of the virtual address, consisting of <process-id, page-number>, is presented to the memory subsystem. The inverted page table is then searched for a match. If a match is found — say, at entry i — then the physical address <i, offset> is generated. If no match is found, then an illegal address access has been attempted.

By keeping information about which virtual-memory page is stored in each physical frame, inverted page tables reduce the amount of physical memory needed to store this information. However, the inverted page table no longer contains complete information about the logical address space of a process, which is required if a referenced page is not currently in memory. For this information to be available, an external page table (one per process) must be kept. Each such table looks like the traditional per-process page table, containing information on where each virtual page is located.

But do external page tables negate the utility of inverted page tables? Since these tables are referenced only when a page fault is occurring, they do not need to be available quickly. Instead, these tables are themselves paged in and out of memory as necessary. Unfortunately, a page fault

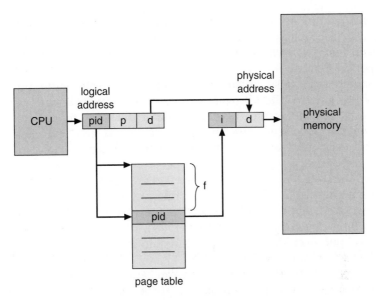

logical address

physical address

CPU

pid | p | d

i | d

physical memory

f

pid

page table

Figure 8.20 Inverted page table.

may now result in the virtual-memory manager causing another page fault as it pages in the external page table it needs to locate the virtual page on the backing store. This special case requires careful handling in the kernel and a delay in the page-lookup processing.

Although this scheme decreases the amount of memory needed to store each page table, it increases the amount of time needed to search the table when a page reference occurs. Because the inverted page table is sorted by a physical address, but lookups occur on virtual addresses, the whole table might need to be searched for a match. This search would take far too long. To alleviate this problem, we use a hash table to limit the search to one — or at most a few — page-table entries. Of course, each access to the hash table adds a memory reference to the procedure, so one virtual-memory reference requires at least two real-memory reads: one for the hash-table entry and one for the page table. To improve performance, we use associative memory registers to hold recently located entries. These registers are searched first, before the hash table is consulted.

8.5.5 Shared Pages

Another advantage of paging is the possibility of *sharing* common code. This consideration is particularly important in a time-sharing environment. Consider a system that supports 40 users, each of whom executes a text editor. If the text editor consists of 150K of code and 50K of data space, we would need 8000K to support the 40 users. If the code is *reentrant,* however, it can be shared, as shown in Figure 8.21. Here we see a three-page editor (each page of size 50K; the large page size is used to simplify the figure) being shared among three processes. Each process has its own data page.

Reentrant code (also called pure code) is non–self-modifying code. If the code is reentrant, then it never changes during execution. Thus, two or more processes can execute the same code at the same time. Each process has its own copy of registers and data storage to hold the data for the process' execution. The data for two different processes will, of course, vary for each process.

Only one copy of the editor needs to be kept in physical memory. Each user's page table maps onto the same physical copy of the editor, but data pages are mapped onto different frames. Thus, to support 40 users, we need only one copy of the editor (150K), plus 40 copies of the 50K of data space per user. The total space required is now 2150K, instead of 8000K — a significant savings.

Other heavily used programs also can be shared: compilers, window systems, database systems, and so on. To be sharable, the code must be

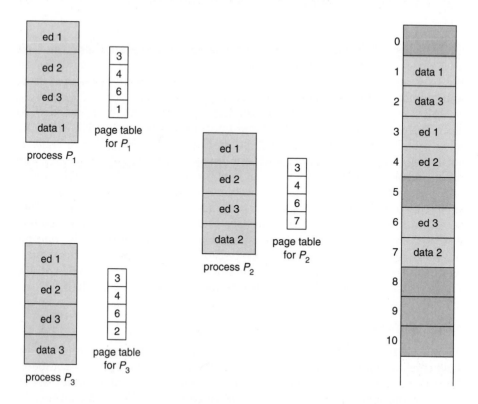

Figure 8.21 Sharing of code in a paging environment.

reentrant. The read-only nature of shared code should not be left to the correctness of the code; the operating system should enforce this property. This sharing of memory between processes on a system is similar to the way threads share the address space of a task, as described in Chapter 4.

Systems that use inverted page tables have difficulty implementing shared memory. Shared memory is usually implemented as two virtual addresses that are mapped to one physical address. This standard method cannot be used, however, as there is only one virtual page entry for every physical page, so one physical page cannot have the two (or more) shared virtual addresses.

8.6   ■   Segmentation

An important aspect of memory management that became unavoidable with paging is the separation of the user's view of memory and the actual physical memory. The user's view of memory is not the same as the actual physical memory. The user's view is mapped onto physical memory. The mapping allows differentiation between logical memory and physical memory.

8.6.1 Basic Method

What is the user's view of memory? Does the user think of memory as a linear array of bytes, some containing instructions and others containing data, or is there some other preferred memory view? There is general agreement that the user or programmer of a system does not think of memory as a linear array of bytes. Rather, the user prefers to view memory as a collection of variable-sized segments, with no necessary ordering among segments (Figure 8.22).

Consider how you think of a program when you are writing it. You think of it as a main program with a set of subroutines, procedures, functions, or modules. There may also be various data structures: tables, arrays, stacks, variables, and so on. Each of these modules or data elements is referred to by name. You talk about "the symbol table," "function Sqrt," "the main program," without caring what addresses in memory these elements occupy. You are not concerned with whether the symbol table is stored before or after the Sqrt function. Each of these segments is of variable length; the length is intrinsically defined by the purpose of the segment in the program. Elements within a segment are identified by their offset from the beginning of the segment: the first statement of the program, the seventeenth entry in the symbol table, the fifth instruction of the Sqrt function, and so on.

Segmentation is a memory-management scheme that supports this user view of memory. A logical address space is a collection of segments. Each

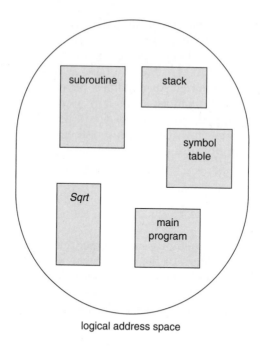

logical address space

Figure 8.22   User's view of a program.

segment has a name and a length. Addresses specify both the segment name and the offset within the segment. The user therefore specifies each address by two quantities: a segment name and an offset. (Contrast this scheme with paging, where the user specified only a single address, which was partitioned by the hardware into a page number and an offset, all invisible to the programmer.)

For simplicity of implementation, segments are numbered and are referred to by a segment number, rather than by a segment name. Thus, a logical address consists of a two tuple:

<segment-number, offset>.

Normally, the user program is compiled, and the compiler automatically constructs segments reflecting the input program. A Pascal compiler might create separate segments for (1) the global variables; (2) the procedure call stack, to store parameters and return addresses; (3) the code portion of each procedure or function; and (4) the local variables of each procedure and function. A FORTRAN compiler might create a separate segment for each common block. Arrays might be assigned separate segments. The loader would take all these segments and assign them segment numbers.

8.6.2 Hardware

Although the user can now refer to objects in the program by a two-dimensional address, the actual physical memory is still, of course, a one-dimensional sequence of bytes. Thus, we must define an implementation to map two-dimensional user-defined addresses into one-dimensional physical addresses. This mapping is effected by a *segment table*. Each entry of the segment table has a segment *base* and a segment *limit*. The segment base contains the starting physical address where the segments resides in memory, whereas the segment limit specifies the length of the segment.

The use of a segment table is illustrated in Figure 8.23. A logical address consists of two parts: a segment number, s, and an offset into that segment, d. The segment number is used as an index into the segment table. The offset d of the logical address must be between 0 and the segment limit. If it is not, we trap to the operating system (logical addressing attempt beyond end of segment). If this offset is legal, it is added to the segment base to produce the address in physical memory of the desired byte. The segment table is thus essentially an array of base−limit register pairs.

As an example, consider the situation shown in Figure 8.24. We have five segments numbered from 0 through 4. The segments are stored in physical memory as shown. The segment table has a separate entry for each segment, giving the beginning address of the segment in physical

Figure 8.23 Segmentation hardware.

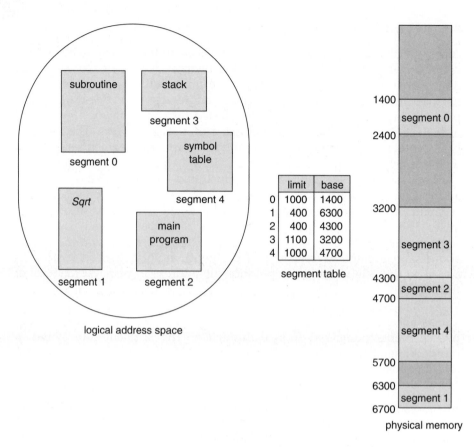

Figure 8.24 Example of segmentation.

memory (the base) and the length of that segment (the limit). For example, segment 2 is 400 bytes long, and begins at location 4300. Thus, a reference to byte 53 of segment 2 is mapped onto location 4300 + 53 = 4353. A reference to segment 3, byte 852, is mapped to 3200 (the base of segment 3) + 852 = 4052. A reference to byte 1222 of segment 0 would result in a trap to the operating system, as this segment is only 1000 bytes long.

8.6.3 Implementation of Segment Tables

Segmentation is closely related to the partition models of memory management presented earlier, the main difference being that one program may consist of several segments. Segmentation is a more complex concept, however, which is why we are describing it after discussing paging. Like the page table, the segment table can be put either in fast registers or in memory. A segment table kept in registers can be referenced quickly; the addition to the base and comparison with the limit can be done simultaneously to save time.

In the case where a program may consist of a large number of segments, it is not feasible to keep the segment table in registers, so we must keep it in memory. A *segment-table base register (STBR)* points to the segment table. Also, because the number of segments used by a program may vary widely, a *segment-table length register (STLR)* is used. For a logical address *(s,d)*, we first check that the segment number *s* is legal (that is, *s* < STLR). Then, we add the segment number to the STBR, resulting in the address (STBR + *s*) in memory of the segment-table entry. This entry is read from memory and we proceed as before: Check the offset against the segment length and compute the physical address of the desired byte as the sum of the segment base and offset.

As occurs with paging, this mapping requires two memory references per logical address, effectively slowing the computer system by a factor of 2, unless something is done. The normal solution is to use a set of associative registers to hold the most recently used segment-table entries. Again, a relatively small set of associative registers can generally reduce the time required for memory accesses to no more than 10 or 15 percent slower than unmapped memory accesses.

8.6.4 Protection and Sharing

A particular advantage of segmentation is the association of protection with the segments. Because the segments represent a semantically defined portion of the program, it is likely that all entries in the segment will be used the same way. Hence, we have some segments that are instructions, whereas other segments are data. In a modern architecture, instructions are non−self-modifying, so instruction segments can be defined as read-only or execute-only. The memory-mapping hardware will check the protection bits associated with each segment-table entry to prevent illegal accesses to memory, such as attempts to write into a read-only segment, or to use an execute-only segment as data. By placing an array in its own segment, the memory-management hardware will automatically check that array indexes are legal and do not stray outside the array boundaries. Thus, many common program errors will be detected by the hardware before they can cause serious damage.

Another advantage of segmentation involves the *sharing* of code or data. Each process has a segment table associated with its process control block, which the dispatcher uses to define the hardware segment table when this process is given the CPU. Segments are shared when entries in the segment tables of two different processes point to the same physical locations. (Figure 8.25).

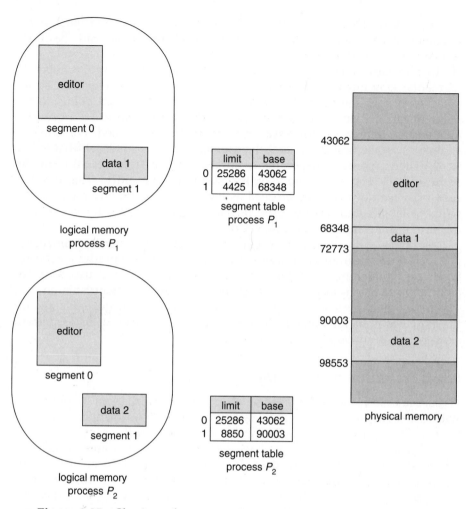

Figure 8.25 Sharing of segments in a segmented memory system.

The sharing occurs at the segment level. Thus, any information can be shared if it is defined to be a segment. Several segments can be shared, so a program composed of several segments can be shared.

For example, consider the use of a text editor in a time-sharing system. A complete editor might be quite large, composed of many segments. These segments can be shared among all users, limiting the physical memory needed to support editing tasks. Rather than n copies of the editor, we need only one copy. For each user, we still need separate, unique segments to store local variables. These segments, of course, would not be shared.

It is also possible to share only parts of programs. For example, common subroutine packages can be shared among many users if they are defined as sharable, read-only segments. Two FORTRAN programs, for instance, may use the same *Sqrt* subroutine, but only one physical copy of the *Sqrt* routine would be needed.

Although this sharing appears simple, there are subtle considerations. Code segments typically contain references to themselves. For example, a conditional jump normally has a transfer address. The transfer address is a segment number and offset. The segment number of the transfer address will be the segment number of the code segment. If we try to share this segment, all sharing processes must define the shared code segment to have the same segment number.

For instance, if we want to share the *Sqrt* routine, and one process wants to make it segment 4 and another wants to make it segment 17, how should the *Sqrt* routine refer to itself? Because there is only one physical copy of *Sqrt*, it must refer to itself in the same way for both users — it must have a unique segment number. As the number of users sharing the segment increases, so does the difficulty of finding an acceptable segment number.

Read-only data segments that contain no physical pointers may be shared as different segment numbers, as may code segments that refer to themselves not directly, but rather only indirectly. For example, conditional branches that specify the branch address as an offset from the current program counter or relative to a register containing the current segment number would allow code to avoid direct reference to the current segment number.

8.6.5   Fragmentation

The long-term scheduler must find and allocate memory for all the segments of a user program. This situation is similar to paging *except* that the segments are of *variable* length; pages are all the same size. Thus, as with the variable-sized partition scheme, memory allocation is a dynamic storage-allocation problem, usually solved with a best-fit or first-fit algorithm.

Segmentation may then cause external fragmentation, when all blocks of free memory are too small to accommodate a segment. In this case, the process may simply have to wait until more memory (or at least a larger hole) becomes available, or compaction may be used to create a larger hole. Because segmentation is by its nature a dynamic relocation algorithm, we can compact memory whenever we want. If the CPU scheduler must wait for one process, due to a memory-allocation problem, it may (or may not) skip through the CPU queue looking for a smaller, lower-priority process to run.

How serious a problem is external fragmentation for a segmentation scheme? Would long-term scheduling with compaction help? The answers to these questions depend mainly on the average segment size. At one extreme, we could define each process to be one segment. This approach reduces to the variable-sized partition scheme. At the other extreme, every byte could be put in its own segment and relocated separately. This arrangement eliminates external fragmentation altogether; however, every byte would need a base register for its relocation, doubling memory use! Of course, the next logical step — fixed-sized, small segments — is paging. Generally, if the average segment size is small, external fragmentation will also be small. (By analogy, consider putting suitcases in the trunk of a car; they never quite seem to fit. However, if you open the suitcases and put the individual items in the trunk, everything fits.) Because the individual segments are smaller than the overall process, they are more likely to fit in the available memory blocks.

8.7 ■ Segmentation with Paging

Both paging and segmentation have their advantages and disadvantages. In fact, of the two most popular microprocessors now being used, the Motorola 68000 line is designed based on a flat address space, whereas the Intel 80X86 family is based on segmentation. Both are merging memory models toward a mixture of paging and segmentation. It is possible to combine these two schemes to improve on each. This combination is best illustrated by two different architectures — the innovative but not widely used MULTICS system and the Intel 386.

8.7.1 MULTICS

In the MULTICS system, a logical address is formed from an 18-bit segment number and a 16-bit offset. Although this scheme creates a 34-bit address space, the segment-table overhead is tolerable; we need only as many segment-table entries as we have segments, as there need not be empty segment-table entries.

However, with segments of 64K words, each of which consists of 36 bits, the average segment size could be large and external fragmentation could be a problem. Even if external fragmentation is not a problem, the search time to allocate a segment, using first-fit or best-fit, could be long. Thus, we may waste memory due to external fragmentation, or waste time due to lengthy searches, or both.

The solution adopted was to *page* the *segments*. Paging eliminates external fragmentation and makes the allocation problem trivial: any empty frame can be used for a desired page. Each page in MULTICS consists of 1K

logical address

Figure 8.26 Paged segmentation on the GE 645 (MULTICS).

words. Thus, the segment offset (16 bits) is broken into a 6-bit page number and a 10-bit page offset. The page number indexes into the page table to give the frame number. Finally, the frame number is combined with the page offset to form a physical address. The translation scheme is shown in Figure 8.26. Notice that the difference between this solution and pure segmentation is that the segment-table entry contains not the base address of the segment, but rather the base address of a *page table* for this segment.

We must now have a separate page table for each segment. However, because each segment is limited in length by its segment-table entry, the page table does not need to be full sized. It requires only as many entries as are actually needed. As with paging, the last page of each segment generally will not be completely full. Thus, we will have, on the average, one-half page of *internal* fragmentation per segment. Consequently, although we have eliminated external fragmentation, we have introduced internal fragmentation and increased table-space overhead.

In truth, even the paged-segmentation view of MULTICS just presented is simplistic. Because the segment number is an 18-bit quantity, we could have up to 262,144 segments, requiring an excessively large segment table. To ease this problem, MULTICS pages the segment table! The segment number (18 bits) is broken into an 8-bit page number and a 10-bit page offset. Hence, the segment table is represented by a page table consisting of up to 2^8 entries. Thus, in general, a logical address in MULTICS is as follows:

segment number		offset	
s_1	s_2	d_1	d_2
8	10	6	10

where s_1 is an index into the page table of the segment table and s_2 is the displacement within the page of the segment table. Now we have found the page containing the segment table we want. Then, d_1 is a displacement into the page table of the desired segment, and finally, d_2 is a displacement into the page containing the word to be accessed (see Figure 8.27).

To ensure reasonable performance, 16 associative registers are available that contain the address of the 16 most recently referred pages. Each register consists of two parts: a key and a value. The key is a 24-bit field that is the concatenation of a segment number and a page number. The value is the frame number.

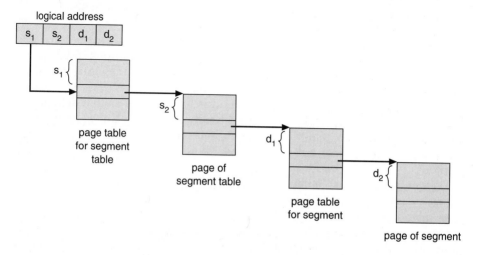

Figure 8.27 Address translation in MULTICS.

8.7.2 OS/2 32-Bit Version

The new IBM OS/2 32-bit version is an operating system running on top of the Intel 386 (and 486) architecture. The 386 uses segmentation with paging for memory management. The maximum number of segments per process is 16K, and each segment can be as large as 4 gigabytes. The page size is 4K bytes. We shall not give a complete description of the memory-management structure of the 386 in this text. Rather, we shall present the major ideas.

The logical address space of a process is divided into two partitions. The first partition consists of up to 8K segments that are private to that process. The second partition consists of up to 8K segments that are shared among all the processes. Information about the first partition is kept in the *local descriptor table (LDT)*, information about the second partition is kept in the *global descriptor table (GDT)*. Each entry in the LDT and GDT table consists of 8 bytes, with detailed information about a particular segment including the base location and length of that segment.

The logical address is a pair (selector, offset), where the selector is a 16-bit number:

s	*g*	*p*
13	1	2

in which *s* designates the segment number, *g* indicates whether the segment is in the GDT or LDT, and *p* deals with protection. The offset is a 32-bit number specifying the location of the byte (word) within the segment in question.

The machine has six segment registers, allowing six segments to be addressed at any one time by a process. It has six 8-byte microprogram registers to hold the corresponding descriptors from either the LDT or GDT. This cache lets the 386 avoid having to read the descriptor from memory for every memory reference.

The physical address on the 386 is 32 bits long and is formed as follows. The select register points to the appropriate entry in the LDT or GDT. The base and limit information about the segment in question are used to generate a *linear address*. First, the limit is used to check for address validity. If the address is not valid, a memory fault is generated, resulting in a trap to the operating system. If it is valid, then the value of the offset is added to the value of the base, resulting in a 32-bit linear address. This address is then translated into a physical address.

As pointed out previously, each segment is paged, and each page is 4K bytes. A page table may thus consist of up to 1 million entries. Because each entry consists of 4 bytes, each process may need up to 4 megabytes of physical address space for the page table alone. Clearly, we would not want to allocate the page table contiguously in main memory. The solution adopted in the 386 is to use a two-level paging scheme. The linear address is divided into a page number consisting of 20 bits, and a page offset consisting of 12 bits. Since we page the page table, the page number is further divided into a 10-bit page directory pointer and a 10-bit page table pointer. The logical address is as follows:

page number		page offset
p_1	p_2	d
10	10	12

The address-translation scheme for this architecture is similar to the scheme shown in Figure 8.19. The Intel address translation is shown in more detail in Figure 8.28. So that the efficiency of physical-memory use can be improved, Intel 386 page tables can be swapped to disk. In this case, an invalid bit is used in the page-directory entry to indicate whether the table to which the entry is pointing is in memory or on disk. If the table is on disk, the operating system can use the other 31 bits to specify the disk location of the table; the table then can be brought into memory on demand.

8.8 ■ Summary

Memory-management algorithms for multiprogrammed operating systems range from the simple single-user system approach to paged segmentation. The greatest determinant of the method used in a particular system is the hardware provided. Every memory address generated by the CPU must be checked for legality and possibly mapped to a physical address. The checking cannot be implemented (efficiently) in software. Hence, we are constrained by the hardware available.

The memory-management algorithms discussed (contiguous allocation, paging, segmentation, and combinations of paging and segmentation) differ in many aspects. The following list indicates some important considerations that you should use in comparing different memory-management strategies:

- **Hardware support:** A simple base register or a pair of base and limit registers is sufficient for the single and multiple partition schemes, whereas paging and segmentation need mapping tables to define the address map.

- **Performance:** As the algorithm becomes more complex, the time required to map a logical address to a physical address increases. For the simple systems, we need only to compare or add to the logical address — operations that are fast. Paging and segmentation can be as

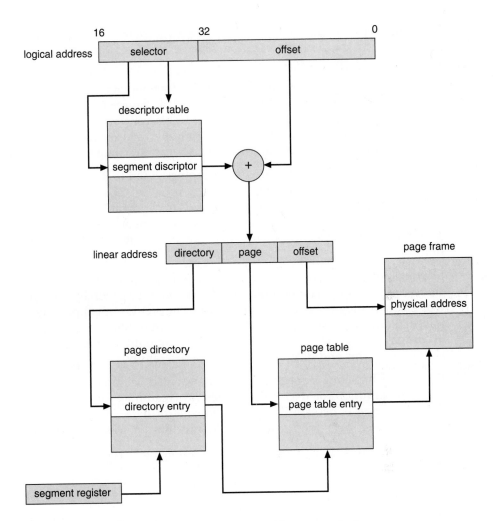

Figure 8.28   Intel 80386 address translation.

fast if the table is implemented in fast registers. If the table is in memory, however, user memory accesses can be degraded substantially. A set of associative registers can reduce the performance degradation to an acceptable level.

● **Fragmentation:** A multiprogrammed system will generally perform more efficiently with a higher level of multiprogramming. For a given set of processes, we can increase the multiprogramming level only by packing more processes into memory. To accomplish this task, we must reduce memory waste or fragmentation. Systems with fixed-sized allocation units, such as the single-partition scheme and paging, suffer from internal fragmentation. Systems with variable-sized allocation units, such as the multiple-partition scheme and segmentation, suffer from external fragmentation.

- **Relocation:** One solution to the external-fragmentation problem is compaction. Compaction involves shifting a program in memory without the program noticing the change. This consideration requires that logical addresses be relocated dynamically, at execution time. If addresses are relocated only at load time, we cannot compact storage.

- **Swapping:** Any algorithm can have swapping added to it. At intervals determined by the operating system, usually dictated by CPU-scheduling policies, processes are copied from main memory to a backing store, and later are copied back to main memory. This scheme allows more processes to be run than can be fit into memory at one time.

- **Sharing:** Another means of increasing the multiprogramming level is to share code and data among different users. Sharing generally requires that either paging or segmentation be used, to provide small packets of information (pages or segments) that can be shared. Sharing is a means of running many processes with a limited amount of memory, but shared programs and data must be designed carefully.

- **Protection:** If paging or segmentation is provided, different sections of a user program can be declared execute-only, read-only, or read−write. This restriction is necessary with shared code or data, and is generally useful in any case to provide simple run-time checks for common programming errors.

■ Exercises

8.1 Explain the difference between logical and physical addresses.

8.2 Explain the following allocation algorithms:

   a. First-fit

   b. Best-fit

   c. Worst-fit

8.3 When a process is rolled out of memory, it loses its ability to use the CPU (at least for a while). Describe another situation where a process loses its ability to use the CPU, but where the process does not get rolled out.

8.4 Explain the difference between internal and external fragmentation.

8.5 Given memory partitions of 100K, 500K, 200K, 300K, and 600K (in order), how would each of the First-fit, Best-fit, and Worst-fit algorithms place processes of 212K, 417K, 112K, and 426K (in order)? Which algorithm makes the most efficient use of memory?

8.6 Consider a system where a program can be separated into two parts: code and data. The CPU knows whether it wants an instruction (instruction fetch) or data (data fetch or store). Therefore, two base−limit register pairs are provided: one for instructions and one for data. The instruction base−limit register pair is automatically read-only, so programs can be shared among different users. Discuss the advantages and disadvantages of this scheme.

8.7 Why are pages sizes always powers of 2?

8.8 Consider a logical address space of eight pages of 1024 words each, mapped onto a physical memory of 32 frames.

   a. How many bits are there in the logical address?

   b. How many bits are there in the physical address?

8.9 Why is it that, on a system with paging, a process cannot access memory it does not own? How could the operating system allow access to other memory? Why should it or should it not?

8.10 Consider a paging system with the page table stored in memory.

   a. If a memory reference takes 200 nanoseconds, how long does a paged memory reference take?

   b. If we add associative registers, and 75 percent of all page-table references are found in the associative registers, what is the effective memory reference time? (Assume that finding a page-table entry in the associative registers takes zero time, if the entry is there.)

8.11 What is the effect of allowing two entries in a page table to point to the same page frame in memory? Explain how this effect could be used to decrease the amount of time needed to copy a large amount of memory from one place to another. What would the effect of updating some byte in the one page be on the other page?

8.12 Why are segmentation and paging sometimes combined into one scheme?

8.13 Describe a mechanism by which one segment could belong to the address space of two different processes.

8.14 Explain why it is easier to share a reentrant module using segmentation than it is to do so when pure paging is used.

8.15 Sharing segments among processes without requiring the same segment number is possible in a dynamically-linked segmentation system.

   a. Define a system that allows static linking and sharing of segments without requiring that the segment numbers be the same.

   b. Describe a paging scheme that allows pages to be shared without requiring that the page numbers be the same.

8.16 Consider the following segment table:

Segment	Base	Length
0	219	600
1	2300	14
2	90	100
3	1327	580
4	1952	96

What are the physical addresses for the following logical addresses?

   a. 0,430

   b. 1,10

   c. 2,500

   d. 3,400

   e. 4,112

8.17 Consider the Intel address translation scheme shown in Figure 8.28.

   a. Describe all the steps that are taken by the Intel 80386 in translating a logical address into a physical address.

   b. What are the advantages to the operating system of hardware that provides such complicated memory translation hardware?

   c. Are there any disadvantages to this address translation system?

8.18 In the IBM/370, memory protection is provided through the use of *keys*. A key is a 4-bit quantity. Each 2K block of memory has a key (the storage key) associated with it. The CPU also has a key (the protection key) associated with it. A store operation is allowed only if both keys are equal, or if either is zero. Which of the following memory-management schemes could be used successfully with this hardware?

   a. Bare machine

   b. Single-user system

c. Multiprogramming with a fixed number of processes

d. Multiprogramming with a variable number of processes

e. Paging

f. Segmentation

Bibliographic Notes

Dynamic storage allocation was discussed by Knuth [1973, Section 2.5], who found through simulation results that first-fit is generally superior to best-fit. Additional discussions were offered by Shore [1975], Bays [1977], Stephenson [1983] and Brent [1989]. An adaptive exact-fit storage-management scheme was presented by Oldehoeft and Allan [1985]. Discussions concerning the 50-percent rule were offered by Knuth [1973].

The concept of paging can be credited to the designers of the Atlas system, which has been described by Kilburn et al. [1961] and Howarth et al. [1961]. The concept of segmentation was first discussed by Dennis [1965]. Paged segmentation was first supported in the GE 645, on which MULTICS was originally implemented [Organick 1972].

Inverted page tables were discussed in an article about the IBM RT storage manager by Chang and Mergen [1988].

Cache memories, including associative memory, were described and analyzed by Smith [1982]. This paper also includes an extensive bibliography on the subject. Hennessy and Patterson [1990] discussed the hardware aspects of TLBs, caches, and MMUs.

The Motorola 68000 microprocessor family was described in Motorola [1989a]. The Intel 8086 was described in Intel [1985a]. The Intel 80386 paging hardware was described in Intel [1986]. Tanenbaum [1992] also discussed Intel 80386 paging. The new Intel 80486 hardware was covered in Intel [1989].

CHAPTER 9

VIRTUAL MEMORY

In Chapter 8, we discussed various memory-management strategies that have been used in computer systems. All these strategies have the same goal: to keep many processes in memory simultaneously to allow multiprogramming. However, they tend to require the entire process to be in memory before the process can execute.

Virtual memory is a technique that allows the execution of processes that may not be completely in memory. The main visible advantage of this scheme is that programs can be larger than physical memory. Further, it abstracts main memory into an extremely large, uniform array of storage, separating logical memory as viewed by the user from physical memory. This technique frees programmers from concern over memory storage limitations. Virtual memory is not easy to implement, however, and may substantially decrease performance if it is used carelessly. In this chapter, we discuss virtual memory in the form of demand paging, and examine its complexity and cost.

9.1 ■ Background

The memory-management algorithms of Chapter 8 are necessary because of one basic requirement: The instructions being executed must be in physical memory. The first approach to meeting this requirement is to place the entire logical address space in physical memory. Overlays and dynamic loading can help ease this restriction, but they generally require special precautions and extra effort by the programmer. This restriction seems both necessary and reasonable, but it is also unfortunate, since it limits the size of a program to the size of physical memory.

In fact, an examination of real programs shows us that, in many cases, the entire program is not needed. For instance,

- Programs often have code to handle unusual error conditions. Since these errors seldom, if ever, occur in practice, this code is almost never executed.

- Arrays, lists, and tables are often allocated more memory than they actually need. An array may be declared 100 by 100 elements, even though it is seldom larger than 10 by 10 elements. An assembler symbol table may have room for 3000 symbols, although the average program has less than 200 symbols.

- Certain options and features of a program may be used rarely. For instance, the routines on U.S. government computers which balance the budget have not been used in years.

Even in those cases where the entire program is needed, it may not all be needed at the same time (such is the case with overlays, for example).

The ability to execute a program that is only partially in memory would have many benefits:

- A program would no longer be constrained by the amount of physical memory that is available. Users would be able to write programs for an extremely large *virtual* address space, simplifying the programming task.

- Because each user program could take less physical memory, more programs could be run at the same time, with a corresponding increase in CPU utilization and throughput, but with no increase in response time or turnaround time.

- Less I/O would be needed to load or swap each user program into memory, so each user program would run faster.

Thus, running a program that is not entirely in memory would benefit both the system and the user.

Virtual memory is the separation of user logical memory from physical memory. This separation allows an extremely large virtual memory to be provided for programmers when only a smaller physical memory is available (Figure 9.1). Virtual memory makes the task of programming much easier, because the programmer no longer needs to worry about the amount of physical memory available, or about what code can be placed in overlays, but can concentrate instead on the problem to be programmed. On systems which support virtual memory, overlays have virtually disappeared.

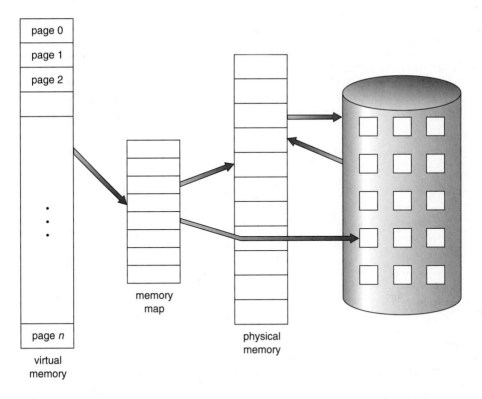

virtual
memory

memory
map

physical
memory

Figure 9.1 Diagram showing virtual memory larger than physical memory.

Virtual memory is commonly implemented by *demand paging*. It can also be implemented in a segmentation system. Several systems provide a paged segmentation scheme, where segments are broken into pages. Thus, the user view is segmentation, but the operating system can implement this view with demand paging. *Demand segmentation* can also be used to provide virtual memory. Burroughs' computer systems have used demand segmentation. The IBM OS/2 operating system also uses demand segmentation. However, segment-replacement algorithms are more complex than are page-replacement algorithms because the segments have variable sizes.

9.2 ■ Demand Paging

A demand-paging system is similar to a paging system with swapping (Figure 9.2). Processes reside on secondary memory (which is usually a disk). When we want to execute a process, we swap it into memory. Rather than swapping the entire process into memory, however, we use a

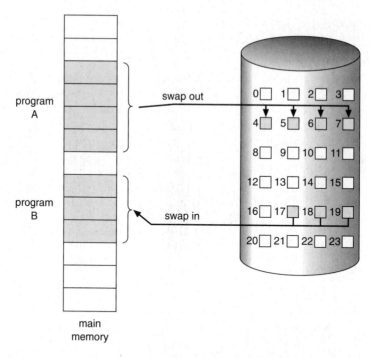

program A

swap out

program B

swap in

main
memory

Figure 9.2   Transfer of a paged memory to contiguous disk space.

lazy swapper. A lazy swapper never swaps a page into memory unless that page will be needed. Since we are now viewing a process as a sequence of pages, rather than one large contiguous address space, the use of the term *swap* is technically incorrect. A swapper manipulates entire processes, whereas a *pager* is concerned with the individual pages of a process. We shall thus use the term *pager,* rather than *swapper,* in connection with demand paging.

When a process is to be swapped in, the pager guesses which pages will be used before the process is swapped out again. Instead of swapping in a whole process, the pager brings only those necessary pages into memory. Thus, it avoids reading into memory pages that will not be used anyway, decreasing the swap time and the amount of physical memory needed.

With this scheme, we need some form of hardware support to distinguish between those pages that are in memory and those pages that are on the disk. The *valid–invalid* bit scheme described in Section 8.5.2 can be used for this purpose. This time, however, when this bit is set to "valid," this value indicates that the associated page is both legal and in memory. If the bit is set to "invalid," this value indicates that the page is either not valid (that is, not in the logical address space of the process), or is valid but is currently on the disk. The page-table entry for a page that is brought into memory is set as usual, but the page-table entry for a page that is not currently in memory is simply marked invalid, or contains the address of the page on disk. This situation is depicted in Figure 9.3.

Notice that marking a page invalid will have no effect if the process never attempts to access that page. Hence, if we guess right and page in all and only those pages that are actually needed, the process will run exactly as though we had brought in all pages. While the process executes and accesses pages that are *memory resident,* execution proceeds normally.

But what happens if the process tries to use a page that was not brought into memory? Access to a page marked invalid causes a *page-fault* trap. The paging hardware, in translating the address through the page table, will notice that the invalid bit is set, causing a trap to the operating system. This trap is the result of the operating system's failure to bring the desired page into memory (in an attempt to minimize disk-transfer

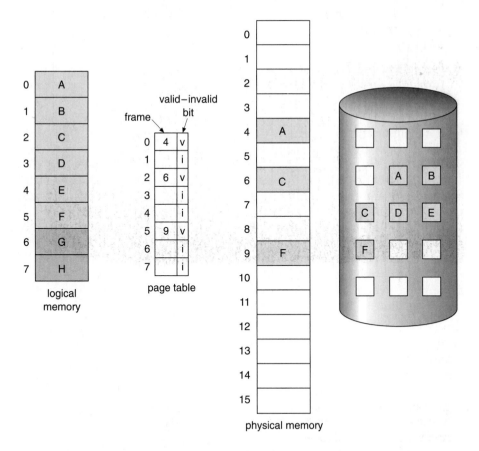

Figure 9.3 Page table when some pages are not in main memory.

overhead and memory requirements), rather than an invalid address error as a result of an attempt to use an illegal memory address (such as an incorrect array subscript). We must therefore correct this oversight. The procedure for handling this page fault is simple (Figure 9.4):

1. We check an internal table (usually kept with the process control block) for this process, to determine whether the reference was a valid or invalid memory access.

2. If the reference was invalid, we terminate the process. If it was valid, but we have not yet brought in that page, we now page in the latter.

3. We find a free frame (by taking one from the free-frame list, for example).

4. We schedule a disk operation to read the desired page into the newly allocated frame.

5. When the disk read is complete, we modify the internal table kept with the process and the page table to indicate that the page is now in memory.

6. We restart the instruction that was interrupted by the illegal address trap. The process can now access the page as though it had always been in memory.

It is important to realize that, because we save the state (registers, condition code, instruction counter) of the interrupted process when the page fault occurs, we can restart the process in *exactly* the same place and state, except that the desired page is now in memory and is accessible. In this way, we are able to execute a process, even though portions of it are not (yet) in memory. When the process tries to access locations that are not in memory, the hardware traps to the operating system (page fault). The operating system reads the desired page into memory and restarts the process as though the page had always been in memory.

In the extreme case, we could start executing a process with *no* pages in memory. When the operating system set the instruction pointer to the first instruction of the process, which is on a non-memory-resident page, the process would immediately fault for the page. After this page was brought into memory, the process would continue to execute, faulting as necessary until every page that it needed was actually in memory. At that point, it could execute with no more faults. This scheme is *pure demand paging*: Never bring a page into memory until it is required.

Theoretically, some programs may access several new pages of memory with each instruction execution, (one page for the instruction and many for data) possibly causing multiple page faults per instruction. This situation would result in unacceptable system performance. Fortunately,

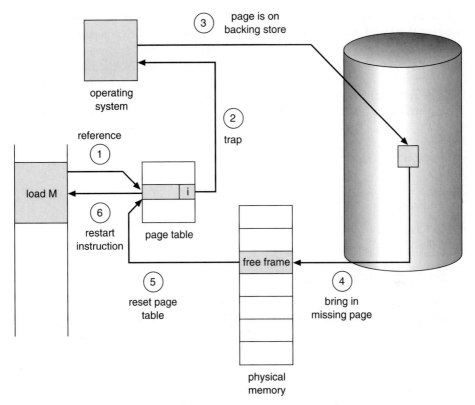

Figure 9.4 Steps in handling a page fault.

analysis of running processes show that this behavior is exceedingly unlikely. Programs tend to have *locality of reference*, described in Section 9.7.1, which results in reasonable performance from demand paging.

The hardware to support demand paging is the same as the hardware for paging and swapping:

- **Page table:** This table has the ability to mark an entry invalid through a valid–invalid bit or special value of protection bits.

- **Secondary memory:** This memory holds those pages not in main memory. The secondary memory is usually a high-speed disk. It is known as the swap device, and the section of disk used for this purpose is known as *swap space* or *backing store*. Swap space allocation is further discussed in Chapter 12.

In addition to this hardware support, considerable software is needed, as we shall see.

Some additional architectural constraints must be imposed. A crucial issue is the need to be able to restart any instruction after a page fault. In most cases, this requirement is easy to meet. A page fault could occur at any memory reference. If the page fault occurs on the instruction fetch, we can restart by fetching the instruction again. If a page fault occurs while we are fetching an operand, we must re-fetch the instruction, decode it again, and then fetch the operand.

As a worst case, consider a three-address instruction such as ADD the content of A to B placing the result in C. The steps to execute this instruction would be

1. Fetch and decode the instruction (ADD).

2. Fetch A.

3. Fetch B.

4. Add A and B.

5. Store the sum in C.

If we faulted when we tried to store in C (because C is in a page not currently in memory), we would have to get the desired page, bring it in, correct the page table, and restart the instruction. The restart would require fetching the instruction again, decoding it again, fetching the two operands again, and then adding again. However, there is really not much repeated work (less than one complete instruction), and the repetition is necessary only when a page fault occurs.

The major difficulty occurs when one instruction may modify several different locations. For example, consider the IBM System 360/370 MVC (move character) instruction, which can move up to 256 bytes from one location to another (possibly overlapping) location. If either block (source or destination) straddles a page boundary, a page fault might occur after the move is partially done. In addition, if the source and destination blocks overlap, the source block may have been modified, in which case we cannot simply restart the instruction.

This problem can be solved in two different ways. In one solution, the microcode computes and attempts to access both ends of both blocks. If a page fault is going to occur, it will happen at this step, before anything is modified. The move can then take place, as we know that no page fault can occur, since all the relevant pages are in memory. The other solution uses temporary registers to hold the values of overwritten locations. If there is a page fault, all the old values are written back into memory before the trap occurs. This action restores memory to its state before the instruction was started, so that the instruction can be repeated.

A similar architectural problem occurs in machines that use special addressing modes, including autodecrement and autoincrement modes (for example, the PDP-11). These addressing modes use a register as a pointer and automatically decrement or increment the register as indicated. Autodecrement automatically decrements the register *before* using its contents as the operand address; autoincrement automatically increments the register *after* using its contents as the operand address. Thus, the instruction

$$MOV (R2)+,-(R3)$$

copies the contents of the location pointed to by register 2 into the location pointed to by register 3. Register 2 is incremented (by 2 for a word, since the PDP-11 is a byte-addressable computer) after it is used as a pointer; register 3 is decremented (by 2) before it is used as a pointer. Now consider what will happen if we get a fault when trying to store into the location pointed to by register 3. To restart the instruction, we must reset the two registers to the values they had before we started the execution of the instruction. One solution is to create a new special status register to record the register number and amount modified for any register that is changed during the execution of an instruction. This status register allows the operating system to "undo" the effects of a partially executed instruction that causes a page fault.

These are by no means the only architectural problems resulting from adding paging to an existing architecture to allow demand paging, but they illustrate some of the difficulties. Paging is added between the CPU and the memory in a computer system. It should be entirely transparent to the user process. Thus, people often assume that paging could be added to any system. Although this assumption is true for a non-demand paging environment, where a page fault represents a fatal error, it is not true in the case where a page fault means only that an additional page must be brought into memory and the process restarted.

9.3 ■ Performance of Demand Paging

Demand paging can have a significant effect on the performance of a computer system. To see why, let us compute the *effective access time* for a demand-paged memory. The memory access time, *ma*, for most computer systems now ranges from 10 to 200 nanoseconds. As long as we have no page faults, the effective access time is equal to the memory access time. If, however, a page fault occurs, we must first read the relevant page from disk, and then access the desired word.

Let p be the probability of a page fault ($0 \leq p \leq 1$). We would expect p to be close to zero; that is, there will be only a few page faults. The *effective* access time is then

$$\text{effective access time} = (1-p) \times ma + p \times \text{page fault time}.$$

To compute the effective access time, we must know how much time is needed to service a page fault. A page fault causes the following sequence to occur:

1. Trap to the operating system.

2. Save the user registers and process state.

3. Determine that the interrupt was a page fault.

4. Check that the page reference was legal and determine the location of the page on the disk.

5. Issue a read from the disk to a free frame:

   a. Wait in a queue for this device until the read request is serviced.

   b. Wait for the device seek and/or latency time.

   c. Begin the transfer of the page to a free frame.

6. While waiting, allocate the CPU to some other user (CPU scheduling; optional).

7. Interrupt from the disk (I/O completed).

8. Save the registers and process state for the other user (if step 6 executed).

9. Determine that the interrupt was from the disk.

10. Correct the page table and other tables to show that the desired page is now in memory.

11. Wait for the CPU to be allocated to this process again.

12. Restore the user registers, process state, and new page table, then resume the interrupted instruction.

Not all of these steps may be necessary in every case. For example, we are assuming that, in step 6, the CPU is allocated to another process while the I/O occurs. This arrangement allows multiprogramming to maintain CPU utilization, but requires additional time to resume the page-fault service routine when the I/O transfer is complete.

In any case, we are faced with three major components of the page-fault service time:

1. Service the page-fault interrupt.

2. Read in the page.

3. Restart the process.

The first and third tasks may be reduced, with careful coding, to several hundred instructions. These tasks may take from 1 to 100 microseconds each. The page-switch time, on the other hand, will probably be close to 24 milliseconds. A typical hard disk has an average latency of 8 milliseconds, a seek of 15 milliseconds and a transfer time of 1 millisecond. Thus, the total paging time would be close to 25 milliseconds, including hardware and software time. Remember also that we are looking at only the device service time. If a queue of processes is waiting for the device (other processes that have caused page faults), we have to add device queueing time as we wait for the paging device to be free to service our request, increasing the time to swap even more.

If we take an average page-fault service time of 25 milliseconds and a memory access time of 100 nanoseconds, then the effective access time in nanoseconds is

$$
\begin{aligned}
\text{effective access time} &= (1-p) \times (100) + p \times (25 \text{ milliseconds}) \\
&= (1-p) \times 100 + p \times 25{,}000{,}000 \\
&= 100 + 24{,}999{,}900 \times p.
\end{aligned}
$$

We see then that the effective access time is directly proportional to the page-fault rate. If one access out of 1000 causes a page fault, the effective access time is 25 microseconds. The computer would be slowed down by a factor of 250 because of demand paging! If we want less than 10-percent degradation, we need

$$
\begin{aligned}
110 &> 100 + 25{,}000{,}000 \times p, \\
10 &> 25{,}000{,}000 \times p, \\
p &< 0.0000004.
\end{aligned}
$$

That is, to keep the slowdown due to paging to a reasonable level, we can allow only less than 1 memory access out of 2,500,000 to page fault.

It is important to keep the page-fault rate low in a demand-paging system. Otherwise, the effective access time increases, slowing process execution dramatically.

One additional aspect of demand paging is the handling and overall use of swap space. Disk I/O to swap space is generally faster than that to the file system. It is faster because swap space is allocated in much larger blocks, and file lookups and indirect allocation methods are not used (see Chapter 12). It is therefore possible for the system to gain better paging throughput, by copying an entire file image into the swap space at process startup, and then to perform demand paging from the swap space. Systems with limited swap space can employ such a different scheme when binary files are used. Demand pages for such files are brought directly from the file system. However, when page replacement is called for, these pages can simply be overwritten (because they are never modified) and read in from the file system again if needed. Yet another option is initially to demand pages from the file system, but to write the pages to swap space as they are replaced. This approach will ensure that only needed pages are ever read from the file system, but all subsequent paging is done from swap space. This method appears to be a good compromise; it is used in BSD UNIX.

9.4 ■ Page Replacement

In our presentation so far, the page-fault rate is not a serious problem, because each page is faulted for at most once, when it is first referenced. This representation is not strictly accurate. Consider that, if a process of 10 pages actually uses only one-half of them, then demand paging saves the I/O necessary to load the five pages that are never used. We could also increase our degree of multiprogramming by running twice as many processes. Thus, if we had 40 frames, we could run eight processes, rather than the four that could run if each required 10 frames (five of which were never used).

If we increase our degree of multiprogramming, we are *over-allocating* memory. If we run six processes, each of which is 10 pages in size, but actually uses only five pages, we have higher CPU utilization and throughput, with 10 frames to spare. It is possible, however, that each of these processes, for a particular data set, may suddenly try to use all 10 of its pages, resulting in a need for 60 frames, when only 40 are available. Although this situation may be unlikely, it becomes much more likely as we increase the multiprogramming level, so that the average memory usage is close to the available physical memory. (In our example, why stop at a multiprogramming level of six, when we can move to a level of seven or eight?)

Over-allocating will show up in the following way. While a user process is executing, a page fault occurs. The hardware traps to the operating system, which checks its internal tables to see that this is a page fault and not an illegal memory access. The operating system determines where the desired page is residing on the disk, but then finds there are *no* free frames on the free-frame list; all memory is in use (Figure 9.5).

The operating system has several options at this point. It could terminate the user process. However, demand paging is something that the operating system is doing to improve the computer system's utilization and throughput. Users should not be aware that their processes are running on a paged system. Paging should be logically transparent to the user. So this option is not the best choice.

We could swap out a process, freeing all its frames, and reducing the level of multiprogramming. This option is a good idea at times, and we

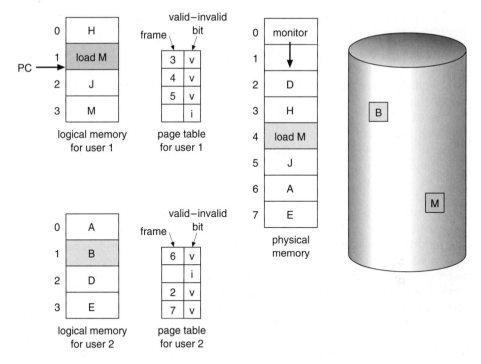

Figure 9.5 Need for page replacement.

consider it further in Section 9.7. First, we shall discuss a more intriguing possibility: *page replacement*.

Page replacement takes the following approach. If no frame is free, we find one that is not currently being used and free it. We can free a frame by writing its contents to swap space, and changing the page table (and all other tables) to indicate that the page is no longer in memory (Figure 9.6). The freed frame can now be used to hold the page for which the process faulted. The page-fault service routine is now modified to include page replacement:

1. Find the location of the desired page on the disk.

2. Find a free frame:

  a. If there is a free frame, use it.

  b. Otherwise, use a page-replacement algorithm to select a *victim* frame.

  c. Write the victim page to the disk; change the page and frame tables accordingly.

3. Read the desired page into the (newly) free frame; change the page and frame tables.

4. Restart the user process.

Notice that, if no frames are free, *two* page transfers (one out and one in) are required. This situation effectively doubles the page-fault service time and will increase the effective access time accordingly.

This overhead can be reduced by the use of a *modify (dirty) bit*. Each page or frame may have a modify bit associated with it in the hardware. The modify bit for a page is set by the hardware whenever any word or byte in the page is written into, indicating that the page has been modified. When we select a page for replacement, we examine its modify bit. If the bit is set, we know that the page has been modified since it was read in from the disk. In this case, we must write that page to the disk. If the modify bit is not set, however, the page has *not* been modified since it was read into memory. Therefore, if the copy of the page on the disk has not been overwritten (by some other page, for example), we can avoid writing the memory page to the disk; it is already there. This technique also applies to read-only pages (for example, pages of binary code). Such

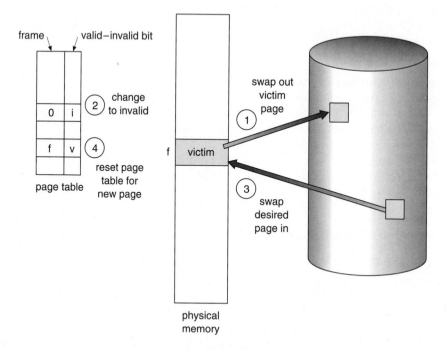

Figure 9.6 Page replacement.

pages cannot be modified; thus, they may be discarded when desired. This scheme can reduce significantly the time to service a page fault, since it reduces I/O time by one-half *if* the page is not modified.

Page replacement is basic to demand paging. It completes the separation between logical memory and physical memory. With this mechanism, a very large virtual memory can be provided for programmers on a smaller physical memory. With non-demand paging, user addresses were mapped into physical addresses, allowing the two sets of addresses to be quite different. All of the pages of a process still must be in physical memory, however. With demand paging, the size of the logical address space is no longer constrained by physical memory. If we have a user process of 20 pages, we can execute it in 10 frames simply by using demand paging, and using a replacement algorithm to find a free frame whenever necessary. If a page that has been modified is to be replaced, its contents are copied to the disk. A later reference to that page will cause a page fault. At that time, the page will be brought back into memory, perhaps replacing some other page in the process.

We must solve two major problems to implement demand paging: We must develop a *frame-allocation algorithm* and a *page-replacement algorithm.* If we have multiple processes in memory, we must decide how many frames to allocate to each process. Further, when page replacement is required, we must select the frames that are to be replaced. Designing appropriate algorithms to solve these problems is an important task, because disk I/O is so expensive. Even slight improvements in demand-paging methods yield large gains in system performance.

9.5 ■ Page-Replacement Algorithms

There are many different page-replacement algorithms. Probably every operating system has its own unique replacement scheme. How do we select a particular replacement algorithm? In general, we want the one with the lowest *page-fault rate.*

We evaluate an algorithm by running it on a particular string of memory references and computing the number of page faults. The string of memory references is called a *reference string.* We can generate reference strings artificially (by a random-number generator, for example) or by tracing a given system and recording the address of each memory reference. The latter choice produces a large number of data (on the order of 1 million addresses per second). To reduce the number of data, we note two things.

First, for a given page size (and the page size is generally fixed by the hardware or system), we need to consider only the page number, not the entire address. Second, if we have a reference to a page p, then any *immediately* following references to page *p* will never cause a page fault. Page *p* will be in memory after the first reference; the immediately following references will not fault.

For example, if we trace a particular process, we might record the following address sequence:

0100, 0432, 0101, 0612, 0102, 0103, 0104, 0101, 0611, 0102, 0103, 0104, 0101, 0610, 0102, 0103, 0104, 0101, 0609, 0102, 0105,

which, at 100 bytes per page, is reduced to the following reference string

1, 4, 1, 6, 1, 6, 1, 6, 1, 6, 1.

To determine the number of page faults for a particular reference string and page-replacement algorithm, we also need to know the number of page frames available. Obviously, as the number of frames available increases, the number of page faults will decrease. For the reference string considered previously, for example, if we had three or more frames, we would have only three faults, one fault for the first reference to each page. On the other hand, with only one frame available, we would have a replacement with every reference, resulting in 11 faults. In general, we expect a curve such as that in Figure 9.7. As the number of frames increases, the number of page faults drops to some minimal level. Of course, adding physical memory increases the number of frames.

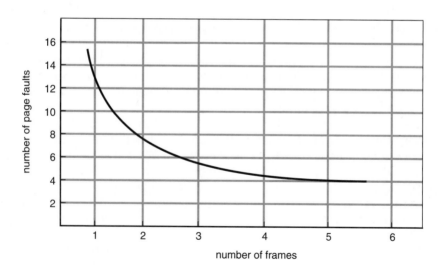

Figure 9.7 Graph of page faults versus the number of frames.

To illustrate the page-replacement algorithms, we shall use the reference string

7, 0, 1, 2, 0, 3, 0, 4, 2, 3, 0, 3, 2, 1, 2, 0, 1, 7, 0, 1

for a memory with three frames.

9.5.1 FIFO Algorithm

The simplest page-replacement algorithm is a FIFO algorithm. A FIFO replacement algorithm associates with each page the time when that page was brought into memory. When a page must be replaced, the oldest page is chosen. Notice that it is not strictly necessary to record the time when a page is brought in. We can create a FIFO queue to hold all pages in memory. We replace the page at the head of the queue. When a page is brought into memory, we insert it at the tail of the queue.

For our example reference string, our three frames are initially empty. The first three references (7, 0, 1) cause page faults, and are brought into these empty frames. The next reference (2) replaces page 7, because page 7 was brought in first. Since 0 is the next reference and 0 is already in memory, we have no fault for this reference. The first reference to 3 results in page 0 being replaced, since it was the first of the three pages in memory (0, 1, and 2) to be brought in. This replacement means that the next reference, to 0, will fault. Page 1 is then replaced by page 0. This process continues as shown in Figure 9.8. Every time a fault occurs, we show which pages are in our three frames. There are 15 faults altogether.

The FIFO page-replacement algorithm is easy to understand and program. However, its performance is not always good. The page replaced may be an initialization module that was used a long time ago and is no longer needed. On the other hand, it could contain a heavily used variable that was initialized early and is in constant use.

reference string

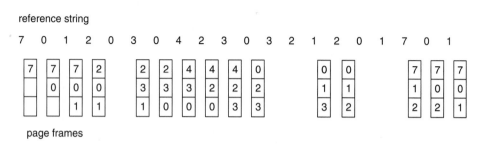

Figure 9.8 FIFO page-replacement algorithm.

Notice that, even if we select for replacement a page that is in active use, everything still works correctly. After we page out an active page to bring in a new one, a fault occurs almost immediately to retrieve the active page. Some other page will need to be replaced to bring the active page back into memory. Thus, a bad replacement choice increases the page-fault rate and slows process execution, but does not cause incorrect execution.

To illustrate the problems that are possible with a FIFO page-replacement algorithm, we consider the reference string

$$1, 2, 3, 4, 1, 2, 5, 1, 2, 3, 4, 5.$$

Figure 9.9 shows the curve of page faults versus the number of available frames. We notice that the number of faults for four frames (10) is *greater* than the number of faults for three frames (nine)! This result is most unexpected and is known as *Belady's anomaly*. Belady's anomaly reflects the fact that, for some page-replacement algorithms, the page-fault rate may *increase* as the number of allocated frames increases. We would expect that giving more memory to a process would improve its performance. In some early research, investigators noticed that this assumption was not always true. Belady's anomaly was discovered as a result.

9.5.2 Optimal Algorithm

One result of the discovery of Belady's anomaly was the search for an *optimal* page-replacement algorithm. An optimal page-replacement algorithm has the lowest page-fault rate of all algorithms. An optimal

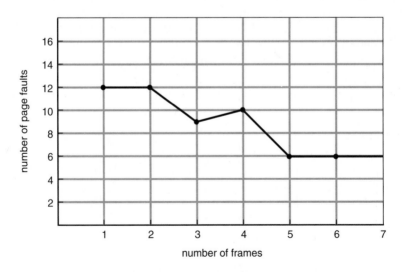

Figure 9.9 Page-fault curve for FIFO replacement on a reference string.

algorithm will never suffer from Belady's anomaly. An optimal page-replacement algorithm exists, and has been called OPT or MIN. It is simply

> Replace the page that will not be used
> for the longest period of time.

Use of this page-replacement algorithm guarantees the lowest possible page-fault rate for a fixed number of frames.

For example, on our sample reference string, the optimal page-replacement algorithm would yield nine page faults, as shown in Figure 9.10. The first three references cause faults that fill the three empty frames. The reference to page 2 replaces page 7, because 7 will not be used until reference 18, whereas page 0 will be used at 5, and page 1 at 14. The reference to page 3 replaces page 1, as page 1 will be the last of the three pages in memory to be referenced again. With only nine page faults, optimal replacement is much better than a FIFO algorithm, which had 15 faults. (If we ignore the first three, which all algorithms must suffer, then optimal replacement is twice as good as FIFO replacement.) In fact, no replacement algorithm can process this reference string in three frames with less than nine faults.

Unfortunately, the optimal page-replacement algorithm is difficult to implement, because it requires future knowledge of the reference string. (We encountered a similar situation with the SJF CPU-scheduling algorithm in Section 5.3.2.) As a result, the optimal algorithm is used mainly for comparison studies. For instance, it may be quite useful to know that, although a new algorithm is not optimal, it is within 12.3 percent of optimal at worst and within 4.7 percent on average.

9.5.3 LRU Algorithm

If the optimal algorithm is not feasible, perhaps an approximation to the optimal algorithm is possible. The key distinction between the FIFO and OPT algorithms (other than looking backward or forward in time) is that the

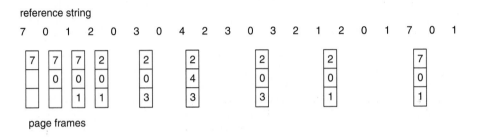

Figure 9.10 Optimal page-replacement algorithm.

reference string

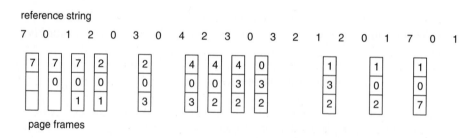

Figure 9.11 LRU page-replacement algorithm.

FIFO algorithm uses the time when a page was brought into memory; the OPT algorithm uses the time when a page is to be *used*. If we use the recent past as an approximation of the near future, then we will replace the page that *has not been used* for the longest period of time (Figure 9.11). This approach is the *least recently used (LRU)* algorithm.

LRU replacement associates with each page the time of that page's last use. When a page must be replaced, LRU chooses that page that has not been used for the longest period of time. This strategy is the optimal page-replacement algorithm looking backward in time, rather than forward. (Strangely, if we let S^R be the reverse of a reference string S, then the page-fault rate for the OPT algorithm on S is the same as the page-fault rate for the OPT algorithm on S^R. Similarly, the page-fault rate for the LRU algorithm on S is the same as the page-fault rate for the LRU algorithm on S^R.)

The result of applying LRU replacement to our example reference string is shown in Figure 9.11. The LRU algorithm produces 12 faults. Notice that the first five faults are the same as the optimal replacement. When the reference to page 4 occurs, however, LRU replacement sees that, of the three frames in memory, page 2 was used least recently. The most recently used page is page 0, and just before that page 3 was used. Thus, the LRU algorithm replaces page 2, not knowing that page 2 is about to be used. When it then faults for page 2, the LRU algorithm replaces page 3 since, of the three pages in memory {0, 3, 4}, page 3 is the least recently used. Despite these problems, LRU replacement with 12 faults is still much better than FIFO replacement with 15.

The LRU policy is often used as a page-replacement algorithm and is considered to be quite good. The major problem is *how* to implement LRU replacement. An LRU page-replacement algorithm may require substantial hardware assistance. The problem is to determine an order for the frames defined by the time of last use. Two implementations are feasible:

- **Counters:** In the simplest case, we associate with each page-table entry a time-of-use field, and add to the CPU a logical clock or counter. The clock is incremented for every memory reference. Whenever a reference to a page is made, the contents of the clock register are copied to the time-of-use field in the page table for that page. In this way, we always have the "time" of the last reference to each page. We replace the page with the smallest time value. This scheme requires a search of the page table to find the LRU page, and a write to memory (to the time-of-use field in the page table) for each memory access. The times must also be maintained when page tables are changed (due to CPU scheduling). Overflow of the clock must be considered.

● **Stack:** Another approach to implementing LRU replacement is to keep a *stack* of page numbers. Whenever a page is referenced, it is removed from the stack and put on the top. In this way, the top of the stack is always the most recently used page and the bottom is the LRU page (Figure 9.12). Because entries must be removed from the middle of the stack, it is best implemented by a doubly linked list, with a head and tail pointer. Removing a page and putting it on the top of the stack then requires changing six pointers at worst. Each update is a little more expensive, but there is no search for a replacement; the tail pointer points to the bottom of the stack, which is the LRU page. This approach is particularly appropriate for software or microcode implementations of LRU replacement.

Neither optimal replacement nor LRU replacement suffers from Belady's anomaly. There is a class of page-replacement algorithms, called *stack algorithms*, that can never exhibit Belady's anomaly. A stack algorithm is an algorithm for which it can be shown that the set of pages in memory for *n*

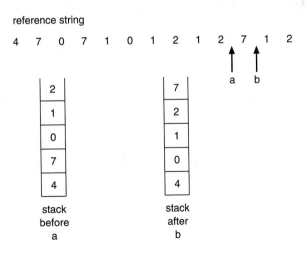

Figure 9.12   Use of a stack to record the most recent page references.

frames is always a *subset* of the set of pages that would be in memory with $n + 1$ frames. For LRU replacement, the set of pages in memory would be the n most recently referenced pages. If the number of frames is increased, these n pages will still be the most recently referenced and so will still be in memory.

Note that neither implementation of LRU would be conceivable without hardware assistance beyond the standard TLB registers. The updating of the clock fields or stack must be done for *every* memory reference. If we were to use an interrupt for every reference, to allow software to update such data structures, it would slow every memory reference by a factor of at least 10, hence slowing every user process by a factor of 10. Few systems could tolerate that level of overhead for memory management.

9.5.4 LRU Approximation Algorithms

Few systems provide sufficient hardware support for true LRU page replacement. Some systems provide no hardware support, and other page-replacement algorithms (such as a FIFO algorithm) must be used. Many systems provide some help, however, in the form of a *reference bit*. The reference bit for a page is set, by the hardware, whenever that page is referenced (either a read or a write to any byte in the page). Reference bits are associated with each entry in the page table.

Initially, all bits are cleared (to 0) by the operating system. As a user process executes, the bit associated with each page referenced is set (to 1) by the hardware. After some time, we can determine which pages have been used and which have not been used by examining the reference bits. We do not know the *order* of use, but we know which pages were used and which were not used. This partial ordering information leads to many page-replacement algorithms that approximate LRU replacement.

9.5.4.1 Additional-Reference-Bits Algorithm

We can gain additional ordering information by recording the reference bits at regular intervals. We can keep an 8-bit byte for each page in a table in memory. At regular intervals (say every 100 milliseconds), a timer interrupt transfers control to the operating system. The operating system shifts the reference bit for each page into the high-order bit of its 8-bit byte, shifting the other bits right 1 bit, discarding the low-order bit. These 8-bit shift registers contain the history of page use for the last eight time periods. If the shift register contains 00000000, then the page has not been used for eight time periods; a page that is used at least once each period would have a shift register value of 11111111.

A page with a history register value of 11000100 has been used more recently than has one with 01110111. If we interpret these 8-bit bytes as unsigned integers, the page with the lowest number is the LRU page, and it can be replaced. Notice that the numbers are not guaranteed to be unique, however. We can either replace (swap out) all pages with the smallest value, or use a FIFO selection among them.

The number of bits of history can be varied, of course, and would be selected (depending on the hardware available) to make the updating as fast as possible. In the extreme case, the number can be reduced to zero, leaving only the reference bit itself. This algorithm is called the *second-chance* page-replacement algorithm.

9.5.4.2 Second-Chance Algorithm

The basic algorithm of second-chance replacement is a FIFO replacement algorithm. When a page has been selected, however, we inspect its reference bit. If the value is 0, we proceed to replace this page. If the reference bit is 1, however, we give that page a second chance and move on to select the next FIFO page. When a page gets a second chance, its reference bit is cleared and its arrival time is reset to the current time. Thus, a page that is given a second chance will not be replaced until all other pages are replaced (or given second chances). In addition, if a page is used often enough to keep its reference bit set, it will never be replaced.

One way to implement the second-chance (sometimes referred to as the clock) algorithm is as a circular queue. A pointer indicates which page is to be replaced next. When a frame is needed, the pointer advances until it finds a page with a 0 reference bit. As it advances, it clears the reference bits (Figure 9.13). Once a victim page is found, the page is replaced and the new page is inserted in the circular queue in that position. Notice that, in the worst case, when all bits are set, the pointer cycles through the whole queue, giving each page a second chance. It clears all the reference bits before selecting the next page for replacement. Second-chance replacement degenerates to FIFO replacement if all bits are set.

9.5.4.3 Enhanced Second-Chance Algorithm

The second-chance algorithm described above can be enhanced by considering both the reference bit and the modify bit (Section 9.4) as an ordered pair. With these 2 bits, we have the following four possible classes:

1. (0,0) neither recently used nor modified - best page to replace

2. (0,1) not recently used but modified - not quite as good, because the page will need to be written out before replacement

3. (1,0) recently used but clean - probably will be used again soon

4. (1,1) recently used and modified - probably will be used again, and write out will be needed before replacing it

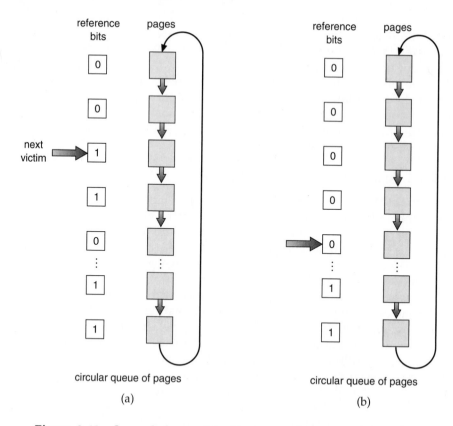

Figure 9.13   Second-chance (clock) page-replacement algorithm.

When page replacement is called for, each page is in one of these four classes. We use the same scheme as the clock algorithm, but instead of examining whether the page to which we are pointing has the reference bit set to 1, we examine the class to which that page belongs. We replace the first page encountered in the lowest nonempty class. Notice that we may have to scan the circular queue several times before we find a page to be replaced.

This algorithm is used in the Macintosh virtual-memory-management scheme. The major difference between this algorithm and the simpler clock algorithm is that here we give preference to those pages that have been modified to reduce the number of I/Os required.

9.5.5   Counting Algorithms

There are many other algorithms that can be used for page replacement. For example, we could keep a counter of the number of references that have been made to each page, and develop the following two schemes.

- LFU **Algorithm:** The *least frequently used (LFU)* page-replacement algorithm requires that the page with the smallest count be replaced. The reason for this selection is that an actively used page should have a large reference count. This algorithm suffers from the situation in which a page is used heavily during the initial phase of a process, but then is never used again. Since it was used heavily, it has a large count and remains in memory even though it is no longer needed. One solution is to shift the counts right by 1 bit at regular intervals, forming an exponentially decaying average usage count.

- MFU **Algorithm:** The *most frequently used (MFU)* page-replacement algorithm is based on the argument that the page with the smallest count was probably just brought in and has yet to be used.

As you might expect, neither MFU nor LFU replacement is common. The implementation of these algorithms is fairly expensive, and they do not approximate OPT replacement very well.

9.5.6 Page Buffering Algorithm

Other procedures are often used in addition to a specific page-replacement algorithm. For example, systems commonly keep a *pool* of free frames. When a page fault occurs, a victim frame is chosen as before. However, the desired page is read into a free frame from the pool before the victim is written out. This procedure allows the process to restart as soon as possible, without waiting for the victim page to be written out. When the victim is later written out, its frame is added to the free-frame pool.

An expansion of this idea is to maintain a list of modified pages. Whenever the paging device is idle, a modified page is selected and is written to the disk. Its modify bit is then reset. This scheme increases the probability that a page will be clean when it is selected for replacement, and will not need to be written out.

Another modification is to keep a pool of free frames, but to remember which page was in each frame. Since the frame contents are not modified when a frame is written to the disk, the old page can be reused directly from the free-frame pool if it is needed before that frame is reused. No I/O is needed in this case. When a page fault occurs, we first check whether the desired page is in the free-frame pool. If it is not, we must select a free frame and read into it.

This technique is used in the VAX/VMS system, with a FIFO replacement algorithm. When the FIFO replacement algorithm mistakenly replaces a page that is still in active use, that page is quickly retrieved from the free-frame buffer, and no I/O is necessary. The free-frame buffer provides protection against the relatively poor, but simple, FIFO replacement algorithm. This method is necessary because the early versions of the VAX did not correctly implement the reference bit.

9.6 ■ Allocation of Frames

How do we allocate the fixed amount of free memory among the various processes? If we have 93 free frames and two processes, how many frames does each process get?

The simplest case of virtual memory is the single-user system. Consider a single-user microcomputer system with 128K memory composed of pages of size 1K. Thus, there are 128 frames. The operating system may take 35K, leaving 93 frames for the user process. Under pure demand paging, all 93 frames would initially be put on the free-frame list. When a user process started execution, it would generate a sequence of page faults. The first 93 page faults would all get free frames from the free-frame list. When the free-frame list was exhausted, a page-replacement algorithm would be used to select one of the 93 in-memory pages to be replaced with the ninety-fourth, and so on. When the process terminated, the 93 frames would once again be placed on the free-frame list.

There are many variations on this simple strategy. We can require that the operating system allocate all its buffer and table space from the free-frame list. When this space is not in use by the operating system, it can be used to support user paging. We could try to keep three free frames reserved on the free-frame list at all times. Thus, when a page fault occurs, there is a free frame available to page into. While the page swap is taking place, a replacement can be selected, which is then written to the disk as the user process continues to execute.

Other variants are also possible, but the basic strategy is clear: The user process is allocated any free frame.

A different problem arises when demand paging is combined with multiprogramming. Multiprogramming puts two (or more) processes in memory at the same time.

9.6.1 Minimum Number of Frames

There are, of course, various constraints on our strategies for the allocations of frames. We cannot allocate more than the total number of available frames (unless there is page sharing). There is also a minimum number of frames that can be allocated. Obviously, as the number of frames allocated to each process decreases, the page fault-rate increases, slowing process execution.

Besides the undesirable performance properties of allocating only a few frames, there is a minimum number of frames that must be allocated. This minimum number is defined by the instruction-set architecture. Remember that, when a page fault occurs before an executing instruction is complete, the instruction must be restarted. Consequently, we must have enough frames to hold all the different pages that any single instruction can reference.

For example, consider a machine in which all memory-reference instructions have only one memory address. Thus, we need at least one frame for the instruction and one frame for the memory reference. In addition, if one-level indirect addressing is allowed (for example, a load instruction on page 16 can refer to an address on page 0, which is an indirect reference to page 23), then paging requires at least three frames per process. Think about what might happen if a process had only two frames.

The minimum number of frames is defined by the computer architecture. For example, the move instruction for the PDP-11 is more than one word for some addressing modes, and thus the instruction itself may straddle two pages. In addition, each of its two operands may be indirect references, for a total of six frames. The worst case for the IBM 370 is probably the MVC instruction. Since the instruction is storage to storage, it takes 6 bytes and can straddle two pages. The block of characters to move and the area to be moved to can each also straddle two pages. This situation would require six frames. (Actually, the worst case is if the MVC instruction is the operand of an EXECUTE instruction that straddles a page boundary; in this case, we need eight frames.)

The worst-case scenario occurs in architectures that allow multiple levels of indirection (for example, each 16-bit word could contain a 15-bit address plus a 1-bit indirect indicator). Theoretically, a simple load instruction could reference an indirect address that could reference an indirect address (on another page) that could also reference an indirect address (on yet another page), and so on, until every page in virtual memory had been touched. Thus, in the worst case, the entire virtual memory must be in physical memory. To overcome this difficulty, we must place a limit on the levels of indirection (for example, limit an instruction to at most 16 levels of indirection). When the first indirection occurs, a counter is set to 16; the counter is then decremented for each successive indirection for this instruction. If the counter is decremented to 0, a trap occurs (excessive indirection). This limitation reduces the maximum number of memory references per instruction to 17, requiring the same number of frames.

The minimum number of frames per process is defined by the architecture, whereas the maximum number is defined by the amount of available physical memory. In between, we are still left with significant choice in frame allocation.

9.6.2 Allocation Algorithms

The easiest way to split m frames among n processes is to give everyone an equal share, m/n frames. For instance, if there are 93 frames and five processes, each process will get 18 frames. The leftover three frames could be used as a free-frame buffer pool. This scheme is called *equal allocation*.

An alternative is to recognize that various processes will need differing amounts of memory. If a small student process of 10K and an interactive database of 127K are the only two processes running in a system with 62 free frames, it does not make much sense to give each process 31 frames. The student process does not need more than 10 frames, so the other 21 are strictly wasted.

To solve this problem, we can use *proportional allocation*. We allocate available memory to each process according to its size. Let the size of the virtual memory for process p_i be s_i, and define

$$S = \Sigma \ s_i.$$

Then, if the total number of available frames is m, we allocate a_i frames to process p_i, where a_i is approximately

$$a_i = s_i/S \times m.$$

Of course, we must adjust each a_i to be an integer, which is greater than the minimum number of frames required by the instruction set, with a sum not exceeding m.

For proportional allocation, we would split 62 frames between two processes, one of 10 pages and one of 127 pages, by allocating four frames and 57 frames, respectively, since

$$10/137 \times 62 \ \simeq \ 4,$$
$$127/137 \times 62 \ \simeq \ 57.$$

In this way, both processes share the available frames according to their "needs," rather than equally.

In both equal and proportional allocation, of course, the allocation to each process may vary according to the multiprogramming level. If the multiprogramming level is increased, each process will lose some frames to provide the memory needed for the new process. On the other hand, if the multiprogramming level decreases, the frames that had been allocated to the departed process can now be spread over the remaining processes.

Notice that, with either equal or proportional allocation, a high-priority process is treated the same as a low-priority process. By its definition, however, we may want to give the high-priority process more memory to speed its execution, to the detriment of low-priority processes.

One approach is to use a proportional allocation scheme where the ratio of frames depends not on the relative sizes of processes, but rather on the processes' priorities, or on a combination of size and priority.

9.6.3 Global Versus Local Allocation

Another important factor in the way frames are allocated to the various processes is page replacement. With multiple processes competing for frames, we can classify page-replacement algorithms into two broad categories: *global replacement* and *local replacement*. Global replacement allows a process to select a replacement frame from the set of all frames, even if that frame is currently allocated to some other process; one process can take a frame from another. Local replacement requires that each process select from only its own set of allocated frames.

For example, consider an allocation scheme where we allow high-priority processes to select frames from low-priority processes for replacement. A process can select a replacement from among its own frames or the frames of any lower-priority process. This approach allows a high-priority process to increase its frame allocation at the expense of the low-priority process.

With a local replacement strategy, the number of frames allocated to a process does not change. With global replacement, a process may happen to select only frames allocated to other processes, thus increasing the number of frames allocated to it (assuming that other processes do not choose *its* frames for replacement).

One problem with a global replacement algorithm is that a process cannot control its own page-fault rate. The set of pages in memory for a process depends not only on the paging behavior of that process, but also on the paging behavior of other processes. Therefore, the same process may perform quite differently (taking 0.5 seconds for one execution and 10.3 seconds for the next execution) due to totally external circumstances. Such is not the case with a local replacement algorithm. Under local replacement, the set of pages in memory for a process is affected by the paging behavior of only that process. For its part, local replacement might hinder a process by not making available to it other, less used pages of memory. Thus, global replacement generally results in greater system throughput, and is therefore the more common method.

9.7 ■ Thrashing

If the number of frames allocated to a low-priority process falls below the minimum number required by the computer architecture, we must suspend that process' execution. We should then page out its remaining pages, freeing all its allocated frames. This provision introduces a swap-in, swap-out level of intermediate CPU scheduling.

In fact, look at any process that does not have "enough" frames. Although it is technically possible to reduce the number of allocated frames to the minimum, there is some (larger) number of pages that are in active use. If the process does not have this number of frames, it will very quickly page fault. At this point, it must replace some page. However, since all its pages are in active use, it must replace a page that will be needed again right away. Consequently, it very quickly faults again, and again, and again. The process continues to fault, replacing pages for which it will then fault and bring back in right away.

This high paging activity is called *thrashing*. A process is thrashing if it is spending more time paging than executing.

9.7.1 Cause of Thrashing

Thrashing results in severe performance problems. Consider the following scenario, which is based on the actual behavior of early paging systems.

The operating system monitors CPU utilization. If CPU utilization is too low, we increase the degree of multiprogramming by introducing a new process to the system. A global page-replacement algorithm is used, replacing pages with no regard to the process to which they belong. Now suppose a process enters a new phase in its execution and needs more frames. It starts faulting and taking pages away from other processes. These processes need those pages, however, and so they also fault, taking pages from other processes. These faulting processes must use the paging device to swap pages in and out. As they queue up for the paging device, the ready queue empties. As processes wait for the paging device, CPU utilization decreases.

The CPU scheduler sees the decreasing CPU utilization, and *increases* the degree of multiprogramming as a result. The new process tries to get started by taking pages from running processes, causing more page faults, and a longer queue for the paging device. As a result, CPU utilization drops even further, and the CPU scheduler tries to increase the degree of multiprogramming even more. Thrashing has occurred and system throughput plunges. The page-fault rate increases tremendously. As a result, the effective memory access time increases. No work is getting done, because the processes are spending all their time paging.

This phenomenon is illustrated in Figure 9.14. CPU utilization is plotted against the degree of multiprogramming. As the degree of multiprogramming increases, CPU utilization also increases, although more slowly, until a maximum is reached. If the degree of multiprogramming is increased even further, thrashing sets in and CPU utilization drops sharply. At this point, to increase CPU utilization and stop thrashing, we must *decrease* the degree of multiprogramming.

The effects of thrashing can be limited by using a *local (or priority) replacement algorithm*. With local replacement, if one process starts thrashing, it cannot steal frames from another process and cause the latter to thrash also. Pages are replaced with regard to the process of which they are a part. However, if processes are thrashing, they will be in the queue

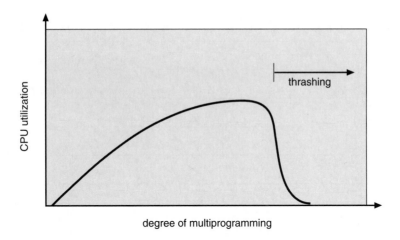

Figure 9.14 Thrashing.

for the paging device most of the time. The average service time for a page fault will increase, due to the longer average queue for the paging device. Thus, the effective access time will increase even for a process that is not thrashing.

To prevent thrashing, we must provide a process as many frames as it needs. But how do we know how many frames it "needs"? There are several techniques. The working-set strategy (discussed in Section 9.7.2) starts by looking at how many frames a process is actually using. This approach defines the *locality model* of process execution.

The locality model states that, as a process executes, it moves from locality to locality. A locality is a set of pages that are actively used together (Figure 9.15). A program is generally composed of several different localities, which may overlap.

For example, when a subroutine is called, it defines a new locality. In this locality, memory references are made to the instructions of the subroutine, its local variables, and a subset of the global variables. When the subroutine is exited, the process leaves this locality, since the local variables and instructions of the subroutine are no longer in active use. We may return to this locality later. Thus, we see that localities are defined by the program structure and its data structures. The locality model states that all programs will exhibit this basic memory reference structure. Note that the locality model is the unstated principle behind the caching discussions so far in this book. If accesses to any types of data were random rather than patterned, caching would be useless.

Suppose that we allocate enough frames to a process to accommodate its current locality. It will fault for the pages in its locality until all these pages are in memory; then, it will not fault again until it changes localities.

Figure 9.15 Locality in a memory reference pattern.

If we allocate fewer frames than the size of the current locality, the process will thrash, since it cannot keep in memory all the pages that it is actively using.

9.7.2 Working-Set Model

The *working-set model* is based on the assumption of locality. This model uses a parameter, Δ, to define the *working-set window*. The idea is to examine the most recent Δ page references. The set of pages in the most recent Δ page references is the *working set* (Figure 9.16). If a page is in active use, it will be in the working set. If it is no longer being used, it will drop from the working set Δ time units after its last reference. Thus, the working set is an approximation of the program's locality.

For example, given the sequence of memory references shown in Figure 9.16, if Δ = 10 memory references, then the working set at time t_1 is {1, 2, 5, 6, 7}. By time t_2, the working set has changed to {3, 4}.

The accuracy of the working set depends on the selection of Δ. If Δ is too small, it will not encompass the entire locality; if Δ is too large, it may overlap several localities. In the extreme, if Δ is infinite, the working set is the set of pages touched during the process execution.

The most important property of the working set is its size. If we compute the working-set size, WSS_i, for each process in the system, we can then consider

$$D = \Sigma \ WSS_i,$$

where D is the total demand for frames. Each process is actively using the pages in its working set. Thus, process i needs WSS_i frames. If the total demand is greater than the total number of available frames ($D > m$), thrashing will occur, because some processes will not have enough frames.

The use of the working-set model is then quite simple. The operating system monitors the working set of each process and allocates to that working set enough frames to provide it with its working-set size. If there are enough extra frames, another process can be initiated. If the sum of the working-set sizes increases, exceeding the total number of available frames, the operating system selects a process to suspend. The process' pages are written out and its frames are relocated to other processes. The suspended process can be restarted later.

This working-set strategy prevents thrashing while keeping the degree of multiprogramming as high as possible. Thus, it optimizes CPU utilization.

The difficulty with the working-set model is keeping track of the working set. The working-set window is a moving window. At each memory reference, a new reference appears at one end and the oldest reference drops off the other end. A page is in the working set if it is referenced anywhere in the working-set window. We can approximate the working-set model with a fixed interval timer interrupt and a reference bit.

page reference table

. . . 2 6 1 5 7 7 7 7 5 1 6 2 3 4 1 2 3 4 4 4 3 4 3 4 4 4 1 3 2 3 4 4 4 3 4 4 4 . . .

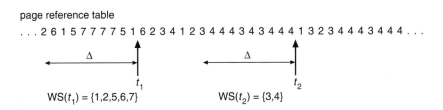

WS(t_1) = {1,2,5,6,7}   WS(t_2) = {3,4}

Figure 9.16 Working-set model.

For example, assume Δ is 10,000 references and we can cause a timer interrupt every 5000 references. When we get a timer interrupt, we copy and clear the reference-bit values for each page. Thus, if a page fault occurs, we can examine the current reference bit and 2 in-memory bits to determine whether a page was used within the last 10,000 to 15,000 references. If it was used, at least 1 of these bits will be on. If it has not been used, these bits will be off. Those pages with at least 1 bit on will be considered to be in the working set. Note that this arrangement is not entirely accurate, because we cannot tell where, within an interval of 5000, a reference occurred. We can reduce the uncertainty by increasing the number of our history bits and the number of interrupts (for example, 10 bits and interrupts every 1000 references). However, the cost to service these more frequent interrupts will be correspondingly higher.

9.7.3 Page-Fault Frequency

The working-set model is successful, and knowledge of the working set can be useful for prepaging (Section 9.8.1), but it seems a clumsy way to control thrashing. The *page-fault frequency (PFF)* strategy takes a more direct approach.

The specific problem is how to prevent thrashing. Thrashing has a high page-fault rate. Thus, we want to control the page-fault rate. When it is too high, we know that the process needs more frames. Similarly, if the page-fault rate is too low, then the process may have too many frames. We can establish upper and lower bounds on the desired page-fault rate (Figure 9.17). If the actual page-fault rate exceeds the upper limit, we allocate that process another frame; if the page-fault rate falls below the lower limit, we remove a frame from that process. Thus, we can directly measure and control the page-fault rate to prevent thrashing.

As with the working-set strategy, we may have to suspend a process. If the page-fault rate increases and no free frames are available, we must select some process and suspend it. The freed frames are then distributed to processes with high page-fault rates.

9.8 ■ Other Considerations

The selections of a replacement algorithm and allocation policy are the major decisions to make for a paging system. There are many other considerations as well.

9.8.1 Prepaging

An obvious property of a pure demand-paging system is the large number of page faults that occur when a process is started. This situation is a result

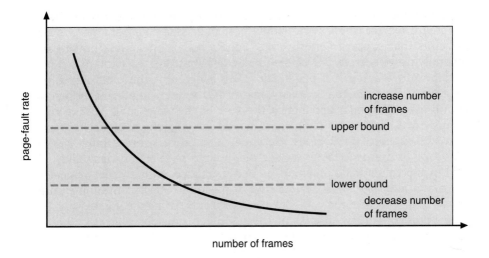

Figure 9.17 Page-fault frequency.

of trying to get the initial locality into memory. The same thing may happen at other times. For instance, when a swapped-out process is restarted, all its pages are on the disk and each must be brought in by its own page fault. *Prepaging* is an attempt to prevent this high level of initial paging. The strategy is to bring into memory at one time all the pages that will be needed.

In a system using the working-set model, for example, we keep with each process a list of the pages in its working set. If we must suspend a process (due to an I/O wait or a lack of free frames), we remember the working set for that process. When the process is to be resumed (I/O completion or enough free frames), we automatically bring its entire working set back into memory before restarting the process.

Prepaging may be an advantage in some cases. The question is simply whether the cost of prepaging is less than the cost of servicing the corresponding page faults. It may well be the case that many of the pages brought back into memory by prepaging are not used. Assume that s pages are prepaged and a fraction α of these s pages are actually used ($0 \leq \alpha \leq 1$). The question is whether the cost of the α saved page faults is greater or less than the cost of prepaging $(1 - \alpha)$ unnecessary pages. If α is close to zero, prepaging loses; if α is close to one, prepaging wins.

9.8.2 Page Size

The designers of an operating system for an existing machine seldom have a choice concerning the page size. However, when new machines are being designed, a decision regarding the best page size must be made. As you might expect, there is no single best page size. Rather, there is a set of factors that support various sizes. Page sizes are invariably powers of 2, generally ranging from 512 (2^9) to 16,384 (2^{14}) bytes.

How do we select a page size? One concern is the size of the page table. For a given virtual memory space, decreasing the page size increases the number of pages, and hence the size of the page table. For a virtual memory of 4 megabytes (2^{22}), there would be 4096 pages of 1024 bytes but only 512 pages of 8192 bytes. Because each active process must have its own copy of the page table, we see that a large page size is desirable.

On the other hand, memory is better utilized with smaller pages. If a process is allocated memory starting at location 00000, continuing until it has as much as it needs, the process probably will not end exactly on a page boundary. Thus, a part of the last page must be allocated (because pages are the units of allocation) but is unused (internal fragmentation). Assuming independence of process size and page size, we would expect that, on the average, one-half of the last page of each process will be wasted. This loss would be only 256 bytes for a page of 512 bytes, but would be 4096 bytes for a page of 8192 bytes. To minimize internal fragmentation, we need a small page size.

Another problem is the time required to read or write a page. I/O time is composed of seek, latency, and transfer times. Transfer time is proportional to the amount transferred (that is, the page size), a fact that would seem to argue for a small page size. Remember from Chapter 2, however, that latency and seek time normally dwarf transfer time. At a transfer rate of 2 megabytes per second, it takes only 0.2 milliseconds to transfer 512 bytes. Latency, on the other hand, is perhaps 8 milliseconds and seek time 20 milliseconds. Of the total I/O time (28.2 milliseconds), therefore, 1 percent is attributable to the actual transfer. Doubling the page size increases I/O time to only 28.4 milliseconds. It takes 28.4 milliseconds to read a single page of 1024 bytes, but 56.4 milliseconds to read the same amount as two pages of 512 bytes each. Thus, a desire to minimize I/O time argues for a larger page size.

With a smaller page size however, total I/O should be reduced, since locality will be improved. A smaller page size allows each page to match program locality more accurately. For example, consider a process of size 200K, of which only one-half (100K) are actually used in an execution. If we have only one large page, we must bring in the entire page, a total of 200K transferred and allocated. If we had pages of only 1 byte, then we could bring in only the 100K that are actually used, resulting in only 100K being transferred and allocated. With a smaller page size, we have better *resolution*, allowing us to isolate only the memory that is actually needed. With a larger page size we must allocate and transfer not only what is needed, but also anything else that happens to be in the page, whether it is needed or not. Thus, a smaller page size should result in less I/O and less total allocated memory.

On the other hand, did you notice that with a page size of 1 byte, we would have a page fault for *each* byte? A process of 200K, using only one-half of that memory, would generate only one page fault with a page size of 200K, but 102,400 page faults for a page size of 1 byte. Each page fault generates the large amount of overhead needed for processing the interrupt, saving registers, replacing a page, queueing for the paging device, and updating tables. To minimize the number of page faults, we need to have a large page size.

The historical trend is toward larger page sizes. Indeed, the first edition of this book (1983) used 4096 bytes as the upper bound on page sizes, and this value was the most common page size in 1990. The Intel 80386 has a page size of 4K; the Motorola 68030 allows page sizes to vary from 256 bytes to 32K. The evolution to larger page sizes is probably the result of CPU speeds and main memory capacity increasing faster than have disk speeds. Page faults are more costly today, in overall system performance, than previously. It is therefore advantageous to increase page sizes to reduce their frequency. Of course, there is more internal fragmentation as a result.

There are other factors to consider (such as the relationship between page size and sector size on the paging device). The problem has no best answer. Some factors (internal fragmentation, locality) argue for a small page size, whereas others (table size, I/O time) argue for a large page size. At least two systems allow two different page sizes. The MULTICS hardware (GE 645) allows pages of either 64 words or 1024 words. The IBM/370 allows pages of either 2K or 4K. The difficulty of picking a page size is illustrated by the fact that MVS on the IBM/370 selected 4K pages, whereas VS/1 selected 2K pages.

9.8.3 Program Structure

Demand paging is designed to be transparent to the user program. In many cases, the user is completely unaware of the paged nature of memory. In other cases, however, system performance can be improved by an awareness of the underlying demand paging.

As a contrived but informative example, assume pages are 128 words in size. Consider a Pascal program whose function is to initialize to 0 each element of a 128 by 128 array. The following code is typical:

```
var A: array [1..128] of array [1..128] of integer;
    for j := 1 to 128
      do for i := 1 to 128
        do A[i][j] := 0;
```

Notice that the array is stored row major. That is, the array is stored $A[1][1]$, $A[1][2]$, ..., $A[1][128]$, $A[2][1]$, $A[2][2]$, ..., $A[128][128]$. For pages of 128 words, each row takes one page. Thus, the proceeding code zeros one word in each page, then another word in each page, and so on. If the operating system allocates less than 128 frames to the entire program, then its execution will result in $128 \times 128 = 16,384$ page faults. Changing the code to

```
var A: array [1..128] of array [1..128] of integer;
    for i := 1 to 128
        do for j := 1 to 128
            do A[i][j] := 0;
```

on the other hand, zeros all the words on one page before starting the next page, reducing the number of page faults to 128.

Careful selection of data structures and programming structures can increase locality and hence lower the page-fault rate and the number of pages in the working set. A stack has good locality since access is always made to the top. A hash table, on the other hand, is designed to scatter references, producing bad locality. Of course, locality of reference is just one measure of the efficiency of the use of a data structure. Other heavily weighed factors include search speed, total number of memory references, and the total number of pages touched.

At a later stage, the compiler and loader can have a significant effect on paging. Separating code and data and generating reentrant code means that code pages can be read-only and hence will never be modified. Clean pages do not have to be paged out to be replaced. The loader can avoid placing routines across page boundaries, keeping each routine completely in one page. Routines that call each other many times can be packed into the same page. This packaging is a variant of the bin-packing problem of operations research: Try to pack the variable-sized load segments into the fixed-sized pages so that interpage references are minimized. Such an approach is particularly useful for large page sizes.

The choice of programming language can affect paging as well. For example, LISP uses pointers frequently, and pointers tend to randomize access to memory. Contrast LISP with PASCAL, which uses few pointers. PASCAL programs will have better locality of reference and therefore generally will execute faster than LISP programs on a virtual memory system.

9.8.4 I/O Interlock

When demand paging is used, we sometimes need to allow some of the pages to be *locked* in memory. One such situation occurs when I/O is done to or from user (virtual) memory. I/O is often implemented by a separate I/O processor. For example, a magnetic-tape controller is generally given the number of bytes to transfer and a memory address for the buffer (Figure 9.18). When the transfer is complete, the CPU is interrupted.

We must be sure the following sequence of events does not occur: A process issues an I/O request, and is put in a queue for that I/O device. Meanwhile, the CPU is given to other processes. These processes cause page faults, and, using a global replacement algorithm, one of them replaces the page containing the memory buffer for the waiting process. The pages are paged out. Some time later, when the I/O request advances to the head of the device queue, the I/O occurs to the specified address. However, this frame is now being used for a different page belonging to another process.

There are two common solutions to this problem. One solution is never to execute I/O to user memory. Instead, data are always copied between system memory and user memory. I/O takes place only between system memory and the I/O device. To write a block on tape, we first copy the block to system memory, and then write it to tape.

This extra copying may result in unacceptably high overhead. Another solution is to allow pages to be *locked* into memory. A lock bit is associated with every frame. If the frame is locked, it cannot be selected for replacement. Under this approach, to write a block on tape, we lock into memory the pages containing the block. The system can then continue as

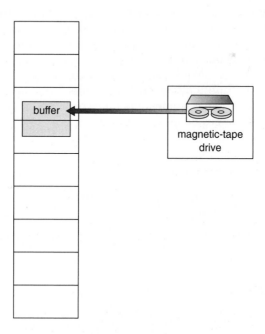

Figure 9.18 Diagram showing why frames used for I/O must be in memory.

usual. Locked pages cannot be replaced. When the I/O is complete, the pages are unlocked.

Another use for a lock bit involves normal page replacement. Consider the following sequence of events. A low-priority process faults. Selecting a replacement frame, the paging system reads the necessary page into memory. Ready to continue, the low-priority process enters the ready queue and waits for the CPU. Since it is a low-priority process, it may not be selected by the CPU scheduler for a while. While the low-priority process waits, a high-priority process faults. Looking for a replacement, the paging system sees a page that is in memory but has not been referenced or modified: the page the low-priority process just brought in. This page looks like a perfect replacement; it is clean and will not need to be written out, and it apparently has not been used for a long time.

Deciding whether the high-priority process should be able to replace the low-priority process is a policy decision. After all, we are simply delaying the low-priority process for the benefit of the high-priority process. On the other hand, we are wasting the effort spent to bring in the page of the low-priority process. If we decide to prevent replacing a newly brought-in page until it can be used at least once, then we can use the lock bit to implement this mechanism. When a page is selected for replacement, its lock bit is turned on and remains on until the faulting process is again dispatched.

Using a lock bit can be dangerous, however, if it gets turned on but never gets turned off. Should this situation occur (due to a bug in the operating system, for example), the locked frame becomes unusable. The Macintosh Operating System provides a page locking mechanism because it is a single-user system, and the overuse of locking would only hurt the user doing the locking. Multi-user systems need to be less trusting of users. For instance, SunOS allows locking "hints," but is free to disregard them if the free page pool becomes too small or if an individual process is requesting too many pages be locked in memory.

9.8.5 Real-Time Processing

The discussions in this chapter have concentrated on providing the best overall utilization of a computer system by optimizing the use of memory. By using memory for active data, and moving inactive data to disk, we increase overall system throughput. However, individual processes may suffer as a result, because they now may take additional page faults during their execution.

Consider a real-time process or thread, as described in Chapter 4. Such a process expects to gain control of the CPU, and to run to completion with a minimum of delays. Virtual memory is the antithesis of real-time computing, because it can introduce unexpected, long-term delays in the execution of a process while pages are brought into memory. Therefore, real-time systems almost never have virtual memory.

In the case of Solaris 2, Sun wanted to allow both time-sharing and real-time computing within a system. To solve the page fault problem, Solaris 2 allows a process to tell the system which pages are important to that process. In addition to allowing "hints" on page use that we have mentioned, the operating system allows privileged users to require pages to be locked into memory. If abused, this mechanism could lock all other processes out of the system. It is necessary to allow real-time processes to have bounded and low dispatch latency.

9.9 ■ Demand Segmentation

Although demand paging is generally considered the most efficient virtual-memory system, a significant amount of hardware is required to implement it. When this hardware is lacking, less efficient means are sometimes devised to provide virtual memory. A case in point is *demand segmentation*. The Intel 80286 does not include paging features, but does have segments. The OS/2 operating system, which runs on this CPU, uses the segmentation hardware to implement demand segmentation as the only possible approximation of demand paging.

OS/2 allocates memory in segments, rather than in pages. It keeps track of these segments through *segment descriptors*, which include information about the segment's size, protections, and location. A process does not need to have all its segments in memory to execute. Instead, the segment descriptor contains a valid bit for each segment to indicate whether the segment is currently in memory. When a process addresses a segment containing either code or data, the hardware checks this valid bit. If the segment is in main memory, the access continues unhindered. If the segment is not in memory, a trap to the operating system occurs (segment fault), just as in demand-paging implementations. OS/2 then swaps out a segment to secondary storage, and brings in the entire requested segment. The interrupted instruction (the one causing the segment fault) then continues.

To determine which segment to replace in case of a segment fault, OS/2 uses another bit in the segment descriptor called *accessed bit*. An accessed bit serves the same purpose as does a reference bit in a demand-paging environment. It is set whenever any byte in the segment is either read or written. A queue is kept containing an entry for each segment in memory. After every time slice, the operating system places at the head of the queue any segments with a set access bit. It then clears all access bits. In this way, the queue stays ordered with the most recently used segments at the head. In addition, OS/2 provides system calls that processes can use to inform the system of those segments that can either be discarded, or must always remain in memory. This information is used to rearrange the entries in the queue. When an invalid-segment trap occurs, the memory-management routines first determine whether there is sufficient free memory space to accommodate the segment. Memory compaction may be done to get rid of external fragmentation. If, after compaction, there is still not sufficient free memory, segment replacement is performed. The segment at the end of the queue is chosen for replacement and is written to swap space. If the newly freed space is large enough to accommodate the requested segment, then the requested segment is read into the vacated segment, the segment descriptor is updated, and the segment is placed at the head of the queue. Otherwise, memory compaction is performed, and the procedure is repeated.

It should be clear that demand segmentation requires considerable overhead. Thus, demand segmentation is not an optimal means for making best use of the resources of a computer system. The alternative on less sophisticated hardware is, however, no virtual memory at all. Given the problems entailed in systems lacking virtual memory, such as those described in Chapter 8, that solution is also lacking. Demand segmentation is therefore a reasonable compromise of functionality given hardware constraints that make demand paging impossible.

9.10 ■ Summary

It is desirable to be able to execute a process whose logical address space is larger than the available physical address space. The programmer can make such a process executable by restructuring it using overlays, but this is generally a difficult programming task. Virtual memory is a technique to allow a large logical address space to be mapped onto a smaller physical memory. Virtual memory allows extremely large processes to be run, and also allows the degree of multiprogramming to be raised, increasing CPU utilization. Further, it frees application programmers from worrying about memory availability.

Pure demand paging never brings in a page until that page is actually referenced. The first reference causes a page fault to the operating-system resident monitor. The operating system consults an internal table to determine where the page is located on the backing store. It then finds a free frame and reads the page in from the backing store. The page table is updated to reflect this change, and the instruction that caused the page fault is restarted. This approach allows a process to run even though its entire memory image is not in main memory at once. As long as the page-fault rate is reasonably low, performance is acceptable.

Demand paging can be used to reduce the number of frames allocated to a process. This arrangement can raise the degree of multiprogramming (allowing more processes to be available for execution at one time) and —

in theory, at least — the CPU utilization of the system. It also allows processes to be run even though their memory requirements exceed the total available physical memory. Such processes run in virtual memory.

If total memory requirements exceed the physical memory, then it may be necessary to replace pages from memory to free frames for new pages. Various page-replacement algorithms are used. FIFO page replacement is easy to program, but suffers from Belady's anomaly. Optimal page replacement requires future knowledge. LRU replacement is an approximation of optimal, but even it may be difficult to implement. Most page-replacement algorithms, such as the second-chance algorithm, are approximations of LRU replacement.

In addition to a page-replacement algorithm, a frame-allocation policy is needed. Allocation can be fixed, suggesting local page replacement, or dynamic, suggesting global replacement. The working-set model assumes that processes execute in localities. The working set is the set of pages in the current locality. Accordingly, each process should be allocated enough frames for its current working set.

If a process does not have enough memory for its working set, it will thrash. Providing enough frames to each process to avoid thrashing may require process swapping and scheduling.

In addition to requiring that we solve the major problems of page replacement and frame allocation, the proper design of a paging system requires that we consider page size, I/O, locking, prepaging, program structure, and other topics. Virtual memory can be thought of as one level of a hierarchy of storage levels in a computer system. Each level has its own access time, size, and cost parameters. A full example of a hybrid, functional virtual-memory system is presented in Chapter 20.

■ Exercises

9.1 When do page faults occur? Describe the actions taken by the operating system when a page fault occurs.

9.2 Assume you have a page reference string for a process with m frames (initially all empty). The page reference string has length p with n distinct page numbers occurring in it. For any page-replacement algorithms,

    a. What is a lower bound on the number of page faults?

    b. What is an upper bound on the number of page faults?

9.3 A certain computer provides its users with a virtual-memory space of 2^{32} bytes. The computer has 2^{18} bytes of physical memory. The virtual memory is implemented by paging, and the page size is 4096 bytes. A user process generates the virtual address 11123456. Explain how the system establishes the corresponding physical location. Distinguish between software and hardware operations.

9.4 Which of the following programming techniques and structures are "good" for a demand-paged environment ? Which are "not good"? Explain your answers.

a. Stack

b. Hashed symbol table

c. Sequential search

d. Binary search

e. Pure code

f. Vector operations

g. Indirection

9.5 Suppose we have a demand-paged memory. The page table is held in registers. It takes 8 milliseconds to service a page fault if an empty page is available or the replaced page is not modified, and 20 milliseconds if the replaced page is modified. Memory access time is 100 nanoseconds.

Assume that the page to be replaced is modified 70 percent of the time. What is the maximum acceptable page-fault rate for an effective access time of no more than 200 nanoseconds?

9.6 Consider the following page-replacement algorithms. Rank these algorithms on a five-point scale from "bad" to "perfect" according to their page-fault rate. Separate those algorithms that suffer from Belady's anomaly from those that do not.

a. LRU replacement

b. FIFO replacement

c. Optimal replacement

d. Second-chance replacement

9.7 When virtual memory is implemented in a computing system, there are certain costs associated with the technique, and certain benefits. List the costs and the benefits. Is it possible for the costs to exceed the benefits? If it is, what measures can be taken to ensure that this does not happen?

9.8 An operating system supports a paged virtual memory, using a central processor with a cycle time of 1 microsecond. Pages have 1000 words, and the paging device is a drum that rotates at 3000 revolutions per minute, and transfers 1 million words per second.

The following statistical measurements were obtained from the system:

- 0.1 percent of all instructions executed accessed a page other than the current page.

- Of the instructions that accessed another page, 80 percent accessed a page already in memory.

- When a new page was required, the replaced page was modified 50 percent of the time.

Calculate the effective instruction time on this system, assuming that the system is running one process only, and that the processor is idle during drum transfers.

9.9 Consider a demand-paging system with the following time-measured utilizations:

CPU utilization	20%
Paging disk	97.7%
Other I/O devices	5%

Which (if any) of the following will (probably) improve CPU utilization? Explain your answer.

a. Install a faster CPU.

b. Install a bigger paging disk.

c. Increase the degree of multiprogramming.

d. Decrease the degree of multiprogramming.

e. Install more main memory.

f. Install a faster hard disk, or multiple controllers with multiple hard disks.

g. Add prepaging to the page fetch algorithms.

h. Increase the page size.

9.10 Consider the two-dimensional array A:

> **var** A: **array** [1..100] **of array** [1..100] **of** *integer*;

where $A[1][1]$ is at location 200, in a paged memory system with pages of size 200. A small process is in page 0 (locations 0 to 199) for manipulating the matrix; thus, every instruction fetch will be from page 0.

For three page frames, how many page faults are generated by the following array-initialization loops, using LRU replacement, and assuming page frame 1 has the process in it, and the other two are initially empty:

a. **for** $j := 1$ **to** 100 **do**
   for $i := 1$ **to** 100 **do**
   $A[i][j] := 0;$

b. **for** $i := 1$ **to** 100 **do**
   for $j := 1$ **to** 100 **do**
   $A[i][j] := 0;$

9.11 Consider the following page reference string:

1, 2, 3, 4, 2, 1, 5, 6, 2, 1, 2, 3, 7, 6, 3, 2, 1, 2, 3, 6.

How many page faults would occur for the following replacement algorithms, assuming one, two, three, four, five, six, or seven frames? Remember all frames are initially empty, so your first unique pages will all cost one fault each.

- LRU replacement

- FIFO replacement

- Optimal replacement

9.12 Suppose that we want to use a paging algorithm that requires a reference bit (such as second-chance replacement or working-set model), but the hardware does not provide one. Sketch how we could simulate a reference bit even if one were not provided by the hardware, or explain why it is not possible to do so. If it is possible, calculate what the cost would be.

9.13 We have devised a new page-replacement algorithm that we think may be optimal. In some contorted test cases, Belady's anomaly occurs. Is the new algorithm optimal? Explain your answer.

9.14 Suppose your replacement policy (in a paged system) consists of regularly examining each page and discarding that page if it has not been used since the last examination. What would you gain and what would you lose by using this policy rather than LRU or second-chance replacement?

9.15 Segmentation is similar to paging, but uses variable-sized "pages." Define two segment-replacement algorithms based on FIFO and LRU page-replacement schemes. Remember that, since segments are not the same size, the segment that is chosen to be replaced may not be big enough to leave enough consecutive locations for the needed segment. Consider strategies for systems where segments cannot be relocated, and those for systems where they can.

9.16 A page-replacement algorithm should minimize the number of page faults. We can do this minimization by distributing heavily used pages evenly over all of memory, rather than having them compete for a small number of page frames. We can associate with each page frame a counter of the number of pages that are associated with that frame. Then, to replace a page, we search for the page frame with the smallest counter.

    a. Define a page-replacement algorithm using this basic idea. Specifically address the problems of (1) What the initial value of the counters is, (2) when counters are increased, (3) when counters are decreased, and (4) how the page to be replaced is selected.

    b. How many page faults occur for your algorithm for the following reference string, for four page frames?

        1, 2, 3, 4, 5, 3, 4, 1, 6, 7, 8, 7, 8, 9, 7, 8, 9, 5, 4, 5, 4, 2.

    c. What is the minimum number of page faults for an optimal page-replacement strategy for the reference string in part b with four page frames?

9.17 Consider a demand-paging system with a paging disk that has an average access and transfer time of 20 milliseconds. Addresses are translated through a page table in main memory, with an access time of 1 microsecond per memory access. Thus, each memory reference through the page table takes two accesses. To improve this time, we have added an associative memory that reduces access time to one memory reference, if the page-table entry is in the associative memory.

    Assume that 80 percent of the accesses are in the associative memory, and that, of the remaining, 10 percent (or 2 percent of the total) cause page faults. What is the effective memory access time?

9.18 Consider a demand-paged computer system where the degree of multiprogramming is currently fixed at four. The system was recently measured to determine utilization of CPU and the paging disk. The results are one of the following alternatives. For each case, what is happening? Can the degree of multiprogramming be increased to increase the CPU utilization? Is the paging helping?

    a. CPU utilization 13 percent; disk utilization 97 percent

    b. CPU utilization 87 percent; disk utilization 3 percent

    c. CPU utilization 13 percent; disk utilization 3 percent

9.19 We have an operating system for a machine that uses base and limit registers, but we have modified the machine to provide a page table.

Can the page tables be set up to simulate base and limit registers? How can they be, or why can they not be?

9.20 What is the cause of thrashing? How does the system detect thrashing? Once it detects thrashing, what can the system do to eliminate this problem?

Bibliographic Notes

Demand paging was first used in the Atlas system, implemented on the Manchester University MUSE computer around 1960 [Kilburn et al. 1961]. Another early demand-paging system was MULTICS, implemented on the GE 645 system [Organick 1972].

Belady et al. [1969] were the first researchers to observe that the FIFO replacement strategy may have the anomaly that bears Belady's name. Mattson et al. [1970] demonstrated that stack algorithms are not subject to Belady's anomaly.

The optimal replacement algorithm was presented by Belady [1966]. It was proved to be optimal by Mattson et al. [1970]. Belady's optimal algorithm is for a fixed allocation; Prieve and Fabry [1976] have an optimal algorithm for situations where the allocation can vary.

The enhanced clock algorithm was discussed by Carr and Hennessy [1981]; it is used in the Macintosh virtual memory-management scheme, and was described by Goldman [1989].

Thrashing was discussed by Denning [1968]. The working-set model was developed by Denning [1968]. Discussions concerning the working-set model were presented by Denning [1980].

The page-fault-rate monitoring scheme was developed by Wulf [1969], who successfully applied this technique to the Burroughs B5500 computer system. Chu and Opderbeck [1976] discussed program behavior and the page-fault-frequency replacement algorithm. Gupta and Franklin [1978] provided a performance comparison between the working-set scheme and the page-fault-frequency replacement scheme.

Demand segmentation and details of OS/2 were described by Iacobucci [1988]. Further information about OS/2 was presented in [Microsoft 1989].

The Intel 80386 paging hardware was described in [Intel 1986]; the Motorola 68030 hardware was covered in [Motorola 1989b]. Virtual-memory management in the VAX/VMS operating system was discussed by Levy and Lipman [1982]. Discussions concerning workstation operating systems and virtual memory are offered by Hagmann [1989].

CHAPTER 10

FILE
SYSTEM
INTERFACE

For most users, the file system is the most visible aspect of an operating system. It provides the mechanism for on-line storage of and access to both data and programs belonging to the operating system and all the users of the computer system. The file system consists of two distinct parts: a collection of *files*, each storing related data, and a *directory structure*, which organizes and provides information about all the files in the system. Some file systems have a third part, *partitions*, which are used to separate physically or logically large collections of directories. In this chapter, we consider the various aspects of files, and the variety of directory structures. We also discuss ways to handle *file protection*, which is necessary in an environment where multiple users have access to files, and where it is usually desirable to control by whom and in what ways files may be accessed. Finally, we discuss the semantics of sharing files among multiple processes.

10.1 ■ File Concept

Computers can store information on several different storage media, such as magnetic disks, magnetic tapes, and optical disks. So that the computer system will be convenient to use, the operating system provides a uniform logical view of information storage. The operating system abstracts from the physical properties of its storage devices to define a logical storage unit, the *file*. Files are mapped, by the operating system, onto physical devices. These storage devices are usually *nonvolatile*, so the contents are persistent through power failures and system reboots.

A file is a named collection of related information that is recorded on secondary storage. From a user's perspective, a file is the smallest allotment of logical secondary storage; that is, data cannot be written to secondary storage unless they are within a file. Commonly, files represent programs (both source and object forms) and data. Data files may be numeric, alphabetic, alphanumeric, or binary. Files may be free-form, such as text files, or may be formatted rigidly. In general, a file is a sequence of bits, bytes, lines, or records whose meaning is defined by the file's creator and user. The concept of a file is thus extremely general.

The information in a file is defined by its creator. Many different types of information may be stored in a file: source programs, object programs, executable programs, numeric data, text, payroll records, graphic images, sound recordings, and so on. A file has a certain defined *structure* according to its type. A *text* file is a sequence of characters organized into lines (and possibly pages); a *source* file is a sequence of subroutines and functions, each of which is further organized as declarations followed by executable statements; an *object* file is a sequence of bytes organized into blocks understandable by the system's linker; an *executable* file is a series of code sections that the loader can bring into memory and execute. The internal structure of files is discussed in Section 10.1.4.

10.1.1 File Attributes

A file is named, for the convenience of its human users, and is referred to by its name. A name is usually a string of characters, such as "example.c". Some systems differentiate between upper- and lower-case characters in names, whereas other systems consider the two cases to be equivalent. When a file is named, it becomes independent of the process, the user, and even the system that created it. For instance, one user might create file "example.c", whereas another user might edit that file by specifying its name. The file's owner might write the file to a floppy disk or magnetic tape, and might read it off onto another system, where it could still be called "example.c".

A file has certain other attributes, which vary from one operating system to another, but typically consist of these:

- **Name**. The symbolic file name is the only information kept in human-readable form.

- **Type**. This information is needed for those systems that support different types.

- **Location**. This information is a pointer to a device and to the location of the file on that device.

- **Size**. The current size of the file (in bytes, words or blocks), and possibly the maximum allowed size are included in this attribute.

- **Protection**. Access-control information controls who can do reading, writing, executing, and so on.

- **Time, date, and user identification**. This information may be kept for (1) creation, (2) last modification, and (3) last use. These data can be useful for protection, security, and usage monitoring.

The information about all files is kept in the directory structure that also resides on secondary storage. It may take from 16 to over 1000 bytes to record this information for each file. In a system with many files, the size of the directory itself may be megabytes. Because directories, like files, must be nonvolatile, they must be stored on the device and brought into memory piecemeal, as needed. We shall discuss the directory-structure organization in Section 10.3

10.1.2 File Operations

A file is an *abstract data type.* To define a file properly, we need to consider the operations that can be performed on files. The operating system provides system calls to create, write, read, reposition, delete, and truncate files. Let us consider what the operating system must do for each of the six basic file operations. It should then be easy to see how similar operations, such as renaming a file, would be implemented.

- **Creating a file**. Two steps are necessary to create a file. First, space in the file system must be found for the file. We shall discuss how to allocate space for the file in Chapter 11. Second, an entry for the new file must be made in the directory. The directory entry records the name of the file and the location in the file system.

- **Writing a file**. To write a file, we make a system call specifying both the name of the file and the information to be written to the file. Given the name of the file, the system searches the directory to find the location of the file. The system must keep a *write* pointer to the location in the file where the next write is to take place. The write pointer must be updated whenever a write occurs.

- **Reading a file**. To read from a file, we use a system call that specifies the name of the file and where (in memory) the next block of the file should be put. Again, the directory is searched for the associated directory entry, and the system needs to keep a *read* pointer to the location in the file where the next read is to take place. Once the read has taken place, the read pointer is updated. Since, in general, a file is either being read or written, most systems keep only one *current-file-position* pointer. Both the read and write operations use this same pointer, saving space and reducing the system complexity.

- **Repositioning within a file**. The directory is searched for the appropriate entry, and the current-file-position is set to a given value. Repositioning within a file does not need to involve any actual I/O. This file operation is also known as a file *seek*.

- **Deleting a file**. To delete a file, we search the directory for the named file. Having found the associated directory entry, we release all file space (so that it can be reused by other files) and erase the directory entry.

- **Truncating a file**. There are occasions when the user wants the attributes of a file to remain the same, but wants to erase the contents of the file. Rather than forcing the user to delete the file and then recreate it, this function allows all attributes to remain unchanged (except for file length) but for the file to be reset to length zero.

These six basic operations certainly comprise the minimal set of required file operations. Other common operations include *appending* new information to the end of an existing file, and *renaming* an existing file. These primitive operations may then be combined to perform other file operations. For instance, creating a *copy* of a file, or copying the file to another I/O device, such as a printer or a display, may be accomplished by creating a new file, and reading from the old and writing to the new. We also want to have operations that allow a user to get and set the various attributes of a file. For example, we may want to have an operation that allows a user to determine the status of a file, such as the file's length, and have an operation that allows a user to set file attributes, such as the file's owner.

Most of the file operations mentioned involve searching the directory for the entry associated with the named file. To avoid this constant searching, many systems will *open* a file when that file first is used actively. The operating system keeps a small table containing information about all open files (the *open-file table*). When a file operation is requested, an index into this table is used, so no searching is required. When the file is no longer actively used, it is *closed* by the process and the operating system removes its entry in the open-file table.

Some systems implicitly open a file when the first reference is made to it. The file is automatically closed when the job or program that opened the file terminates. Most systems, however, require that a file be opened explicitly by the programmer with a system call (**open**) before that file can be used. The **open** operation takes a file name and searches the directory, copying the directory entry into the open-file table, assuming the file protections allow such access. The **open** system call will typically return a pointer to the entry in the open-file table. This pointer, not the actual file name, is used in all I/O operations, avoiding any further searching, and simplifying the system-call interface.

The implementation of the **open** and **close** operations in a multiuser environment, such as UNIX, is more complicated. In such a system, several users may open the file at the same time. Typically, the operating system uses two levels of internal tables. There is a per-process table of all the files that each process has open. Stored in this table is information regarding the use of the file by the process. For instance, the current file pointer for each file is found here, indicating the location in the file which the next **read** or **write** call will affect.

Each entry in the per-process table in turn points to a systemwide open-file table. The systemwide table contains information that is process independent, such as the location of the file on disk, access dates, and file size. Once a file is opened by one process, another process executing an **open** call simply results in a new entry being added to the process' open file table with a new current file pointer, and a pointer to the appropriate entry in the systemwide table. Typically, the open-file table also has an *open count* associated with each file, indicating the number of processes which have the file open. Each **close** decreases this count, and when the count reaches zero, the file is no longer in use, and the file's entry is removed from the open file table. In summary, there are several pieces of information associated with an open file.

- **File pointer**. On systems that do not include a file offset as part of the **read** and **write** system calls, the system must track the last read/write location as a current-file-position pointer. This pointer is unique to each process operating on the file, and therefore must be kept separate from the on-disk file attributes.

- **File open count**. As files are closed, the operating system must reuse its open-file table entries, or it could run out of space in the table. Because multiple processes may open a file, the system must wait for the last file close before removing the open-file table entry. This counter tracks the number of opens and closes, and reaches zero on the last close. The system can then remove the entry.

- **Disk location of the file**. Most file operations require the system to modify data within the file. The information needed to locate the file on disk is kept in memory to avoid having to read it from disk for each operation.

Some operating systems provide facilities for locking sections of an open file for multiprocess access, to share sections of a file among several processes, and even to map sections of a file into memory on virtual-memory systems. This last function is called *memory mapping* a file and allows a part of the virtual address space to be logically associated with a section of a file. Reads and writes to that memory region are then treated as reads and writes to the file, greatly simplifying file use. Closing the file results in all the memory-mapped data being written back to disk and removed from the virtual memory of the process. Multiple processes may be allowed to map the same file into the virtual memory of each, to allow sharing of data. Writes by any of the processes modify the data in virtual memory and can be seen by all others that map the same section of the file. Given our knowledge of virtual memory from Chapter 9, it should be clear how the sharing of memory-mapped sections of memory is implemented: Each sharing process' virtual-memory map points to the same page of physical memory — the page that holds a copy of the disk block. This memory sharing is illustrated in Figure 10.1. So that access to the shared data is coordinated, the processes involved might use one of the mechanisms for achieving mutual exclusion described in Chapter 6.

10.1.3 File Types

One major consideration in designing a file system, and the entire operating system, is whether the operating system should recognize and support file types. If an operating system recognizes the type of a file, it can then operate on the file in reasonable ways. For example, a common mistake occurs when a user tries to print the binary-object form of a

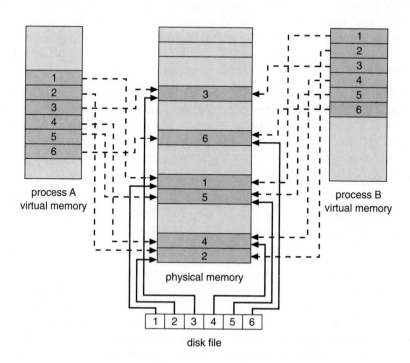

Figure 10.1 Memory-mapped files.

program. This attempt normally produces garbage, but can be prevented *if* the operating system has been told that the file is a binary-object program.

A common technique for implementing file types is to include the type as part of the file name. The name is split into two parts — a name and an *extension*, usually separated by a period character (Figure 10.2). In this way, the user and the operating system can tell from the name alone what the type of a file is. For example, in MS-DOS, a name can consist of up to eight characters followed by a period and terminated by an up-to-three-character extension. The system uses the extension to indicate the type of the file and the type of operations that can be done on that file. For instance, only a file with a ".com", ".exe", or ".bat" extension can be executed. The ".com" and ".exe" files are two forms of binary executable files, whereas a ".bat" file is a *batch* file containing, in ASCII format,

File type	Usual extension	Function
Executable	exe, com, bin or none	ready-to-run machine-language program
Object	obj, o	compiled, machine language, not linked
Source code	c, p, pas, f77, asm, a	source code in various languages
Batch	bat, sh	commands to the command interpreter
Text	txt, doc	textual data, documents
Word processor	wp, tex, rrf, etc	various word-processor formats
Library	lib, a	libraries of routines for programmers
Print or view	ps, dvi, gif	ASCII or binary file in a format for printing or viewing
Archive	arc, zip, tar	related files grouped into one file, sometimes compressed, for archiving or storage

Figure 10.2 Common file types.

commands to the operating system. MS-DOS recognizes only a few extensions, but application programs also use them to indicate file types in which they are interested. For example, assemblers expect source files to have an ".asm" extension, and the WordPerfect wordprocessor expects its file to end with ".wp". These extensions are not required, but a user may specify a file without the extension (to save typing), and the application will look for a file with the given name and the extension it expects. Because these extensions are not supported by the operating system, they can be considered as "hints" to applications which operate on them.

Another example of the utility of file types comes from the TOPS-20 operating system. If the user tries to execute an object program whose source file has been modified (edited) since the object file was produced, the source file will be recompiled automatically. This function ensures that the user always runs an up-to-date object file. Otherwise, the user could waste a significant amount of time executing the old object file. Notice that, for this function to be possible, the operating system must be able to discriminate the source file from the object file, to check the time that each file was last modified or created, and to determine the language of the source program (in order to use the correct compiler).

Consider the Apple Macintosh operating system. In this system, each file has a type, such as "text" or "pict". Each file also has a creator attribute containing the name of the program that created it. This attribute is set by the operating system during the create call, so its use is enforced and supported by the system. For instance, a file produced by a word processor has the word processor's name as its creator. When the user opens that file, by double-clicking the mouse on the icon representing the file, the word processor is invoked automatically, and the file is loaded, ready to be edited.

The UNIX operating system is unable to provide such a feature because it uses a crude *magic number* stored at the beginning of some files to indicate roughly the type of the file: executable program, batch file (known as a shell script), postscript file, and so on. Not all files have magic numbers, so system features cannot be based solely on this type information. UNIX does not record the name of the creating program, either. UNIX also allows file name extension hints, but these extensions are not enforced or depended on by the operating system; they are mostly to aid users in determining the type of contents of the file.

10.1.4 File Structure

File types also may be used to indicate the internal structure of the file. As mentioned in Section 10.1.3, source and object files have structures that match the expectations of the programs that read them. Further, certain files must conform to a required structure that is understood by the operating system. For example, the operating system may require that an executable file have a specific structure so that it can determine where in memory to load the file and what the location of the first instruction is. Some operating systems extend this idea into a set of system-supported file structures, with sets of special operations for manipulating files with those structures.

DEC's popular VMS operating system has a file system that does support multiple file structures. It defines three file structures. On other systems, such as those of IBM, many different access methods are supported, and choosing the right one for a particular application is a major design problem.

The above discussion brings us to one of the disadvantages of having the operating system support multiple file structures: The resulting size of the operating system is cumbersome. If the operating system defines five different file structures, it needs to contain the code to support these file structures. In addition, every file may need to be definable as one of the file types supported by the operating system. Severe problems may result from new applications that require information structured in ways not supported by the operating system.

For example, assume that a system supports two types of files: text files (composed of ASCII characters separated by a carriage return and line feed) and executable binary files. Now, if we (as users) want to define an encrypted file to protect our files from being read by unauthorized people, we may find neither file type to be appropriate. The encrypted file is not ASCII text lines, but rather is (apparently) random bits. Although it may appear to be a binary file, it is not executable. As a result, we may have to circumvent or misuse the operating system's file-types mechanism, or to modify or abandon our encryption scheme.

Some operating systems impose (and support) a minimal number of file structures. This approach has been adopted in UNIX, MS-DOS, and others. UNIX considers each file to be a sequence of 8-bit bytes; no interpretation of these bits is made by the operating system. This scheme provides maximum flexibility, but little support. Each application program must include its own code to interpret an input file into the appropriate structure. However, all operating systems must support at least one structure — that of an executable file — so that the system is able to load and run programs.

Another example of an operating system that supports a minimal number of file structures is the Macintosh operating system, which expects executables to contain two parts: a *resource fork* and a *data fork*. The resource fork contains information of interest to the user. For instance, it holds the labels of any buttons displayed by the program. A foreign user may want to relabel these buttons in his own language, and the Macintosh operating system provides tools to allow modification of the data in the resource fork. The data fork contains the program code and data that the user may not change. To accomplish the same task on a UNIX or MS-DOS system, the programmer would need to change and recompile the source code, unless she created her own user-changeable data file. The moral of this example is that it is useful for an operating system to support structures that will be used frequently, and that will save the programmer substantial effort. Too few structures make programming inconvenient, whereas too many cause operating-system bloat and programmer confusion.

10.1.5 Internal File Structure

Internally, locating an offset within a file can be complicated for the operating system. Recall from Chapter 2 that disk systems typically have a well-defined block size determined by the size of a sector. All disk I/O is performed in units of one block (physical record), and all blocks are the same size. It is unlikely that the physical record size will exactly match the length of the desired logical record. Logical records may even vary in length. *Packing* a number of logical records into physical blocks is a common solution to this problem.

For example, the UNIX operating system defines all files to be simply a stream of bytes. Each byte is individually addressable by its offset from the beginning (or end) of the file. In this case, the logical record is 1 byte. The file system automatically packs and unpacks bytes into physical disk blocks (say, 512 bytes per block) as necessary.

The logical record size, physical block size, and packing technique determine how many logical records are in each physical block. The packing can be done either by the user's application program or by the operating system.

In either case, the file may be considered to be a sequence of blocks. All the basic I/O functions operate in terms of blocks. The conversion from logical records to physical blocks is a relatively simple software problem.

Notice that disk space being always allocated in blocks has the result that, in general, some portion of the last block of each file may be wasted. If each block is 512 bytes, then a file of 1949 bytes would be allocated four blocks (2048 bytes); the last 99 bytes would be wasted. The wasted bytes allocated to keep everything in units of blocks (instead of bytes) is *internal fragmentation*. All file systems suffer from internal fragmentation; the larger the block size, the greater the internal fragmentation.

10.2 ■ Access Methods

Files store information. When it is used, this information must be accessed and read into computer memory. There are several ways that the information in the file can be accessed. Some systems provide only one access method for files. On other systems, such as those of IBM, many different access methods are supported, and choosing the right one for a particular application is a major design problem.

10.2.1 Sequential Access

The simplest access method is *sequential access*. Information in the file is processed in order, one record after the other. This mode of access is by far the most common, for example, editors and compilers usually access files in this fashion.

The bulk of the operations on a file are reads and writes. A read operation reads the next portion of the file and automatically advances a file pointer, which tracks the I/O location. Similarly, a write appends to the end of the file and advances to the end of the newly written material (the new end of file). Such a file can be reset to the beginning, and, on some systems, a program may be able to skip forward or backward n records, for some integer n (perhaps only for $n = 1$). Sequential access is depicted in Figure 10.3. Sequential access is based on a tape model of a file, and works as well on sequential-access devices as it does on random-access ones.

10.2.2 Direct Access

Another method is *direct access* (or *relative access*). A file is made up of fixed-length *logical records* that allow programs to read and write records rapidly in no particular order. The direct access method is based on a disk model of a file, since disks allow random access to any file block. For direct access, the file is viewed as a numbered sequence of blocks or records. A direct-access file allows arbitrary blocks to be read or written. Thus, we may read block 14, then read block 53, and then write block 7. There are no restrictions on the order of reading or writing for a direct-access file.

Direct-access files are of great use for immediate access to large amounts of information. Databases are often of this type. When a query concerning a particular subject arrives, we compute which block contains the answer, and then read that block directly to provide the desired information.

Figure 10.3 Sequential-access file.

For example, on an airline-reservation system, we might store all the information about a particular flight (for example, flight 713) in the block identified by the flight number. Thus, the number of available seats for flight 713 is stored in block 713 of the reservation file. To store information about a larger set, such as people, we might compute a hash function on the people's names, or search a small in-core index to determine a block to read and search.

The file operations must be modified to include the block number as a parameter. Thus, we have *read n*, where *n* is the block number, rather than *read next*, and *write n*, rather than *write next*. An alternative approach is to retain *read next* and *write next*, as with sequential access, and to add an operation, *position file to n*, where *n* is the block number. Then, to effect a *read n*, we would *position to n* and then *read next*.

The block number provided by the user to the operating system is normally a *relative block number*. A relative block number is an index relative to the beginning of the file. Thus, the first relative block of the file is 0, the next is 1, and so on, even though the actual absolute disk address of the block may be 14703 for the first block, and 3192 for the second. The use of relative block numbers allows the operating system to decide where the file should be placed (called the allocation problem, as discussed in Chapter 11), and helps to prevent the user from accessing portions of the file system that may not be part of his file. Some systems start their relative block numbers at 0; others start at 1.

Given a logical record length L, a request for record N is turned into an I/O request for L bytes at location $L + (N - 1)$ within the file. Since logical records are of a fixed size, it is also easy to read, write, or delete a record.

Not all operating systems support both sequential and direct access for files. Some systems allow only sequential file access; others allow only direct access. Some systems require that a file be defined as sequential or direct when it is created; such a file can be accessed only in a manner consistent with its declaration. Notice, however, that it is easy to simulate sequential access on a direct-access file. If we simply keep a variable cp, which defines our current position, then we can simulate sequential file operations, as shown in Figure 10.4. On the other hand, it is extremely inefficient and clumsy to simulate a direct-access file on a sequential-access file.

10.2.3 Other Access Methods

Other access methods can be built on top of a direct-access method. These additional methods generally involve the construction of an *index* for the file. The index, like an index in the back of a book, contains pointers to the various blocks. To find an entry in the file, we first search the index, and then use the pointer to access the file directly and to find the desired entry.

Sequential access	Implementation for direct access
reset	cp := 0;
read next	read cp;
	cp := cp+1;
write next	write cp;
	cp := cp+1;

Figure 10.4 Simulation of sequential access on a direct-access file.

For example, a retail-price file might list the universal product codes (UPCs) for items, with the associated prices. Each entry consists of a 10-digit UPC and a six-digit price, for a 16-byte entry. If our disk has 1024 bytes per block, we can store 64 entries per block. A file of 120,000 entries would occupy about 2000 blocks (2 million bytes). By keeping the file sorted by UPC, we can define an index consisting of the first UPC in each block. This index would have 2000 entries of 10 digits each, or 20,000 bytes, and thus could be kept in memory. To find the price of a particular item, we can (binary) search the index. From this search, we would know exactly which block contains the desired entry and access that block. This structure allows us to search a large file doing little I/O.

With large files, the index file itself may become too large to be kept in memory. One solution is to create an index for the index file. The primary index file would contain pointers to secondary index files, which would point to the actual data items.

For example, IBM's indexed sequential access method (ISAM) uses a small master index that points to disk blocks of a secondary index. The secondary index blocks point to the actual file blocks. The file is kept sorted on a defined key. To find a particular item, we first make a binary search of the master index, which provides the block number of the secondary index. This block is read in, and again a binary search is used to find the block containing the desired record. Finally, this block is searched sequentially. In this way, any record can be located from its key by at most two direct-access reads. Figure 10.5 shows a similar situation as implemented by VMS index and relative files.

10.3 ■ Directory Structure

The file systems of computers can be extensive. Some systems store thousands of files on hundreds of gigabytes of disk. To manage all these data, we need to organize them. This organization is usually done in two

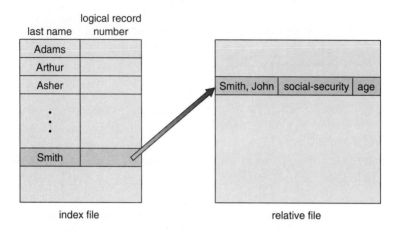

Figure 10.5   Example of index and relative files.

parts.   First, the file system is broken into *partitions*, also known as *minidisks* in the IBM world or *volumes* in the PC and Macintosh arenas. Typically, each disk on a system contains at least one partition, which is a low-level structure in which files and directories reside.   Sometimes, partitions are used to provide several separate areas within one disk, each treated as a separate storage device, whereas other systems allow partitions to be larger than a disk to group disks into one logical structure. In this way, the user needs to be concerned with only the logical directory and file structure, and can ignore completely the problems of physically allocating space for files.   For this reason partitions can be thought of as virtual disks.

Second, each partition contains information about files within it.   This information is kept in entries in a *device directory* or *volume table* of contents. The device directory (more commonly known simply as a "directory") records information — such as name, location, size, and type — for all files on that partition.   Figure 10.6 shows the typical file-system organization.

The directory can be viewed as a symbol table that translates file names into their directory entries.   If we take such a view, then it becomes apparent that the directory itself can be organized in many ways. We want to be able to insert entries, to delete entries, to search for a named entry, and to list all the entries in the directory. In Chapter 11, we discuss the appropriate data structures that can be used in the implementation of the directory structure.   In this section, we examine several schemes for defining the logical structure of the directory system.   When considering a particular directory structure, we need to keep in mind the operations that are to be performed on a directory:

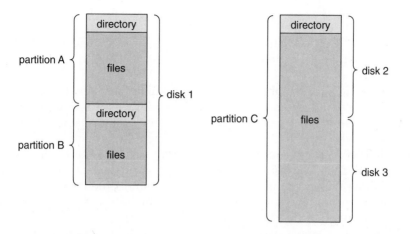

Figure 10.6 A typical file-system organization.

- **Search for a file**. We need to be able to search a directory structure to find the entry for a particular file. Since files have symbolic names and similar names may indicate a relationship between files, we may want to be able to find all files whose names match a particular pattern.

- **Create a file**. New files need to be created and added to the directory.

- **Delete a file**. When a file is no longer needed, we want to remove it from the directory.

- **List a directory**. We need to be able to list the files in a directory, and the contents of the directory entry for each file in the list.

- **Rename a file**. Because the name of a file represents its contents to its users, the name must be changeable when the contents or use of the file changes. Renaming a file may also allow its position within the directory structure to be changed.

- **Traverse the file system**. It is useful to be able to access every directory, and every file within a directory structure. For reliability, it is a good idea to save the contents and structure of the entire file system at regular intervals. This saving often consists of copying all files to magnetic tape. This technique provides a backup copy in case of system failure or if the file is simply no longer in use. In this case, the file can be copied to tape, and the disk space of that file released for reuse by another file.

In Sections 10.3.1 to 10.3.5, we describe the most common schemes for defining the logical structure of a directory.

10.3.1 Single-Level Directory

The simplest directory structure is the single-level directory. All files are contained in the same directory, which is easy to support and understand (Figure 10.7).

A single-level directory has significant limitations, however, when the number of files increases or when there is more than one user. Since all files are in the same directory, they must have unique names. If we have two users who call their data file *test*, then the unique-name rule is violated. (For example, in one programming class, 23 students called the program for their second assignment *prog2*; another 11 called it *assign2*.) Although file names are generally selected to reflect the content of the file, they are often limited in length. The MS-DOS operating system allows only 11-character file names; UNIX allows 255 characters.

Even with a single user, as the number of files increases, it becomes difficult to remember the names of all the files, so as to create only files with unique names. It is not uncommon for a user to have hundreds of files on one computer system and an equal number of additional files on another system. In such an environment, keeping track of so many files is a daunting task.

10.3.2 Two-Level Directory

The major disadvantage to a single-level directory is the confusion of file names between different users. The standard solution is to create a *separate* directory for each user.

In the two-level directory structure, each user has her own user file directory (UFD). Each UFD has a similar structure, but lists only the files of a single user. When a user job starts or a user logs in, the system's master file directory (MFD) is searched. The master file directory is indexed by user name or account number, and each entry points to the UFD for that user (Figure 10.8).

When a user refers to a particular file, only his own UFD is searched. Thus, different users may have files with the same name, as long as all the file names within each UFD are unique.

Figure 10.7   Single-level directory.

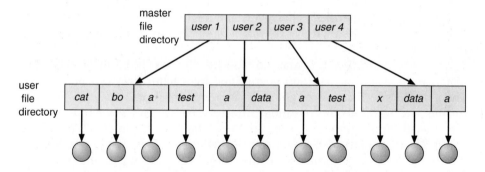

Figure 10.8 Two-level directory structure.

To create a file for a user, the operating system searches only that user's UFD to ascertain whether another file of that name exists. To delete a file, the operating system confines its search to the local UFD; thus, it cannot accidentally delete another user's file that has the same name.

The user directories themselves must be created and deleted as necessary. A special system program is run with the appropriate user name and account information. The program creates a new user file directory and adds an entry for it to the master file directory. The execution of this program might be restricted to system administrators. The allocation of disk space for user directories can be handled with the techniques discussed in Chapter 11 for files themselves.

The two-level directory structure solves the name-collision problem, but it still has problems. This structure effectively isolates one user from another. This isolation is an advantage when the users are completely independent, but is a disadvantage when the users *want* to cooperate on some task and to access one another's files. Some systems simply do not allow local user files to be accessed by other users.

If access is to be permitted, one user must have the ability to name a file in another user's directory. To name a particular file uniquely in a two-level directory, we must give both the user name and the file name. A two-level directory can be thought of as a tree, or at least an inverted tree, of height 2. The root of the tree is the master file directory. Its direct descendants are the UFDs. The descendants of the user file directories are the files themselves. The files are the leaves of the tree. Specifying a user name and a file name defines a path in the tree from the root (the master file directory) to a leaf (the specified file). Thus, a user name and a file name define a *path name*. Every file in the system has a path name. To name a file uniquely, a user must know the path name of the file desired.

For example, if user A wishes to access her own test file named *test*, she can simply refer to *test*. To access the test file of user B (with directory-entry name *userb*), however, she might have to refer to */userb/test*. Every system has its own syntax for naming files in directories other than the user's own.

There is additional syntax to specify the partition of a file. For instance, in MS-DOS a partition is specified by a letter followed by a colon. Thus, a file specification might be "C:\userb\test". Some systems go even further and separate the partition, directory name, and file name parts of the specification. For instance, in VMS, the file "login.com" might be specified as: "u:[sst.jdeck]login.com;1", where "u" is the name of the partition, "sst" is the name of the directory, "jdeck" is the name of subdirectory, and "1", is the version number. Other systems simply treat the partition name as part of the directory name. The first name given is that of the partition, and the rest is the directory and file. For instance, "/u/pbg/test" might specify partition "u", directory "pbg", and file "test".

A special case of this situation occurs in regard to the system files. Those programs provided as a part of the system (loaders, assemblers, compilers, utility routines, libraries, and so on) are generally defined as files. When the appropriate commands are given to the operating system, these files are read by the loader and are executed. Many command interpreters act by simply treating the command as the name of a file to load and execute. As the directory system is defined presently, this file name would be searched for in the current user file directory. One solution would be to copy the system files into each user file directory. However, copying all the system files would be enormously wasteful of space. (If the system files require 5 megabytes, then supporting 12 users would require 5 × 12 = 60 megabytes just for copies of the system files.)

The standard solution is to complicate the search procedure slightly. A special user directory is defined to contain the system files (for example, user 0). Whenever a file name is given to be loaded, the operating system first searches the local user file directory. If the file is found, it is used. If it is not found, the system automatically searches the special user directory that contains the system files. The sequence of directories searched when a file is named is called the *search path*. This idea can be extended, such that the search path contains an unlimited list of directories to search when a command name is given. This method is the one most used in UNIX and MS-DOS.

10.3.3 Tree-Structured Directories

Once we have seen how to view a two-level directory as a two-level tree, the natural generalization is to extend the directory structure to a tree of arbitrary height (Figure 10.9). This generalization allows users to create their own subdirectories and to organize their files accordingly. The MS-DOS system, for instance, is structured as a tree. In fact a tree is the most common directory structure. The tree has a root directory. Every file in the

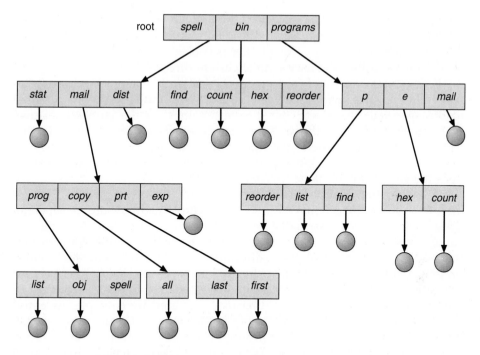

Figure 10.9 Tree-structured directory structure.

system has a unique path name. A path name is the path from the root, through all the subdirectories, to a specified file.

A directory (or subdirectory) contains a set of files or subdirectories. A directory is simply another file, but it is treated in a special way. All directories have the same internal format. One bit in each directory entry defines the entry as a file (0) or as a subdirectory (1). Special system calls are used to create and delete directories.

In normal use, each user has a *current directory*. The current directory should contain most of the files that are of current interest to the user. When reference is made to a file, the current directory is searched. If a file is needed that is not in the current directory, then the user must either specify a path name or change the current directory to be the directory holding that file. To change the current directory to a different directory, a system call is provided that takes a directory name as a parameter and uses it to redefine the current directory. Thus, the user can change his current directory whenever he desires. From one **change directory** system call to the next, all **open** system calls search the current directory for the specified file.

The initial current directory of a user is designated when the user job starts or the user logs in. The operating system searches the accounting file (or some other predefined location) to find an entry for this user (for accounting purposes). In the accounting file is a pointer to (or the name of) the user's initial directory. This pointer is copied to a local variable for this user, which specifies the user's initial current directory.

Path names can be of two types: *absolute* path names or *relative* path names. An absolute path name begins at the root and follows a path down to the specified file, giving the directory names on the path. A relative path name defines a path from the current directory. For example, in the tree-structured file system of Figure· 10.9, if the current directory is *root/spell/mail*, then the relative path name *prt/first* refers to the same file as does the absolute path name *root/spell/mail/prt/first*.

Allowing the user to define his own subdirectories permits him to impose a structure on his files. This structure might result in separate directories for files associated with different topics (for example, a subdirectory was created to hold the text of this book) or different forms of information (for example, the directory *programs* may contain source programs; the directory *bin* may store all the binaries).

An interesting policy decision in a tree-structured directory structure is how to handle the deletion of a directory. If a directory is empty, its entry in its containing directory can simply be deleted. However, suppose the directory to be deleted is not empty, but contains several files, or possibly subdirectories. One of two approaches can be taken. Some systems, such as MS-DOS, will not delete a directory unless it is empty. Thus, to delete a directory, the user must first delete all the files in that directory. If there are any subdirectories, this procedure must be applied recursively to them, so that they can be deleted also. This approach may result in a substantial amount of work.

An alternative approach, such as that taken by the UNIX **rm** command, is to provide the option that, when a request is made to delete a directory, all that directory's files and subdirectories are also to be deleted. Note that either approach is fairly easy to implement; the choice is one of policy. The latter policy is more convenient, but more dangerous, because an entire directory structure may be removed with one command. If that command was issued in error, a large number of files and directories would need to be restored from backup tapes.

With a tree-structured directory system, files of other users can be accessed easily. For example, user B can access files of user A by specifying their path names. User B can specify either an absolute or a relative path name. Alternatively, user B could change her current directory to be user A's directory, and access the files by their file names. Some systems also allow users to define their own search paths. In this case, user B could define her search path to be (1) her local directory, (2) the system file directory, and (3) user A's directory, in that order. As long as the name of a file of user A did not conflict with the name of a local file or system file, it could be referred to simply by its name.

Note that a path to a file in a tree-structured directory can be longer than that in a two-level directory. To allow users to access programs without having to remember these long paths, the Macintosh operating system automates the search for executable programs. It maintains a file, called the "Desktop File", containing the name and location of all executable programs it has seen. When a new hard disk or floppy disk is added to the system, or the network is accessed, the operating system traverses the directory structure, searching for executable programs on the device and recording the pertinent information. This mechanism supports the double-click execution functionality described previously. A double-click on a file causes its creator attribute to be read, and the "Desktop File" to be searched for a match. Once the match is found, the appropriate executable program is started with the clicked-on file as its input.

10.3.4 Acyclic-Graph Directories

Consider two programmers who are working on a joint project. The files associated with that project can be stored in a subdirectory, separating them from other projects and files of the two programmers. But since both programmers are equally responsible for the project, both want the subdirectory to be in their own directories. The common subdirectory should be *shared*. A shared directory or file will exist in the file system in two (or more) places at once. Notice that a shared file (or directory) is not the same as two copies of the file. With two copies, each programmer can view the copy rather than the original, but if one programmer changes the file, the changes will not appear in the other's copy. With a shared file, there is only *one* actual file, so any changes made by one person would be immediately visible to the other. This form of sharing is particularly important for shared subdirectories; a new file created by one person will automatically appear in all the shared subdirectories.

A tree structure prohibits the sharing of files or directories. An *acyclic graph* allows directories to have shared subdirectories and files (Figure 10.10). The *same* file or subdirectory may be in two different directories. An acyclic graph (that is, a graph with no cycles) is a natural generalization of the tree-structured directory scheme.

In a situation where several people are working as a team, all the files to be shared may be put together into one directory. The user file directories of all the team members would each contain this directory of shared files as a subdirectory. Even when there is a single user, his file organization may require that some files be put into several different subdirectories. For example, a program written for a particular project should be both in the directory of all programs and in the directory for that project.

Shared files and subdirectories can be implemented in several ways. A common way, exemplified by many of the UNIX systems, is to create a new

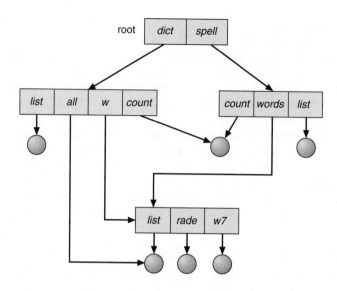

Figure 10.10   Acyclic-graph directory structure.

directory entry called a *link*. A link is effectively a pointer to another file or subdirectory. For example, a link may be implemented as an absolute or relative path name (a *symbolic link*). When a reference to a file is made, we search the directory. The directory entry is marked as a link and the name of the real file (or directory) is given. We *resolve* the link by using the path name to locate the real file. Links are easily identified by their format in the directory entry, (or by their having a special type on systems that support types) and are effectively named indirect pointers. The operating system ignores these links when traversing directory trees to preserve the acyclic structure of the system.

The other approach to implementing shared files is simply to duplicate all information about them in both sharing directories. Thus, both entries are identical and equal. A link is clearly different from the original directory entry; thus, the two are not equal. Duplicate directory entries, however, make the original and the copy indistinguishable. A major problem with duplicate directory entries is maintaining consistency if the file is modified.

An acyclic-graph directory structure is more flexible than is a simple tree structure, but is also more complex. Several problems must be considered carefully. Notice that a file may now have multiple absolute path names. Consequently, distinct file names may refer to the same file. This situation is similar to the aliasing problem for programming languages. If we are trying to traverse the entire file system (to find a file, to accumulate statistics on all files, or to copy all files to backup storage), this problem becomes significant, since we do not want to traverse shared structures more than once.

Another problem involves deletion. When can the space allocated to a shared file be deallocated and reused? One possibility is to remove the file whenever anyone deletes it, but this action may leave dangling pointers to the now-nonexistent file. Worse, if the remaining file pointers contain actual disk addresses, and the space is subsequently reused for other files, these dangling pointers may point into the middle of other files.

In a system where sharing is implemented by symbolic links, this situation is somewhat easier to handle. The deletion of a link does not need to affect the original file; only the link is removed. If the file entry itself is deleted, the space for the file is deallocated, leaving the links dangling. We can search for these links and remove them also, but unless a list of the associated links is kept with each file, this search can be expensive. Alternatively, we can leave the links until an attempt is made to use them. At that time, we can determine that the file of the name given by the link does not exist, and can fail to resolve the link name; the access is treated just like any other illegal file name. (In this case, the system designer should consider carefully what to do when a file is deleted and another file of the same name is created, before a symbolic link to the original file is used.) In the case of UNIX, symbolic links are left when a file is deleted, and it is up to the user to realize that the original file is gone or has been replaced.

Another approach to deletion is to preserve the file until all references to it are deleted. To implement this approach, we must have some mechanism for determining that the last reference to the file has been deleted. We could keep a list of all references to a file (directory entries or symbolic links). When a link or a copy of the directory entry is established, a new entry is added to the file-reference list. When a link or directory entry is deleted, we remove its entry on the list. The file is deleted when its file-reference list is empty.

The trouble with this approach is the variable and potentially large size of the file-reference list. However, we really do not need to keep the entire list — we need to keep only a count of the *number* of references. A new link or directory entry increments the reference count; deleting a link or entry decrements the count. When the count is 0, the file can be deleted; there are no remaining references to it. The UNIX operating system uses this approach for nonsymbolic links, or *hard links*, keeping a reference count in the file information block (or inode, see Section 19.7.2). By effectively prohibiting multiple references to directories, we maintain an acyclic-graph structure.

To avoid these problems, some systems do not allow shared directories or links. For example, in MS-DOS, the directory structure is a tree structure, rather than an acyclic graph, thereby avoiding the problems associated with file deletion in an acyclic-graph directory structure.

10.3.5 General Graph Directory

One serious problem with using an acyclic graph structure is ensuring that there are no cycles. If we start with a two-level directory and allow users to create subdirectories, a tree-structured directory results. It should be fairly easy to see that simply adding new files and subdirectories to an existing tree-structured directory preserves the tree-structured nature. However, when we add links to an existing tree-structured directory, the tree structure is destroyed, resulting in a simple graph structure (Figure 10.11).

The primary advantage of an acyclic graph is the relative simplicity of the algorithms to traverse the graph and to determine when there are no more references to a file. We want to avoid traversing shared sections of an acyclic graph twice, mainly for performance reasons. If we have just searched a major shared subdirectory for a particular file, without finding that file, we want to avoid searching that subdirectory again; the second search would be a waste of time.

If cycles are allowed to exist in the directory, we likewise want to avoid searching any component twice, for reasons of correctness as well as performance. A poorly designed algorithm might result in an infinite loop continually searching through the cycle and never terminating. One solution is to arbitrarily limit the number of directories which will be accessed during a search.

A similar problem exists when we are trying to determine when a file can be deleted. As with acyclic-graph directory structures, a 0 in the reference count means that there are no more references to the file or

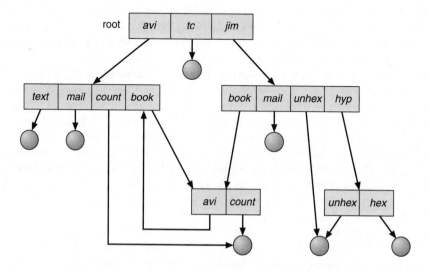

Figure 10.11 General graph directory.

directory, and the file can be deleted. However, it is also possible, when cycles exist, that the reference count may be nonzero, even when it is no longer possible to refer to a directory or file. This anomaly results from the possibility of self-referencing (a cycle) in the directory structure. In this case, it is generally necessary to use *garbage collection* to determine when the last reference has been deleted and the disk space can be reallocated. Garbage collection involves traversing the file system, marking everything that can be accessed. Then, a second pass collects everything that is not marked onto a list of free space. (A similar marking procedure can be used to ensure that a traversal or search will cover everything in the file system once and only once.) Garbage collection for a disk-based file system, however, is extremely time-consuming and is thus seldom attempted.

Garbage collection is necessary only because of possible cycles in the graph. Thus, an acyclic-graph structure is much easier to work with. The difficulty is to avoid cycles, as new links are added to the structure. How do we know when a new link will complete a cycle? There are algorithms to detect cycles in graphs; however, they are computationally expensive, especially when the graph is on disk storage. Generally, tree directory structures are more common than are acyclic-graph structures.

10.4 ■ Protection

When information is kept in a computer system, a major concern is its protection from both physical damage (*reliability*) and improper access (*protection*).

Reliability is generally provided by duplicate copies of files. Many computers have systems programs that automatically (or through computer-operator intervention) copy disk files to tape at regular intervals (once per day or week or month) to maintain a copy should a file system be accidentally destroyed. File systems can be damaged by hardware problems (such as errors in reading or writing), power surges or failures, head crashes, dirt, temperature extremes, and vandalism. Files may be deleted accidentally. Bugs in the file-system software can also cause file contents to be lost. Reliability is covered in more detail in Chapter 12.

Protection can be provided in many ways. For a small single-user system, we might provide protection by physically removing the floppy disks and locking them in a desk drawer or file cabinet. In a multiuser system, however, other mechanisms are needed.

10.4.1 Types

The need for protecting files is a direct result of the ability to access files. On systems that do not permit access to the files of other users, protection is not needed. Thus, one extreme would be to provide complete protection by prohibiting access. The other extreme is to provide free access with no protection. Both of these approaches are too extreme for general use. What is needed is *controlled access*.

Protection mechanisms provide controlled access by limiting the types of file access that can be made. Access is permitted or denied depending on several factors, one of which is the type of access requested. Several different types of operations may be controlled:

- **Read**. Read from the file.

- **Write**. Write or rewrite the file.

- **Execute**. Load the file into memory and execute it.

- **Append**. Write new information at the end of the file.

- **Delete**. Delete the file and free its space for possible reuse.

- **List**. List the name and attributes of the file.

Other operations, such as renaming, copying, or editing the file, may also be controlled. For many systems, however, these higher-level functions (such as copying) may be implemented by a system program that makes lower-level system calls. Protection is provided at only the lower level. For instance, copying a file may be implemented simply by a sequence of read requests. In this case, a user with read access can also cause the file to be copied, printed, and so on.

Many different protection mechanisms have been proposed. Each scheme has its advantages and disadvantages and must be selected as appropriate for its intended application. A small computer system that is used by only a few members of a research group may not need the same types of protection as will a large corporate computer that is used for research, finance, and personnel operations. A complete treatment of the protection problem is deferred to Chapter 13.

10.4.2 Access Lists and Groups

The most common approach to the protection problem is to make access dependent on the identity of the user. Various users may need different types of access to a file or directory. The most general scheme to implement identity-dependent access is to associate with each file and directory an *access list*, specifying the user name and the types of access allowed for each user. When a user requests access to a particular file, the operating system checks the access list associated with that file. If that user is listed for the requested access, the access is allowed. Otherwise, a protection violation occurs, and the user job is denied access to the file.

The main problem with access lists is their length. If we want to allow everyone to read a file, we must list all users with read access. This technique has two undesirable consequences:

- Constructing such a list may be a tedious and unrewarding task, especially if we do not know in advance the list of users in the system.

- The directory entry that previously was of fixed size needs now to be of variable size, resulting in space management being more complicated.

These problems can be resolved by use of a condensed version of the access list.

To condense the length of the access list, many systems recognize three classifications of users in connection with each file:

- **Owner**. The user who created the file is the owner.

- **Group**. A set of users who are sharing the file and need similar access is a group, or workgroup.

- **Universe**. All other users in the system constitute the universe.

As an example, consider a person, Sara, who is writing a new book. She has hired three graduate students (Jim, Dawn, and Jill) to help with the project. The text of the book is kept in a file named *book*. The protection associated with this file is as follows:

- Sara should be able to invoke all operations on the file.

- Jim, Dawn, and Jill should be able only to read and write the file; they should not be allowed to delete the file.

- All others users should be able to read the file. (Sara is interested in letting as many people as possible read the text so that she can obtain appropriate feedback.)

To achieve such a protection, we must create a new group, say *text*, with members Jim, Dawn, and Jill. The name of the group *text* must be then associated with the file *book*, and the access right must be set in accordance with the policy we have outlined.

Note that, for this scheme to work properly, group membership must be controlled tightly. This control can be accomplished in a number of different ways. For example, in the UNIX system, groups can be created and modified by only the manager of the facility (or by any superuser). Thus, this control is achieved through human interaction. In the VMS system, with each file, an *access list* (also known as an *access control list*) may be associated, listing those users who can access the file. The owner of the file can create and modify this list. Access lists are discussed further in Section 13.4.2.

With this more limited protection classification, only three fields are needed to define protection. Each field is often a collection of bits, each of which either allows or prevents the access associated with it. For example, the UNIX system defines three fields of 3 bits each: **rwx**, where **r** controls read access, **w** controls write access, and **x** controls execution. A separate field is kept for the file owner, for the owner's group and for all other users. In this scheme, 9 bits per file are needed to record protection information. Thus, for our example, the protection fields for the file *book* are as follows; For the owner Sara, all 3 bits are set; for the group *text*, the **r** and **w** bits are set; and for the universe, only the **r** bit is set.

Notice, however, that this scheme is not as general as is the access-list scheme. To illustrate our point, let us return to the book example. Suppose that Sara wants to exclude Jason from the list of people who can read the text. She cannot do so with the basic protection scheme outlined.

10.4.3 Other Protection Approaches

There is another approach to the protection problem, which is to associate a password with each file. Just as access to the computer system itself is often controlled by a password, access to each file can be controlled by a password. If the passwords are chosen randomly and changed often, this scheme may be effective in limiting access to a file to only those users who know the password. There are, however, several disadvantages to this scheme. First, if we associate a separate password with each file, the number of passwords that a user needs to remember may become large, making the scheme impractical. If only one password is used for all the files, then, once it is discovered, all files are accessible. Some systems (for example, TOPS-20) allow a user to associate a password with a subdirectory, rather than with an individual file, to deal with this problem. The IBM VM/CMS operating system allows three passwords for a minidisk: one each for read, write, and multiwrite access. Second, commonly, only one password is associated with each file. Thus, protection is on an all-or-nothing basis. To provide protection on a more detailed level, we must use multiple passwords.

Limited file protection is also currently available on single user systems, such as MS-DOS and Macintosh operating system. These operating systems, when originally designed, essentially ignored dealing with the protection problem. However, since these systems are being placed on networks where file sharing and communication is necessary, protection mechanisms are having to be retrofitted into the operating system. Note that it is almost always easier to design a feature into an new operating system than it is to add a feature to an existing one. Such updates are usually less effective and are not seamless.

-rw-rw-r--	1 pbg	staff	31200	Sep	3 08:30	intro.ps
drwx------	5 pbg	staff	512	Jul	8 09:33	private/
drwxrwxr-x	2 pbg	staff	512	Jul	8 09:35	doc/
drwxrwx---	2 pbg	student	512	Aug	3 14:13	student-proj/
-rw-r--r--	1 pbg	staff	9423	Feb	24 1993	program.c
-rwxr-xr-x	1 pbg	staff	20471	Feb	24 1993	program
drwx--x--x	4 pbg	faculty	512	Jul	31 10:31	lib/
drwx------	3 pbg	staff	1024	Aug	29 06:52	mail/
drwxrwxrwx	3 pbg	staff	512	Jul	8 09:35	test/

Figure 10.12   A sample directory listing.

We note that, in a multilevel directory structure, we need not only to protect individual files, but also to protect collections of files contained in a subdirectory; that is, we need to provide a mechanism for directory protection. The directory operations that must be protected are somewhat different from the file operations. We want to control the creation and deletion of files in a directory. In addition, we probably want to control whether a user can determine the existence of a file in a directory. Sometimes, knowledge of the existence and name of a file may be significant in itself. Thus, listing the contents of a directory must be a protected operation. Therefore, if a path name refers to a file in a directory, the user must be allowed access to both the directory and the file. In systems where files may have numerous path names (such as acyclic or general graphs), a given user may have different access rights to a file, depending on the path name used.

10.4.4 An Example: UNIX

In the UNIX system, directory protection is handled similarly to file protection. That is, associated with each subdirectory are three fields — owner, group, and universe — each consisting of the 3 bits **rwx**. Thus, a user can list the content of a subdirectory only if the **r** bit is set in the appropriate field. Similarly, a user can change his current directory to another current directory (say *foo*) only if the **x** bit associated with the *foo* subdirectory is set in the appropriate field.

A sample directory listing from a UNIX environment is shown in Figure 10.12. The first field describes the file or directory's protection. A **d** as the first character indicates a subdirectory. Also shown are the number of links to the file, the owner's name, the group's name, the size of the file in unit of bytes, the creation date, and finally the file's name (with optional extension).

10.5 ■ Consistency Semantics

Consistency semantics is an important criterion for evaluation of any file system that supports sharing of files. It is a characterization of the system that specifies the semantics of multiple users accessing a shared file simultaneously. In particular, these semantics should specify when modifications of data by one user are observable by other users.

For the following discussion, we assume that a series of file accesses (that is, reads and writes) attempted by a user to the same file, is always enclosed between the **open** and **close** operations. We call the series of accesses between an **open** and **close** operation a *file session*. To illustrate the concept, we sketch several prominent examples of consistency semantics.

10.5.1 UNIX Semantics

The UNIX file system (see Chapter 17) uses the following consistency semantics:

- Writes to an open file by a user are visible immediately to other users that have this file open at the same time.

- There is a mode of sharing where users share the pointer of current location into the file. Thus, the advancing of the pointer by one user affects all sharing users. Here, a file has a single image that interleaves all accesses, regardless of their origin.

These semantics lend themselves to an implementation where a file is associated with a single physical image that is accessed as an exclusive resource. Contention for this single image results in user processes being delayed.

10.5.2 Session Semantics

The Andrew file system (see Chapter 17) uses the following consistency semantics:

- Writes to an open file by a user are not visible immediately to other users that have the same file open simultaneously.

- Once a file is closed, the changes made to it are visible only in sessions starting later. Already-open instances of the file do not reflect these changes.

According to these semantics, a file may be associated temporarily with several (possibly different) images at the same time. Consequently, multiple users are allowed to perform both read and write accesses concurrently on their image of the file, without delay. Notice that almost no constraints are enforced on scheduling accesses.

10.5.3 Immutable-Shared-Files Semantics

A different, unique approach is that of *immutable shared files*. Once a file is declared as shared by its creator, it cannot be modified. An immutable file has two important properties: Its name may not be reused and its contents may not be altered. Thus, the name of an immutable file signifies that the contents of the file are fixed, rather than the file being a container for variable information. The implementation of these semantics in a distributed system (Chapter 17) is simple, since the sharing is disciplined (read-only).

10.6 ■ Summary

A file is an abstract data type defined and implemented by the operating system. It is a sequence of logical records. A logical record may be a byte, a line (fixed or variable length), or a more complex data item. The operating system may specifically support various record types or may leave that support to the application program.

The major task for the operating system is to map the logical file concept onto physical storage devices such as magnetic tape or disk. Since the physical record size of the device may not be the same as the logical record size, it may be necessary to block logical records into physical records. Again, this task may be supported by the operating system or left for the application program.

Tape-based file systems are constrained; most file systems are disk-based. Tapes are commonly used for data transport between machines, or for backup or archival storage.

Each device in a file system keeps a volume table of contents or device directory listing the location of the files on the device. In addition, it is useful to create directories to allow files to be organized. A single-level directory in a multiuser system causes naming problems, since each file must have a unique name. A two-level directory solves this problem by creating a separate directory for each user. Each user has her own directory, containing her own files.

The directory lists the files by name, and includes such information as the file's location on the disk, length, type, owner, time of creation, time of last use, and so on.

The natural generalization of a two-level directory is a tree-structured directory. A tree-structured directory allows a user to create subdirectories to organize his files. Acyclic-graph directory structures allow subdirectories and files to be shared, but complicate searching and deletion. A general graph structure allows complete flexibility in the sharing of files and directories, but sometimes requires garbage collection to recover unused disk space.

Since files are the main information-storage mechanism in most computer systems, file protection is needed. Access to files can be controlled separately for each type of access: read, write, execute, append, list directory, and so on. File protection can be provided by passwords, by access lists, or by special ad hoc techniques.

File systems are often implemented in a layered or modular structure. The lower levels deal with the physical properties of storage devices. Upper levels deal with symbolic file names and logical properties of files. Intermediate levels map the logical file concepts into physical device properties.

■ Exercises

10.1 Consider a file system where a file can be deleted and its disk space reclaimed while links to that file still exist. What problems may occur if a new file is created in the same storage area or with the same absolute path name? How can these problems be avoided?

10.2 Some systems automatically delete all user files when a user logs off or a job terminates, unless the user explicitly requests that they be kept; other systems keep all files unless the user explicitly deletes them. Discuss the relative merits of each approach.

10.3 Why do some systems keep track of the type of a file, while others leave it to the user or simply do not implement multiple file types? Which system is "better"?

10.4 Similarly, some systems support many types of structures for a file's data, while others simply support a stream of bytes. What are the advantages and disadvantages?

10.5 What are the advantages and disadvantages of recording the name of the creating program with the file's attributes (as is done in the Macintosh operating system)?

10.6 Could you simulate a multilevel directory structure with a single-level directory structure in which arbitrarily long names can be used? If your answer is yes, explain how you can do so, and contrast this scheme with the multilevel directory scheme. If your answer is no, explain what prevents your simulation's success. How would your answer change if file names were limited to seven characters?

10.7 Explain the purpose of the **open** and **close** operations.

10.8 Some systems automatically open a file when it is referenced for the first time, and close the file when the job terminates. Discuss the advantages and disadvantages of this scheme as compared to the more traditional one, where the user has to open and close the file explicitly.

10.9 Give an example of an application in which data in a file should be accessed in the following order:

  a. Sequentially

  b. Randomly

10.10 Some systems provide file sharing by maintaining a single copy of a file; other systems maintain several copies, one for each of the users sharing the file. Discuss the relative merits of each approach.

10.11 In some systems, a subdirectory can be read and written by an authorized user, just as ordinary files can be.

  a. Describe the protection problems that could arise.

  b. Suggest a scheme for dealing with each of the protection problems you named in part a.

10.12 Consider a system that supports 5000 users. Suppose that you want to allow 4990 of these users to be able to access one file.

  a. How would you specify this protection scheme in UNIX?

  b. Could you suggest another protection scheme that can be used more effectively for this purpose than the scheme provided by UNIX?

10.13 Researchers have suggested that, instead of having an access list associated with each file (specifying which users can access the file, and how), we should have a *user control list* associated with each user (specifying which files a user can access, and how). Discuss the relative merits of these two schemes.

Bibliographic Notes

General discussions concerning file systems were offered by Grosshans [1986]. Golden and Pechura [1986] described the structure of microcomputer file systems. Database systems and their file structures were described in full in Korth and Silberschatz [1991].

A multilevel directory structure was first implemented on the MULTICS system [Organick 1972]. Most operating systems now implement multilevel directory structures. These include UNIX [Ritchie and Thompson 1974], the Apple Macintosh operating system [Apple 1991], and MS-DOS [Microsoft 1991].

The MS-DOS file system was described in Norton and Wilton [1988]. That of VAX VMS was covered in Kenah el al. [1988], and Digital [1981]. The Network File System (NFS) was designed by Sun Microsystems, and allows directory structures to be spread across networked computer systems. Discussions concerning NFS were presented in Sandberg et al. [1985], Sandberg [1987], and Sun Microsystems [1990]. NFS is fully described in Chapter 17. The immutable-shared-files semantics was described by Schroeder et al. [1985].

Interesting research is ongoing in the area of file-system interfaces. Several papers in USENIX [1992a] discussed the issues of file naming and attributes. For example, the Plan 9 operating system from AT&T Bell Laboratories makes all objects look like file systems. Thus, to display a list of processes on a system, a user simply lists the contents of the /proc directory. Similarly, to display the time of day, a user needs only to type the file /dev/time.

CHAPTER 11

FILE
SYSTEM
IMPLEMENTATION

As we saw in Chapter 10, the file system provides the mechanism for on-line storage and access to both data and programs. The file system resides permanently on *secondary storage*, which has the main requirement that it must be able to hold a large amount of data, permanently. This chapter is primarily concerned with issues concerning file storage and access on the most common secondary-storage medium, the disk. We explore ways to allocate disk space, to recover freed space, to track the locations of data, and to interface other parts of the operating system to secondary storage. Performance issues are considered throughout the chapter.

11.1 ■ File-System Structure

Disks provide the bulk of secondary storage on which a file system is maintained. To improve I/O efficiency, I/O transfers between memory and disk are performed in units of *blocks*. Each block is one or more sectors. Depending on the disk drive, sectors vary from 32 bytes to 4096 bytes; usually, they are 512 bytes. Disks have two important characteristics that make them a convenient medium for storing multiple files:

1. They can be rewritten in place; it is possible to read a block from the disk, to modify the block, and to write it back into the same place.

2. We can access directly any given block of information on the disk. Thus, it is simple to access any file either sequentially or randomly,

and switching from one file to another requires only moving the read−write heads and waiting for the disk to revolve.

We discuss disk structure in great detail in Chapter 12.

11.1.1 File-System Organization

To provide an efficient and convenient access to the disk, the operating system imposes a *file system* to allow the data to be stored, located, and retrieved easily. A file system poses two quite different design problems. The first problem is defining how the file system should look to the user. This task involves the definition of a file and its attributes, operations allowed on a file, and the directory structure for organizing the files. Next, algorithms and data structures must be created to map the logical file system onto the physical secondary-storage devices.

The file system itself is generally composed of many different levels. The structure shown in Figure 11.1 is an example of a layered design. Each level in the design uses the features of lower levels to create new features for use by higher levels.

The lowest level, the *I/O control*, consists of *device drivers* and interrupt handlers to transfer information between memory and the disk system. A device driver can be thought of as a translator. Its input consists of high-level commands such as "retrieve block 123." Its output consists of low-level, hardware-specific instructions, which are used by the hardware controller, which interfaces the I/O device to the rest of the system. The

Figure 11.1   Layered file system.

device driver usually writes specific bit patterns to special locations in the I/O controller's memory to tell the controller on which device location to act and what actions to take.

The *basic file system* needs only to issue generic commands to the appropriate device driver to read and write physical blocks on the disk. Each physical block is identified by its numeric disk address (for example, drive 1, cylinder 73, surface 2, sector 10).

The *file-organization module* knows about files and their logical blocks, as well as physical blocks. By knowing the type of file allocation used and the location of the file, the file-organization module can translate logical block addresses to physical block addresses for the basic file system to transfer. Each file's logical blocks are numbered from 0 (or 1) through N, whereas the physical blocks containing this data usually do not match the logical numbers, so a translation is needed to locate each block. The file-organization module also includes the free-space manager, which tracks unallocated blocks and provides these blocks to the file-organization module when requested.

Finally, the *logical file system* uses the directory structure to provide the file-organization module with the information the latter needs, given a symbolic file name. The logical file system is also responsible for protection and security, as was discussed in Chapter 10 and will be further discussed in Chapter 13.

To create a new file, an application program calls the logical file system. The logical file system knows the format of the directory structures. To create a new file, it reads the appropriate directory into memory, updates it with the new entry, and writes it back to the disk. A directory can be treated exactly as a file — one with a type field indicating that it is a directory. Thus, the logical file system can call the file-organization module to map the directory I/O into disk-block numbers, which are passed on to the basic file system and I/O control system.

Once the directory has been updated, the logical file system can use it to perform I/O. When a file is opened, the directory structure is searched for the desired file entry. It would be possible to search the directory structure for every I/O operation, but that would be inefficient. To speed the search, the operating system generally keeps in memory a table, referred to as the *open-file* table, consisting of information about all the currently opened files (Figure 11.2).

The first reference to a file (normally an **open**) causes the directory structure to be searched and the directory entry for this file to be copied into the table of opened files. The index into this table is returned to the user program, and all further references are made through the index (a *file descriptor* or *file control block*), rather than with a symbolic name. Consequently, as long as the file is not closed, all directory lookups are done on the open-file table. All changes to the directory entry are made to the open-file table in memory. When the file is closed by all users that

index	file name	permissions	access dates	pointer to disk block
0	TEST.C	rw rw rw	...	→
1	MAIL.TXT	rw		→
2				
.				
.				
.				
n				

Figure 11.2 A typical open-file table.

have opened it, the updated entry is copied back to the disk-based directory structure.

Some systems complicate this scheme even further by using multiple levels of in-memory tables. For example, in the BSD UNIX file system, each process has an open-file table that merely points to a systemwide open-file table, which in turn points to a table of active *inodes*. The active-inodes table is an in-memory cache of inodes currently in use, and includes the inode index fields that point to the on-disk data blocks. In this way, once a file is opened, all but the actual data blocks are in memory for rapid access by any process accessing the file. The BSD UNIX system is typical in its use of caches wherever disk I/O can be saved. Its cache hit rate of 85 percent shows that these techniques are well worth implementing. The BSD UNIX system is described fully in Chapter 19. The open-file table is detailed in Section 10.1.2.

11.1.2 File-System Mounting

Just as a file must be **open**ed before it is used, a file system must be *mount*ed before it can be available to processes on the system. The mount procedure is straightforward. The operating system is given the name of the device, and the location within the file structure at which to attach the file system (called the *mount point*). For instance, on a UNIX system, a file system containing user's home directories might be mounted as /*home*; then, to access the directory structure within that file system, one could precede the directory names with /*home*, as in /*home/jane*. Mounting that file system under /*users* would result in the path name /*users/jane* to reach the same directory.

Next, the operating system verifies that the device contains a valid file system. It does so by asking the device driver to read the device directory and verifying that the directory has the expected format. Finally, the operating system notes in its directory structure that a file system is mounted at the specified mount point. This scheme enables the operating system to traverse its directory structure, switching among file systems as appropriate.

Consider the actions of the Macintosh Operating System. Whenever the system encounters a disk for the first time (hard disks are found at boot time, floppy disks are seen when they are inserted into the drive), the Macintosh Operating System searches for a file system on the device. If it finds one, it automatically mounts the file system at the root level, adding a folder icon on the screen labeled with the name of the file system (as stored in the device directory). The user is then able to click on the icon and thus to display the newly mounted file system.

File system mounting is further discussed in Sections 17.6.2 and 19.7.5.

11.2 ■ Allocation Methods

The direct-access nature of disks allows us flexibility in the implementation of files. In almost every case, many files will be stored on the same disk. The main problem is how to allocate space to these files so that disk space is utilized effectively and files can be accessed quickly. Three major methods of allocating disk space are in wide use: *contiguous*, *linked*, and *indexed*. Each method has its advantages and disadvantages. Accordingly, some systems (such as Data General's RDOS for its Nova line of computers) support all three. More common, a system will use one particular method for all files.

11.2.1 Contiguous Allocation

The *contiguous* allocation method requires each file to occupy a set of contiguous blocks on the disk. Disk addresses define a linear ordering on the disk. Notice that, with this ordering, accessing block $b + 1$ after block b normally requires no head movement. When head movement is needed (from the last sector of one cylinder to the first sector of the next cylinder), it is only one track. Thus, the number of disk seeks required for accessing contiguously allocated files is minimal, as is seek time when a seek is finally needed. The IBM VM/CMS operating system uses contiguous allocation because it provides such good performance.

Contiguous allocation of a file is defined by the disk address and length (in block units) of the first block. If the file is n blocks long, and starts at location b, then it occupies blocks b, $b + 1$, $b + 2$, ..., $b + n - 1$. The directory entry for each file indicates the address of the starting block and the length of the area allocated for this file (Figure 11.3).

Accessing a file that has been allocated contiguously is easy. For sequential access, the file system remembers the disk address of the last block referenced and, when necessary, reads the next block. For direct access to block i of a file that starts at block b, we can immediately access

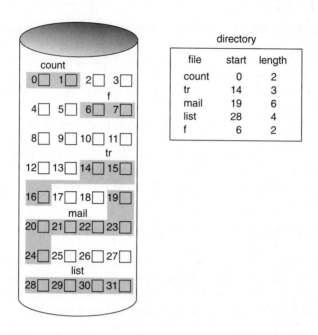

Figure 11.3 Contiguous allocation of disk space.

block $b + i$. Thus, both sequential and direct access can be supported by contiguous allocation.

One difficulty with contiguous allocation is finding space for a new file. The implementation of the free-space management system, discussed in Section 11.3, determines how this task is accomplished. Any management system can be used, but some are slower than others.

The contiguous disk-space-allocation problem can be seen to be a particular application of the general *dynamic storage-allocation* problem discussed in Section 8.4, which is how to satisfy a request of size n from a list of free holes. *First-fit* and *best-fit* are the most common strategies used to select a free hole from the set of available holes. Simulations have shown that both first-fit and best-fit are more efficient than worst-fit in terms of both time and storage utilization. Neither first-fit nor best-fit is clearly best in terms of storage utilization, but first-fit is generally faster.

These algorithms suffer from *external fragmentation*. As files are allocated and deleted, the free disk space is broken into little pieces. External fragmentation exists whenever free space is broken into chunks. It becomes a problem when the largest contiguous chunk is insufficient for a request; storage is fragmented into a number of holes, no one of which is large enough to store the data. Depending on the total amount of disk storage and the average file size, external fragmentation may be either a minor or a major problem.

Some older microcomputer systems used contiguous allocation on floppy disks. To prevent loss of significant amounts of disk space to external fragmentation, the user had to run a repacking routine that copied the entire file system onto another floppy disk or onto a tape. The original floppy disk was then freed completely, creating one large contiguous free space. The routine then copied the files back onto the floppy disk by allocating contiguous space from this one large hole. This scheme effectively *compacts* all free space into one contiguous space, solving the fragmentation problem. The cost of this compaction is time. Copying all the files from a disk to compact space may take hours and may be necessary on a weekly basis. During this *down time*, normal system operation cannot continue, so such compaction is avoided at all costs on production machines.

There are other problems with contiguous allocation. A major problem is determining how much space is needed for a file. When the file is created, the total amount of space it will need must be found and allocated. How does the creator (program or person) know the size of the file to be created? In some cases, this determination may be fairly simple (copying an existing file, for example); in general, however, the size of an output file may be difficult to estimate.

If we allocate too little space to a file, we may find that that file cannot be extended. Especially with a best-fit allocation strategy, the space on both sides of the file may be in use. Hence, we cannot make the file larger in place. Two possibilities then exist. First, the user program can be terminated, with an appropriate error message. The user must then allocate more space and run the program again. These repeated runs may be costly. To prevent them, the user will normally overestimate the amount of space needed, resulting in considerable wasted space.

The other possibility is to find a larger hole, to copy the contents of the file to the new space, and to release the previous space. This series of actions may be repeated as long as space exists, although it can also be time-consuming. Notice, however, that in this case the user never needs to be informed explicitly about what is happening; the system continues despite the problem, although more and more slowly.

Even if the total amount of space needed for a file is known in advance, preallocation may be inefficient. A file that grows slowly over a long period (months or years) must be allocated enough space for its final size, even though much of that space may be unused for a long time. The file therefore has a large amount of *internal fragmentation*.

To avoid several of these drawbacks, some operating systems use a modified contiguous allocation scheme, where a contiguous chunk of space is allocated initially, and then, when that amount is not large enough, another chunk of contiguous space, an *extent*, is added to the initial allocation. The location of a file's blocks is then recorded as a location and a block count, plus a link to the first block of the next extent. On some systems, the owner of the file can set the extent size, but this setting results in inefficiencies if the owner is incorrect. Internal fragmentation can still be a problem if the extents are too large, and external fragmentation can be a problem as extents of varying sizes are allocated and deallocated.

11.2.2 Linked Allocation

Linked allocation solves all problems of contiguous allocation. With linked allocation, each file is a linked list of disk blocks; the disk blocks may be scattered anywhere on the disk. The directory contains a pointer to the first and last blocks of the file. For example, a file of five blocks might start at block 9, continue at block 16, then block 1, block 10, and finally block 25 (Figure 11.4). Each block contains a pointer to the next block. These pointers are not made available to the user. Thus, if each block is 512 bytes, and a disk address (the pointer) requires 4 bytes, then the user sees blocks of 508 bytes.

To create a new file, we simply create a new entry in the directory. With linked allocation, each directory entry has a pointer to the first disk block of the file. This pointer is initialized to *nil* (the end-of-list pointer value) to signify an empty file. The size field is also set to 0. A write to the file causes a free block to be found via the free-space management

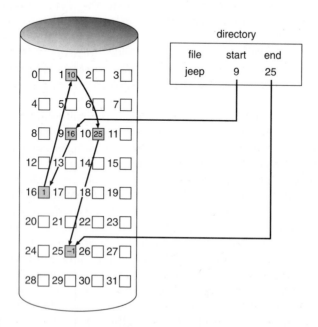

Figure 11.4 Linked allocation of disk space.

system, and this new block is then written to, and is linked to the end of the file. To read a file, we simply read blocks by following the pointers from block to block.

There is no external fragmentation with linked allocation, and any free block on the free-space list can be used to satisfy a request. Notice also that there is no need to declare the size of a file when that file is created. A file can continue to grow as long as there are free blocks. Consequently, it is never necessary to compact disk space.

Linked allocation does have disadvantages, however. The major problem is that it can be used effectively for only sequential-access files. To find the ith block of a file, we must start at the beginning of that file, and follow the pointers until we get to the ith block. Each access to a pointer requires a disk read, and sometimes a disk seek. Consequently, it is inefficient to support a direct-access capability for linked allocation files.

Another disadvantage to linked allocation is the space required for the pointers. If a pointer requires 4 bytes out of a 512-byte block, then 0.78 percent of the disk is being used for pointers, rather than for information. Each file requires slightly more space than it otherwise would.

The usual solution to this problem is to collect blocks into multiples, called *clusters*, and to allocate the clusters rather than blocks. For instance, the file system may define a cluster as 4 blocks, and operate on the disk in only cluster units. Pointers then use a much smaller percentage of the file's disk space. This method allows the logical-to-physical block mapping to remain simple, but improves disk throughput (fewer disk head seeks) and decreases the space needed for block allocation and free-list management. The cost of this approach is an increase in internal fragmentation, because more space is wasted if a cluster is partially full than when a block is partially full. Clusters can be used to optimize disk access for many other algorithms, so they are used in most operating systems.

Yet another problem is reliability. Since the files are linked together by pointers scattered all over the disk, consider what would happen if a pointer were lost or damaged. A bug in the operating-system software or a disk hardware failure might result in picking up the wrong pointer. This error could result in linking into the free-space list or into another file. One partial solution is to use doubly linked lists or to store the file name and relative block number in each block; however, these schemes require even more overhead for each file.

An important variation on the linked allocation method is the use of a *file-allocation table (FAT)*. This simple but efficient method of disk-space allocation is used by the MS-DOS and OS/2 operating systems. A section of disk at the beginning of each partition is set aside to contain the table. The table has one entry for each disk block, and is indexed by block number. The FAT is used much as is a linked list. The directory entry contains the block number of the first block of the file. The table entry indexed by that block number then contains the block number of the next block in the file. This chain continues until the last block, which has a special end-of-file value as the table entry. Unused blocks are indicated by a 0 table value. Allocating a new block to a file is a simple matter of finding the first 0-valued table entry, and replacing the previous end-of-file value with the address of the new block. The 0 is then replaced with the end-of-file value. An illustrative example is the FAT structure of Figure 11.5 for a file consisting of disk blocks 217, 618, and 3311.

Note that the FAT allocation scheme can result in a significant number of head seeks, unless the FAT is cached. The disk head must move to the start of the partition to read the FAT and find the location of the block in question, then move to the location of the block itself. In the worst case, both moves occur for each block. A benefit is that random access is optimized, because the disk head can find the location of any block by reading the information in the FAT.

11.2.3 Indexed Allocation

Linked allocation solves the external-fragmentation and size-declaration problems of contiguous allocation. However, linked allocation cannot support efficient direct access, since the pointers to the blocks are scattered

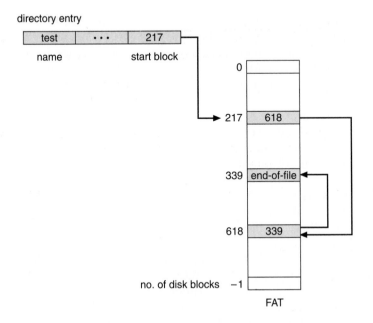

Figure 11.5 File-allocation table.

with the blocks themselves all over the disk and need to be retrieved in order. Indexed allocation solves this problem by bringing all the pointers together into one location: the *index block*.

Each file has its own index block, which is an array of disk-block addresses. The *i*th entry in the index block points to the *i*th block of the file. The directory contains the address of the index block (Figure 11.6). To read the *i*th block, we use the pointer in the *i*th index-block entry to find and read the desired block. This scheme is similar to the paging scheme described in Chapter 8.

When the file is created, all pointers in the index block are set to *nil*. When the *i*th block is first written, a block is obtained from the free-space manager, and its address is put in the *i*th index-block entry.

Indexed allocation supports direct access, without suffering from external fragmentation, because any free block on the disk may satisfy a request for more space.

Indexed allocation does suffer from wasted space. The pointer overhead of the index block is generally greater than the pointer overhead of linked allocation. Consider a common case in which we have a file of only one or two blocks. With linked allocation, we lose the space of only one pointer per block (one or two pointers). With indexed allocation, an entire index block must be allocated, even if only one or two pointers will be non-*nil*.

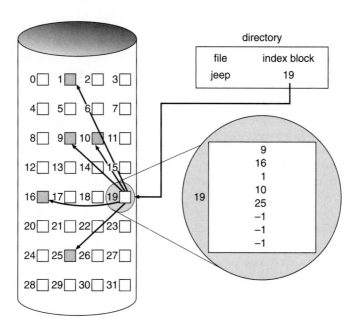

Figure 11.6 Indexed allocation of disk space.

This point raises the question of how large the index block should be. Every file must have an index block, so we want the index block to be as small as possible. If the index block is too small, however, it will not be able to hold enough pointers for a large file, and a mechanism will have to be available to deal with this issue:

- **Linked scheme**. An index block is normally one disk block. Thus, it can be read and written directly by itself. To allow for large files, we may link together several index blocks. For example, an index block might contain a small header giving the name of the file, and a set of the first 100 disk-block addresses. The next address (the last word in the index block) is *nil* (for a small file) or is a pointer to another index block (for a large file).

- **Multilevel index**. A variant of the linked representation is to use a separate index block to point to the index blocks, which point to the file blocks themselves. To access a block, the operating system uses the first-level index to find the second-level index to find the desired data block. This approach could be continued to a third or fourth level, depending on the desired maximum file size. With 2048-byte blocks (through clustering), we can get 512 4-byte pointers into an index block. Two levels of indexes allow 4,194,304 data blocks, which allows a file of up to 8.5 gigabytes. This number of bytes currently exceeds the physical capacity of an individual disk drive.

- **Combined scheme**. Another alternative, used in the BSD UNIX system, is to keep the first, say, 15 pointers of the index block in the file's index block (or inode). (The directory entry points to the inode, as discussed in Section 19.7.) The first 12 of these pointers point to *direct blocks*; that is, they contain addresses of blocks that contain data of the file. Thus, the data for small (no more than 12 blocks) files do not need a separate index block. If the block size is 4K, then up to 48K of data may be accessed directly. The next three pointers point to *indirect blocks*. The first indirect block pointer is the address of a *single indirect block*. The single indirect block is an index block, containing not data, but rather the addresses of blocks that do contain data. Then there is a *double indirect block* pointer, which contains the address of a block that contains the addresses of blocks that contain pointers to the actual data blocks. The last pointer would contain the address of a *triple indirect block*. Under this method, the number of blocks that can be allocated to a file exceeds the amount of space addressable by the 4-byte file pointers used by the operating system or passed in system calls. The 32-bit file pointer reaches only 2^{32} bytes, or 4 gigabytes. An inode is shown in Figure 11.7.

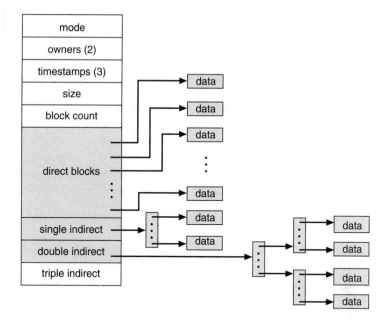

Figure 11.7   The UNIX inode.

Note that indexed allocation schemes suffer from some of the same performance problems as does linked allocation. Specifically, the index blocks can be cached in memory, but the data blocks may be spread all over a partition.

11.2.4 Performance

The allocation methods that we have discussed vary in their storage efficiency and data-block access times. Both are important criteria in selecting the proper method or methods for an operating system to implement.

One difficulty in comparing the performance of the various systems is determining how the systems will be used. A system with mostly sequential access should use a method different from that for a system with mostly random access. For any type of access, contiguous allocation requires only one access to get a disk block. Since we can easily keep the initial address of the file in memory, we can calculate immediately the disk address of the ith block (or the next block) and read it directly.

For linked allocation, we can also keep the address of the next block in memory and read it directly. This method is fine for sequential access; for direct access, however, an access to the ith block might require i disk reads. This problem indicates why linked allocation should not be used for an application requiring direct access.

As a result, some systems support direct-access files by using contiguous allocation and sequential access by linked allocation. For these systems, the type of access to be made must be declared when the file is created. A file created for sequential access will be linked and cannot be used for direct access. A file created for direct access will be contiguous and can support both direct access and sequential access, but its maximum length must be declared when it is created. Notice that, in this case, the operating system must have appropriate data structures and algorithms to support *both* allocation methods. Files can be converted from one type to another by the creation of a new file of the desired type, into which the contents of the old file are copied. The old file may then be deleted, and the new file renamed.

Indexed allocation is more complex. If the index block is already in memory, then the access can be made directly. However, keeping the index block in memory requires considerable space. If this memory space is not available, then we may have to read first the index block and then the desired data block. For a two-level index, two index-block reads might be necessary. For an extremely large file, accessing a block near the end of the file would require reading in all the index blocks to follow the pointer chain before the data block finally could be read. Thus, the performance of indexed allocation depends on the index structure, on the size of the file, and on the position of the block desired.

Some systems combine contiguous allocation with indexed allocation by using contiguous allocation for small files (up to three or four blocks), and automatically switching to an indexed allocation if the file grows large. Since most files are small, and contiguous allocation is efficient for small files, average performance can be quite good.

For instance, the version of UNIX from Sun Microsystems was changed in 1991 to improve performance in the file-system allocation algorithm. The performance measurements indicated that the maximum disk throughput on a typical workstation (12-MIPS Sparcstation1) took 50 percent of the CPU and produced a disk bandwidth of only 1.5 megabytes per second. To improve performance, Sun made changes to allocate space in very large clusters (56K) whenever possible. This allocation reduced external fragmentation, and thus seek and latency times. In addition, the disk-reading routines were optimized to read in these large clusters. The inode structure was left unchanged. These changes, plus the use of read-ahead and free-behind (discussed in Section 11.5.2) resulted in 25 percent less CPU being used for somewhat improved throughput.

Many other optimizations are possible and are in use. Given the disparity between CPU and disk speed, it is not unreasonable to add thousands of extra instructions to the operating system to save just a few disk head movements. Furthermore, this disparity is increasing over time, to the point where hundreds of thousands of instructions reasonably could be used to optimize head movements. For example, research is proceeding on the use of artificial-intelligence algorithms to analyze past disk-access patterns so as to predict future ones.

11.3 ∎ Free-Space Management

Since there is only a limited amount of disk space, it is necessary to reuse the space from deleted files for new files, if possible. (Write-once optical disks only allow one write to any given sector, and thus such reuse is not physically possible.) To keep track of free disk space, the system maintains a *free-space list*. The free-space list records all disk blocks that are *free* — those not allocated to some file or directory. To create a file, we search the free-space list for the required amount of space, and allocate that space to the new file. This space is then removed from the free-space list. When a file is deleted, its disk space is added to the free-space list. The free-space list, despite its name, might not be implemented as a list, as we shall discuss.

11.3.1 Bit Vector

Frequently, the free-space list is implemented as a *bit map* or *bit vector*. Each block is represented by 1 bit. If the block is free, the bit is 1; if the block is allocated, the bit is 0.

For example, consider a disk where blocks 2, 3, 4, 5, 8, 9, 10, 11, 12, 13, 17, 18, 25, 26, and 27 are free, and the rest of the blocks are allocated. The free-space bit map would be

001111001111110001100000011100000 ...

The main advantage of this approach is that it is relatively simple and efficient to find the first free block, or n consecutive free blocks on the disk. Indeed, many computers supply bit-manipulation instructions that can be used effectively for that purpose. For example, the Intel 80386 and 80486 and Motorola 68020 through 68040 microprocessors (the processors that power recent IBM PC compatibles and Macintosh systems, respectively) have instructions that return the offset in a word of the first bit with the value 1. In fact, the Apple Macintosh Operating System uses the bit-vector method to allocate disk space. To find the first free block, the Macintosh Operating System checks sequentially each word in the bit map to see whether that value is not 0, since a 0-valued word has all 0 bits and represents a set of allocated blocks. The first non0 word is scanned for the first 1 bit, which is the location of the first free block. The calculation of the block number is

(number of bits per word) * (number of 0-value words) + offset of first 1 bit

Again, we see hardware features driving software functionality. Unfortunately, bit vectors are inefficient unless the entire vector is kept in main memory (and is written to disk occasionally for recovery needs). Keeping it in main memory is possible for smaller disks, such as on microcomputers, but not for larger ones. A now-common 1.3-gigabyte disk with 512-byte blocks would need a bit map of over 310K to track its free blocks. Clustering the blocks in intervals of four reduces this number to 78K per disk.

11.3.2 Linked List

Another approach is to link together all the free disk blocks, keeping a pointer to the first free block in a special location on the disk and caching it in memory. This first block contains a pointer to the next free disk block, and so on. In our example (Section 11.3.1), we would keep a pointer to block 2, as the first free block. Block 2 would contain a pointer to block 3, which would point to block 4, which would point to block 5, which would point to block 8, and so on (Figure 11.8). However, this scheme is not efficient; to traverse the list, we must read each block, which requires substantial I/O time. Fortunately, traversing the free list is not a frequent action. Usually, the operating system simply needs a free block so that it can allocate that block to a file, so the first block in the free list is used. Note that the FAT method incorporates free-block accounting into the allocation data structure. No separate method is needed.

11.3.3 Grouping

A modification of the free-list approach is to store the addresses of n free blocks in the first free block. The first $n-1$ of these blocks are actually free. The last block contains the addresses of another n free blocks, and so on. The importance of this implementation is that the addresses of a large number of free blocks can be found quickly, unlike in the standard linked-list approach.

11.3.4 Counting

Another approach is to take advantage of the fact that, generally, several contiguous blocks may be allocated or freed simultaneously, particularly when space is allocated with the contiguous allocation algorithm or through clustering. Thus, rather than keeping a list of n free disk

free-space list head

Figure 11.8   Linked free-space list on disk.

addresses, we can keep the address of the first free block and the number n of free contiguous blocks that follow the first block. Each entry in the free-space list then consists of a disk address and a count. Although each entry requires more space than would a simple disk address, the overall list will be shorter, as long as the count is generally greater than 1.

11.4 ■ Directory Implementation

The selection of directory-allocation and directory-management algorithms has a large effect on the efficiency, performance and reliability of the file system. Therefore, it is important to understand the tradeoffs involved in these algorithms.

11.4.1 Linear

The simplest method of implementing a directory is to use a linear list of file names with pointers to the data blocks. A linear list of directory entries requires a linear search to find a particular entry. This method is simple to program but is time-consuming to execute. To create a new file, we must first search the directory to be sure that no existing file has the same name. Then, we add a new entry at the end of the directory. To delete a file, we search the directory for the named file, then release the space allocated to it. To reuse the directory entry, we can do one of several things. We can mark the entry as unused (by assigning it a special name, such as an all-blank name, or with a used–unused bit in each entry), or we can attach it to a list of free directory entries. A third alternative is to copy the last entry in the directory into the freed location, and to decrease the length of the directory. A linked list can also be used to decrease the time to delete a file.

The real disadvantage of a linear list of directory entries is the linear search to find a file. Directory information is used frequently, and a slow implementation of access to it would be noticed by users. In fact, many operating systems implement a software cache to store the most recently used directory information. A cache hit avoids constantly rereading the information from disk. A sorted list allows a binary search and decreases the average search time. However, the search algorithm is more complex to program. In addition, the requirement that the list must be kept sorted may complicate creating and deleting files, since we may have to move substantial amounts of directory information to maintain a sorted directory. (However, notice that if we want to be able to produce a list of all files in a directory sorted by file name, we do not have to sort separately before listing.) A linked binary tree might help here.

11.4.2 Hash Table

Another data structure that has been used for a file directory is a *hash table*. In this method, a linear list stores the directory entries, but a hash data structure is also used. The hash table takes a value computed from the file name and returns a pointer to the file name in the linear list. Therefore, it can greatly decrease the directory search time. Insertion and deletion are also fairly straightforward, although some provision must be made for *collisions* — situations where two file names hash to the same location. The major difficulties with a hash table are the generally fixed size of the hash table and the dependence of the hash function on the size of the hash table.

For example, assume that we establish a hash table of 64 entries. The hash function converts file names into integers from 0 to 63, probably by a final operation that uses the remainder of a division by 64. If we later try to create a sixty-fifth file, we must enlarge the directory hash table — say, to 128 entries. As a result, we need a new hash function, which must map file names to the range 0 to 127, and we must reorganize the existing directory entries to reflect their new hash-function values. Alternately, each hash entry can be a linked list instead of an individual value, and we can resolve collisions by adding the new entry to the linked list. Lookups are somewhat slowed, because resolving a name to a pointer might require stepping through the linked list of the hash entry to find the correct entry.

11.5 ■ Efficiency and Performance

Now that we have discussed the block-allocation and directory-management options, we can further consider their effect on performance and efficient disk use. Disks tend to be a major bottleneck in system performance, since they are the slowest main computer component. In this section, we discuss a variety of techniques used to improve the efficiency and performance of secondary storage.

11.5.1 Efficiency

The efficient use of disk space is heavily dependent on the disk allocation and directory algorithms in use. For instance, UNIX inodes are preallocated on a partition. Even an "empty" disk has a percentage of its space lost to inodes. However, by preallocating the inodes and spreading them across the partition, we improve the file system's performance. This improved performance is a result of the UNIX allocation and free-space algorithms, which try to keep a file's data blocks near that file's inode block to reduce seek time.

As another example, let us reconsider the clustering scheme discussed in Section 11.2, which aids in file-seek and file-transfer performance at the cost of internal fragmentation. To reduce this fragmentation, BSD UNIX varies the cluster size as a file grows. Large clusters are used where they can be filled, and small clusters are used for small files and the last cluster of a file. This system is described in Chapter 19.

Also requiring consideration are the types of data normally kept in a file's directory (or inode) entry. Commonly, a "last write date" is recorded to supply information to the user and to determine whether the file needs to be backed up. Some systems also keep a "last access date," so that a user can determine when the file was last read. The result of keeping this information is that, whenever the file is read, a field in the directory structure needs to be written to. This change requires the block to be read into memory, a section changed, and the block written back out to disk, because operations on disks occur only in block (or cluster) chunks. So, any time a file is opened for reading, its directory entry must be read and written as well. This requirement can be inefficient for frequently accessed files, so we must weigh its benefit against its performance cost when designing a file system. Generally, *every* data item associated with a file needs to be considered for its affect on efficiency and performance.

As an example, consider how efficiency is affected by the size of the pointers used to access data. Most systems use either 16- or 32-bit pointers throughout the operating system. These pointer sizes limit the length of a file to either 2^{16} (64K), or 2^{32} bytes (4 gigabytes). Some systems implement 64-bit pointers to increase this limit to 2^{64} bytes, which is a very large number indeed. However, 64-bit pointers take more space to store, and in turn make the allocation and free-space management methods (linked lists, indexes, and so on) use more disk space.

One of the difficulties in choosing a pointer size, or indeed any fixed allocation size within an operating system, is planning for the effects of changing technology. Consider that the first IBM PC XT had a 5-megabyte hard drive, and an MS-DOS file system that could support only 32 megabytes. (Each FAT entry was 12 bits, pointing to an 8K cluster.) As disk capacities increased, larger disks had to be split into 32-megabyte partitions, because the file system could not track blocks beyond 32 megabytes. As hard disks of over 100-megabyte capacities became common, the disk data structures and algorithms in MS-DOS had to be modified to allow larger file systems. (Each FAT entry was expanded to 16 bits.) The initial file-system decisions were made for efficiency reasons; however, with the advent of MS-DOS, Version 4, millions of computer users were inconvenienced when they had to switch to the new, larger file system.

As another example, consider the evolution of Sun's Solaris operating system. Originally, many data structures were of fixed lengths, allocated at system startup. These structures included the process table and the open-file table. When the process table became full, no more processes could be created. When the file table became full, no more files could be opened. The system would fail to provide services to the users. These table sizes could be increased only by recompiling the kernel and rebooting the system. Since the release of Solaris 2, almost all kernel structures are allocated dynamically, eliminating these artificial limits on system performance. Of course, the algorithms that manipulate these tables are more complicated, and the operating system is a little slower because it must dynamically allocate and deallocate table entries, but that price is the usual one for more functional generality.

11.5.2 Performance

Once the basic disk methods are selected, there are still several ways to improve performance. As noted in Chapter 2, some disk controllers include enough local memory to create an on-board *cache* that may be sufficiently large to store an entire track at a time. Once a seek is performed, the track is read into the disk cache starting at the sector under the disk head (alleviating latency time). The disk controller then transfers any sector requests to the operating system. Once blocks make it from the disk controller into main memory, the operating system may cache the blocks there. Some systems maintain a separate section of main memory for a *disk cache*, where blocks are kept under the assumption that they will be used again shortly. LRU is a reasonable general-purpose algorithm for block replacement. Other systems (such as Sun's version of UNIX) treat all unused physical memory as a buffer pool that is shared by the paging system and the disk-block caching system. A system performing many I/O operations will use most of its memory as a block cache, whereas a system executing many programs will use more memory as paging space.

Some systems optimize their disk cache by using different replacement algorithms, depending on the access type of the file. A file being read or written sequentially should not have its blocks replaced in LRU order, because the most recently used block will be used last, or perhaps never again. Instead, sequential access may be optimized by techniques known as *free-behind* and *read-ahead*. Free-behind removes a block from the buffer as soon as the next block is requested. The previous blocks are not likely to be used again and waste buffer space. With read-ahead, a requested block and several subsequent blocks are read and cached. It is likely that these blocks will be requested after the current block is processed. Retrieving these blocks from the disk in one transfer and caching them saves a considerable amount of time. Even a track cache on the controller may not eliminate the need for read-ahead on a multiprogrammed system, since some other process may request a transfer at another track before the next sequential request takes place.

Another method of using main memory to improve performance is common on personal computers. A section of memory is set aside and treated as a *virtual disk*, or RAM *disk*. In this case, a RAM disk device driver accepts all the standard disk operations, but performs those operations on the memory section, instead of on a disk. All disk operations can then be executed on this RAM disk and, except for the lightning-fast speed, users will not notice a difference. Unfortunately, RAM disks are useful for only temporary storage, since a power failure or a reboot of the system will usually erase them. Commonly, temporary files such as intermediate compiler files are stored there.

The difference between a RAM disk and a disk cache is that the contents of the RAM disk are totally user controlled, whereas those of the disk cache are under the control of the operating system. For instance, a RAM disk will stay empty until the user (or programs, at a user's direction) creates files there. Figure 11.9 shows the possible caching locations in a system.

11.6 ■ Recovery

Since files and directories are kept both in main memory and on disk, care must taken to ensure that system failure does not result in loss of data or in data inconsistency.

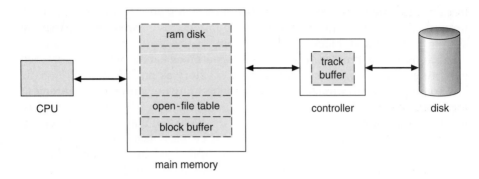

Figure 11.9 Various disk-caching locations.

11.6.1 Consistency Checking

As discussed in Section 11.4, part of the directory information is kept in main memory (cache) so as to speed up access. The directory information in main memory is generally more up to date than is the corresponding information on the disk, because the write of cached directory information to disk does not necessarily occur as soon as the update takes place.

Consider the possible effect of a computer crash. In this case, the table of opened files is generally lost, and with it any changes in the directories of opened files. This event can leave the file system in an inconsistent state: The actual state of some files is not as described in the directory structure. Frequently, a special program is run at reboot time to check for and correct disk inconsistencies.

The *consistency checker* compares the data in the directory structure with the data blocks on disk, and tries to fix any inconsistencies it finds. The allocation and free-space management algorithms dictate what types of problems the checker can find, and how successful it will be in fixing those problems. For instance, if linked allocation is used and there is a link from any block to its next block, then the entire file can be reconstructed from the data blocks, and the directory structure can be recreated. The loss of a directory entry on an indexed allocation system could be disastrous, because the data blocks have no knowledge of one another. For this reason, UNIX caches directory entries for reads, but any data write that results in an inode update generally causes the inode block to be written to disk before the data themselves are.

11.6.2 Backup and Restore

Because magnetic disks fail and loss of data may occur, care must be taken to ensure that the data are not lost forever. To this end, system programs can be used to *back up* data from disk to another storage device, usually a floppy disk, magnetic tape, or optical disk. Recovery from the loss of an individual file, or of an entire disk, may then be a matter of *restoring* the data from backup.

To minimize the copying needed, we can use information from each file's directory entry. For instance, if the backup program knows when the last backup of a file was done, and the file's last write date in the directory indicates that the file has not changed since then, then the file does not need to be copied again. A typical backup schedule may then be as follows:

- **Day 1**. Copy to a backup medium all files from the disk.

- **Day 2**. Copy to another medium all files changed since day 1.

- **Day 3**. Copy to another medium all files changed since day 2.

.

.

.

- **Day N**. Copy to another medium all files changed since day $N-1$. Then go back to Day 1.

The new cycle can have its backup written over the previous set, or onto a new set of backup media. In this manner, we can restore an entire disk by starting restores with the backup from day 1 and continuing through day N. Of course, the larger N is, the more tapes or disks need to be read for a complete restore. An added advantage of this backup cycle is that we can restore any file accidently deleted during the cycle by retrieving the deleted file from the backup of the previous day. The length of the cycle is a compromise between the amount of backup medium needed and the number of days back from which a restore can be done.

11.7 ■ Summary

The file system resides permanently on *secondary storage*, which has the main requirement that it must be able to hold a large amount of data, permanently. The most common secondary-storage medium is the disk.

Files can be allocated space on the disk in three ways: through contiguous, linked, or indexed allocation. Contiguous allocation can suffer from external fragmentation. Direct-access files cannot be supported with linked allocation. Indexed allocation may require substantial overhead for its index block. There are many ways in which these algorithms can be optimized. Contiguous space may be enlarged through extents to increase flexibility and to decrease external fragmentation. Indexed allocation can be done in clusters of multiple blocks to increase throughput and to reduce the number of index entries needed. Indexing in large clusters is similar to contiguous allocation with extents.

Free-space allocation methods also influence the efficiency of use of disk space, the performance of the file system, and the reliability of secondary storage. The methods used include bit vectors and linked lists. Optimizations include grouping, counting, and the FAT, which places the linked list in one location.

The   directory-management   routines   must   consider   efficiency, performance, and reliability. A hash table is the most frequently used method; it is fast and efficient. Unfortunately, damage to the table or a system crash could result in the directory information not corresponding to the disk's contents. A *consistency checker* — a systems program — can be used to repair the damage.

■   Exercises

11.1 Consider a file currently consisting of 100 blocks. Assume that the file control block (and the index block, in the case of indexed allocation) is already in memory. Calculate how many disk I/O operations are required for contiguous, linked, and indexed (single-level) allocation strategies, if, for one block, the following conditions hold. In the contiguous-allocation case, assume that there is no room to grow in the beginning, but there is room to grow in the end. Assume that the block information to be added is stored in memory.

   a. The block is added at the beginning.

   b. The block is added in the middle.

   c. The block is added at the end.

   d. The block is removed from the beginning.

   e. The block is removed from the middle.

   f. The block is removed from the end.

11.2 Consider a system where free space is kept in a free-space list.

   a. Suppose that the pointer to the free-space list is lost. Can the system reconstruct the free-space list? Explain your answer.

   b. Suggest a scheme to ensure that the pointer is never lost as a result of memory failure.

11.3 What problems could occur if a system allowed a file system to be mounted simultaneously at more than one location?

11.4 Why must the bit map for file allocation be kept on mass storage, rather than in main memory?

11.5 Consider a system that supports the strategies of contiguous, linked, and indexed allocation. What criteria should be used in deciding which strategy is best utilized for a particular file?

11.6 Consider a file system on a disk that has both logical and physical block sizes of 512 bytes. Assume that the information about each file is already in memory. For each of the three allocation strategies (contiguous, linked, and indexed), answer these questions:

 a. How is the logical-to-physical address mapping accomplished in this system? (For the indexed allocation, assume that a file is always less than 512 blocks long.)

 b. If we are currently at logical block 10 (the last block accessed was block 10) and want to access logical block 4, how many physical blocks must be read from the disk?

11.7 One problem with contiguous allocation is that the user must preallocate enough space for each file. If the file grows to be larger than the space allocated for it, special actions must be taken. One solution to this problem is to define a file structure consisting of an initial contiguous area (of a specified size). If this area is filled, the operating system automatically defines an overflow area that is linked to the initial contiguous area. If the overflow area is filled, another overflow area is allocated. Compare this implementation of a file with the standard contiguous and linked implementations.

11.8 Fragmentation on a storage device could be eliminated by recompaction of the information. Typical disk devices do not have relocation or base registers (such as are used when memory is to be compacted), so how can we relocate files? Give three reasons why recompacting and relocation of files often are avoided.

11.9 How do caches help improve performance? Why do systems not use more or larger caches if they are so useful?

11.10 In what situations would using memory as a RAM disk be more useful than using it as a disk cache?

11.11 Why is it advantageous for the user for an operating system to dynamically allocate its internal tables? What are the penalties to the operating system for doing so?

11.12 Consider the following backup scheme:

- **Day 1**. Copy to a backup medium all files from the disk.

- **Day 2**. Copy to another medium all files changed since day 1.

- **Day 3**. Copy to another medium all files changed since day 1.

This contrasts to the schedule given in Section 11.6.2 by having all subsequent backups copy all files modified since the first full backup. What are the benefits of this system over the one in Section 11.6.2? Are restore operations made easier or more difficult? Explain your answer.

Bibliographic Notes

The Apple Macintosh disk-space management scheme was discussed in Apple [1987, 1991]. The MS-DOS FAT system was explained in Norton and Wilton [1988], and the OS/2 description is found in [Iacobucci 1988]. These operating systems use the Motorola MC68000 family [Motorola 1989a] and the Intel 8086 [Intel 1985a, 1985b, 1986, 1990] CPUs, respectively. IBM allocation methods were described in Deitel [1990]. The internals of the BSD UNIX system were covered in full in Leffler et al. [1989]. McVoy and Kleiman [1991] presented optimizations to these methods made in SunOS.

Disk file allocation based on the buddy system was discussed by Koch [1987]. A file-organization scheme that guarantees retrieval in one access was discussed by Larson and Kajla [1984].

Disk caching was discussed by McKeon [1985] and Smith [1985]. Caching in the experimental Sprite operating system was described in Nelson et al. [1988]. General discussions concerning mass-storage technology were offered by Chi [1982] and Hoagland [1985]. Folk and Zoellick [1987] covered the gamut of file structures.

CHAPTER 12

SECONDARY STORAGE STRUCTURE

The file system can be logically viewed as consisting of three parts. In Chapter 10, we saw the user and programmer interface to the file system. In Chapter 11, we described the internal data structures and algorithms used by the operating system to implement this interface. In this chapter we discuss the lowest level of the file system — the secondary storage structure. We first describe disk-head-scheduling algorithms. Next we discuss disk formatting, and management of boot blocks, damaged blocks, and swap space. We end with coverage of disk reliability and stable-storage.

12.1 ■ Disk Structure

Disks provide the bulk of secondary storage for modern computer systems. Magnetic tape was used as an early secondary-storage medium. Although it is relatively permanent, and can hold large numbers of data, magnetic tape is slow in comparison to the access time of main memory. Even more important, magnetic tape is limited to sequential access. Thus, it is unsuitable for providing the random access needed by files. Tapes are currently used mainly for backup, for storage of infrequently used information, and as a medium for transferring information from one system to another.

Information on the disk is referenced by a multipart address, which includes the drive number, the surface, the track, and the sector. All the tracks on one drive that can be accessed without the heads being moved (the equivalent tracks on the different surfaces) constitute a *cylinder*.

Within a track, information is stored in sectors. IBM mainframes allow the user to select the size of the sector, but most other disks have a sector size fixed by hardware. A *sector* is the smallest unit of information that can be read from or written to the disk. Depending on the disk drive, sectors vary from 32 bytes to 4096 bytes; usually, they are 512 bytes. There are 4 to 32 sectors per track, and from 20 to 1500 tracks per disk surface. To access a sector, we must specify the surface, track, and sector. To help the disk drive to locate its sector location, the drive records sector marks between the sectors. The read−write heads are moved to the correct track (seek time) and are electronically switched to the correct surface; then, we wait (latency time) for the requested sector to rotate below the heads. Seek time is dependent on the time it takes for the disk heads to move, so the farther apart the tracks are, the longer the seek time is.

I/O transfers between memory and disk are performed in units of one or more sectors, called *blocks*, to improve I/O efficiency. Addressing a particular block requires a track (or cylinder) number, a surface number, and a sector number. Thus, the disk can be viewed as a three-dimensional array of blocks. Commonly, this array is treated by the operating system as a one-dimensional array of blocks. Typically, block addresses increase through all blocks on a track, then through all the tracks in a cylinder, and finally from cylinder 0 to the last cylinder on the disk. We use s to denote the number of sectors per track, and t to denote the number of tracks per cylinder; clearly, we can convert from a disk address of cylinder i, surface j, sector k to a one-dimensional block number b, by

$$b = k + s \times (j + i \times t).$$

Notice that, with this mapping, accessing block $b + 1$ when the last block accessed was b requires a seek only when b was the last block of one cylinder and $b + 1$ is the first block of the next cylinder. Even in this case, the head is moved only one track.

12.2 ■ Disk Scheduling

Because most jobs depend heavily on the disk for program loading and input and output files, it is important that disk service be as fast as possible. The operating system can improve on the average disk service time by scheduling the requests for disk access.

Disk speed is composed of three parts. To access a block on the disk, the system must first move the head to the appropriate track or cylinder. This head movement is called a *seek*, and the time to complete it is *seek time*. Once the head is at the right track, it must wait until the desired block rotates under the read−write head. This delay is *latency* time. Finally, the actual transfer of data between the disk and main memory can take place. This last part is *transfer* time. The total time to service a disk request is the sum of the seek time, latency time, and transfer time.

As we discussed in Chapter 2, every I/O device, including each disk drive, has a queue of pending requests. Whenever a process needs I/O to or from the disk, it issues a system call to the operating system. The request specifies several pieces of necessary information:

- Whether this operation is input or output

- What is the disk address (a block number, translated by the file organization module into drive, cylinder, surface, and sector coordinates)

- What is the memory address to copy to or from

- What is the amount of information to be transferred (a byte count)

If the desired disk drive and controller are available, the request can be serviced immediately. However, while the drive or controller is serving one request, any additional requests, normally from other processes, will need to be queued.

For a multiprogramming system with many processes, the disk queue may often be nonempty. Thus, when a request is complete, we must pick a new request from the queue and service it. A disk service requires a move of the head to the desired track, then a wait for latency, and finally a transfer of the data.

12.2.1 FCFS Scheduling

The simplest form of disk scheduling is, of course, *first-come, first-served (FCFS)* scheduling. This algorithm is easy to program and is intrinsically fair. However, it may not provide the best (average) service. Consider, for example, an ordered disk queue with requests involving tracks

$$98, 183, 37, 122, 14, 124, 65, \text{ and } 67,$$

listed first (98) to last (67). If the read–write head is initially at track 53, it will first move from 53 to 98, then to 183, 37, 122, 14, 124, 65, and finally to 67, for a total head movement of 640 tracks. This schedule is diagrammed in Figure 12.1.

The problem with this schedule is illustrated by the wild swing from 122 to 14 and then back to 124. If the requests for tracks 37 and 14 could be serviced together, before or after the requests at 122 and 124, the total head movement could be decreased substantially and the average time to service each request would decrease, improving disk throughput.

queue = 98, 183, 37, 122, 14, 124, 65, 67
head starts at 53

Figure 12.1 FCFS disk scheduling.

12.2.2 SSTF Scheduling

It seems reasonable to service together all requests close to the current head position, before moving the head far away to service another request. This assumption is the basis for the *shortest-seek-time-first* (SSTF) disk-scheduling algorithm. The SSTF algorithm selects the request with the minimum seek time from the current head position. Since seek time is generally proportional to the track difference between the requests, we implement this approach by moving the head to the closest track in the request queue.

For our example request queue, the closest request to the initial head position (53) is at track 65. Once we are at track 65, the next closest request is at track 67. At this point, the distance to track 37 is 30, whereas the distance to 98 is 31. Therefore, the request at track 37 is closer and is served next. Continuing, we service the request at track 14, then 98, 122, 124, and finally at 183 (Figure 12.2). This scheduling method results in a total head movement of only 236 tracks — little more than one-third of the distance needed for FCFS scheduling. This algorithm would result in a substantial improvement in average disk service.

SSTF scheduling is essentially a form of shortest-job-first (SJF) scheduling, and, like SJF scheduling, it may cause *starvation* of some requests. Remember that, in a real system, requests may arrive at any time. Assume that we have two requests in the queue, for 14 and 186. If a request near 14 arrives while we are servicing that request, it will be serviced next, making the request at 186 wait. While this request is being serviced, another request close to 14 could arrive. In theory, a continual stream of requests near one another could arrive, causing the request for

queue = 98, 183, 37, 122, 14, 124, 65, 67
head starts at 53

Figure 12.2 SSTF disk scheduling.

track 186 to wait indefinitely. This scenario is statistically unlikely, but is possible.

Finally, the SSTF algorithm, although a substantial improvement over the FCFS algorithm, is not optimal. For example, if we move the head from 53 to 37, even though the latter is not closest, and then to 14, before turning around to service 65, 67, 98, 122, 124, and 183, we can reduce the total head movement to 208 tracks.

12.2.3 SCAN Scheduling

Recognition of the dynamic nature of the request queue leads to the SCAN algorithm. The read−write head starts at one end of the disk, and moves toward the other end, servicing requests as it reaches each track, until it gets to the other end of the disk. At the other end, the direction of head movement is reversed and servicing continues. The head continuously scans the disk from end to end. We again use our example.

Before applying SCAN to scheduling,

98, 183, 37, 122, 14, 124, 65, and 67

we need to know the direction of head movement, in addition to the head's last position. If the head was moving toward 0, the head movement would service 37 and 14 as it moved to 0. At track 0, the head would reverse and move to the other end of the disk, servicing the requests at 65, 67, 98, 122, 124, and 183 as it moves (Figure 12.3). If a request arrives in the queue just in front of the head, it will be serviced almost immediately, whereas a request arriving just behind the head will have to wait until the

Figure 12.3   SCAN disk scheduling.

head moves to the end of the disk, reverses direction, and returns, before being serviced.

The SCAN algorithm is sometimes called the *elevator algorithm,* since it is similar to the behavior of elevators as they service requests to move from floor to floor in a building.   Another analogy is that of shoveling snow from a sidewalk during a snowstorm.   Starting from one end, we remove snow as we move toward the other end. As we move, new snow falls behind us. At the far end, we reverse direction and remove the newly fallen snow behind us.

Assuming a uniform distribution of requests for tracks, consider the density of requests when the head reaches one end and reverses direction. At this point, there are relatively few requests immediately behind the head, since these tracks have recently been serviced. The heaviest density of requests is at the other end of the disk. These requests have also waited the longest.

12.2.4 C-SCAN Scheduling

A variant of SCAN scheduling that is designed to provide a more uniform wait time is C-SCAN (circular SCAN) scheduling. As does SCAN scheduling, C-SCAN scheduling moves the head from one end of the disk to the other, servicing requests as it goes. When it reaches the other end, however, it immediately returns to the beginning of the disk, without servicing any requests on the return trip (Figure 12.4). The C-SCAN scheduling algorithm essentially treats the disk as though it were circular, with the last track adjacent to the first one.

queue = 98, 183, 37, 122, 14, 124, 65, 67
head starts at 53

Figure 12.4 C-SCAN disk scheduling.

12.2.5 LOOK Scheduling

Notice that, as we described them, both SCAN and C-SCAN scheduling always move the head from one end of the disk to the other. In practice, neither algorithm is implemented in this way. More commonly, the head is only moved as far as the last request in each direction. As soon as there are no requests in the current direction, the head movement is reversed. These versions of SCAN and C-SCAN scheduling are called LOOK scheduling (look for a request before moving in that direction) and C-LOOK scheduling (Figure 12.5).

12.2.6 Selecting a Disk-Scheduling Algorithm

Given so many disk-scheduling algorithms, how do we choose a particular algorithm? SSTF scheduling is common and has a natural appeal. The SCAN and C-SCAN scheduling algorithms are more appropriate for systems that place a heavy load on the disk. It is possible to define an optimal algorithm, but the computation needed for an optimal schedule may not justify the savings over SSTF or SCAN scheduling.

With any scheduling algorithm, however, performance depends heavily on the number and types of requests. In particular, if the queue seldom has more than one outstanding request, then all scheduling algorithms are effectively equivalent. In this case, FCFS scheduling is also a reasonable algorithm.

Notice also that the requests for disk service can be greatly influenced by the file-allocation method. A program reading a contiguously allocated

Figure 12.5   C-LOOK disk scheduling.

file will generate several requests that are close together on the disk, resulting in limited head movement. A linked or indexed file, on the other hand, may include blocks that are widely scattered on the disk, resulting in better disk-space utilization at the expense of head movement.

The location of directories and index blocks also is important. Since every file must be opened to be used, and opening a file requires searching the directory structure, the directories will be accessed frequently. Placing the directories halfway between the inner and outer edge of the disk, rather than at either end, can significantly reduce disk-head movement. For instance, if a directory entry is in the first sector and a file's data are in the last sector, then the disk head needs to move the entire width of the disk. If the directory entry is more toward the middle, the head will have to move at most one-half the width.

It should be clear that, as a result of these considerations, the disk-scheduling algorithm, like all others, should be written as a separate module of the operating system, allowing it to be removed and to be replaced with a different algorithm if necessary. Either FCFS or SSTF scheduling is a reasonable initial choice. In fact disk controller manufacturers have been helping operating system designers by moving head scheduling algorithms into the hardware itself. The operating system sends requests to the controller in FCFS order, and the controller queues them and executes them in some more optimal order. Unfortunately, if the operating system is unaware of the controller's methodology, the operating system may be ordering the requests in a way it expects to be optimal, and the controller may be rearranging them into the order it likes best. The result could be decreased, rather than increased, performance!

12.3 ■ Disk Management

There are several other aspects of disk management for which an operating system is responsible. Here we discuss disk initialization, booting from disk, and bad-block recovery.

12.3.1 Disk Formatting

When a magnetic disk is manufactured, it is essentially a blank slate, just a platter or platters of magnetically changeable medium. Before the computer can make use of the disk, the disk must be broken into the sectors that the computer can understand. This process is called *physical formatting*. When formatted, a disk consists of a set of sectors on each track the head can address. Each sector has a header containing the sector number (so the disk knows when it has found the correct sector) and space for an *error correcting code* (ECC). When data are written to the sector, the ECC is updated with a value calculated from the values of each byte written into the sector. When the sector is read, the ECC is recalculated and is compared with the stored value. If the stored and calculated numbers are different, the data are corrupted and the disk sector may be bad (see Section 12.3.3). This calculation and comparison are done automatically by the controller.

Most hard disks come physically formatted from the factory. The operating system still needs to partition and to *format logically* a disk before it can use that disk. This logical formatting writes an initial, blank directory onto the disk, and may install a FAT, inodes, free space lists, or any other information the system needs to track the disk's contents. Some database systems do not require their partitions to be logically formatted. Rather, they use the raw disk and bypass all the operating system I/O calls. This bypassing results in performance gain at the cost of duplicating some operating-system code.

12.3.2 Boot Block

For a computer to start running — for instance, when it is powered up or rebooted — it needs to have an initial program to run. This initial program, or *bootstrap program*, tends to be simple. It initializes all aspects of the system, from CPU registers to device controllers to memory contents. The bootstrap program must know how to load the operating system and to start it executing. To accomplish this goal, the bootstrap program must locate the operating system kernel, load it into memory, and jump to an initial address.

How does the computer know the location of the bootstrap program to start it running? Some systems, such as the Apple Macintosh, store most of the bootstrap in read-only memory (ROM) . This location is convenient, because ROM needs no initialization, and so is always available. The problem is that changing the bootstrap requires changing the ROM hardware chips. For this reason, most systems store a little of the bootstrap in ROM, and store the remainder in the *boot blocks* at a fixed location on a disk. This disk is known as the *boot disk* or *system disk*; the system cannot function without it.

The code stored in ROM requests the block transfer from the disk controller (no device drivers are loaded at this point), loads data from the boot blocks into memory, and starts executing the new code. Changes to the boot program are made by rewriting of the boot blocks. The program stored in the boot blocks is more sophisticated than is the one stored in the ROM, and is able to load the entire operating system from a nonfixed location on disk, and to start the operating system running. It may be able to do so with very little code. For example, the IBM PC uses one 512-byte block for its boot program (Figure 12.6).

12.3.3 Bad Blocks

Because disks have moving parts and small tolerances (recall that the magnetic-disk read−write head floats just above the disk surface), they are prone to failure. Sometimes, the failure is complete, and the disk needs to be replaced, and its contents restored from backup media to the replacement. More frequently, one or more blocks become unreadable and unwritable. Most disks even come from the factory with *bad blocks*. Depending on the disk and controller in use, these blocks are handled in a variety of ways.

On the IBM PC family with IDE drives, bad blocks must be handled manually. The **format** command finds bad blocks when the disk is logically formatted, and writes a special value into the FAT entries to tell

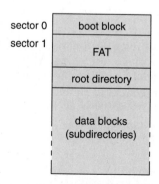

Figure 12.6 MS-DOS disk layout.

the allocation routines not to use those blocks. If blocks go bad during normal operation, a special program is run manually to search for new bad blocks and to lock them away as before. Data that resided on the bad blocks usually are lost.

The SCSI disk and controller, used in high-end PCs and most workstations, are smarter about bad-block recovery. The controller keeps a list of bad blocks on the disk, initialized during physical format and updated over the life of the disk. The controller also sets aside sectors not available to the operating system. For each bad sector, the controller can be told to replace it logically with a sector from this pool. This scheme is known as *slipping* or *forwarding* the sector. Thus, the operating system might request a write of sector 10 on track 12, but the controller would notice that sector is bad and would instead write sector 27 on track 153. A typical bad-sector transaction might then be as follows:

- The operating system requests sector 5, track 20.

- The controller calculates the ECCs and finds the sector is bad. It reports this finding to the operating system.

- The next time that the system is rebooted, a special command is run to tell the SCSI controller to replace the bad sector with a good one.

- The next time the system requests sector 5, track 20, the request is translated into the replacement sector's address by the controller.

Note that such a redirection by the controller could invalidate any optimization by the disk-scheduling algorithm! As a solution, some disks place replacement sectors in each cylinder, and then try to *slip* a sector with another from the same cylinder. Since a low percentage of sectors is bad, little performance is actually lost. An alternative is to move the disk-scheduling algorithm into the disk controller, since it knows the "real" location of all blocks on the disk.

The reason that the correction is not done totally automatically is that the data in the bad block usually are lost, and the file must be repaired either manually or through a file restoration.

12.4 ■ Swap-Space Management

Swap-space management is another low-level task of the operating system. Virtual memory requires the use of disk as an extension of memory. Unfortunately, disk access is much slower than memory access. Because swap space has a large impact on system performance, its design and implementation are focused on providing the best throughput for the virtual memory system. In this section we discuss how swap space is used, where swap space is located on disk, and how the swap space is managed.

12.4.1 Swap-Space Use

Swap space is used in various ways by different operating systems, depending upon the implemented memory management algorithms. For instance, systems which implement swapping may use swap space to hold the entire process image, including the code and data sections. Paging systems may simply store pages which have been pushed out of main memory. The amount of swap space needed on a system can therefore vary depending on the amount of memory it is backing and the way in which it is used. On personal computers, only a few megabytes of disk space may be needed. On UNIX workstations and minicomputers, tens or hundreds of megabytes may be used.

Some operating systems, such as UNIX, allow the use of multiple swap spaces. These extra swap spaces are usually put on separate disks, so the load placed on the I/O system by paging and swapping can be balanced over the system's I/O devices.

Note that it is safer to overestimate than to underestimate swap space, because if a system runs out of swap space it may be forced to abort processes or crash entirely. Overestimation results in wasted disk space which could otherwise be used for files, but does no other harm.

12.4.2 Swap-Space Location

There are two places a swap space can reside. Swap space can be carved out of the normal file system, or can be a separate disk partition. If the swap space is simply a large file within the file system (as in Microsoft Windows), normal file system routines can be used to create and destroy it, name it, and allocate its space. Adding another swap space is as easy as creating another file. This approach is therefore easy to implement. Unfortunately, it is also inefficient. Navigating the directory structure and the disk allocation data structures takes time, and (potentially) extra disk accesses. External fragmentation may also greatly increase swap space read and write times as reading an entire process image can require multiple seeks. Performance can be optimized by using caches to hold the block location information, and using special tools to allocate sequential blocks for this file, but still there is the added cost of traversing the in-cache data structures.

More commonly, swap space is created in a separate disk partition. No file system or directory structure is placed on this space. Rather, separate swap-space management algorithms are used to allocate and deallocate the blocks. The advantage of this method is its speed. The algorithms are optimized for very fast storage and retrieval of data, rather than storage efficiency. Internal fragmentation is increased, but this tradeoff is acceptable because data in swap space generally live for much shorter amounts of time than files in the file system, and this data is accessed much more frequently than that in the file system. Unfortunately, this raw method requires that space be set aside during file system creation. Adding more swap space can only be done by destroying extant file systems or adding new disks.

Some systems are flexible and allow both raw and file-system based swap spaces. Solaris 2 is an example of this. The policy and implementation are separate, allowing the machine's administrator to decide which type to use. The tradeoff is between convenience of allocation and management, and system performance.

12.4.3 Swap-Space Management

As an example of the methods used to manage swap space, we now follow the evolution of swapping and paging in UNIX. As fully discussed in Chapter 19, UNIX started with an implementation of swapping. Entire processes were written to swap space or read into memory, contiguously, at one time. UNIX moved to a combination of swapping and paging as paging hardware became available.

In 4.3BSD, swap space is allocated to a process when the process is started. Enough space is set aside to hold the instruction pages (known as the *text pages*, or the *text segment*) and the *data segment* of the process. In this way, a process will generally not run out of swap space while it executes. When a process starts, its text is paged in from the file system. These pages are written out to swap as needed, and read back in from there, so the file system is consulted once for each text page. Pages from the data segment are read in from the file system, or created (if they are uninitialized), and are written to swap space and paged back in as needed. One optimization is that processes with the same text pages (for instance, two users running the same editor) share these pages, both in physical memory and in swap space. If one process has already paged the blocks in from the file system and out to the swap space, the other process can get them directly from the swap space.

Two per-process *swap maps* are used by the kernel to track swap space use. The text segment is a fixed size, so its swap space is allocated in 512K chunks, except for the last chunk which holds the remainder of the pages, in 1K increments (Figure 12.7).

The data segment swap map is more complicated, because the data segment can grow over time. The map is of fixed size, but contains swap addresses for blocks of varying size. Given index i, a block pointed to by swap map entry i is of size $i * 16K$, to a maximum of 2 megabytes. This data structure is shown in Figure 12.8. (The block size minimum and maximum are variable, and can be changed at system reboot.) If the last block is full and the process grows, a new block is allocated in swap space. This scheme results in small processes using only small blocks and

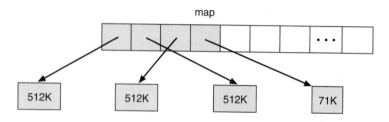

Figure 12.7 4.3BSD text segment swap map.

minimizing fragmentation. The blocks of large processes can be quickly found, and the swap map remains rather small.

In Solaris 1 (SunOS 4), some changes were made to standard UNIX methods to improve efficiency and reflect technological changes. When a process executes, text segment pages are brought in from the file system, accessed in main memory, and thrown away if selected for pageout. It is more efficient to read a page back in from the file system than to write it and then read it from swap space.

More changes were made in Solaris 2. The largest change is in the time of swap-space allocation. Solaris 2 allocates swap space only when a page is forced out of memory, not when the page is allocated. This is an improvement on modern systems which have more main memory than older systems, and tend to page less.

12.5 ■ Disk Reliability

Disks used to be the least reliable component of a system. They still have relatively high failure rates, and their failure causes a loss of data and significant downtime while the disk is replaced and data are restored. The recovery in case of a disk crash may take hours, as backup copies of the data on tape are transferred to the disk. Under normal circumstances, these restored data are not a precise image of the disk when it crashed. Backups are usually performed daily or weekly, meaning that any changes to the data since the last backup are lost if a disk crashes. Improving disk speed and reliability is therefore an important topic in current research.

Several improvements in disk-use techniques have been proposed. These methods involve the use of multiple disks working cooperatively. To improve speed, researchers have developed *disk striping* (or interleaving), a technique now in use on a few systems. A group of disks is treated as one storage unit, with each block broken into several subblocks. Each subblock is stored on a separate disk. The time required to transfer one block into memory decreases drastically, since the disks

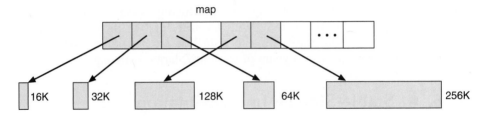

Figure 12.8 4.3BSD data segment swap map.

transfer their subblocks in parallel, fully utilizing their *I/O bandwidth*, or transfer capacity. This decrease is especially notable if the disks are *synchronized* such that there is no latency between the subblock-access on each drive. This advantage is also magnified if many small, inexpensive disks are used in place of a few, large, expensive disks. The access rate improves because seeks occur in parallel and more data can be transferred after the seek.

This idea was the basis for the development of redundant arrays of inexpensive disks (RAID), which improves performance, especially the price–performance ratio, and provides for the duplication of data to improve reliability. Redundancy can be organized in various ways, with differing performance and cost efficiencies.

The simplest RAID organization, called *mirroring* or *shadowing*, consists of keeping a duplicate copy of each disk. This solution is, of course, costly, because twice as many disks are used to store the same number of data. In the most complex RAID organization, *block interleaved parity*, data are written to each disk in the array in a block unit, just as in more normal configurations. However, an extra block of parity data is written. This parity block is the parity of all the equivalent blocks on each disk in the array. For instance, if there are eight disks in the array, then sector 0 of disks 1 through 7 have their parity computed and stored on disk 8. The computation takes place on a bit level for each byte, just as memory parity is computed. If one disk crashes, one of the data bits is essentially erased (an *erasure error*), but can be recomputed from the other data bits plus the parity. Thus, a single disk crash no longer results in loss of data (although multiple simultaneous crashes do have that result).

Of course, use of RAID improves speed by virtue of the use of multiple disks and controllers. This gain is less than that realized from pure disk striping, however, since the parity block must also be read or written for each block access, and the parity computation must be performed. We can decrease this overhead by distributing the parity over all disks, rather than setting aside one parity disk. Since the tradeoff between speed and reliability is a reasonable one, RAID use is becoming more common, with many vendors either researching or producing RAID hardware and software. It has been shown that, with an array of 100 inexpensive disks and 10 parity disks, the mean time to data loss (MTDL) of the array is 90 years, compared to the 2 or 3 years of standard, large, expensive disks.

12.6 ■ Stable-Storage Implementation

In Chapter 6, we introduced the concept of a write-ahead log, which required the availability of stable storage. Information residing in stable storage is *never* lost. To implement such a storage, we need to replicate the needed information on more than nonvolatile storage media (usually disk) with independent failure modes. We also need to update the information in a controlled manner to ensure that failure during data transfer does not damage the needed information. For the remainder of this section, we will discuss the issue of how the storage media can be protected from failure during data transfer.

Block transfer between memory and disk storage can result in:

- **Successful completion:** The transferred information arrived safely at its destination.

- **Partial failure:** A failure occurred in the midst of transfer and the destination block has incorrect information.

- **Total failure:** The failure occurred sufficiently early during the transfer so that the destination block remains intact.

We require that if a data-transfer failure occurs, the system detects it and invokes a recovery procedure to restore the block to a consistent state. To do so, the system must maintain two physical blocks for each logical block. An output operation is executed as follows:

1. Write the information onto the first physical block.

2. When the first write successfully completes, write the same information onto the second physical block.

3. The output is complete only after the second write successfully completes.

During recovery from a failure, each pair of physical blocks is examined. If both are the same and no detectable error exists, then no further actions are necessary. If one block contains a detectable error, then we replace its content with the value of the second block. If both blocks contain no detectable error, but they differ in content, then we replace the content of the first block with the value of the second. This recovery procedure ensures that a write to stable storage either succeeds completely or results in no change. The attempt to write to stable storage succeeds only if all copies are written.

This procedure can be extended easily to allow the use of an arbitrarily large number of copies of each block of stable storage. Although a large number of copies further reduces the probability of a failure, it is usually reasonable to simulate stable storage with only two copies.

12.7 ■ Summary

Disk systems are the major secondary-storage I/O device on most computers. Requests for disk I/O are generated both by the file system and by virtual-memory systems. Each request specifies the address on the disk to be referenced, which is in the form of a block number. The lower levels of the file-system manager convert this address into the hardware-level partition, cylinder, surface, and sector number.

Moving-head disk-scheduling algorithms are designed to minimize total head movement; they include the FCFS, SSTF, SCAN, C-SCAN, LOOK, and C-LOOK algorithms.

Disk efficiency is still an active area of research. For instance, Hewlett-Packard is experimenting with making disk controllers smarter, and the University of California at Berkeley has a log-based file system that uses the extreme approach of treating the disk as though it were a sequential-access device, greatly reducing disk seeks and fragmentation.

In order to reduce fragmentation the system can back up and restore the entire disk or partition. The blocks are read from their scattered locations, and the restore writes them back more contiguously. Some systems (such as MS-DOS) have utilities that will scan the disk and then move blocks around to decrease the fragmentation. The performance increases realized from these techniques can be large, but the system is generally unusable while the techniques operate.

The operating system also must manage the disk blocks. First, a disk must be formatted to create the blocks on the raw hardware. Then boot blocks are added to store the system's boot-strap code. Finally, when a block becomes corrupt, the system must have a way to logically replace that block with another, good block.

Because efficient swap space use is a key to performance, systems frequently bypass the file system structure and use disk blocks more directly to store memory pages which do not fit within physical memory. Some systems just use a file within the file system for this, but there can be a performance penalty. Other systems allow the user or system administrator to make the decision by providing both options.

The write-ahead log scheme requires the availability of stable storage. To implement such a storage, we need to replicate the needed information on more than one nonvolatile storage media (usually disk) with independent failure modes. We also need to update the information in a controlled manner to ensure that failure during data transfer does not damage the needed information.

■   Exercises

12.1 All the disk-scheduling disciplines, except FCFS scheduling, are not truly fair (starvation may occur).

   a. Explain why this assertion is true.

   b. Describe a scheme to ensure fairness.

   c. Explain why fairness is an important goal in a time-sharing system.

12.2 Suppose that the head of a moving-head disk with 200 tracks, numbered 0 to 199, is currently serving a request at track 143 and has just finished a request at track 125.   The queue of requests is kept in the FIFO order:

$$86, 147, 91, 177, 94, 150, 102, 175, 130.$$

What is the total number of head movements needed to satisfy these requests for the following disk-scheduling algorithms?

   a. FCFS scheduling

   b. SSTF scheduling

   c. SCAN scheduling

   d. LOOK scheduling

   e. C-SCAN scheduling

12.3 Write a monitor-type program (see Chapter 6) for disk scheduling using the SCAN and C-SCAN disk-scheduling algorithms.

12.4 When the average queue length is small, all the disk-scheduling algorithms reduce to FCFS scheduling. Explain why this assertion is true.

12.5 Compare the throughput of C-SCAN and SCAN scheduling, assuming a uniform distribution of requests.

12.6 Is disk scheduling, other than FCFS scheduling, useful in a single-user environment?   Explain your answer.

12.7 SSTF scheduling tends to favor mid-range cylinders over the innermost and outermost cylinders. Explain why this assertion is true.

12.8 Requests are not usually uniformly distributed. For example, the cylinders on which the file directory structures reside are accessed more frequently than are most files. Suppose that you know that 50 percent of the requests are for a small fixed number of cylinders.

    a. Which of the scheduling algorithms discussed in this chapter would be best?

    b. Can you suggest a new scheduling algorithm for this case? If you can, describe your algorithm.

12.9 Why is latency optimization usually not employed in disk scheduling? How would the standard algorithms (FCFS, SSTF, SCAN, and C-SCAN scheduling) be modified to include latency optimization?

12.10 How would the use of a RAM disk affect your selection of a disk-scheduling algorithm? What factors would you need to consider?

12.11 Why is it important to try to balance file system I/O among the disks and controllers on a system in a multitasking environment?

12.12 What are the tradeoffs involved in re-reading code pages from the file system rather than using swap space to store them?

12.13 Is there any way to implement truly stable storage? Explain your answer.

Bibliographic Notes

Discussions concerning magnetic-disk technology were presented by Freedman [1983], and Harker et al. [1981]. Optical disks were covered by Kenville [1982], Fujitani [1984], O'Leary and Kitts [1985], Gait [1988], and Olsen and Kenly [1989]. Ammon et al. [1985] discussed a high-speed, large-capacity "jukebox" optical-disk system. Discussions of floppy disks were offered by Pechura and Schoeffler [1983] and Sarisky [1983]. Discussions of redundant arrays of inexpensive disks (RAID) were presented by Patterson et al. [1988] and Chen and Patterson [1990]. Disk system architectures for high performance computing are discussed by Katz et al. [1989]. Nelson and Cheng [1992] compared the performance of IPI and SCSI disks and controllers in a real system.

    A complete survey of all the various disk-scheduling algorithms, and a comparative analysis of these algorithms was presented by Teorey and Pinkerton [1972]. The comparison was done using simulations, and it was recommended that either SCAN or C-SCAN scheduling should be used, depending on the load. Wilhelm [1976] and Hofri [1980] compared the FCFS and the SSTF seek disk-scheduling algorithms. A continuum of disk-scheduling algorithms was presented by Geist and Daniel [1987].

The Loge project [English and Stepanov 1992] experimented with adding intelligence to the disk controller. The log-based file system, which works hard to make disk access sequential, was discussed in Rosenblum and Ousterhout [1991]. Both of these projects are the topics of continuing research.

PART FOUR

PROTECTION AND SECURITY

Protection mechanisms provide controlled access by limiting the types of file access that can be made by the various users. Protection must also be available to ensure that besides the files, memory segments, CPU, and other resources can be operated on by only those processes that have gained proper authorization from the operating system.

Protection is provided by a mechanism that controls the access of programs, processes, or users to the resources defined by a computer system. This mechanism must provide a means for specification of the controls to be imposed, together with a means of enforcement.

The security system prevents unauthorized access to a system, and ensuing malicious destruction or alteration of data. Security ensures the authentication of users of the system to protect the integrity of the information stored in the system (both data and code), as well as the physical resources of the computer system.

CHAPTER 13

PROTECTION

The various processes in an operating system must be protected from one another's activities. For that purpose, various mechanisms exist that can be used to ensure that the files, memory segments, CPU, and other resources can be operated on by only those processes that have gained proper authorization from the operating system.

Protection refers to a mechanism for controlling the access of programs, processes, or users to the resources defined by a computer system. This mechanism must provide a means for specification of the controls to be imposed, together with some means of enforcement. We distinguish between protection and *security*, which is a measure of confidence that the integrity of a system and its data will be preserved. Security assurance is a much broader topic than is protection, and we address it in Chapter 14.

In this chapter, we examine the problem of protection in great detail, and develop a unifying model for implementing protection.

13.1 ■ Goals of Protection

As computer systems have become more sophisticated and pervasive in their applications, the need to protect their integrity has also grown. Protection was originally conceived as an adjunct to multiprogramming operating systems, so that untrustworthy users might safely share a common logical name space, such as a directory of files, or share a common physical name space, such as memory. Modern protection concepts have evolved to increase the reliability of any complex system that makes use of shared resources.

There are several reasons for providing protection. Most obvious is the need to prevent mischievous, intentional violation of an access restriction by a user. Of more general importance, however, is the need to ensure that each program component active in a system uses system resources only in ways consistent with the stated policies for the uses of these resources. This requirement is an absolute one for a reliable system.

Protection can improve reliability by detecting latent errors at the interfaces between component subsystems. Early detection of interface errors can often prevent contamination of a healthy subsystem by a subsystem that is malfunctioning. An unprotected resource cannot defend against use (or misuse) by an unauthorized or incompetent user. A protection-oriented system provides means to distinguish between authorized and unauthorized usage.

The role of protection in a computer system is to provide a *mechanism* for the enforcement of the *policies* governing resource use. These policies can be established in a variety of ways. Some are fixed in the design of the system, whereas others are formulated by the management of a system. Still others are defined by the individual users to protect their own files and programs. A protection system must have the flexibility to enforce a variety of policies that can be declared to it.

Policies for resource use may vary, depending on the application, and they may be subject to change over time. For these reasons, protection can no longer be considered solely as a matter of concern to the designer of an operating system. It should also be available as a tool for the applications programmer, so that resources created and supported by an applications subsystem can be guarded against misuse. In this chapter, we describe the protection mechanisms the operating system should provide, so that an application designer can use them in designing her own protection software.

One important principle is the separation of *policy* from *mechanism*. Mechanisms determine how something will be done. In contrast, policies decide *what* will be done. The separation of policy and mechanism is important for flexibility. Policies are likely to change from place to place or time to time. In the worst case, every change in policy would require a change in the underlying mechanism. General mechanisms are more desirable, because a change in a policy would then require the modification of only some system parameters or tables.

13.2 ■ Domain of Protection

A computer system is a collection of processes and objects. By *objects*, we mean both hardware objects (such as the CPU, memory segments, printers, disks, and tape drives), and software objects (such as files, programs, and semaphores). Each object has a unique name that differentiates it from all other objects in the system, and each can be accessed only through well-defined and meaningful operations. Objects are essentially *abstract data types*.

The operations that are possible may depend on the object. For example, a CPU can only be executed on. Memory segments can be read and written, whereas a card reader can only be read. Tape drives can be read, written, and rewound. Data files can be created, opened, read, written, closed, and deleted; program files can be read, written, executed, and deleted.

Obviously, a process should be allowed to access only those resources it has been authorized to access. Furthermore, at any time, it should be able to access only those resources that it currently requires to complete its task. This requirement, commonly referred to as the *need-to-know* principle, is useful in limiting the amount of damage a faulty process can cause in the system. For example, when process p invokes procedure A, the procedure should be allowed to access only its own variables and the formal parameters passed to it; it should not be able to access all the variables of process p. Similarly, consider the case where process p invokes a compiler to compile a particular file. The compiler should not be able to access any arbitrary files, but only a well-defined subset of files (such as the source file, listing file, and so on) related to the file to be compiled. Conversely, the compiler may have private files used for accounting or optimization purposes, which process p should not be able to access.

13.2.1 Domain Structure

To facilitate this scheme, we introduce the concept of a *protection domain*. A process operates within a protection domain, which specifies the resources that the process may access. Each domain defines a set of objects and the types of operations that may be invoked on each object. The ability to execute an operation on an object is an *access right*. A *domain* is a collection of access rights, each of which is an ordered pair *<object-name, rights-set>*. For example, if domain D has the access right <file F, {read,write}>, then a process executing in domain D can both read and write file F; it cannot, however, perform any other operation on that object.

Domains do not need to be disjoint; they may share access rights. For example, in Figure 13.1, we have three domains: D_1, D_2, and D_3. The access right <O_4, {print}> is shared by both D_2 and D_3, implying that a process executing in either one of these two domains can print object O_4. Note that a process must be executing in domain D_1 to read and write object O_1. On the other hand, only processes in domain D_3 may execute object O_1.

The association between a process and a domain may be either static (if the set of resources available to a process is fixed throughout the latter's lifetime) or dynamic. As might be expected, the problems inherent in

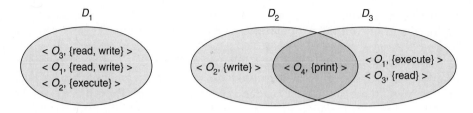

D_1 D_2 D_3

< O_3, {read, write} >
< O_1, {read, write} >
< O_2, {execute} >

< O_2, {write} >

< O_4, {print} >

< O_1, {execute} >
< O_3, {read} >

Figure 13.1 System with three protection domains.

establishing dynamic protection domains require more careful solution than do the simpler problems of the static case.

If the association between processes and domains is fixed, and we want to adhere to the need-to-know principle, then a mechanism must be available to change the content of a domain. A process may execute in two different phases. For example, it may need read access in one phase and write access in another. If a domain is static, we must define the domain to include both read and write access. However, this arrangement provides more rights than are needed in each of the two phases, since we have read access in the phase where we need only write access, and vice versa. Thus, the need-to-know principle is violated. We must allow the contents of a domain to be modified, so that it always reflects the minimum necessary access rights.

If the association is dynamic, a mechanism is available to allow a process to switch from one domain to another. We may also want to allow the content of a domain to be changed. If we cannot change the content of a domain, we can provide the same effect by creating a new domain with the changed content, and switching to that new domain when we want to change the domain content.

We note that a domain can be realized in a variety of ways:

- Each *user* may be a domain. In this case, the set of objects that can be accessed depends on the identity of the user. Domain switching occurs when the user is changed — generally when one user logs out and another user logs in.

- Each *process* may be a domain. In this case, the set of objects that can be accessed depends on the identity of the process. Domain switching corresponds to one process sending a message to another process, and then waiting for a response.

- Each *procedure* may be a domain. In this case, the set of objects that can be accessed corresponds to the local variables defined within the procedure. Domain switching occurs when a procedure call is made.

We shall discuss domain switching in greater detail later on in this chapter.

13.2.2 Examples

Consider the standard dual-mode (monitor-user mode) model of operating-system execution. When a process executes in monitor mode, it can execute privileged instructions and thus gain complete control of the computer system. On the other hand, if the process executes in user mode, it can invoke only nonprivileged instructions. Consequently, it can execute only within its predefined memory space. These two modes protect the operating system (executing in monitor domain) from the user processes (executing in user domain). In a multiprogrammed operating system, two protection domains are insufficient, since users also want to be protected from one another. Therefore, a more elaborate scheme is needed. We illustrate this scheme by examining two influential operating systems — UNIX and MULTICS — to see how these concepts have been implemented there.

13.2.2.1 UNIX

In the UNIX operating system, a domain is associated with the user. Switching the domain corresponds to changing the user identification temporarily. This change is accomplished through the file system as follows. An owner identification and a domain bit (known as the *setuid bit*) are associated with each file. When a user (with *user-id* = *A*) starts executing a file owned by *B*, whose associated domain bit is *off*, the *user-id* of the process is set to *A*. When the setuid bit is *on*, the user-id is set to that of the owner of the file: *B*. When the process exits, this temporary user-id change ends.

There are other common methods used to change domains in operating systems in which user-ids are used for domain definition, because almost all systems need to provide such a mechanism. This mechanism is used when an otherwise privileged facility needs to be made available to the general user population. For instance, it might be desirable to allow users to access a network without letting them write their own networking programs. In such a case, on a UNIX system, the setuid bit on a networking program would be set, causing the user-id to change when the program is run. The user-id would change to that of a user with network access privilege (such as "root," the most powerful user-id). One problem with this method is that if a user manages to create a file with user-id "root" and with its setuid bit on, that user can become "root" and do anything and everything on the system. The setuid mechanism is discussed further in Chapter 19.

An alternative to this method used on other operating systems is to place privileged programs in a special directory. The operating system would be designed to change the user-id of any program run from this directory, either to the equivalent of "root" or to the user-id of the owner of the directory. This eliminates the setuid problem of secret setuid programs, because all these programs are in one location. This method is less flexible than that used in UNIX, however.

Even more restrictive, and thus more protective, are systems that simply do not allow a change of user-id. In these instances, special techniques must be used to allow users access to privileged facilities. For instance, a *daemon* process may be started at boot time and run as a special user-id. Users then run a separate program, which sends requests to this process whenever they need to use the facility. This method is used by the TOPS-20 operating system.

In any of these systems, great care must be taken in writing privileged programs. Any oversight or carelessness can result in a total lack of protection on the system. Generally, these programs are the first to be attacked by people trying to break into a system; unfortunately, the attackers are frequently successful. For instance, there are many instances where security has been breached on UNIX systems because of the setuid feature. We discuss security in Chapter 14.

13.2.2.2 MULTICS

In the MULTICS system, the protection domains are organized hierarchically into a ring structure. Each ring corresponds to a single domain (Figure 13.2). The rings are numbered from 0 to 7. Let D_i and D_j be any two domain rings. If $j < i$, then D_i is a subset of D_j. That is, a process executing in domain D_j has more privileges than does a process executing in domain D_i. A process executing in domain D_0 has the most privileges. If there are only two rings, this scheme is equivalent to the monitor-user mode of

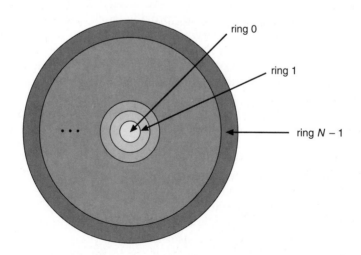

Figure 13.2 MULTICS ring structure.

execution, where monitor mode corresponds to D_0 and user mode corresponds to D_1.

MULTICS has a segmented address space; each segment is a file. Each segment is associated with one of the rings. A segment description includes an entry that identifies the ring number. In addition, it includes three access bits to control reading, writing, and execution. The association between segments and rings is a policy decision with which we are not concerned in this book. With each process, a *current-ring-number* counter is associated, identifying the ring in which the process is executing currently. When a process is executing in ring i, it cannot access a segment associated with ring j, $j < i$. It can, however, access a segment associated with ring k, $k \geq i$. The type of access, however, is restricted, according to the access bits associated with that segment.

Domain switching in MULTICS occurs when a process crosses from one ring to another by calling a procedure in a different ring. Obviously, this switch must be done in a controlled manner; otherwise, a process can start executing in ring 0, and no protection will be provided. To allow controlled domain switching, we modify the ring field of the segment descriptor to include the following:

- **Access bracket:** A pair of integers, $b1$ and $b2$, such that $b1 \leq b2$.

- **Limit:** An integer $b3$, such that $b3 > b2$.

- **List of gates:** Identifies the entry points (gates) at which the segments may be called.

If a process executing in ring i calls a procedure (segment) with access bracket $(b1, b2)$, then the call is allowed if $b1 \leq i \leq b2$, and the current ring number of the process remains i. Otherwise, a trap to the operating system occurs, and the situation is handled as follows:

- If $i < b1$, then the call is allowed to occur, because we have a transfer to a ring (domain) with fewer privileges. However, if parameters are passed that refer to segments in a lower ring (that is, segments that are not accessible to the called procedure), then these segments must be copied into an area that can be accessed by the called procedure.

- If $i > b2$, then the call is allowed to occur only if $b3$ is less than or equal to i, and the call has been directed to one of the designated entry points in the list of gates. This scheme allows processes with limited access rights to call procedures in lower rings that have more access rights, but only in a carefully controlled manner.

The main disadvantage of the ring (hierarchical) structure is that it does not allow us to enforce the need-to-know principle. In particular, if an object must be accessible in domain D_j but not accessible in domain D_i, then we must have $j < i$. But this requirement means that every segment accessible in D_i is also accessible in D_j.

The MULTICS protection system is generally more complex and less efficient than are those used in current operating systems. If protection interferes with the ease of use of the system, or significantly decreases system performance, then its use must be weighed carefully against the purpose of the system. For instance, it would be reasonable to have a complex protection system on a computer used by a university to process students' grades, and also used by students for class work. A similar protection system would not be suited to a computer being used for number crunching in which performance is of utmost importance. It would therefore be of benefit to separate the mechanism from the protection policy, allowing the same system to have complex or simple protection depending on the needs of its users. To separate mechanism from policy, we require more general models of protection.

13.3 ■ Access Matrix

Our model of protection can be viewed abstractly as a matrix, called an *access matrix*. The rows of the access matrix represent domains, and the columns represent objects. Each entry in the matrix consists of a set of access rights. Because objects are defined explicitly by the column, we can omit the object name from the access right. The entry **access**(i,j) defines the set of operations that a process, executing in domain D_i, can invoke on object O_j.

To illustrate these concepts, we consider the access matrix shown in Figure 13.3. There are four domains and four objects: three files (F_1, F_2, F_3), and one laser printer. When a process executes in domain D_1, it can

object domain	F_1	F_2	F_3	printer
D_1	read		read	
D_2				print
D_3		read	execute	
D_4	read write		read write	

Figure 13.3   Access matrix.

read files F_1 and F_3. A process executing in domain D_4 has the same privileges as it does in domain D_1, but in addition, it can also write onto files F_1 and F_3. Note that the laser printer can be accessed only by a process executing in domain D_2.

The access-matrix scheme provides us with the mechanism for specifying a variety of policies. The mechanism consists of implementing the access matrix and ensuring that the semantic properties we have outlined indeed hold. More specifically, we must ensure that a process executing in domain D_i can access only those objects specified in row i, and then only as allowed by the access-matrix entries.

Policy decisions concerning protection can be implemented by the access matrix. The policy decisions involve which rights should be included in the (i,j)th entry. We must also decide the domain in which each process executes. This last policy is usually decided by the operating system.

The users normally decide the contents of the access-matrix entries. When a user creates a new object O_j, the column O_j is added to the access matrix with the appropriate initialization entries, as dictated by the creator. The user may decide to enter some rights in some entries in column j and other rights in other entries, as needed.

The access matrix provides an appropriate mechanism for defining and implementing strict control for both the static and dynamic association between processes and domains. When we switch a process from one domain to another, we are executing an operation (switch) on an object (the domain). We can control domain switching by including domains among the objects of the access matrix. Similarly, when we change the content of the access matrix, we are performing an operation on an object: the access matrix. Again, we can control these changes by including the access matrix itself as an object. Actually, since each entry in the access

object domain	F_1	F_2	F_3	laser printer	D_1	D_2	D_3	D_4
D_1	read		read			switch		
D_2				print			switch	switch
D_3		read	execute					
D_4	read write		read write		switch			

Figure 13.4 Access matrix of Figure 13.3 with domains as objects.

matrix may be modified individually, we must consider each entry in the access matrix as an object to be protected.

Now, we need to consider only the operations that are possible on these new objects (domains and the access matrix), and decide how we want processes to be able to execute these operations.

Processes should be able to switch from one domain to another. Domain switching from domain D_i to domain D_j is allowed to occur if and only if the access right *switch* ϵ **access**(i, j). Thus, in Figure 13.4, a process executing in domain D_2 can switch to domain D_3 or to domain D_4. A process in domain D_4 can switch to D_1, and one in domain D_1 can switch to domain D_2.

Allowing controlled change to the contents of the access-matrix entries requires three additional operations: **copy, owner,** and **control**.

The ability to copy an access right from one domain (row) of the access matrix to another is denoted by an asterisk (*) appended to the access right. The *copy* right allows the copying of the access right only within the column (that is, for the object) for which the right is defined. For example, in Figure 13.5(a), a process executing in domain D_2 can copy the read operation into any entry associated with file F_2. Hence, the access matrix of Figure 13.5(a) can be modified to the access matrix shown in Figure 13.5(b).

object \ domain	F_1	F_2	F_3
D_1	execute		write*
D_2	execute	read*	execute
D_3	execute		

(a)

object \ domain	F_1	F_2	F_3
D_1	execute		write*
D_2	execute	read*	execute
D_3	execute	read	

(b)

Figure 13.5 Access matrix with *copy* rights.

There are two variants to this scheme:

1. A right is copied from **access**(i, j) to **access**(k, j); it is then removed from **access**(i, j); this action is a *transfer* of a right, rather than a copy.

2. Propagation of the *copy* right may be limited. That is, when the right R^* is copied from **access**(i, j) to **access**(k, j), only the right R (not R^*) is created. A process executing in domain D_k cannot further copy the right R.

A system may select only one of these three *copy* rights, or it may provide all three by identifying them as separate rights: *copy*, *transfer*, and *limited copy*.

The *copy* right allows a process to copy some rights from an entry in one column to another entry in the same column. We also need a mechanism to allow addition of new rights and removal of some rights. The *owner* right controls these operations. If **access**(i, j) includes the *owner* right, then a process executing in domain D_i can add and remove any right in any entry in column j. For example, in Figure 13.6(a), domain D_1 is the

object domain	F_1	F_2	F_3
D_1	owner execute		write
D_2		read* owner	read* owner write*
D_3	execute		

(a)

object domain	F_1	F_2	F_3
D_1	owner execute		
D_2		owner read* write*	read* owner write*
D_3		write	write

(b)

Figure 13.6   Access matrix with *owner* rights.

owner of F_1, and thus can add and delete any valid right in column F_1. Similarly, domain D_2 is the owner of F_2 and F_3, and thus can add and remove any valid right within these two columns. Thus, the access matrix of Figure 13.6(a) can be modified to the access matrix shown in Figure 13.6(b).

The *copy* and *owner* rights allow a process to change the entries in a column. A mechanism is also needed to change the entries in a row. The *control* right is applicable to only domain objects. If **access**(*i*, *j*) includes the *control* right, then a process executing in domain D_i can remove any access right from row *j*. For example, suppose that, in Figure 13.4, we include the *control* right in **access**(D_2, D_4). Then, a process executing in domain D_2 could modify domain D_4, as shown in Figure 13.7.

Although the *copy* and *owner* rights provide us with a mechanism to limit the propagation of access rights, they do not, however, provide us with the appropriate tools for preventing the propagation of information (that is, disclosure of information). The problem of guaranteeing that no information initially held in an object can migrate outside of its execution environment is called the *confinement problem*. This problem is in general unsolvable (see Bibliographic Notes for references).

These operations on the domains and the access matrix are not in themselves particularly important. What is more important is that they illustrate the ability of the access-matrix model to allow the implementation and control of dynamic protection requirements. New objects and new domains can be created dynamically and included in the access-matrix model. However, we have shown only that the basic mechanism is here; the policy decisions concerning which domains are to have access to which objects in which ways must be made by the system designers and users.

domain \ object	F_1	F_2	F_3	laser printer	D_1	D_2	D_3	D_4
D_1	read		read			switch		
D_2				print			switch	switch control
D_3		read	execute					
D_4	write		write	switch				

Figure 13.7 Modified access matrix of Figure 13.4.

13.4 ■ Implementation of Access Matrix

How can the access matrix be implemented effectively? In general, the matrix will be sparse; that is, most of the entries will be empty. Although there are data-structure techniques available for representing sparse matrices, they are not particularly useful for this application, because of the way in which the protection facility is used.

13.4.1 Global Table

The simplest implementation of the access matrix is a global table consisting of a set of ordered triples <domain, object, rights-set>. Whenever an operation M is executed on an object O_j within domain D_i, the global table is searched for a triple $<D_i, O_j, R_k>$, where $M \in R_k$. If this triple is found, the operation is allowed to continue; otherwise, an exception (error) condition is raised. This implementation suffers from several drawbacks. The table is usually large and thus cannot be kept in main memory, so additional I/O is needed. Virtual-memory techniques are often used for managing this table. In addition, it is difficult to take advantage of special groupings of objects or domains. For example, if a particular object can be read by everyone, it must have a separate entry in every domain.

13.4.2 Access Lists for Objects

Each column in the access matrix can be implemented as an access list for one object, as described in Section 10.4.2. Obviously, the empty entries can be discarded. The resulting list for each object consists of ordered pairs <domain, rights-set>, which define all domains with a nonempty set of access rights for that object.

This approach can be extended easily to define a list plus a *default* set of access rights. When an operation M on an object O_j is attempted in domain D_i, we search the access list for object O_j, looking for an entry $<D_i, R_k>$ with $M \in R_k$. If the entry is found, we allow the operation; if it is not, we check the default set. If M is in the default set, we allow the access. Otherwise, access is denied and an exception condition occurs. Note that, for efficiency, we may check the default set first, and then search the access list.

13.4.3 Capability Lists for Domains

Rather than associating the columns of the access matrix with the objects as access lists, we can associate each row with its domain. A *capability list* for a domain is a list of objects together with the operations allowed on those objects. An object is often represented by its physical name or address, called a *capability*. To execute operation M on object O_j, the process executes the operation M, specifying the capability (pointer) for object O_j as a parameter. Simple *possession* of the capability means that access is allowed.

The capability list is associated with a domain, but is never directly accessible to a process executing in that domain. Rather, the capability list is itself a protected object, maintained by the operating system and accessed by the user only indirectly. Capability-based protection relies on the fact that the capabilities are never allowed to migrate into any address space directly accessible by a user process (where they could be modified). If all capabilities are secure, the object they protect is also secure against unauthorized access.

Capabilities were originally proposed as a kind of secure pointer, to meet the need for resource protection that was foreseen as multiprogrammed computer systems came of age. The idea of an inherently protected pointer (from the point of view of a user of a system) provides a foundation for protection that can be extended up to the applications level.

To provide inherent protection, we must distinguish capabilities from other kinds of objects, and must interpret them by an abstract machine on which higher-level programs run. Capabilities are usually distinguished from other data in one of two ways:

- Each object has a *tag* to denote its type as either a capability or as accessible data. The tags themselves must not be directly accessible by an applications program. Hardware or firmware support may be used to enforce this restriction. Although only 1 bit is necessary to distinguish between capabilities and other objects, more bits are often used. This extension allows all objects to be tagged with their types by the hardware. Thus, the hardware can distinguish integers, floating-point numbers, pointers, Booleans, characters, instructions, capabilities, and uninitialized values by their tags.

- Alternatively, the address space associated with a program can be split into two parts. One part is accessible to the program and contains the program's normal data and instructions. The other part, containing the capability list, is accessible by only the operating system. A segmented memory space (Section 8.6) is useful to support this approach.

Several capability-based protection systems have been developed; we describe them briefly in Section 13.6. The Mach operating system also uses a version of capability-based protection; it is described in great detail in Chapter 20.

13.4.4 A Lock–Key Mechanism

The *lock–key scheme* is a compromise between access lists and capability lists. Each object has a list of unique bit patterns, called *locks*. Similarly, each domain has a list of unique bit patterns, called *keys*. A process executing in a domain can access an object only if that domain has a key that matches one of the locks of the object.

As capability lists must be, the list of keys for a domain must be managed by the operating system on behalf of the domain. Users are not allowed to examine or modify the list of keys (or locks) directly.

13.4.5 Comparison

Access lists correspond directly to the needs of the users. When a user creates an object, she can specify which domains can access the object, as well as the operations allowed. However, because access-rights information for a particular domain is not localized, determining the set of access rights for each domain is difficult. In addition, every access to the object must be checked, requiring a search of the access list. In a large system with long access lists, this search can be time-consuming.

Capability lists do not correspond directly to the needs of the users; they are useful, however, for localizing information for a particular process. The process attempting access must present a capability for that access. Then, the protection system needs only to verify that the capability is valid. Revocation of capabilities, however, may be inefficient (Section 13.5).

The lock–key mechanism is a compromise between these two schemes. The mechanism can be both effective and flexible, depending on the length of the keys. The keys can be passed freely from domain to domain. In addition, access privileges may be effectively revoked by the simple technique of changing some of the keys associated with the object (Section 13.5).

Most systems use a combination of access lists and capabilities. When a process first tries to access an object, the access list is searched. If access is denied, an exception condition occurs. Otherwise, a capability is created and is attached to the process. Additional references use the capability to demonstrate swiftly that access is allowed. After the last access, the capability is destroyed. This strategy is used in the MULTICS system and in the CAL system; these systems use both access lists and capability lists.

As an example, consider a file system. Each file has an associated access list. When a process opens a file, the directory structure is searched to find the file, access permission is checked, and buffers are allocated. All this information is recorded in a new entry in a file table associated with the process. The operation returns an index into this table for the newly opened file. All operations on the file are made by specification of the index into the file table. The entry in the file table then points to the file and its buffers. When the file is closed, the file-table entry is deleted. Since the file table is maintained by the operating system, it cannot be corrupted by the user. Thus, the only files that the user can access are those that have been opened. Since access is checked when the file is opened, protection is ensured. This strategy is used in the UNIX system.

Note that the right to access *must* still be checked on each access, and the file-table entry has a capability only for the allowed operations. If a file is opened for reading, then a capability for read access is placed in the file-table entry. If an attempt is made to write onto the file, the system determines this protection violation by comparing the requested operation with the capability in the file-table entry.

13.5 ■ Revocation of Access Rights

In a dynamic protection system, it may sometimes be necessary to revoke access rights to objects that are shared by different users. Various questions about revocation may arise:

- **Immediate versus delayed:** Does revocation occur immediately, or is it delayed? If revocation is delayed, can we find out when it will take place?

- **Selective versus general:** When an access right to an object is revoked, does it affect *all* the users who have an access right to that object, or can we specify a select group of users whose access rights should be revoked?

- **Partial versus total:** Can a subset of the rights associated with an object be revoked, or must we revoke all access rights for this object?

- **Temporary versus permanent:** Can access be revoked permanently (that is, the revoked access right will never again be available), or can access be revoked and later be obtained again?

With an access-list scheme, revocation is easy. The access list is searched for the access right(s) to be revoked, and they are deleted from the list. Revocation is immediate, and can be general or selective, total or partial, and permanent or temporary.

Capabilities, however, present a much more difficult revocation problem. Since the capabilities are distributed throughout the system, we must find them before we can revoke them. There are several different schemes for implementing revocation for capabilities, including the following:

- **Reacquisition**. Periodically, capabilities are deleted from each domain. If a process wants to use a capability, it may find that that capability has been deleted. The process may then try to reacquire the capability. If access has been revoked, the process will not be able to reacquire the capability.

- **Back-pointers**. A list of pointers is maintained with each object, pointing to all capabilities associated with that object. When revocation is required, we can follow these pointers, changing the capabilities as necessary. This scheme has been adopted in the MULTICS system. It is quite general, although it is a costly implementation.

- **Indirection**. The capabilities do not point to the objects directly, but instead point indirectly. Each capability points to a unique entry in a global table, which in turn points to the object. We implement revocation by searching the global table for the desired entry and deleting it. When an access is attempted, the capability is found to point to an illegal table entry. Table entries can be reused for other capabilities without difficulty, since both the capability and the table entry contain the unique name of the object. The object for a capability and its table entry must match. This scheme was adopted in the CAL system. It does not allow selective revocation.

- **Keys**. A key is a unique bit pattern that can be associated with each capability. This key is defined when the capability is created, and it can be neither modified nor inspected by the process owning that capability. A *master key* associated with each object can be defined or replaced with the **set-key** operation. When a capability is created, the current value of the master key is associated with the capability. When the capability is exercised, its key is compared to the master key. If the keys match, the operation is allowed to continue; otherwise, an exception condition is raised. Revocation replaces the master key with a new value by the **set-key** operation, invalidating all previous capabilities for this object.

  Note that this scheme does not allow selective revocation, since only one master key is associated with each object. If we associate a list of keys with each object, then selective revocation can be implemented. Finally, we can group all keys into one global table of keys. A capability is valid only if its key matches some key in the global table. We implement revocation by removing the matching key from the table. With this scheme, a key can be associated with several objects, and several keys can be associated with each object, providing maximum flexibility.

  In key-based schemes, the operations of defining keys, inserting them into lists, and deleting them from lists should not be available to all users. In particular, it would be reasonable to allow only the owner of an object to set the keys for that object. This choice, however, is a policy decision that the protection system can implement, but should not define.

13.6 ■ Capability-Based Systems

In this section, we briefly survey two capability-based protection systems. These systems vary in their complexity and in the type of policies that can be implemented on them. Neither of them is widely used, but they are interesting proving grounds for protection theories.

13.6.1 Hydra

Hydra is a capability-based protection system that provides considerable flexibility. The system provides a fixed set of possible access rights that are known to and interpreted by the system. These rights include such basic forms of access as the right to read, write, or execute a memory segment. In addition, the system provides the means for a user (of the protection system) to declare additional rights. The interpretation of user-defined rights is performed solely by the user's program, but the system provides access protection for the use of these rights, as well as for the use of system-defined rights. The facilities provided by this system are interesting, and constitute a significant development in protection technology.

Operations on objects are defined procedurally. The procedures that implement such operations are themselves a form of object, and are accessed indirectly by capabilities. The names of user-defined procedures must be identified to the protection system if it is to deal with objects of the user-defined type. When the definition of an object is made known to Hydra, the names of operations on the type become *auxiliary rights*. Auxiliary rights can be described in a capability for an instance of the type. For a process to perform an operation on a typed object, the capability it holds for that object must contain the name of the operation being invoked among its auxiliary rights. This restriction enables discrimination of access rights to be made on an instance-by-instance and process-by-process basis.

Another interesting concept is *rights amplification*. This scheme allows certification of a procedure as *trustworthy* to act on a formal parameter of a specified type, on behalf of any process that holds a right to execute the procedure. The rights held by a trustworthy procedure are independent of, and may exceed, the rights held by the calling process. However, it is necessary neither to regard such a procedure as universally trustworthy (the procedure is not allowed to act on other types, for instance), nor to extend trustworthiness to any other procedures or program segments that might be executed by a process.

Amplification is useful in allowing implementation procedures access to the representation variables of an abstract data type. If a process holds a capability to a typed object A, for instance, this capability may include an auxiliary right to invoke some operation P, but would not include any of the so-called kernel rights, such as read, write, or execute, on the segment that represents A. Such a capability gives a process a means of indirect access (through the operation P) to the representation of A, but only for specific purposes.

On the other hand, when a process invokes the operation P on an object A, the capability for access to A may be amplified as control passes to the code body of P. This amplification may be necessary, to allow P the right to access the storage segment representing A, to implement the operation that P defines on the abstract data type. The code body of P may be allowed to read or to write to the segment of A directly, even though the calling process cannot. On return from P, the capability for A is restored to its original, unamplified state. This case is a typical one in which the rights held by a process for access to a protected segment must change dynamically, depending on the task to be performed. The dynamic adjustment of rights is performed to guarantee consistency of a programmer-defined abstraction. Amplification of rights can be stated explicitly in the declaration of an abstract type to the Hydra system.

When a user passes an object as an argument to a procedure, it may be necessary to ensure that the procedure cannot modify the object. We can implement this restriction readily by passing an access right that does not have the modification (write) right. However, if amplification may occur, the right to modify may be reinstated. Thus, the user-protection requirement can be circumvented. In general, of course, a user may trust that a procedure indeed performs its task correctly. This assumption, however, is not always correct, because of hardware or software errors. Hydra solves this problem by restricting amplifications.

The procedure call mechanism of Hydra was designed as a direct solution to the *problem of mutually suspicious subsystems*. This problem is defined as follows. Suppose that a program is provided that can be invoked as a service by a number of different users (for example, a sort routine, a compiler, a game). When users invoke this service program, they take the risk that the program will malfunction and will either damage the given data, or will retain some access right to the data to be used (without authority) later. Similarly, the service program may have some private files (for accounting purposes, for example) that should not be accessed directly by the calling user program. Hydra provides mechanisms for directly dealing with this problem.

A Hydra subsystem is built on top of its protection kernel and may require protection of its own components. A subsystem interacts with the kernel through calls on a set of kernel-defined primitives that defines access rights to resources defined by the subsystem. Policies for use of these resources by user processes can be defined by the subsystem designer, but are enforceable by use of the standard access protection afforded by the capability system.

A programmer can make direct use of the protection system, after acquainting himself with its features in the appropriate reference manual. Hydra provides a large library of system-defined procedures that can be called by user programs. A user of the Hydra system would explicitly incorporate calls on these system procedures into the code of his programs, or would use a program translator that had been interfaced to Hydra.

13.6.2 Cambridge CAP System

A different approach to capability-based protection has been taken in the design of the Cambridge CAP system. CAP's capability system is simpler and superficially less powerful than that of Hydra. However, closer examination shows that it too can be used to provide secure protection of user-defined objects. In CAP, there are two kinds of capabilities. The ordinary kind is called a *data capability*. It can be used to provide access to objects, but the only rights provided are the standard read, write, or execute of the individual storage segments associated with the object. Data capabilities are interpreted by microcode in the CAP machine.

A so-called *software capability* is protected by, but not interpreted by, the CAP microcode. It is interpreted by a *protected* (that is, a privileged) procedure, which may be written by an applications programmer as part of a subsystem. A particular kind of rights amplification is associated with a protected procedure. When executing the code body of such a procedure, a process temporarily acquires the rights to read or write the contents of a software capability itself. This specific kind of rights amplification corresponds to an implementation of the **seal** and **unseal** primitives on capabilities (see Bibliographic Notes for references). Of course, this privilege is still subject to type verification to ensure that only software capabilities for a specified abstract type are allowed to be passed to any such procedure. Universal trust is not placed in any code other than the CAP machine's microcode.

The interpretation of a software capability is left completely to the subsystem, through the protected procedures it contains. This scheme allows a variety of protection policies to be implemented. Although a programmer can define her own protected procedures (any of which might be incorrect), the security of the overall system cannot be compromised. The basic protection system will not allow an unverified, user-defined, protected procedure access to any storage segments (or capabilities) that do not belong to the protection environment in which it resides. The most serious consequence of an insecure protected procedure is a protection breakdown of the subsystem for which that procedure has responsibility.

The designers of the CAP system have noted that the use of software capabilities has allowed them to realize considerable economies in formulating and implementing protection policies commensurate with the requirements of abstract resources. However, a subsystem designer who wants to make use of this facility cannot simply study a reference manual, as is the case with Hydra. Instead, he must learn the principles and techniques of protection, since the system provides him with no library of procedures to be used.

13.7 ■ Language-Based Protection

To the degree that protection is provided in existing computer systems, it has usually been achieved through the device of an operating-system kernel, which acts as a security agent to inspect and validate each attempt to access a protected resource. Since comprehensive access validation is potentially a source of considerable overhead, either we must give it hardware support to reduce the cost of each validation, or we must accept that the system designer may be inclined to compromise the goals of protection. It is difficult to satisfy all these goals if the flexibility to implement various protection policies is restricted by the support mechanisms provided or if protection environments are made larger than necessary to secure greater operational efficiency.

As operating systems have become more complex, and particularly as they have attempted to provide higher-level user interfaces, the goals of protection have become much more refined. In this refinement, we find that the designers of protection systems have drawn heavily on ideas that originated in programming languages and especially on the concepts of abstract data types and objects. Protection systems are now concerned not only with the identity of a resource to which access is attempted but also with the functional nature of that access. In the newest protection systems, concern for the function to be invoked extends beyond a set of system-defined functions, such as standard file access methods, to include functions that may be user-defined as well.

Policies for resource use may also vary, depending on the application, and they may be subject to change over time. For these reasons, protection can no longer be considered as a matter of concern to only the designer of an operating system. It should also be available as a tool for use by the applications designer, so that resources of an applications subsystem can be guarded against tampering or the influence of an error.

At this point, programming languages enter the picture. Specifying the desired control of access to a shared resource in a system is making a declarative statement about the resource. This kind of statement can be integrated into a language by an extension of its typing facility. When protection is declared along with data typing, the designer of each subsystem can specify its requirements for protection, as well as its need for use of other resources in a system. Such a specification should be given directly as a program is composed, and in the language in which the program itself is stated. There are several significant advantages to this approach:

1. Protection needs are simply declared, rather than programmed as a sequence of calls on procedures of an operating system.

2. Protection requirements may be stated independently of the facilities provided by a particular operating system.

3. The means for enforcement do not need to be provided by the designer of a subsystem.

4. A declarative notation is natural because access privileges are closely related to the linguistic concept of data type.

There is a variety of techniques that can be provided by a programming language implementation to enforce protection, but any of these must depend on some degree of support from an underlying machine and its operating system. For example, suppose a language were used to generate code to run on the Cambridge CAP system. On this system, every storage reference made on the underlying hardware occurs indirectly through a capability. This restriction prevents any process from accessing a resource outside of its protection environment at any time. However, a program may impose arbitrary restrictions on how a resource may be used during execution of a particular code segment by any process. We can implement such restrictions most readily by using the software capabilities provided by CAP. A language implementation might provide standard, protected procedures to interpret software capabilities that would realize the protection policies that could be specified in the language. This scheme puts policy specification at the disposal of the programmers, while freeing them from the details of implementing its enforcement.

Even if a system does not provide a protection kernel as powerful as those of Hydra or CAP, there are still mechanisms available for implementing protection specifications given in a programming language. The principal distinction is that the *security* of this protection will not be as great as that supported by a protection kernel, because the mechanism must rely on more assumptions about the operational state of the system. A compiler can separate references for which it can certify that no protection violation could occur from those for which a violation might be possible, and can treat them differently. The security provided by this form of protection rests on the assumption that the code generated by the compiler will not be modified prior to or during its execution.

What, then, are the relative merits of enforcement based solely on a kernel, as opposed to enforcement provided largely by a compiler?

- **Security:** Enforcement by a kernel provides a greater degree of security of the protection system itself than does the generation of protection-checking code by a compiler. In a compiler-supported scheme, security rests on correctness of the translator, on some underlying mechanism of storage management that protects the segments from which compiled code is executed, and, ultimately, on the security of files from which a program is loaded. Some of these same considerations also apply to a software-supported protection kernel, but to a lesser degree, since the kernel may reside in fixed physical storage segments and may be loaded from only a designated file. With a tagged capability system, in which all address computation is performed either by hardware or by a fixed microprogram, even greater security is possible. Hardware-supported protection is also relatively immune to protection violations that might occur as a result of either hardware or system software malfunction.

- **Flexibility:** There are limits to the flexibility of a protection kernel in implementing a user-defined policy, although it may supply adequate facilities for the system to provide enforcement for its own policies. With a programming language, protection policy can be declared and enforcement provided as needed by an implementation. If a language does not provide sufficient flexibility, it can be extended or replaced, with less perturbation of a system in service than would be caused by the modification of an operating-system kernel.

- **Efficiency:** The greatest efficiency is obtained when enforcement of protection is supported directly by hardware (or microcode). Insofar as software support is required, language-based enforcement has the advantage that static access enforcement can be verified off-line at compile time. Also, since the enforcement mechanism can be tailored by an intelligent compiler to meet the specified need, the fixed overhead of kernel calls can often be avoided.

In summary, the specification of protection in a programming language allows the high-level description of policies for the allocation and use of resources. A language implementation can provide software for protection enforcement when automatic hardware-supported checking is unavailable. In addition, it can interpret protection specifications to generate calls on whatever protection system is provided by the hardware and the operating system.

One way of making protection available to the application program is through the use of *software capability* that could be used as an object of computation. Inherent in this concept is the idea that certain program components might have the privilege of creating or examining these software capabilities. A capability-creating program would be able to execute a primitive operation that would seal a data structure, rendering the latter's contents inaccessible to any program components that did not hold either the seal or the unseal privileges. They might copy the data structure, or pass its address to other program components, but they could not gain access to its contents. The reason for introducing such software capabilities is to bring a protection mechanism into the programming language. The only problem with the concept as proposed is that the use of the **seal** and **unseal** operations takes a procedural approach to specifying protection. A nonprocedural or declarative notation seems a preferable way to make protection available to the applications programmer.

What is needed is a safe, dynamic access-control mechanism for distributing capabilities to system resources among user processes. If it is to contribute to the overall reliability of a system, the access-control mechanism should be safe to use. If it is to be useful in practice, it should also be reasonably efficient. This requirement has led to the development of a number of language constructs that allow the programmer to declare various restrictions on the use of a specific managed resource (see the Bibliographic Notes for appropriate references). These constructs provide mechanisms for three functions:

1. Distributing capabilities safely and efficiently among customer processes: In particular, mechanisms ensure that a user process will use the managed resource only if it was granted a capability to that resource.

2. Specifying the type of operations that a particular process may invoke on an allocated resource (for example, a reader of a file should be allowed only to read the file, whereas a writer should be able both to read and to write): It should not be necessary to grant the same set of rights to every user process, and it should be impossible for a process to enlarge its set of access rights, except with the authorization of the access control mechanism.

3. Specifying the order in which a particular process may invoke the various operations of a resource (for example, a file must be opened before it can be read): It should be possible to give two processes different restrictions on the order in which they can invoke the operations of the allocated resource.

The incorporation of protection concepts into programming languages, as a practical tool for system design, is at present in its infancy. It is likely that protection will become a matter of greater concern to the designers of new systems with distributed architectures and increasingly stringent requirements on data security. Then, the importance of suitable language notations in which to express protection requirements will be recognized more widely.

13.8 ■ Summary

Computer systems contain many objects. These objects need to be protected from misuse. Objects may be hardware (such as memory, CPU time, or I/O devices) or software (such as files, programs, and abstract data types). An access right is permission to perform an operation on an object. A domain is a set of access rights. Processes execute in domains and may use any of the access rights in the domain to access and manipulate objects.

The access matrix is a general model of protection. The access matrix provides a mechanism for protection without imposing a particular protection policy on the system or its users. The separation of policy and mechanism is an important design property.

The access matrix is sparse. It is normally implemented either as access lists associated with each object, or as capability lists associated with each domain. We can include dynamic protection in the access-matrix model by considering domains and the access matrix itself as objects.

Real systems are much more limited, and tend to provide protection for only files. UNIX is representative, providing read, write, and execution protection separately for the owner, group, and general public for each file. MULTICS uses a ring structure in addition to file access. Hydra, the Cambridge CAP system, and Mach are capability systems that extend protection to user-defined software objects.

■ Exercises

13.1 What are the main differences between capability lists and access lists?

13.2 A Burroughs B7000/B6000 MCP file can be tagged as sensitive data. When such a file is deleted, its storage area is overwritten by some random bits. For what purpose would such a scheme be useful?

13.3 In a ring-protection system, level 0 has the greatest access to objects and level n (greater than zero) has fewer access rights. The access rights of a program at a particular level in the ring structure are considered as a set of capabilities. What is the relationship between the capabilities of a domain at level j and a domain at level i to an object (for $j > i$)?

13.4 Consider a computer system in which "computer games" can be played by students only between 10 P.M. and 6 A.M., by faculty members between 5 P.M. and 8 A.M., and by the computer center staff at all times. Suggest a scheme for implementing this policy efficiently.

13.5 The RC 4000 system (and other systems) have defined a tree of processes (called a process tree) such that all the descendants of a process are given resources (objects) and access rights by their ancestors only. Thus, a descendant can never have the ability to do anything that its ancestors cannot do. The root of the tree is the operating system, which has the ability to do anything. Assume the set of access rights was represented by an access matrix, A. $A(x,y)$ defines the access rights of process x to object y. If x is a descendant of z, what is the relationship between $A(x,y)$ and $A(z,y)$ for an arbitrary object y?

13.6 What hardware features are needed in a computer system for efficient capability manipulation? Can these be used for memory protection?

13.7 Consider a computing environment where a unique number is associated with each process and each object in the system. Suppose that we allow a process with number n to access an object with number m only if $n > m$. What type of protection structure do we have?

13.8 What protection problems may arise if a shared stack is used for parameter passing?

13.9 Consider a computing environment where a process is given the privilege of accessing an object only n times. Suggest a scheme for implementing this policy.

13.10 If all the access rights to an object are deleted, the object can no longer be accessed. At this point, the object should also be deleted, and the space it occupies should be returned to the system. Suggest an efficient implementation of this scheme.

13.11 What is the need-to-know principle? Why is it important for a protection system to adhere to this principle?

13.12 Why is it difficult to protect a system in which users are allowed to do their own I/O?

13.13 Capability lists are usually kept within the address space of the user. How does the system ensure that the user cannot modify the contents of the list?

Bibliographic Notes

The access-matrix model of protection between domains and objects was developed by Lampson [1969, 1971]. Popek [1974], Saltzer and Schroeder [1975] provided excellent surveys on the subject of protection. Harrison et al. [1976] used a formal version of this model to enable them to prove mathematically properties of a protection system.

The concept of a capability evolved from Iliffe's and Jodeit's *codewords*, which were implemented in the Rice University computer [Iliffe and Jodeit 1962]. The term *capability* was introduced by Dennis and Van Horn [1966].

The Hydra system was described by Wulf et al. [1981]. The CAP system was described by Needham and Walker [1977]. Organick [1972] discussed the MULTICS ring protection system.

Revocation was discussed by Redell and Fabry [1974], Cohen and Jefferson [1975], and Ekanadham and Bernstein [1979]. The principle of separation of policy and mechanism was advocated by the designer of Hydra [Levin et al. 1975]. The confinement problem was first discussed by Lampson [1973], and was further examined by Lipner [1975].

The use of higher-level languages for specifying access control was suggested first by Morris [1973], who proposed the use of the *seal* and *unseal* operation discussed in Section 13.7. Kieburtz and Silberschatz [1978, 1983], and McGraw and Andrews [1979], proposed various language constructs for dealing with general dynamic resource-management schemes. Jones and Liskov [1978] considered the problem of how a static access-control scheme can be incorporated in a programming language that supports abstract data types.

CHAPTER 14

SECURITY

Protection, as we have discussed it in Chapter 13, is strictly an *internal* problem: How do we provide controlled access to programs and data stored in a computer system? Security, on the other hand, requires not only an adequate protection system, but also consideration of the *external* environment within which the system operates. Internal protection is not useful if the operator's console is exposed to unauthorized personnel, or if files (stored, for example, on tapes and disks) can simply be removed from the computer system and taken to a system with no protection. These security problems are essentially management, not operating-system, problems.

The information stored in the system (both data and code), as well as the physical resources of the computer system, need to be protected from unauthorized access, malicious destruction or alteration, and accidental introduction of inconsistency. In this chapter, we examine the ways in which information may be misused or intentionally made inconsistent. We then present mechanisms to guard against this occurrence.

14.1 ■ The Security Problem

In Chapter 13, we discussed various mechanisms that the operating system can provide (with an appropriate aid from the hardware) that will allow users to protect their resources (usually programs and data). These mechanisms work well as long as the users of the system do not try to circumvent the intended use of and access to these resources. Unfortunately, in reality, this situation is seldom realized. When it is not, security comes into play. We say that a system is secure if its resources are utilized and accessed as intended under all circumstances. Unfortunately, it is not generally possible to achieve total security. Nonetheless, mechanisms must be available to make security breaches a rare occurrence, rather than the norm.

Security violations (misuse) of the system can be categorized as being either intentional (malicious) or accidental. It is easier to protect against accidental misuse than to protect against malicious misuse. Among the forms of malicious access are the following:

- Unauthorized reading of data (theft of information)

- Unauthorized modification of data

- Unauthorized destruction of data

Absolute protection of the system from malicious abuse is not possible, but the cost to the perpetrator can be made sufficiently high to deter most if not all attempts to access, without proper authority, the information residing in the system.

To protect the system, we must take security measures at two levels:

- **Physical:** The site or sites containing the computer systems must be physically secured against armed or surreptitious entry by intruders.

- **Human:** Users must be authorized carefully to reduce the chance of any such user giving access to an intruder in exchange for a bribe or other favors.

Security at both levels must be maintained to ensure operating system security. A weakness at a high level of security (physical or human) allows circumvention of strict low-level (operating system) security measures.

It is worthwhile, in many applications, to devote a considerable effort to the security of the computer system. Large commercial systems containing payroll or other financial data are inviting targets to thieves. Systems that contain data pertaining to corporate operations may be of interest to unscrupulous competitors. Furthermore, loss of such data, whether via accident or fraud, can seriously impair the ability of the corporation to function.

On the other hand, the system hardware must provide protection (as discussed in Chapter 13) to allow for the implementation of security features. For instance, MS-DOS and Macintosh OS provide little security because the hardware for which they were originally designed for did not provide memory or I/O protection. Now that the hardware has become sufficiently sophisticated to provide protection, the designers of these operating systems are struggling to add security. Unfortunately, adding a feature to a functional system is a much more difficult and challenging task than is designing and implementing the feature before the system is built.

In the remainder of this chapter, we shall address security at the operating-system level. Security at the physical and human levels, although important, is far beyond the scope of this text. Security within the operating system is implemented at several levels, ranging from passwords for access to the system to the isolation of concurrent processes running within the system. The file system also provides some degree of protection.

14.2 ■ Authentication

A major security problem for operating systems is the *authentication* problem. The protection system depends on an ability to identify the programs and processes that are executing. This ability, in turn, eventually rests on our power to identify each user of the system. A user normally identifies himself. How do we determine if a user's identity is authentic? Generally, authentication is based on some combination of three sets of items: user possession (a key or card), user knowledge (a user identifier and password), and a user attribute (fingerprint, retina pattern, or signature).

The most common approach to authenticating a user identity is the use of user *passwords*. When the user identifies herself by user-id or account name, she is asked for a password. If the user-supplied password matches the password stored in the system, the system assumes that the user is legitimate.

Passwords are often used to protect objects in the computer system, in the absence of more complete protection schemes. They can be considered a special case of either keys or capabilities. For instance, a password could be associated with each resource (such as a file). Whenever a request is made to use the resource, the password must be given. If the password is correct, access is granted. Different passwords may be associated with different access rights. For example, different passwords may be used for reading, appending, and updating a file.

Although there are some problems associated with the use of passwords, they are nevertheless extremely common, because they are easy to understand and use. The problems with passwords are related to the difficulty of keeping a password secret. Passwords can be compromised by being guessed, accidentally exposed, or illegally transferred from an authorized user to an unauthorized one, as we show next.

There are two common ways to guess a password. One is for the intruder (either human or program) to know the user or have information about the user. All too frequently, people use obvious information (such as the name of their cat or spouse) as their password. The other way is brute-force; trying all possible combinations of letters, numbers, and punctuation until the password is found. Short passwords do not leave enough choices to prevent a password from being guessed by repeated trials. For example, a four-decimal password provides only 10,000 variations. On the average, guessing 5000 times would produce the password. If a program could be written that would try a password every 1 millisecond, it would then take only about 5 seconds to guess a password. Longer passwords are less susceptible to being guessed by enumeration, and systems that allow uppercase and lowercase letters, numbers, and all punctuation characters to be used in passwords make the task of guessing the password much more difficult. Of course users must take advantage of the large password space and not just use lower-case letters.

The failure of password security due to exposure can result from visual or electronic monitoring. An intruder could look over the shoulder of a user when the user is logging in, and can learn the password easily. Alternatively, anyone with access to the network on which a computer resides could seamlessly add a network monitor, allowing her to watch all data being transferred on the network, including user-ids and passwords. Exposure is a particularly severe problem if the password is written down where it can be read or lost. As we shall see, some systems force the user to select hard-to-remember or long passwords. Taken to extreme, this can cause a user to record the password, providing much worse security than when the system allows easy passwords!

The final method of password compromise is the result of human nature. Most computer installations have the rule that users are not allowed to share accounts. This rule is sometimes implemented for accounting reasons, but often it is used to aid in security. For instance, if one user-id was shared by several users, and a security breach occurred from that user-id, then it is impossible to know who was using that user-id at the time, or even if it was one of the authorized users. With one user per user-id, the user could be questioned directly about the use of that account. Sometimes, users break account-sharing rules to help out friends or circumvent accounting, and this behavior can result in a system being accessed by unauthorized users, possibly harmful ones.

Passwords can be either system-generated or user-selected. System-generated passwords may be difficult to remember, and thus may be commonly written down. User-selected passwords, however, are often easy to guess (the user's name or favorite car, for example). At some sites, administrators occasionally check user passwords and notify the users if the password is too short or easy to guess. Some systems also *age* passwords, forcing users to change them at regular intervals (every month, for instance). This method is not foolproof either, since users may easily toggle between two passwords.

Several variants on the simple password scheme can be used. For example, the password can be changed frequently. In the extreme, the password is changed for each session. A new password is selected (either by the system or by the user) at the end of *each* session, and that password must be used for the next session. Note that, even if a password is misused, it can be used only once, and its use prevents the legitimate user from using it. Consequently, the legitimate user discovers the security violation at the next session, when he uses a now-invalid password. Steps can then be taken to repair the broached security.

Another approach is to have a set of paired passwords. When a session begins, the system randomly selects and presents one part of a password pair; the user must supply the other part. This approach can be generalized to the use of an algorithm as a password. The algorithm might be an integer function, for example. The system selects a random integer and presents it to the user. The user applies the function and replies with the result of the function. The system also applies the function. If the two results match, access is allowed.

One problem with all these approaches is the difficulty of keeping the password (or list of password pairs, or algorithms) secret. The UNIX system uses a variant of the algorithmic password to avoid the necessity of keeping its password list secret. Each user has a password. The system contains a function that is very difficult (the designers hope impossible) to invert, but simple to compute. That is, given a value x, it is easy to compute the function value $f(x)$. Given a function value $f(x)$, however, it is impossible to compute x. This function is used to encode all passwords. Only the encoded passwords are stored. When a user presents a password, it is encoded and compared against the stored encoded password. Even if the stored encoded password is seen, it cannot be decoded, so the password cannot be determined. Thus, the password file does not need to be kept secret.

The flaw in this method is that the system no longer has control over the passwords. Although the passwords are encrypted, anyone with a copy of the password file may run fast encryption routines against it, encrypting each word in a dictionary, for instance, and comparing the results against the passwords. If the user has selected a password that is also a word in the dictionary, the password is cracked. On sufficiently fast computers, or even on clusters of slow computers, such a comparison may only take a few hours. For this reason, new versions of UNIX hide the password entries. On current UNIX systems, it is a good idea for users to use combination passwords, such as two dictionary words separated by a punctuation character. Such passwords do not easily succumb to algorithmic guessing techniques because the result is a very large space (number of words in the dictionary squared) which needs to be encrypted to try to match such passwords. To avoid the dictionary encryption method, some systems disallow the use of dictionary words as passwords.

14.3 ■ Program Threats

In an environment where a program written by one user may be used by another user, there is an opportunity for misuse, which may result in unexpected behavior. Below, we describe two common methods for achieving this.

14.3.1 Trojan Horse

Many systems have mechanisms for allowing programs written by users to be executed by other users. If these programs are executed in a domain that provides the access rights of the executing user, they may misuse these rights. Inside a text-editor program, for example, there may be code to search the file to be edited for certain keywords. If any are found, the entire file may be copied to a special area accessible to the creator of the text editor. A code segment that misuses its environment is called a *Trojan horse*. The Trojan-horse problem is exacerbated by long search paths (such as are common on UNIX systems). The search path lists the set of directories to search when an ambiguous program name is given. The path is searched for a file of that name and the file is executed. All the directories in the search path must be secure, or a Trojan horse could be slipped into the user's path and executed accidentally.

For instance, consider the use of the "." character in a search path. The "." tells the shell to include the current directory in the search. Thus, if a user has "." in her search path, has set her current directory to a friend's directory, and enters the name of a normal system command, the command may be executed from the friend's directory instead. The program would run within the user's domain, allowing the program to do anything that the user is allowed to do, including deleting the user's files for instance.

14.3.2 Trap Door

The designer of a program or system might leave a hole in the software that only he is capable of using. This type of security breach was shown in the movie "War Games." For instance, the code might check for a specific user identifier or password and circumvent normal security procedures. There have been cases of programmers being arrested for embezzling from banks by including rounding errors in their code, and having the occasional half-cent credited to their accounts. This account crediting can add up to quite a large amount of money, considering the number of transactions a bank executes!

A clever trap door could be included in a compiler. The compiler could generate standard object code as well as a trap door, regardless of the source code being compiled. This activity is particularly nefarious, since a search of the source code of the program would not reveal any problems. Only the source code of the compiler would contain the information. Trap doors pose a difficult problem because, to detect them, we would have to analyze all the source code for all components of a system. Given that software systems may consist of millions of lines of code, this analysis is not done frequently.

14.4 ■ System Threats

Most operating systems provide a means for processes to spawn other processes. In such an environment, it is possible to create a situation where operating-system resources and user files are misused. The two most common methods for doing this are worms and viruses, which are discussed below.

14.4.1 Worms

A *worm* is a process that uses the spawn mechanism to clobber system performance. The worm spawns copies of itself, using up system resources and perhaps locking out system use by all other processes. On computer networks, worms are particularly potent, since they may reproduce themselves among systems and thus shut down the entire network. Such an event occurred in 1988 to UNIX systems on the worldwide *Internet* network, causing millions of dollars of lost system and programmer time.

The Internet links thousands of government, academic, research, and industrial computers internationally and serves as the infrastructure for electronic exchange of scientific information. At the close of the work day of November 2, 1988, Robert Tappan Morris, Jr., a first-year Cornell graduate student, unleashed a worm program on one or more hosts connected to the Internet. Targeting Sun Microsystems' Sun 3 workstations and VAX computers running variants of 4 BSD UNIX, the worm quickly spread over great distances and within a few hours of its release had consumed system resources to the point of bringing down the infected machines.

Although Morris designed the self-replicating program for rapid reproduction and distribution, features of the UNIX networking environment provided the means to propagate the worm throughout the system. It is likely that Morris chose for initial infection an Internet host left open for and accessible to outside users. From there, the worm program exploited flaws in the UNIX operating system's security routines and took advantage of UNIX utilities that simplify resource sharing in local area networks to gain unauthorized access to thousands of other connected sites. Morris' methods of attack are outlined next.

The worm was made up of two programs, a *grappling hook* (also called *bootstrap* or *vector*) program and the main program. Named *l1.c*, the grappling hook consisted of 99 lines of C code compiled and run on each machine it accessed. Once established on the system under attack, the grappling hook connected to the machine where it originated and uploaded a copy of the main worm onto the "hooked" system (see Figure 14.1). The main program proceeded to search for other machines to which the newly infected system could connect easily. In these actions, Morris exploited a UNIX networking utility, *rsh*, for easy remote task execution. By setting up special files that list host−login name pairs, users can omit entering a password each time they access a remote account on the paired list. The worm searched these special files for site names that would allow remote execution without a password. Where remote shells were established, the worm program was uploaded and began executing anew.

The attack via remote access was one of three infection methods built into the worm. The other two methods involved operating system bugs in the UNIX *finger* and *sendmail* programs. The *finger* utility functions as an electronic telephone directory; the command

finger username@sitename

returns a person's real and login names, along with other information that the user may have provided, such as office and home addresses and telephone numbers, research plan, or their birthdays. *Finger* runs as a background process (daemon) at each BSD site and responds to queries throughout the Internet. The point vulnerable to malicious entry involved reading input without checking bounds for overflow. Morris' program

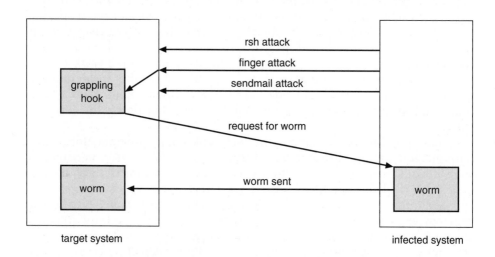

Figure 14.1 The Morris Internet worm.

queried *finger* with a 536-byte string crafted to exceed the buffer allocated for input and to overwrite the stack frame. Instead of returning to the *main* routine it was in before Morris' call, the *finger* daemon was routed to a procedure within the invading 536-byte string now residing on the stack. The new procedure executed */bin/sh*, which, if successful, provided the worm a remote shell on the machine under attack.

The bug exploited in *sendmail* also involved utilizing a daemon process for malicious entry. *Sendmail* routes electronic mail in a network environment. Debugging code in the utility permits testers to verify and display the state of the mail system. The debugging option is useful to system administrators and is often left on as a background process. Morris included in his attack arsenal a call to *debug*, which, instead of specifying a user address, as would be normal in testing, issued a set of commands that mailed and executed a copy of the grappling-hook program.

Once in place, the main worm proceeded in systematic attempts to discover user passwords. It began by trying simple cases of no password or passwords constructed of account–user name combinations, to comparisons with an internal dictionary of 432 favorite password choices, to the final stage of trying each word in the standard UNIX on-line dictionary as a possible password. This elaborate and efficient three-stage password-cracking algorithm enabled the worm to gain further access to other user accounts on the infected system. The worm then searched for *rsh* data files in these newly broken accounts. Any *rsh* entries were tried, and, as described previously, the worm could then gain access to user accounts on remote systems.

With each new access, the worm program searched for already active copies of itself. If it found one, the new copy exited, except for every seventh instance. Had the worm exited on all duplicate sightings, it might have remained undetected. Allowing every seventh duplicate to proceed (possibly to confound efforts to stop its spread by baiting with "fake" worms) created a wholesale infestation of Sun and VAX systems on the Internet.

The very features of the UNIX network environment that assisted the worm's propagation also helped to stop its advance. Ease of electronic communication, mechanisms to copy source and binary files to remote machines and access to both source code and human expertise allowed cooperative efforts to develop solutions to proceed apace. By the evening of the next day, November 3, methods of halting the invading program were circulated to system administrators via the Internet. Within days, specific software patches for the exploited security flaws were available.

One natural response is to question Morris' motives in unleashing the worm. The action has been characterized as both a harmless prank gone awry and a serious criminal offense. Based on the complexity of starting the attack, it is unlikely that the worm's release or the scope of its spread was unintentional. The worm program took elaborate steps to cover its tracks and to repel efforts to stop its spread. Yet the program contained no code aimed at damaging or destroying the systems on which it ran. The author clearly had the expertise to include such commands; in fact, data structures were present in the bootstrap code that could have been used to transfer Trojan horse or virus programs (see Section 14.4.2). The actual behavior of the program may lead to interesting observations, but does not provide a sound basis for inferring motive. What is not open to speculation, however, is the legal outcome: A federal court convicted Morris and handed down a sentence of 3 years probation, 400 hours of community service, and a $10,000 fine. Morris' legal costs probably were in excess of $100,000.

14.4.2 Viruses

Another form of computer attack is a *virus*. Like worms, viruses are designed to spread into other programs and can wreak havoc in a system, including modifying or destroying files and causing system crashes and program malfunctions. Whereas a worm is structured as a complete, standalone program, a virus is a fragment of code embedded in a legitimate program. Viruses are a major problem for computer users, especially users of microcomputer systems. Multiuser computers, generally, are not prone to viruses because the executable programs are protected from writing by the operating system. Even if a virus does infect a program, its powers are limited because other aspects of the system are protected. Single-user systems have no such protections and, as a result, a virus has free run.

Viruses usually spread by users downloading viral programs from public bulletin boards or exchanging floppy disks containing an infection. A case from February 1992 involving two Cornell University students provides an illustration. The students had developed three Macintosh game programs with an embedded virus that they distributed to worldwide software archives via the Internet. The virus was discovered when a mathematics professor in Wales downloaded the games, and antivirus programs on his system alerted him to an infection. Some 200 other users had also downloaded the games. Although the virus was not designed to destroy data, it could spread to application files and cause such problems as long delays and program malfunctions. The authors were easy to trace, since the games had been mailed electronically from a Cornell account. New York state authorities arrested the students on misdemeanor charges of computer tampering and may have since filed additional charges.

In another incident, a programmer in California being divorced by his wife gave her a disk to load on a disputed computer. The disk contained a virus and erased all the files on the system. The husband was arrested and charged with destruction of property.

On occasion, upcoming viral infections are announced in high-profile media events. Such was the case with the Michelangelo virus, that was scheduled to erase infected hard disk files on March 6, 1992, the Renaissance artist's five hundred seventeenth birthday. Because of the extensive publicity surrounding the virus, most U.S. sites had located and destroyed the virus before it was activated, so it caused little or no damage. Such cases both alert the general public to and alarm them about the virus problem. Antivirus programs are currently very good sellers. Most commercial packages are effective against only particular, known viruses. They work by searching all the programs on a system for the specific pattern of instructions known to make up the virus. When they find a known pattern, they remove the instructions, "disinfecting" the program. These commercial packages have catalogs of hundreds of viruses for which they search.

The best protection against computer viruses is prevention, or the practice of *safe computing*. Purchasing unopened software from vendors and avoiding free or pirated copies from public sources or floppy-disk exchange is the safest route to preventing infection. However, even new copies of legitimate software applications are not immune to virus infection.

Another safeguard, while not preventing infection, does permit early detection. A user must begin by completely reformatting the hard disk, especially the boot sector, which is often targeted for viral attack. Only secure software is uploaded, and a checksum for each file is calculated. The checksum list must be then be kept free from unauthorized access. Following any system reboot, a program can recompute the checksums and compare them to the original list; any differences serve as a warning of possible infection. Because they usually work among systems, worms and viruses are generally considered to pose security, rather than protection, problems.

14.5 ■ Threat Monitoring

The security of a system can be improved by two management techniques. One is *threat monitoring*. The system can check for suspicious patterns of activity in an attempt to detect a security violation. A common example of this scheme is a time-sharing system that counts the number of incorrect passwords given when a user is trying to log in. More than a few incorrect attempts may signal an attempt to guess a password.

Another common technique is an *audit log*. An audit log simply records the time, user, and type of all accesses to an object. After security has been violated, the audit log can be used to determine how and when the problem occurred and perhaps the amount of damage done. This information can be useful, both for recovery from the violation and, possibly, in the development of better security measures to prevent future problems. Unfortunately, logs can become large, and logging uses system resources which are then unavailable to the users.

Rather than log system activities, we can scan the system periodically for security holes. These scans can be done when the computer is relatively unused, and therefore have less effect than logging. Such a scan can check a variety of aspects of the system:

- Short or easy-to-guess passwords

- Unauthorized set-uid programs, if the system supports this mechanism

- Unauthorized programs in system directories

- Unexpected long-running processes

- Improper directory protections, on both user and system directories

- Improper protections on system data files, such as the password file, device drivers, or even the operating-system kernel itself

- Dangerous entries in the program search path (for example, Trojan horse as discussed in Section 14.3.1)

- Changes to system programs; we can detect unexpected changes by keeping a list of the checksum values of all system programs, and comparing this list against the current checksum values of the programs — checksums do not change unless the contents of the file have changed

Any problems found by a security scan can either be fixed automatically or be reported to the managers of the system.

Networked computers are much more susceptible to security attacks than are standalone systems. Rather than attacks from a known set of access points, such as directly connected terminals, we face attacks from an unknown and very large set of access points — a potentially severe security problem. To a lesser extent, systems connected to telephone lines via modems are also more exposed.

In fact, the U.S. federal government considers systems to be only as secure as is their most far-reaching connection. For instance, a top-security system may be accessed only from within a building also considered top-secure. The system loses the top-secure rating if any form of communication can occur outside that environment. Some government facilities take extreme security precautions. The connectors into which a terminal plugs to communicate with the secure computer are locked in a safe in the office when the terminal is not being used. A person needs to know a physical lock combination, as well as authentication information for the computer itself, to gain access to the computer.

14.6   ■   Encryption

The various provisions that an operating system may make for authorization may not offer sufficient protection for highly sensitive data. Moreover, as computer networks gain popularity, more sensitive (classified) information is being transmitted over channels where eavesdropping and message interception are possible. To keep such sensitive information secure, we need mechanisms to allow a user to protect data transferred over the network.

Encryption is one common method of protecting information transmitted over unreliable links. The basic mechanism works as follows:

1. The information (text) is *encrypted* (encoded) from its initial readable form (called *clear text*), to an internal form (called *cipher text*). This internal text form, although readable, does not make any sense.

2. The cipher text can be stored in a readable file, or transmitted over unprotected channels.

3. To make sense of the cipher text, the receiver must *decrypt* (decode) it back into clear text.

Even if the encrypted information is accessed by an unauthorized person, it will be useless unless it can be decoded. The main issue is the development of encryption schemes that are impossible (or at least exceedingly difficult) to break.

There is a variety of methods to accomplish this task. The most common ones provide a general encryption algorithm E, a general decryption algorithm D, and a secret key (or keys) to be supplied for each application. Let E_k and D_k denote the encryption and decryption algorithms, respectively, for a particular application with a key k. Then the encryption algorithm must satisfy the following properties for any message m:

1. $D_k(E_k(m)) = m$.

2. Both E_k and D_k can be computed efficiently.

3. The security of the system depends only on the secrecy of the key, and not on the secrecy of the algorithms E and D.

One such scheme, called the *Data Encryption Standard*, was recently adopted by the National Bureau of Standards. This scheme suffers from the *key-distribution* problem: Before communication can take place, the secret keys must be sent securely to both the sender and receiver. This task cannot be done effectively in a communication-network environment. A solution to this problem is to use a *public key-encryption* scheme. Each user has both a public and a private key, and two users can communicate knowing only each other's public key.

An algorithm based on this concept follows. This algorithm is believed to be almost unbreakable. The public encryption key is a pair (e,n); the private key is a pair (d,n), where e, d, and n are positive integers. Each message is represented as an integer between 0 and $n - 1$. (A long message is broken into a series of smaller messages, each of which can be represented as such an integer.) The functions E and D are defined as

$$E(m) = m^e \bmod n = C,$$
$$D(C) = C^d \bmod n.$$

The main problem is choosing the encryption and decryption keys. The integer n is computed as the product of two large (100 or more digits) randomly chosen prime numbers p and q with

$$n = p \times q.$$

The value of d is chosen to be a large, randomly chosen integer relatively prime to $(p - 1) \times (q - 1)$. That is, d satisfies

greatest common divisor$[d, (p - 1) \times (q - 1)] = 1.$

Finally, the integer e is computed from p, q, and d to be the *multiplicative inverse* of d modulo $(p - 1) \times (q - 1)$. That is, e satisfies

$$e \times d \bmod (p - 1) \times (q - 1) = 1.$$

We should point out that, although n is publicly known, p and q are not. This condition is allowed because of the well-known fact that it is difficult to factor n. Consequently, the integers d and e cannot be guessed easily.

Let us illustrate this scheme with an example. Let $p = 5$ and $q = 7$. Then, $n = 35$ and $(p - 1) \times (q - 1) = 24$. Since 11 is relatively prime to 24, we can choose $d = 11$; and since $11 \times 11 \bmod 24 = 121 \bmod 24 = 1$, $e = 11$. Suppose now that $m = 3$. Then,

$$C = m^e \bmod n = 3^{11} \bmod 35 = 12,$$

and

$$C^d \bmod n = 12^{11} \bmod 35 = 3 = m.$$

Thus, if we encode m using e, we can decode m using d.

14.7 ■ Summary

Protection is an internal problem. Security must consider both the computer system and the environment (people, buildings, businesses, valuable objects, and threats) within which the system is used.

The data stored in the computer system need to be protected from unauthorized access, malicious destruction or alteration, and accidental introduction of inconsistency. It is easier to protect against accidental loss of data consistency than to protect against malicious access to the data. Absolute protection of the information stored in a computer system from malicious abuse is not possible, but the cost to the perpetrator can be made sufficiently high to deter most, if not all, attempts to access that information without proper authority.

The various authorization provisions in a computer system may not be sufficient protection for highly sensitive data. In such cases, data may be *encrypted*. It is not possible for encrypted data to be read unless the reader knows how to decipher (*decrypt*) the encrypted data.

■ Exercises

14.1 A password may become known to other users in a variety of ways. Is there a simple method for detecting that such an event has occurred? Explain your answer.

14.2 The list of all passwords is kept within the operating system. Thus, if a user manages to read this list, password protection is no longer provided. Suggest a scheme that will avoid this problem. (Hint: Use different internal and external representations.)

14.3 An experimental addition to UNIX allows a user to connect a *watchdog* program to a file, such that the watchdog is invoked whenever a program requests access to the file. The watchdog then either grants or denies access to the file. Discuss the pros and cons of using watchdogs for security.

14.4 The UNIX program, COPS, scans a given system for possible security holes and alerts the user to possible problems. What are the potential hazards of using such a system for security? How can these problems be limited or eliminated?

14.5 Discuss ways by which managers of systems connected to the Internet could have limited or eliminated the damage done by the worm. What are the drawbacks of making such changes to the way in which the system operates?

14.6 Argue for or against the sentence handed down against Robert Morris, Jr., for his creation and execution of the Internet worm.

14.7 Make a list of security concerns for a computer system for a bank. For each item on your list, state whether this concern relates to physical security, human security, or operating-system security.

14.8 What are the advantages of encrypting data stored in the computer system?

Bibliographic Notes

General discussions concerning security were offered by Hsiao et al. [1979], Landwehr [1981], Denning [1982], Pfleeger [1989], and Russell and Gangemi [1991]. The U.S. federal government is, of course, concerned about security. It publishes the *Orange Book*, which describes a set of security levels, and the features that an operating system must have to qualify for each security rating. Reading it is a good starting point for understanding security concerns. Also of general interest is the the text by Lobel [1986].

Issues concerning the design and verification of secure systems were discussed by Rushby [1981] and Silverman [1983]. A security kernel for a multiprocessor microcomputer was described by Schell [1983]. A distributed secure system was described by Rushby and Randell [1983].

Morris and Thompson [1979] discussed password security. Morshedian [1986] presented methods to fight password pirates. Password authentication with insecure communications was considered by Lamport [1981]. The issue of password cracking was discussed by Seely [1989]. The issue of computer breakins was discussed by Lehmann [1987] and Reid [1987].

Discussions concerning UNIX security were offered by Grampp and Morris [1984], Wood and Kochan [1985], Farrow [1986a, 1986b], Filipski and Hanko [1986], Hecht et al. [1988], Kramer [1988], and Garfinkel and Spafford [1991]. Bershad and Pinkerton [1988] presented the watchdogs extension to BSD UNIX. The COPS security-scanning package for UNIX was written by Dan Farmer at Purdue University. It is available to users on the Internet via the *ftp* program from host ftp.uu.net in directory /pub/security/cops.

Spafford [1989] presented a detailed technical discussion of the Internet worm. The Spafford article appeared with three others in a special section on the Internet worm in *Communications of the ACM*, Volume 32, Number 6, June 1989.

Diffie and Hellman [1976, 1979] were the first researchers to propose the use of the public key-encryption scheme. The algorithm presented in

Section 14.6, which is based on the public key-encryption scheme, was developed by Rivest et al. [1978]. Lempel [1979], Simmons [1979], Gifford [1982], Denning [1982], and Ahituv et al. [1987] concerned the use of cryptography in computer systems. Discussions concerning protection of digital signatures were offered by Akl [1983], Davies [1983], and Denning [1983, 1984].

PART FIVE

DISTRIBUTED SYSTEMS

A distributed system is a collection of processors that do not share memory or a clock. Instead, each processor has its own local memory, and the processors communicate with each other through various communication lines. The processors in a distributed system vary in size and function. They may include small microprocessors, workstations, minicomputers, and large general-purpose computer systems.

A distributed system provides the user with access to the various resources that the system maintains. Access to a shared resource allows computation speedup, and improved data availability and reliability.

A distributed file system is a file-service system whose users, servers, and storage devices are dispersed among the various sites of a distributed system. Accordingly, service activity has to be carried out across the network; instead of a single centralized data repository, there are multiple and independent storage devices.

A distributed system must provide various mechanisms for process synchronization and communication, for dealing with the deadlock problem, and for dealing with a variety of failures that are not encountered in a centralized system.

CHAPTER 15

NETWORK STRUCTURES

A recent trend in computer systems is to distribute computation among several physical processors. There are basically two schemes for building such systems. In a *multiprocessor* (tightly coupled) system, the processors share memory and a clock, and communication usually takes place through the shared memory. In a *distributed* (loosely coupled) system, the processors do not share memory or a clock. Instead, each processor has its own local memory. The processors communicate with one another through various communication networks, such as high-speed buses or telephone lines. In this chapter, we discuss the general structure of distributed systems and the networks that interconnect them. Detailed discussions are given in Chapters 16 to 18.

15.1 ■ Background

A distributed system is a collection of loosely coupled processors interconnected by a communication network. From the point of view of a specific processor in a distributed system, the rest of the processors and their respective resources are *remote*, whereas its own resources are *local*.

The processors in a distributed system may vary in size and function. They may include small microprocessors, workstations, minicomputers, and large general-purpose computer systems. These processors are referred to by a number of different names, such as *sites*, *nodes*, *computers*, *machines*, *hosts*, and so on, depending on the context in which they are mentioned. We mainly use the term *site*, to indicate a location of machines and *host* to refer to a specific system at a site. Generally, one host at one site, the *server*, has a resource that another host at another site, the *client* (or user), would like to use. The purpose of the distributed system is to provide an efficient and convenient environment for this type of sharing of resources. A distributed system is shown in Figure 15.1.

A distributed operating system provides users with access to the various resources that the system provides. By *resources*, we mean both hardware (such as printers and tape drives) and software (such as files and programs). Access to these resources is controlled by the operating system. There are basically two complementary schemes for providing such a service:

- **Network operating systems:** The users are aware of the multiplicity of machines, and need to access these resources by either logging into the appropriate remote machine, or transferring data from the remote machine to their own machines.

- **Distributed operating systems:** The users do not need to be aware of the multiplicity of machines. They access remote resources in the same manner as they do local resources.

Before discussing these two types of operating systems, we shall examine why such systems are useful, and what the structure of the underlying computer network is. In Chapter 16, we present detailed discussions concerning the structure of these two types of operating systems.

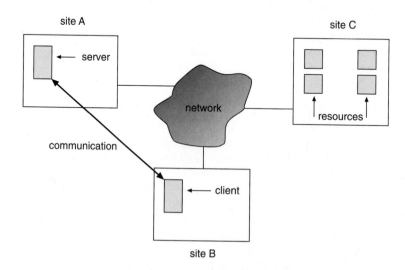

Figure 15.1 A distributed system.

15.2 ■ Motivation

There are four major reasons for building distributed systems: *resource sharing, computation speedup, reliability,* and *communication.* In this section, we briefly elaborate on each of them.

15.2.1 Resource Sharing

If a number of different sites (with different capabilities) are connected to one another, then a user at one site may be able to use the resources available at another. For example, a user at site A may be using a laser printer available at only site B. Meanwhile, a user at B may access a file that resides at A. In general, resource sharing in a distributed system provides mechanisms for sharing files at remote sites, processing information in a distributed database, printing files at remote sites, using remote specialized hardware devices (such as a high-speed array processor), and performing other operations.

15.2.2 Computation Speedup

If a particular computation can be partitioned into a number of subcomputations that can run concurrently, then the availability of a distributed system may allow us to distribute the computation among the various sites, to run the computation concurrently. In addition, if a particular site is currently overloaded with jobs, some of them may be moved to other, lightly loaded, sites. This movement of jobs is called *load sharing.* Automated load sharing, in which the distributed operating system automatically moves jobs, is still uncommon in commercial systems. It remains an active research area, however.

15.2.3 Reliability

If one site fails in a distributed system, the remaining sites can potentially continue operating. If the system is composed of a number of large autonomous installations (that is, general-purpose computers), the failure of one of them should not affect the rest. If, on the other hand, the system is composed of a number of small machines, each of which is responsible for some crucial system function (such as terminal character I/O or the file system), then a single failure may halt the operation of the whole system. In general, if enough redundancy exists in the system (in both hardware and data), the system can continue with its operation, even if some of its sites have failed.

The failure of a site must be detected by the system, and appropriate action may be needed to recover from the failure. The system must no longer use the services of that site. In addition, if the function of the failed site can be taken over by another site, the system must ensure that the transfer of function occurs correctly. Finally, when the failed site recovers or is repaired, mechanisms must be available to integrate it back into the system smoothly. As we shall see in the following chapters, these actions present difficult issues with many possible solutions.

15.2.4 Communication

When several sites are connected to one another by a communication network, the users at different sites have the opportunity to exchange information. At a low level, *messages* are passed between systems in a manner similar to the single-computer message system discussed in Section 4.6. Given message passing, all the higher-level functionality found in standalone systems can be expanded to encompass the distributed system. Such functions include file transfer, login, mail, and remote procedure calls (RPCs).

The advantage of a distributed system is that these functions can be carried out over great distances. A project can be performed by two people at geographically separate sites. By transferring the files of the project, logging in to each other's remote systems to run programs, and exchanging mail to coordinate the work, the users are able to minimize the limitations inherent in long-distance work. In fact, this book was written in such a manner.

Taken together, the advantages of distributed systems have resulted in an industry-wide trend toward *downsizing*. Many companies are replacing their mainframes with networks of workstations or personal computers. The advantages to the companies include a better "bang for the buck" (better functionality for the cost), flexibility in locating resources and expanding facilities, better user interfaces, and easier maintenance.

Obviously, an operating system that was designed as a collection of processes that communicate through a message system (such as the Accent system) can be extended more easily to a distributed system than can a nonmessage passing system. For instance, MS-DOS is not easily integrated into a network because its kernel is interrupt based and lacks any support for message passing.

15.3 ■ Topology

The sites in the system can be connected physically in a variety of ways. Each configuration has advantages and disadvantages. We describe briefly the most common configurations implemented, and compare them with respect to the following criteria:

- **Basic cost:** How expensive is it to link the various sites in the system?

- **Communication cost:.** How long does it take to send a message from site A to site B?

- **Reliability:** If a link or a site in the system fails, can the remaining sites still communicate with one another?

The various topologies are depicted as graphs whose nodes correspond to sites. An edge from node A to node B corresponds to a direct connection between the two sites.

15.3.1 Fully Connected Networks

In a *fully connected network*, each site is directly linked with all other sites in the system (Figure 15.2). The basic cost of this configuration is high, since a direct communication line must be available between every two sites. The basic cost grows as the square of the number of sites. In this environment, however, messages between the sites can be sent fast; a message needs to use only one link to travel between any two sites. In addition, such systems are reliable, since many links must fail for the system to become partitioned. A system is *partitioned* if it has been split into two (or more) subsystems that lack any connection between them.

15.3.2 Partially Connected Networks

In a *partially connected network*, direct links exist between some, but not all, pairs of sites (Figure 15.3). Hence, the basic cost of this configuration is lower than that of the fully connected network. However, a message from one site to another may have to be sent through several intermediate sites, resulting in slower communication. For example, in the system depicted in

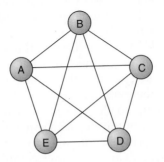

Figure 15.2   Fully connected network.

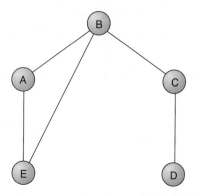

Figure 15.3 Partially connected network.

Figure 15.3, a message from site A to site D must be sent through sites B and C.

In addition, a partially connected system is not as reliable as is a fully connected network. The failure of one link may partition the network. For the example in Figure 15.3, if the link from *B* to *C* fails, then the network is partitioned into two subsystems. One subsystem includes sites A, B, and E; the second subsystem includes sites C and D. The sites in one partition cannot communicate with the sites in the other. So that this possibility is minimized, each site is usually linked to at least two other sites. For example, if we add a link from A to D, the failure of a single link cannot result in the partition of the network.

15.3.3 Hierarchical Networks

In a *hierarchical network,* the sites are organized as a tree (Figure 15.4). This organization is commonly used for corporate networks. Individual offices are linked to the local main office. Main offices are linked to regional offices; regional offices are linked to corporate headquarters.

Each site (except the root) has a unique parent, and some (possibly zero) number of children. The basic cost of this configuration is generally less than that of the partially connected scheme. In this environment, a parent and child communicate directly. Siblings may communicate with each other only through their common parent. A message from one sibling to another must be sent up to the parent, and then down to the sibling. Similarly, cousins can communicate with each other only through their common grandparent. This configuration matches well with the generalization that systems near each other communicate more than those that are distant. For instance, systems within a building are more likely to transfer data than those at separate installations.

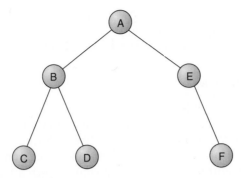

Figure 15.4 Tree-structured network.

If a parent site fails, then its children can no longer communicate with each other or with other processors. In general, the failure of any node (except a leaf) partitions the network into several disjoint subtrees.

15.3.4 Star Networks

In a *star network*, one of the sites in the system is connected to all other sites (Figure 15.5). None of the other sites are connected to any other. The basic cost of this system is linear in the number of sites. The communication cost is also low, because a message from process A to B requires at most two transfers (from A to the central site, and then from the central site B). This simple transfer scheme, however, may not ensure speed, since the central site may become a bottleneck. Consequently, though the number of message transfers needed is low, the time required

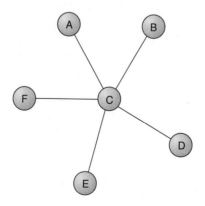

Figure 15.5 Star network.

to send these messages may be high. In many star systems, therefore, the central site is completely dedicated to the message-switching task.

If the central site fails, the network is completely partitioned.

15.3.5 Ring Networks

In a *ring network,* each site is physically connected to exactly two other sites (Figure 15.6a). The ring can be either unidirectional or bidirectional. In a unidirectional architecture, a site can transmit information to only one of its neighbors. All sites must send information in the same direction. In a bidirectional architecture, a site can transmit information to both of its neighbors. The basic cost of a ring is linear in the number of sites. However, the communication cost can be high. A message from one site to another travels around the ring until it reaches its destination. In a unidirectional ring, this process could require $n - 1$ transfers. In a bidirectional ring, at most $n/2$ transfers are needed.

In a bidirectional ring, two links must fail before the network will be partitioned. In a unidirectional ring, a single site failure (or link failure) would partition the network. One remedy is to extend the architecture by providing double links, as depicted in Figure 15.6b. The IBM token ring network is a ring network.

15.3.6 Multiaccess Bus Networks

In a *multiaccess bus network,* there is a single shared link (the bus). All the sites in the system are directly connected to that link, which may be

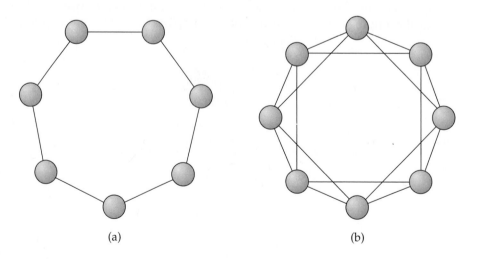

(a)   (b)

Figure 15.6   Ring networks. (a) Single links. (b) Double links.

organized as a straight line (Figure 15.7a) or as a ring (Figure 15.7b). The sites can communicate with each other directly through this link. The basic cost of the network is linear in the number of sites. The communication cost is quite low, unless the link becomes a bottleneck. Notice that this network topology is similar to that of the star network with a dedicated central site. The failure of one site does not affect communication among the rest of the sites. However, if the link fails, the network is partitioned completely. The ubiquitous Ethernet network, used by many institutions worldwide, is based on the multiaccess bus model.

15.3.7 Hybrid Networks

It is common for networks of differing types to be connected together. For example, within a site, a multiaccess bus such as Ethernet may be used, but between sites, a hierarchy may be used. Communications in such an environment can be tricky because the multiple protocols must be translated to one another and the routing of data is more complicated.

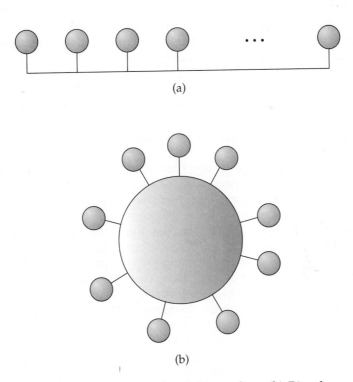

(a)

(b)

Figure 15.7 Bus network. (a) Linear bus. (b) Ring bus.

15.4 ■ Network Types

There are basically two types of networks: *local-area networks* and *wide-area networks*. The main difference between the two is the way in which they are geographically distributed. Local-area networks are composed of processors that are distributed over small geographical areas, such as a single building or a number of adjacent buildings. Wide-area networks, on the other hand, are composed of a number of autonomous processors that are distributed over a large geographical area (such as the United States). These differences imply major variations in the speed and reliability of the communications network, and are reflected in the distributed operating-system design.

15.4.1 Local-Area Networks

Local-area networks (LANs) emerged in the early 1970s, as a substitute for large mainframe computer systems. It had become apparent that, for many enterprises, it is more economical to have a number of small computers, each with its own self-contained applications, rather than a single large system. Because each small computer is likely to need a full complement of peripheral devices (such as disks and printers), and because some form of data sharing is likely to occur in a single enterprise, it was a natural step to connect these small systems into a network.

LANs are usually designed to cover a small geographical area (such as a single building, or a few adjacent buildings) and are generally used in an office environment. All the sites in such systems are close to one another, so the communication links tend to have a higher speed and lower error rate than do their counterparts in wide-area networks. So that this higher speed and reliability can be attained, high-quality (expensive) cables are needed. It is also possible to use the cable exclusively for data network traffic. Over longer distances, the cost of using high-quality cable is enormous, and the exclusive use of the cable tends to be prohibitive.

The most common links in a local-area network are twisted pair, baseband coaxial cable, broadband coaxial cable, and fiber optics. The most common configurations are multiaccess bus, ring, and star networks. Communication speeds range from 1 megabyte per second, for networks such as Appletalk and IBM's slow token ring, to 1 gigabit per second for experimental optical networks. Ten megabits per second is most common, and is the speed of Ethernet. Recently, the optical-fiber−based FDDI network has been increasing its market share. This network is token based and runs at 100 megabits per second.

A typical LAN may consist of a number of different minicomputers or workstations, various shared peripheral devices (such as laser printers or magnetic-tape units), and one or more gateways (specialized processors)

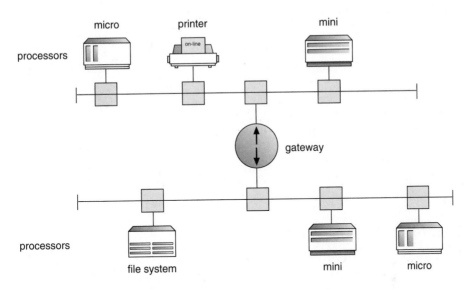

Figure 15.8   Local-area network.

that provide access to other networks (Figure 15.8). An Ethernet scheme is commonly used to construct LANs. There is no central controller in an Ethernet network, because it is a multiaccess bus, so new hosts can be added easily to the network.

15.4.2 Wide-Area Networks

Wide-area networks (WANs) emerged in the late 1960s, mainly as an academic research project to provide efficient communication between sites, allowing hardware and software to be shared conveniently and economically by a wide community of users. The first WAN to be designed and developed was the *Arpanet*. Work on the Arpanet began in 1968. The Arpanet has grown from a four-site experimental network to a worldwide network of networks, the Internet, comprising thousands of computer systems. Recently, several commercial networks have also appeared on the market. The Telenet system is available within the continental United States; the Datapac system is available in Canada. These networks provide their customers with the ability to access a wide range of hardware and software computing resources.

Because the sites in a WAN are physically distributed over a large geographical area, the communication links are by default relatively slow and unreliable. Typical links are telephone lines, microwave links, and satellite channels. These communication links are controlled by special

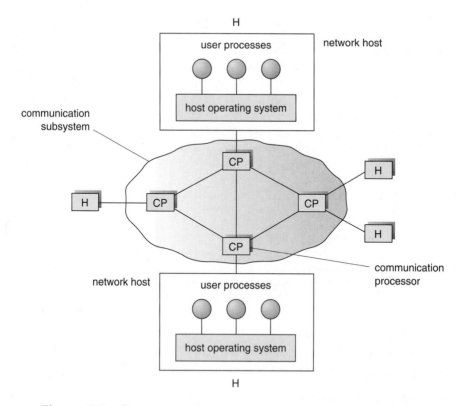

Figure 15.9 Communication processors in a wide-area network.

communication processors (Figure 15.9), which are responsible for defining the interface through which the sites communicate over the network, as well as for transferring information among the various sites.

As an example, let us consider the Internet WAN. The system provides an ability for hosts at geographically separated sites to communicate with one another. The host computers typically differ from one another in type, speed, word length, operating system, and so on. Hosts are generally on LANs, which are in turn connected to the Internet via regional networks. The regional networks, such as NSFnet in the Northeast United States, are interlinked with *routers* (described in Section 15.5.2) to form the worldwide network. Connections between networks frequently use a telephone-system service called T1, which provides a transfer rate of 1.544 megabits per second. The routers control the path each message takes through the net. This routing may be either dynamic, to increase communications efficiency, or static, to reduce security risks or to allow communications charges to be computed.

Other WANs in operation use standard telephone lines as their primary means of communication. *Modems* are the devices that accept digital data from the computer side and convert it to the analog signals that the telephone system uses. A modem at the destination site converts the analog signal back to digital and the destination receives the data. The UNIX news network, UUCP, allows systems to communicate with each other at predetermined times, via modems, to exchange messages. The messages are then routed to other nearby systems and in this way either are propagated to all hosts on the network (public messages) or are transferred to their destination (private messages). WANs are generally slower than LANs; their transmission rates range from 1200 bits per second to over 1 megabit per second.

15.5 ■ Communication

Now that we have discussed the physical aspects of networking, we turn to the internal workings. The designer of a *communication* network must address four basic issues:

- **Naming and name resolution:** How do two processes locate each other to communicate?

- **Routing strategies:** How are messages sent through the network?

- **Connection strategies:** How do two processes send a sequence of messages?

- **Contention:** The network is a shared resource, so how do we resolve conflicting demands for its use?

In Sections 15.5.1 through 15.5.4, we elaborate each of these issues.

15.5.1 Naming and Name Resolution

The first component of network communication is the naming of the systems in the network. For a process at site A to exchange information with a process at site B, they must be able to specify each other. Within a computer system, each process has a process-id, and messages may be addressed with the process-id. Because networked systems share no memory, they initially have no knowledge of the host of their target process, or even if the other process exists.

To solve this problem, processes on remote systems are generally identified by the pair <host name, identifier>, where "host name" is a name unique within the network, and "identifier" may be a process-id or other unique number within that host. A "host name" is usually an alphanumeric identifier, rather than a number, to make it easier for users to specify. For instance, site A might have hosts named "homer," "marge," "bart," and "lisa." "Bart" is certainly easier to remember than is "12814831100."

Names are convenient for humans to use, but computers prefer numbers for speed and simplicity. For this reason, there must be a mechanism to *resolve* the host name into a host-id which describes the destination system to the networking hardware. This resolve mechanism is similar to the name-to-address binding which occurs during program compilation, linking, loading, and execution (Chapter 8). In the case of host names, there are two possibilities. First, every host may have a data file containing the names and addresses of all the other hosts reachable on the network (similar to binding at compile time). The problem with this model is that adding or removing a host from the network requires updating the data files on all the hosts. The alternative is to distribute the information among systems on the network. The network must then use a protocol to distribute and retrieve the information. This scheme is like execution-time binding. The first method was the original method used on the Internet, but as the Internet grew it became untenable, and the second method, the *domain name service* (DNS) is now in use.

DNS specifies the naming structure of the hosts, as well as name to address resolution. Hosts on the Internet are logically addressed with a multipart host. Names progress from the most specific to the most general part of the address, with periods separating the fields. For instance, "bob.cs.brown.edu" refers to host "bob" in the Department of Computer Science at Brown University. Generally, the system resolves addresses by examining the host name components in reverse order. Each component has a *name server* (simply a process on a system) that accepts a name and returns the address of the name server responsible for that name. As the final step, the name server for the host in question is contacted and a host-id is returned. For our example system, "bob.cs.brown.edu," the following steps would be taken as result of a request made by a process on system A to communicate with "bob.cs.brown.edu":

1. The kernel of system A issues a request to the name server for the "edu" domain, asking for the address of the name server for "brown.edu." The name server for the "edu" domain must be at a known address, so that it can be queried. (Other top-level domains include "com" for commercial sites, "org" for organizations, and one for each country connected to the network (for systems specified by their country rather than organization type)).

2. The "edu" name server returns the address of the host on which the "brown.edu" name server resides.

3. The kernel on system A then queries the name server at this address and asks about "cs.brown.edu."

4. An address again is returned, and a request to that address for "bob.cs.brown.edu" finally returns an *Internet address* host-id for that host (for example, 128.148.31.100).

This protocol may seem inefficient, but local caches are usually kept at each name server to speed the process. For example, the "edu" name server would have "brown.edu" in its cache, and would inform system A that it can resolve two portions of the name, returning a pointer to the "cs.brown.edu" name server. Of course, the contents of these caches must be refreshed over time in case the name server is moved or its address changes. In fact, this service is such an important one that there are many optimizations in the protocol, and many safeguards. Consider what would happen if the primary "edu" name server crashed. It is possible that no "edu" hosts would be able to have their addresses resolved, making them all unreachable! The solution is the use of secondary, backup, name servers to duplicate the contents of the primary servers.

Before the domain name service was introduced, all hosts on the Internet needed copies of a file that contained the names and addresses of each host on the network. All changes to this file had to be registered at one site (host SRI-NIC), and periodically all hosts had to copy the updated file from SRI-NIC to be able to contact new systems or find hosts whose addresses changed. Under the domain name service, each name server site is responsible for updating the host information for that domain. For instance, any host changes at Brown University are the responsibility of the name server for "brown.edu," and do not have to be reported anywhere else. DNS lookups will automatically retrieve the updated information because "brown.edu" is contacted directly. Within domains, there can be autonomous subdomains to distribute further the responsibility for host name and host-id changes.

Generally, it is the responsibility of the operating system to accept from its processes a message destined for <host name, identifier>, and to transfer that message to the appropriate host. The kernel on the destination host is then responsible for transferring the message to the process named by the identifier. This exchange is by no means trivial, and is described later in Section 15.5.3.

15.5.2 Routing Strategies

When a process at site A wants to communicate with a process at site B, how is the message sent? If there is only one physical path from A to B (such as in a star or hierarchical network), the message must be sent through that path. However, if there are multiple physical paths from A to B, then several routing options exist. Each site has a *routing table*, indicating the alternative paths that can be used to send a message to other sites. The table may include information about the speed and cost of the various communication paths, and it may be updated as necessary, either manually or via programs that exchange routing information. The three most common routing schemes are *fixed routing*, *virtual routing*, and *dynamic routing*:

- **Fixed routing:** A path from A to B is specified in advance and does not change unless a hardware failure disables this path. Usually, the shortest path is chosen, so that communication costs are minimized.

- **Virtual circuit:** A path from A to B is fixed for the duration of one *session*. Different sessions involving messages from A to B may have different paths. A session could be as short as a file transfer or as long as a remote-login period.

- **Dynamic routing:** The path used to send a message from site A to site B is chosen only when a message is sent. Because the decision is made dynamically, separate messages may be assigned different paths. Site A will make a decision to send the message to site C; C, in turn, will decide to send it to site D, and so on. Eventually, a site will deliver the message to B. Usually a site sends a message to another site on that link that is the least used at that particular time.

There are tradeoffs among these three schemes. Fixed routing cannot adapt to link failures or load changes. In other words, if a path has been established between A and B, the messages must be sent along this path, even if the path is down or is used heavily while another possible path is used lightly. We can partially remedy this problem by using virtual circuits, and can avoid it completely by using dynamic routing. Fixed routing and virtual circuits ensure that messages from A to B will be delivered in the order in which they were sent. In dynamic routing, messages may arrive out of order. We can remedy this problem by appending a sequence number to each message.

Note that dynamic routing is the most complicated to set up and run. It is the best way to manage routing in complicated environments, however. UNIX provides both static routing for use on hosts within simple networks, and dynamic routing for complicated network environments. It is also possible to mix the two. Within a site, the hosts may just need to know how to reach the system that connects the local network to other networks (such as companywide networks or the Internet). Such a host is known as a *gateway*. These individual hosts would have a static route to the gateway. The gateway itself would use dynamic routing to be able to reach any host on the rest of the network.

A *router* is the entity within the computer system responsible for routing messages. A router can be a host computer with routing software, or a special-purpose device. Either way, a router must have at least two network connections, or else it would have nowhere to route messages. A router decides whether any given message needs to be passed from the network on which it is received to any other network connected to the router. It makes this determination by examining the destination Internet address of the message. The router examines its tables to determine the location of the destination host, or at least of the network to which to send the message toward the destination host. In the case of static routing, this table is changed only by manual update (a new file is loaded onto the router). With dynamic routing, a *routing protocol* is used between routers to inform them of network changes and to allow them to update their routing tables automatically.

15.5.3 Connection Strategies

Once messages are able to reach their destinations, processes may institute communications "sessions" to exchange information. There are a number of different ways to connect pairs of processes that want to communicate over the network. The three most common schemes are *circuit switching, message switching,* and *packet switching*:

- **Circuit switching:** If two processes want to communicate, a permanent physical link is established between them. This link is allocated for the duration of the communication, and no other process can use that link during this period (even if the two processes are not actively communicating for a while). This scheme is similar to that used in the telephone system. Once a communication line has been opened between two parties (that is, party A calls party B), no one else can use this circuit, until the communication is terminated explicitly (for example, when one of the parties hangs up).

- **Message switching:** If two processes want to communicate, a *temporary* link is established for the duration of one message transfer. Physical links are allocated dynamically among correspondents as needed, and are allocated for only short periods. Each message is a block of data, with system information (such as the source, the destination, and error-correction codes) that allows the communication network to deliver the message to the destination correctly. This scheme is similar to the post-office mailing system. Each letter is considered a message that contains both the destination address and source (return) address. Note that many messages (from different users) can be shipped over the same link.

- **Packet switching:** Messages are generally of variable length. To simplify the system design, we commonly implement communication with fixed-length messages called *packets*, *frames*, or *datagrams*. One logical message may have to be divided into a number of packets. Each packet may be sent to its destination separately, and therefore must include a source and destination address with its data. Each packet may take a different path through the network. The packets must be reassembled into messages as they arrive.

There are obvious tradeoffs among these schemes. Circuit switching requires set-up time, but incurs less overhead for shipping each message, and may waste network bandwidth. Message and packet switching, on the other hand, require less set-up time, but incur more overhead per message. Also, in packet switching, each message must be divided into packets and later reassembled. Packet switching is the most common method used on data networks because it makes the best use of network bandwidth and it is not harmful for data to be broken into packets, possibly routed separately, and reassembled at the destination. Doing the same with an audio signal (say, a telephone communication) could cause great confusion if not done carefully.

15.5.4 Contention

Depending on the network topology, a link may connect more than two sites in the computer network, so it is possible that several sites will want to transmit information over a link simultaneously. This difficulty occurs mainly in a ring or multiaccess bus network. In this case, the transmitted information may become scrambled and must be discarded. The sites must be notified about the problem, so that they can retransmit the information. If no special provisions are made, this situation may be repeated, resulting in degraded performance. Several techniques have been developed to avoid repeated collisions, including *collision detection*, *token passing*, and *message slots*.

- **CSMA/CD:** Before transmitting a message over a link, a site must listen to determine whether another message is currently being transmitted over that link; this technique is called *carrier sense with multiple access* (*CSMA*). If the link is free, the site can start transmitting. Otherwise, it must wait (and continue to listen) until the link is free. If two or more sites begin transmitting at exactly the same time (each thinking that no other site is using the link), then they will register a *collision detection* (*CD*) and will stop transmitting. Each site will try again after some random time interval. Note that, when site A starts transmitting over a link, it must listen continuously to detect collisions with messages from other sites. The main problem with this approach is that, when the system is very busy, many collisions may occur, and thus performance may be degraded. Nevertheless, CSMA/CD has been used successfully in the Ethernet system, the most common network system. (The Ethernet protocol is defined by the IEEE 802.3 standard.) To limit the number of collisions, the number of hosts per Ethernet network must be limited. Adding more hosts to a congested network could result in poor network throughput. As systems get faster, they are able to send more packets per time segment. As a result, the number of systems per Ethernet segment generally is decreasing, to keep networking performance reasonable.

- **Token passing:** A unique message type, known as a *token*, continuously circulates in the system (usually a ring structure). A site that wants to transmit information must wait until the token arrives. It removes the token from the ring and begins to transmit its messages. When the site completes its round of message passing, it retransmits the token. This action, in turn, allows another site to receive and remove the token, and to start its message transmission. If the token gets lost, then the systems must detect the loss and generate a new token. They usually do that by declaring an *election*, to elect a unique site where a new token will be generated. Later, in Section 18.6, we present one election algorithm. A token-passing scheme has been adopted by the IBM and HP/Apollo systems. The benefit of a token-passing network is that performance is constant. Adding new systems to a network may lengthen the time a system waits for the token, but it will not cause a large performance decrease as may happen on Ethernet. On lightly loaded networks, however, Ethernet is more efficient, because systems may send messages at any time.

- **Message slots:** A number of fixed-length message slots continuously circulate in the system (usually a ring structure). Each slot can hold a fixed-sized message and control information (such as what the source and destination are, and whether the slot is empty or full). A site that is ready to transmit must wait until an empty slot arrives. It then inserts its message into the slot, setting the appropriate control information. The slot with its message then continues in the network. When it arrives at a site, that site inspects the control information to determine whether the slot contains a message for this site. If not, that site recirculates the slot and message. Otherwise, it removes the message, resetting the control information to indicate that the slot is empty. The site can then either use the slot to send its own message or release the slot. Because a slot can contain only fixed-sized messages, a single logical message may have to be broken down into several smaller packets, each of which is sent in a separate slot. This scheme has been adopted in the experimental Cambridge Digital Communication Ring.

15.6 ■ Design Strategies

When designing a communication network, we must deal with the inherent complexity of coordinating asynchronous operations communicating in a potentially slow and error-prone environment. It is also essential that the systems on the network agree on a protocol or a set of protocols for determining host names, locating hosts on the network, establishing connections, and so on. We can simplify the design problem (and related implementation) by partitioning the problem into multiple layers. Each layer on one system communicates with the equivalent layer on other systems. Each layer may have its own protocols, or may be a logical segmentation. The protocols may be implemented in hardware or software. For instance, Figure 15.10 shows the logical communications between two computers, with the three lowest-level layers implemented in hardware. Following the International Standards Organization (ISO), we refer to the layers with the following descriptions:

1. **Physical layer:** The physical layer is responsible for handling both the mechanical and electrical details of the physical transmission of a bit stream. At the physical layer, the communicating systems must agree on the electrical representation of a binary 0 and 1, so that when data are sent as a stream of electrical signals, the receiver is able to interpret the data properly as binary data. This layer is implemented in the hardware of the networking device.

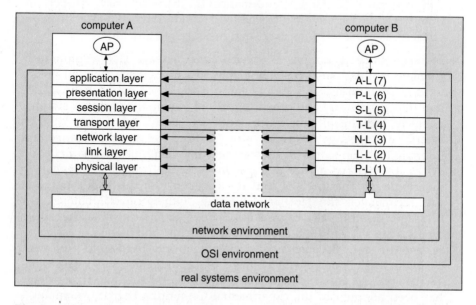

Figure 15.10 Two computers communicating via the ISO network model.

2. **Data-link layer:** The data-link layer is responsible for handling the *frames,* or fixed-length parts of packets, including any error detection and recovery that occurred in the physical layer.

3. **Network layer:** The network layer is responsible for providing connections and for routing packets in the communication network, including handling the address of outgoing packets, decoding the address of incoming packets, and maintaining routing information for proper response to changing load levels. Routers work at this layer.

4. **Transport layer:** The transport layer is responsible for low-level access to the network and for transfer of messages between the clients, including partitioning messages into packets, maintaining packet order, controlling flow, and generating physical addresses.

5. **Session layer:** The session layer is responsible for implementing sessions, or process-to-process communications protocols. Typically, these protocols are the actual communications for remote logins, and for file and mail transfers.

6. **Presentation layer:** The presentation layer is responsible for resolving the differences in formats among the various sites in the network, including character conversions, and half duplex–full duplex modes (character echoing).

7. **Application layer:** The application layer is responsible for interacting directly with the users. This layer deals with file transfer, remote-login protocols, and electronic mail, as well as with schemas for distributed databases.

Figure 15.11 summarizes the ISO *protocol stack* (a set of cooperating protocols), showing the physical flow of data. As mentioned, logically each layer of a protocol stack communicates with the equivalent layer on other systems. But physically, a message starts at or above the application layer, and is passed through each lower level in turn. Each of these layers may modify the message and include message header data for the equivalent layer on the receiving side. Finally, the message makes it to the data-network layer and is transferred as one or more packets (Figure 15.12). These data are received by the data link layer of the target system, and the message is moved up through the protocol stack, being analyzed, modified, and stripped of headers as it progresses. It finally reaches the application layer for use by the receiving process.

The ISO model formalizes some of the earlier work done in network protocols, but was developed in late 1970s and is not yet in widespread use. Part of the basis for ISO is the more timeworn and widely used protocol stack developed under UNIX for use in the Arpanet (which became the Internet.)

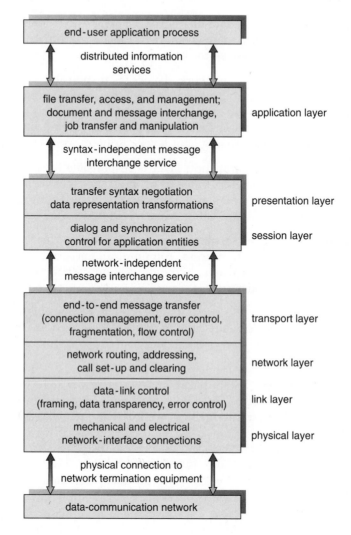

Figure 15.11 The ISO protocol layer summary.

Most Internet sites still communicate via the *Transmission Control Protocol/Internet Protocol,* commonly known as TCP/IP. The TCP/IP protocol stack has fewer layers than does the ISO model. Theoretically, because it combines several functions in each layer, it is more difficult to implement but more efficient than ISO networking. The TCP/IP stack (with its ISO correspondence) is shown in Figure 15.13. The IP protocol is responsible for transmitting IP *datagrams,* the basic unit of information, across a TCP/IP internet. TCP uses IP to transport a reliable stream of information between two processes. The other common internet transmission protocol is UDP/IP.

The *User Datagram Protocol (UDP)* is an unreliable, connectionless transport protocol. It uses IP to transfer the packets, but adds error correction and a protocol *port* address to specify the process on the remote system for which the packet is destined.

15.7 ■ Networking Example

We shall now return to the name-resolution issue raised in Section 15.5.1, and shall examine its operation with respect to the TCP/IP protocol stack on the Internet. We consider the processing needed to transfer a packet between hosts on different Ethernet networks.

In a TCP/IP network, every host has a name and an associated 32-bit Internet number (host-id). Both of these must be unique, and, so that the name space can be managed, they are segmented. The name is hierarchical (as explained in Section 15.5.1), describing the host name and then the organizations with which the host is associated. The host-id is split into a network number and a host number. The proportion of the split varies, depending on the size of the network. Once a network number is assigned by the Internet administrators, the site with that number is free to assign host-ids.

The sending system checks its routing tables to locate a router to send the packet on its way. The routers use the network part of the host-id to transfer the packet from its source network to the destination network.

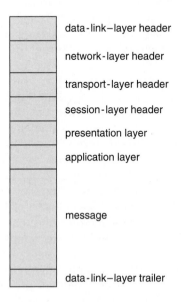

data-link–layer header

network-layer header

transport-layer header

session-layer header

presentation layer

application layer

message

data-link–layer trailer

Figure 15.12 An ISO network message.

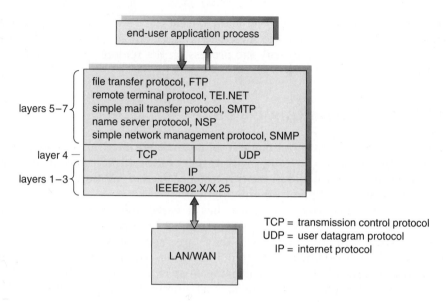

Figure 15.13   The TCP/IP protocol layer summary.

The destination system then receives the packet. The packet may be a complete message, or it may just be a component of a message, with more packets needed before the message is reassembled and passed to the TCP/UDP layer for transmission to the destination process.

Now we know how a packet moves from its source network to its destination. Within a network, how does a packet move from sender (host or router) to receiver? Every Ethernet device has a unique byte number assigned to it for addressing. Two devices communicate with each other only with this number. Periodically, the kernel generates a UDP packet containing the host-id and Ethernet number of the system. This packet is *broadcast* to all other systems on that Ethernet network. A broadcast uses a special network address (usually, the maximum address) to signal that all hosts should receive and process the packet. The broadcast is not resent by gateways, so only systems on the local network receive them. On receipt of this message, every host retrieves this id pair from the UDP packet and caches the pair in an internal table. This sequence is the *Address Resolution Protocol (ARP)*. The cache entries are *aged*, so that they eventually get removed from the cache if a renewing broadcast is not received. In this way hosts that are removed from a network are eventually "forgotten."

Once an Ethernet device has announced its host-id and address, communication can begin. A process may specify the name of a host with which to communicate. The kernel takes that name and determines the

Internet number of the target, using a DNS lookup. The message is passed from the application layer, through the software layers, and to the hardware layer. At the hardware layer, the packet (or packets) has the Ethernet address at its start, and a trailer at the end to indicate the end of the packet and containing a *checksum* for detection of packet damage (Figure 15.14). The packet is placed on the network by the Ethernet device. Note that the data section of the packet may contain some or all of the data of the original message, but may also contain some of the upper-level headers that compose the message. In other words, all parts of the original message must be sent from source to destination, and all headers above the 802.3 layer (data-link layer) are included as data in the Ethernet packets.

If the destination is on the same local network as the source, the system can look in its ARP cache, can find the Ethernet address of the host, and can place the packet on the wire. The destination Ethernet device then sees its address in the packet and reads in the packet, passing it up the protocol stack.

If the destination system is on a network different from that of the source, the source system finds an appropriate router on its network and sends the packet there. Routers then pass the packet along the WAN until it reaches its destination network. The router that connects the destination network checks its ARP cache, finds the Ethernet number of the destination, and sends the packet to that host. Through all of these

Figure 15.14   An Ethernet packet.

transfers, the data-link−layer header may change as the Ethernet address of the next router in the chain is used, but the other headers of the packet remain the same until the packet is received and they are processed by the protocol stack, finally being passed to the receiving process by the kernel.

15.8 ■ Summary

A distributed system is a collection of processors that do not share memory or a clock. Instead, each processor has its own local memory, and the processors communicate with one another through various communication lines, such as high-speed buses or telephone lines. The processors in a distributed system vary in size and function. They may include small microprocessors, workstations, minicomputers, and large general-purpose computer systems.

The processors in the system are connected through a communication network, which can be configured in a number of different ways. The network may be fully or partially connected. It may be a tree, a star, a ring, or a multiaccess bus. The communication-network design must include routing and connection strategies, and must solve the problems of contention and security.

Principally, there are two types of distributed systems: LANs and WANs. The main difference between the two is in the way they are distributed geographically. LANs are composed of processors that are distributed over small geographical areas, such as a single building or a few adjacent buildings. WANs are composed of autonomous processors that are distributed over a large geographical area (such as the United States).

Protocol stacks, as specified by network layering models, massage the message, adding information to it to ensure that it reaches its destination. A naming system such as DNS must be used to translate from a host name to network address, and another protocol (such as ARP) may be needed to translate the network number to a network device address (an Ethernet address, for instance). If systems are on separate networks, routers are needed to pass packets from source network to destination network.

■ Exercises

15.1 Contrast the various network topologies in terms of reliability.

15.2 Why do most WANs employ only a partially connected topology?

15.3 What are the main differences between a WAN and a LAN?

15.4 What network configuration would best suit the following environments?

a. A dormitory floor

b. A university campus

c. A state

d. A nation

15.5 Even though the ISO model of networking specifies seven layers of functionality, most computer systems use fewer layers to implement a network. Why do they use fewer layers? What problems could the use of fewer layers cause?

15.6 Explain why a doubling of the speed of the systems on an Ethernet segment may result in decreased network performance. What changes could be made to ameliorate the problem?

15.7 Under what circumstances is a token-ring network more effective than an Ethernet network?

15.8 Why would it be a bad idea for gateways to pass broadcast packets between networks? What would be the advantages of doing so?

15.9 In what ways is using a name server better than using static host tables? What are the problems and complications associated with name servers? What methods could be used to decrease the amount of traffic name servers generate to satisfy translation requests?

15.10 Of what use is an address resolution protocol? Why is the use of such a protocol better than making each host read each packet to determine to whom it is destined? Does a token-ring network need such a protocol?

Bibliographic Notes

Tanenbaum [1988] and Halsall [1992] provided general overviews of computer networks. Fortier [1989] presented a detailed discussion of networking hardware and software.

The Internet and several other networks were discussed in Quarterman and Hoskins [1986]. The Internet and its protocols was described in Comer [1991] and Comer and Stevens [1991, 1993]. UNIX network programming was described thoroughly in Stevens [1990]. The general state of networks has been given in Quarterman [1990].

Feng [1981] surveyed the various network topologies. Boorstyn and Frank [1977] and Gerla and Kleinrock [1977] discussed topology design problems. Day and Zimmerman [1983] discussed the OSI model.

A special issue of *Computer Networks* [December 1979] included nine papers on LANs covering such subjects as hardware, software, simulation, and examples. A taxonomy and extensive list of LANs were presented by Thurber and Freeman [1980]. Stallings [1984] discussed various types of ring-structured LANs.

Reliable communication in the presence of failures was discussed by Birman and Joseph [1987]. Integrating security in a large distributed system was discussed by Satyanarayanan [1989].

CHAPTER 16

DISTRIBUTED-SYSTEM STRUCTURES

In this chapter, we discuss the general structure of distributed systems. We contrast the main differences in operating-system design between these types of systems and the centralized systems with which we were concerned previously.

16.1 ■ Network-Operating Systems

A *network operating system* provides an environment where users, who are aware of the multiplicity of machines, can access remote resources by either logging into the appropriate remote machine, or transferring data from the remote machine to their own machines.

16.1.1 Remote Login

An important function of a network operating system is to allow users to log in remotely on another computer. The Internet provides the *telnet* facility for this purpose. To illustrate this facility, let us suppose that a user at Brown University wishes to compute on "cs.utexas.edu," a computer that is located at the University of Texas. To do so, the user must have a valid account on that machine. To log in remotely, the user issues the command

telnet cs.utexas.edu

This command results in a connection being formed between the local machine at Brown University and the "cs.utexas.edu" computer. After this connection has been established, the networking software creates a transparent, bidirectional link such that all characters entered by the user are sent to a process on "cs.utexas.edu," and all the output from that process is sent back to the user. The process on the remote machine asks the user for a login name and a password. Once the correct information has been received, the process acts as a proxy for the user, who can compute on the remote machine just as any local user can.

16.1.2 Remote File Transfer

Another major function of a network operating system is to provide a mechanism for file transfer from one machine to another. In such an environment, each computer maintains its own local file system. If a user at one site (say, "cs.brown.edu") wants to access a file located on another computer (say, "cs.utexas.edu"), then the file must be copied explicitly from the computer at Texas to the computer at Brown.

The Internet provides a mechanism for such a transfer with the File Transfer Protocol (FTP) program. Suppose that a user on cs.brown.edu wants to copy a file *paper.tex* that resides on cs.utexas.edu into a local file *my-paper.tex*. The user must first invoke the FTP program, by executing

ftp cs.utexas.edu

The program then asks the user for the login name and a password. Once the correct information has been received, the user must connect to the subdirectory where the file *paper.tex* resides, and then copy the file by executing

get *paper.tex my-paper.tex*

In this scheme, the file location is not transparent to the user; users must know exactly where each file is. Moreover, there is no real file sharing, because a user can only copy a file from one site to another. Thus, several copies of the same file may exist, resulting in a waste of space. In addition, if these copies are modified, the various copies will be inconsistent.

Notice that, in our example, the user at Brown university must have login permission on "cs.utexas.edu." FTP also provides a way to allow a user who does not have an account on the Texas computer to copy files remotely. This remote copying is accomplished through the "anonymous ftp" method, which works as follows. The file to be copied (that is, *paper.tex*) must be placed in a special subdirectory (say *ftp*) with the protection set to allow the public to read the file. A user who wishes to copy the file uses the **ftp** command as before. When the user is asked for the login name, the user supplies the name "anonymous," and an arbitrary password.

Once anonymous login is accomplished, care must be taken by the system to ensure that this partially authorized user does not access inappropriate files. Generally, the user is allowed to access only those files that are in the directory tree of user "anonymous." Any files placed here are accessible to any anonymous users, subject to the usual file-protection scheme used on that machine. Anonymous users, however, cannot access files outside of this directory tree.

The FTP mechanism is implemented in a manner similar to telnet. There is a daemon on the remote site that watches for connection requests to the system's FTP port. Login authentication is accomplished, and the user is allowed to execute commands remotely. Unlike the telnet daemon, which executes any command for the user, the FTP daemon responds only to a predefined set of file-related commands. These include:

- **get:** Transfer a file from the remote machine to the local machine

- **put:** Transfer from the local machine to the remote machine

- **ls** or **dir:** List files in the current directory on the remote machine

- **cd:** Change the current directory on the remote machine

There are also various commands to change transfer modes (for binary or ASCII files) and to determine connection status.

An important point about telnet and FTP is that they require the user to change paradigms. FTP requires the user to know a command set entirely different from the normal operating-system commands. Telnet requires a smaller shift, in which the user must know appropriate commands on the remote system. For instance, a user on a UNIX machine who telnets to a VMS machine must switch to VMS commands for the duration of the telnet session. Facilities are more convenient for users if they do not require the use of a different set of commands. Distributed operating systems are designed to ameliorate this problem.

16.2 ■ Distributed-Operating Systems

In a distributed operating system, the users access remote resources in the same manner as they do local resources. Data and process migration from one site to another is under the control of the distributed operating system.

16.2.1 Data Migration

Suppose that a user on site A wants to access data (such as a file) that reside at site B. There are two basic methods for the system to transfer the data. One approach is to transfer the entire file to site A. From that point on, all access to the file is local. When the user no longer needs access to the file, a copy of the file (if it has been modified) is sent back to site B. Even if only a modest change has been made to a large file, all the data must be transferred. This mechanism can be thought of as an automated FTP system. This approach was used in the Andrew file system, as will be discussed in Chapter 17, but it was found to be too inefficient.

The other approach is to transfer to site A only those portions of the file that are actually *necessary* for the immediate task. If another portion is required later, another transfer will take place. When the user no longer wants to access the file, any part of it that has been modified must be sent back to site B. (Note the similarity to demand paging.) The Sun Microsystems' Network File System (NFS) protocol uses this method (see Chapter 17), as do newer versions of Andrew.

Clearly, if only a small part of a large file is being accessed, the latter approach is preferable. If significant portions of the file are being accessed, it is more efficient to copy the entire file.

Note that it is not sufficient merely to transfer data from one site to another. The system must also perform various data translations if the two sites involved are not directly compatible (for instance, if they use different character-code representations or represent integers with a different number or order of bits).

16.2.2 Computation Migration

In some circumstances, it may be more efficient to transfer the computation, rather than the data, across the system. For example, consider a job that needs to access various large files that reside at different sites, to obtain a summary of those files. It would be more efficient to access the files at the sites where they reside and then to return the desired results to the site that initiated the computation. Generally, if the time to transfer the data is longer than the time to execute the remote command, the remote command should be used.

Such a computation can be carried out in a number of different ways. Suppose that process P wants to access a file at site A. Access to the file is carried out at site A, and could be initiated by a *remote procedure call*, or RPC. An RPC uses a datagram protocol (UDP on the internet) to execute a routine on a remote system (Section 16.3.1). Process P invokes a predefined procedure at site A. The procedure executes appropriately, and then returns the results to P.

Alternatively, process P can send a *message* to site A. The operating system at site A would then create a new process Q whose function is to carry out the designated task. When process Q completes its execution, it sends the needed result back to P via the message system. Note that, in this scheme, process P may execute concurrently with process Q and in fact may have several processes running concurrently on several sites.

Both methods could be used to access several files residing at various sites. One remote procedure call might result in the invocation of another remote procedure call, or even in the transfer of messages to another site. Similarly, process Q could, during the course of its execution, send a message to another site, which in turn would create another process. This process might either send a message back to Q or repeat the cycle.

16.2.3 Process Migration

A logical extension to computation migration is process migration. When a process is submitted for execution, it is not always executed at the site in which it is initiated. It may be advantageous to execute the entire process, or parts of it, at different sites. This scheme may be used for several reasons:

- **Load balancing:** The processes (or subprocesses) may be distributed across the network to even the workload.

- **Computation speedup:** If a single process can be divided into a number of subprocesses that may run concurrently on different sites, then the total process turnaround time can be reduced.

- **Hardware preference:** The process may have characteristics that make it more suitable for execution on some specialized processor (such as matrix inversion on an array processor, rather than on a microprocessor).

- **Software preference:** The process may require software that is available at only a particular site, and either the software cannot be moved, or it is less expensive to move the process.

- **Data access:** Just as in computation migration, if the data being used in the computation are numerous, it may be more efficient to have a process run remotely, rather than to transfer all the data locally.

There are basically two complementary techniques that can be used to move processes in a computer network. In the first, the system can attempt to hide the fact that the process has migrated from the client. This scheme has the advantage that the user does not need to code his program explicitly to accomplish the migration. This method is usually employed for achieving load balancing and computation speedup among homogeneous systems, as they do not need user input to help them execute programs remotely.

The other approach is to allow (or require) the user to specify explicitly how the process should migrate. This method is usually employed in a situation when the process must be moved to satisfy a hardware or software preference.

16.3 ■ Remote Services

Consider a user who needs access to data located at some other site. For example, a user may wish to find out the total number of lines, words and characters in a file located at another site A. The request for doing so is handled by a remote server at site A, who accesses the file, computes the desired result, and eventually transfers the actual data back to the user.

One way to achieve this transfer is through the *remote-service* method. Requests for accesses are delivered to the server. The server machine performs the accesses, and their results are forwarded back to the user. There is a direct correspondence between accesses and traffic to and from the server. Access requests are translated to messages for the servers, and server replies are packed as messages sent back to the users. Every access is handled by the server and results in network traffic. For example, a read results in a request message being sent to the server, and a reply to the user with the requested data.

16.3.1 Remote Procedure Calls

One of the most common forms of remote service is the *remote procedure call* (*RPC*) paradigm, which we discussed briefly in Section 4.6.3. The RPC was designed as a way to abstract the procedure-call mechanism for use between systems with network connections. It is similar in many respects to the IPC mechanism described in Section 4.6, and is usually built on top of such a system. Because we are dealing with an environment where the processes are executing on separate systems, we must use a *message-based* communication scheme to provide remote service. In contrast to the IPC facility, the messages exchanged for RPC communication are well structured, and are thus no longer just packets of data. They are addressed to an RPC daemon listening to a *port* on the remote system, and contain an identifier of the function to execute and the parameters to pass to that function. The function is then executed as requested, and any output is sent back to the requester in a separate message.

A *port* is simply a number included at the start of a message packet. Whereas a system normally has one network address, it can have many ports within that address to differentiate the many network services it supports. If a remote process needs a service, it addresses its messages to the proper port. For instance, if a system wished to allow other systems to be able to list the current users on it, it would have a daemon supporting such an RPC attached to a port, say port 3027. Any remote system could obtain the needed information (that is, the list of current users) by sending an RPC message to port 3027 on the server; the data would be received in a reply message.

The RPC mechanism is common on networked systems, so there are several issues that we should discuss in regard to its operation. One important issue is that of the semantics of a call. Whereas local procedure calls fail only under extreme circumstances, RPCs can fail, or be duplicated and executed more than once, due to common network errors. Because we are dealing with message transfer over unreliable communication links, it is much easier for an operating system to ensure that a message was acted on at most once, than it is to ensure that the message was acted on exactly once. Because local procedure calls have the latter meaning, most systems attempt to duplicate that functionality. They do so by attaching to each message a timestamp. The server must keep a history of all the timestamps of messages it has already processed, or a history large enough to ensure that repeated messages are detected. Incoming messages that have a timestamp already in the history are ignored. Generation of these timestamps is discussed in Section 18.1.

Another important issue concerns the communication between server and client. With standard procedure calls, some form of binding takes place during link, load, or execution time (see Chapter 8), such that a procedure call's name is replaced by the memory address of the procedure call. The RPC scheme requires a similar binding of the client and the server port, but how does a client know the port numbers on the server? Neither system has full information about the other because they do not share memory. Two approaches are common. First, the binding information may be predecided, in the form of fixed port addresses. At compile time, an RPC call has a fixed port number associated with it. Once a program is compiled, the server cannot change the port number of the requested service. Second, binding can be done dynamically by a rendezvous mechanism. Typically, an operating system provides a rendezvous (also called a matchmaker) daemon on a fixed RPC port. A client then sends a message, containing the name of the RPC, to the rendezvous daemon requesting the port address of the RPC it needs to execute. The port number is returned, and the RPC calls may be sent to that port until the process terminates (or the server crashes). This method requires the extra overhead of the initial request, but is more flexible than the first approach. A sample interaction is shown in Figure 16.1.

The remote procedure calls scheme is useful in implementing a distributed file system (see Chapter 17). Such a system can be implemented as a set of RPC daemons and clients. The messages are addressed to the DFS port on a server on which a file operation is to take place. The message contains the disk operation to be performed. Disk operations might be **read, write, rename, delete,** or **status,** corresponding to the usual file-related system calls. The return message contains any data resulting from that call, which is executed by the DFS daemon on behalf of the client. For instance, a message might contain a request to transfer a whole file to a client, or be limited to simple block requests. In the latter case, several such requests might be needed if a whole file is to be transferred.

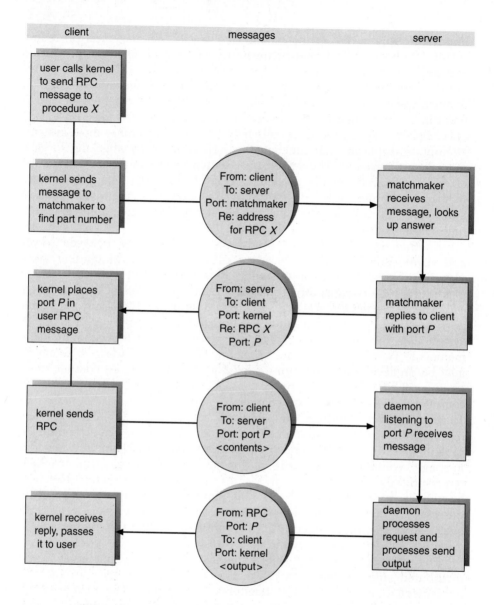

Figure 16.1 Execution of a remote procedure call (RPC).

16.3.2 Threads

Distributed systems often utilize both threads and RPCs. Threads may be used to send and receive messages while other operations within the task continue asynchronously. For instance, a daemon might have many threads waiting to receive request messages, with a single message being picked up by a thread and processed concurrently with other threads doing the same. Researchers are studying how the use of threads can make RPCs more lightweight. One improvement over conventional RPC takes advantage of the fact that a server thread that blocks waiting for a new request has little significant context information. In a scheme sometimes referred to as *implicit receive,* a thread that has completed a job disappears. The kernel then simply creates a new thread to handle incoming requests. It also writes the message onto the server's address space and sets up the stack so that the new thread can access the message. A thread created on an as "needed" basis to respond to a new RPC can be called a *pop-up thread.* This technique improves performance because it is cheaper to start a new thread than to restore an existing one. Because no threads block waiting for new work, no context has to be saved, or restored. Additional time is saved because incoming RPCs do not have to be copied to a buffer within a server thread.

It has been shown that a significant number of RPCs in distributed systems are to processes on the same machine as the caller. RPC can be made more lightweight if highly efficient communication is enabled via shared memory between threads in different processes that are running on the same machine. On starting up, a server thread, *ST,* exports its interface to the kernel. Defined in the interface are those procedures that are callable, their parameters, and other related features. A client thread, *CT,* that imports this interface will receive a unique identifier that it will use later to make the call. To make a call to *ST, CT* pushes the arguments onto an *argument stack,* which is a data structure shared by both *ST* and *CT.* As part of the call, *ST* also puts the unique identifier in a register. Once the kernel observes this placement, it knows that the call is not remote, but rather is local. The kernel then puts the client in the server's address space and initiates *CT's* execution of *ST's* procedure. Because the arguments are already in place and do not have to be copied, local RPCs handled in this manner show an improved performance time over conventional RPCs.

Let us illustrate the use of threads in a distributed environment by examining a specific threads package available through the Open Software Foundation's Distributed Computing Environment (DCE). DCE is important because almost all major UNIX vendors have agreed to add it to their UNIX implementations as a way of standardizing the network functionality and protocols and allow better interoperability between systems. It will also be used by Microsoft's Windows/NT. The DCE package provides, for user convenience, a large number of calls. In this chapter, we consider the most significant; we group them into the following five categories:

1. Thread-management calls: **create, exit, join, detach**

2. Synchronization calls: **mutex_init, mutex_destroy, mutex_lock, mutex_trylock, mutex_unlock**

3. Condition-variable   calls: **cond_init,**   **cond_destroy,**   **cond_wait,**
   cond_signal, cond_broadcast

4. Scheduling calls: **setscheduler, getscheduler, setprio, getprio**

5. Kill-thread calls: **cancel, setcancel**

We now briefly discuss each of these.

The four thread-management calls create new threads and allow them to exit on completing a request. The call **join,** which is similar to the UNIX system call **wait,** permits a parent to wait for its child. If a parent thread need not wait for the child, it may decline to do so with **detach.**

Access to shared data can be synchronized through the use of *mutex,* which is a variant of a binary semaphore (see Chapter 6). Mutexes in DCE can be created (initiated) or destroyed dynamically. A mutex is either in a locked or unlocked state. Three operations are defined on mutexes, **mutex_lock, mutex_trylock,** and **mutex_unlock.** A lock attempt succeeds on only an unlocked mutex; once locked, the mutex is confined to a single atomic action. Conversely, a mutex is unlocked by **mutex_unlock;** if several threads are waiting on the mutex, only a single thread is released. The **mutex_trylock** call attempts to lock a mutex. If that mutex is already locked, then this call returns a status code indicating that it did not lock, and the thread issuing the call is not blocked. If that mutex is unlocked, then the call returns a success status code.

DCE also provides the condition variable feature found in most thread packages. This feature functions in much the same way as do the condition variables in monitors (Chapter 6). A condition variable works in conjunction with a mutex but has a significantly different use. To illustrate, let us suppose that a thread A has locked a mutex m1 to gain entry to a critical region. Once there, the thread discovers that it cannot continue executing until another thread B has executed and has modified data in that critical region. Thread A would normally lock a second mutex m2 for that purpose. This second locking, however, would result in a deadlock, because thread B cannot enter the critical region to change the data for which A is waiting.

Rather than locking mutex m2, thread A could lock a condition variable. This condition-variable locking would automatically unlock mutex m1 if the setting of the lock by thread A results in a wait. When thread B changes the desired data, it issues a wakeup call that activates the waiting thread A.

Like mutexes, condition variables can also be created and deleted dynamically. The capacity to wait on a condition variable is provided by **cond_wait.** DCE provides two types of wakeup operations: **cond_signal** resumes the execution of only a single waiting thread, whereas **cond_broadcast** resumes the execution of all threads that are waiting on the condition variable.

Another category of calls we consider comprises scheduling calls. The set of scheduling calls in the DCE package allow the scheduling algorithms and priorities to be set and read. A number of preemptive and nonpreemptive scheduling algorithms are available, including round robin and FIFO.

The threads package provides calls for killing threads. The system call **cancel** enacts an attempt to kill another thread. That thread can use the **setcancel** call either to allow or to disallow the kill attempt.

16.4 ■ Robustness

A distributed system may suffer from various types of hardware failure. The failure of a link, the failure of a site, and the loss of a message are the most common failures. To ensure that the system is robust, we must *detect* any of these failures, *reconfigure* the system so that computation may continue, and *recover* when a site or a link is repaired.

16.4.1 Failure Detection

In an environment with no shared memory, it is generally not possible to differentiate among link failure, site failure, and message loss. We can usually detect that one of these failures has occurred, but we may not be able to identify what kind of failure it is. Once a failure has been detected, appropriate action must be taken, depending on the particular application.

To detect link and site failure, we use a *handshaking* procedure. Suppose that sites A and B have a direct physical link between them. At fixed intervals, both sites send each other an *I-am-up* message. If site A does not receive this message within a predetermined time period, it can assume that site B has failed, that the link between A and B has failed, or that the message from B has been lost. At this point, site A has two choices. It can wait for another time period to receive an *I-am-up* message from B, or it can send an *Are-you-up?* message to B.

If site A does not receive an *I-am-up* message or a reply to its inquiry, the procedure can be repeated. The only conclusion that site A can draw safely is that some type of failure has occurred.

Site A can try to differentiate between link failure and site failure by sending an *Are-you-up?* message to B by another route (if one exists). If and when B receives this message, it immediately replies positively. This positive reply tells A that B is up, and that the failure is in the direct link between them. Since it is not known in advance how long it will take the message to travel from A to B and back, a *time-out* scheme must be used. At the time A sends the *Are-you-up?* message, it specifies a time interval during which it is willing to wait for the reply from B. If A receives the reply message within that time interval, then it can safely conclude that B is up. If, however, it does not receive the reply message within the time interval (that is, a time-out occurs), then A may conclude only that one or more of the following situations has occurred:

1. Site B is down.

2. The direct link (if one exists) from A to B is down.

3. The alternative path from A to B is down.

4. The message has been lost.

Site A cannot, however, decide which of these events has indeed occurred.

16.4.2 Reconfiguration

Suppose that site A has discovered, through the mechanism described in the previous section, that a failure has occurred. It must then initiate a procedure that will allow the system to reconfigure and to continue its normal mode of operation.

- If a direct link from A to B has failed, this information must be broadcast to every site in the system, so that the various routing tables can be updated accordingly.

- If the system believes that a site has failed (because that site can be reached no longer), then every site in the system must be so notified, so that they will no longer attempt to use the services of the failed site. The failure of a site that serves as a central coordinator for some activity (such as deadlock detection) requires the election of a new coordinator. Similarly, if the failed site is part of a logical ring, then a new logical ring must be constructed. Note that, if the site has not failed (that is, if it is up but cannot be reached), then we may have the undesirable situation where two sites serve as the coordinator. When the network is partitioned, the two coordinators (each for its own partition) may initiate conflicting actions. For example, if the coordinators are responsible for implementing mutual exclusion, we may have a situation where two processes may be executing simultaneously in their critical sections.

16.4.3 Recovery from Failure

When a failed link or site is repaired, it must be integrated into the system gracefully and smoothly.

- Suppose that a link between A and B has failed. When it is repaired, both A and B must be notified. We can accomplish this notification by continuously repeating the handshaking procedure, described in Section 16.4.1.

- Suppose that site B has failed. When it recovers, it must notify all other sites that it is up again. Site B then may have to receive from the other sites various information to update its local tables; for example, it may need routing table information, a list of sites that are down, or undelivered messages and mail. Note that, if the site has not failed, but simply could not be reached, then this information is still required.

16.5 ■ Design Issues

It has been the challenge of many designers to make the multiplicity of processors and storage devices transparent to the users. Ideally, a distributed system should look to its users like a conventional, centralized system. The user interface of a transparent distributed system should not distinguish between local and remote resources. That is, users should be able to access remote distributed systems as though the latter were local, and it should be the responsibility of the distributed system to locate the resources and to arrange for the appropriate interaction.

Another aspect of transparency is user mobility. It would be convenient to allow users to log in to any machine in the system, and not to force them to use a specific machine. A transparent distributed system facilitates user mobility by bringing over the user's environment (for example, home directory) to wherever she logs in. Both the Andrew file system from CMU and Project Athena from MIT provide this functionality on a large scale. NFS can provide this transparency on a smaller scale.

We use the term *fault tolerance* in a broad sense. Communication faults, machine failures (of type fail-stop), storage-device crashes, and decays of storage media are all considered to be faults that should be tolerated to some extent. A fault-tolerant system should continue to function, perhaps in a degraded form, when faced with these failures. The degradation can be in performance, in functionality, or in both. It should be, however, proportional, in some sense, to the failures that cause it. A system that grinds to a halt when only a few of its components fail is certainly not fault tolerant. Unfortunately, fault tolerance is difficult to implement. Most commercial systems provide only limited tolerance. For instance, the DEC VAXcluster allows multiple computers to share a set of disks. If a system crashes, users may still access their information from another system. Of course, if a disk fails, all the systems will lose access. But in this case, RAID can be used to ensure continued access to the data even in the event of a failure (Section 12.5).

The capability of a system to adapt to increased service load is called *scalability*. Systems have bounded resources and can become completely saturated under increased load. For example, regarding a file system, saturation occurs either when a server's CPU runs at a high utilization rate, or when disks are almost full. Scalability is a relative property, but it can be measured accurately. A scalable system should react more gracefully to increased load than does a nonscalable one. First, its performance should degrade more moderately than that of a nonscalable system. Second, its resources should reach a saturated state later, when compared with a nonscalable system. Even perfect design cannot accommodate an ever growing load. Adding new resources might solve the problem, but it might generate additional indirect load on other resources (for example, adding machines to a distributed system can clog the network and increase service loads). Even worse, expanding the system can incur expensive design modifications. A scalable system should have the potential to grow without these problems. In a distributed system, the ability to scale up gracefully is of special importance, since expanding the network by adding new machines or interconnecting two networks is commonplace. In short, a scalable design should withstand high service load, accommodate growth of the user community, and enable simple integration of added resources.

Fault tolerance and scalability are related to each other. A heavily loaded component can become paralyzed and behave like a faulty component. Also, shifting the load from a faulty component to that component's backup can saturate the latter. Generally, having spare resources is essential for ensuring reliability as well as for handling peak loads gracefully. An inherent advantage that a distributed system has is a potential for fault tolerance and scalability because of the multiplicity of resources. However, inappropriate design can obscure this potential. Fault-tolerance and scalability considerations call for a design demonstrating distribution of control and data.

Very large-scale distributed systems, to a great extent, are still only theoretical. There are no magic guidelines to ensure the scalability of a system. It is easier to point out why current designs are not scalable. We shall discuss several designs that pose problems, and shall propose possible solutions, all in the context of scalability.

One principle for designing very large-scale systems is the principle that the service demand from any component of the system should be bounded by a constant that is independent of the number of nodes in the system. Any service mechanism whose load demand is proportional to the size of the system is destined to become clogged once the system grows beyond a certain size. Adding more resources would not alleviate such a problem. The capacity of this mechanism simply limits the growth of the system.

Central control schemes and central resources should not be used to build scalable (and fault-tolerant) systems. Examples of centralized entities are central authentication servers, central naming servers, and central file servers. Centralization is a form of functional asymmetry among machines constituting the system. The ideal alternative is a configuration that is functionally symmetric; that is, all the component machines have an equal role in the operation of the system, and hence each machine has some degree of autonomy. Practically, it is virtually impossible to comply with such a principle. For instance, incorporating diskless machines violates functional symmetry, since the workstations depend on a central disk. However, autonomy and symmetry are important goals to which we should aspire.

The practical approximation to symmetric and autonomous configuration is *clustering*. The system is partitioned into a collection of semiautonomous clusters. A cluster consists of a set of machines and a dedicated cluster server. So that cross-cluster resource references will be relatively infrequent, each machine's requests should be satisfied by its own cluster server most of the time. Of course, this scheme depends on the ability to localize resource references and to place the component units appropriately. If the cluster is well balanced — that is, if the server in charge suffices to satisfy all the cluster demands — it can be used as a modular building block to scale up the system.

A major problem in the design of any service is the process structure of the server. Servers are supposed to operate efficiently in peak periods, when hundreds of active clients need to be served simultaneously. A single-process server is certainly not a good choice, since whenever a request necessitates disk I/O, the whole service will be blocked. Assigning a process for each client is a better choice; however, the expense of frequent context switches between the processes must be considered. A related problem occurs because all the server processes need to share information. It appears that one of the best solutions for the server architecture is the use of lightweight processes or threads, which we discussed in Section 4.5. The abstraction presented by a group of lightweight processes is that of multiple threads of control associated with some shared resources. Usually, a lightweight process is not bound to a particular client. Instead, it serves single requests of different clients. Scheduling threads can be preemptive or nonpreemptive. If threads are allowed to run to completion (nonpreemptive), then their shared data do not need to be protected explicitly. Otherwise, some explicit locking mechanism must be used. It is clear that some form of lightweight-processes scheme is essential for servers to be scalable.

16.6 ■ Summary

A distributed system provides the user with access to the various resources the system provides. Access to a shared resource can be provided by data migration, computation migration, or job migration. A distributed file system must address two major issues: transparency (does a user access all files in the same manner regardless of where they are in the network?) and locality (where do files reside in the system?).

A distributed file system is built on top of lower-level networking functions. The most common lower-level function is the remote procedure call (RPC) mechanism. An RPC is a structured message addressed to an RPC daemon listening to a *port* on the remote system, and contains an identifier of the function to execute and the parameters to pass to that function. The function is then executed as requested, and any output is sent back to the requester in a separate message. Threads can be used to make the destination process easier to write and more efficient, as one thread can process a request from beginning to end while its fellow threads are doing the same for other requests.

A distributed system may suffer from various types of hardware failure. For the system to be fault tolerant, it must detect failures and reconfigure the system. When the failure is repaired, the system must be reconfigured again.

■ Exercises

16.1 What are the advantages and disadvantages of making the computer network transparent to the user?

16.2 What are the formidable problems that designers must solve to implement a network transparent system?

16.3 Process migration within a heterogeneous network is usually impossible, given the differences in architectures and operating systems. Describe a method for process migration across different architectures running:

a. The same operating system

b. Different operating systems

16.4 To build a robust distributed system, you must know what kinds of failures can occur.

a. List possible types of failure in a distributed system.

b. Specify which items in your list also are applicable to a centralized system.

16.5 Is it always crucial to know that the message you have sent has arrived at its destination safely? If your answer is "yes," explain why. If your answer is "no," give appropriate examples.

16.6 Present an algorithm for reconstructing a logical ring after a process in the ring fails.

16.7 Consider a distributed system with two sites, A and B. Consider whether site A can distinguish among the following:

a. B goes down.

b. The link between A and B goes down.

c. B is extremely overloaded and response time is 100 times longer than normal.

What implications does your answer have for recovery in distributed systems?

Bibliographic Notes

Forsdick et al. [1978] and Donnelley [1979] discussed operating systems for computer networks. A survey of distributed operating systems was offered by Tanenbaum and Van Renesse [1985].

Discussions concerning distributed operating-system structures have been offered by Popek and Walker [1985] (the Locus system), Cheriton and Zwaenepoel [1983] (the V kernel), Ousterhout et al. [1988] (the Sprite network operating system), Balkovich et al. [1985] (Project Athena) and Tanenbaum et al. [1990] and Mullender et al. [1990] (the Amoeba distributed operating system). A comparison of Amoeba and Sprite is offered by Douglis et al. [1991].

Discussions concerning load balancing and load sharing were presented by Chow and Abraham [1982], Eager et al. [1986], and Ferguson et al. [1988]. Discussions concerning process migration were presented by Eager et al. [1986], Zayas [1987], Smith [1988], Jul et al. [1988], Artsy [1989a], Douglis and Ousterhout [1987, 1989], and Eskicioglu [1990]. A special issue on process migration was edited by Artsy [1989b].

Schemes for sharing idle workstations in a distributed shared computing environment are presented by Nichols [1987], Mutka and Livny [1987], and Litzkow et al. [1988].

Reliable communication in the presense of failures was discussed by Birman and Joseph [1987]. The principle that the service demand from any component of the system should be bounded by a constant that is independent of the number of nodes in the system was first advanced by Barak and Kornatzky [1987].

CHAPTER 17

DISTRIBUTED FILE SYSTEMS

In the previous chapter, we discussed network construction and the low-level protocols needed for messages to be transferred between systems. Now we discuss one use of this infrastructure. A *distributed file system* (DFS) is a distributed implementation of the classical time-sharing model of a file system, where multiple users share files and storage resources (Chapter 10). The purpose of a DFS is to support the same kind of sharing when the files are physically dispersed among the various sites of a distributed system.

In this chapter, we discuss the various ways a DFS can be designed and implemented. First, we discuss common concepts on which DFSs are based. Then, we illustrate our concepts by examining the UNIX United, NFS, Andrew, Sprite, and Locus DFSs. We take this approach to the presentation because distributed systems is an active research area, and the many design tradeoffs we shall illuminate are still being examined. By exploring these example systems, we hope to provide a sense of the considerations involved in designing an operating system, and also to indicate current areas of operating-system research.

17.1 ■ Background

A distributed system is a collection of loosely coupled machines interconnected by a communication network. We use the term *machine* to denote either a mainframe or a workstation. From the point of view of a specific machine in a distributed system, the rest of the machines and their respective resources are *remote,* whereas the machine's own resources are referred to as *local.*

To explain the structure of a DFS, we need to define the terms *service, server,* and *client.* A *service* is a software entity running on one or more machines and providing a particular type of function to a priori unknown clients. A *server* is the service software running on a single machine. A *client* is a process that can invoke a service using a set of operations that forms its *client interface.* Sometimes, a lower-level interface is defined for the actual cross-machine interaction, which we refer to as the *intermachine interface.*

Using this terminology, we say that a file system provides file services to clients. A client interface for a file service is formed by a set of primitive *file operations,* such as create a file, delete a file, read from a file, and write to a file. The primary hardware component that a file server controls is a set of local secondary-storage devices (usually, magnetic disks), on which files are stored, and from which they are retrieved according to the client requests.

A DFS is a file system whose clients, servers, and storage devices are dispersed among the machines of a distributed system. Accordingly, service activity has to be carried out across the network, and instead of a single centralized data repository, there are multiple and independent storage devices. As will become evident, the concrete configuration and implementation of a DFS may vary. There are configurations where servers run on dedicated machines, as well as configurations where a machine can be both a server and a client. A DFS can be implemented as part of a distributed operating system, or alternatively by a software layer whose task is to manage the communication between conventional operating systems and file systems. The distinctive features of a DFS are the multiplicity and autonomy of clients and servers in the system.

Ideally, a DFS should look to its clients like a conventional, centralized file system. The multiplicity and dispersion of its servers and storage devices should be made transparent. That is, the client interface of a DFS should not distinguish between local and remote files. It is up to the DFS to locate the files and to arrange for the transport of the data. A transparent DFS facilitates user mobility by bringing over the user's environment (that is, home directory) to wherever a user logs in.

The most important *performance* measurement of a DFS is the amount of time needed to satisfy various service requests. In conventional systems, this time consists of disk access time and a small amount of CPU processing time. In a DFS, however, a remote access has the additional overhead attributed to the distributed structure. This overhead includes the time needed to deliver the request to a server, as well as the time for getting the response across the network back to the client. For each direction, in addition to the actual transfer of the information, there is the CPU overhead of running the communication protocol software. The performance of a

DFS can be viewed as another dimension of the DFS's transparency. That is, the performance of an ideal DFS would be comparable to that of a conventional file system.

The fact that a DFS manages a set of dispersed storage devices is the DFS's key distinguishing feature. The overall storage space managed by a DFS is composed of different, and remotely located, smaller storage spaces. Usually, there is correspondence between these constituent storage spaces and sets of files. We use the term *component unit* to denote the smallest set of files that can be stored on a single machine, independently from other units. All files belonging to the same component unit must reside in the same location.

17.2 ■ Naming and Transparency

Naming is a mapping between logical and physical objects. For instance, users deal with logical data objects represented by file names, whereas the system manipulates physical blocks of data, stored on disk tracks. Usually, a user refers to a file by a textual name. The latter is mapped to a lower-level numerical identifier that in turn is mapped to disk blocks. This multilevel mapping provides users with an abstraction of a file that hides the details of how and where on the disk the file is actually stored.

In a *transparent* DFS, a new dimension is added to the abstraction: that of hiding where in the network the file is located. In a conventional file system, the range of the naming mapping is an address within a disk. In a DFS, this range is augmented to include the specific machine on whose disk the file is stored. Going one step further with the concept of treating files as abstractions leads to the possibility of *file replication*. Given a file name, the mapping returns a set of the locations of this file's replicas. In this abstraction, both the existence of multiple copies and their location are hidden.

17.2.1 Naming Structures

There are two related notions regarding name mappings in a DFS that need to be differentiated:

- **Location transparency:** The name of a file does not reveal any hint of the file's physical storage location.

- **Location independence:** The name of a file does not need to be changed when the file's physical storage location changes.

Both definitions are relative to the level of naming discussed previously, since files have different names at different levels (that is, user-level textual names, and system-level numerical identifiers). A location-independent naming scheme is a dynamic mapping, since it can map the same file name to different locations at two different times. Therefore, location independence is a stronger property than is location transparency.

In practice, most of the current DFSs provide a static, location-transparent mapping for user-level names. These systems, however, do not support file *migration;* that is, changing the location of a file automatically is impossible. Hence, the notion of location independence is quite irrelevant for these systems. Files are associated permanently with a specific set of disk blocks. Files and disks can be moved between machines manually, but file migration implies an automatic, operating-system initiated action. Only Andrew (Section 17.6.3) and some experimental file systems support location independence and file mobility. Andrew supports file mobility mainly for administrative purposes. A protocol provides migration of Andrew's component units to satisfy high-level user requests, without changing either the user-level names, or the low-level names of the corresponding files.

There are a few aspects that can further differentiate location independence and static location transparency:

- Divorcing data from location, as exhibited by location independence, provides better abstraction for files. A file name should denote the file's most significant attributes, which are its contents, rather than its location. Location-independent files can be viewed as logical data containers that are not attached to a specific storage location. If only static location transparency is supported, the file name still denotes a specific, although hidden, set of physical disk blocks.

- Static location transparency provides users with a convenient way to share data. Users can share remote files by simply naming the files in a location-transparent manner, as though the files were local. Nevertheless, sharing the storage space is cumbersome, because logical names are still statically attached to physical storage devices. Location independence promotes sharing the storage space itself, as well as the data objects. When files can be mobilized, the overall, system-wide storage space looks like a single, virtual resource. A possible benefit of such a view is the ability to balance the utilization of disks across the system.

- Location independence separates the naming hierarchy from the storage-devices hierarchy and from the intercomputer structure. By contrast, if static location transparency is used (although names are transparent), we can easily expose the correspondence between component units and machines. The machines are configured in a pattern similar to the naming structure. This may restrict the architecture of the system unnecessarily and conflict with other considerations. A server in charge of a root directory is an example of a structure that is dictated by the naming hierarchy and contradicts decentralization guidelines.

Once the separation of name and location has been completed, files residing on remote server systems may be accessed by various clients. In fact, these clients may be *diskless* and rely on servers to provide all files, including the operating-system kernel. Special protocols are needed for the boot sequence, however. Consider the problem of getting the kernel to a diskless workstation. The diskless workstation has no kernel, so it cannot use the DFS code to retrieve the kernel. Instead, a special boot protocol, stored in read-only memory (ROM) on the client, is invoked. It enables networking and retrieves only one special file (the kernel or boot code) from a fixed location. Once the kernel is copied over the network and loaded, its DFS makes all the other operating-system files available. The advantages of diskless clients are many, including lower cost (because no disk is needed on each machine) and greater convenience (when an operating-system upgrade occurs, only the server copy needs to be modified, rather than all the clients as well). The disadvantages are the added complexity of the boot protocols and the performance loss resulting from the use of a network rather than of a local disk.

The current trend is toward clients with local disks. Disk drives are increasing in capacity and decreasing in cost rapidly, with new generations appearing every year or so. The same cannot be said for networks, which evolve every 5 to 10 years. Overall, systems are growing more quickly than are networks, so extra efforts are needed to limit network access to improve system throughput.

17.2.2 Naming Schemes

There are three main approaches to naming schemes in a DFS. In the simplest approach, files are named by some combination of their host name and local name, which guarantees a unique systemwide name. In Ibis, for instance, a file is identified uniquely by the name *host:local-name*, where *local-name* is a UNIX-like path. This naming scheme is neither location transparent nor location independent. Nevertheless, the same file operations can be used for both local and remote files. The structure of the DFS is a collection of isolated component units that are entire conventional file systems. In this first approach, component units remained isolated, although means are provided to refer to a remote file. We do not consider this scheme any further in this text.

The second approach was popularized by Sun's Network File System (NFS). NFS is the file system component of ONC+, a networking package which will be supported by many UNIX vendors. NFS provides means to attach remote directories to local directories, thus giving the appearance of a coherent directory tree. Early NFS versions only allowed previously mounted remote directories to be accessed transparently. With the advent of the *automount* feature, mounts occur on-demand based on a table of mount points and file structure names. There is also some integration of components to support transparent sharing. This integration, however, is limited and is not uniform, because each machine may attach different remote directories to its tree. The resulting structure is versatile. Usually, it is a forest of UNIX trees with shared subtrees.

Total integration of the component file systems is achieved using the third approach. A single global name structure spans all the files in the system. Ideally, the composed file-system structure should be isomorphic to the structure of a conventional file system. In practice, however, there are many special files (for example, UNIX device files and machine-specific binary directories) that make this goal difficult to attain. We shall examine different variations of this approach in our discussions of UNIX United, Locus, Sprite, and Andrew in Section 17.6.

An important criterion for evaluation of the naming structures is their administrative complexity. The most complex and most difficult structure to maintain is the NFS structure. Because any remote directory can be attached anywhere onto the local directory tree, the resulting hierarchy can be highly unstructured. The effect of a server becoming unavailable is that some arbitrary set of directories on different machines becomes unavailable. In addition, a separate accreditation mechanism is used to control which machine is allowed to attach which directory to its tree. This mechanism can lead to the situation in which, on one client, a user can access a remote directory tree, whereas on another client, access is denied to that user.

17.2.3 Implementation Techniques

Implementation of transparent naming requires a provision for the mapping of a file name to the associated location. Keeping this mapping manageable calls for aggregating sets of files into component units, and providing the mapping on a component unit basis rather than on a single-file basis. This aggregation serves administrative purposes as well. UNIX-like systems use the hierarchical directory tree to provide name-to-location mapping, and to aggregate files recursively into directories.

To enhance the availability of the crucial mapping information, we can use methods such as replication, local caching, or both. As we already noted, location independence means that the mapping changes over time; hence, replicating the mapping renders a simple yet consistent update of this information impossible. A technique to overcome this obstacle is to introduce low-level, *location-independent file identifiers*. Textual file names are mapped to lower-level file identifiers that indicate to which component unit the file belongs. These identifiers are still location independent. They can be replicated and cached freely without being invalidated by migration of component units. A second level of mapping, which maps component units to locations and needs a simple yet consistent update mechanism, is the inevitable price. Implementing UNIX-like directory trees using these low-level, location-independent identifiers makes the whole hierarchy invariant under component unit migration. The only aspect that does change is the component unit-location mapping.

A common way to implement these low-level identifiers is to use structured names. These names are bit strings that usually have two parts. The first part identifies the component unit to which the file belongs; the second part identifies the particular file within the unit. Variants with more parts are possible. The invariant of structured names, however, is that individual parts of the name are unique at all times only within the context of the rest of the parts. We can obtain uniqueness at all times by taking care not to reuse a name that is still used, by adding sufficiently more bits (this method is used in Andrew), or by using a timestamp as one of the parts of the name (as done in Apollo Domain). Another way to view this process is that we are taking a location-transparent system, such as Ibis, and adding another level of abstraction to produce a location-independent naming scheme.

The use of the techniques of aggregation of files into component units, and of lower-level location-independent file identifiers, is exemplified in Andrew and Locus.

17.3 ■ Remote File Access

Consider a user who requests access to a remote file. Assuming that the server storing the file was located by the naming scheme, the actual data transfer to satisfy the user request for the remote access must take place.

One way to achieve this transfer is through a *remote-service* mechanism, where requests for accesses are delivered to the server, the server machine performs the accesses, and their results are forwarded back to the user. One of the most common ways of implementing remote service is the *remote procedure call (RPC)* paradigm, which we discussed in Section 16.3.1. We note that there is a direct analogy between disk-access methods in conventional file systems and the remote-service method in a DFS. The remote-service method is analogous to performing a disk access for each access request.

To ensure reasonable performance of a remote-service mechanism, we can use a form of *caching*. In conventional file systems, the rationale for caching is to reduce disk I/O (thereby increasing performance), whereas in DFSs, the goal is to reduce both network traffic and disk I/O. In the following, we discuss various issues concerning the implementation of caching in a DFS, and contrast the latter with the basic remote-service paradigm.

17.3.1 Basic Caching Scheme

The concept of caching is simple. If the data needed to satisfy the access request are not already cached, then a copy of those data is brought from the server to the client system. Accesses are performed on the cached copy. The idea is to retain recently accessed disk blocks in the cache, so that repeated accesses to the same information can be handled locally, without additional network traffic. A replacement policy (for example, least recently used) is used to keep the cache size bounded. There is no direct correspondence between accesses and traffic to the server. Files are still identified with one master copy residing at the server machine, but copies of (parts of) the file are scattered in different caches. When a cached copy is modified, the changes need to be reflected on the master copy to preserve the relevant consistency semantics. The problem of keeping the cached copies consistent with the master file is the *cache-consistency problem*, which will be discussed in Section 17.3.4. Observant readers will realize that DFS caching could just as easily be called *network virtual memory*: It acts similarly to demand-paged virtual memory, except that the backing store is not a local disk, but rather is a remote server.

The granularity of the cached data can vary from blocks of a file to an entire file. Usually, more data are cached than are needed to satisfy a single access, so that many accesses can be served by the cached data. This procedure is much like disk read-ahead (Section 11.5.2). The Andrew system caches files in large chunks (64K). The other systems discussed in this chapter support caching of individual blocks driven by clients' demands. Increasing the caching unit increases the hit ratio, but also increases the miss penalty because each miss requires more data to be transferred. It also increases the potential for consistency problems. Selecting the unit of caching involves considering parameters such as the network transfer unit and the RPC protocol service unit (in case an RPC protocol is used). The network transfer unit (for Ethernet, a packet) is about 1.5K, so larger units of cached data need to be disassembled for delivery and reassembled on reception.

Block size and the total cache size are obviously of importance for block-caching schemes. In UNIX-like systems, common block sizes are 4K or 8K. For large caches (over 1 megabyte), large block sizes (over 8K) are beneficial. For smaller caches, large block sizes are less beneficial because they result in fewer blocks in the cache.

17.3.2 Cache Location

Now we turn to the issue of where the cached data should be stored. Disk caches have one clear advantage over main memory cache — reliability. Modifications to cached data are lost in a crash if the cache is kept in volatile memory. Moreover, if the cached data are kept on disk, they are still there during recovery and there is no need to fetch them again. On the other hand, main-memory caches have several advantages of their own:

- Main-memory caches permit workstations to be diskless.

- Data can be accessed more quickly from a cache in main memory than from one on a disk.

- The current technology trend is toward bigger and less expensive memories. The achieved performance speedup is predicted to outweigh the advantages of disk caches.

- The server caches (the ones used to speed up disk I/O) will be in main memory regardless of where user caches are located; by using main-memory caches on the user machine too, we can build a single caching mechanism for use by both servers and users (as is done in Sprite).

Many remote-access implementations can be thought of as a hybrid of caching and remote service. In NFS and Locus, for instance, the implementation is based on remote service but is augmented with caching for performance. On the other hand, Sprite's implementation is based on caching, but under certain circumstances a remote service method is adopted. Thus, when we evaluate the two methods, we actually evaluate to what degree one method is emphasized over the other.

17.3.3 Cache Update Policy

The policy used to write modified data blocks back to the server's master copy has critical effect on the system's performance and reliability. The simplest policy is to write data through to disk as soon as they are placed on any cache. The advantage of *write-through* is its reliability. Little information is lost when a client system crashes. However, this policy requires each write access to wait until the information is sent to the server, which results in poor write performance. Caching with write-through is equivalent to using remote service for write accesses and exploiting caching only for read accesses. NFS provides write-through access.

An alternate write policy is to delay updates to the master copy. Modifications are written to the cache and then are written through to the server at a later time. This policy has two advantages over write-through. First, because writes are to the cache, write accesses complete much more quickly. Second, data may be overwritten before they are written back, in which case all but the last update never needs to be written at all. Unfortunately, *delayed-write* schemes introduce reliability problems, since unwritten data will be lost whenever a user machine crashes.

There are several variations of the delayed-write policy that differ in when modified data blocks are flushed to the server. One alternative is to flush a block when it is about to be ejected from the client's cache. This option can result in good performance, but some blocks can reside in the client's cache a long time before they are written back to the server. A compromise between this alternative and the write-through policy is to scan the cache at regular intervals and to flush blocks that have been modified since the last scan, just as UNIX scans its local cache. Sprite uses this policy with a 30-second interval.

Yet another variation on delayed-write is to write data back to the server when the file is closed. This policy, *write-on-close*, is used in the Andrew system. In the case of files that are open for short periods or are modified rarely, this policy does not significantly reduce network traffic. In addition, the write-on-close policy requires the closing process to delay while the file is written through, which reduces the performance advantages of delayed writes. The performance advantages of this policy over delayed-write with more frequent flushing are apparent for files that are open for long periods and are modified frequently.

17.3.4 Consistency

A client machine is faced with the problem of deciding whether or not a locally cached copy of the data is consistent with the master copy (and hence can be used). If the client machine determines that its cached data are out of date, accesses can no longer be served by those cached data. An up-to-date copy of the data needs to be cached. There are two approaches to verify the validity of cached data:

- **Client-initiated approach:** The client initiates a validity check in which it contacts the server and checks whether the local data are consistent with the master copy. The frequency of the validity check is the crux of this approach and determines the resulting consistency semantics. It can range from a check before every access, to a check on only first access to a file (on file open, basically). Every access that is coupled with a validity check is delayed, compared with an access served immediately by the cache. Alternatively, a check can be initiated every fixed interval of time. Depending on its frequency, the validity check can load both the network and the server.

- **Server-initiated approach:** The server records, for each client, the (parts of) files that it caches. When the server detects a potential inconsistency, it must react. A potential for inconsistency occurs when a file is cached by two different clients in conflicting modes. If session semantics (Section 10.5.2) are implemented, then, whenever a server receives a request to close a file that has been modified, it should react by notifying the clients to consider the cached data invalid and discard that data. Clients having this file open at that time discard their copy when the current session is over. Other clients discard their copy at once. Under session semantics, the server does not need to be informed about opens of already cached files. The server's reaction is triggered only by the close of a writing session, and hence only this kind of session is delayed. In Andrew, session semantics are implemented, and a server-initiated method, called *callback*, is employed (Section 17.6.3).

On the other hand, if a more restrictive consistency semantics, such as UNIX semantics (Section 10.5.1), is implemented, the server must play a more active role. The server must be notified whenever a file is opened and the intended mode (read or write mode) must be indicated for every open. Assuming such notification, the server can act when it detects a file that is opened simultaneously in conflicting modes by disabling caching for that particular file (as done in Sprite). Actually, disabling caching results in switching to a remote-service mode of operation.

17.3.5 A Comparison of Caching and Remote Service

Essentially, the choice between caching and remote service trades off a potentially increased performance with decreased simplicity. We evaluate this tradeoff by listing the advantages and disadvantages of the two methods:

- A substantial number of the remote accesses can be handled efficiently by the local cache when caching is used. Capitalizing on locality in file-access patterns makes caching even more attractive. Thus, most of the remote accesses will be served as fast as will local ones. Moreover, servers are contacted only occasionally, rather than for each access. Consequently, server load and network traffic are reduced, and the potential for scalability is enhanced. By contrast, every remote access is handled across the network when the remote-service method is used. The penalty in network traffic, server load, and performance is obvious.

- Total network overhead in transmitting big chunks of data (as is done in caching) is lower than when series of responses to specific requests are transmitted (as in the remote-service method).

- Disk-access routines on the server may be better optimized if it is known that requests are always for large, contiguous segments of data, rather than for random disk blocks.

- The cache-consistency problem is the major drawback of caching. In access patterns that exhibit infrequent writes, caching is superior. However, when writes are frequent, the mechanisms employed to overcome the consistency problem incur substantial overhead in terms of performance, network traffic, and server load.

- So that caching will confer a benefit, execution should be carried out on machines that have either local disks or large main memories. Remote access on diskless, small-memory-capacity machines should be done through the remote-service method.

- In caching, since data are transferred en masse between the server and client, rather than in response to the specific needs of a file operation, the lower intermachine interface is quite different from the upper-user interface. The remote-service paradigm, on the other hand, is just an extension of the local file-system interface across the network. Thus, the intermachine interface mirrors the local user-file-system interface.

17.4 ■ Stateful versus Stateless Service

There are two approaches to server-side information. Either the server tracks each file being accessed by each client, or it simply provides blocks as they are requested by the client without knowledge of the blocks' usage.

The typical scenario of a *stateful file service* is as follows. A client must perform an open on a file before accessing that file. The server fetches some information about the file from its disk, stores it in its memory, and gives the client a connection identifier that is unique to the client and the open file. (In UNIX terms, the server fetches the inode and gives the client a file descriptor, which serves as an index to an in-core table of inodes.) This identifier is used for subsequent accesses until the session ends. A stateful service is characterized as a connection between the client and the server during a session. Either on closing the file, or by a garbage-collection mechanism, the server must reclaim the main-memory space used by clients who are no longer active.

The advantage of stateful service is increased performance. File information is cached in main memory and can be accessed easily via the connection identifier, thereby saving disk accesses. In addition, a stateful server would know whether a file were open for sequential access and could therefore read ahead the next blocks. Stateless servers cannot do so, since they have no knowledge of the purpose of the client's requests. The key point regarding fault tolerance in a stateful service approach is that main-memory information is kept by the server about its clients.

A *stateless file server* avoids this state information by making each request self-contained. That is, each request identifies the file and the position in the file (for read and write accesses) in full. The server does not need to keep a table of open files in main memory, although it usually does so for efficiency reasons. Moreover, there is no need to establish and terminate a connection by open and close operations. They are totally redundant, since each file operation stands on its own and is not considered as part of a session. A client process would open a file, and that open would not result in a remote message being sent. Reads and writes would, of course, take place as remote messages (or cache lookups). The final close by the client would again result in only a local operation.

The distinction between stateful and stateless service becomes evident when we consider the effects of a crash occurring during a service activity. A stateful server loses all its volatile state in a crash. Ensuring the graceful recovery of such a server involves restoring this state — usually by a recovery protocol based on a dialog with clients. Less graceful recovery requires that the operations that were underway when the crash occurred, be aborted. A different problem is caused by client failures. The server needs to become aware of such failures, so that it can reclaim space allocated to record the state of crashed client processes. This phenomenon is sometimes referred to as *orphan detection and elimination*.

A stateless server avoids these problems, since a newly reincarnated server can respond to a self-contained request without any difficulty. Therefore, the effects of server failures and recovery are almost unnoticeable. There is no difference between a slow server and a recovering server from a client's point of view. The client keeps retransmitting its request if it receives no response.

The penalty for using the robust stateless service is longer request messages, and slower processing of requests, since there is no in-core information to speed the processing. In addition, stateless service imposes additional constraints on the design of the DFS. First, since each request identifies the target file, a uniform, systemwide, low-level naming scheme should be used. Translating remote to local names for each request would cause even slower processing of the requests. Second, since clients retransmit requests for file operations, these operations must be *idempotent;* that is, each operation must have the same effect and return the same output if executed several times consecutively. Self-contained read and write accesses are idempotent, as long as they use an absolute byte count to indicate the position within the file they access and do not rely on an incremental offset (as done in UNIX **read** and **write** system calls). However, we must be careful when implementing destructive operations (such as delete a file) to make them idempotent too.

In some environments, a stateful service is a necessity. If the server employs the server-initiated method for cache validation, it cannot provide stateless service, since it maintains a record of which files are cached by which clients.

The way UNIX uses file descriptors and implicit offsets is inherently stateful. Servers must maintain tables to map the file descriptors to inodes, and store the current offset within a file. This is why NFS, which employs a stateless service, does not use file descriptors, and does include an explicit offset in every access.

17.5 ■ File Replication

Replication of files on different machines is a useful redundancy for improving availability. Multimachine replication can benefit performance too, since selecting a nearby replica to serve an access request results in shorter service time.

The basic requirement of a replication scheme is that different replicas of the same file reside on failure-independent machines. That is, the availability of one replica is not affected by the availability of the rest of the replicas. This obvious requirement implies that replication management is inherently a location-opaque activity. Provisions for placing a replica on a particular machine must be available.

It is desirable to hide the details of replication from users. It is the task of the naming scheme to map a replicated file name to a particular replica. The existence of replicas should be invisible to higher levels. However, the replicas must be distinguished from one another by different lower-level names. Another transparency issue is providing replication control at higher levels. Replication control includes determination of the degree of replication and of the placement of replicas. Under certain circumstances, it is desirable to expose these details to users. Locus, for instance, provides users and system administrators with mechanisms to control the replication scheme.

The main problem associated with replicas is their update. From a user's point of view, replicas of a file denote the same logical entity, and thus an update to any replica must be reflected on all other replicas. More precisely, the relevant consistency semantics must be preserved when accesses to replicas are viewed as virtual accesses to the replicas' logical files. If consistency is not of primary importance, it can be sacrificed for availability and performance. This option is an incarnation of a fundamental tradeoff in the area of fault tolerance. The choice is between preserving consistency at all costs, thereby creating a potential for indefinite blocking, and sacrificing consistency under some (we hope rare) circumstance of catastrophic failures for the sake of guaranteed progress. Among the surveyed systems, Locus employs replication extensively and sacrifices consistency in the case of network partition, for the sake of availability of files for both read and write accesses (see Section 17.6.5 for details).

As an illustration of these concepts, we describe the replication scheme of Ibis, which uses a variation of the primary-copy approach. The domain of the name mapping is a pair <primary-replica-identifier, local-replica-

identifier>. Since there may be no replica locally, a special value is used in
that case. Thus, the mapping is relative to a machine. If the local replica is
the primary one, the pair contains two identical identifiers. Ibis supports
demand replication, which is an automatic replication-control policy
(similar to whole-file caching). Under demand replication, reading a
nonlocal replica causes it to be cached locally, thereby generating a new
nonprimary replica. Updates are performed on only the primary copy and
cause all other replicas to be invalidated by sending appropriate messages.
Atomic and serialized invalidation of all nonprimary replicas is not
guaranteed. Hence, a stale replica may be considered valid. To satisfy
remote write accesses, we migrate the primary copy to the requesting
machine.

17.6   ■   Example Systems

In this section, we illustrate the common concepts on which DFSs are based
by examining five different and interesting DFSs: UNIX United, Sun NFS,
Andrew, Sprite, and Locus.

17.6.1 UNIX United

The *UNIX United* project from the University of Newcastle upon Tyne,
England, is one of the earliest attempts to scale up the UNIX file system to a
distributed one without modifying the UNIX kernel. In UNIX United, a
software subsystem is added to each of a set of interconnected UNIX
systems (referred to as *component* or *constituent* systems), to construct a
distributed system that is functionally indistinguishable from a
conventional centralized UNIX system. The system is presented in two
levels of detail. First, an overview of UNIX United is given. Then, the
implementation, the Newcastle Connection layer, is examined and issues
regarding networking and internetworking are discussed.

17.6.1.1 Overview

Any number of interlinked UNIX systems can be joined to compose a UNIX
United system. Their naming structures (for files, devices, directories, and
commands) are joined together into a single naming structure, in which
each component system is, for all intents and purposes, just a directory.
Ignoring for the moment questions regarding accreditation and access
control, the resulting system is one where each user can read or write any
file, use any device, execute any command, or inspect any directory,
regardless of the system to which it belongs.

   The component unit is a complete UNIX directory tree belonging to a
certain machine. The position of these component units in the naming
hierarchy is arbitrary. They can appear in the naming structure in positions

subservient to other component units (directly or through intermediary directories).

Roots of component units are assigned names so that they become accessible and distinguishable externally. A file system's own root is still referred to as "/" and still serves as the starting point of all path names starting with a "/". However, a subservient file system can access its superior system by referring to its own root parent (that is, "/.."). Therefore, there is only one root that is its own parent and that is not assigned a string name — namely, the root of the composite name structure, which is just a virtual node needed to make the whole structure a single tree. Under this convention, there is no notion of absolute path name. Each path name is relative to some context, either to the current working directory or to the current component unit.

In Figure 17.1, *unix1*, *unix2*, *unix3*, and *unix4* are names of component systems. As an illustration of the relative path names, note that within the *unix1* system, file *f2* on the system *unix2* is referred to as /../unix2/f2. Within the *unix3* system, this file is referred to as /../../unix2/f2. Now, suppose that the current root ("/") is as shown by the arrow. Then, file *f3* is referred to as /f3, file *f1* is referred to as /../f1, file *f2* is referred to as /../../unix2/f2, and finally file *f4* is referred to as /../../unix2/dir/unix4/f4.

Observe that users are aware of the upward boundaries of their current component unit, since they must use the "../" syntax whenever they wish to ascend outside of their current machine. Hence, UNIX United does not provide complete location transparency.

The traditional root directories (for example, /dev, /temp) are maintained for each machine separately. Because of the relative naming scheme they are named, from within a component system, in exactly the same manner as in a conventional UNIX.

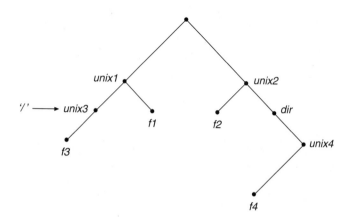

Figure 17.1 Example of a UNIX United directory structure.

Each component system has its own set of named users and its own administrator (superuser). The latter is responsible for the accreditation for users of his own system, as well as for that of remote users. A remote user's identifier is prefixed with the name of the user's original system for uniqueness. Accesses are governed by the standard UNIX file-protection mechanisms, even if they cross components' boundaries. That is, there is no need for users to log in separately, or to provide passwords, when they access remote files. However, users wishing to access files in a remote system must arrange with the specific system administrator separately.

It is often convenient to set the naming structure so as to reflect organizational hierarchy of the environment in which the system exists.

17.6.1.2 The Newcastle Connection

The Newcastle Connection is a (user-level) software layer incorporated in each component system. This connection layer separates the UNIX kernel on one hand, and the user-level programs on the other hand (see Figure 17.2). It intercepts all system calls concerning files, and filters out those that have to be redirected to remote systems. Also, the connection layer accepts system calls that have been directed to it from other systems. Remote layers communicate by the means of an RPC protocol.

The connection layer preserves the same UNIX system-call interface as that of the UNIX kernel, in spite of the extensive remote activity that the system carries out. The penalty of preserving the kernel intact is that the service is implemented as user-level daemon processes, which slow down remote operation.

Each connection layer stores a partial skeleton of the overall naming structure. Obviously, each system stores locally its own file system. In addition, each system stores fragments of the overall name structure that relate it to its neighboring systems in the naming structure (that is, systems that can be reached via traversal of the naming tree without passing through another system). In Figure 17.3, we show the partial skeletons of the hierarchy of the file systems of Figure 17.1 as maintained by the systems *unix1*, *unix2*, and *unix3*, respectively (only the relevant parts are shown).

Figure 17.2 Schematic view of UNIX United architecture.

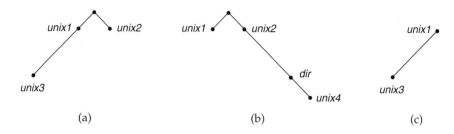

Figure 17.3 The file system of (a) *unix1*, (b) *unix2*, and (c) *unix3*.

The fragments maintained by different systems overlap and hence must remain consistent, a requirement that makes changing the overall structure an infrequent event. Some leaves of the partial structure stored locally correspond to remote roots of other parts of the global file system. These leaves are specially marked, and contain addresses of the appropriate storage sites of the descending file systems. Path-name traversals have to be continued remotely when such marked leaves are encountered, and, in fact, can span several systems until the target file is located. Once a name is resolved and the file is opened, that file is accessed using file descriptors. The connection layer marks descriptors that refer to remote files, and keeps network addresses and routing information for them in a per-process table.

The actual remote file accesses are carried out by a set of file-server processes on the target system. Each client has its own file server process with which it communicates directly. The initial connection is established with the aid of a *spawner* process that has a standard fixed name that makes it callable from any external process. This spawner process performs the remote access-rights checks according to a machine-user identification pair. Also, it converts this identification to a valid local name. So that UNIX semantics will be preserved, once a client process forks, its file service process forks as well. This service scheme does not excel in terms of robustness. Special recovery actions have to be taken in case of simultaneous server and client failures. However, the connection layer attempts to mask and isolate failures resulting from the fact that the system is a distributed one.

17.6.2 The Sun Network File System

The Network File System (NFS) is both an implementation and a specification of a software system for accessing remote files across LANs (or even WANs). NFS is part of ONC+, which most UNIX vendors are supporting. The implementation is part of the Solaris operating system, which is a modified version of UNIX SVR4, running on Sun workstations and other hardware. It uses the unreliable datagram protocol (UDP/IP protocol) and Ethernet (or another networking system). The specification and the implementation are intertwined in our description of NFS. Whenever a level of detail is needed, we refer to the Sun implementation; whenever the description is general enough, it applies to the specification also.

17.6.2.1 Overview

NFS views a set of interconnected workstations as a set of independent machines with independent file systems. The goal is to allow some degree of sharing among these file systems (on explicit request) in a transparent manner. Sharing is based on server–client relationship. A machine may be, and often is, both a client and a server. Sharing is allowed between any pair of machines, rather than with only dedicated server machines. To ensure machine independence, sharing of a remote file system affects only the client machine and no other machine.

So that a remote directory will be accessible in a transparent manner from a particular machine — say, from *M1* — a client of that machine has to carry out a mount operation first. The semantics of the operation are that a remote directory is mounted over a directory of a local file system. Once the mount operation is completed, the mounted directory looks like an integral subtree of the local file system, replacing the subtree descending from the local directory. The local directory becomes the name of the root of the newly mounted directory. Specification of the remote directory as an argument for the mount operation is done in a nontransparent manner; the location (that is, host name) of the remote directory has to be provided. However, from then on, users on machine *M1* can access files in the remote directory in a totally transparent manner.

To illustrate file mounting, we consider the file system depicted in Figure 17.4, where the triangles represent subtrees of directories that are of interest. In this figure, three independent file systems of machines named *U*, *S1*, and *S2* are shown. At this point, at each machine, only the local files can be accessed. In Figure 17.5(a), the effects of the mounting of *S1:/usr/shared* over *U:/usr/local* are shown. This figure depicts the view users

Figure 17.4   Three independent file systems.

on U have of their file system. Observe that they can access any file within the *dir1* directory, for instance, using the prefix */usr/local/dir1* on U after the mount is complete. The original directory */usr/local* on that machine is no longer visible.

Subject to access-rights accreditation, potentially any file system, or a directory within a file system, can be mounted remotely on top of any local directory. Diskless workstations can even mount their own roots from servers.

Cascading mounts are also permitted. That is, a file system can be mounted over another file system that is not a local one, but rather is a remotely mounted one. However, a machine is affected by only those mounts that it has itself invoked.

By mounting a remote file system, the client does not gain access to other file systems that were, by chance, mounted over the former file system. Thus, the mount mechanism does not exhibit a transitivity property. In Figure 17.5(b), we illustrate cascading mounts by continuing with our previous example. The figure shows the result of mounting *S2:/dir2/dir3* over *U:/usr/local/dir1*, which is already remotely mounted from *S1*. Users can access files within *dir3* on U using the prefix */usr/local/dir1*. If a shared file system is mounted over a user's home directories on all machines in a network, a user can log in to any workstation and get his home environment. This property is referred to as *user mobility*.

One of the design goals of NFS was to operate in a heterogeneous environment of different machines, operating systems, and network architectures. The NFS specification is independent of these media and thus encourages other implementations. This independence is achieved through the use of RPC primitives built on top of an External Data Representation (XDR) protocol used between two implementation-independent interfaces. Hence, if the system consists of heterogeneous machines and file systems that are properly interfaced to NFS, file systems of different types can be mounted both locally and remotely.

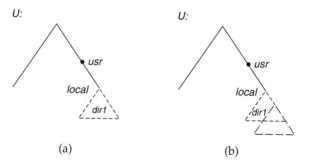

(a)   (b)

Figure 17.5 Mounting in NFS. (a) Mounts. (b) Cascading mounts.

The NFS specification distinguishes between the services provided by a mount mechanism and the actual remote-file-access services. Accordingly, two separate protocols are specified for these services; a *mount protocol*, and a protocol for remote file accesses called the NFS *protocol*. The protocols are specified as sets of RPCs. These RPCs are the building blocks used to implement transparent remote file access.

17.6.2.2 The Mount Protocol

The mount protocol is used to establish the initial logical connection between a server and a client. In Sun's implementation, each machine has a server process, outside the kernel, performing the protocol functions.

A mount operation includes the name of the remote directory to be mounted and the name of the server machine storing it. The mount request is mapped to the corresponding RPC and is forwarded to the mount server running on the specific server machine. The server maintains an *export list* (the */etc/exports* in UNIX, which can be edited by only a superuser), which specifies local file systems that it exports for mounting, along with names of machines that are permitted to mount them. Unfortunately, this list has a maximum length, so NFS is limited in scalability. Recall that any directory within an exported file system can be mounted remotely by an accredited machine. Hence, a component unit is such a directory. When the server receives a mount request that conforms to its export list, it returns to the client a *file handle* that serves as the key for further accesses to files within the mounted file system. The file handle contains all the information that the server needs to distinguish an individual file it stores. In UNIX terms, the file handle consists of a file-system identifier, and an inode number to identify the exact mounted directory within the exported file system.

The server also maintains a list of the client machines and the corresponding currently mounted directories. This list is used mainly for administrative purposes — for instance, for notifying all clients that the server is going down. Adding and deleting an entry in this list is the only way that the server state can be affected by the mount protocol.

Usually, a system has a static mounting preconfiguration that is established at boot time (*/etc/fstab* in UNIX); however, this layout can be modified. Besides the actual mount procedure, the mount protocol includes several other procedures, such as unmount and return export list.

17.6.2.3 The NFS Protocol

The NFS protocol provides a set of RPCs for remote file operations. The procedures support the following operations:

- Searching for a file within a directory

- Reading a set of directory entries
- Manipulating links and directories
- Accessing file attributes
- Reading and writing files

These procedures can be invoked only after a file handle for the remotely mounted directory has been established.

The omission of open and close operations is intentional. A prominent feature of NFS servers is that they are *stateless*. Servers do not maintain information about their clients from one access to another access. There are no parallels to UNIX's open-files table or file structures on the server side. Consequently, each request has to provide a full set of arguments, including a unique file identifier and an absolute offset inside the file for the appropriate operations. The resulting design is robust; no special measures need to be taken to recover a server after a crash. File operations need to be idempotent for this purpose.

Maintaining the list of clients mentioned above seems to violate the statelessness of the server. However, it is not essential for the correct operation of the client or the server, and hence this list does not need to be restored after a server crash. Consequently, it might include inconsistent data and is treated only as a hint.

A further implication of the stateless-server philosophy and a result of the synchrony of an RPC is that modified data (including indirection and status blocks) must be committed to the server's disk before results are returned to the client. That is, a client can cache write blocks, but when it flushes them to the server, it assumes that they have reached the server's disks. Thus, a server crash and recover will be invisible to a client; all blocks that the server is managing for the client will be intact. The consequent performance penalty can be large, because the advantages of caching are lost. In fact, there are several products now on the market that specifically address this NFS problem by providing fast stable storage (usually memory with battery backup) in which to store blocks written by NFS. These blocks remain intact even after system crash, and are written from this stable storage to disk periodically.

A single NFS write procedure call is guaranteed to be atomic, and also is not intermixed with other write calls to the same file. The NFS protocol, however, does not provide concurrency-control mechanisms. A **write** system call may be broken down into several RPC writes, because each NFS write or read call can contain up to 8K of data and UDP packets are limited to 1500 bytes. As a result, two users writing to the same remote file may get their data intermixed. The claim is that, because lock management is inherently stateful, a service outside the NFS should provide locking (and Solaris does). Users are advised to coordinate access to shared files using mechanisms outside the scope of NFS.

17.6.2.4 The NFS Architecture

The NFS architecture consists of three major layers; it is depicted schematically in Figure 17.6. The first layer is the UNIX file-system interface, based on the **open, read, write,** and **close** calls, and file descriptors.

The second layer is called *Virtual File System (VFS)* layer; it serves two important functions:

- It separates file-system generic operations from their implementation by defining a clean VFS interface. Several implementations for the VFS interface may coexist on the same machine, allowing transparent access to different types of file systems mounted locally.

- The VFS is based on a file representation structure called a *vnode* that contains a numerical designator for a file that is networkwide unique. (Recall that UNIX inodes are unique within only a single file system.) The kernel maintains one vnode structure for each active node (file or directory).

Thus, the VFS distinguishes local files from remote ones, and local files are further distinguished according to their file-system types.

Similarly to standard UNIX, the kernel maintains a table (*/etc/mtab* in UNIX) recording the details of the mounts in which it took part as a client. Further, the vnodes for each directory that is mounted over are kept in

Figure 17.6 Schematic view of the NFS architecture.

memory at all times and are marked, so that requests concerning such directories will be redirected to the corresponding mounted file systems via the mount table. Essentially, the vnode structures, complemented by the mount table, provide a pointer for every file to its parent file system, as well as to the file system over which it is mounted.

The VFS activates file-system–specific operations to handle local requests according to their file-system types, and calls the NFS protocol procedures for remote requests. File handles are constructed from the relevant vnodes and are passed as arguments to these procedures. The layer implementing the NFS protocol is the bottom layer of the architecture and is called the NFS service layer.

As an illustration of the architecture, let us trace how an operation on an already-open remote file is handled (follow the example on Figure 17.6). The client initiates the operation by a regular system call. The operating-system layer maps this call to a VFS operation on the appropriate vnode. The VFS layer identifies the file as a remote one and invokes the appropriate NFS procedure. An RPC call is made to the NFS service layer at the remote server. This call is reinjected to the VFS layer on the remote system, which finds that it is local and invokes the appropriate file-system operation. This path is retraced to return the result. An advantage of this architecture is that the client and the server are identical; thus, a machine may be a client, or a server, or both.

The actual service on each server is performed by several kernel processes that provide a temporary substitute to a lightweight process (threads) facility.

17.6.2.5 Path-Name Translation

We do path-name translation by breaking the path into component names and performing a separate NFS *lookup* call for every pair of component name and directory vnode. Once a mount point is crossed, every component lookup causes a separate RPC to the server (see Figure 17.7). This expensive path-name–traversal scheme is needed, since each client has a unique layout of its logical name space, dictated by the mounts it performed. It would have been much more efficient to hand a server a path name and to receive a target vnode once a mount point was encountered. At any point, however, there can be another mount point for the particular client of which the stateless server is unaware.

So that lookup is faster, a directory name lookup cache on the client's side holds the vnodes for remote directory names. This cache speeds up references to files with the same initial path name. The directory cache is discarded when attributes returned from the server do not match the attributes of the cached vnode.

Recall that mounting a remote file system on top of another already-mounted remote file system (cascading mount) is allowed in NFS. However,

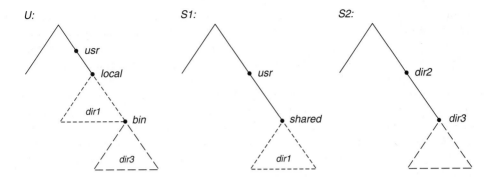

Figure 17.7   Path-name translation.

a server cannot act as an intermediary between a client and another server. Instead, a client must establish a direct server–client connection with the second server by directly mounting the desired directory. When a client has a cascading mount, more than one server can be involved in a path-name traversal. However, each component lookup is performed between the original client and some server. Therefore, when a client does a lookup on a directory on which the server has mounted a file system, the client sees the underlying directory, instead of the mounted directory.

17.6.2.6 Remote Operations

With the exception of opening and closing files, there is almost one-to-one correspondence between the regular UNIX system calls for file operations and the NFS protocol RPCs. Thus, a remote file operation can be translated directly to the corresponding RPC. Conceptually, NFS adheres to the remote-service paradigm, but in practice buffering and caching techniques are employed for the sake of performance. There is no direct correspondence between a remote operation and an RPC. Instead, file blocks and file attributes are fetched by the RPCs and are cached locally. Future remote operations use the cached data, subject to consistency constraints.

There are two caches: file-blocks cache and file-attribute (inode-information) cache. On a file open, the kernel checks with the remote server whether to fetch or revalidate the cached attributes. The cached file blocks are used only if the corresponding cached attributes are up to date. The attribute cache is updated whenever new attributes arrive from the server. Cached attributes are (by default) discarded after 60 seconds. Both read-ahead and delayed-write techniques are used between the server and the client. Clients do not free delayed-write blocks until the server confirms that the data have been written to disk. In contrast to the system used in Sprite, delayed-write is retained even when a file is opened concurrently, in conflicting modes. Hence, UNIX semantics are not preserved.

Tuning the system for performance makes it difficult to characterize the consistency semantics of NFS. New files created on a machine may not be visible elsewhere for 30 seconds. It is indeterminate whether writes to a file at one site are visible to other sites that have this file open for reading. New opens of that file observe only the changes that have already been flushed to the server. Thus, NFS provides neither strict emulation of UNIX semantics, nor the session semantics of Andrew.   In spite of these drawbacks, the utility and high performance of the mechanism makes it the most widely used, multivendor distributed system in operation.

17.6.3 Andrew

Andrew is a distributed computing environment that has been under development since 1983 at Carnegie Mellon University. As such, it is one of the newest DFSs. The Andrew file system (AFS) constitutes the underlying information-sharing mechanism among clients of the environment. A commercial implementation of AFS, known as DFS, is part of the DCE distributed computing environment from the OSF organization. Many UNIX vendors, as well as Microsoft, have announced support for this system.   One of the most formidable attributes of Andrew is scalability: The Andrew system is targeted to span over 5000 workstations.

17.6.3.1 Overview

Andrew distinguishes between *client machines* (sometimes referred to as workstations) and dedicated *server machines*. Servers and clients alike run the 4.2BSD UNIX operating system and are interconnected by an internet of LANs.

Clients are presented with a partitioned space of file names: a *local name space* and a *shared name space*. Dedicated servers, collectively called *Vice*, after the name of the software they run, present the shared name space to the clients as a homogeneous, identical, and location transparent file hierarchy. The local name space is the root file system of a workstation, from which the shared name space descends. Workstations run the *Virtue* protocol to communicate with Vice, and are required to have local disks where they store their local name space. Servers collectively are responsible for the storage and management of the shared name space. The local name space is small, is distinct for each workstation, and contains system programs essential for autonomous operation and better performance. Also local are temporary files and files that the workstation owner, for privacy reasons, explicitly wants to store locally.

Viewed at a finer granularity, clients and servers are structured in clusters interconnected by a WAN. Each cluster consists of a collection of workstations on a LAN, and a representative of Vice called a *cluster server*, and is connected to the WAN by a *router*. The decomposition into clusters is done primarily to address the problem of scale. For optimal performance, workstations should use the server on their own cluster most of the time, thereby making cross-cluster file references relatively infrequent.

The file-system architecture was based on consideration of scale, too. The basic heuristic was to offload work from the servers to the clients, in light of experience indicating that server CPU speed is the system's bottleneck. Following this heuristic, the key mechanism selected for remote file operations is to cache files in large chunks (64K). This feature reduces file-open latency, and allows reads and writes to be directed to the cached copy without frequently involving the servers.

There are additional issues in Andrew's design that we shall not discuss here; briefly, they are these:

- **Client mobility:** Clients are able to access any file in the shared name space from any workstation. The only effect clients may notice when accessing files from other than their usual workstations is some initial performance degradation due to the caching of files.

- **Security:** The Vice interface is considered as the boundary of trustworthiness, because no client programs are executed on Vice machines. Authentication and secure-transmission functions are provided as part of a connection-based communication package, based on the RPC paradigm. After mutual authentication, a Vice server and a client communicate via encrypted messages. Encryption is performed by hardware devices or (more slowly) in software. Information about clients and groups is stored in a protection database that is replicated at each server.

- **Protection:** Andrew provides *access lists* for protecting directories and the regular UNIX bits for file protection. The access list may contain information about those users that are allowed to access a directory, as well as information about those users that are *not* allowed to access a directory. Thus, with this scheme, it is simple to specify that everyone except, say, Jim can access a directory. Andrew supports the access types read, write, lookup, insert, administer, lock, and delete.

- **Heterogeneity:** Defining a clear interface to Vice is a key for integration of diverse workstation hardware and operating system. So that heterogeneity is facilitated, some files in the local */bin* directory are symbolic links pointing to machine-specific executable files residing in Vice.

17.6.3.2 The Shared Name Space

Andrew's shared name space is constituted of component units called *volumes.* Andrew's volumes are unusually small component units. Typically, they are associated with the files of a single client. Few volumes reside within a single disk partition, and they may grow (up to a quota) and shrink in size. Conceptually, volumes are glued together by a mechanism similar to the UNIX mount mechanism. However, the granularity difference is significant, since in UNIX only an entire disk partition (containing a file system) can be mounted. Volumes are a key administrative unit and play a vital role in identifying and locating an individual file.

A Vice file or directory is identified by a low-level identifier called a *fid.* Each Andrew directory entry maps a path-name component to a fid. A fid is 96 bits long and has three equal-length components: a *volume number*, a *vnode number*, and a *uniquifier.* The vnode number is used as an index into an array containing the inodes of files in a single volume. The uniquifier allows reuse of vnode numbers, thereby keeping certain data structures compact. Fids are location transparent; therefore, file movements from server to server do not invalidate cached directory contents.

Location information is kept on a volume basis in a *volume-location database* replicated on each server. A client can identify the location of every volume in the system by querying this database. It is the aggregation of files into volumes that makes it possible to keep the location database at a manageable size.

To balance the available disk space and utilization of servers, volumes need to be migrated among disk partitions and servers. When a volume is shipped to its new location, its original server is left with temporary forwarding information, so that the location database does not need to be updated synchronously. While the volume is being transferred, the original server still can handle updates, which are shipped later to the new server. At some point, the volume is briefly disabled so that the recent modifications can be processed; then, the new volume becomes available again at the new site. The volume-movement operation is atomic; if either server crashes, the operation is aborted.

Read-only replication at the granularity of an entire volume is supported for system-executable files and for seldom-updated files in the upper levels of the Vice name space. The volume-location database specifies the server containing the only read−write copy of a volume and a list of read-only replication sites.

17.6.3.3 File Operations and Consistency Semantics

The fundamental architectural principle in Andrew is the caching of entire files from servers. Accordingly, a client workstation interacts with Vice servers only during opening and closing of files, and even this interaction is not always necessary. No remote interaction is caused by reading or writing files (in contrast to the remote-service method). This key distinction has far-reaching ramifications for performance, as well as for semantics of file operations.

The operating system on each workstation intercepts file-system calls and forwards them to a client-level process on that workstation. This process, called *Venus*, caches files from Vice when they are opened, and stores modified copies of files back on the servers from which they came when they are closed. Venus may contact Vice only when a file is opened or closed; reading and writing of individual bytes of a file are performed directly on the cached copy and bypass Venus. As a result, writes at some sites are not visible immediately at other sites.

Caching is further exploited for future opens of the cached file. Venus assumes that cached entries (files or directories) are valid unless notified otherwise. Therefore, Venus does not need to contact Vice on a file open to validate the cached copy. The mechanism to support this policy, called *callback*, dramatically reduces the number of cache-validation requests received by servers. It works as follows. When a client caches a file or a directory, the server updates its state information recording this caching. We say that the client has a callback on that file. The server notifies the client before allowing a modification to the file by another client. In such a case, we say that the server removes the callback on the file for the former client. A client can use a cached file for open purposes only when the file has a callback. If a client closes a file after modifying it, all other clients caching this file lose their callbacks. Therefore, when these clients open the file later, they have to get the new version from the server.

Reading and writing bytes of a file are done directly by the kernel without Venus intervention on the cached copy. Venus regains control when the file is closed and, if the file has been modified locally, Venus updates the file on the appropriate server. Thus, the only occasions in which Venus contacts Vice servers are on opens of files that either are not in the cache or have had their callback revoked, and on closes of locally modified files.

Basically, Andrew implements session semantics. The only exceptions are file operations other than the primitive read and write (such as protection changes at the directory level), which are visible everywhere on the network immediately after the operation completes.

In spite of the callback mechanism, a small amount of cached validation traffic is still present, usually to replace callbacks lost because of machine or network failures. When a workstation is rebooted, Venus considers all cached files and directories suspect, and generates a cache-validation request for the first use of each such entry.

The callback mechanism forces each server to maintain callback information and each client to maintain validity information. If the amount of callback information maintained by a server is excessive, the server can break callbacks and reclaim some storage by unilaterally notifying clients and revoking the validity of their cached files. There is a potential for inconsistency if the callback state maintained by Venus gets out of sync with the corresponding state maintained by the servers.

Venus also caches contents of directories and symbolic links, for path-name translation. Each component in the path name is fetched, and a callback is established for it if it is not already cached, or if the client does not have a callback on it. Lookups are done locally by Venus on the fetched directories using fids. There is no forwarding of requests from one server to another. At the end of a path-name traversal, all the intermediate directories and the target file are in the cache with callbacks on them. Future open calls to this file will involve no network communication at all, unless a callback is broken on a component of the path name.

The only exceptions to the caching policy are modifications to directories that are made directly on the server responsible for that directory for reasons of integrity. There are well-defined operations in the Vice interface for such purposes. Venus reflects the changes in its cached copy to avoid refetching the directory.

17.6.3.4 Implementation

Client processes are interfaced to a UNIX kernel with the usual set of system calls. The kernel is modified slightly to detect references to Vice files in the relevant operations and to forward the requests to the client-level Venus process at the workstation.

Venus carries out path-name translation component by component, as was described above. It has a mapping cache that associates volumes to server locations in order to avoid server interrogation for an already-known volume location. If a volume is not present in this cache, Venus contacts any server to which it already has a connection, requests the location information, and enters that information into the mapping cache. Unless Venus already has a connection to the server, it establishes a new connection. It then uses this connection to fetch the file or directory. Connection establishment is needed for authentication and security purposes. When a target file is found and cached, a copy is created on the local disk. Venus then returns to the kernel, which opens the cached copy and returns its handle to the client process.

The UNIX file system is used as a low-level storage system for both servers and clients. The client cache is a local directory on the workstation's disk. Within this directory are files whose names are placeholders for cache entries. Both Venus and server processes access UNIX files directly by the latter's inodes to avoid the expensive path-name−to-inode translation routine (*namei*). Because the internal inode interface is not visible to client-level processes (both Venus and server processes are client-level processes), an appropriate set of additional system calls was added.

Venus manages two separate caches: one for status and the other for data. It uses a simple least recently used (LRU) algorithm to keep each of them bounded in size. When a file is flushed from the cache, Venus notifies the appropriate server to remove the callback for this file. The status cache is kept in virtual memory to allow rapid servicing of **stat** (file status returning) system calls. The data cache is resident on the local disk, but the UNIX I/O buffering mechanism does some caching of disk blocks in memory that is transparent to Venus.

A single client-level process on each file server services all file requests from clients. This process uses a lightweight-process package with nonpreemptable scheduling to service many client requests concurrently. The RPC package is integrated with the lightweight-process package, thereby allowing the file server to be concurrently making or servicing one RPC per lightweight process. RPC is built on top of a low-level datagram abstraction. Whole file transfer is implemented as a side effect of these RPC calls. There is one RPC connection per client, but there is no a priori binding of lightweight processes to these connections. Instead, a pool of lightweight processes services client requests on all connections. The use of a single multithreaded server process allows the caching of data structures needed to service requests. On the other hand, a crash of a single server process has the disastrous effect of paralyzing this particular server.

17.6.4 Sprite

Sprite is an experimental distributed operating system under development at the University of California at Berkeley. Its main research thrusts have been in the areas of network file systems, process migration, and high-performance file systems. Sprite runs on Sun and DEC workstations and is used for day-to-day computing by a few dozen students, faculty, and staff.

17.6.4.1 Overview

Sprite designers envision the next generation of workstations as powerful machines with vast physical memory. The configuration for which Sprite is targeted is large and fast disks concentrated on a few server machines servicing the storage needs of hundreds of diskless workstations. The workstations are interconnected by several LANs. Because file caching is used, the large physical memories will compensate for the lack of local disks.

The interface that Sprite provides in general, and to the file system in particular, is much like the one provided by UNIX. The file system appears as a single UNIX tree encompassing all files and devices in the network, making them equally and transparently accessible from every workstation. The location transparency in Sprite is complete; there is no way to discern a file's network location from that file's name.

Unlike NFS, Sprite enforces consistency of shared files. Each **read** system call is guaranteed to return the most up-to-date data for a file, even if it is being opened concurrently by several remote processes. Thus, Sprite emulates a single time-sharing UNIX system in a distributed environment.

A unique feature of the Sprite file system is its interplay with the virtual-memory system. Most versions of UNIX use a special disk partition as a swapping area for virtual-memory purposes. In contrast, Sprite uses ordinary files, called *backing files,* to store the data and stacks of running processes. The basis for this design is that it simplifies process migration and enables flexibility and sharing of the space allocated for swapping. Backing files are cached in the main memories of servers, just like any other file. The designers claim that clients should be able to read random pages from server's (physical) cache faster than they can from local disks, which means that a server with a large cache may provide better paging performance than will local disk.

The virtual memory and file system share the same cache and negotiate on how to divide it according to their conflicting needs. Sprite allows the file cache on each machine to grow and shrink in response to changing demands of the machine's virtual memory and file system. This scheme is similar to Apollo's Domain operating system, which has a dynamically sized swap space.

We briefly mention a few other features of Sprite. In contrast to UNIX, where only code can be shared among processes, Sprite provides a mechanism for sharing an address space between client processes on a single workstation. A process-migration facility, which is transparent to clients as well as to the migrated process, is also provided.

17.6.4.2 Prefix Tables

Sprite presents its client with a single file-system hierarchy. The hierarchy is composed of several subtrees called *domains* (the Sprite term for component units), with each server providing storage for one or more domains. Each machine maintains a server map called a *prefix table,* whose function is to map domains to servers. The mapping is built and updated dynamically by a broadcast protocol that places a message on the network for all other network members to read. We first describe how the tables are used during name lookups, and later describe how the tables change dynamically.

Each entry in a prefix table corresponds to one of the domains. It contains the name of the topmost directory in the domain (called the prefix for the domain), the network address of the server storing the domain, and a numeric designator identifying the domain's root directory for the storing server. Typically, this designator is an index into the server table of open files; it saves repeating expensive name translation.

Every lookup operation for an absolute path name starts with the client searching its prefix table for the longest prefix matching the given file name. The client strips the matching prefix from the file name and sends the remainder of the name to the selected server along with the designator from the prefix-table entry. The server uses this designator to locate the root directory of the domain, and then proceeds by usual UNIX path-name translation for the remainder of the file name. If the server succeeds in completing the translation, it replies with a designator for the open file.

There are several cases where the server does not complete the lookup operation:

- When the server encounters an absolute path name in a symbolic link, it immediately returns to the client the absolute path name. The client looks up the new name in its prefix table and initiates another lookup with a new server.

- A path name can ascend past the root of a domain (because of a parent ".." component). In such a case, the server returns the remainder of the path name to the client. The latter combines the remainder with the prefix of the domain that was just exited to form a new absolute path name.

- A path name can also descend into a new domain. This descent can happen when an entry for a domain is absent from the table, and as a result the prefix of the domain above the missing domain is the longest matching prefix. The selected server cannot complete the path-name traversal, since the latter descends outside its domain. Alternatively, when a root of a domain is beneath a working directory and a file in that domain is referred to with a relative path name, the server also cannot complete the translation. The solution to these situations is to place a marker to indicate domain boundaries (a mount point, in NFS terms). The marker is a special kind of file called a *remote link*. Similar to a symbolic link, its content is a file name — its own name in this case. When a server encounters a remote link, it returns the file name to the client.

Relative path names are treated much as they are in conventional UNIX. When a process specifies a new working directory, the prefix mechanism is used to open the working directory and both its server address and designator are saved in the process's state. When a lookup operation detects a relative path name, it sends the path name directly to the server for the current working directory, along with the directory's designator. Hence, from the server's point of view, there is no difference between relative and absolute name lookups.

So far, the key difference from mappings based on the UNIX mount mechanism was the initial step of matching the file name against the prefix table, instead of looking it up component by component. Systems (such as NFS and conventional UNIX) that employ a name-lookup cache create a similar effect of avoiding the component-by-component lookup once the cache holds the appropriate information.

Prefix tables are a unique mechanism mainly because of the way they evolve and change. When a remote link is encountered by the server, this indicates to the server that the client lacks an entry for a domain — the domain whose remote link was encountered. To obtain the missing prefix information, the client must broadcast a file name. A *broadcast* is a network message that is seen by all the computer systems on the network. The server storing that file responds with the prefix-table entry for this file, including the string to use as a prefix, the server's address, and the descriptor corresponding to the domain's root. The client then can fill in the details in its prefix table.

Initially, each client starts with an empty prefix table. The broadcast protocol is invoked to find the entry for the root domain. More entries are added gradually as needed; a domain that has never been accessed will not appear in the table.

The server locations kept in the prefix table are hints that are corrected when found to be wrong. Hence, if a client tries to open a file and gets no response from the server, it invalidates the prefix-table entry and attempts a broadcast query. If the server has become available again, it responds to the broadcast and the prefix-table entry is reestablished. This same mechanism also works if the server reboots at a different network address, or if its domains are moved to other servers.

The prefix mechanism ensures that, whenever a server storing a domain is functioning, the domain's files can be opened and accessed from any machine regardless of the status of the servers of domains above the particular domain. Essentially, the built-in broadcast protocol enables dynamic configuration and a certain degree of robustness. Also, when a prefix for a domain exists in a client's table, a direct client–server connection is established as soon as the client attempts to open a file in that domain (in contrast to path-name traversal schemes).

A machine with a local disk that wishes to keep private some local files can place an entry for the private domain in its prefix table and refuse to respond to broadcast queries about that domain. One of the uses of this provision can be for the directory *usr/tmp*, which holds temporary files generated by many UNIX programs. Every workstation needs access to *usr/tmp*. But workstations with local disks would probably prefer to use their own disk for the temporary space. Recall that the designers of Sprite expect reads from a server cache to be faster than those from a local disk, but do not predict this relationship for writes. They can set up their *usr/tmp* domains for private use, with a network file server providing a public version of the domain for diskless clients. All broadcast queries for */usr/tmp* would be handled by the public server.

A primitive form of read-only replication can also be provided. It can be arranged that servers storing a replicated domain give different clients different prefix entries (standing for different replicas) for the same domain. The same technique can be used for sharing binary files by different hardware types of machines.

Since the prefix tables bypass part of the directory-lookup mechanism, the permission checking done during lookup is bypassed too. The effect is that all programs implicitly have search permission along all the paths denoting prefixes of domains. If access to a domain is to be restricted, it must be restricted at or below the root of the domain.

17.6.4.3 Caching and Consistency

An important aspect of the Sprite file-system design is the extent of the use of caching techniques. Capitalizing on the large main memories and advocating diskless workstations, file caches are stored in memory, instead of on local disks (as in Andrew). Caching is used by both client and server workstations. The caches are organized on a block basis, rather than on a file basis (as in Andrew). The size of the blocks is currently 4K. Each block in the cache is virtually addressed by the file designator and a block location within the file. Using virtual addresses instead of physical disk addresses enables clients to create new blocks in the cache and to locate any block without the file inode being brought from the server.

When a read kernel call is invoked to read a block of a file, the kernel first checks its cache and returns the information from the cache, if it is present. If the block is not in the cache, the kernel reads it from disk (if the file is locally stored), or requests it from the server; in either case, the block is added to the cache, replacing the least recently used block. If the block is requested from the server, the server checks its own cache before issuing a disk I/O request, and adds the block to its cache, if the block was not already there. Currently, Sprite does not use read-ahead to speed up sequential read (in contrast to NFS).

A delayed-write approach is used to handle file modification. When an application issues a write kernel call, the kernel simply writes the block into its cache and returns to the application. The block is not written through to the server's cache or the disk until it is ejected from the cache, or 30 seconds have elapsed since the block was last modified. Hence, a block written on a client machine will be written to the server's cache in at most 30 seconds, and will be written to the server's disk after an additional 30 seconds. This policy results in better performance in exchange for the possibility of recent changes being lost in a crash.

Sprite employs a version-number scheme to enforce consistency of shared files. The version number of a file is incremented whenever a file is opened in write mode. When a client opens a file, it obtains from the server the file's current version number, which the client compares to the version number associated with the cached blocks for that file. If they are different, the client discards all cached blocks for the file and reloads its cache from the server when the blocks are needed. Because of the delayed-write policy, the server does not always have the current file data. Servers handle this situation by keeping track of the last writer for each file. When a client other than the last writer opens the file, the server forces the last writer to write back all its modified data blocks to the server's cache.

When a server detects (during an open operation) that a file is open on two or more workstations and that at least one of them is writing the file, it disables client caching for that file. All subsequent reads and writes go through the server, which serializes the accesses. Caching is disabled on a file basis, resulting in only clients with open files being affected. Obviously, a substantial degradation of performance occurs when caching is disabled. A noncachable file becomes cachable again when it has been closed by all clients. A file may be cached simultaneously by several active readers.

This approach depends on the server being notified whenever a file is opened or closed. This notification requirement prohibits performance optimizations such as name caching in which clients open files without contacting the file servers. Essentially, the servers are used as centralized control points for cache consistency. To fulfill this function, they must maintain state information about open files.

17.6.5 Locus

Locus is a project at the University of California at Los Angeles to build a full-scale distributed operating system. The system is upward-compatible with UNIX, but unlike those in NFS, UNIX United, and other UNIX-based distributed systems, the extensions are major and necessitate an entirely new kernel, rather than a modified one.

17.6.5.1 Overview

The Locus file system presents to clients and applications a single tree-structure naming hierarchy. This structure covers all objects (files, directories, executable files, and devices) of all the machines in the system. Locus names are fully transparent; it is not possible to discern from a name of an object the object's location in the network. To a first approximation, there is almost no way to distinguish the Locus name structure from a standard UNIX tree.

A Locus file may correspond to a set of copies distributed on different sites. An additional transparency dimension is introduced since it is the system's responsibility to keep all copies up to date and to ensure that access requests are served by the most recent available version. Clients may have control over both the number and location of replicated files. Conversely, clients may prefer to be totally unaware of the replication scheme. In Locus, file replication serves mainly to increase availability for reading purposes in the event of failures and partitions. A primary-copy approach is adopted for modifications.

Locus adheres to the same file-access semantics with which standard UNIX presents clients. Locus provides these semantics in the distributed and replicated environment in which it operates. Alternate mechanisms of advisory and enforced locking of files and parts of files are also offered. Moreover, atomic updates of files are supported by **commit** and **abort** system calls.

Operation during failures and network partitions is emphasized in Locus' design. As long as a copy of a file is available, read requests can be served, and it is still guaranteed that the version read is the most recent available one. Automatic mechanisms update stale copies of files at the time of the merge of the latter's storage site to a partition.

Emphasis on high performance in the design of Locus led to the incorporation of networking functions (such as formatting, queuing, transmitting, and retransmitting messages) into the operating system. Specialized remote-operations protocols were devised for kernel-to-kernel communication, in contrast to the prevalent approach of using the RPC protocol, or some other existing protocol. The reduction of the number of network layers has achieved high performance for remote operations. On the other hand, this specialized protocol hampers the portability of Locus to different networks and file systems.

An efficient but limited process facility called *server processes* (lightweight processes) was created for serving remote requests. These processes have no nonprivileged address space. All their code and stacks are resident in the operating-system nucleus; they can call internal system routines directly, and can share some data. These processes are assigned to serve network requests that accumulate in a system queue. The system is configured with some number of these processes, but that number is automatically and dynamically altered during system operation.

17.6.5.2 The Name Structure

The logical name structure disguises both location and replication details from clients and applications. In effect, logical filegroups are joined together to form this unified structure. Physically, a logical filegroup is mapped to multiple *physical containers* (called also *packs*) that reside at various sites and that store replicas of the files of that filegroup. The pair <logical-filegroup-number, inode number>, which is referred to as a file's *designator*, serves as a globally unique low-level name for a file. Observe that the designator itself hides both location and replication details.

Each site has a consistent and complete view of the logical name structure. A logical mount table is replicated globally and contains an entry for each logical filegroup. An entry records the file designator of the directory over which the filegroup is logically mounted, and indication of which site is currently responsible for access synchronization within the filegroup. We shall explain the function of this site later in this section. In addition, each site that stores a copy of the directory over which a subtree is mounted must keep that directory's inode in memory with an indication that it is mounted over. Keeping the inode in memory is done so that any access from any site to that directory will be caught, allowing the standard UNIX mount indirection to function (via the logical mount table, Section 11.1.2). A protocol, implemented within the **mount** and **unmount** Locus system calls, performs update of the logical mount tables on all sites, when necessary.

On the physical level, physical containers correspond to disk partitions and are assigned pack numbers that, together with a logical filegroup number, identify an individual pack. One of the packs is designated as the *primary copy*. A file must be stored at the site of the primary copy, and in addition can be stored at any subset of the other sites where there exists a pack corresponding to its filegroup. Thus, the primary copy stores the filegroup completely, whereas the rest of the packs might be partial.

Replication is especially useful for directories in the high levels of the name hierarchy. Such directories exhibit mostly read-only characteristics and are crucial for path-name translation of most files.

The various copies of a file are assigned the same inode number on all the filegroup's packs. Consequently, a pack has an empty inode slot for all files that it does not store. Data-page numbers may be different on different packs; hence, reference over the network to data pages use logical page numbers rather than physical ones. Each pack has a mapping of these logical numbers to its physical numbers. So that automatic replication management will be facilitated, each inode of a file copy contains a version number, determining which copy dominates other copies.

Each site has a container table, which maps logical filegroup numbers to disk locations for the filegroups that have packs locally on this site. When requests for accesses to files stored locally arrive at a site, the system consults this table to map the file designator to a local disk address.

Although globally unique file naming is important most of the time, there are certain files and directories that are hardware and site specific (that is, */bin*, which is hardware specific, and */dev*, which is site specific). Locus provides transparent means for translating references to these traditional file names to hardware- and site-specific files.

17.6.5.3 File Operations

Locus' approach to file operations is certainly a departure from the prevalent client–server model. Providing replicated files with synchronous access necessitates an additional function. Locus distinguishes three logical roles in file accesses, each one potentially performed by a different site:

- **Using site (US):** The US issues the requests to open and access a remote file.

- **Storage site (SS):** The SS is the site selected to serve the requests.

- **Current synchronization site (CSS):** The CSS enforces global synchronization policy for a filegroup, and selects an SS for each open request referring to a file in the filegroup. There is at most one CSS for each filegroup in any set of communicating sites (that is, a partition). The CSS maintains the version number and a list of physical containers for every file in the filegroup.

We now describe the open, read, write, close, commit, and abort operations, as they are carried out by the US, SS, and CSS entities. Related synchronization issues are described separately in the next subsection.

Opening a file commences as follows. The US determines the relevant CSS by looking up the filegroup in the logical mount table, and then forwards the open request to the CSS. The CSS polls potential SSs for that file to decide which one of them will act as the real SS. In its polling messages, the CSS includes the version number for the particular file, so that the potential SS can, by comparing this number to their own, decide whether or not their copy is up to date. The CSS selects an SS by considering the responses it received from the candidate sites, and sends the selected SS identity to the US. Both the CSS and the SS allocate in-core inode structures for the opened file. The CSS needs this information to make future synchronization decisions, and the SS maintains the inode to serve forthcoming accesses efficiently.

After a file is open, read requests are sent directly to the SS without the CSS intervention. A read request contains the designator of the file, the logical number of the needed page within that file, and a guess as to where the in-core inode is stored in the SS. Once the inode is found, the SS translates the logical page number to a physical number, and a standard low-level routine is called to allocate a buffer and to obtain the appropriate page from disk. The buffer is queued on the network queue for transmission as a response to the US, where it is stored in a kernel buffer. Once a page is fetched to the US, further **read** calls are serviced from the kernel buffer. As in the case of local disk reads, read-ahead is useful to speed up sequential reads, at both the US and the SS.

If a process loses its connection with a file that it is reading remotely, the system attempts to reopen a different copy of the same version of the file.

Translating a path name into a file designator proceeds by a seemingly conventional path-name traversal mechanism, since path names are regular UNIX path names, with no exceptions (unlike UNIX United). Every lookup of a component of the path name within a directory involves opening the directory and reading from it. Observe that there is no parallel to NFS's remote lookup operation, and that the actual directory searching is performed by the client, rather than by the server.

A directory opened for path-name searching is open not for normal read, but instead for an internal unsynchronized read. The distinction is that no global synchronization is needed, and no locking is done while the reading is performed; that is, updates to the directory can occur while the search is ongoing. When the directory is local, the CSS is not even informed of such access.

In Locus, a primary-copy policy is employed for file modification. The CSS has to select the primary-copy pack site as the SS for an open for a write. The act of modifying data takes on two forms. If the modification does not include the entire page, the old page is read from the SS using the read protocol. If the change involves the entire page, a buffer is set up at the US without any reads. In either case, after changes are made, possibly by delayed-write, the page is sent back to the SS. All modified pages must be flushed to the SS before a modified file can be closed.

If a file is closed by the last client process at a US, the SS and CSS must be informed so that they can deallocate in-core inode structures, and so that the CSS can alter state data that might affect its next synchronization decision.

Commit and abort system calls are provided, and closing a file commits it. If a file is open for modification by more than one process, the changes are not made permanent until one of the processes issues a commit system call or until all the processes close the file.

When a file is modified, shadow pages are allocated at the SS. The in-core copy of the disk inode is updated to point to these new shadow pages. The disk inode is kept intact, pointing to the original pages. The atomic commit operation consists of replacing the disk inode with the in-core inode. After that point, the file contains the new information. To abort a set of changes, we merely discard the in-core inode information and free up the disk space used to record the changes. The US function never deals with actual disk pages, but rather deals with logical pages. Thus, the entire shadow-page mechanism is implemented at the SS and is transparent to the US.

Locus deals with file modification by first committing the change to the primary copy. Later, messages are sent to all other SSs of the modified file, as well as to the CSS. At minimum, these messages identify the modified file and contain the new version number (to prevent attempts to read the old versions). At this point, it is the responsibility of these additional SSs to bring their files up to date by propagating the entire file or just the changes. A queue of propagation requests is kept within the kernel at each site, and a kernel process services the queue efficiently by issuing appropriate read requests. This propagation procedure uses the standard commit mechanism. Thus, if contact with the file containing the newer version is lost, the local file is left with a coherent copy, albeit one still out of date.

Given this commit mechanism, we are always left with either the original file or a completely changed file, but never with a partially made change, even in the face of site failures.

17.6.5.4 Synchronized Accesses to Files

Locus tries to emulate conventional UNIX semantics on file accesses in a distributed environment. In standard UNIX, multiple processes are permitted to have the same file open concurrently. These processes issue **read** and **write** system calls, and the system guarantees that each successive operation sees the effects of the ones that precede it. We can implement this scheme fairly easily by having the processes share the same operating-system data structures and caches, and by using locks on data structures to serialize requests. Since remote tasking is supported in Locus, such situations can arise when the sharing processes do not co-reside on the same machine and hence complicate the implementation significantly.

There are two sharing modes to consider. First, in UNIX, several processes descending from the same ancestor process can share the same current position (offset) in a file. A single token scheme is devised to preserve this special mode of sharing. A site can proceed to execute system calls that need the offset only when the token is present.

Second, in UNIX, the same in-core inode for a file can be shared by several processes. In Locus, the situation is much more complicated, since the inode of the file can be cached at several sites. Also, data pages are cached at multiple sites. A multiple-data-tokens scheme is used to synchronize sharing of the file's inode and data. A single exclusive-writer, multiple-readers policy is enforced. Only a site with the write token for a file may modify the file, and any site with a read token can read the file. Both token schemes are coordinated by token managers operating at the corresponding storage sites.

The cached data pages are guaranteed to contain valid data only when the file's data token is present. When the write data token is taken from that site, the inode is copied back to the SS, as are all modified pages. Since arbitrary changes may have occurred to the file when the token was not present, all cached buffers are invalidated when the token is released. When a data token is granted to a site, both the inode and data pages need to be fetched from the SS. There are some exceptions to this policy. Some attribute reading and writing calls (for example, **stat**), as well as directory reading and modifying (for example, **lookup**) calls are not subject to the synchronization constraints. These calls are sent directly to the SS, where the changes are made, committed, and propagated to all storage and using sites.

This mechanism guarantees consistency; each access sees the most recent data. A different issue regarding access synchronization is serializability of accesses. To this end, Locus offers facilities for locking entire files or parts of them. Locking can be advisory (checked only as a result of a locking attempt), or enforced (checked on all reads and writes). A process can choose either to fail if it cannot immediately get a lock, or to wait for the lock to be released.

17.6.5.5 Operation in a Faulty Environment

The basic approach in Locus is to maintain, within a single partition, strict synchronization among copies of a file, so that all clients of that file within that partition see the most recent version.

The primary-copy approach eliminates the possibility of conflicting updates, since the primary copy must be in the client's partition to allow an update. However, the problem of detecting updates and propagating them to all the copies remains, especially since updates are allowed in a partitioned network. During normal operation, the commit protocol ascertains proper detection and propagation of updates, as was described in the last subsection. However, a more elaborate scheme has to be employed by recovering sites that wish to bring their packs up to date. To this end, the system maintains a *commit count* for each filegroup, enumerating each commit of every file in the filegroup. Each pack has a *lower-water mark (LWM)* that is a commit-count value, up to which the system guarantees that all prior commits are reflected in the pack. Also, the primary copy pack keeps a complete list of all the recent commits in secondary storage. When a pack joins a partition, it contacts the primary copy site, and checks whether its LWM is within the recent commit-list bounds. If it is, the pack site schedules a kernel process, which brings the pack to a consistent state by performing the missing updates. If the primary pack is not available, writing is disallowed in this partition, but reading is possible after a new CSS is chosen. The new CSS communicates with the partition members so that it will be informed of the most recent available (in the partition) version of each file in the filegroup. Once the new CSS accomplishes this objective, other pack sites can reconcile themselves with it. As a result, all communicating sites see the same view of the filegroup, and this view is as complete as possible, given a particular partition. Note that, since updates are allowed within the partition with the primary copy, and reads are allowed in the rest of the partitions, it is possible to read out-of-date replicas of a file. Thus, Locus sacrifices consistency for the ability to continue and both to update and to read files in a partitioned environment.

When a pack is too far out of date (that is, its LWM indicates a value prior to the earliest commit-count value in the primary-copy commit list), the system invokes an application-level process to bring the filegroup up to date. At this point, the system lacks sufficient knowledge of the most recent commits to redo the changes. Instead, the site must inspect the entire inode space to determine which files in its pack are out of date.

When a site is lost from an operational Locus network, a clean-up procedure is necessary. Essentially, once a site has decided that a particular site is unavailable, it must invoke failure handling for all the resources that the processes were using at that site. This substantial cleaning procedure is the penalty of the state information kept by all three sites participating in file access.

Since directory updates are not restricted to being applied to the primary copy, conflicts among updates in different partitions may arise. However, because of the simple nature of directory-entry modification, an automatic reconciliation procedure is devised. This procedure is based on comparing the inodes and string-name pairs of replicas of the same directory. The most extreme action taken is when the same name string corresponds to two different inodes. The file's name is altered slightly, and the file's owner is notified by electronic mail.

17.7 ■ Summary

A DFS is a file-service system whose clients, servers, and storage devices are dispersed among the various sites of a distributed system. Accordingly, service activity has to be carried out across the network; instead of a single centralized data repository, there are multiple and independent storage devices.

Ideally, a DFS should look to its clients like a conventional, centralized file system. The multiplicity and dispersion of its servers and storage devices should be made transparent. That is, the client interface of a DFS should not distinguish between local and remote files. It is up to the DFS to locate the files and to arrange for the transport of the data. A transparent DFS facilitates client mobility by bringing over the client's environment to the site where a client logs in.

There are several approaches to naming schemes in a DFS. In the simplest approach, files are named by some combination of their host name and local name, which guarantees a unique systemwide name. Another approach, popularized by NFS, provides means to attach remote directories to local directories, thus giving the appearance of a coherent directory tree.

Requests to access a remote file are usually handled by two complementary methods. With remote service, requests for accesses are delivered to the server. The server machine performs the accesses, and their results are forwarded back to the client. With *caching*, if the data needed to satisfy the access request are not already cached, then a copy of those data is brought from the server to the client. Accesses are performed on the cached copy. The idea is to retain recently accessed disk blocks in the cache, so that repeated accesses to the same information can be handled locally, without additional network traffic. A replacement policy is used to keep the cache size bounded. The problem of keeping the cached copies consistent with the master file is the *cache-consistency problem*.

There are two approaches to server-side information. Either the server tracks each file being accessed by each client, or it simply provides blocks as they are requested by the client without knowledge of their use. These approaches are the stateful versus stateless service paradigms.

Replication of files on different machines is a useful redundancy for improving availability. Multimachine replication can benefit performance too, since selecting a nearby replica to serve an access request results in shorter service time.

■ Exercises

17.1 What are the benefits of a DFS when compared to a file system in a centralized system?

17.2 Which of the example DFSs would handle a large, multiclient database application most efficiently? Explain your answer.

17.3 Under which circumstances would a client prefer a location-transparent DFS? Under which would she prefer a location-independent DFS? Discuss the reasons for these preferences.

17.4 What aspects of a distributed system would you select for a system running on a totally reliable network?

17.5 Compare and contrast the techniques of caching disk blocks locally, on a client system, and remotely, on a server.

17.6 What are the benefits of mapping objects into virtual memory, as Apollo Domain does? What are the detriments?

Bibliographic Notes

A distributed file service based on optimistic concurrency control was described by Mullender and Tanenbaum [1985]. Discussions concerning consistency and recovery control for replicated files were offered by Davcev and Burkhard [1985]. Management of replicated files in a UNIX environment is covered by Brereton [1986] and Purdin et al. [1987]. Wah [1984] discussed the issue of file placement on distributed computer systems.

UNIX United was described by Brownbridge et al. [1982]. The Locus system was discussed by Popek and Walker [1985]. The Sprite system was described by Ousterhout et al. [1988], and Nelson et al. [1988]. Sun's Network File System (NFS) was presented in Sandberg et al. [1985], Sandberg [1987], and Sun Microsystems [1990]. The Andrew system was discussed by Morris et al. [1986], Howard et al. [1988], and Satyanarayanan [1990]. The Apollo Domain system was discussed by Leach et al. [1982].

A detailed survey of mainly centralized file servers was given in Svobodova [1984]. The emphasis there is on support of atomic transactions, and not on location transparency and naming.

CHAPTER 18

DISTRIBUTED COORDINATION

In Chapter 6, we described various mechanisms that allow processes to synchronize their actions. We also discussed a number of schemes to ensure the atomicity property of a transaction that executes either in isolation or concurrently with other transactions. In Chapter 7 we described various methods that an operating system can use to deal with the deadlock problem. In this chapter, we examine how the centralized synchronization mechanisms can be extended to a distributed environment. We also discuss various methods for handling deadlocks in a distributed system.

18.1 ■ Event Ordering

In a centralized system, it is always possible to determine the order in which two events have occurred, since there is a single common memory and clock. In many applications, it is of utmost importance to be able to determine order. For example, in a resource-allocation scheme, we specify that a resource can be used only *after* the resource has been granted. In a distributed system, however, there is no common memory and no common clock. Therefore, it is sometimes impossible to say which of two events occurred first. The *happened-before* relation is only a partial ordering of the events in distributed systems. Since the ability to define a total ordering is crucial in many applications, we present a distributed algorithm for extending the *happened-before* relation to a consistent total ordering of all the events in the system.

18.1.1 The Happened-Before Relation

Since we are considering only sequential processes, all events executed in a single process are totally ordered. Also, by the law of causality, a message can be received only after it has been sent. Therefore, we can define the *happened-before* relation (denoted by →) on a set of events as follows (assuming that sending and receiving a message constitutes an event):

1. If A and B are events in the same process, and A was executed before B, then A → B.

2. If A is the event of sending a message by one process and B is the event of receiving that message by another process, then A → B.

3. If A → B and B → C then A → C.

Since an event cannot happen before itself, the → relation is an irreflexive partial ordering.

If two events, A and B, are not related by the → relation (that is, A did not happen before B, and B did not happen before A), then we say that these two events were executed *concurrently*. In this case, neither event can causally affect the other. If, however, A → B, then it is possible for event A to affect event B causally.

The definitions of concurrency and of *happened-before* can best be illustrated by a space–time diagram, such as that in Figure 18.1. The horizontal direction represents space (that is, different processes), and the vertical direction represents time. The labeled vertical lines denote processes (or processors). The labeled dots denote events. A wavy line denotes a message sent from one process to another. From this diagram, it is clear that events A and B are concurrent if and only if no path exists either from A to B or from B to A.

For example, consider Figure 18.1. Some of the events related by the *happened-before* relation are

$$p_1 \rightarrow q_2,$$
$$r_0 \rightarrow q_4,$$
$$q_3 \rightarrow r_1,$$
$$p_1 \rightarrow q_4 \quad \text{(since } p_1 \rightarrow q_2 \text{ and } q_2 \rightarrow q_4\text{).}$$

Some of the concurrent events in the system are

$$q_0 \text{ and } p_2,$$
$$r_0 \text{ and } q_3,$$
$$r_0 \text{ and } p_3,$$
$$q_3 \text{ and } p_3.$$

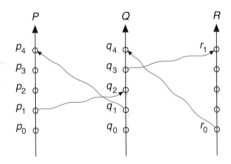

Figure 18.1   Relative time for three concurrent processes.

We cannot know which of two concurrent events, such as q_0 and p_2, happened first. However, since neither event can affect the other (there is no way for one of them to know whether the other has occurred yet), it is not important which of them happened first. It is important only that any processes that care about the order of two concurrent events agree on some order.

18.1.2 Implementation

To determine that an event A happened before an event B, we need either a common clock or a set of perfectly synchronized clocks. Since, in a distributed system neither of these is available, we must define the *happened-before* relation without the use of physical clocks.

We associate with each system event a *timestamp*. We can then define the *global ordering* requirement: For every pair of events A and B, if A → B, then the timestamp of A is less than the timestamp of B. Below we will see that the converse does not need to be true.

How do we enforce the global ordering requirement in a distributed environment? We define within *each* process P_i a *logical clock*, LC_i. The logical clock can be implemented as a simple counter that is incremented between any two successive events executed within a process. Since the logical clock has a monotonically increasing value, it assigns a unique number to every event, and if an event A occurs before event B in process P_i, then $LC_i(A) < LC_i(B)$. The timestamp for an event is the value of the logical clock for that event. Clearly, this scheme ensures that, for any two events in the same process, the global ordering requirement is met.

Unfortunately, this scheme does not ensure that the global ordering requirement is met across processes. To illustrate the problem, we consider two processes P_1 and P_2 that communicate with each other. Suppose that P_1 sends a message to P_2 (event A) with $LC_1(A) = 200$, and P_2 receives the message (event B) with $LC_2(B) = 195$ (because the processor for P_2 is slower than the processor for P_1 and so its logical clock ticks slower). This situation violates our requirement, since A → B, but the timestamp of A is greater than the timestamp of B.

To resolve this difficulty, we require a process to advance its logical clock when it receives a message whose timestamp is greater than the current value of its logical clock. In particular, if process P_i receives a message (event B) with timestamp t and $LC_i(B) \leq t$, then it should advance its clock such that $LC_i(B) = t+1$. Thus, in our example, when P_2 receives the message from P_1, it will advance its logical clock such that $LC_2(B) = 201$.

Finally, to realize a total ordering, we need only to observe that, with our timestamp ordering scheme, if the timestamps of two events A and B are the same, then the events are concurrent. In this case, we may use process identity numbers to break ties and to create a total ordering. The use of timestamps is discussed later in this chapter.

18.2 ■ Mutual Exclusion

In this section, we present a number of different algorithms for implementing mutual exclusion in a distributed environment. We assume that the system consists of n processes, each of which resides at a different processor. To simplify our discussion, we assume that processes are numbered uniquely from 1 to n, and that there is a one-to-one mapping between processes and processors (that is, each process has its own processor).

18.2.1 Centralized Approach

In a centralized approach to providing mutual exclusion, one of the processes in the system is chosen to coordinate the entry to the critical section. Each process that wants to invoke mutual exclusion sends a *request* message to the coordinator. When the process receives a *reply* message from the coordinator, it can proceed to enter its critical section. After exiting its critical section, the process sends a *release* message to the coordinator and proceeds with its execution.

On receiving a *request* message, the coordinator checks to see whether some other process is in its critical section. If no process is in its critical section, the coordinator immediately sends back a *reply* message. Otherwise, the request is queued. When the coordinator receives a *release* message, it removes one of the request messages from the queue (in accordance with some scheduling algorithm) and sends a *reply* message to the requesting process.

It should be clear that this algorithm ensures mutual exclusion. In addition, if the scheduling policy within the coordinator is fair (such as first-come, first-served scheduling), no starvation can occur. This scheme requires three messages per critical-section entry: a *request*, a *reply*, and a *release*.

If the coordinator process fails, then a new process must take its place. In Section 18.6, we describe various algorithms for electing a unique new coordinator. Once a new coordinator has been elected, it must poll all the processes in the system, to reconstruct its *request* queue. Once the queue has been constructed, the computation may resume.

18.2.2 Fully Distributed Approach

If we want to distribute the decision making across the entire system, then the solution is far more complicated. We present an algorithm that is based on the event-ordering scheme described in Section 18.1.

When a process P_i wants to enter its critical section, it generates a new timestamp, *TS*, and sends the message *request*(P_i, *TS*) to all other processes in the system (including itself). On receiving a *request* message, a process may reply immediately (that is, send a *reply* message back to P_i), or it may defer sending a reply back (because it is already in its critical section, for example). A process that has received a *reply* message from all other processes in the system can enter its critical section, queueing incoming requests and deferring them. After exiting its critical section, the process sends *reply* messages to all its deferred requests.

The decision whether process P_i replies immediately to a *request*(P_j, *TS*) message or defers its reply is based on three factors:

1. If process P_i is in its critical section, then it defers its reply to P_j.

2. If process P_i does *not* want to enter its critical section, then it sends a reply immediately to P_j.

3. If process P_i wants to enter its critical section but has not yet entered it, then it compares its own *request* timestamp with the timestamp *TS* of the incoming request made by process P_j. If its own *request* timestamp is greater than *TS*, then it sends a reply immediately to P_j (P_j asked first). Otherwise, the reply is deferred.

This algorithm exhibits the following desirable behavior:

- Mutual exclusion is obtained.

- Freedom from deadlock is ensured.

- Freedom from starvation is ensured, since entry to the critical section is scheduled according to the timestamp ordering. The timestamp ordering ensures that processes are served in a first-come, first-served order.

- The number of messages per critical-section entry is $2 \times (n - 1)$. This number is the minimum number of required messages per critical-section entry when processes act independently and concurrently.

To illustrate how the algorithm functions, we consider a system consisting of processes P_1, P_2, and P_3. Suppose that processes P_1 and P_3 want to enter their critical sections. Process P_1 then sends a message *request* (P_1, timestamp = 10) to processes P_2 and P_3, while process P_3 sends a message *request* (P_3, timestamp = 4) to processes P_1 and P_2. The timestamps 4 and 10 were obtained from the logical clocks described in Section 18.1. When process P_2 receives these *request* messages, it replies immediately. When process P_1 receives the *request* from process P_3 it replies immediately, since the timestamp (10) on its own *request* message is greater than the timestamp (4) for process P_3. When process P_3 receives the *request* from process P_1, it defers its reply, since the timestamp (4) on its *request* message is less than the timestamp (10) for the message of process P_1. On receiving replies from both process P_1 and process P_2, process P_3 can enter its critical section. After exiting its critical section, process P_3 sends a reply to process P_1, which can then enter its critical section.

Note that this scheme requires the participation of all the processes in the system. This approach has three undesirable consequences:

1. The processes need to know the identity of all other processes in the system. When a new process joins the group of processes participating in the mutual-exclusion algorithm, the following actions need to be taken:

   a. The process must receive the names of all the other processes in the group.

   b. The name of the new process must be distributed to all the other processes in the group.

   This task is not as trivial as it may seem, since some *request* and *reply* messages may be circulating in the system when the new process joins the group. The interested reader is referred to the Bibliographic Notes for more details.

2. If one of the processes fails, then the entire scheme collapses. We can resolve this difficulty by continuously monitoring the state of all the processes in the system. If one process fails, then all other processes are notified, so that they will no longer send *request* messages to the failed process. When a process recovers, it must initiate the procedure that allows it to rejoin the group.

3. Processes that have not entered their critical section must pause frequently to assure other processes that they intend to enter the critical section. This protocol is therefore suited for small, stable sets of cooperating processes.

18.2.3 Token-Passing Approach

Another method of providing mutual exclusion is to circulate a token among the processes in the system. A *token* is a special type of message that is passed around the system. Possession of the token entitles the holder to enter the critical section. Since there is only a single token in the system, only one process can be in its critical section at a time.

We assume that the processes in the system are *logically* organized in a ring structure. The physical communication network does not need to be a ring. As long as the processes are connected to one another, it is possible to implement a logical ring. To implement mutual exclusion, we pass the token around the ring. When a process receives the token, it may enter its critical section, keeping the token. After the process exits its critical section, the token is passed around again. If the process receiving the token does not want to enter its critical section, it passes the token to its neighbor. This scheme is similar to algorithm 1 in Chapter 6, but a token is substituted for a shared variable.

Since there is only a single token, only one process at a time can be in its critical section. In addition, if the ring is unidirectional, freedom from starvation is ensured. The number of messages required to implement mutual exclusion may vary from one message per entry, in the case of high contention (that is, every process wants to enter its critical section), to an infinite number of messages, in the case of low contention (that is, no process wants to enter its critical section).

Two types of failure must be considered. First, if the token is lost, an election must be called to generate a new token. Second, if a process fails, a new logical ring must be established. There are several different algorithms for election and for reconstructing a logical ring. In Section 18.6, we present an election algorithm. The development of an algorithm for reconstructing the ring is left to you in Exercise 18.6.

18.3 ■ Atomicity

In Chapter 6, we introduced the concept of an atomic transaction, which is a program unit that must be executed *atomically*. That is, either all the operations associated with it are executed to completion, or none are performed. When we are dealing with a distributed system, it becomes much more complicated to ensure the atomicity property of a transaction, as compared to in a centralized system. This difficulty occurs because several sites may be participating in the execution of a single transaction. The failure of one of these sites, or the failure of a communication link connecting these sites, may result in erroneous computations.

It is the function of the *transaction coordinator* of a distributed system to ensure that the execution of the various transactions in the distributed system preserves atomicity. Each site has its own local transaction coordinator that is responsible for coordinating the execution of all the transactions initiated at that site. For each such transaction, the coordinator is responsible for the following:

- Starting the execution of the transaction

- Breaking the transaction into a number of subtransactions, and distributing these subtransactions to the appropriate sites for execution

- Coordinating the termination of the transaction, which may result in the transaction being committed at all sites or aborted at all sites

We assume that each local site maintains a log for recovery purposes.

18.3.1 The Two-Phase Commit Protocol

For atomicity to be ensured, all the sites in which a transaction T executed must agree on the final outcome of the execution. T must either commit at all sites or it must abort at all sites. To ensure this property, the transaction coordinator of T must execute a *commit protocol*. Among the simplest and most widely used commit protocols is the *two-phase commit (2PC)* protocol, which we discuss here.

Let T be a transaction initiated at site S_i, and let the transaction coordinator at S_i be C_i. When T completes its execution — that is, when all the sites at which T has executed inform C_i that T has completed — then C_i starts the 2PC protocol.

- **Phase 1:** C_i adds the record <prepare T> to the log and forces the record onto stable storage. It then sends a prepare T message to all sites at which T executed. On receiving such a message, the transaction manager at that site determines whether it is willing to commit its portion of T. If the answer is no, it adds a record <no T> to the log, and then it responds by sending an abort T message to C_i. If the answer is yes, it adds a record <ready T> to the log, and forces all the log records corresponding to T onto stable storage. The transaction manager then replies with a ready T message to C_i.

- **Phase 2:** When C_i receives responses to the prepare T message from all the sites, or when a prespecified interval of time has elapsed since the prepare T message was sent out, C_i can determine whether the transaction T can be committed or aborted. Transaction T can be committed if C_i received a ready T message from all the participating sites. Otherwise, transaction T must be aborted. Depending on the verdict, either a record <commit T> or a record <abort T> is added to the log and is forced onto stable storage. At this point, the fate of the transaction has been sealed. Following this, the coordinator sends either a commit T or an abort T message to all participating sites. When a site receives that message, it records the message in the log.

A site at which T executed can unconditionally abort T at any time prior to its sending the message ready T to the coordinator. The ready T message is, in effect, a promise by a site to follow the coordinator's order to commit T or to abort T. The only situation in which a site can make such a promise is if the needed information is stored in stable storage. Otherwise, if the site crashes after sending ready T, it may be unable to make good on its promise.

Since unanimity is required to commit a transaction, the fate of T is sealed as soon as at least one site responds abort T. Since the coordinator site S_i is one of the sites at which T executed, the coordinator can decide unilaterally to abort T. The final verdict regarding T is determined at the time the coordinator writes that verdict (commit or abort) to the log and forces it to stable storage. In some implementations of the 2PC protocol, a site sends an acknowledge T message to the coordinator at the end of the second phase of the protocol. When the coordinator receives the acknowledge T message from all the sites, it adds the record <complete T> to the log.

18.3.2 Failure Handling in 2PC

We now examine in detail how 2PC responds to various types of failures. As we shall see, one major disadvantage of the 2PC protocol is that coordinator failure may result in blocking, where a decision either to commit or to abort T may have to be postponed until C_i recovers.

18.3.2.1 Failure of a Participating Site

When a participating site S_k recovers from a failure, it must examine its log to determine the fate of those transactions that were in the midst of execution when the failure occurred. Let T be one such transaction. We consider each of the possible cases:

- The log contains a <commit T> record. In this case, the site executes **redo**(T).

- The log contains an <abort T> record. In this case, the site executes **undo**(T).

- The log contains a <ready T> record. In this case, the site must consult C_i to determine the fate of T. If C_i is up, it notifies S_k regarding whether T committed or aborted. In the former case, it executes **redo**(T); in the latter case, it executes **undo**(T). If C_i is down, S_k must try to find the fate of T from other sites. It does so by sending a **query-status** T message to all the sites in the system. On receiving such a message, a site must consult its log to determine whether T has executed there, and if so, whether T committed or aborted. It then notifies S_k about this outcome. If no site has the appropriate information (that is, whether T committed or aborted), then S_k can neither abort nor commit T. The decision concerning T is postponed until S_k can obtain the needed information. Thus, S_k must periodically resend the **query-status** message to the other sites. It does so until a site recovers that contains the needed information. Note that the site at which C_i resides always has the needed information.

- The log contains no control records (abort, commit, ready) concerning T.   The absence of control records implies that S_k failed before responding to the prepare T message from C_i. Since the failure of S_k precludes the sending of such a response, by our algorithm C_i must abort T. Hence, S_k must execute **undo**(T).

18.3.2.2 Failure of the Coordinator

If the coordinator fails in the midst of the execution of the commit protocol for transaction T, then the participating sites must decide on the fate of T. We shall see that, in certain cases, the participating sites cannot decide whether to commit or abort T, and therefore it is necessary for these sites to wait for the recovery of the failed coordinator.

- If an active site contains a <commit T> record in its log, then T must be committed.

- If an active site contains an <abort T> record in its log, then T must be aborted.

- If some active site does *not* contain a <ready T> record in its log, then the failed coordinator C_i cannot have decided to commit T. We can draw this conclusion because a site that does not have a <ready T> record in its log cannot have sent a ready T message to C_i. However, the coordinator may have decided to abort T, but not to commit T. Rather than wait for C_i to recover, it is preferable to abort T.

- If none of the preceding cases holds, then all active sites must have a <ready T> record in their logs, but no additional control records (such as <abort *T*> or <commit *T*>). Since the coordinator has failed, it is impossible to determine whether a decision has been made, or what that decision is, until the coordinator recovers. Thus, the active sites must wait for C_i to recover. Since the fate of *T* remains in doubt, *T* may continue to hold system resources. For example, if locking is used, *T* may hold locks on data at active sites. Such a situation is undesirable because it may take hours or days before C_i is again active. During this time other transactions may be forced to wait for *T*. As a result, data are unavailable not only on the failed site (C_i) but on active sites as well. The number of unavailable data increases as the downtime of C_i grows. This situation is called the *blocking* problem, because *T* is blocked pending the recovery of site C_i.

18.3.2.3 Failure of the Network

When a link fails, all the messages that are in the process of being routed through the link do not arrive at their destination intact. From the viewpoint of the sites connected throughout that link, it appears that the other sites have failed. Thus, our previous schemes apply here as well.

When a number of links fail, the network may partition. In this case, two possibilities exist. The coordinator and all its participants may remain in one partition; in this case, the failure has no effect on the commit protocol. Alternatively, the coordinator and its participants may belong to several partitions; in this case, messages between the participant and the coordinator are lost, reducing the case to a link failure, as discussed.

18.4 ■ Concurrency Control

In this section, we show how certain of the concurrency-control schemes discussed in Chapter 6 can be modified so that they can be used in a distributed environment.

It is the function of the *transaction manager* of a distributed database system to manage the execution of those transactions (or subtransactions) that access data stored in a local site. Note that each such transaction may be either a local transaction (that is, a transaction that only executes at that site) or part of a global transaction (that is, a transaction that executes at several sites). Each transaction manager is responsible for maintaining a log for recovery purposes, and for participating in an appropriate concurrency-control scheme to coordinate the concurrent execution of the transactions executing at that site. As we shall see, the concurrency schemes described in Chapter 6 need to be modified to accommodate the distribution of transactions.

18.4.1 Locking Protocols

The two-phase locking protocols described in Chapter 6 can be used in a distributed environment. The only change that needs to be incorporated is in the way the lock manager is implemented. In this section, we present several possible schemes, the first of which deals with the case where no data replication is allowed. The other schemes are applicable to the more general case where data can be replicated in several sites. As in Chapter 6, we shall assume the existence of the *shared* and *exclusive* lock modes.

18.4.1.1 Nonreplicated Scheme

If no data are replicated in the system, then the locking schemes described in Section 6.9 can be applied as follows. Each site maintains a local lock manager whose function is to administer the lock and unlock requests for those data items that are stored in that site. When a transaction wishes to lock data item Q at site S_i, it simply sends a message to the lock manager at site S_i requesting a lock (in a particular lock mode). If data item Q is locked in an incompatible mode, then the request is delayed until that request can be granted. Once it has been determined that the lock request can be granted, the lock manager sends a message back to the initiator indicating that the lock request has been granted.

The scheme has the advantage of simple implementation. It requires two message transfers for handling lock requests, and one message transfer for handling unlock requests. However, deadlock handling is more complex. Since the lock and unlock requests are no longer made at a single site, the various deadlock-handling algorithms discussed in Chapter 7 must be modified, as will be discussed in Section 18.5.

18.4.1.2 Single-Coordinator Approach

Under the single-coordinator approach, the system maintains a *single* lock manager that resides in a *single* chosen site, say S_i. All lock and unlock requests are made at site S_i. When a transaction needs to lock a data item, it sends a lock request to S_i. The lock manager determines whether the lock can be granted immediately. If so, it sends a message to that effect to the site at which the lock request was initiated. Otherwise, the request is delayed until it can be granted, at which time a message is sent to the site at which the lock request was initiated. The transaction can read the data item from *any* one of the sites at which a replica of the data item resides. In the case of a **write,** all the sites where a replica of the data item resides must be involved in the writing.

The scheme has the following advantages:.

- **Simple implementation:** This scheme requires two messages for handling lock requests, and one message for handling unlock requests.

- **Simple deadlock handling:** Since all lock and unlock requests are made at one site, the deadlock-handling algorithms discussed in Chapter 7 can be applied directly to this environment.

The disadvantages of the scheme include the following:

- **Bottleneck:** The site S_i becomes a bottleneck, since all requests must be processed there.
- **Vulnerability:** If the site S_i fails, the concurrency controller is lost. Either processing must stop or a recovery scheme must be used.

A compromise between these advantages and disadvantages can be achieved through a *multiple-coordinator approach,* in which the lock-manager function is distributed over several sites.

Each lock manager administers the lock and unlock requests for a subset of the data items. Each lock manager resides in a different site. This distribution reduces the degree to which the coordinator is a bottleneck, but it complicates deadlock handling, since the lock and unlock requests are not made at one single site.

18.4.1.3 Majority Protocol

The majority protocol is a modification of the nonreplicated data scheme that we presented earlier. The system maintains a lock manager at each site. Each manager manages the locks for all the data or replicas of data stored at that site. When a transaction wishes to lock a data item Q, which is replicated in n different sites, it must send a lock request to more than one-half of the n sites in which Q is stored. Each lock manager determines whether the lock can be granted immediately (as far as it is concerned). As before, the response is delayed until the request can be granted. The transaction does not operate on Q until it has successfully obtained a lock on a majority of the replicas of Q.

This scheme deals with replicated data in a decentralized manner, thus avoiding the drawbacks of central control. However, it suffers from its own disadvantages:

- **Implementation:** The majority protocol is more complicated to implement than the previous schemes. It requires $2(n/2 + 1)$ messages for handling lock requests, and $(n/2 + 1)$ messages for handling unlock requests.
- **Deadlock handling:** Since the lock and unlock requests are not made at one site, the deadlock-handling algorithms must be modified (see Section 18.5). In addition, it is possible for a deadlock to occur even if only one data item is being locked. To illustrate, consider a system

with four sites and full replication. Suppose that transactions T_1 and T_2 wish to lock data item Q in exclusive mode. Transaction T_1 may succeed in locking Q at sites S_1 and S_3, while transaction T_2 may succeed in locking Q at sites S_2 and S_4. Each then must wait to acquire the third lock, and hence a deadlock has occurred.

18.4.1.4 Biased Protocol

The biased protocol is based on a model similar to that of the majority protocol. The difference is that requests for shared locks are given more favorable treatment than are requests for exclusive locks. The system maintains a lock manager at each site. Each manager manages the locks for all the data items stored at that site. *Shared* and *exclusive* locks are handled differently.

- **Shared locks:** When a transaction needs to lock data item Q, it simply requests a lock on Q from the lock manager at one site containing a replica of Q.

- **Exclusive locks:** When a transaction needs to lock data item Q, it requests a lock on Q from the lock manager at all sites containing a replica of Q.

As before, the response to the request is delayed until the request can be granted.

The scheme has the advantage of imposing less overhead on **read** operations than does the majority protocol. This advantage is especially significant in common cases in which the frequency of **reads** is much greater than is the frequency of **writes**. However, the additional overhead on **writes** is a disadvantage. Furthermore, the biased protocol shares the majority protocol's disadvantage of complexity in handling deadlock.

18.4.1.5 Primary Copy

In the case of data replication, we may choose one of the replicas as the primary copy. Thus, for each data item Q, the primary copy of Q must reside in precisely one site, which we call the *primary site of Q*.

When a transaction needs to lock a data item Q, it requests a lock at the primary site of Q. As before, the response to the request is delayed until the request can be granted.

Thus, the primary copy enables concurrency control for replicated data to be handled in a manner similar to that for unreplicated data. This method of handling allows for a simple implementation. However, if the primary site of Q fails, Q is inaccessible even though other sites containing a replica may be accessible.

18.4.2 Timestamping

The principal idea behind the timestamping scheme discussed in Section 6.9 is that each transaction is given a *unique* timestamp that is used in deciding the serialization order. Our first task, then, in generalizing the centralized scheme to a distributed scheme is to develop a scheme for generating unique timestamps. Once this scheme has been developed, our previous protocols can be applied directly to the nonreplicated environment.

18.4.2.1 Generation of Unique Timestamps

There are two primary methods for generating unique timestamps, one centralized and one distributed. In the centralized scheme, a single site is chosen for distributing the timestamps. The site can use a logical counter or its own local clock for this purpose.

In the distributed scheme, each site generates a unique local timestamp using either a logical counter or the local clock. The global unique timestamp is obtained by concatenation of the unique local timestamp with the site identifier, which must be unique (Figure 18.2). The order of concatenation is important! We use the site identifier in the least significant position to ensure that the global timestamps generated in one site are not always greater than those generated in another site. Compare this technique for generating unique timestamps with the one we presented in Section 18.1.2 for generating unique names.

We may still have a problem if one site generates local timestamps at a faster rate than do other sites. In such a case, the fast site's logical counter will be larger than that of other sites. Therefore, all timestamps generated by the fast site will be larger than those generated by other sites. What is needed is a mechanism to ensure that local timestamps are generated fairly across the system. To accomplish the fair generation of timestamps, we define within each site S_i a *logical clock* (LC_i), which generates the unique local timestamp. The logical clock can be implemented as a counter that is

local unique timestamp   site identifier

global unique identifier

Figure 18.2 Generation of unique timestamps.

incremented after a new local timestamp is generated. To ensure that the various logical clocks are synchronized, we require that a site S_i advance its logical clock whenever a transaction T_i with timestamp $<x,y>$ visits that site and x is greater than the current value of LC_i. In this case, site S_i advances its logical clock to the value $x + 1$.

If the system clock is used to generate timestamps, then timestamps are assigned fairly provided that no site has a system clock that runs fast or slow. Since clocks may not be perfectly accurate, a technique similar to that used for logical clocks must be used to ensure that no clock gets far ahead or far behind another clock.

18.4.2.2   Timestamp-Ordering Scheme

The basic timestamp scheme introduced in Section 6.9 can be extended in a straightforward manner to a distributed system. As in the centralized case, cascading rollbacks may result if no mechanism is used to prevent a transaction from reading a data item value that is not yet committed. To eliminate cascading rollbacks, we can combine the basic timestamp scheme of Section 6.9 with the 2PC protocol of Section 18.3 to obtain a protocol that ensures serializability with no cascading rollbacks. We leave the development of such an algorithm to you.

The basic timestamp scheme just described suffers from the undesirable property that conflicts between transactions are resolved through rollbacks, rather than through waits. To alleviate this problem, we can buffer the various **read** and **write** operations (that is, *delay* them) until a time when we are assured that these operations can take place without causing aborts. A **read**(x) operation by T_i must be delayed if there exists a transaction T_j that will perform a **write**(x) operation but has not yet done so, and $\text{TS}(T_j) < \text{TS}(T_i)$. Similarly, a **write**(x) operation by T_i must be delayed if there exists a transaction T_j that will perform either **read**(x) or **write**(x) operation and $\text{TS}(T_j) < \text{TS}(T_i)$. There are various methods for ensuring this property. One such method, called the *conservative timestamp-ordering scheme*, requires each site to maintain a **read** and **write** queue consisting of all the **read** and **write** requests, respectively, that are to be executed at the site and that must be delayed to preserve the above property. We shall not present the scheme here. Rather, we leave the development of the algorithm to you.

18.5 ■ Deadlock Handling

The deadlock-prevention, deadlock-avoidance, and deadlock-detection algorithms presented in Chapter 7 can be extended so that they can also be used in a distributed system. In the following, we describe several of these distributed algorithms.

18.5.1 Deadlock Prevention

The deadlock-prevention and deadlock-avoidance algorithms presented in Chapter 7 can also be used in a distributed system, provided that appropriate modifications are made. For example, we can use the resource-ordering deadlock-prevention technique by simply defining a *global* ordering among the system resources. That is, all resources in the entire system are assigned unique numbers, and a process may request a resource (at any processor) with unique number i only if it is not holding a resource with a unique number greater than i. Similarly, we can use the banker's algorithm in a distributed system by designating one of the processes in the system (the *banker*) as the process that maintains the information necessary to carry out the banker's algorithm. Every resource request must be channeled through the banker.

These two schemes can be used in dealing with the deadlock problem in a distributed environment. The first scheme is simple to implement and requires little overhead. The second scheme can also be implemented easily, but it may require too much overhead. The banker may become a bottleneck, since the number of messages to and from the banker may be large. Thus, the banker's scheme does not seem to be of practical use in a distributed system.

In this section, we present a new deadlock-prevention scheme that is based on a timestamp-ordering approach with resource preemption. For simplicity, we consider only the case of a single instance of each resource type.

To control the preemption, we assign a unique priority number to each process. These numbers are used to decide whether a process P_i should wait for a process P_j. For example, we can let P_i wait for P_j if P_i has a priority higher than that of P_j; otherwise P_i is rolled back. This scheme prevents deadlocks because, for every edge $P_i \rightarrow P_j$ in the wait-for graph, P_i has a higher priority than P_j. Thus, a cycle cannot exist.

One difficulty with this scheme is the possibility of starvation. Some processes with extremely low priority may always be rolled back. This difficulty can be avoided through the use of timestamps. Each process in the system is assigned a unique timestamp when it is created. Two complementary deadlock-prevention schemes using timestamps have been proposed:

- **The wait–die scheme:** This approach is based on a nonpreemptive technique. When process P_i requests a resource currently held by P_j, P_i is allowed to wait only if it has a smaller timestamp than does P_j (that is, P_i is older than P_j). Otherwise, P_i is rolled back (dies). For example, suppose that processes P_1, P_2, and P_3 have timestamps 5, 10, and 15, respectively. If P_1 requests a resource held by P_2, P_1 will wait. If P_3 requests a resource held by P_2, P_3 will be rolled back.

- **The wound−wait scheme:** This approach is based on a preemptive technique and is a counterpart to the wait−die system. When process P_i requests a resource currently held by P_j, P_i is allowed to wait only if it has a larger timestamp than does P_j (that is, P_i is younger than P_j). Otherwise, P_j is rolled back (P_j is *wound* by P_i). Returning to our previous example, with processes P_1, P_2, and P_3, if P_1 requests a resource held by P_2, then the resource will be preempted from P_2 and P_2 will be rolled back. If P_3 requests a resource held by P_2, then P_3 will wait.

Both schemes can avoid starvation, provided that, when a process is rolled back, it is *not* assigned a new timestamp. Since timestamps always increase, a process that is rolled back will eventually have the smallest timestamp. Thus, it will not be rolled back again. There are, however, significant differences in the way the two schemes operate.

- In the wait−die scheme, an older process must wait for a younger one to release its resource. Thus, the older the process gets, the more it tends to wait. By contrast, in the wound−wait scheme, an older process never waits for a younger process.

- In the wait−die scheme, if a process P_i dies and is rolled back because it requested a resource held by process P_j, then P_i may reissue the same sequence of requests when it is restarted. If the resource is still held by P_j, then P_i will die again. Thus, P_i may die several times before acquiring the needed resource. Contrast this series of events with what happens in the wound−wait scheme. Process P_i is wounded and rolled back because P_j requested a resource it holds. When P_i is restarted and requests the resource now being held by P_j, P_i waits. Thus, there are fewer rollbacks in the wound−wait scheme.

The major problem with these two schemes is that unnecessary rollbacks may occur.

18.5.2 Deadlock Detection

The deadlock-prevention algorithm may preempt resources even if no deadlock has occurred. To prevent unnecessary preemptions, we can use a deadlock-detection algorithm. We construct a wait-for graph describing the resource-allocation state. Since we are assuming only a single resource of each type, a cycle in the wait-for graph represents a deadlock.

The main problem in a distributed system is deciding how to maintain the wait-for graph. We elaborate this problem by describing several common techniques to deal with this issue. These schemes require that each site keep a *local* wait-for graph. The nodes of the graph correspond to all the processes (local as well as nonlocal) that are currently either holding or requesting any of the resources local to that site. For example, in Figure 18.3 we have a system consisting of two sites, each maintaining its local wait-for graph. Note that processes P_2 and P_3 appear in both graphs, indicating that the processes have requested resources at both sites.

These local wait-for graphs are constructed in the usual manner for local processes and resources. When a process P_i in site A needs a resource held by process P_j in site B, a request message is sent by P_i to site B. The edge $P_i \rightarrow P_j$ is then inserted in the local wait-for graph of site B.

Clearly, if any local wait-for graph has a cycle, deadlock has occurred. On the other hand, the fact that there are no cycles in any of the local wait-for graphs does not mean that there are no deadlocks. To illustrate this problem, we consider the system depicted in Figure 18.3. Each wait-for graph is acyclic; nevertheless, a deadlock exists in the system. To prove that a deadlock has not occurred, we must show that the *union* of all local graphs is acyclic. The graph (shown in Figure 18.4) that we obtain by taking the union of the two wait-for graphs of Figure 18.3 does indeed contain a cycle, implying that the system is in a deadlock state.

There are a number of different methods for organizing the wait-for graph in a distributed system. We shall describe several common schemes.

18.5.2.1 Centralized Approach

In the centralized approach, a global wait-for graph is constructed as the union of all the local wait-for graphs. It is maintained in a *single* process: the *deadlock-detection coordinator*. Since there is communication delay in the system, we must distinguish between two types of wait-for graphs. The *real* graph describes the real but unknown state of the system at any instance in time, as would be seen by an omniscient observer. The *constructed* graph is an approximation generated by the coordinator during the execution of its algorithm. Obviously, the constructed graph must be generated such that, whenever the detection algorithm is invoked, the

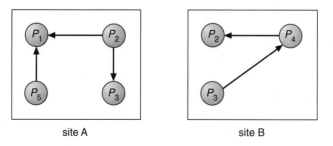

site A   site B

Figure 18.3 Two local wait-for graphs.

reported results are correct in a sense that, if a deadlock exists, then it is reported properly, and if a deadlock is reported, then the system is indeed in a deadlock state. As we shall show, it is not easy to construct such correct algorithms.

There are three different options (points in time) when the wait-for graph may be constructed:

1. Whenever a new edge is inserted or removed in one of the local wait-for graphs

2. Periodically, when a number of changes have occurred in a wait-for graph

3. Whenever the coordinator needs to invoke the cycle-detection algorithm

Let us consider option 1. Whenever an edge is either inserted or removed in a local graph, the local site must also send a message to the coordinator to notify it of this modification. On receiving such a message, the coordinator updates its global graph. Alternatively, a site can send a number of such changes in a single message periodically. Returning to our previous example, the coordinator process will maintain the global wait-for graph as depicted in Figure 18.4. When site B inserts the edge $P_3 \rightarrow P_4$ in its local wait-for graph, it also sends a message to the coordinator. Similarly, when site A deletes the edge $P_5 \rightarrow P_1$, because P_1 has released a resource that was requested by P_5, an appropriate message is sent to the coordinator.

When the deadlock-detection algorithm is invoked, the coordinator searches its global graph. If a cycle is found, a victim is selected to be rolled back. The coordinator must notify all the sites that a particular process has been selected as victim. The sites, in turn, roll back the victim process.

Note that, in this scheme (option 1), unnecessary rollbacks may occur, as a result of two situations:

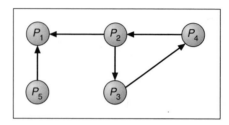

Figure 18.4 Global wait-for graph for Figure 18.3.

- *False cycles* may exist in the global wait-for graph. To illustrate this point, we consider a snapshot of the system as depicted in Figure 18.5. Suppose that P_2 releases the resource it is holding in site A, resulting in the deletion of the edge $P_1 \to P_2$ in A. Process P_2 then requests a resource held by P_3 at site B, resulting in the addition of the edge $P_2 \to P_3$ in B. If the *insert* $P_2 \to P_3$ message from B arrives before the *delete* $P_1 \to P_2$ message from A, the coordinator may discover the false cycle $P_1 \to P_2 \to P_3 \to P_1$ after the *insert* (but before the *delete*). Deadlock recovery may be initiated, although no deadlock has occurred.

- Unnecessary rollbacks may also result when a *deadlock* has indeed occurred and a victim has been picked, but at the same time one of the processes was aborted for reasons unrelated to the deadlock (such as the process exceeding its allocated time). For example, suppose that site A in Figure 18.3 decides to abort P_2. At the same time, the coordinator has discovered a cycle and picked P_3 as a victim. Both P_2 and P_3 are now rolled back, although only P_2 needed to be rolled back.

Note that the same problems are inherited in solutions employing the other two options (that is, options 2 and 3).

Let us now present a centralized deadlock-detection algorithm, using option 3, which detects all deadlocks that actually occur, and does not detect false deadlocks. To avoid the report of false deadlocks, we require that requests from different sites be appended with unique identifiers (timestamps). When process P_i, at site A, requests a resource from P_j, at site B, a request message with timestamp TS is sent. The edge $P_i \to P_j$ with the label TS is inserted in the local wait-for of A. This edge is inserted in the local wait-for graph of B only if B has received the request message and cannot immediately grant the requested resource. A request from P_i to P_j in the same site is handled in the usual manner; no timestamps are associated with the edge $P_i \to P_j$. The detection algorithm is then as follows:

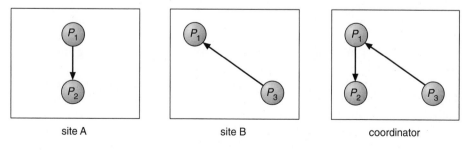

site A   site B   coordinator

Figure 18.5   Local and global wait-for graphs.

1. The controller sends an initiating message to each site in the system.

2. On receiving this message, a site sends its local wait-for graph to the coordinator. Note that each of these wait-for graphs contains all the local information the site has about the state of the real graph. The graph reflects an instantaneous state of the site, but it is not synchronized with respect to any other site.

3. When the controller has received a reply from each site, it constructs a graph as follows:

   a. The constructed graph contains a vertex for every process in the system.

   b. The graph has an edge $P_i \rightarrow P_j$ if and only if (1) there is an edge $P_i \rightarrow P_j$ in one of the wait-for graphs, or (2) an edge $P_i \rightarrow P_j$ with some label TS appears in more than one wait-for graph.

We assert that, if there is a cycle in the constructed graph, then the system is in a deadlock state. If there is no cycle in the constructed graph, then the system was not in a deadlock state when the detection algorithm was invoked as result of the initiating messages sent by the coordinator (in step 1).

18.5.2.2 Fully Distributed Approach

In the *fully distributed* deadlock-detection algorithm, all controllers share equally the responsibility for detecting deadlock. In this scheme, every site constructs a wait-for graph that represents a part of the total graph, depending on the dynamic behavior of the system. The idea is that, if a deadlock exists, a cycle will appear in (at least) one of the partial graphs. We present one such algorithm, which involves construction of partial graphs in every site.

Each site maintains its own local wait-for graph. A local wait-for graph in this scheme differs from the one described earlier in that we add one additional node P_{ex} to the graph. An arc $P_i \rightarrow P_{ex}$ exists in the graph if P_i is waiting for a data item in another site being held by *any* process. Similarly, an arc $P_{ex} \rightarrow P_j$ exists in the graph if there exists a process at another site that is waiting to acquire a resource currently being held by P_j in this local site.

To illustrate this situation, we consider the two local wait-for graphs of Figure 18.3. The addition of the node P_{ex} in both graphs results in the local wait-for graphs shown in Figure 18.6.

If a local wait-for graph contains a cycle that does not involve node P_{ex}, then the system is in a deadlock state. If, however, there exists a cycle involving P_{ex}, then this implies that there is a *possibility* of a deadlock. To

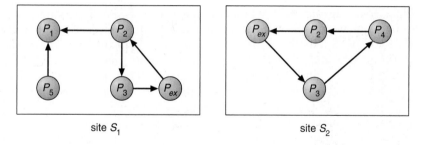

Figure 18.6   Augmented local wait-for graphs of Figure 18.3.

ascertain whether a deadlock does exist, we must invoke a distributed deadlock-detection algorithm.

Suppose that, at site S_i, the local wait-for graph contains a cycle involving node P_{ex}. This cycle must be of the form

$$P_{ex} \to P_{k_1} \to P_{k_2} \to \cdots \to P_{k_n} \to P_{ex},$$

which indicates that transaction P_{k_n} in site S_i is waiting to acquire a data item located in some other site — say, S_j. On discovering this cycle, site S_i sends to site S_j a deadlock-detection message containing information about that cycle.

When site S_j receives this deadlock-detection message, it updates its local wait-for graph with the new information. Then, it searches the newly constructed wait-for graph for a cycle not involving P_{ex}. If one exists, a deadlock is found and an appropriate recovery scheme is invoked. If a cycle involving P_{ex} is discovered, then S_j transmits a deadlock-detection message to the appropriate site — say, S_k. Site S_k, in return, repeats the procedure. Thus, after a finite number of rounds, either a deadlock is discovered, or the deadlock-detection computation halts.

To illustrate this procedure, we consider the local wait-for graphs of Figure 18.6. Suppose that site S_1 discovers the cycle

$$P_{ex} \to P_2 \to P_3 \to P_{ex}.$$

Since P_3 is waiting to acquire a data item in site S_2, a deadlock-detection message describing that cycle is transmitted from site S_1 to site S_2. When site S_2 receives this message, it updates its local wait-for graph, obtaining the wait-for graph of Figure 18.7. This graph contains the cycle

$$P_2 \to P_3 \to P_4 \to P_2,$$

which does not include node P_{ex}. Therefore, the system is in a deadlock state and an appropriate recovery scheme must be invoked.

Note that the outcome would be the same if site S_2 discovered the cycle first in its local wait-for graph and sent the deadlock-detection message to site S_1. In the worst case, both sites will discover the cycle at about the same time, and two deadlock-detection messages will be sent: one by S_1 to S_2 and another by S_2 to S_1. This situation results in unnecessary message transfer and overhead in updating the two local wait-for graphs and searching for cycles in both graphs.

To reduce message traffic, we assign to each transaction P_i a unique identifier, which we denote by $ID(P_i)$. When site S_k discovers that its local wait-for graph contains a cycle involving node P_{ex} of the form

$$P_{ex} \to P_{K_1} \to P_{K_2} \to \cdots \to P_{K_n} \to P_{ex},$$

it sends a deadlock-detection message to another site only if

$$ID(P_{K_n}) < ID(P_{K_1}).$$

Otherwise, site S_k continues its normal execution, leaving the burden of initiating the deadlock-detection algorithm to some other site.

To illustrate this scheme, we consider again the wait-for graphs maintained at sites S_1 and S_2 of Figure 18.6. Suppose that

$$ID(P_1) < ID(P_2) < ID(P_3) < ID(P_4).$$

Let both sites discover these local cycles at about the same time. The cycle in site S_1 is of the form

$$P_{ex} \to P_2 \to P_3 \to P_{ex}.$$

Since $ID(P_3) > ID(P_2)$, site S_1 does not send a deadlock-detection message to site S_2.

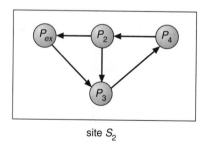

site S_2

Figure 18.7 Augmented local wait-for graph in site S_2 of Figure 18.6.

The cycle in site S_2 is of the form

$$P_{ex} \to P_3 \to P_4 \to P_2 \to P_{ex}.$$

Since $ID(P_2) < ID(P_3)$, site S_2 does send a deadlock-detection message to site S_1, which, on receiving the message, updates its local wait-for graph. Site S_1 then searches for a cycle in the graph and discovers that the system is in a deadlock state.

18.6 ■ Election Algorithms

As we pointed out in Section 18.3, many distributed algorithms employ a coordinator process that performs functions needed by the other processes in the system. These functions include enforcing mutual exclusion, maintaining a global wait-for graph for deadlock detection, replacing a lost token, or controlling an input or output device in the system. If the coordinator process fails due to the failure of the site at which it resides, the system can continue execution only by restarting a new copy of the coordinator on some other site. The algorithms that determine where a new copy of the coordinator should be restarted are called *election* algorithms.

Election algorithms assume that a unique priority number is associated with each active process in the system. For ease of notation, we assume that the priority number of process P_i is i. To simplify our discussion, we assume a one-to-one correspondence between processes and sites, and thus refer to both as processes. The coordinator is always the process with the largest priority number. Hence, when a coordinator fails, the algorithm must elect that active process with the largest priority number. This number must be sent to each active process in the system. In addition, the algorithm must provide a mechanism for a recovered process to identify the current coordinator.

In this section, we present two interesting examples of election algorithms for two different configurations of distributed systems. The first algorithm is applicable to systems where every process can send a message to every other process in the system. The second algorithm is applicable to systems organized as a ring (logically or physically). Both algorithms require n^2 messages for an election, where n is the number of processes in the system. We assume that a process that has failed knows on recovery that it indeed has failed and thus takes appropriate actions to rejoin the set of active processes.

18.6.1 The Bully Algorithm

Suppose that process P_i sends a request that is not answered by the coordinator within a time interval T. In this situation, it is assumed that the coordinator has failed, and P_i tries to elect itself as the new coordinator. This task is completed through the following algorithm.

Process P_i sends an election message to every process with a higher priority number. Process P_i then waits for a time interval T for an answer from any one of these processes.

If no response is received within time T, P_i assumes that all processes with numbers greater than i have failed, and elects itself the new coordinator. Process P_i restarts a new copy of the coordinator and sends a message to inform all active processes with priority numbers less than i that P_i is the new coordinator.

However, if an answer is received, P_i begins a time interval T', waiting to receive a message informing it that a process with a higher priority number has been elected. (Some other process is electing itself coordinator, and should report the results within time T'.) If no message is sent within T', then the process with a higher number is assumed to have failed, and process P_i should restart the algorithm.

If P_i is not the coordinator, then, at any time during execution, P_i may receive one of the following two messages from process P_j:

1. P_j is the new coordinator ($j > i$). Process P_i, in turn, records this information.

2. P_j started an election ($j < i$). Process P_i sends a response to P_j and begins its own election algorithm, provided that P_i has not already initiated such an election.

The process that completes its algorithm has the highest number and is elected as the coordinator. It has sent its number to all active processes with smaller numbers. After a failed process recovers, it immediately begins execution of the same algorithm. If there are no active processes with higher numbers, the recovered process forces all processes with lower numbers to let it become the coordinator process, even if there is a currently active coordinator with a lower number. For this reason, the algorithm is termed the *bully* algorithm.

Let us demonstrate the operation of the algorithm with a simple example of a system consisting of processes P_1 through P_4. The operations are as follows:

1. All processes are active; P_4 is the coordinator process.

2. P_1 and P_4 fail. P_2 determines P_4 has failed by sending a request that is not answered within time T. P_2 then begins its election algorithm by sending a request to P_3.

3. P_3 receives the request, responds to P_2, and begins its own algorithm by sending an election request to P_4.

4. P_2 receives P_3's response, and begins waiting for an interval T'.

5. P_4 does not respond within an interval T, so P_3 elects itself the new coordinator, and sends the number 3 to P_2 and P_1 (which P_1 does not receive, since it has failed).

6. Later, when P_1 recovers, it sends an election request to P_2, P_3, and P_4.

7. P_2 and P_3 respond to P_1 and begin their own election algorithms. P_3 will again be elected, using the same events as before.

8. Finally, P_4 recovers and notifies P_1, P_2, and P_3 that it is the current coordinator. (P_4 sends no election requests, since it is the process with the highest number in the system.)

18.6.2 Ring Algorithm

The *ring* algorithm assumes that the links are unidirectional, and that processes send their messages to their right neighbors. The main data structure used by the algorithm is the *active list*, a list that contains the priority numbers of all active processes in the system when the algorithm ends; each process maintains its own active list. The algorithm works as follows:

1. If process P_i detects a coordinator failure, it creates a new active list that is initially empty. It then sends a message *elect(i)* to its right neighbor, and adds the number i to its active list.

2. If P_i receives a message *elect(j)* from the process on the left, it must respond in one of three ways:

   a. If this is the first *elect* message it has seen or sent, P_i creates a new active list with the numbers i and j. It then sends the message *elect(i)*, followed by the message *elect(j)*.

   b. If $i \neq j$ (that is, the message received does not contain P_i's number), then P_i adds j to its active list and forwards the message to its right neighbor.

   c. If $i = j$ (that is, P_i receives the message *elect(i)*), then the active list for P_i now contains the numbers of all the active processes in the system. Process P_i can now determine the largest number in the active list to identify the new coordinator process.

This algorithm does not specify how a recovering process determines the number of the current coordinator process. One solution would be to require a recovering process to send an inquiry message. This message is forwarded around the ring to the current coordinator, which in turn sends a reply containing its number.

18.7 ■ Reaching Agreement

For a system to be reliable, we need a mechanism that allows a set of processes to agree on a common "value." There are several reasons why such an agreement may not take place. First, the communication medium may be faulty, resulting in lost or garbled messages. Second, the processes themselves may be faulty, resulting in unpredictable process behavior. The best we can hope for, in this case, is that processes fail in a clean way, stopping their execution without deviating from their normal execution pattern. In the worst case, processes may send garbled or incorrect messages to other processes, or even collaborate with other failed processes in an attempt to destroy the integrity of the system.

This problem has been expressed as the *Byzantine generals problem*. Several divisions of the Byzantine army, each commanded by its own general, surround an enemy camp. The Byzantine generals must reach a common agreement on whether or not to attack the enemy at dawn. It is crucial that all generals agree, since an attack by only some of the divisions would result in defeat. The various divisions are geographically dispersed and the generals can communicate with one another only via messengers who run from camp to camp. There are at least two major reasons why the generals may not be able to reach an agreement:

- Messengers may get caught by the enemy and thus may be unable to deliver their messages. This situation corresponds to unreliable communication in a computer system, and is discussed further in Section 18.7.1.

- Generals may be *traitors*, trying to prevent the *loyal* generals from reaching an agreement. This situation corresponds to faulty processes in a computer system, and is discussed further in Section 18.7.2.

18.7.1 Unreliable Communications

Let us assume that, if processes fail, they do so in a clean way, and that the communication medium is unreliable. Suppose that process P_i at site A, which has sent a message to process P_j at site B, needs to know whether P_j has received the message so that it can decide how to proceed with its computation. For example, P_i may decide to compute a function S if P_j has received its message, or to compute a function F if P_j has not received the message (because of some hardware failure).

To detect failures, we can use a *time-out* scheme similar to the one described in Section 16.4.1. When P_i sends out a message, it also specifies a time interval during which it is willing to wait for an acknowledgment message from P_j. When P_j receives the message, it immediately sends an acknowledgment to P_i. If P_i receives the acknowledgment message within the specified time interval, it can safely conclude that P_j has received its message. If, however, a time-out occurs, then P_i needs to retransmit its message and to wait for an acknowledgment. This procedure continues until P_i either gets the acknowledgment message back, or is notified by the system that site B is down. In the first case, it will compute S; in the latter case, it will compute F. Note that, if these are the only two viable alternatives, P_i must wait until it has been notified that one of the situations has occurred.

Suppose now that P_j also needs to know that P_i has received its acknowledgment message, to decide on how to proceed with its computation. For example, P_j may want to compute S only if it is assured that P_i got its acknowledgment. In other words, P_i and P_j will compute S if and only if both have agreed on it. It turns out that, in the presence of failure, it is not possible to accomplish this task. More precisely, it is not possible in a distributed environment for processes P_i and P_j to agree completely on their respective states.

Let us prove this claim. Suppose that there exists a minimal sequence of message transfers such that, after the messages have been delivered, both processes agree to compute S. Let m' be the last message sent by P_i to P_j. Since P_i does not know whether its message will arrive at P_j (since the message may be lost due to a failure), P_i will execute S regardless of the outcome of the message delivery. Thus, m' could be removed from the sequence without affecting the decision procedure. Hence, the original sequence was not minimal, contradicting our assumption and showing that there is no sequence. The processes can never be sure that both will compute S.

18.7.2 Faulty Processes

Let us assume that the communication medium is reliable but that processes can fail in unpredictable ways. Consider a system of n processes, of which no more than m are faulty. Suppose that each process P_i has some private value of V_i. We wish to devise an algorithm that allows each nonfaulty process P_i to construct a vector $X_i = A_{i,1}, A_{i,2}, ..., A_{i,n})$ such that

1. If P_j is a nonfaulty process, then $A_{i,j} = V_j$.
2. If P_i and P_j are both nonfaulty processes, then $X_i = X_j$.

There are many solutions to this problem. These solutions share the following properties:

1. A correct algorithm can be devised only if $n \geq 3 \times m + 1$.
2. The worst-case delay for reaching agreement is proportionate to $m + 1$ message-passing delays.

3. The number of messages required for reaching agreement is large. No single process is trustworthy, so all processes must collect all information and make their own decisions.

Rather than presenting a general solution, which would be complicated, we present an algorithm for the simple case where $m = 1$ and $n = 4$. The algorithm requires two rounds of information exchange:

1. Each process sends its private value to the other three processes.

2. Each process sends the information it has obtained in the first round to all other processes.

A faulty process obviously may refuse to send messages. In this case, a nonfaulty process can choose an arbitrary value and pretend that that value was sent by that process.

Once these two rounds are completed, a nonfaulty process P_i can construct its vector $X_i = (A_{i,1}, A_{i,2}, A_{i,3}, A_{i,4})$ as follows:

1. $A_{i,i} = V_i$.

2. For $j \neq i$, if at least two of the three values reported for process P_j (in the two rounds of exchange) agree, then the majority value is used to set the value of $A_{i,j}$. Otherwise, a default value, say *nil*, is used to set the value of $A_{i,j}$.

18.8 ■ Summary

In a distributed system with no common memory and no common clock, it is sometimes impossible to determine the exact order in which two events occur. The happened-before relation is only a partial ordering of the events in distributed systems. Timestamps can be used to provide a consistent event ordering in a distributed system.

Mutual exclusion in a distributed environment can be implemented in a variety of ways. In a centralized approach, one of the processes in the system is chosen to coordinate the entry to the critical section. In the fully distributed approach, the decision making is distributed across the entire system. A distributed algorithm, which is applicable to ring-structured network, is the token-passing approach.

For atomicity to be ensured, all the sites in which a transaction T executed must agree on the final outcome of the execution. T either commits at all sites or aborts at all sites. To ensure this property, the transaction coordinator of T must execute a *commit* protocol. The most widely used commit protocol is the 2PC protocol.

The various concurrency-control schemes that can be used in a centralized system can be modified for use in a distributed environment. In the case of locking protocols, the only change that needs to be incorporated is in the way that the lock manager is implemented. In the case of timestamping and validation schemes, the only needed change is the development of a mechanism for generating unique *global* timestamps. The mechanism can either concatenate a local timestamp with the site identification or advance local clocks whenever a message arrives that has a larger timestamp.

The primary method for dealing with deadlocks in a distributed environment is deadlock detection. The main problem is deciding how to maintain the wait-for graph. Different methods for organizing the wait-for graph include a centralized approach and a fully distributed approach.

Some of the distributed algorithms require the use of a coordinator. If the coordinator fails owing to the failure of the site at which it resides, the system can continue execution only by restarting a new copy of the coordinator on some other site. It does so by maintaining a backup coordinator that is ready to assume responsibility if the coordinator fails. Another approach is to choose the new coordinator after the coordinator has failed. The algorithms that determine where a new copy of the coordinator should be restarted are called *election* algorithms. Two algorithms, the bully algorithm and a ring algorithm, can be used to elect a new coordinator in case of failures.

■ Exercises

18.1 Discuss the advantages and disadvantages of the two methods we presented for generating globally unique timestamps.

18.2 Your company is building a computer network, and you are asked to write an algorithm for achieving distributed mutual exclusion. Which scheme will you use? Explain your choice.

18.3 Why is deadlock detection much more expensive in a distributed environment than it is in a centralized environment?

18.4 Your company is building a computer network, and you are asked to develop a scheme for dealing with the deadlock problem.

    a. Would you use a deadlock-detection scheme, or a deadlock-prevention scheme?

    b. If you were to use a deadlock-prevention scheme, which one would you use? Explain your choice.

    c. If you were to use a deadlock-detection scheme, which one would you use? Explain your choice.

18.5 Consider the following *hierarchical* deadlock-detection algorithm, in which the global wait-for graph is distributed over a number of different *controllers*, which are organized in a tree. Each nonleaf controller maintains a wait-for graph that contains relevant information from the graphs of the controllers in the subtree below it. In particular, let S_A, S_B, and S_C be controllers such that S_C is the lowest common ancestor of S_A and S_B (S_C must be unique, since we are dealing with a tree). Suppose that node T_i appears in the local wait-for graph of controllers S_A and S_B. Then, T_i must also appear in the local wait-for graph of

- Controller S_C

- Every controller in the path from S_C to S_A

- Every controller in the path from S_C to S_B

In addition, if T_i and T_j appear in the wait-for graph of controller S_D and there exists a path from T_i to T_j in the wait-for graph of one of the children of D, then an edge $T_i \rightarrow T_j$ must be in the wait-for graph of S_D.

Show that, if a cycle exists in any of the wait-for graphs, then the system is deadlocked.

18.6 Derive an election algorithm for bidirectional rings that is more efficient than the one presented in this chapter. How many messages are needed for n processes?

18.7 Consider a failure that occurs during two-phase commit for a transaction. For each possible failure, explain how two-phase commit ensures transaction atomicity despite the failure.

Bibliographic Notes

The distributed algorithm for extending the happened-before relation to a consistent total ordering of all the events in the system (Section 18.1) was developed by Lamport [1978a].

The first general algorithm for implementing mutual exclusion in a distributed environment was developed by Lamport [1978a] also. Lamport's scheme requires $3 \times (n - 1)$ messages per critical-section entry. Subsequently, Ricart and Agrawala [1981] proposed a distributed algorithm that requires only $2 \times (n - 1)$ messages. Their algorithm was presented in Section 18.2.2. A square root algorithm for distributed mutual exclusion was presented by Maekawa [1985]. The token-passing algorithm for ring-structured systems presented in Section 18.2.3 was developed by Le Lann [1977]. Discussions concerning mutual exclusion in computer networks were presented by Carvalho and Roucairol [1983]. An efficient and fault-tolerant solution of distributed mutual exclusion was presented by Agrawal and El Abbadi [1991]. A simple taxonomy for distributed mutual exclusion algorithms was presented by Raynal [1991].

The issue of distributed synchronization was discussed by Reed and Kanodia [1979] (shared-memory environment), Lamport [1978a, 1978b], and Schneider [1982] (totally disjoint processes). A distributed solution to the dining-philosophers problem was presented by Chang [1980].

The 2PC protocol was developed by Lampson and Sturgis [1976] and Gray [1978]. Mohan and Lindsay [1983] discussed two modified versions of 2PC, called presume commit and presume abort, that reduce the overhead of 2PC by defining default assumption regarding the fate of transactions.

Papers dealing with the problems of implementing the transaction concept in a distributed database were presented by Gray [1981], Traiger et al. [1982], and Spector and Schwarz [1983]. Comprehensive discussions covering distributed concurrency control were offered by Bernstein et al. [1987].

Rosenkrantz et al. [1978] reported the timestamp distributed deadlock-prevention algorithm. The fully distributed deadlock-detection scheme presented in Section 18.5.2 was developed by Obermarck [1982]. The hierarchical deadlock-detection scheme of Exercise 18.3 appeared in Menasce and Muntz [1979]. A survey of deadlock detection in distributed systems is offered by Knapp [1987] and Singhal [1989].

The Byzantine generals problem was discussed by Lamport et al. [1982] and Pease et al. [1980]. The bully algorithm was presented by Garcia-Molina [1982]. The election algorithm for a ring-structured system was written by Le Lann [1977].

PART SIX

CASE STUDIES

The various concepts described in this book can now be drawn together by describing real operating systems. Two UNIX-based operating systems are covered in detail — Berkeley 4.3BSD and Mach. These operating systems were chosen in part because UNIX at one time was almost small enough to understand and yet is not a toy operating system. Most of its internal algorithms were selected for *simplicity*, not for speed or sophistication. UNIX is readily available to departments of computer science, so many students may have access to it. Mach gives us an opportunity to study a modern operating system that provides compatibility with 4.3BSD but has a vastly different design and implementation.

In addition to Berkeley 4.3BSD and Mach, we briefly discuss several other highly influential operating systems. The order of presentation has been chosen to highlight the similarities and differences of the systems; it is not strictly chronological, and does not reflect the relative importance of the system.

CHAPTER 19

THE
UNIX
SYSTEM

Although operating-system concepts can be considered in purely theoretical terms, it is often useful to see how they are implemented in practice. This chapter presents an in-depth examination of the 4.3BSD operating system, a version of UNIX, as an example of the various concepts presented in this book. By examining a complete, real system, we can see how the various concepts discussed in this book relate both to one another and to practice. We consider first a brief history of UNIX, and present the system's user and programmer interfaces. Then, we discuss the internal data structures and algorithms used by the UNIX kernel to support the user−programmer interface.

19.1 ■ History

The first version of UNIX was developed in 1969 by Ken Thompson of the Research Group at Bell Laboratories to use an otherwise idle PDP-7. He was soon joined by Dennis Ritchie. Thompson, Ritchie, and other members of the Research Group produced the early versions of UNIX.

Ritchie had previously worked on the MULTICS project, and MULTICS had a strong influence on the newer operating system. Even the name UNIX is merely a pun on MULTICS. The basic organization of the file system, the idea of the command interpreter (the shell) as a user process, the use of a separate process for each command, the original line-editing characters (# to erase the last character and @ to erase the entire line), and numerous other features came directly from MULTICS. Ideas from various other operating systems, such as from MIT's CTSS and the XDS-940 system, were also used.

Ritchie and Thompson worked quietly on UNIX for many years. Their work on the first version allowed them to move it to a PDP-11/20, for a second version. A third version resulted from their rewriting most of the operating system in the systems-programming language C, instead of the previously used assembly language. C was developed at Bell Laboratories to support UNIX. UNIX was also moved to larger PDP-11 models, such as the 11/45 and 11/70. Multiprogramming and other enhancements were added when it was rewritten in C and moved to systems (such as the 11/45) that had hardware support for multiprogramming.

As UNIX developed, it became widely used within Bell Laboratories and gradually spread to a few universities. The first version widely available outside Bell Laboratories was Version 6, released in 1976. (The version number for early UNIX systems corresponds to the edition number of the UNIX *Programmer's Manual* that was current when the distribution was made; the code and the manuals were revised independently.)

In 1978, Version 7 was distributed. This UNIX system ran on the PDP-11/70 and the Interdata 8/32, and is the ancestor of most modern UNIX systems. In particular, it was soon ported to other PDP-11 models and to the VAX computer line. The version available on the VAX was known as 32V. Research has continued since then.

After the distribution of Version 7 in 1978, the UNIX Support Group (USG) assumed administrative control and responsibility from the Research Group for distributions of UNIX within AT&T, the parent organization for Bell Laboratories. UNIX was becoming a product, rather than simply a research tool. The Research Group has continued to develop their own version of UNIX, however, to support their own internal computing. Next came Version 8, which included a facility called the *stream I/O system* that allows flexible configuration of kernel IPC modules. It also contained RFS, a remote file system similar to Sun's NFS. Next came Versions 9 and 10 (the latter version, released in 1989, is available only within Bell Laboratories).

USG mainly provided support for UNIX within AT&T. The first external distribution from USG was System III, in 1982. System III incorporated features of Version 7, and 32V, and also of several UNIX systems developed by groups other than Research. Features of UNIX/RT, a real-time UNIX system, as well as numerous portions of the Programmer's Work Bench (PWB) software tools package were included in System III.

USG released System V in 1983; it is largely derived from System III. The divestiture of the various Bell operating companies from AT&T has left AT&T in a position to market System V aggressively. USG was restructured as the UNIX System Development Laboratory (USDL), which released UNIX System V Release 2 (V.2) in 1984. UNIX System V Release 2, Version 4 (V.2.4) added a new implementation of virtual memory with copy-on-write paging and shared memory. USDL was in turn replaced by AT&T

Information Systems (ATTIS), which distributed System V Release 3 (V.3) in 1987. V.3 adapts the V8 implementation of the stream I/O system and makes it available as STREAMS. It also includes RFS, an NFS-like remote file system.

The small size, modularity, and clean design of early UNIX systems led to UNIX-based work at numerous other computer-science organizations, such as at Rand, BBN, the University of Illinois, Harvard, Purdue, and even DEC. The most influential of the non-Bell Laboratories and non−AT&T UNIX development groups, however, has been the University of California at Berkeley.

The first Berkeley VAX UNIX work was the addition in 1978 of virtual memory, demand paging, and page replacement to 32V by Bill Joy and Ozalp Babaoglu to produce 3BSD UNIX. This version was the first implementation of any of these facilities on any UNIX system. The large virtual-memory space of 3BSD allowed the development of very large programs, such as Berkeley's own Franz LISP. The memory-management work convinced the Defense Advanced Research Projects Agency (DARPA) to fund Berkeley for the development of a standard UNIX system for government use; 4BSD UNIX was the result.

The 4BSD work for DARPA was guided by a steering committee that included many notable people from the UNIX and networking communities. One of the goals of this project was to provide support for the DARPA Internet networking protocols (TCP/IP). This support was provided in a general manner. It is possible in 4.2BSD to communicate uniformly among diverse network facilities, including local-area networks (such as Ethernets and token rings) and wide-area networks (such as NSFNET). This implementation was the most important reason for the current popularity of these protocols. It was used as the basis for the implementations of many vendors of UNIX computer systems, and even other operating systems. It permitted the Internet to grow from 60 connected networks in 1984 to more than 8000 networks and an estimated 10 million users in 1993.

In addition, Berkeley adapted many features from contemporary operating systems to improve the design and implementation of UNIX. Many of the terminal line-editing functions of the TENEX (TOPS-20) operating system were provided by a new terminal driver. A new user interface (the C Shell), a new text editor (ex/vi), compilers for Pascal and LISP, and many new systems programs were written at Berkeley. For 4.2BSD, certain efficiency improvements were inspired by the VMS operating system.

UNIX software from Berkeley is released in *Berkeley Software Distributions*. It is convenient to refer to the Berkeley VAX UNIX systems following 3BSD as 4BSD, although there were actually several specific releases, most notably 4.1BSD and 4.2BSD. The generic numbers BSD and 4BSD are used for the PDP-11 and VAX distributions of Berkeley UNIX. 4.2BSD, first

610 ■ Chapter 19: The UNIX System

distributed in 1983, was the culmination of the original Berkeley DARPA UNIX project. 2.9BSD is the equivalent version for PDP-11 systems.

In 1986, 4.3BSD was released. It was so similar to 4.2BSD that its manuals described 4.2BSD more comprehensively than the 4.2BSD manuals did. It did include numerous internal changes, however, including bug fixes and performance improvements. Some new facilities also were added, including support for the Xerox Network System protocols.

4.3BSD Tahoe was the next version, released in 1988. It included various new developments, such as improved networking congestion control and TCP/IP performance. Also, disk configurations were separated from the device drivers, and are now read off the disks themselves. Expanded time-zone support is also included. 4.3BSD Tahoe was actually developed on and for the CCI Tahoe system (Computer Console, Inc., Power 6 computer), rather than for the usual VAX base. The corresponding PDP-11 release is 2.10.1BSD, which is distributed by the USENIX Association, which also publishes the 4.3BSD manuals. The 4.32BSD Reno release saw the inclusion of an implementation of ISO/OSI networking.

The last Berkeley release, 4.4BSD, was finalized in June of 1993. It includes new X.25 networking support, and POSIX standard compliance. It also has a radically new file system organization, with a new virtual file system interface and support for *stackable* file systems, allowing file systems to be layered on top of each other for easy inclusion of new features. An implementation of NFS is also included in the release (Chapter 17), as is a new log-based file system (see Chapter 12). The 4.4BSD virtual memory system is derived from Mach (described in the next chapter). Several other changes, such as enhanced security and improved kernel structure, are also included. With the release of version 4.4, Berkeley has halted its research efforts.

4BSD was the operating system of choice for VAXes from its initial release (1979) until the release of Ultrix, DEC's BSD implementation. 4BSD is still the best choice for many research and networking installations. Many organizations would buy a 32V license and order 4BSD from Berkeley without even bothering to get a 32V tape.

The current set of UNIX systems is not limited to those by Bell Laboratories, AT&T, and Berkeley, however. Sun Microsystems helped popularize the BSD flavor of UNIX by shipping it on their workstations. As UNIX has grown in popularity, it has been moved to many different computers and computer systems. A wide variety of UNIX, and UNIX-like, operating systems have been created. DEC supports its UNIX (called Ultrix) on its workstations and is replacing Ultrix with another UNIX-derived operating system, OSF/1; Microsoft rewrote UNIX for the Intel 8088 family and called it XENIX, and its new Windows/NT operating system is heavily influenced by UNIX; IBM has UNIX (AIX) on its PCs, workstations, and mainframes. In fact, UNIX is available on almost all general-purpose computers; it runs on personal computers, workstations, minicomputers, mainframes, and supercomputers, from Apple Macintosh IIs to Cray IIs. Because of its wide availability, it is used in environments ranging from academic to military to manufacturing process control. Most of these systems are based on Version 7, System III, 4.2BSD, or System V.

The wide popularity of UNIX with computer vendors has made UNIX the most portable of operating systems, and has made it possible for users to expect a UNIX environment independent of any specific computer manufacturer. But the large number of implementations of the system has led to remarkable variation in the programming and user interfaces distributed by the vendors. For true vendor independence, application-program developers need consistent interfaces. Such interfaces would allow all "UNIX" applications to run on all UNIX systems, which is certainly not the current situation. This issue has become important as UNIX has become the preferred program-development platform for applications ranging from databases to graphics and networking, and has led to a strong market demand for UNIX standards.

There are several standardization projects underway, starting with the *lusr/group 1984 Standard* sponsored by the UniForum industry user's group. Since then, many official standards bodies have continued the effort, including IEEE and ISO (the POSIX standard). The X/Open Group international consortium completed XPG3, a Common Application Environment, which subsumes the IEEE interface standard. Unfortunately, XPG3 is based on a draft of the ANSI C standard, rather than the final specification, and therefore needs to be redone. The XPG4 is due out in 1993. In 1989, the ANSI standards body standardized the C programming language, producing an ANSI C specification that vendors were quick to adopt. As these projects continue, the variant flavors of UNIX will converge and there will be one programming interface to UNIX, allowing UNIX to become even more popular. There are in fact two separate sets of powerful UNIX vendors working on this problem: the AT&T-guided UNIX International (UI) and the Open Software Foundation (OSF) have both agreed to follow the POSIX standard. Recently, many of the vendors involved in those two groups have agreed on further standardization (the COSE agreement) on the Motif window environment, and ONC+ (which includes Sun RPC and NFS) and DCE network facilities (which includes AFS and an RPC package).

AT&T replaced its ATTIS group in 1989 with the UNIX Software Organization (USO), which shipped the first merged UNIX, System V Release 4. This system combines features from System V, 4.3BSD, and Sun's SunOS, including long file names, the Berkeley file system, virtual memory management, symbolic links, multiple access groups, job control, and reliable signals; it also conforms to the published POSIX standard, POSIX.1. After USO produced SVR4, it became an independent AT&T subsidiary named Unix System Laboratories (USL); in 1993, it was purchased by Novell, Inc.

Figure 19.1 summarizes the relationships among the various versions of UNIX.

The UNIX system has grown from a personal project of two Bell Laboratories employees to an operating system being defined by multinational standardization bodies. Yet this system is still of interest to academia. We believe that UNIX has become and will remain an important

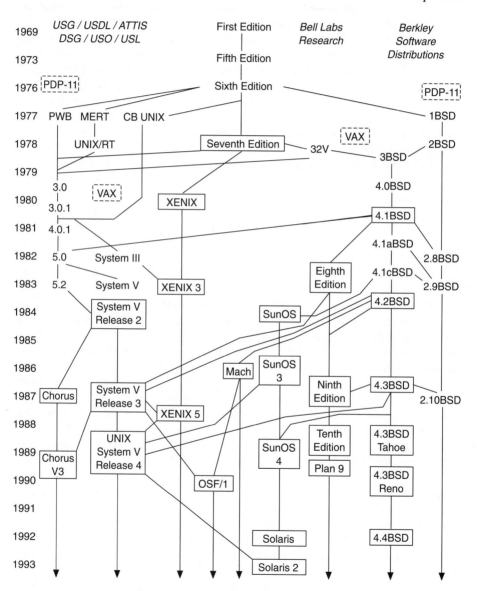

Figure 19.1   History of UNIX versions.

part of operating-system theory and practice. UNIX is an excellent vehicle for academic study. For example, the Tunis operating system, the Xinu operating system, and the Minix operating system are based on the concepts of UNIX, but were developed explicitly for classroom study. There is a plethora of ongoing UNIX-related research systems, including Mach, Chorus, Comandos, and Roisin. The original developers, Ritchie and Thompson, were honored in 1983 by the Association for Computing Machinery Turing award for their work on UNIX.

The specific UNIX version used in this chapter is the VAX version of 4.3BSD. This system is used because it implements many interesting operating-system concepts, such as demand paging with clustering, and networking. It has also been influential in other UNIX systems, in standards, and in networking developments. The VAX implementation is used because 4.3BSD was developed on the VAX and that machine still represents a convenient point of reference, despite the recent proliferation of implementations on other hardware (such as the Motorola 68040 and 88000, the Intel i486, the Sun SPARC, DEC Alpha, HP Precision, and the MIPS R4000 CPUs).

19.2 ■ Design Principles

UNIX as designed to be a time-sharing system. The standard user interface (the shell) is simple and can be replaced by another, if desired. The file system is a multilevel tree, which allows users to create their own subdirectories. Each user data file is simply a sequence of bytes.

Disk files and I/O devices are treated as similarly as possible. Thus, device dependencies and peculiarities are kept in the kernel as much as possible; even in the kernel, most of them are confined to the device drivers.

UNIX supports multiple processes. A process can easily create new processes. CPU scheduling is a simple priority algorithm. 4.3BSD uses demand paging as a mechanism to support memory-management and CPU-scheduling decisions. Swapping is used if a system is suffering from excess paging.

Because UNIX was originated first by one programmer, Ken Thompson, and then by another, Dennis Ritchie, as a system for their own convenience, it was small enough to understand. Most of the algorithms were selected for *simplicity*, not for speed or sophistication. The intent was to have the kernel and libraries provide a small set of facilities that was sufficiently powerful to allow a person to build a more complex system if one were needed. UNIX's clean design has resulted in many imitations and modifications.

Although the designers of UNIX had a significant amount of knowledge about other operating systems, UNIX had no elaborate design spelled out before its implementation. This flexibility appears to have been one of the key factors in the development of the system. Some design principles were involved, however, even though they were not made explicit at the outset.

The UNIX system was designed by programmers for programmers. Thus, it has always been interactive, and facilities for program development have always been a high priority. Such facilities include the program *make* (which can be used to check to see which of a collection of source files for a program need to be compiled, and then to do the compiling) and the *Source Code Control System (SCCS)* (which is used to keep successive versions of files available without having to store the entire contents of each step).

The operating system is written mostly in C, which was developed to support UNIX, since neither Thompson nor Ritchie enjoyed programming in assembly language. The avoidance of assembly language was also necessary because of the uncertainty about the machine or machines on which UNIX would be run. It has greatly simplified the problems of moving UNIX from one hardware system to another.

From the beginning, UNIX development systems have had all the UNIX sources available on-line, and the developers have used the systems under development as their primary systems. This pattern of development has greatly facilitated the discovery of deficiencies and their fixes, as well as of new possibilities and their implementations. It has also encouraged the plethora of UNIX variants existing today, but the benefits have outweighed the disadvantages: if something is broken, it can be fixed at a local site; there is no need to wait for the next release of the system. Such fixes, as well as new facilities, may be incorporated into later distributions.

The size constraints of the PDP-11 (and earlier computers used for UNIX) have forced a certain elegance. Where other systems have elaborate algorithms for dealing with pathological conditions, UNIX just does a controlled crash called *panic*. Instead of attempting to cure such conditions, UNIX tries to prevent them. Where other systems would use brute force or macro-expansion, UNIX mostly has had to develop more subtle, or at least simpler, approaches.

These early strengths of UNIX produced much of its popularity, which in turn produced new demands that challenged those strengths. UNIX was used for tasks such as networking, graphics, and real-time operation, which did not always fit into its original text-oriented model. Thus, changes were made to certain internal facilities and new programming interfaces were added. These new facilities, and others — particularly window interfaces — required large amounts of code to support them, radically increasing the size of the system. For instance, networking and windowing both doubled the size of the system. This pattern in turn pointed out the continued strength of UNIX — whenever a new development occurred in the industry, UNIX could usually absorb it, but still remain UNIX.

19.3 ■ Programmer Interface

As do most computer systems, UNIX consists of two separable parts: the kernel and the systems programs. We can view the UNIX operating system as being layered, as shown in Figure 19.2. Everything below the system-call interface and above the physical hardware is the *kernel*. The kernel provides the file system, CPU scheduling, memory management, and other operating-system functions through system calls. Systems programs use the kernel-supported system calls to provide useful functions, such as compilation and file manipulation.

System calls define the *programmer interface* to UNIX; the set of systems programs commonly available defines the *user interface*. The programmer and user interface define the context that the kernel must support.

System calls in VAX 4.2BSD are made by a trap to location 40 of the VAX interrupt vectors. Parameters are passed to the kernel on the hardware stack; the kernel returns values in registers R0 and R1. Register R0 may also return an error code. The carry bit distinguishes a normal return from an error return.

This level of detail is seldom seen by a UNIX programmer, fortunately. Most systems programs are written in C, and the UNIX *Programmer's Manual* presents all system calls as C functions. A system program written in C for 4.3BSD on the VAX can generally be moved to another 4.3BSD system and simply recompiled, even though the two systems may be quite different. The details of system calls are known only to the compiler. This feature is a major reason for the portability of UNIX programs.

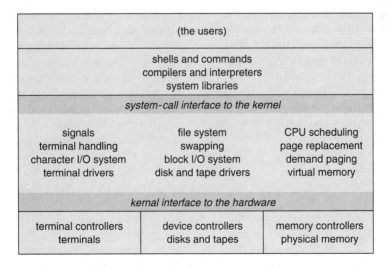

Figure 19.2 4.3BSD layer structure.

System calls for UNIX can be roughly grouped into three categories: file manipulation, process control, and information manipulation. In Chapter 3, we listed a fourth category, device manipulation, but since devices in UNIX are treated as (special) files, the same system calls support both files and devices (although there is an extra system call for setting device parameters).

19.3.1 File Manipulation

A *file* in UNIX is a sequence of bytes. Different programs expect various levels of structure, but the kernel does not impose a structure on files. For instance, the convention for text files is lines of ASCII characters separated by a single newline character (which is the linefeed character in ASCII), but the kernel knows nothing of this convention.

Files are organized in tree-structured *directories*. Directories are themselves files that contain information on how to find other files. A *path name* to a file is a text string that identifies a file by specifying a path through the directory structure to the file. Syntactically, it consists of individual file-name elements separated by the slash character. For example, in */usr/local/font*, the first slash indicates the root of the directory tree, called the *root* directory. The next element, *usr*, is a subdirectory of the root, *local* is a subdirectory of *usr*, and *font* is a file or directory in the directory *local*. Whether *font* is an ordinary file or a directory cannot be determined from the path-name syntax.

UNIX has both *absolute path names* and *relative path names*. Absolute path names start at the root of the file system and are distinguished by a slash at the beginning of the path name; */usr/local/font* is an absolute path name. Relative path names start at the *current directory*, which is an attribute of the process accessing the path name. Thus, *local/font* indicates a file or directory named *font* in the directory *local* in the current directory, which might or might not be */usr*.

A file may be known by more than one name in one or more directories. Such multiple names are known as *links*, and all links are treated equally by the operating system. 4.3BSD also supports *symbolic links*, which are files containing the path name of another file. The two kinds of links are also known as *hard links* and *soft links*. Soft (symbolic) links, unlike hard links, may point to directories and may cross file-system boundaries.

The file name "." in a directory is a hard link to the directory itself. The file name ".." is a hard link to the parent directory. Thus, if the current directory is */user/jlp/programs*, then *../bin/wdf* refers to */user/jlp/bin/wdf*.

Hardware devices have names in the file system. These *device special files* or *special files* are known to the kernel as device interfaces, but are nonetheless accessed by the user by much the same system calls as are other files.

Figure 19.3 shows a typical UNIX file system. The root (/) normally contains a small number of directories as well as *vmunix*, the binary boot image of the operating system; */dev* contains the device special files, such as */dev/console, /dev/lp0, /dev/mt0*, and so on; */bin* contains the binaries of the essential UNIX systems programs. Other binaries may be in */usr/bin* (for applications systems programs, such as text formatters), */usr/ucb* (for systems programs written by Berkeley rather than by AT&T), or */usr/local/bin* (for systems programs written at the local site). Library files — such as the C, Pascal, and FORTRAN subroutine libraries — are kept in */lib* (or */usr/lib* or */usr/local/lib*).

The files of users themselves are stored in a separate directory for each user, typically in */user*. Thus, the user directory for *carol* would normally be in */user/carol*. For a large system, these directories may be further grouped to ease administration, creating a file structure with */user/prof/avi* and */user/staff/carol*. Administrative files and programs, such as the password file, are kept in */etc*. Temporary files can be put in */tmp*, which is normally erased during system boot, or in */usr/tmp*.

Each of these directories may have considerably more structure. For example, the font-description tables for the troff formatter for the Merganthaler 202 typesetter are kept in */usr/lib/troff/dev202*. All the conventions concerning the location of specific files and directories have been defined by programmers and their programs; the operating-system kernel needs only */etc/init*, which is used to initialize terminal processes, to be operable.

System calls for basic file manipulation are **creat, open, read, write, close, unlink,** and **trunc.** The **creat** system call, given a path name, creates an (empty) file (or truncates an existing one). An existing file is opened by the **open** system call, which takes a path name and a mode (such as read, write, or read−write) and returns a small integer, called a *file descriptor.* A file descriptor may then be passed to a **read** or **write** system call (along with a buffer address and the number of bytes to transfer) to perform data transfers to or from the file. A file is closed when its file descriptor is passed to the **close** system call. The **trunc** call reduces the length of a file to 0.

A file descriptor is an index into a small table of open files for this process. Descriptors start at 0 and seldom get higher than 6 or 7 for typical programs, depending on the maximum number of simultaneously open files.

Each **read** or **write** updates the current offset into the file, which is associated with the file-table entry and is used to determine the position in the file for the next **read** or **write**. The **lseek** system call allows the position to be reset explicitly. It also allows the creation of sparse files (files with "holes" in them). The **dup** and **dup2** system calls can be used to produce a new file descriptor that is a copy of an existing one. The **fcntl** system call can also do that, and in addition can examine or set various parameters of

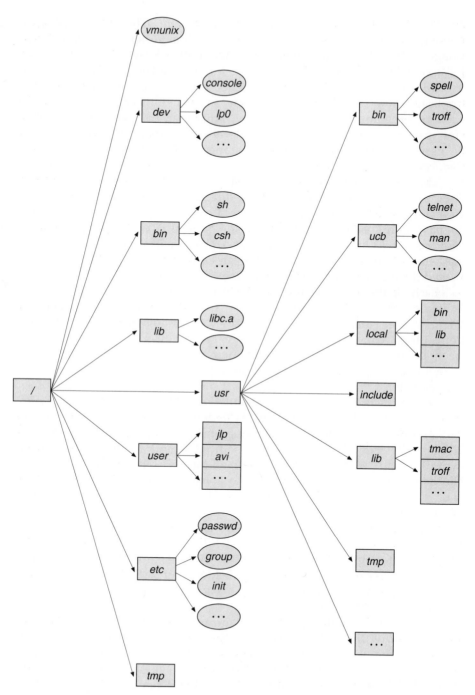

Figure 19.3 Typical UNIX directory structure.

an open file. For example, it can make each succeeding **write** to an open file append to the end of that file. There is an additional system call, **ioctl,** for manipulating device parameters. It can set the baud rate of a serial port, or rewind a tape, for instance.

Information about the file (such as its size, protection modes, owner, and so on) can be obtained by the **stat** system call. Several system calls allow some of this information to be changed: **rename** (change file name), **chmod** (change the protection mode), and **chown** (change the owner and group). Many of these system calls have variants that apply to file descriptors instead of file names. The **link** system call makes a hard link for an existing file, creating a new name for an existing file. A link is removed by the **unlink** system call; if it is the last link, the file is deleted. The **symlink** system call makes a symbolic link.

Directories are made by the **mkdir** system call and are deleted by **rmdir**. The current directory is changed by **cd**.

Although it is possible to use the standard file calls (**open** and others) on directories, it is inadvisable to do so, since directories have an internal structure that must be preserved. Instead, another set of system calls is provided to open a directory, to step through each file entry within the directory, to close the directory, and to perform other functions; these are **opendir, readdir, closedir,** and others.

19.3.2 Process Control

A *process* is a program in execution. Processes are identified by their *process identifier*, which is an integer. A new process is created by the **fork** system call. The new process consists of a copy of the address space of the original process (the same program and the same variables with the same values). Both processes (the parent and the child) continue execution at the instruction after the **fork** with one difference: The return code for the **fork** is zero for the new (child) process, whereas the (nonzero) process identifier of the child is returned to the parent.

Typically, the **execve** system call is used after a fork by one of the two processes to replace that process' virtual memory space with a new program. The **execve** system call loads a binary file into memory (destroying the memory image of the program containing the **execve** system call) and starts its execution.

A process may terminate by using the **exit** system call, and its parent process may wait for that event by using the **wait** system call. If the child process crashes, the system simulates the **exit** call. The **wait** system call provides the process id of a terminated child so that the parent can tell which of possibly many children terminated. A second system call, **wait3,** is similar to **wait** but also allows the parent to collect performance statistics about the child. Between the time the child exits, and the time the parent completes one of the **wait** system calls, the child is *defunct*. A defunct process can do nothing, but exists merely so that the parent can collect its status information. If the parent process of a defunct process exits before a child, the defunct process is inherited by the *init* process (which in turn **wait**s on it) and becomes a *zombie* process. A typical use of these facilities is shown in Figure 19.4.

The simplest form of communication between processes is by *pipes,* which may be created before the **fork,** and whose endpoints are then set up between the **fork** and the **execve.** A pipe is essentially a queue of bytes between two processes. The pipe is accessed by a file descriptor, like an ordinary file. One process writes into the pipe, and the other reads from the pipe. The size of the original pipe system was fixed by the system. With 4.3BSD, pipes are implemented on top of the socket system, which has variable-sized buffers. Reading from an empty pipe or writing into a full pipe causes the process to be blocked until the state of the pipe changes. Special arrangements are needed for a pipe to be placed between a parent and child (so only one is reading and one is writing).

All user processes are descendants of one original process, called *init* (which has process identifier 1). Each terminal port available for interactive use has a *getty* process forked for it by *init*. The *getty* process initializes terminal line parameters and waits for a user's *login name*, which it passes through an **execve** as an argument to a *login* process. The *login* process collects the user's password, encrypts the password, and compares the result to an encrypted string taken from the file */etc/passwd*. If the comparison is successful, the user is allowed to log in. The *login* process executes a *shell*, or command interpreter, after setting the numeric *user identifier* of the process to that of the user logging in. (The shell and the user identifier are found in */etc/passwd* by the user's login name.) It is with this shell that the user ordinarily communicates for the rest of the login session; the shell itself forks subprocesses for the commands the user tells it to execute.

The user identifier is used by the kernel to determine the user's permissions for certain system calls, especially those involving file

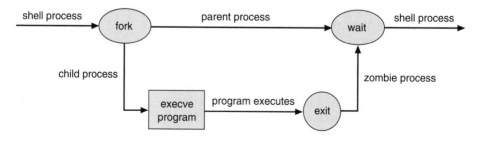

Figure 19.4 A shell forks a subprocess to execute a program.

accesses. There is also a *group identifier*, which is used to provide similar privileges to a collection of users. In 4.3BSD a process may be in several groups simultaneously. The *login* process puts the shell in all the groups permitted to the user by the files */etc/passwd* and */etc/group*.

There are actually two user identifiers used by the kernel: the *effective user identifier* is the identifier used to determine file access permissions. If the file of a program being loaded by an **execve** has the **setuid** bit set in its inode, the effective user identifier of the process is set to the user identifier of the owner of the file, whereas the *real user identifier* is left as it was. This scheme allows certain processes to have more than ordinary privileges while still being executable by ordinary users. The **setuid** idea was patented by Dennis Ritchie (U.S. Patent 4,135,240) and is one of the distinctive features of UNIX. There is a similar **setgid** bit for groups. A process may determine its real and effective user identifier with the **getuid** and **geteuid** calls, respectively. The **getgid** and **getegid** calls determine the process identifier and group identifier, respectively. The rest of a process' groups may be found with the **getgroups** system call.

19.3.3 Signals

Signals are a facility for handling exceptional conditions similar to software interrupts. There are 20 different signals, each corresponding to a distinct condition. A signal may be generated by a keyboard interrupt, by an error in a process (such as a bad memory reference), or by a number of asynchronous events (such as timers or job-control signals from the shell). Almost any signal may also be generated by the **kill** system call.

The *interrupt* signal, SIGINT, is used to stop a command before that command completes. It is usually produced by the ˆC character (ASCII 3). As of 4.2BSD, the important keyboard characters are defined by a table for each terminal and can be redefined easily. The *quit* signal, SIGQUIT, is usually produced by the \ character (ASCII 28). The *quit* signal both stops the currently executing program and dumps its current memory image to a file named *core* in the current directory. The core file can be used by debuggers. SIGILL is produced by an illegal instruction and SIGSEGV by an attempt to address memory outside of the legal virtual-memory space of a process.

Arrangements can be made either for most signals to be ignored (to have no effect), or for a routine in the user process (a signal handler) to be called. A signal handler may safely do one of two things before returning from catching a signal: call the **exit** system call, or modify a global variable. There is one signal (the *kill* signal, number 9, SIGKILL) that cannot be ignored or caught by a signal handler. SIGKILL is used, for example, to kill a runaway process that is ignoring other signals such as SIGINT or SIGQUIT.

Signals can be lost: If another signal of the same kind is sent before a previous signal has been accepted by the process to which it is directed, the first signal will be overwritten and only the last signal will be seen by the process. In other words, a call to the signal handler tells a process that there has been at least one occurance of the signal. Also, there is no relative priority among UNIX signals. If two different signals are sent to the same process at the same time, it is indeterminate which one the process will receive first.

Signals were originally intended to deal with exceptional events. As is true of the use of most other features in UNIX, however, signal use has steadily expanded. 4.1BSD introduced job control, which uses signals to start and stop subprocesses on demand. This facility allows one shell to control multiple processes: starting, stopping, and backgrounding them as the user wishes. 4.3BSD added the SIGWINCH signal, invented by Sun Microsystems, for informing a process that the window in which output is being displayed has changed size. Signals are also used to deliver urgent data from network connections.

Users also wanted more reliable signals, and a bug fix in an inherent race condition in the old signals implementation. Thus, 4.2BSD also brought with it a race-free, reliable, separately implemented signal capability. It allows individual signals to be blocked during critical sections, and has a new system call to let a process sleep until interrupted. It is similar to hardware-interrupt functionality. This capability is now part of the POSIX standard.

19.3.4 Process Groups

Groups of related processes frequently cooperate to accomplish a common task. For instance, processes may create, and communicate over, pipes. Such a set of processes is termed a *process group*, or a *job*. Signals may be sent to all processes in a group. A process usually inherits its process group from its parent, but the **setpgrp** system call allows a process to change its group.

Process groups are used by the C shell to control the operation of multiple jobs. Only one process group may use a terminal device for I/O at any time. This *foreground* job has the attention of the user on that terminal while all other nonattached jobs (*background* jobs) perform their function without user interaction. Access to the terminal is controlled by process group signals. Each job has a *controlling terminal* (again, inherited from its parent). If the process group of the controlling terminal matches the group of a process, that process is in the foreground, and is allowed to perform I/O. If a nonmatching (background) process attempts the same, a SIGTTIN or SIGTTOU signal is sent to its process group. This signal usually results in the process group freezing until it is foregrounded by the user, at which point it receives a SIGCONT signal, indicating that the process can perform the I/O. Similarly, a SIGSTOP may be sent to the foreground process group to freeze it.

19.3.5 Information Manipulation

System calls exist to set and return both an interval timer (**getitimer/setitimer**) and the current time (**gettimeofday/settimeofday**) in microseconds. In addition, processes can ask for their process identifier (**getpid**), their group identifier (**getgid**), the name of the machine on which they are executing (**gethostname**), and many other values.

19.3.6 Library Routines

The system-call interface to UNIX is supported and augmented by a large collection of library routines and header files. The header files provide the definition of complex data structures used in system calls. In addition, a large library of functions provides additional program support.

For example, the UNIX I/O system calls provide for the reading and writing of blocks of bytes. Some applications may want to read and write only 1 byte at a time. Although it would be possible to read and write 1 byte at a time, that would require a system call for each byte — a very high overhead. Instead, a set of standard library routines (the standard I/O package accessed through the header file *<stdio.h>*) provides another interface, which reads and writes several thousand bytes at a time using local buffers, and transfers between these buffers (in user memory) when I/O is desired. Formatted I/O is also supported by the standard I/O package.

Additional library support is provided for mathematical functions, network access, data conversion, and so on. The 4.3BSD kernel supports over 150 system calls; the C program library has over 300 library functions. Although the library functions eventually result in system calls where necessary (for example, the *getchar* library routine will result in a **read** system call if the file buffer is empty), it is generally unnecessary for the programmer to distinguish between the basic set of kernel system calls and the additional functions provided by library functions.

19.4   ■   User Interface

Both the programmer and the user of a UNIX system deal mainly with the set of systems programs that have been written and are available for execution. These programs make the necessary system calls to support their function, but the system calls themselves are contained within the program and do not need to be obvious to the user.

The common systems programs can be grouped into several categories; most of them are file or directory oriented. For example, the system programs to manipulate directories are *mkdir* to create a new directory, *rmdir* to remove a directory, *cd* to change the current directory to another, and *pwd* to print the absolute path name of the current (working) directory.

The *ls* program lists the names of the files in the current directory. Any of 18 options can ask that properties of the files be displayed also. For example, the *-l* option asks for a long listing, showing the file name, owner, protection, date and time of creation, and size. The *cp* program creates a new file that is a copy of an existing file. The *mv* program moves a file from one place to another in the directory tree. In most cases, this move simply requires a renaming of the file; if necessary, however, the file is copied to the new location and the old copy is deleted. A file is deleted by the *rm* program (which makes an **unlink** system call).

To display a file on the terminal, a user can run *cat*. The *cat* program takes a list of files and concatenates them, copying the result to the standard output, commonly the terminal. On a high-speed cathode-ray tube (CRT) display, of course, the file may speed by too fast to be read. The *more* program displays the file one screen at a time, pausing until the user types a character to continue to the next screen. The *head* program displays just the first few lines of a file; *tail* shows the last few lines.

These are the basic systems programs widely used in UNIX. In addition, there are a number of editors (*ed, sed, emacs, vi,* and so on), compilers (C, Pascal, FORTRAN, and so on), and text formatters (troff, TEX, scribe, and so on). There are also programs for sorting (*sort*) and comparing files (*cmp, diff*), looking for patterns (*grep, awk*), sending mail to other users (*mail*), and many other activities.

19.4.1 Shells and Commands

Both user-written and systems programs are normally executed by a command interpreter. The command interpreter in UNIX is a user process like any other. It is called a *shell*, as it surrounds the kernel of the operating system. Users can write their own shell, and there are, in fact, several shells in general use. The *Bourne shell*, written by Steve Bourne, is probably the most widely used — or, at least, it is the most widely available. The C *shell*, mostly the work of Bill Joy, a founder of Sun Microsystems, is the most popular on BSD systems. The Korn shell, by Dave Korn, has become popular because it combines the features of the Bourne shell and the C shell.

The common shells share much of their command-language syntax. UNIX is normally an interactive system. The shell indicates its readiness to accept another command by typing a prompt, and the user types a command on a single line. For instance, in the line

$$\% \; ls \; -l$$

the percent sign is the usual C shell prompt, and the *ls -l* (typed by the user) is the (long) list-directory command. Commands can take arguments, which the user types after the command name on the same line, separated by white space (spaces or tabs).

Although there are a few commands built into the shells (such as *cd*), a typical command is an executable binary object file. A list of several directories, the *search path*, is kept by the shell. For each command, each of the directories in the search path is searched, in order, for a file of the same name. If a file is found, it is loaded and executed. The search path can be set by the user. The directories */bin* and */usr/bin* are almost always in the search path, and a typical search path on a BSD system might be

$$(\ . \ /home/prof/avi/bin \quad /usr/local/bin \quad /usr/ucb \quad /bin \quad /usr/bin \ )$$

The *ls* command's object file is */bin/ls*, and the shell itself is */bin/sh* (the Bourne shell) or */bin/csh* (the C shell).

Execution of a command is done by a **fork** system call followed by an **execve** of the object file. The shell usually then does a **wait** to suspend its own execution until the command completes (Figure 19.4). There is a simple syntax (an ampersand [&] at the end of the command line) to indicate that the shell should *not* wait for the completion of the command. A command left running in this manner while the shell continues to interpret further commands is said to be a *background* command, or to be running in the background. Processes for which the shell *does* wait are said to run in the *foreground*.

The C shell in 4.3BSD systems provides a facility called *job control* (partially implemented in the kernel), as mentioned previously. Job control allows processes to be moved between the foreground and the background. The processes can be stopped and restarted on various conditions, such as a background job wanting input from the user's terminal. This scheme allows most of the control of processes provided by windowing or layering interfaces, but requires no special hardware. Job control is also useful in window systems, such as the X Window System developed at MIT. Each window is treated as a terminal, allowing multiple processes to be in the foreground (one per window) at any one time. Of course, background processes may exist on any of the windows. The Korn shell also supports job control, and it is likely that job control (and process groups) will be standard in future versions of UNIX.

19.4.2 Standard I/O

Processes can open files as they like, but most processes expect three file descriptors (numbers 0, 1, and 2) to be open when they start. These file descriptors are inherited across the **fork** (and possibly the **execve**) that created the process. They are known as *standard input* (0), *standard output* (1), and *standard error* (2). All three are frequently open to the user's terminal. Thus, the program can read what the user types by reading standard input, and the program can send output to the user's screen by writing to standard output. The standard-error file descriptor is also open for writing and is used for error output; standard output is used for ordinary output. Most programs can also accept a file (rather than a terminal) for standard input and standard output. The program does not care where its input is coming from and where its output is going. This is one of the elegant design features of UNIX.

The common shells have a simple syntax for changing what files are open for the standard I/O streams of a process. Changing a standard file is called *I/O redirection*. The syntax for I/O redirection is shown in Figure 19.5. In this example, the *ls* command produces a listing of the names of files in the current directory, the *pr* command formats that list into pages suitable for a printer, and the *lpr* command spools the formatted output to a printer, such as */dev/lp0*. The subsequent command forces all output and all error messages to be redirected to a file. Without the ampersand, error messages appear on the terminal.

19.4.3 Pipelines, Filters, and Shell Scripts

The first three commands of Figure 19.5 could have been coalesced into the one command

$$\% \; ls \mid pr \mid lpr$$

Each vertical bar tells the shell to arrange for the output of the preceding command to be passed as input to the following command. A pipe is used to carry the data from one process to the other. One process writes into one end of the pipe, and another process reads from the other end. In the example, the write end of one pipe would be set up by the shell to be the standard output of *ls,* and the read end of the pipe would be the standard input of *pr;* there would be another pipe between *pr* and *lpr*.

Command	Meaning of command
% ls > filea	direct output of *ls* to file *filea*
% pr < filea > fileb	input from *filea* and output to *fileb*
% lpr < fileb	input from *fileb*
%	
% make program >& errs	save both standard output and standard error in a file

Figure 19.5 Standard I/O redirection.

A command such as *pr* that passes its standard input to its standard output, performing some processing on it, is called a *filter*. Many UNIX commands can be used as filters. Complicated functions can be pieced together as pipelines of common commands. Also, common functions, such as output formatting, do not need to be built into numerous commands, because the output of almost any program can be piped through *pr* (or some other appropriate filter).

Both of the common UNIX shells are also programming languages, with shell variables and the usual higher-level programming-language control constructs (loops, conditionals). The execution of a command is analogous to a subroutine call. A file of shell commands, a *shell script*, can be executed like any other command, with the appropriate shell being invoked automatically to read it. *Shell programming* thus can be used to combine ordinary programs conveniently for sophisticated applications without the necessity of any programming in conventional languages.

This external user view is commonly thought of as the definition of UNIX, yet it is the most easily changed definition. Writing a new shell with a quite different syntax and semantics would greatly change the user view while not changing the kernel or even the programmer interface. Several menu-driven and iconic interfaces for UNIX now exist, and the X Window System is rapidly becoming a standard. The heart of UNIX is, of course, the kernel. This kernel is much more difficult to change than is the user interface, because all programs depend on the system calls that it provides to remain consistent. Of course, new system calls can be added to increase functionality, but programs must then be modified to use the new calls.

19.5 ■ Process Management

A major design problem for operating systems is the representation of processes. One substantial difference between UNIX and many other systems is the ease with which multiple processes can be created and manipulated. These processes are represented in UNIX by various control blocks. There are no system control blocks accessible in the virtual address space of a user process; control blocks associated with a process are stored in the kernel. The information in these control blocks is used by the kernel for process control and CPU scheduling.

19.5.1 Process Control Blocks

The most basic data structure associated with processes is the *process structure*. A process structure contains everything that the system needs to know about a process when the process is swapped out, such as its unique process identifier, scheduling information (such as the priority of the process), and pointers to other control blocks. There is an array of process structures whose length is defined at system linking time. The process structures of ready processes are kept linked together by the scheduler in a doubly linked list (the ready queue), and there are pointers from each process structure to the process' parent, to its youngest living child, and to various other relatives of interest, such as a list of processes sharing the same program code (text).

The *virtual address space* of a user process is divided into text (program code), data, and stack segments. The data and stack segments are always in the same address space, but may grow separately, and usually in opposite directions: most frequently, the stack grows down as the data grow up toward it. The text segment is sometimes (as on an Intel 8086 with separate instruction and data space) in an address space different from the data and stack, and is usually read-only. The debugger puts a text segment in read-write mode to be able to allow insertion of breakpoints.

Every process with sharable text (almost all, under 4.3BSD) has a pointer from its process structure to a *text structure*. The text structure records how many processes are using the text segment, including a pointer into a list of their process structures, and where the page table for the text segment can be found on disk when it is swapped. The text structure itself is always resident in main memory: an array of such structures is allocated at system link time. The text, data, and stack segments for the processes may be swapped. When the segments are swapped in, they are paged.

The *page tables* record information on the mapping from the process' virtual memory to physical memory. The process structure contains pointers to the page table, for use when the process is resident in main memory, or the address of the process on the swap device, when the process is swapped. There is no special separate page table for a shared text segment; every process sharing the text segment has entries for its pages in the process' page table.

Information about the process that is needed only when the process is resident (that is, not swapped out) is kept in the *user structure* (or *u structure*), rather than in the process structure. The u structure is mapped read-only into user virtual address space, so user processes can read its contents. It is writable by the kernel. On the VAX, a copy of the VAX PCB is kept here for saving the process' general registers, stack pointer, program counter, and page-table base registers when the process is not running. There is space to keep system-call parameters and return values. All user and group identifiers associated with the process (not just the effective user identifier kept in the process structure) are kept here. Signals, timers, and quotas have data structures here. Of more obvious relevance to the ordinary user, the current directory and the table of open files are maintained in the user structure.

Every process has both a user and a system phase. Most ordinary work is done in *user mode*, but, when a system call is made, it is performed in *system mode.* The system and user phases of a process never execute simultaneously. When a process is executing in system mode, a *kernel stack* for that process is used, rather than the user stack belonging to that process. The kernel stack for the process immediately follows the user structure: The kernel stack and the user structure together compose the *system data segment* for the process. The kernel has its own stack for use when it is not doing work on behalf of a process (for instance, for interrupt handling).

Figure 19.6 illustrates how the process structure is used to find the various parts of a process.

The **fork** system call allocates a new process structure (with a new process identifier) for the child process, and copies the user structure. There is ordinarily no need for a new text structure, as the processes share their text; the appropriate counters and lists are merely updated. A new page table is constructed, and new main memory is allocated for the data and stack segments of the child process. The copying of the user structure preserves open file descriptors, user and group identifiers, signal handling, and most similar properties of a process.

The **vfork** system call does *not* copy the data and stack to the new process; rather, the new process simply shares the page table of the old one. A new user structure and a new process structure are still created. A common use of this system call is by a shell to execute a command and to

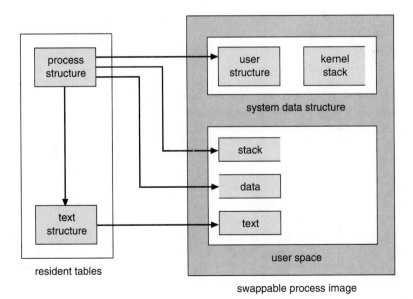

Figure 19.6 Finding parts of a process using the process structure.

wait for its completion. The parent process uses **vfork** to produce the child process. Because the child process wishes to use an **execve** immediately to change its virtual address space completely, there is no need for a complete copy of the parent process. Such data structures as are necessary for manipulating pipes may be kept in registers between the **vfork** and the **execve**. Files may be closed in one process without affecting the other process, since the kernel data structures involved depend on the user structure, which is not shared. The parent is suspended when it calls **vfork** until the child either calls **execve** or terminates, so that the parent will not change memory that the child needs.

When the parent process is large, **vfork** can produce substantial savings in system CPU time. However, it is a fairly dangerous system call, since any memory change occurs in both processes until the **execve** occurs. An alternative is to share all pages by duplicating the page table, but to mark the entries of both page tables as *copy-on-write*. The hardware protection bits are set to trap any attempt to write in these shared pages. If such a trap occurs, a new frame is allocated and the shared page is copied to the new frame. The page tables are adjusted to show that this page is no longer shared (and therefore no longer needs to be write-protected), and execution can resume.

An **execve** system call creates no new process or user structure; rather, the text and data of the process are replaced. Open files are preserved (although there is a way to specify that certain file descriptors are to be closed on an **execve**). Most signal-handling properties are preserved, but arrangements to call a specific user routine on a signal are canceled, for obvious reasons. The process identifier and most other properties of the process are unchanged.

19.5.2 CPU Scheduling

CPU scheduling in UNIX is designed to benefit interactive processes. Processes are given small CPU time slices by a priority algorithm that reduces to round-robin scheduling for CPU-bound jobs.

Every process has a *scheduling priority* associated with it; larger numbers indicate lower priority. Processes doing disk I/O or other important tasks have priorities less than "pzero" and cannot be killed by signals. Ordinary user processes have positive priorities and thus are all less likely to be run than are any system process, although user processes can set precedence over one another through the *nice* command.

The more CPU time a process accumulates, the lower (more positive) its priority becomes, and vice versa, so there is negative feedback in CPU scheduling and it is difficult for a single process to take all the CPU time. Process aging is employed to prevent starvation.

Older UNIX systems used a 1-second quantum for the round-robin scheduling. 4.3BSD reschedules processes every 0.1 second and recomputes priorities every second. The round-robin scheduling is accomplished by the *timeout* mechanism, which tells the clock interrupt driver to call a kernel subroutine after a specified interval; the subroutine to be called in this case causes the rescheduling and then resubmits a *timeout* to call itself again. The priority recomputation is also timed by a subroutine that resubmits a *timeout* for itself.

There is no preemption of one process by another in the kernel. A process may relinquish the CPU because it is waiting on I/O or because its time slice has expired. When a process chooses to relinquish the CPU, it goes to sleep on an *event*. The kernel primitive used for this purpose is called *sleep* (not to be confused with the user-level library routine of the same name). It takes an argument, which is by convention the address of a kernel data structure related to an *event* that the process wants to occur before that process is awakened. When the event occurs, the system process that knows about it calls *wakeup* with the address corresponding to the event, and *all* processes that had done a *sleep* on the same address are put in the ready queue to be run.

For example, a process waiting for disk I/O to complete will *sleep* on the address of the buffer header corresponding to the data being transferred. When the interrupt routine for the disk driver notes that the transfer is complete, it calls *wakeup* on the buffer header. The interrupt uses the kernel stack for whatever process happened to be running at the time, and the *wakeup* is done from that system process.

The process that actually does run is chosen by the scheduler. *Sleep* takes a second argument, which is the scheduling priority to be used for this purpose. This priority argument, if less than "pzero", also prevents the process from being awakened prematurely by some exceptional event, such as a *signal*.

When a signal is generated, it is left pending until the system half of the affected process next runs. This event usually happens soon, since the signal normally causes the process to be awakened if the process has been waiting for some other condition.

There is no memory associated with events, and the caller of the routine that does a *sleep* on an event must be prepared to deal with a premature return, including the possibility that the reason for waiting has vanished.

There are *race conditions* involved in the event mechanism. If a process decides (because of checking a flag in memory, for instance) to sleep on an event, and the event occurs before the process can execute the primitive that does the actual sleep on the event, the process sleeping may then sleep forever. We prevent this situation by raising the hardware processor priority during the critical section so that no interrupts can occur, and thus only the process desiring the event can run until it is sleeping. Hardware processor priority is used in this manner to protect critical regions throughout the kernel, and is the greatest obstacle to porting UNIX to multiple processor machines. However, this problem has not prevented such ports from being done repeatedly.

Many processes such as text editors are I/O bound and usually will be scheduled mainly on the basis of waiting for I/O. Experience suggests that the UNIX scheduler performs best with I/O-bound jobs, as can be observed when there are several CPU-bound jobs, such as text formatters or language interpreters, running.

What has been referred to here as *CPU scheduling* corresponds closely to the *short-term scheduling* of Chapter 4, although the negative-feedback property of the priority scheme provides some long-term scheduling in that it largely determines the long-term *job mix*. Medium-term scheduling is done by the swapping mechanism described in Section 19.6.

19.6 ■ Memory Management

Much of UNIX's early development was done on a PDP-11. The PDP-11 has only eight segments in its virtual address space, and each of these are at most 8192 bytes. The larger machines, such as the PDP-11/70, allow separate instruction and address spaces, which effectively double the address space and number of segments, but this address space is still relatively small. In addition, the kernel was even more severely constrained due to dedication of one data segment to interrupt vectors, another to point at the per-process system data segment, and yet another for the UNIBUS (system I/O bus) registers. Further, on the smaller PDP-11s, total physical memory was limited to 256K. The total memory resources were insufficient to justify or support complex memory-management algorithms. Thus, UNIX swapped entire process memory images.

19.6.1 Swapping

Pre-3BSD UNIX systems use swapping exclusively to handle memory contention among processes: If there is too much contention, processes are swapped out until enough memory is available. Also, a few large processes can force many small processes out of memory, and a process larger than nonkernel main memory cannot be run at all. The system data segment (the *u* structure and kernel stack) and the user data segment (text [if nonsharable], data, and stack) are kept in contiguous main memory for swap-transfer efficiency, so external fragmentation of memory can be a serious problem.

Allocation of both main memory and swap space is done first-fit. When the size of a process' memory image increases (due to either stack expansion or data expansion), a new piece of memory big enough for the whole image is allocated. The memory image is copied, the old memory is freed, and the appropriate tables are updated. (An attempt is made in some systems to find memory contiguous to the end of the current piece, to avoid some copying.) If no single piece of main memory is large enough, the process is swapped out such that it will be swapped back in with the new size.

There is no need to swap out a sharable text segment, because it is read-only, and there is no need to read in a sharable text segment for a process when another instance is already in core. That is one of the main reasons for keeping track of sharable text segments: less swap traffic. The other reason is the reduced amount of main memory required for multiple processes using the same text segment.

Decisions regarding which processes to swap in or out are made by the *scheduler process* (also known as the *swapper*). The *scheduler* wakes up at least once every 4 seconds to check for processes to be swapped in or out. A process is more likely to be swapped out if it is idle, has been in main memory a long time, or is large; if no obvious candidates are found, other processes are picked by age. A process is more likely to be swapped in if it has been swapped out a long time, or is small. There are checks to prevent thrashing, basically by not letting a process be swapped out if it has not been in memory for a certain amount of time.

If jobs do not need to be swapped out, the process table is searched for a process deserving to be brought in (determined by how small the process is and how long it has been swapped out). If there is not enough memory available, processes are swapped out until there is.

In 4.3BSD, swap space is allocated in pieces that are multiples of a power of 2 and a minimum size (for example, 32 pages), up to a maximum that is determined by the size of the swap-space partition on the disk. If several logical disk partitions may be used for swapping, they should be the same size, for this reason. The several logical disk partitions should also be on separate disk arms to minimize disk seeks.

Many UNIX systems still use the swapping scheme just described. All Berkeley UNIX systems, on the other hand, depend primarily on paging for memory-contention management, and depend only secondarily on swapping. A scheme similar in outline to the traditional one is used to determine which processes get swapped in or out, but the details differ and the influence of swapping is less.

19.6.2 Paging

Berkeley introduced paging to UNIX with 3BSD. VAX 4.2BSD is a demand-paged virtual-memory system. External fragmentation of memory is eliminated by paging. (There is, of course, internal fragmentation, but it is negligible with a reasonably small page size.) Swapping can be kept to a minimum because more jobs can be kept in main memory, because paging allows execution with only parts of each process in memory.

Demand paging is done in a straightforward manner. When a process needs a page and the page is not there, a page fault to the kernel occurs, a frame of main memory is allocated, and the proper disk page is read into the frame.

There are a few optimizations. If the page needed is still in the page table for the process, but has been marked invalid by the page-replacement process, it can be marked valid and used without any I/O transfer. Pages can similarly be retrieved from the list of free frames. When most processes are started, many of their pages are prepaged and are put on the free list for recovery by this mechanism. Arrangements may also be made for a process to have no prepaging on startup, but that is seldom done, as it results in more page-fault overhead, being closer to pure demand paging.

If the page has to be fetched from disk, it must be locked in memory for the duration of the transfer. This locking ensures that the page will not be selected for page replacement. Once the page is fetched and mapped properly, it must remain locked if raw physical I/O is being done on it.

The *page-replacement* algorithm is more interesting. The VAX has no hardware memory page-reference bit. This lack makes many memory-management algorithms, such as page-fault frequency, unusable. 4.2BSD uses a modification of the *second chance* (clock) algorithm described in Section 9.5.4. The map of all nonkernel main memory (the *core map* or *cmap*) is swept linearly and repeatedly by a software *clock hand*. When the clock hand reaches a given frame, if the frame is marked as in use by some software condition (for example, physical I/O is in progress using it), or the frame is already free, the frame is left untouched, and the clock hand sweeps to the next frame. Otherwise, the corresponding text or process page-table entry for this frame is located. If the entry is already invalid, the frame is added to the free list; otherwise, the page-table entry is made invalid but reclaimable (that is, if it does not get paged out by the next time it is wanted, it can just be made valid again). 4.3BSD Tahoe added support for systems which do implement the reference bit. On such systems, one pass of the clock turns the reference bit off, and a second pass places those pages whose reference bits remain off onto the free list for replacement. Of course, if the page is dirty (the VAX *does* have a dirty bit), it must first be written to disk before being added to the free list. Pageouts are done in clusters to improve performance.

There are checks to make sure that the number of valid data pages for a process does not fall too low, and to keep the paging device from being flooded with requests. There is also a mechanism by which a process may limit the amount of main memory it uses.

The LRU clock hand is implemented in the *pagedaemon,* which is process 2 (remember that the *scheduler* is process 0, and *init* is process 1). This process spends most of its time sleeping, but a check is done several times per second (scheduled by a *timeout*) to see if action is necessary; if it is, process 2 is awakened. Whenever the number of free frames falls below a threshold, *lotsfree*, the *pagedaemon* is awakened; thus, if there is always a large amount of free memory, the *pagedaemon* imposes no load on the system, because it never runs.

The sweep of the clock hand each time the *pagedaemon* process is awakened (that is, the number of frames scanned, which is usually more than the number paged out), is determined both by the number of frames lacking to reach *lotsfree* and by the number of frames that the *scheduler* has determined are needed for various reasons (the more frames needed, the longer the sweep). If the number of frames free rises to *lotsfree* before the expected sweep is completed, the hand stops and the *pagedaemon* process sleeps. The parameters that determine the range of the clock-hand sweep are determined at system startup according to the amount of main memory, such that *pagedaemon* does not use more than 10 percent of all CPU time.

If the *scheduler* decides that the paging system is overloaded, processes will be swapped out whole until the overload is relieved. This swapping usually happens only if several conditions are met: load average is high, free memory has fallen below a low limit, *minfree*; and the average memory available over recent time is less than a desirable amount, *desfree*, where *lotsfree* > *desfree* > *minfree*. In other words, only a chronic shortage of memory with several processes trying to run will cause swapping, and even then free memory has to be extremely low at the moment. (An excessive paging rate or a need for memory by the kernel itself may also enter into the calculations, in rare cases.) Processes may be swapped by the *scheduler*, of course, for other reasons (such as simply for not running for a long time).

The parameter *lotsfree* is usually one-quarter of the memory in the map that the clock hand sweeps, and *desfree* and *minfree* are usually the same across different systems, but are limited to fractions of available memory.

Every process' text segment is by default shared and read-only. This scheme is practical with paging, because there is no external fragmentation, and the swap space gained by sharing more than offsets the negligible amount of overhead involved, as the kernel virtual space is large.

CPU scheduling, swapping, and paging interact: the lower the priority of a process, the more likely that its pages will be paged out and the more likely that it will be swapped in its entirety.

The age preferences in choosing processes to swap guard against thrashing, but paging does so more effectively. Ideally, processes will not be swapped out unless they are idle, because each process will need only a small working set of pages in main memory at any one time, and the *pagedaemon* will reclaim unused pages for use by other processes.

The amount of memory the process will need is some fraction of that process' total virtual size, up to one-half if that process has been swapped out for a long time.

The VAX 512-byte hardware pages are too small for I/O efficiency, so they are clustered in groups of two so that all paging I/O is actually done in 1024-byte chunks. In other words, the effective page size is not necessarily identical to the hardware page size of the machine, although it must be a multiple of the hardware page size.

19.7 ■ File System

The UNIX file system supports two main objects: files and directories. Directories are just files with a special format, so the representation of a file is the basic UNIX concept.

19.7.1 Blocks and Fragments

Most of the file system is taken up by *data blocks*, which contain whatever the users have put in their files. Let us consider how these data blocks are stored on the disk.

The hardware disk sector is usually 512 bytes. A block size larger than 512 bytes is desirable for speed. However, because UNIX file systems usually contain a very large number of small files, much larger blocks would cause excessive internal fragmentation. That is why the earlier 4.1BSD file system was limited to a 1024-byte (1K) block.

The 4.2BSD solution is to use *two* block sizes for files which have no indirect blocks: all the blocks of a file are of a large *block* size (such as 8K), except the last. The last block is an appropriate multiple of a smaller *fragment* size (for example, 1024) to fill out the file. Thus, a file of size 18,000 bytes would have two 8K blocks and one 2K fragment (which would not be filled completely).

The *block* and *fragment* sizes are set during file-system creation according to the intended use of the file system: If many small files are expected, the fragment size should be small; if repeated transfers of large files are expected, the basic block size should be large. Implementation details force a maximum block-to-fragment ratio of 8 : 1, and a minimum block size of 4K, so typical choices are 4096 : 512 for the former case and 8192 : 1024 for the latter.

Suppose data are written to a file in transfer sizes of 1K bytes, and the block and fragment sizes of the file system are 4K and 512 bytes. The file system will allocate a 1K fragment to contain the data from the first transfer. The next transfer will cause a new 2K fragment to be allocated. The data from the original fragment must be copied into this new fragment, followed by the second 1K transfer. The allocation routines do attempt to find the required space on the disk immediately following the existing fragment so that no copying is necessary, but, if they cannot do so, up to seven copies may be required before the fragment becomes a block. Provisions have been made for programs to discover the block size for a file so that transfers of that size can be made, to avoid fragment recopying.

19.7.2 Inodes

A file is represented by an *inode* (Figure 11.7). An inode is a record that stores most of the information about a specific file on the disk. The name *inode* (pronounced *EYE node*) is derived from "index node" and was originally spelled "i-node"; the hyphen fell out of use over the years. The term is also sometimes spelled "I node".

The inode contains the user and group identifiers of the file, the times of the last file modification and access, a count of the number of hard links (directory entries) to the file, and the type of the file (plain file, directory, symbolic link, character device, block device, or socket). In addition, the inode contains 15 pointers to the disk blocks containing the data contents of the file. The first 12 of these pointers point to *direct blocks;* that is, they contain addresses of blocks that contain data of the file. Thus, the data for small files (no more than 12 blocks) can be referenced immediately, because a copy of the inode is kept in main memory while a file is open. If the block size is 4K, then up to 48K of data may be accessed directly from the inode.

The next three pointers in the inode point to *indirect blocks*. If the file is large enough to use indirect blocks, the indirect blocks are each of the major block size; the fragment size applies to only data blocks. The first indirect block pointer is the address of a *single indirect block*. The single indirect block is an index block, containing not data, but rather the addresses of blocks that do contain data. Then, there is a *double-indirect-block pointer*, the address of a block that contains the addresses of blocks that contain pointers to the actual data blocks. The last pointer would contain the address of a *triple indirect block*; however, there is no need for it. The minimum block size for a file system in 4.2BSD is 4K, so files with as many as 2^{32} bytes will use only double, not triple, indirection. That is, as each block pointer takes 4 bytes, we have 49,152 bytes accessible in direct blocks, 4,194,304 bytes accessible by a single indirection, and 4,294,967,296 bytes reachable through double indirection, for a total of 4,299,210,752 bytes, which is larger than 2^{32} bytes. The number 2^{32} is significant because the file offset in the file structure in main memory is kept in a 32-bit word. Files therefore cannot be larger than 2^{32} bytes. Since file pointers are signed integers (for seeking backward and forward in a file), the actual maximum file size is 2^{32-1} bytes. Two gigabytes is large enough for most purposes.

19.7.3 Directories

There is no distinction between plain files and directories at this level of implementation; directory contents are kept in data blocks, and directories are represented by an inode in the same way as plain files. Only the inode type field distinguishes between plain files and directories. Plain files are not assumed to have a structure, however, whereas directories have a specific structure. In Version 7, file names were limited to 14 characters, so directories were a list of 16-byte entries: 2 bytes for an inode number and 14 bytes for a file name.

In 4.2BSD, file names are of variable length, up to 255 bytes, so directory entries are also of variable length. Each entry contains first the length of the entry, then the file name and the inode number. This variable-length entry makes the directory management and search routines more complex, but greatly improves the ability of users to choose meaningful names for their files and directories, with no practical limit on the length of the name.

The first two names in every directory are "." and "..". New directory entries are added to the directory in the first space available, generally after the existing files. A linear search is used.

The user refers to a file by a path name, whereas the file system uses the inode as its definition of a file. Thus, the kernel has to map the supplied user path name to an inode. The directories are used for this mapping.

First, a starting directory is determined. If the first character of the path name is "/", the starting directory is the root directory. If the path name starts with any character other than a slash, the starting directory is the current directory of the current process. The starting directory is checked for proper file type and access permissions, and an error is returned if necessary. The inode of the starting directory is always available.

The next element of the path name, up to the next "/", or to the end of the path name, is a file name. The starting directory is searched for this name, and an error is returned if the name is not found. If there is yet another element in the path name, the current inode must refer to a directory, and an error is returned if it does not, or if access is denied. This directory is searched as was the previous one. This process continues until the end of the path name is reached and the desired inode is returned. This step-by-step process is needed because at any directory a mount point (or symbolic link, see below) may be encountered, causing the translation to move to a different directory structure for continuation.

Hard links are simply directory entries like any other. We handle symbolic links for the most part by starting the search over with the path name taken from the contents of the symbolic link. We prevent infinite loops by counting the number of symbolic links encountered during a path-name search and returning an error when a limit (eight) is exceeded.

Nondisk files (such as devices) do not have data blocks allocated on the disk. The kernel notices these file types (as indicated in the inode) and calls appropriate drivers to handle I/O for them.

Once the inode is found by, for instance, the **open** system call, a *file structure* is allocated to point to the inode. The file descriptor given to the user refers to this file structure. 4.3BSD added a *directory name cache* to hold recent directory-to-inode translations. This improvement greatly increased file system performance.

19.7.4 Mapping of a File Descriptor to an Inode

System calls that refer to open files indicate the file by passing a file descriptor as an argument. The file descriptor is used by the kernel to index a table of open files for the current process. Each entry of the table contains a pointer to a file structure. This file structure in turn points to the inode; see Figure 19.7. The open file table has a fixed length which is only settable at boot time. Therefore, there is a fixed limit on the number of concurrently open files in a system.

The **read** and **write** system calls do not take a position in the file as an argument. Rather, the kernel keeps a *file offset*, which is updated by an appropriate amount after each **read** or **write** according to the number of data actually transferred. The offset can be set directly by the **lseek** system call. If the file descriptor indexed an array of inode pointers instead of file pointers, this offset would have to be kept in the inode. Because more than one process may open the same file, and each such process needs its

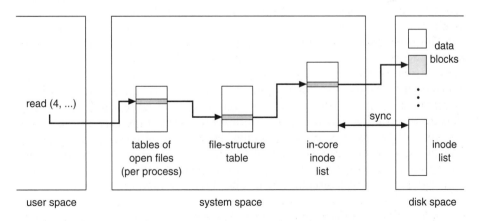

Figure 19.7 File-system control blocks.

own offset for the file, keeping the offset in the inode is inappropriate. Thus, the file structure is used to contain the offset.

File structures are inherited by the child process after a **fork,** so several processes may share the *same* offset location for a file.

The *inode structure* pointed to by the file structure is an in-core copy of the inode on the disk. The in-core inode has a few extra fields, such as a reference count of how many file structures are pointing at it, and the file structure has a similar reference count for how many file descriptors refer to it. When a count becomes zero, the entry is no longer needed and may be reclaimed and reused.

19.7.5 Disk Structures

The file system that the user sees is supported by data on a mass storage device — usually, a disk. The user ordinarily knows of only one file system, but this one logical file system may actually consist of several *physical* file systems, each on a different device. Because device characteristics differ, each separate hardware device defines its own physical file system. In fact, it is generally desirable to partition large physical devices, such as disks, into multiple *logical* devices. Each logical device defines a physical file system. Figure 19.8 illustrates how a directory structure is partitioned into file systems, which are mapped onto logical devices, which are partitions of physical devices. The sizes and locations of these partitions were coded into device drivers in earlier systems, but are maintained on the disk by 4.3BSD.

Partitioning a physical device into multiple file systems has several benefits. Different file systems can support different uses. Although most partitions would be used by the file system, at least one will be necessary for a swap area for the virtual-memory software. Reliability is improved, because software damage is generally limited to only one file system. We can improve efficiency by varying the file-system parameters (such as the block and fragment sizes) for each partition. Also, separate file systems prevent one program from using all available space for a large file, because files cannot be split across file systems. Finally, disk backups are done per partition, and it is faster to search a backup tape for a file if the partition is smaller. Restoring the full partition from tape is also faster.

The actual number of file systems on a drive varies according to the size of the disk and the purpose of the computer system as a whole. One file system, the *root file system,* is always available. Other file systems may be *mounted* — that is, integrated into the directory hierarchy of the root file system.

A bit in the inode structure indicates that the inode has a file system mounted on it. A reference to this file causes the *mount table* to be searched to find the device number of the mounted device. The device number is

| logical file system | file systems | logical devices | physical devices |

Figure 19.8 Mapping of a logical file system to physical devices.

used to find the inode of the root directory of the mounted file system, and that inode is used. Conversely, if a path-name element is ".." and the directory being searched is the root directory of a file system that is mounted, the mount table is searched to find the inode it is mounted on, and that inode is used.

Each file system is a separate system resource and represents a set of files. The first sector on the logical device is the *boot block*, possibly containing a primary bootstrap program, which may be used to call a secondary bootstrap program residing in the next 7.5K. A system needs only one partition containing boot-block data, but duplicates may be installed via privileged programs by the systems manager, to allow booting when the primary copy is damaged. The *superblock* contains static parameters of the file system. These parameters include the total size of the file system, the block and fragment sizes of the data blocks, and assorted parameters that affect allocation policies.

19.7.6 Implementations

The user interface to the file system is simple and well defined, allowing the implementation of the file system itself to be changed without significant effect on the user. The file system was changed between Version 6 and Version 7, and again between Version 7 and 4BSD. For Version 7, the size of inodes doubled, the maximum file and file-system sizes increased, and the details of free-list handling and superblock information changed. At that time also, *seek* (with a 16-bit offset) became *lseek* (with a 32-bit offset), to allow specification of offsets in larger files, but few other changes were visible outside the kernel.

In 4.0BSD, the size of blocks used in the file system was increased from 512 bytes to 1024 bytes. Although this increased size produced increased internal fragmentation on the disk, it doubled throughput, due mainly to the greater number of data accessed on each disk transfer. This idea was later adopted by System V, along with a number of other ideas, device drivers, and programs.

4.2BSD added the Berkeley Fast File System, which increased speed, and was accompanied by new features. Symbolic links required new system calls. Long file names necessitated the new directory system calls to traverse the now-complex internal directory structure. Finally, the **truncate** calls were added. The Fast File System was a success, and is now found in most implementations of UNIX. Its performance is made possible by its layout and allocation policies, which we discuss next. In Section 11.2.4, we discussed changes made in SunOS to further increase disk throughput.

19.7.7 Layout and Allocation Policies

The kernel uses a <*logical device number, inode number*> pair to identify a file. The logical device number defines the file system involved. The inodes in the file system are numbered in sequence. In the Version 7 file system, all inodes are in an array immediately following a single superblock at the beginning of the logical device, with the data blocks following the inodes. The *inode number* is effectively just an index into this array.

With the Version 7 file system, a block of a file can be anywhere on the disk between the end of the inode array and the end of the file system. Free blocks are kept in a linked list in the superblock. Blocks are pushed onto the front of the free list, and are removed from the front as needed to serve new files or to extend existing files. Thus, the blocks of a file may be arbitrarily far from both the inode and one another. Furthermore, the more a file system of this kind is used, the more disorganized the blocks in a file become. We can reverse this process only by reinitializing and restoring the entire file system, which is not a convenient task to perform. This process was described in Section 11.6.2.

Another difficulty is that the reliability of the file system is suspect. For speed, the superblock of each mounted file system is kept in memory. Keeping the superblock in memory allows the kernel to access a superblock quickly, especially for using the free list. Every 30 seconds, the superblock is written to the disk, to keep the in-core and disk copies synchronized (by the update program, using the **sync** system call). However, it is not uncommon for system bugs or hardware failures to cause a system crash, which destroys the in-core superblock between updates to the disk. Then, the free list on disk does not reflect accurately the state of the disk; to reconstruct it, we must perform a lengthy examination of all blocks in the file system. Note that this problem still remains in the new file system.

The 4.2BSD file-system implementation is radically different from that of Version 7. This reimplementation was done primarily to improve efficiency and robustness, and most such changes are invisible outside the kernel. There were other changes introduced at the same time, such as symbolic links and long file names (up to 255 characters), that are visible at both the system-call and the user levels. Most of the changes required for these features were not in the kernel, however, but rather were in the programs that use them.

Space allocation is especially different. The major new concept in 4.3BSD is the *cylinder group*. The cylinder group was introduced to allow localization of the blocks in a file. Each cylinder group occupies one or more consecutive cylinders of the disk, so that disk accesses within the cylinder group require minimal disk head movement. Every cylinder group has a superblock, a cylinder block, an array of inodes, and some data blocks (Figure 19.9).

The superblock is identical in each cylinder group, so that it can be recovered from any one of them in the event of disk corruption. The *cylinder block* contains dynamic parameters of the particular cylinder group. These include a bit map of free data blocks and fragments, and a bit map

Figure 19.9   4.3BSD cylinder group.

of free inodes. Statistics on recent progress of the allocation strategies are also kept here.

The header information in a cylinder group (the superblock, the cylinder block, and the inodes) is not always at the beginning of the cylinder group. If it were, the header information for every cylinder group might be on the same disk platter; a single disk head crash could wipe out all of them. Therefore, each cylinder group has its header information at a different offset from the beginning of the group.

It is common for the directory-listing command *ls* to read all the inodes of every file in a directory, making it desirable for all such inodes to be close together. For this reason, the inode for a file is usually allocated from the same cylinder group as is the inode of the file's parent directory. Not everything can be localized, however, so an inode for a new directory is put in a *different* cylinder group from that of its parent directory. The cylinder group chosen for such a new directory inode is that with the greatest number of unused inodes.

To reduce disk head seeks involved in accessing the data blocks of a file, we allocate blocks from the same cylinder group as often as possible. Because a single file cannot be allowed to take up all the blocks in a cylinder group, a file exceeding a certain size (such as 2 megabytes) has further block allocation redirected to a different cylinder group, the new group being chosen from among those having more than average free space. If the file continues to grow, allocation is again redirected (at each megabyte) to yet another cylinder group. Thus, all the blocks of a small file are likely to be in the same cylinder group, and the number of long head seeks involved in accessing a large file is kept small.

There are two levels of disk-block-allocation routines. The global policy routines select a desired disk block according to the considerations already discussed. The local policy routines use the specific information recorded in the cylinder blocks to choose a block near the one requested. If the requested block is not in use, it is returned. Otherwise, the block rotationally closest to the one requested in the same cylinder, or a block in a different cylinder but in the same cylinder group, is returned. If there are no more blocks in the cylinder group, a quadratic rehash is done among all the other cylinder groups to find a block; if that fails, an exhaustive search is done. If enough free space (typically 10 percent) is left in the file system, blocks usually are found where desired, the quadratic rehash and exhaustive search are not used, and performance of the file system does not degrade with use.

Because of the increased efficiency of the Fast File System, typical disks are now utilized at 30 percent of their raw transfer capacity. This percentage is a marked improvement over that realized with the Version 7 file system, which used about 3 percent of the bandwidth.

4.3BSD Tahoe introduced the Fat Fast File System, which allows the number of inodes per cylinder group, the number of cylinders per cylinder group, and the number of distinguished rotational positions to be set when the file system is created. 4.3BSD used to set these parameters according to the disk hardware type.

19.8   ■   I/O System

One of the purposes of an operating system is to hide the peculiarities of specific hardware devices from the user. For example, the file system presents a simple consistent storage facility (the file) independent of the underlying disk hardware. In UNIX, the peculiarities of I/O devices are also hidden from the bulk of the kernel itself by the *I/O system*. The I/O system consists of a buffer caching system, general device driver code, and drivers for specific hardware devices. Only the device driver knows the peculiarities of a specific device. The major parts of the I/O system are diagrammed in Figure 19.10.

There are three main kinds of I/O in 4.3BSD: block devices, character devices, and the *socket* interface. The socket interface, together with its protocols and network interfaces, will be treated in Section 19.9.1.

Block devices include disks and tapes. Their distinguishing characteristic is that they are directly addressable in a fixed block size — usually, 512 bytes. A block-device driver is required to isolate details of tracks, cylinders, and so on, from the rest of the kernel. Block devices are accessible directly through appropriate device special files (such as /dev/rp0), but are more commonly accessed indirectly through the file system. In either case, transfers are buffered through the *block buffer cache*, which has a profound effect on efficiency.

Character devices include terminals and line printers, but also almost everything else (except network interfaces) that does not use the block buffer cache. For instance, /dev/mem is an interface to physical main memory, and /dev/null is a bottomless sink for data and an endless source

system-call interface to the kernel					
socket	plain file	cooked block interface	raw block interface	raw tty interface	cooked TTY
protocols	file system				line discipline
network interface	block-device driver			character-device driver	
the hardware					

Figure 19.10   4.3BSD kernel I/O structure.

of end-of-file markers. Some devices, such as high-speed graphics interfaces, may have their own buffers or may always do I/O directly into the user's data space; because they do not use the block buffer cache, they are classed as character devices.

Terminals and terminal-like devices use *C-lists*, which are buffers smaller than those of the block buffer cache.

Block devices and *character* devices are the two main device classes. Device drivers are accessed by one of two arrays of entry points. One array is for block devices; the other is for character devices. A device is distinguished by a class (block or character) and a *device number*. The device number consists of two parts. The *major device number* is used to index the array for character or block devices to find entries into the appropriate device driver. The *minor device number* is interpreted by the device driver as, for example, a logical disk partition or a terminal line.

A device driver is connected to the rest of the kernel only by the entry points recorded in the array for its class, and by its use of common buffering systems. This segregation is important for portability, and also for system configuration.

19.8.1 Block Buffer Cache

The block devices use a block buffer cache. The buffer cache consists of a number of buffer headers, each of which can point to a piece of physical memory, as well as to a device number and a block number on the device. The buffer headers for blocks not currently in use are kept in several linked lists, one each for

- Buffers recently used, linked in LRU order (the LRU list)
- Buffers not recently used, or without valid contents (the AGE list)
- EMPTY buffers with no physical memory associated with them

The buffers in these lists are also hashed by device and block number for search efficiency.

When a block is wanted from a device (a read), the cache is searched. If the block is found, it is used, and no I/O transfer is necessary. If it is not found, a buffer is chosen from the AGE list, or the LRU list if AGE is empty. Then the device number and block number associated with it are updated, memory is found for it if necessary, and the new data are transferred into it from the device. If there are no empty buffers, the LRU buffer is written to its device (if it is modified) and the buffer is reused.

On a write, if the block in question is already in the buffer cache, the new data are put in the buffer (overwriting any previous data), the buffer header is marked to indicate the buffer has been modified, and no I/O is immediately necessary. The data will be written when the buffer is needed for other data. If the block is not found in the buffer cache, an empty buffer is chosen (as with a read) and a transfer is done to this buffer.

Writes are periodically forced for dirty buffer blocks to minimize potential file-system inconsistencies after a crash.

The number of data in a buffer in 4.3BSD is variable, up to a maximum over all file systems, usually 8K. The minimum size is the paging-cluster size, usually 1024 bytes. Buffers are page-cluster aligned, and any page cluster may be mapped into only one buffer at a time, just as any disk block may be mapped into only one buffer at a time. The EMPTY list holds buffer headers which are used if a physical memory block of 8K is split to hold multiple, smaller blocks. Headers are needed for these blocks and are retrieved from EMPTY.

The number of data in a buffer may grow as a user process writes more data following those already in the buffer. When this increase in the data occurs, a new buffer large enough to hold all the data is allocated, and the original data are copied into it, followed by the new data. If a buffer shrinks, a buffer is taken off the empty queue, excess pages are put in it, and that buffer is released to be written to disk.

Some devices, such as magnetic tapes, require blocks to be written in a certain order, so facilities are provided to force a synchronous write of buffers to these devices, in the correct order. Directory blocks are also written synchronously, to forestall crash inconsistencies. Consider the chaos that could occur if many changes were made to a directory, but the directory entries themselves were not updated.

The size of the buffer cache can have a profound effect on the performance of a system, because, if it is large enough, the percentage of cache hits can be high and the number of actual I/O transfers low.

There are some interesting interactions among the buffer cache, the file system, and the disk drivers. When data are written to a disk file, they are buffered in the cache, and the disk driver sorts its output queue according to disk address. These two actions allow the disk driver to minimize disk head seeks and to write data at times optimized for disk rotation. Unless synchronous writes are required, a process writing to disk simply writes into the buffer cache, and the system asynchronously writes the data to disk when convenient. The user process sees very fast writes. When data are read from a disk file, the block I/O system does some read-ahead; however, writes are much nearer to asynchronous than are reads. Thus, output to the disk through the file system is often faster than is input for large transfers, counter to intuition.

19.8.2 Raw Device Interfaces

Almost every block device also has a character interface, and these are called *raw device interfaces*. Such an interface differs from the *block interface* in that the block buffer cache is bypassed.

Each disk driver maintains a queue of pending transfers. Each record in the queue specifies whether it is a read or a write, a main memory address for the transfer (usually in 512-byte increments), a device address for the transfer (usually the address of a disk sector), and a transfer size (in sectors). It is simple to map the information from a block buffer to what is required for this queue.

It is almost as simple to map a piece of main memory corresponding to part of a user process' virtual address space. This mapping is what a raw disk interface, for instance, does. Unbuffered transfers directly to or from a user's virtual address space are thus allowed. The size of the transfer is limited by the physical devices, some of which require an even number of bytes.

The kernel accomplishes transfers for swapping and paging simply by putting the appropriate request on the queue for the appropriate device. No special swapping or paging device driver is needed.

The 4.2BSD file-system implementation was actually written and largely tested as a user process that used a raw disk interface, before the code was moved into the kernel. In an interesting about-face, the Mach operating system (Chapter 20) has no file system per se. File systems can be implemented as user-level tasks.

19.8.3 C-Lists

Terminal drivers use a character buffering system. This system involves keeping small blocks of characters (usually 28 bytes) in linked lists. There are routines to enqueue and dequeue characters for such lists. Although all free character buffers are kept in a single free list, most device drivers that use them limit the number of characters that may be queued at one time for any given terminal line.

A **write** system call to a terminal enqueues characters on a list for the device. An initial transfer is started, and interrupts cause dequeuing of characters and further transfers.

Input is similarly interrupt driven. Terminal drivers typically support *two* input queues, however, and conversion from the first (raw queue) to the other (canonical queue) is triggered by the interrupt routine putting an end-of-line character on the raw queue. The process doing a read on the device is then awakened, and its system phase does the conversion; the characters thus put on the canonical queue are then available to be returned to the user process by the read.

It is also possible to have the device driver bypass the canonical queue and return characters directly from the raw queue. This mode of operation is known as *raw mode*. Full-screen editors, and other programs that need to react to every keystroke, use this mode.

19.9 ■ Interprocess Communication

Many tasks can be accomplished in isolated processes, but many others require interprocess communication. Isolated computing systems have long served for many applications, but networking is increasingly important. With the increasing use of personal workstations, resource sharing is becoming more common. Interprocess communication has not traditionally been one of UNIX's strong points.

Most UNIX systems have not permitted *shared memory* because the PDP-11 hardware did not encourage it. System V does support a shared-memory facility, and one was planned for 4.2BSD, but was not implemented due to time constraints. Solaris 2 supports shared memory, as do many other current versions of UNIX. In any case, shared memory presents a problem in a networked environment, because network accesses can never be as fast as memory accesses on the local machine. Although we could, of course, pretend that memory was shared between two separate machines by copying data across a network transparently, the major benefit of shared memory (speed) would be lost.

19.9.1 Sockets

The *pipe* (discussed in Section 19.4.3) is the IPC mechanism most characteristic of UNIX. A pipe permits a reliable unidirectional byte stream between two processes. It is traditionally implemented as an ordinary file, with a few exceptions. It has no name in the file system, being created instead by the **pipe** system call. Its size is fixed, and when a process attempts to write to a full pipe, the process is suspended. Once all data previously written into the pipe have been read out, writing continues at the beginning of the file (pipes are not true circular buffers). One benefit of the small size (usually 4096 bytes) of pipes is that pipe data are seldom actually written to disk; they usually are kept in memory by the normal block buffer cache.

In 4.3BSD, pipes are implemented as a special case of the *socket* mechanism. The socket mechanism provides a general interface not only to facilities such as pipes, which are local to one machine, but also to networking facilities. Even on the same machine, a pipe can be used only by two processes related through use of the **fork** system call. The socket mechanism can be used by unrelated processes.

A socket is an endpoint of communication. A socket in use usually has an *address* bound to it. The nature of the address depends on the *communication domain* of the socket. A characteristic property of a domain is that processes communicating in the same domain use the same *address format*. A single socket can communicate in only one domain.

The three domains currently implemented in 4.3BSD are the UNIX domain (AF_UNIX), the Internet domain (AF_INET), and the XEROX Network Services (NS) domain (AF_NS). The address format of the UNIX domain is ordinary file-system path names, such as */alpha/beta/gamma*. Processes communicating in the Internet domain use DARPA Internet communications protocols (such as TCP/IP) and Internet addresses, which consist of a 32-bit host number and a 32-bit port number (representing a rendezvous point on the host).

There are several *socket types*, which represent classes of services. Each type may or may not be implemented in any communication domain. If a type is implemented in a given domain, it may be implemented by one or more protocols, which may be selected by the user:

- **Stream sockets:** These sockets provide reliable, duplex, sequenced data streams. No data are lost or duplicated in delivery, and there are no record boundaries. This type is supported in the Internet domain by the TCP protocol. In the UNIX domain, pipes are implemented as a pair of communicating stream sockets.

- **Sequenced packet sockets:** These sockets provide data streams like those of stream sockets, except that record boundaries are provided. This type is used in the XEROX AF_NS protocol.

- **Datagram sockets:** These sockets transfer messages of variable size in either direction. There is no guarantee that such messages will arrive in the same order they were sent, or that they will be unduplicated, or that they will arrive at all, but the original message (record) size is preserved in any datagram that does arrive. This type is supported in the Internet domain by the UDP protocol.

- **Reliably delivered message sockets:** These sockets transfer messages that are guaranteed to arrive, and that otherwise are like the messages transferred using datagram sockets. This type is currently unsupported.

- **Raw sockets:** These sockets allow direct access by processes to the protocols that support the other socket types. The protocols accessible include not only the uppermost ones, but also lower-level protocols. For example, in the Internet domain, it is possible to reach TCP, IP beneath that, or an Ethernet protocol beneath that. This capability is useful for developing new protocols.

The socket facility has a set of system calls specific to it. The **socket** system call creates a socket. It takes as arguments specifications of the communication domain, the socket type, and the protocol to be used to support that type. The value returned is a small integer called a *socket* *descriptor*, which is in the same name space as file descriptors. The socket descriptor indexes the array of open "files" in the *u* structure in the kernel, and has a file structure allocated for it. The 4.3BSD file structure may point to a *socket* structure instead of to an inode. In this case, certain socket information (such as the socket's type, message count, and the data in its input and output queues) is kept directly in the socket structure.

For another process to address a socket, the socket must have a name. A name is bound to a socket by the **bind** system call, which takes the socket descriptor, a pointer to the name, and the length of the name as a byte string. The contents and length of the byte string depend on the address format. The **connect** system call is used to initiate a connection. The arguments are syntactically the same as those for **bind;** the socket descriptor represents the local socket and the address is that of the foreign socket to which the attempt to connect is made.

Many processes that communicate using the socket IPC follow the *client–server model*. In this model, the *server* process provides a *service* to the *client* process. When the service is available, the server process listens on a well-known address, and the client process uses **connect,** as described previously, to reach the server.

A server process uses **socket** to create a socket and **bind** to bind the well-known address of its service to that socket. Then, it uses the **listen** system call to tell the kernel that it is ready to accept connections from clients, and to specify how many pending connections the kernel should queue until the server can service them. Finally, the server uses the **accept** system call to accept individual connections. Both **listen** and **accept** take as an argument the socket descriptor of the original socket. **Accept** returns a new socket descriptor corresponding to the new connection; the original socket descriptor is still open for further connections. The server usually uses **fork** to produce a new process after the **accept** to service the client while the original server process continues to listen for more connections.

There are also system calls for setting parameters of a connection and for returning the address of the foreign socket after an **accept**.

When a connection for a socket type such as a stream socket is established, the addresses of both endpoints are known and no further addressing information is needed to transfer data. The ordinary **read** and **write** system calls may then be used to transfer data.

The simplest way to terminate a connection and to destroy the associated socket is to use the **close** system call on its socket descriptor. We may also wish to terminate only one direction of communication of a duplex connection; the **shutdown** system call can be used for this purpose.

Some socket types, such as datagram sockets, do not support connections; instead, their sockets exchange datagrams that must be addressed individually. The system calls **sendto** and **recvfrom** are used for such connections. Both take as arguments a socket descriptor, a buffer pointer and the length, and an address-buffer pointer and length. The address buffer contains the address to send to for **sendto** and is filled in with the address of the datagram just received by **recvfrom**. The number of data actually transferred is returned by both system calls.

The **select** system call can be used to multiplex data transfers on several file descriptors and/or socket descriptors. It can even be used to allow one server process to listen for client connections for many services and to **fork** a process for each connection as the connection is made. The server does a **socket, bind,** and **listen** for each service, and then does a **select** on all the socket descriptors. When **select** indicates activity on a descriptor, the server does an **accept** on it and forks a process on the new descriptor returned by **accept,** leaving the parent process to do a **select** again.

19.9.2 Network Support

Almost all current UNIX systems support the UUCP network facilities, which are mostly used over dial-up telephone lines to support the UUCP mail network and the USENET news network. These are, however, rudimentary networking facilities, as they do not support even remote login, much less remote procedure call or distributed file systems. These facilities are also almost completely implemented as user processes, and are not part of the operating system proper.

4.3BSD supports the DARPA Internet protocols UDP, TCP, IP, and ICMP on a wide range of Ethernet, token-ring, and ARPANET interfaces. The framework in the kernel to support this is intended to facilitate the implementation of further protocols, and all protocols are accessible via the socket interface. The first version of the code was written by Rob Gurwitz of BBN as an add-on package for 4.1BSD.

The International Standards Organization's (ISO) Open System Interconnection (OSI) Reference Model for networking prescribes seven layers of network protocols and strict methods of communication between them. An implementation of a protocol may communicate only with a peer entity speaking the same protocol at the same layer, or with the protocol-protocol interface of a protocol in the layer immediately above or below in the same system. The ISO networking model is implemented in 4.3BSD Reno and 4.4BSD.

The 4.3BSD networking implementation, and to a certain extent the *socket* facility, is more oriented toward the ARPANET Reference Model (ARM). The ARPANET in its original form served as a proof of concept for many networking concepts, such as packet switching and protocol layering. The ARPANET was retired in 1988 because the hardware that supported it was no longer state of the art. Its successors, such as the NSFNET and the Internet, are even larger, and serve as a communications utility for researchers and as a testbed for Internet gateway research. The ARM predates the ISO model; the ISO model was in large part inspired by the ARPANET research.

Although the ISO model is often interpreted as requiring a limit of one protocol communicating per layer, the ARM allows several protocols in the same layer. There are only four protocol layers in the ARM, plus

- **Process/Applications:** This layer subsumes the application, presentation, and session layers of the ISO model. Such user-level programs as the File Transfer Protocol (FTP) and Telnet (remote login) exist at this level.

- **Host-Host:** This layer corresponds to ISO's transport and the top part of its network layers. Both the Transmission Control Protocol (TCP) and the Internet Protocol (IP) are in this layer, with TCP on top of IP. TCP corresponds to an ISO transport protocol, and IP performs the addressing functions of the ISO network layer.

- **Network Interface:** This layer spans the lower part of the ISO network layer and all of the data-link layer. The protocols involved here depend on the physical network type. The ARPANET uses the IMP-Host protocols, whereas an Ethernet uses Ethernet protocols.

- **Network Hardware:** The ARM is primarily concerned with software, so there is no explicit network hardware layer; however, any actual network will have hardware corresponding to the ISO hardware layer.

The networking framework in 4.3BSD is more generalized than is either the ISO model or the ARM, although it is most closely related to the ARM; see Figure 19.11.

User processes communicate with network protocols (and thus with other processes on other machines) via the *socket* facility, which corresponds to the ISO Session layer, as it is responsible for setting up and controlling communications.

Sockets are supported by *protocols* — possibly by several, layered one on another. A protocol may provide services such as reliable delivery, suppression of duplicate transmissions, flow control, or addressing, depending on the socket type being supported and the services required by any higher protocols.

A protocol may communicate with another protocol or with the network interface that is appropriate for the network hardware. There is little restriction in the general framework on what protocols may communicate with what other protocols, or on how many protocols may be layered on top of one another. The user process may, by means of the raw socket type, directly access any layer of protocol from the uppermost used to support one of the other socket types, such as streams, down to a raw network interface. This capability is used by routing processes and also for new protocol development.

ISO reference model	ARPANET reference model	4.2BSD layers	example layering
application	process applications	user programs and libraries	telnet
presentation			
session		sockets	sock_stream
transport	host–host	protocol	TCP
network			IP
data link	network interface	network interfaces	Ethernet driver
hardware	network hardware	network hardware	interlan controller

Figure 19.11 Network reference models and layering.

There tends to be one *network-interface* driver per network controller type. The network interface is responsible for handling characteristics specific to the local network being addressed. This arrangement ensures that the protocols using the interface do not need to be concerned with these characteristics.

The functions of the network interface depend largely on the *network hardware,* which is whatever is necessary for the network to which it is connected. Some networks may support reliable transmission at this level, but most do not. Some networks provide broadcast addressing, but many do not.

The socket facility and the networking framework use a common set of memory buffers, or *mbuf*s. These are intermediate in size between the large buffers used by the block I/O system and the C-lists used by character devices. An *mbuf* is 128 bytes long, 112 bytes of which may be used for data; the rest is used for pointers to link the *mbuf* into queues and for indicators of how much of the data area is actually in use.

Data are ordinarily passed between layers (socket-protocol, protocol-protocol, or protocol-network interface) in *mbuf*s. This ability to pass the buffers containing the data eliminates some data copying, but there is still frequently a need to remove or add protocol headers. It is also convenient and efficient for many purposes to be able to hold data that occupy an area the size of the memory-management page. Thus, it is possible for the data of an *mbuf* to reside not in the *mbuf* itself, but rather elsewhere in memory. There is an *mbuf* page table for this purpose, as well as a pool of pages dedicated to *mbuf* use.

19.10 ■ Summary

The early advantages of UNIX were that this system was written in a high-level language, was distributed in source form, and had provided powerful operating-system primitives on an inexpensive platform. These advantages led to UNIX's popularity at educational, research, and government institutions, and eventually in the commercial world. This popularity first produced many strains of UNIX with variant and improved facilities. Market pressures are currently leading to the consolidation of these versions. One of the most influential versions is 4.3BSD, developed at Berkeley for the VAX, and later ported to many other platforms.

UNIX provides a file system with tree-structured directories. Files are supported by the kernel as unstructured sequences of bytes. Direct access and sequential access are supported through system calls and library routines.

Files are stored as an array of fixed-size data blocks with perhaps a trailing fragment. The data blocks are found by pointers in the inode. Directory entries point to inodes. Disk space is allocated from cylinder groups to minimize head movement and to improve performance.

UNIX is a multiprogrammed system. Processes can easily create new processes with the **fork** system call. Processes can communicate with pipes or, more generally, sockets. They may be grouped into jobs that may be controlled with signals.

Processes are represented by two structures: the process structure and the user structure. CPU scheduling is a priority algorithm with dynamically computed priorities that reduces to round-robin scheduling in the extreme case.

4.3BSD memory management is swapping supported by paging. A *pagedaemon* process uses a modified second-chance page-replacement algorithm to keep enough free frames to support the executing processes.

Page and file I/O uses a block buffer cache to minimize the amount of actual I/O. Terminal devices use a separate character buffering system.

Networking support is one of the most important features in 4.3BSD. The socket concept provides the programming mechanism to access other processes, even across a network. Sockets provide an interface to several sets of protocols.

■ Exercises

19.1 What are the major differences between 4.3BSD UNIX and SYSVR3? Is one system "better" than the other? Explain your answer.

19.2 How were the design goals of UNIX different from those of other operating systems during the early stages of UNIX development?

19.3 Why are there many different versions of UNIX currently available? In what ways is this diversity an advantage to UNIX? In what ways is it a disadvantage?

19.4 What are the advantages and disadvantages of writing an operating system in a high-level language, such as C?

19.5 In what circumstances is the system-call sequence **fork execve** most appropriate? When is **vfork** preferable?

19.6 Does 4.3BSD UNIX give scheduling priority to I/O or CPU-bound processes? For what reason does it differentiate between these categories, and why is one given priority over the other? How does it know which of these categories fits a given process?

19.7 Early UNIX systems used swapping for memory management, whereas 4.3BSD used paging and swapping. Discuss the advantages and disadvantages of the two memory methods.

19.8 Describe the modifications to a file system that the 4.3BSD kernel makes when a process requests the creation of a new file */tmp/foo* and writes to that file sequentially until the file size reaches 20K.

19.9 Directory blocks in 4.3BSD are written synchronously when they are changed. Consider what would happen if they were written asynchronously. Describe the state of the file system if a crash occurred after all the files in a directory were deleted but before the directory entry was updated on disk.

19.10 Describe the process that is needed to recreate the free list after a crash in 4.1BSD.

19.11 What effects on system performance would the following changes to 4.3BSD have? Explain your answers.

    a. The merging of the block buffer cache and the process paging space

    b. Clustering disk I/O into larger chunks

    c. Implementing and using shared memory to pass data between processes, rather than using RPC or sockets

    d. Using the ISO seven-layer networking model, rather than the ARM network model

19.12 What socket type should be used to implement an intercomputer file-transfer program? What type should be used for a program that periodically tests to see whether another computer is up on the network? Explain your answer.

Bibliographic Notes

The best general description of the distinctive features of UNIX is still that presented by Ritchie and Thompson [1974]. Much of the history of UNIX was given in Ritchie [1979]. A critique of UNIX was offered by Blair et al. [1985]. The two main modern versions of UNIX are 4.3BSD and System V. System V internals were described at length in Bach [1987]. The authoritative treatment of the design and implementation of 4.3BSD is that by Leffler et al. [1989].

Possibly the best book on general programming under UNIX, especially on the use of the shell and facilities such as *yacc* and *sed*, is that by Kernighan and Pike [1984]. Systems programming was covered by Stevens [1992]. Another text of interest is [Bourne 1983]. The programming language of choice under UNIX is C [Kernighan and Ritchie 1988]. C is also the system's implementation language. The Bourne shell was described in Bourne [1978]. The Korn shell was described in Korn [1983].

The set of documentation that comes with UNIX systems is called the *UNIX Programmer's Manual* (UPM) and is traditionally organized in two volumes. Volume 1 contains short entries for every command, system call, and subroutine package in the system, and is also available on-line via the *man* command. Volume 2, *Supplementary Documents* (usually divided into Volumes 2A and 2B for convenience of binding), contains assorted papers relevant to the system and manuals for those commands or packages too complex to describe in one or two pages. Berkeley systems add Volume 2C to contain documents concerning Berkeley-specific features.

The Version 7 file system was described in Thompson [1978], and the 4.2BSD file system was described in McKusick et al. [1984]. A crash-resistant UNIX file system was described by Anyanwu and Marshall [1986]. The basic reference for process-management is Thompson [1978]. The 3BSD memory-management system was described in Babaoglu and Joy [1981], and some 4.3BSD memory-management developments were described in McKusick and Karels [1988]. The I/O system was described in Thompson [1978].

A description of the UNIX operating-system security was given by Grampp and Morris [1984] and by Wood and Kochan [1985].

Two useful papers on communications under 4.2BSD are those by Leffler et al. [1978, 1983], both in UPM Volume 2C.

The *ISO Reference Model* was given in [ISO 1981]. The *ARPANET Reference Model* was set forth in Cerf and Cain [1983]. The Internet and its protocols were described in Comer [1991], Comer and Stevens [1991, 1993]. UNIX network programming was described thoroughly in Stevens [1990]. The general state of networks was given in Quarterman [1990].

There are many useful papers in the two special issues of *The Bell System Technical Journal* on UNIX [BSTJ 1978, BSTJ 1984]. Other papers of interest have appeared at various USENIX conferences and are available in the proceedings of those conferences, as well as in the USENIX-refereed journal, *Computer Systems*.

Several textbooks describing variants of the UNIX system are those by Holt [1983], discussing the Tunis operating system; Comer [1984, 1987], discussing the Xinu operating system; and Tanenbaum [1987], describing the Minix operating system.

CHAPTER 20

THE
MACH
SYSTEM

The Mach operating system is designed to incorporate the many recent innovations in operating-system research to produce a fully functional, technically advanced system. Unlike UNIX, which was developed without regard for multiprocessing, Mach incorporates multiprocessing support throughout. Its multiprocessing support is also exceedingly flexible, ranging from shared memory systems to systems with no memory shared between processors. Mach is designed to run on computer systems ranging from one to thousands of processors. In addition, Mach is easily ported to many varied computer architectures. A key goal of Mach is to be a distributed system capable of functioning on heterogeneous hardware.

Although many experimental operating systems are being designed, built, and used, Mach is better able to satisfy the needs of the masses than the others are because it offers full compatibility with UNIX 4.3BSD. As such, it provides a unique opportunity for us to compare two functionally similar, but internally dissimilar, operating systems. The order and contents of the presentation of Mach is different from that of UNIX to reflect the differing emphasis of the two systems. There is no section on the user interface, because that component is similar in 4.3BSD when running the BSD server. As we shall see, Mach provides the ability to layer emulation of other operating systems as well, and they can even run concurrently.

20.1 ■ History

Mach traces its ancestry to the Accent operating system developed at Carnegie Mellon University (CMU). Although Accent pioneered a number of novel operating system concepts, its utility was limited by its inability to execute UNIX applications and its strong ties to a single hardware architecture that made it difficult to port. Mach's communication system and philosophy are derived from Accent, but many other significant portions of the system (for example, the virtual memory system, task and thread management) were developed from scratch. An important goal of the Mach effort was support for multiprocessors.

Mach's development followed an evolutionary path from BSD UNIX systems. Mach code was initially developed inside the 4.2BSD kernel, with BSD kernel components being replaced by Mach components as the Mach components were completed. The BSD components were updated to 4.3BSD when that became available. By 1986, the virtual memory and communication subsystems were running on the DEC VAX computer family, including multiprocessor versions of the VAX. Versions for the IBM RT/PC and for SUN 3 workstations followed shortly. 1987 saw the completion of the Encore Multimax and Sequent Balance multiprocessor versions, including task and thread support, as well as the first official releases of the system, Release 0 and Release 1.

Through Release 2, Mach provides compatibility with the corresponding BSD systems by including much of BSD's code in the kernel. The new features and capabilities of Mach make the kernels in these releases larger than the corresponding BSD kernels. Mach 3 (Figure 20.1) moves the BSD code outside of the kernel, leaving a much smaller *microkernel*. This system implements only basic Mach features in the kernel; all UNIX-specific code has been evicted to run in user-mode servers. Excluding UNIX-specific code from the kernel allows replacement of BSD with another operating system, or the simultaneous execution of multiple operating-system interfaces on top of the microkernel. In addition to BSD, user-mode implementations have been developed for DOS, the Macintosh

Figure 20.1   Mach 3 structure.

operating system, and OSF/1. This approach has similarities to the *virtual-machine* concept, but the virtual machine is defined by software (the Mach kernel interface), rather than by hardware. As of Release 3.0, Mach became available on a wide variety of systems, including single-processor SUN, Intel, IBM, and DEC machines, and multiprocessor DEC, Sequent, and Encore systems.

Mach was propelled into the forefront of industry attention when the Open Software Foundation (OSF) announced in 1989 that it would use Mach 2.5 as the basis for its new operating system, OSF/1. The initial release of OSF/1 occurred a year later, and now competes with UNIX System V, Release 4, the operating system of choice among *UNIX International (UI)* members. OSF members include key technological companies such as IBM, DEC, and HP. Mach 2.5 is also the basis for the operating system on the *NeXT* workstation, the brainchild of Steve Jobs, of Apple Computer fame. OSF is evaluating Mach 3 as the basis for a future operating-system release, and research on Mach continues at CMU and OSF, and elsewhere.

20.2 ■ Design Principles

The Mach operating system was designed to provide basic mechanisms that most current operating systems lack. The goal is to design an operating system that is BSD compatible and, in addition, excels in the following areas.

- Support for diverse architectures, including multiprocessors with varying degrees of shared memory access: Uniform Memory Access (UMA), Non-Uniform Memory Access (NUMA), and No Remote Memory Access (NORMA)

- Ability to function with varying intercomputer network speeds, from wide-area networks to high-speed local-area networks and tightly coupled multiprocessors

- Simplified kernel structure, with a small number of abstractions; in turn these abstractions are sufficiently general to allow other operating systems to be implemented on top of Mach

- Distributed operation, providing network transparency to clients and an object-oriented organization both internally and externally

- Integrated memory management and interprocess communication, to provide both efficient communication of large numbers of data, and communication-based memory management

- Heterogeneous system support, to make Mach widely available and interoperable among computer systems from multiple vendors

The designers of Mach have been heavily influenced by BSD (and by UNIX in general), whose benefits include

- A simple programmer interface, with a good set of primitives and a consistent set of interfaces to system facilities

- Easy portability to a wide class of uniprocessors

- An extensive library of utilities and applications

- The ability to combine utilities easily via pipes

Of course, BSD was seen as having several drawbacks that need to be redressed:

- A kernel that has become the repository of many redundant features — and that consequently is difficult to manage and modify

- Original design goals that made it difficult to provide support for multiprocessors, distributed systems, and shared program libraries; for instance, because the kernel was designed for uniprocessors, it has no provisions for locking code or data that other processors might be using

- Too many fundamental abstractions, providing too many similar, competing means to accomplish the same task

It should be clear that the development of Mach continues to be a huge undertaking. The benefits of such a system are equally large, however. The operating system runs on many existing uni- and multiprocessor architectures, and can be easily ported to future ones. It makes research easier, because computer scientists can add features via user-level code, instead of having to write their own tailor-made operating system. Areas of experimentation include operating systems, databases, reliable distributed systems, multiprocessor languages, security, and distributed artificial intelligence. In its current instantiation, the Mach system is usually as efficient as are other major versions of UNIX when performing similar tasks.

20.3 ■ System Components

To achieve the design goals of Mach, the developers reduced the operating-system functionality to a small set of basic abstractions, out of which all other functionality can be derived. The Mach approach is to place as little as possible within the kernel, but to make what is there powerful enough that all other features can be implemented at user level.

Mach's design philosophy is to have a simple, extensible kernel, concentrating on communication facilities. For instance, all requests to the kernel, and all data movement among processes, are handled through one communication mechanism. By limiting all data operations to one mechanism, Mach is able to provide systemwide protection to its users by protecting the communications mechanism. Optimizing this one communications path can result in significant performance gains, and is simpler than trying to optimize several paths. Mach is extensible, because many traditionally kernel-based functions can be implemented as user-level servers. For instance, all pagers (including the default pager) can be implemented externally and called by the kernel for the user.

Mach is an example of an *object-oriented* system where the data and the operations that manipulate that data are encapsulated into an abstract object. Only the operations of the object are able to act on the entities defined in it. The details of how these operations are implemented are hidden, as are the internal data structures. Thus, a programmer can use an object only by invoking its defined, exported operations. A programmer can change the internal operations without changing the interface definition, so changes and optimizations do not affect other aspects of system operation. The object-oriented approach supported by Mach allows objects to reside anywhere in a network of Mach systems, transparent to the user. The *port* mechanism, discussed later in this section, makes all of this possible.

Mach's primitive abstractions are the heart of the system, and are as follows:

- A **task** is an execution environment that provides the basic unit of resource allocation. A task consists of a virtual address space and protected access to system resources via ports. A task may contain one or more threads.

- A **thread** is the basic unit of execution, and must run in the context of a task (which provides the address space). All threads within a task share the tasks' resources (ports, memory, and so on). There is no notion of a "process" in Mach. Rather, a traditional process would be implemented as a task with a single thread of control.

- A **port** is the basic object reference mechanism in Mach, and is implemented as a kernel-protected communication channel. Communication is accomplished by sending messages to ports; messages are queued at the destination port if no thread is immediately ready to receive them. Ports are protected by kernel-managed capabilities, or *port rights*; a task must have a port right to send a message to a port. The programmer invokes an operation on an object by *sending* a message to a port associated with that object. The object being represented by a port *receives* the messages.

- A **port set** is a group of ports sharing a common message queue. A thread can receive messages for a port set, and thus service multiple ports. Each received message identifies the individual port (within the set) that it was received from; the receiver can use this to identify the object referred to by the message.

- A **message** is the basic method of communication between threads in Mach. It is a typed collection of data objects; for each object, it may contain the actual data or a pointer to out-of-line data. Port rights are passed in messages; passing port rights in messages is the only way to move them among tasks. (Passing a port right in shared memory does not work, because the Mach kernel will not permit the new task to use a right obtained in this manner.)

- A **memory object** is a source of memory; tasks may access it by mapping portions (or the entire object) into their address spaces. The object may be managed by a user-mode *external memory manager*. One example is a file managed by a file server; however, a memory object can be any object for which memory-mapped access makes sense. A mapped buffer implementation of a UNIX pipe is one example.

Figure 20.2 illustrates these abstractions, which we shall elaborate in the remainder of this chapter.

An unusual feature of Mach, and a key to the system's efficiency, is the blending of memory and interprocess-communication features. Whereas some other distributed systems (such as Solaris, with its NFS features) have special-purpose extensions to the file system to extend it over a network, Mach provides a general-purpose, extensible merger of memory and messages at the heart of its kernel. This feature not only allows Mach to be used for distributed and parallel programming, but also helps in the implementation of the kernel itself.

Mach connects memory management and communication (IPC) by allowing each to be used in the implementation of the other. Memory management is based on the use of *memory objects*. A memory object is represented by a port (or ports), and IPC messages are sent to this port to request operations (for example, *pagein, pageout*) on the object. Because IPC is used, memory objects may reside on remote systems and be accessed transparently. The kernel caches the contents of memory objects in local memory. Conversely, memory-management techniques are used in the implementation of message passing. Where possible, Mach passes messages by moving pointers to shared memory objects, rather than by copying the object itself.

IPC tends to involve considerable system overhead and is generally less efficient than is communication accomplished through shared memory, for intrasystem messages. Because Mach is a message-based kernel, it is important that message handling be carried out efficiently. Most of the

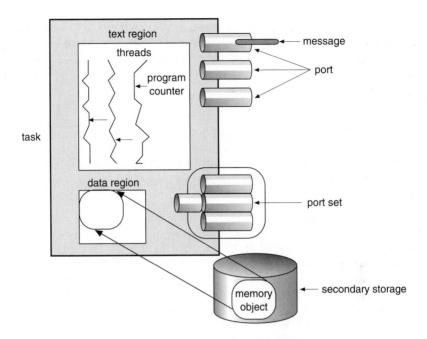

Figure 20.2 Mach's basic abstractions.

inefficiency of message handling in traditional operating systems is due to either the copying of messages from one task to another (if the message is intracomputer) or low network transfer speed (for intercomputer messages). To solve these problems, Mach uses virtual-memory remapping to transfer the contents of large messages. In other words, the message transfer modifies the receiving task's address space to include a copy of the message contents. *Virtual copy*, or *copy-on-write*, techniques are used to avoid or delay the actual copying of the data. There are several advantages to this approach:

- Increased flexibility in memory management to user programs

- Greater generality, allowing the virtual copy approach to be used in tightly and loosely coupled computers

- Improved performance over UNIX message passing

- Easier task migration; because ports are location independent, a task and all its ports can be moved from one machine to another; all tasks that previously communicated with the moved task can continue to do so because they reference a task by only its ports and communicate via messages to these ports

We shall detail the operation of process management, IPC, and memory management. Then, we shall discuss Mach's chameleonlike ability to support multiple operating-system interfaces.

20.4 ■ Process Management

A *task* can be thought of as a traditional process that does not have an instruction pointer or a register set. A task contains a virtual address space, a set of port rights, and accounting information. A task is a passive entity that does nothing unless it has one or more *thread*s executing in it.

20.4.1 Basic Structure

A task containing one thread is similar to a UNIX process. Just as a **fork** system call produces a new UNIX process, Mach creates a new task to emulate this behavior. The new task's memory is a duplicate of the parent's address space, as dictated by the *inheritance attributes* of the parent's memory. The new task contains one thread, which is started at the same point as the creating **fork** call in the parent. Threads and tasks may also be suspended and resumed.

Threads are especially useful in server applications, which are common in UNIX, since one task can have multiple threads to service multiple requests to the task. They also allow efficient use of parallel computing resources. Rather than having one process on each processor (with the corresponding performance penalty and operating-system overhead), a task may have its threads spread among parallel processors. Threads also add efficiency to user-level programs. For instance, in UNIX, an entire process must wait when a page fault occurs, or when a system call is executed. In a task with multiple threads, only the thread that causes the page fault or executes a system call is delayed; all other threads continue executing. Because Mach has kernel-supported threads (see Section 4.5), the threads have some cost associated with them. They must have supporting data structures in the kernel, and more complex kernel-scheduling algorithms must be provided. These algorithms and thread states are discussed in Section 4.5.

At the user level, threads may be in one of two states.

- **Running:** The thread is either executing or waiting to be allocated a processor. A thread is considered to be running even if it is blocked within the kernel (waiting for a page fault to be satisfied, for instance).

- **Suspended:** The thread is neither executing on a processor nor waiting to be allocated a processor. A thread can resume its execution only if it is returned to the running state.

These two states are also associated with a task. An operation on a task affects all threads in a task, so suspending a task involves suspending all the threads in it. Task and thread suspensions are separate, independent mechanisms, however, so resuming a thread in a suspended task does not resume the task.

Mach provides primitives from which thread-synchronization tools can be built. This primitives provision is consistent with Mach's philosophy of providing minimum yet sufficient functionality in the kernel. The Mach IPC facility can be used for synchronization, with processes exchanging messages at rendezvous points. Thread-level synchronization is provided by calls to start and stop threads at appropriate times. A *suspend count* is kept for each thread. This count allows multiple suspend calls to be executed on a thread, and only when an equal number of resume calls occur is the thread resumed. Unfortunately, this feature has its own limitation. Because it is an error for a start call to be executed before a stop call (the suspend count would become negative), these routines cannot be used to synchronize shared data access. However, *wait* and *signal* operations associated with semaphores, and used for synchronization, can be implemented via the IPC calls. This method will be discussed in Section 20.5.

20.4.2 The C Threads Package

Mach provides low-level but flexible routines instead of polished, large, and more restrictive functions. Rather than making programmers work at this low level, Mach provides many higher-level interfaces for programming in C and other languages. For instance, the C *Threads* package provides multiple threads of control, shared variables, mutual exclusion for critical sections, and condition variables for synchronization. In fact, C Threads is one of the major influences of the POSIX P Threads standard, which many operating systems are being modified to support. As a result there are strong similarities between the C Threads and P Threads programming interfaces. The thread-control routines include calls to perform these tasks:

- Create a new thread within a task, given a function to execute and parameters as input. The thread then executes concurrently with the creating thread, which receives a thread identifier when the call returns.

- Destroy the calling thread, and return a value to the creating thread.

- Wait for a specific thread to terminate before allowing the calling thread to continue. This call is a synchronization tool, much like the UNIX **wait** system calls.

- Yield use of a processor, signaling that the scheduler may run another thread at this point. This call is also useful in the presence of a preemptive scheduler, as it can be used to relinquish the CPU voluntarily before the time quantum (scheduling interval) expires if a thread has no use for the CPU.

Mutual exclusion is achieved through the use of spinlocks, as were discussed in Chapter 6. The routines associated with mutual exclusion are these:

- The routine *mutex_alloc* dynamically creates a mutex variable.

- The routine *mutex_free* deallocates a dynamically created mutex variable.

- The routine *mutex_lock* locks a mutex variable. The executing thread loops in a spinlock until the lock is attained. A deadlock results if a thread with a lock tries to lock the same mutex variable. Bounded waiting is not guaranteed by the C Threads package. Rather, it is dependent on the hardware instructions used to implement the mutex routines.

- The routine *mutex_unlock* unlocks a mutex variable, much like the typical *signal* operation of a semaphore.

General synchronization without busy waiting can be achieved through the use of *condition variables*, which can be used to implement a *condition critical region* or a *monitor*, as was described in Chapter 6. A condition variable is associated with a mutex variable, and reflects a Boolean state of that variable. The routines associated with general synchronization are these:

- The routine *condition_alloc* dynamically allocates a condition variable.

- The routine *condition_free* deletes a dynamically created condition variable allocated as result of *condition_alloc*.

- The routine *condition_wait* unlocks the associated mutex variable, and blocks the thread until a *condition_signal* is executed on the condition variable, indicating that the event being waited for may have occurred. The mutex variable is then locked, and the thread continues. A *condition_signal* does not guarantee that the condition still holds when the unblocked thread finally returns from its *condition_wait* call, so the awakened thread must loop, executing the *condition_wait* routine until it is unblocked and the condition holds.

As an example of the C Threads routines, consider the bounded-buffer synchronization problem of Section 6.5.1. The producer and consumer are

repeat
>   ...
>   produce an item into *nextp*
>   ...
>   **mutex_lock**(*mutex*);
>   **while**(*full*)
>   **condition_wait**(*nonfull, mutex*);
>   ...
>   add *nextp* to buffer
>   ...
>   **condition_signal**(*nonempty*);
>   **mutex_unlock**(*mutex*);
> **until** *false*;

Figure 20.3   The structure of the producer process.

represented as threads that access the common bounded-buffer pool. We use a mutex variable to protect the buffer while it is being updated. Once we have exclusive access to the buffer, we use condition variables to block the producer thread if the buffer is full, and to block the consumer thread if the buffer is empty. Although this program normally would be written in the C language on a Mach system, we shall use the familiar Pascal-like syntax of previous chapters for clarity. As in Chapter 6, we assume that the buffer consists of n slots, each capable of holding one item. The *mutex* semaphore provides mutual exclusion for accesses to the buffer pool and is initialized to the value 1. The *empty* and *full* semaphores count the number of empty and full buffers, respectively. The semaphore *empty* is initialized to the value n; the semaphore *full* is initialized to the value 0. The condition variable *nonempty* is true while the buffer has items in it, and *nonfull* is true if the buffer has an empty slot.

The first step includes the allocation of the mutex and condition variables:

>   **mutex_alloc**(*mutex*);
>   **condition_alloc**(*nonempty, nonfull*);

The code for the producer thread is shown in Figure 20.3; the code for the consumer thread is shown in Figure 20.4. When the program terminates, the mutex and condition variables need to be deallocated:

>   **mutex_free**(*mutex*);
>   **condition_free**(*nonempty, nonfull*);

```
repeat
    mutex_lock(mutex);
    while(empty)
        condition_wait(nonempty, mutex);
        ...
    remove an item from the buffer to nextc
        ...
    condition_signal(nonfull);
    mutex_unlock(mutex);
        ...
    consume the item in nextc
        ...
until false;
```

Figure 20.4   The structure of the consumer process.

20.4.3 The CPU Scheduler

The CPU scheduler for a thread-based multiprocessor operating system is more complex than are its process-based relatives. There are generally more threads in a multithreaded system than there are processes in a multitasking system. Keeping track of multiple processors is also difficult, and is a relatively new area of research. Mach uses a simple policy to keep the scheduler manageable. Only threads are scheduled, so no knowledge of tasks is needed in the scheduler. All threads compete equally for resources, including time quanta.

Each thread has an associated priority number ranging from 0 through 127, which is based on the exponential average of its usage of the CPU. That is, a thread that recently used the CPU for a large amount of time has the lowest priority. Mach uses the priority to place the thread in one of 32 global run queues. These queues are searched in priority order for waiting threads when a processor becomes idle. Mach also keeps per-processor, or local, run queues. A local run queue is used for threads that are bound to an individual processor. For instance, a device driver for a device connected to an individual CPU must run on only that CPU.

Instead of there being a central dispatcher that assigns threads to processors, each processor consults the local and global run queues to select the appropriate next thread to run. Threads in the local run queue have absolute priority over those in the global queues, because it is assumed that they are performing some chore for the kernel. The run queues (like most other objects in Mach) are locked when they are modified to avoid simultaneous changes by multiple processors. To speed dispatching of threads on the global run queue, Mach maintains a list of idle processors.

Additional scheduling difficulties arise from the multiprocessor nature of Mach. A fixed time quantum is not appropriate because there may be fewer runable threads than there are available processors, for instance. It would be wasteful to interrupt a thread with a context switch to the kernel when that thread's quantum runs out, only to have the thread be placed right back in the running state. Thus, instead of using a fixed-length quantum, Mach varies the size of the time quantum inversely with the total number of threads in the system. It keeps the time quantum over the entire system constant, however. For example, in a system with 10 processors, 11 threads, and a 100-millisecond quantum, a context switch needs to occur on each processor only once per second to maintain the desired quantum.

Of course, there are still complications to be considered. Even relinquishing the CPU while waiting for a resource is more difficult than it is on traditional operating systems. First, a call must be issued by a thread to alert the scheduler that the thread is about to block. This alert avoids race conditions and deadlocks, which could occur when the execution takes place in a multiprocessor environment. A second call actually causes the thread to be moved off the run queue until the appropriate event occurs. There are many other internal thread states that are used by the scheduler to control thread execution.

20.4.4 Exception Handling

Mach was designed to provide a single, simple, consistent exception-handling system, with support for standard as well as user-defined exceptions. To avoid redundancy in the kernel, Mach uses kernel primitives whenever possible. For instance, an exception handler is just another thread in the task in which the exception occurs. Remote procedure call (RPC) messages are used to synchronize the execution of the thread causing the exception (the "victim") and that of the handler, and to communicate information about the exception between the victim and handler. Mach exceptions are also used to emulate the BSD *signal* package, as described later in this section.

Disruptions to normal program execution come in two varieties: internally generated *exceptions* and external *interrupts*. Interrupts are asynchronously generated disruptions of a thread or task, whereas exceptions are caused by the occurrence of unusual conditions during a thread's execution. Mach's general-purpose exception facility is used for error detection and debugger support. This facility is also useful for other reasons, such as taking a core dump of a bad task, allowing tasks to handle their own errors (mostly arithmetic), and emulating instructions not implemented in hardware.

Mach supports two different granularities of exception handling. Error handling is supported by per-thread exception handling, whereas debuggers use per-task handling. It makes little sense to try to debug only one thread, or to have exceptions from multiple threads invoke multiple debuggers. Aside from this distinction, the only other difference between the two types of exceptions lies in their inheritance from a parent task. Taskwide exception-handling facilities are passed from the parent to child tasks, so debuggers are able to manipulate an entire tree of tasks. Error handlers are not inherited, and default to no handler at thread- and task-creation time. Finally, error handlers take precedence over debuggers if the exceptions occur simultaneously. The reason for this approach is that error handlers are normally part of the task, and therefore should execute normally even in the presence of a debugger.

Exception handling proceeds as follows:

- The victim thread causes notification of an exception's occurrence via a *raise* RPC message being sent to the handler.

- The victim then calls a routine to wait until the exception is handled.

- The handler receives notification of the exception, usually including information about the exception, the thread, and the task causing the exception.

- The handler performs its function according to the type of exception. The handler's action involves *clearing* the exception, causing the victim to resume, or *terminating* the victim thread.

To support the execution of BSD programs, Mach needs to support BSD-style signals. Signals provide software generated interrupts and exceptions. Unfortunately, signals are of limited functionality in multithreaded operating systems. The first problem is that, in UNIX, a signal's handler must be a routine in the process receiving the signal. If the signal is caused by a problem in the process itself (for example, a division by zero), the problem cannot be remedied, because a process has limited access to its own context. A second, more troublesome aspect of signals is that they were designed for only single-threaded programs. For instance, it makes no sense for all threads in a task to get a signal, but how can a signal be seen by only one thread?

Because the signal system must work correctly with multithreaded applications for Mach to run 4.3BSD programs, signals could not be abandoned. Producing a functionally correct signal package required several rewrites of the code, however! A final problem with UNIX signals is that they can be lost. This loss occurs when another signal of the same type occurs before the first is handled. Mach exceptions are queued as a result of their RPC implementation.

Externally generated signals, including those sent from one BSD process to another, are processed by the BSD server section of the Mach 2.5 kernel.

Their behavior is therefore the same as it is under BSD. Hardware exceptions are a different matter, because BSD programs expect to receive hardware exceptions as signals. Therefore, a hardware exception caused by a thread must arrive at the thread as a signal. So that this result is produced, hardware exceptions are converted to exception RPCs. For tasks and threads that do not make explicit use of the Mach exception-handling facility, the destination of this RPC defaults to an in-kernel task. This task has only one purpose: Its thread runs in a continuous loop, receiving these exception RPCs. For each RPC, it converts the exception into the appropriate signal, which is sent to the thread that caused the hardware exception. It then completes the RPC, clearing the original exception condition. With the completion of the RPC, the initiating thread reenters the run state. It immediately sees the signal and executes its signal-handling code. In this manner, all hardware exceptions begin in a uniform way — as exceptions RPCs. Threads not designed to handle such exceptions, however, receive the exceptions as they would on a standard BSD system — as signals. In Mach 3.0, the signal-handling code is moved entirely into a server, but the overall structure and flow of control is similar to those of Mach 2.5.

20.5 ■ Interprocess Communication

Most commercial operating systems, such as UNIX, provide communication between processes, and between hosts with fixed, global names (internet addresses). There is no location independence of facilities, because any remote system needing to use a facility must know the name of the system providing that facility. Usually, data in the messages are untyped streams of bytes. Mach simplifies this picture by sending messages between location-independent ports. The messages contain typed data for ease of interpretation. All BSD communication methods can be implemented with this simplified system.

The two components of Mach IPC are *ports* and *messages*. Almost everything in Mach is an object, and all objects are addressed via their communications ports. Messages are sent to these ports to initiate operations on the objects by the routines that implement the objects. By depending on only ports and messages for all communication, Mach delivers location independence of objects and security of communication. Data independence is provided by the NetMsgServer task, as discussed later. Mach ensures security by requiring that message senders and receivers have *rights*. A right consists of a port name and a capability (send or receive) on that port, and is much like a capability in object-oriented systems. There can be only one task with receive rights to any given port, but many tasks may have send rights. When an object is created, its creator also allocates a port to represent the object, and obtains the access rights to that port. Rights can be given out by the creator of the object (including the kernel), and are passed in messages. If the holder of a receive right sends that right in a message, the receiver of the message gains the right and the sender loses it. A task may allocate ports to allow access to any objects it owns, or for communication. The destruction of either a port or the holder of the receive right causes the revocation of all rights to that port, and the tasks holding send rights can be notified if desired.

20.5.1 Ports

A port is implemented as a protected, bounded queue within the kernel of the system on which the object resides. If a queue is full, a sender may abort the send, wait for a slot to become available in the queue, or have the kernel deliver the message for it.

There are several system calls to provide the port functionality:

- Allocate a new port in a specified task and give the caller's task all access rights to the new port. The port name is returned.

- Deallocate a task's access rights to a port. If the task holds the receive right, the port is destroyed and all other tasks with send rights are, potentially, notified.

- Get the current status of a task's port.

- Create a backup port, which is given the receive right for a port if the task containing the receive right requests its deallocation (or terminates).

When a task is created, the kernel creates several ports for it. The function *task_self* returns the name of the port that represents the task in calls to the kernel. For instance, for a task to allocate a new port, it would call *port_allocate* with *task_self* as the name of the task that will own the port. Thread creation results in a similar *thread_self* thread kernel port. This scheme is similar to the standard process-id concept found in UNIX. Another port created for a task is returned by *task_notify*, and is the name of the port to which the kernel will send event-notification messages (such as notifications of port terminations).

Ports can also be collected into *port set*s. This facility is useful if one thread is to service requests coming in on multiple ports (for example, for multiple objects). A port may be a member of at most one port set at a time, and, if a port is in a set, it may not be used directly to receive messages. Instead, the message will be routed to the port set's queue. A port set may not be passed in messages, unlike a port. Port sets are objects that serve a purpose similar to the 4.3BSD **select** system call, but they are more efficient.

20.5.2 Messages

A message consists of a fixed-length header and a variable number of typed data objects. The header contains the destination's port name, the name of the reply port to which return messages should be sent, and the length of the message (see Figure 20.5). The data in the message (*in-line* data) were limited to less than 8K in Mach 2.5 systems, but Mach 3.0 has no limit. Any data exceeding that limit must be sent in multiple messages, or more likely via reference by a pointer in a message (*out-of-line* data, as we shall describe shortly). Each data section may be a simple type (numbers or characters), port rights, or pointers to out-of-line data. Each section has an associated type, so that the receiver can unpack the data correctly even if it uses a byte ordering different from that used by the sender. The kernel also inspects the message for certain types of data. For instance, the kernel must process port information within a message, either by translating the port name into an internal port data structure address, or by forwarding it for processing to the NetMsgServer, as we shall explain.

The use of pointers in a message provides the means to transfer the entire address space of a task in one single message. The kernel also must process pointers to out-of-line data, as a pointer to data in the sender's address space would be invalid in the receiver's — especially if the sender and receiver reside on different systems! Generally, systems send messages

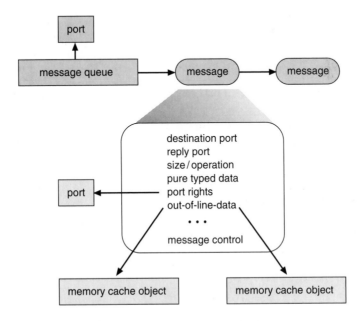

Figure 20.5 Mach messages.

by copying the data from the sender to the receiver. Because this technique can be inefficient, especially in the case of large messages, Mach optimizes this procedure. The data referenced by a pointer in a message being sent to a port on the same system are not copied between the sender and the receiver. Instead, the address map of the receiving task is modified to include a copy-on-write copy of the pages of the message. This operation is *much* faster than a data copy, and makes message passing efficient. In essence, message passing is implemented via virtual-memory management.

In Version 2.5, this operation was implemented in two phases. A pointer to a region of memory caused the kernel to map that region of memory into its own space temporarily, setting the sender's memory map to copy-on-write mode to ensure that any modifications did not affect the original version of the data. When a message was received at its destination, the kernel moved its mapping to the receiver's address space, using a newly allocated region of virtual memory within that task.

In Version 3, this process was simplified. The kernel creates a data structure that would be a copy of the region if it were part of an address map. On receipt, this data structure is added to the receiver's map and becomes a copy accessible to the receiver.

The newly allocated regions in a task do not need to be contiguous with previous allocations, so Mach virtual memory is said to be *sparse*, consisting of regions of data separated by unallocated addresses. A full message transfer is shown in Figure 20.6.

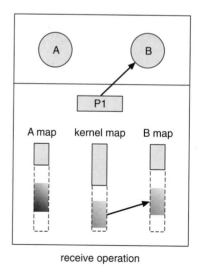

send operation   receive operation

Figure 20.6 Mach message transfer.

20.5.3 The NetMsgServer

For a message to be sent between computers, the destination of a message must be located, and the message must be transmitted to the destination. UNIX traditionally leaves these mechanisms to the low-level network protocols, which require the use of statically assigned communication endpoints (for example, the port number for services based on TCP or UDP). One of Mach's tenets is that all objects within the system are location independent, and that the location is transparent to the user. This tenet requires Mach to provide location-transparent naming and transport to extend IPC across multiple computers. This naming and transport are performed by the *Network Message Server* or NetMsgServer, a user-level capability-based networking daemon that forwards messages between hosts. It also provides a primitive networkwide name service that allows tasks to register ports for lookup by tasks on any other computer in the network. Mach ports can be transferred only in messages, and messages must be sent to ports; the primitive name service solves the problem of transferring the first port that allows tasks on different computers to exchange messages. Subsequent IPC interactions are fully transparent; the NetMsgServer tracks all rights and out-of-line memory passed in intercomputer messages, and arranges for the appropriate transfers. The NetMsgServers maintain among themselves a distributed database of port rights that have been transferred between computers and of the ports to which these rights correspond.

The kernel uses the NetMsgServer when a message needs to be sent to a port that is not on the kernel's computer. Mach's kernel IPC is used to transfer the message to the local NetMsgServer. The NetMsgServer then uses whatever network protocols are appropriate to transfer the message to its peer on the other computer; the notion of a NetMsgServer is protocol-independent, and NetMsgServers have been built that use various protocols. Of course, the NetMsgServers involved in a transfer must agree on the protocol used. Finally, the NetMsgServer on the destination computer uses that kernel's IPC to send the message to the correct destination task. The ability to extend local IPC transparently across nodes is supported by the use of proxy ports. When a send right is transferred from one computer to another, the NetMsgServer on the destination computer creates a new port, or proxy, to represent the original port at the destination. Messages sent to this proxy are received by the NetMsgServer and are forwarded transparently to the original port; this procedure is one example of how the NetMsgServers cooperate to make a proxy indistinguishable from the original port.

Because Mach is designed to function in a network of heterogeneous systems, it must provide a way to send between systems data that are formatted in a way that is understandable by both the sender and receiver. Unfortunately, computers vary the format in which they store types of data. For instance, an integer on one system might take 2 bytes to store, and the most significant byte might be stored before the least significant one. Another system might reverse this ordering. The NetMsgServer therefore uses the type information stored in a message to translate the data from the sender's to the receiver's format. In this way, all data are represented correctly when they reach their destination.

The NetMsgServer on a given computer accepts RPCs that add, look up, and remove network ports from the NetMsgServer's name service. As a security precaution, a port value provided in an add request must match that in the remove request for a thread to ask for a port name to be removed from the database.

As an example of the NetMsgServer's operation, consider a thread on node A sending a message to a port that happens to be in a task on node B. The program simply sends a message to a port to which it has a send right. The message is first passed to the kernel, which delivers it to its first recipient, the NetMsgServer on node A. The NetMsgServer then contacts (through its database information) the NetMsgServer on node B and sends the message. The NetMsgServer on node B then presents the message to the kernel with the appropriate local port for node B. The kernel finally provides the message to the receiving task when a thread in that task executes a *msg_receive* call. This sequence of events is shown in Figure 20.7.

Mach 3.0 provides an alternative to the NetMsgServer as part of its improved support for NORMA multiprocessors. The NORMA IPC subsystem

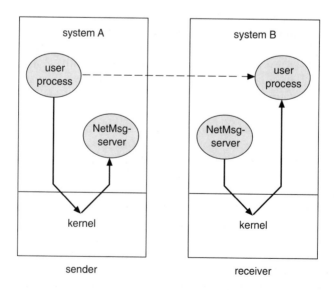

Figure 20.7 Network IPC forwarding by NetMsgServer.

of Mach 3.0 implements functionality similar to the NetMsgServer directly in the Mach kernel, providing much more efficient internode IPC for multicomputers with fast interconnection hardware. For example, the time-consuming copying of messages between the NetMsgServer and the kernel is eliminated. Use of NORMA IPC does not exclude use of the NetMsgServer; the NetMsgServer can still be used to provide MACH IPC service over networks that link a NORMA multiprocessor to other computers. In addition to NORMA IPC, Mach 3.0 also provides support for memory management across a NORMA system, and the ability for a task in such a system to create child tasks on nodes other than its own. These features support the implementation of a single-system-image operating system on a NORMA multiprocessor; the multiprocessor behaves like one large system, rather than like an assemblage of smaller systems (for both users and applications).

20.5.4 Synchronization Through IPC

The IPC mechanism is extremely flexible, and is used throughout Mach. For example, it may be used for thread synchronization. A port may be used as a synchronization variable, and may have n messages sent to it for n resources. Any thread wishing to use a resource executes a receive call on that port. The thread will receive a message if the resource is available; otherwise, it will wait on the port until a message is available there. To return a resource after use, the thread can send a message to the port. In this regard, receiving is equivalent to the semaphore operation *wait*, and sending is equivalent to *signal*. This method can be used for synchronizing semaphore operations among threads in the same task, but cannot be used for synchronization among tasks, because only one task may have receive rights to a port. For more general-purpose semaphores, a simple daemon may be written that implements the same method.

20.6 ■ Memory Management

Given the object-oriented nature of Mach, it is not surprising that a principle abstraction in Mach is the *memory object*. Memory objects are used to manage secondary storage, and generally represent files, pipes, or other data that are mapped into virtual memory for reading and writing (Figure 20.8). Memory objects may be backed by user-level memory managers, which take the place of the more traditional kernel-incorporated virtual-memory pager found in other operating systems. In contrast to the traditional approach of having the kernel provide management of secondary storage, Mach treats secondary-storage objects (usually files) as it does all other objects in the system. Each object has a port associated

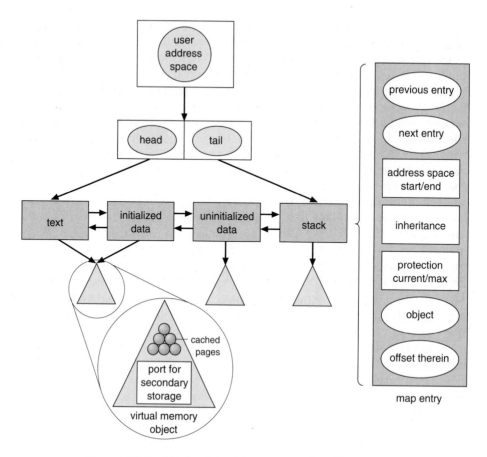

Figure 20.8 Mach virtual memory task address map.

with it, and may be manipulated by messages being sent to its port. Memory objects — unlike the memory-management routines in monolithic, traditional kernels — allow easy experimentation with new memory-manipulation algorithms.

20.6.1 Basic Structure

The virtual address space of a task is generally *sparse*, consisting of many holes of unallocated space. For instance, a memory-mapped file is placed in some set of addresses. Large messages are also transferred as shared memory segments. For each of these segments, a section of virtual-memory address is used to provide the threads with access to the message. As new items are mapped or removed from the address space, holes of unallocated memory appear in the address space.

Mach makes no attempt to compress the address space, although a task may fail (crash) if it has no room for a requested region in its address space. Given that address spaces are 4 gigabytes or more, this limitation is not currently a problem. However, maintaining a regular page table for a 4 gigabyte address space for each task, especially one with holes in it, would use excessive amounts of memory (1 megabyte or more). The key to sparse address spaces is that page-table space is used for only currently allocated regions. When a page fault occurs, the kernel must check to see whether the page is in a valid region, rather than simply indexing into the page table and checking the entry. Although the resulting lookup is more complex, the benefits of reduced memory-storage requirements and simpler address-space maintenance make the approach worthwhile.

Mach also has system calls to support standard virtual-memory functionality, including the allocation, deallocation, and copying of virtual memory. When allocating a new virtual-memory object, the thread may provide an address for the object or may let the kernel choose the address. Physical memory is not allocated until pages in this object are accessed. The object's backing store is managed by the default pager (discussed in Section 20.6.2). Virtual-memory objects are also allocated automatically when a task receives a message containing out-of-line data.

Associated system calls return information about a memory object in a task's address space, change the access protection of the object, and specify how an object is to be passed to child tasks at the time of their creation (shared, copy-on-write, or not present).

20.6.2 User-Level Memory Managers

A secondary-storage object is usually mapped into the virtual address space of a task. Mach maintains a cache of memory-resident pages of all mapped objects, as in other virtual-memory implementations. However, a page fault occurring when a thread accesses a nonresident page is executed as a message to the object's port. The concept of a memory object being created and serviced by nonkernel tasks (unlike threads, for instance, which are created and maintained by only the kernel) is important. The end result is that, in the traditional sense, memory can be paged by user-written memory managers. When the object is destroyed, it is up to the memory manager to write back any changed pages to secondary storage. No assumptions are made by Mach about the content or importance of memory objects, so the memory objects are independent of the kernel.

There are several circumstances in which user-level memory managers are insufficient. For instance, a task allocating a new region of virtual memory might not have a memory manager assigned to that region, since it does not represent a secondary-storage object (but must be paged), or a memory manager could fail to perform pageout. Mach itself also needs a memory manager to take care of its memory needs. For these cases, Mach provides a *default memory manager*. The Mach 2.5 default memory manager uses the standard file system to store data that must be written to disk, rather than requiring a separate swap space, as in 4.3BSD. In Mach 3.0 (and OSF/1), the default memory manager is capable of using either files in a standard filesystem or dedicated disk partitions. The default memory manager has an interface similar to that of the user-level ones, but with some extensions to support its role as the memory manager that can be relied on to perform pageout when user-level managers fail to do so.

Pageout policy is implemented by an internal kernel thread, the *pageout daemon*. A paging algorithm based on FIFO with second chance (Section 9.5.4) is used to select pages for replacement. The selected pages are sent to the appropriate manager (either user level or default) for actual pageout. A user-level manager may be more intelligent than the default manager, and may implement a different paging algorithm suitable to the object it is backing (that is, by selecting some other page and forcibly paging it out). If a user-level manager fails to reduce the resident set of pages when asked to do so by the kernel, the default memory manager is invoked and it pages out the user-level manager to reduce the user-level manager's resident set size. Should the user-level manager recover from the problem that prevented it from performing its own pageouts, it will touch these pages (causing the kernel to page them in again), and can then page them out as it sees fit.

If a thread needs access to data in a memory object (for instance, a file), it invokes the *vm_map* system call. Included in this system call is a port which identifies the object, and the memory manager which is responsible for the region. The kernel executes calls on this port when data are to be read or written in that region. An added complexity is that the kernel makes these calls asynchronously, since it would not be reasonable for the kernel to be waiting on a user-level thread. Unlike the situation with pageout, the kernel has no recourse if its request is not satisfied by the external memory manager. The kernel has no knowledge of the contents of an object or of how that object must be manipulated.

Memory managers are responsible for the consistency of the contents of a memory object mapped by tasks on different machines (tasks on a single machine share a single copy of a mapped memory object). Consider a situation in which tasks on two different machines attempt to modify the same page of an object concurrently. It is up to the manager to decide whether these modifications must be serialized. A conservative manager implementing strict memory consistency would force the modifications to be serialized by granting write access to only one kernel at a time. A more sophisticated manager could allow both accesses to proceed concurrently (for example, if the manager knew that the two tasks were modifying distinct areas within the page, and that it could merge the modifications successfully at some future time). Note that most external memory managers written for Mach (for example, those implementing mapped files) do not implement logic for dealing with multiple kernels, due to the complexity of such logic.

When the first *vm_map* call is made on a memory object, the kernel sends a message to the memory manager port passed in the call, invoking the *memory_manager_init* routine, which the memory manager must provide as part of its support of a memory object. The two ports passed to the memory manager are a *control port* and a *name port*. The control port is used by the memory manager to provide data to the kernel (for example, pages to be made resident). Name ports are used throughout Mach. They do not receive messages, but rather are used simply as a point of reference and comparison. Finally, the memory object must respond to a *memory_manager_init* call with a *memory_object_set_attributes* call to indicate that it is ready to accept requests. When all tasks with send rights to a memory object relinquish those rights, the kernel deallocates the object's ports, thus freeing the memory manager and memory object for destruction.

There are several kernel calls that are needed to support external memory managers. The *vm_map* call has already been discussed in the paragraph above. There are also commands to get and set attributes and to provide page-level locking when it is required (for instance, after a page fault has occurred but before the memory manager has returned the appropriate data). Another call is used by the memory manager to pass a page (or multiple pages, if read-ahead is being used) to the kernel in response to a page fault. This call is necessary since the kernel invokes the memory manager asynchronously. There are also several calls to allow the memory manager to report errors to the kernel.

The memory manager itself must provide support for several calls so that it can support an object. We have already discussed *memory_object_init* and others. When a thread causes a page fault on a memory object's page, the kernel sends a *memory_object_data_request* to the memory object's port on behalf of the faulting thread. The thread is placed in wait state until the memory manager either returns the page in a *memory_object_data_provided* call, or returns an appropriate error to the kernel. Any of the pages that have been modified, or any *precious pages* that the kernel needs to remove from resident memory (due to page aging, for instance), are sent to the memory object via *memory_object_data_write*. Precious pages are pages that may not have been modified, but that cannot be discarded as they otherwise would, because the memory manager no longer retains a copy. The memory manager declares these pages to be precious and expects the kernel to return them when they are removed from memory. Precious pages save unnecessary duplication and copying of memory.

Again, there are several other calls for locking, protection information and modification, and the other details with which all virtual memory systems must deal.

In the current version, Mach does not allow external memory managers to affect the page-replacement algorithm directly. Mach does not export the memory-access information that would be needed for an external task to select the least recently used page, for instance. Methods of providing such information are currently under investigation. An external memory manager is still useful for a variety of reasons, however:

- It may reject the kernel's replacement victim if it knows of a better candidate (for instance, MRU page replacement).

- It may monitor the memory object it is backing, and request pages to be paged out before the memory usage invokes Mach's pageout daemon.

- It is especially important in maintaining consistency of secondary storage for threads on multiple processors, as we shall show in Section 20.6.3.

- It can control the order of operations on secondary storage, to enforce consistency constraints demanded by database management systems. For example, in transaction logging, transactions must be written to a log file on disk before they modify the database data.

- It can control mapped file access.

20.6.3 Shared Memory

Mach uses shared memory to reduce the complexity of various system facilities, as well as to provide these features in an efficient manner. Shared memory generally provides extremely fast interprocess communication, reduces overhead in file management, and helps to support multiprocessing and database management. Mach does not use shared memory for all these traditional shared-memory roles, however. For instance, all threads in a task share that task's memory, so no formal shared-memory facility is needed within a task. However, Mach must still provide traditional shared memory to support other operating-system constructs, such as the UNIX **fork** system call.

It is obviously difficult for tasks on multiple machines to share memory, and to maintain data consistency. Mach does not try to solve this problem directly; rather, it provides facilities to allow the problem to be solved. Mach supports consistent shared memory only when the memory is shared by tasks running on processors that share memory. A parent task is able to declare which regions of memory are to be *inherited* by its children, and which are to be readable−writable. This scheme is different from copy-on-write inheritance, in which each task maintains its own copy of any changed pages. A writable object is addressed from each task's address map, and all changes are made to the same copy. The threads within the tasks are responsible for coordinating changes to memory so that they do not interfere with one another (by writing to the same location concurrently). This coordination may be done through normal synchronization methods: critical sections or mutual-exclusion locks.

For the case of memory shared among separate machines, Mach allows the use of external memory managers. If a set of unrelated tasks wishes to share a section of memory, the tasks may use the same external memory manager and access the same secondary-storage areas through it. The implementor of this system would need to write the tasks and the external pager. This pager could be as simple or as complicated as needed. A simple implementation would allow no readers while a page was being written to. Any write attempt would cause the pager to invalidate the page in all tasks currently accessing it. The pager would then allow the write and would revalidate the readers with the new version of the page. The readers would simply wait on a page fault until the page again became available. Mach provides such a memory manager: the Network Memory Server (NetMemServer). For multicomputers, the NORMA configuration of Mach 3.0 provides similar support as a standard part of the kernel. This XMM subsystem allows multicomputer systems to use external memory managers that do not incorporate logic for dealing with multiple kernels; the XMM subsystem is responsible for maintaining data consistency among multiple kernels that share memory, and makes these kernels appear to be a single kernel to the memory manager. The XMM subsystem also implements virtual copy logic for the mapped objects that it manages. This virtual copy logic includes both copy-on-reference among multicomputer kernels, and sophisticated copy-on-write optimizations.

20.7   ■   Programmer Interface

There are several levels at which a programmer may work within Mach. There is, of course, the system-call level, which, in Mach 2.5, is equivalent to the 4.3BSD system-call interface. Version 2.5 includes most of 4.3BSD as one thread in the kernel. A BSD system call traps to the kernel and is serviced by this thread on behalf of caller, much as standard BSD would handle it. The emulation is not multithreaded, so it has limited efficiency.

Mach 3.0 has moved from the single-server model to support of multiple servers. It has therefore become a true microkernel without the full features normally found in a kernel. Rather, full functionality can be provided via emulation libraries, servers, or a combination of the two. In keeping with the definition of a microkernel, the emulation libraries and servers run outside the kernel at user level. In this way, multiple operating systems can run concurrently on one Mach 3.0 kernel.

An emulation library is a set of routines that lives in a read-only part of a program's address space. Any operating-system calls the program makes are translated into subroutine calls to the library. Single-user operating systems, such as MS-DOS and the Macintosh operating system, have been implemented solely as emulation libraries. For efficiency reasons, the emulation library lives in the address space of the program needing its functionality, but in theory could be a separate task.

More complex operating systems are emulated through the use of libraries and one or more servers. System calls that cannot be implemented in the library are redirected to the appropriate server. Servers can be multithreaded for improved efficiency. BSD and OSF/1 are implemented as single multithreaded servers. Systems can be decomposed into multiple servers for greater modularity.

Functionally, a system call starts in a task, and passes through the kernel before being redirected, if appropriate, to the library in the task's address space or to a server. Although this extra transfer of control will decrease the efficiency of Mach, this decrease is somewhat ameliorated by the ability for multiple threads to be executing BSD-like code concurrently.

At the next higher programming level is the C *Threads* package. This package is a run-time library that provides a C language interface to the basic Mach threads primitives. It provides convenient access to these primitives, including routines for the forking and joining of threads, mutual exclusion through mutex variables (Section 20.4.2), and synchronization through use of condition variables. Unfortunately, it is not appropriate for the C Threads package to be used between systems that share no memory (NORMA systems), since it depends on shared memory to implement its constructs. There is currently no equivalent of C Threads for NORMA systems. Other run-time libraries have been written for Mach, including threads support for other languages.

Although the use of primitives makes Mach flexible, it also makes many programming tasks repetitive. For instance, significant amounts of code are associated with sending and receiving messages in each task that uses messages (which, in Mach, is most tasks). The designers of Mach therefore provide an interface generator (or stub generator) called *MIG*. MIG is essentially a compiler that takes as input a definition of the interface to be used (declarations of variables, types and procedures), and generates the RPC interface code needed to send and receive the messages fitting this definition and to connect the messages to the sending and receiving threads.

20.8 ■ Summary

The Mach operating system is designed to incorporate the many recent innovations in operating-system research to produce a fully functional, technically advanced operating system.

The Mach operating system was designed with the following three critical goals in mind:

- Emulate 4.3BSD UNIX so that the executable files from a UNIX system can run correctly under Mach.

- Have a modern operating system that supports many memory models, and parallel and distributed computing.

- Design a kernel that is simpler and easier to modify than is 4.3BSD.

As we have shown in this chapter, Mach is well on its way to achieving these goals.

Mach 2.5 includes 4.3BSD in its kernel, which provides the emulation needed but enlarges the kernel. This 4.3BSD code has been rewritten to provide the same 4.3 functionality, but to use the Mach primitives. This change allows the 4.3BSD support code to run in user space on a Mach 3.0 system.

Mach uses lightweight processes, in the form of multiple threads of execution within one task (or address space), to support multiprocessing and parallel computation. Its extensive use of messages as the only communications method ensures that protection mechanisms are complete and efficient. By integrating messages with the virtual-memory system, Mach also ensures that messages can be handled efficiently. Finally, by having the virtual-memory system use messages to communicate with the daemons managing the backing store, Mach provides great flexibility in the design and implementation of these memory-object-managing tasks.

By providing low-level, or primitive, system calls from which more complex functions may be built, Mach reduces the size of the kernel while permitting operating-system emulation at the user level, much like IBM's virtual-machine systems.

■ Exercises

20.1 What three features of Mach make it appropriate for distributed processing?

20.2 Name two ways that port sets are useful in implementing parallel programs.

20.3 Consider an application that maintains a database of information, and provides facilities for other tasks to add, delete, and query the database. Give three configurations of ports, threads, and message types that could be used to implement this system. Which is the best? Explain your answer.

20.4 Give the outline of a task that would migrate subtasks (tasks it creates) to other systems. Include information about how it would decide when to migrate tasks, which tasks to migrate, and how the migration would take place.

20.5 Name two types of applications for which you would use the MIG package.

20.6 Why would someone use the low-level system calls, instead of the C Threads package?

20.7 Why are external memory managers not able to replace the internal page-replacement algorithms? What information would need to be made available to the external managers for them to make page-replacement decisions? Why would providing this information violate the principle behind the external managers?

20.8 Why is it difficult to implement mutual exclusion and condition variables in an environment where like-CPUs do not share any memory? What approach and mechanism could be used to make such features available on a NORMA system?

20.9 What are the advantages to rewriting the 4.3BSD code as an external, user-level library, rather than leaving it as part of the Mach kernel? Are there any disadvantages? Explain your answer.

Bibliographic Notes

The Accent operating system was described by Rashid and Robertson [1981]. An historical overview of the progression from an even earlier system, RIG, through Accent to Mach was given by Rashid [1986]. General discussions concerning the Mach model are offered by Tevanian and Smith [1989].

Accetta et al. [1986] presented an overview of the original design of Mach. The Mach scheduler was described in detail by Tevanian et al. [1987a] and Black [1990]. An early version of the Mach shared memory and memory-mapping system was presented by Tevanian et al. [1987b].

The most current description of the C Threads package appears in Cooper and Draves [1987]; MIG was described by Draves et al. [1989]. An overview of these packages' functionality and a general introduction to programming in Mach was presented by Walmer and Thompson [1989] and Boykin et al. [1993].

Black et al. [1988] discussed the Mach exception-handling facility. A multithreaded debugger based on this mechanism was described in Caswell and Black [1989].

A series of talks about Mach sponsored by the OSF UNIX consortium is available on videotape from OSF. Topics include an overview, threads, networking, memory management, many internal details, and some example implementations of Mach. The slides from these talks were given in [OSF 1989].

On systems where USENET News is available (most educational institutions in the United States, and some overseas), the news group *comp.os.mach* is used to exchange information on the Mach project and its components.

An overview of the microkernel structure of Mach 3.0, complete with performance analysis of Mach 2.5 and 3.0 compared to other systems, was given in Black et al. [1992]. Details of the kernel internals and interfaces of Mach 3.0 were provided in Loepere [1992]. Tanenbaum [1992] presented a comparison of Mach and Amoeba. Discussions concerning parallelization in Mach and 4.3BSD are offered by Boykin and Langerman [1990].

Ongoing research was presented at USENIX Mach and Micro-kernel Symposia [USENIX 1990, USENIX 1991, and USENIX 1992b]. Active research areas include virtual memory, real time, and security [McNamee and Armstrong 1990].

CHAPTER 21

HISTORICAL PERSPECTIVE

In Chapter 1, we presented a short historical survey of the development of operating systems. That survey was brief and lacked detail, since the fundamental concepts of operating systems (CPU scheduling, memory management, processes, and so on) had not yet been presented. By now, however, you understand the basic concepts. We are thus in a position to examine how our concepts have been applied in several older and highly influential operating systems. Some of them (such as the XDS-940 or the THE system) were one-of-a-kind systems; others (such as OS/360) are widely used. The order of presentation has been chosen to highlight the similarities and differences of the systems, and is not strictly chronological or ordered by importance. The serious student of operating systems should be familiar with all these systems.

The treatment of each system is brief, but each section contains references to further reading. The papers, written by the designers of the systems, are important both for their technical content, and for their style and flavor.

21.1 ■ Atlas

The Atlas operating system [Kilburn et al. 1961, Howarth et al. 1961] was designed at the University of Manchester in England in the late 1950s and early 1960s. Many of its basic features, which were novel at the time, have become standard parts of modern operating systems. Device drivers were a major part of the system. In addition, system calls were added by a set of special instructions called *extra codes*.

Atlas was a batch operating system with spooling. Spooling allowed the system to schedule jobs according to the availability of peripheral devices, such as magnetic tape units, paper tape readers, paper tape punches, line printers, card readers, or card punches.

The most remarkable feature of Atlas, however, was its memory management. Core memory was new and expensive at the time. Many computers, like the IBM 650, used a drum for primary memory. The Atlas system used a drum for its main memory, but had a small amount of core memory that was used as a cache for the drum. Demand paging was used to transfer information between core memory and the drum automatically.

The Atlas system used a British computer with 48-bit words. Addresses were 24 bits, but were encoded in decimal, which allowed only 1 million words to be addressed. At that time, this was a very large address space. The physical memory for Atlas was a 98K word drum and 16K words of core. Memory was divided into 512-word pages, providing 32 frames in physical memory. An associative memory of 32 registers implemented the mapping from a virtual address to a physical address.

If a page fault occurred, a page-replacement algorithm was invoked. One memory frame was always kept empty, so that a drum transfer could start immediately. The page-replacement algorithm attempted to predict the future memory-accessing behavior based on past behavior. A reference bit for each frame was set whenever the frame was accessed. The reference bits were read into memory every 1024 instructions. The last 32 values of the reference bit were used to define the time since the last reference (t_1) and the interval between the last two references (t_2). Pages were chosen for replacement in the following order:

1. Any page with $t_1 > t_2 + 1$. This page is considered to be no longer in use.

2. If $t_1 \leq t_2$ for all pages, then replace that page with the largest $t_2 - t_1$.

The page-replacement algorithm assumes that programs access memory in loops. If the time between the last two references is t_2, then another reference is expected t_2 time units later. If a reference does not occur ($t_1 > t_2$), it is assumed that the page is no longer being used, and the page is replaced. If all pages are still in use, then the page that will not be needed for the longest time is replaced. The time to the next reference is expected to be $t_2 - t_1$.

21.2 ■ XDS-940

The XDS-940 operating system [Lichtenberger and Pirtle 1965] was designed at the University of California at Berkeley. Like the Atlas system, it used paging for memory management. Unlike the Atlas system, the XDS-940 was a time-shared system.

The paging was used only for relocation; it was not used for demand paging. The virtual memory of any user process was only 16K words, whereas the physical memory was 64K words. Pages were 2K words each. The page table was kept in registers. Since physical memory was larger than virtual memory, several user processes could be in memory at the same time. The number of users could be increased by sharing of pages when the pages contained read-only reentrant code. Processes were kept on a drum and were swapped in and out of memory as necessary.

The XDS-940 system was constructed from a modified XDS-930. The modifications were typical of the changes made to a basic computer to allow an operating system to be written properly. A user-monitor mode was added. Certain instructions, such as I/O and Halt, were defined to be privileged. An attempt to execute a privileged instruction in user mode would trap to the operating system.

A system-call instruction was added to the user-mode instruction set. This instruction was used to create new resources, such as files, allowing the operating system to manage the physical resources. Files, for example, were allocated in 256-word blocks on the drum. A bit map was used to manage free drum blocks. Each file had an index block with pointers to the actual data blocks. Index blocks were chained together.

The XDS-940 system also provided system calls to allow processes to create, start, suspend, and destroy subprocesses. A user programmer could construct a system of processes. Separate processes could share memory for communication and synchronization. Process creation defined a tree structure, where a process is the root and its subprocesses are nodes below it in the tree. Each of the subprocesses could, in turn, create more subprocesses.

21.3 ■ THE

The THE operating system [Dijkstra 1968, McKeag and Wilson 1976 (Chapter 3)] was designed at the Technische Hogeschool at Eindhoven in the Netherlands. It was a batch system running on a Dutch computer, the EL X8, with 32K of 27-bit words. The system was mainly noted for its clean design, particularly its layer structure, and its use of a set of concurrent processes employing semaphores for synchronization.

Unlike the XDS-940 system, however, the set of processes in the THE system was static. The operating system itself was designed as a set of cooperating processes. In addition, five user processes were created, which served as the active agents to compile, execute, and print user programs. When one job was finished, the process would return to the input queue to select another job.

A priority CPU-scheduling algorithm was used. The priorities were recomputed every 2 seconds and were inversely proportional to the amount of CPU time used recently (in the last 8 to 10 seconds). This scheme gave higher priority to I/O-bound processes and to new processes.

Memory management was limited by the lack of hardware support. However, since the system was limited and user programs could be written only in Algol, a software paging scheme was used. The Algol compiler automatically generated calls to system routines, which made sure the requested information was in memory, swapping if necessary. The backing store was a 512K word drum. A 512-word page was used, with an LRU page-replacement strategy.

Another major concern of the THE system was deadlock control. The banker's algorithm was used to provide deadlock avoidance.

Closely related to the THE system is the Venus system [Liskov 1972]. The Venus system was also a layer-structure design, using semaphores to synchronize processes. The lower levels of the design were implemented in microcode, however, providing a much faster system. The memory management was changed to a paged-segmented memory. The system was also designed as a time-sharing system, rather than a batch system.

21.4 ■ RC 4000

The RC 4000 system, like the THE system, was notable primarily for its design concepts. It was designed for the Danish RC 4000 computer by Regenecentralen, particularly by Brinch Hansen [1970, 1973 (Chapter 8)]. The objective was not to design a batch system, or a time-sharing system, or any other specific system. Rather, the goal was to create an operating-system nucleus, or kernel, on which a complete operating system could be built. Thus, the system structure was layered, and only the lower levels — the kernel — were provided.

The kernel supported a collection of concurrent processes. Processes were supported by a round-robin CPU scheduler. Although processes could share memory, the primary communication and synchronization mechanism was the *message system* provided by the kernel. Processes could communicate with each other by exchanging fixed-sized messages of eight words in length. All messages were stored in buffers from a common buffer pool. When a message buffer was no longer required, it was returned to the common pool.

A *message queue* was associated with each process. It contained all the messages that had been sent to that process, but had not yet been received. Messages were removed from the queue in FIFO order. The system supported four primitive operations, which were executed atomically:

- **send-message** (**in** *receiver,* **in** *message,* **out** *buffer*)

- **wait-message** (**out** *sender,* **out** *message,* **out** *buffer*)

- **send-answer** (**out** *result,* **in** *message,* **in** *buffer*)

- **wait-answer** (**out** *result,* **out** *message,* **in** *buffer*)

The last two operations allowed processes to exchange several messages at a time.

These primitives required that a process service its message queue in a FIFO order, and that it block itself while other processes were handling its messages. To remove these restrictions, the developers provided two additional communication primitives. They allowed a process to wait for the arrival of the next message or to answer and service its queue in any order:

- **wait-event** (**in** *previous-buffer,* **out** *next-buffer,* **out** *result*)

- **get-event** (**out** *buffer*)

I/O devices were also treated as processes. The device drivers were code that converted the device interrupts and registers into messages. Thus, a process would write to a terminal by sending that terminal a message. The device driver would receive the message and output the character to the terminal. An input character would interrupt the system and transfer to a device driver. The device driver would create a message from the input character and send it to a waiting process.

21.5 ■ CTSS

The CTSS (Compatible Time-Sharing System) system [Corbato et al. 1962] was designed at MIT as an experimental time-sharing system. It was implemented on an IBM 7090 and eventually supported up to 32 interactive users. The users were provided with a set of interactive commands, which allowed them to manipulate files and to compile and run programs through a terminal.

The 7090 had a 32K memory, made up of 36-bit words. The monitor used 5K words, leaving 27K for the users. User memory images were swapped between memory and a fast drum. CPU scheduling employed a multilevel-feedback-queue algorithm. The time quantum for level i was 2^i time units. If a program did not finish its CPU burst in one time quantum, it was moved down to the next level of the queue, giving it twice as much time. The program at the highest level (with the shortest quantum) was run first. The initial level of a program was determined by its size, so that the time quantum was at least as long as the swap time.

CTSS was extremely successful, and continued to be used as late as 1972. Although it was quite limited, it succeeded in demonstrating that time sharing was a convenient and practical mode of computing. One result of CTSS was increased development of time-sharing systems. Another result was the development of MULTICS.

21.6 ■ MULTICS

The MULTICS operating system [Corbato and Vyssotsky 1965, Organick 1972] was designed at MIT as a natural extension of CTSS. CTSS and other early time-sharing systems were so successful that there was an immediate desire to proceed quickly to bigger and better systems. As larger computers became available, the designers of CTSS set out to create a time-sharing *utility*. Computing service would be provided like electrical power. Large computer systems would be connected by telephone wires to terminals in offices and homes throughout a city. The operating system would be a time-shared system running continuously with a vast file system of shared programs and data.

MULTICS was designed by a team from MIT, GE (which later sold its computer department to Honeywell), and Bell Laboratory (which dropped out of the project in 1969). The basic GE 635 computer was modified to a new computer system called the GE 645, mainly by the addition of paged-segmentation memory hardware.

A virtual address was composed of an 18-bit segment number and a 16-bit word offset. The segments were then paged in 1K word pages. The second-chance page-replacement algorithm was used.

The segmented virtual address space was merged into the file system; each segment was a file. Segments were addressed by the name of the file. The file system itself was a multilevel tree structure, allowing users to create their own subdirectory structures.

Like CTSS, MULTICS used a multilevel feedback queue for CPU scheduling. Protection was accomplished by an access list associated with each file and a set of protection rings for executing processes. The system, which was written almost entirely in PL/1, comprised about 300,000 lines of code. It was extended to a multiprocessor system, allowing a CPU to be taken out of service for maintenance while the system continued running.

21.7 ■ OS/360

The longest line of operating-system development is undoubtedly that for IBM computers. The early IBM computers, such as the IBM 7090 and the IBM 7094, are prime examples of the development of common I/O subroutines, followed by a resident monitor, privileged instructions, memory protection, and simple batch processing. These systems were developed separately, often by each site independently. As a result, IBM was faced with many different computers, with different languages and different system software.

The IBM/360 was designed to alter this situation. The IBM/360 was designed as a family of computers spanning the complete range from small business machines to large scientific machines. Only one set of software would be needed for these systems, which all used the same operating system: OS/360 [Mealy et al. 1966]. This arrangement was supposed to reduce the maintenance problems for IBM and to allow users to move programs and applications freely from one IBM system to another.

Unfortunately, OS/360 tried to be all things for all people. As a result, it did none of its tasks especially well. The file system included a type field that defined the type of each file, and different file types were defined for fixed-length and variable-length records and for blocked and unblocked files. Contiguous allocation was used, so the user had to guess the size of each output file. The Job Control Language (JCL) added parameters for every possible option, making it incomprehensible to the average user.

The memory-management routines were hampered by the architecture. Although a base-register addressing mode was used, the program could access and modify the base register, so that absolute addresses were generated by the CPU. This arrangement prevented dynamic relocation; the program was bound to physical memory at load time. Two separate versions of the operating system were produced: OS/MFT used fixed regions and OS/MVT used variable regions.

The system was written in assembly language by thousands of programmers, resulting in millions of lines of code. The operating system itself required large amounts of memory for its code and tables. Operating-system overhead often consumed one-half of the total CPU cycles. Over the years, new versions were released to add new features and to fix errors. However, fixing one error often caused another in some remote part of the system, so that the number of known errors in the system was fairly constant.

Virtual memory was added to OS/360 with the change to the IBM 370 architecture. The underlying hardware provided a segmented-paged virtual memory. New versions of OS used this hardware in different ways. OS/VS1 created one large virtual address space, and ran OS/MFT in that virtual memory. Thus, the operating system itself was paged, as well as user programs. OS/VS2 Release 1 ran OS/MVT in virtual memory. Finally, OS/VS2 Release 2, which is now called MVS, provided each user with his own virtual memory.

MVS is still basically a batch operating system. The CTSS system was run on an IBM 7094, but MIT decided that the address space of the 360, IBM's successor to the 7094, was too small for MULTICS, so they switched vendors. IBM then decided to create its own time-sharing system, TSS/360 [Lett and

Konigsford 1968]. Like MULTICS, TSS/360 was supposed to be a large time-shared utility. The basic 360 architecture was modified in the model 67 to provide virtual memory. Several sites purchased the 360/67 in anticipation of TSS/360.

TSS/360 was delayed, however, so other time-sharing systems were developed as temporary systems until TSS/360 was available. A time-sharing option (TSO) was added to OS/360. IBM's Cambridge Scientific Center developed CMS as a single-user system and CP/67 to provide a virtual machine to run it on [Meyer and Seawright 1970, Parmelee et al. 1972].

When TSS/360 was eventually delivered, it was a failure. It was too large and too slow. As a result, no site would switch from its temporary system to TSS/360. Today, time sharing on IBM systems is largely provided either by TSO under MVS or by CMS under CP/67 (renamed VM).

What went wrong with TSS/360 and MULTICS? Part of the problem was that these were advanced systems, and were too large and too complex to be understood. Another problem was the assumption that computing power would be available from a large, remote computer by time sharing. It now appears that most computing will be done by small individual machines — personal computers — not by large, remote time-shared systems that try to be all things to all users.

21.8 ■ Other Systems

There are, of course, other operating systems, and most of them have interesting properties. The MCP operating system for the Burroughs computer family [McKeag and Wilson 1976] was the first to be written in a system programming language. It also supported segmentation and multiple CPUs. The SCOPE operating system for the CDC 6600 [McKeag and Wilson 1976] was also a multi-CPU system. The coordination and synchronization of the multiple processes were surprisingly well designed. Tenex [Bobrow et al. 1972] was an early demand-paging system for the PDP-10, which has had a great influence on subsequent time-sharing systems, such as TOPS-20 for the DEC-20. The VMS operating system for the VAX is based on the RSX operating system for the PDP-11. CP/M was the most common operating system for 8-bit microcomputer systems, few of which exist today; MS-DOS is the most common system for 16-bit microcomputers. Graphical user interfaces, or GUIs, are becoming more popular in order to make computers easier to use. The Macintosh Operating System and Microsoft Windows are the two leaders in this area.

APPENDIX

THE NACHOS SYSTEM

By Thomas E. Anderson

University of California, Berkeley

I hear and I forget, I see and I remember,

I do and I understand.

-- Chinese proverb

A good way to gain a deeper understanding of modern operating-system concepts is to get your hands dirty — to take apart the code for an operating system to see how it works at a low level, to build significant pieces of the operating system yourself, and to observe the effects of your work. An operating-system course project provides this opportunity to see how you can use basic concepts to solve real-world problems. Course projects can also be valuable in many other areas of computer science, from compilers and databases to graphics and robotics. But a project is particularly important for operating systems, where many of the concepts are best learned by example and experimentation.

That is why we created *Nachos,* an instructional operating system intended for use as the course project for an undergraduate or first-year graduate course in operating systems. Nachos includes code for a simple but complete working operating system, a machine simulator that allows it to be used in a normal UNIX workstation environment, and a set of sample assignments. Nachos lets anyone explore all the major components of a modern operating system described in this book, from threads and process synchronization, to file systems, to multiprogramming, to virtual memory, to networking. The assignments ask you to design and implement a significant piece of functionality in each of these areas.

Nachos is distributed without charge. It currently runs on both Digital Equipment Corporation MIPS UNIX workstations and Sun SPARC workstations; ports to other machines are in progress. See Section A.4 to learn how to obtain a copy of Nachos.

Here, we give an overview of the Nachos operating system and the machine simulator, and describe our experiences with the example assignments. Of necessity, Nachos is evolving continually, because the field of operating systems is evolving continually. Thus, we can give only a snapshot of Nachos; in Section A.4 we explain how to obtain more up to date information.

A.1 ■ Overview

Many of the earliest operating-system course projects were designed in response to the development of UNIX in the mid-1970s. Earlier operating systems, such as MULTICS and OS/360, were far too complicated for an undergraduate to understand, much less to modify, in one semester.

Even UNIX itself is too complicated for that purpose, but UNIX showed that the core of an operating system can be written in only a few dozen pages, with a few simple but powerful interfaces. However, recent advances in operating systems, hardware architecture, and software engineering have caused many operating-systems projects developed over the past two decades to become out-of-date. Networking and distributed applications are now commonplace. Threads are crucial for the construction of both operating systems and higher-level concurrent applications. And the cost–performance tradeoffs among memory, CPU speed, and secondary storage are now different from those imposed by core memory, discrete logic, magnetic drums, and card readers.

Nachos is intended to help people learn about these modern systems concepts. Nachos illustrates and takes advantage of modern operating-systems technology, such as threads and remote procedure calls; recent hardware advances, such as RISCs and the prevalence of memory hierarchies; and modern software-design techniques, such as protocol layering and object-oriented programming.

In designing Nachos, we faced constantly the tradeoff between simplicity and realism in choosing what code to provide as part of the baseline system, and what to leave for the assignments. We believe that a course project must achieve a careful balance among the time that students spend reading code, that they spend designing and implementing, and that they spend learning new concepts. At one extreme, we could have provided nothing but bare hardware, leaving a *tabula rasa* for students to build an entire operating system from scratch. This approach is impractical, given the scope of topics to cover. At the other extreme, starting with code that is too realistic would make it easy to lose sight of key ideas in a forest of details.

Our approach was to build the simplest possible implementation for each subsystem of Nachos; this provides a working example — albeit an overly simplistic one — of the operation of each component of an operating system. The baseline Nachos operating-system kernel includes a thread manager, a file system, the ability to run user programs, and a simple network mailbox. As a result of our emphasis on simplicity, the baseline kernel comprises about 2500 lines of code, about one-half of which are devoted to interface descriptions and comments. (The hardware simulator takes up another 2500 lines, but you do not need to understand the details of its operation to do the assignments.) It is thus practical to read, understand, and modify Nachos during a single semester course. By contrast, building a project around a system like UNIX would add realism, but the UNIX 4.3BSD file system *by itself*, even excluding the device drivers, comprises roughly 5000 lines of code. Since a typical course will spend only about 2 to 3 weeks of the semester on file systems, size makes UNIX impractical as a basis for an undergraduate operating-system course project.

We have found that the baseline Nachos kernel can demystify a number of operating-system concepts that are difficult to understand in the abstract. Simply reading and walking through the execution of the baseline system can answer numerous questions about how an operating system works at a low level, such as:

- How do all the pieces of an operating system fit together?

- How does the operating system start a thread? How does it start a process?

- What happens when one thread context switches to another thread?

- How do interrupts interact with the implementation of critical sections?

- What happens on a system call? What happens on a page fault?

- How does address translation work?

- Which data structures in a file system are on disk, and which are in memory?

- What data need to be written to disk when a user creates a file?

- How does the operating system interface with I/O devices?

- What does it mean to build one layer of a network protocol on another?

Of course, reading code by itself can be a boring and pointless exercise; we addressed this problem by keeping the code as simple as possible, and by designing assignments that modify the system in fundamental ways. Because we start with working code, the assignments can focus on the more interesting aspects of operating-system design, where tradeoffs exist and there is no single right answer.

A.2 ■ Nachos Software Structure

Before we discuss the sample assignments in detail, we first outline the structure of the Nachos software. Figure A.1 illustrates how the major pieces in Nachos fit together. Like many earlier instructional operating systems, Nachos runs on a *simulation* of real hardware. Originally, when operating-system projects were first being developed in the 1970s and early 1980s, the reason for using a simulator was to make better use of scarce hardware resources. Without a simulator, each student would need her

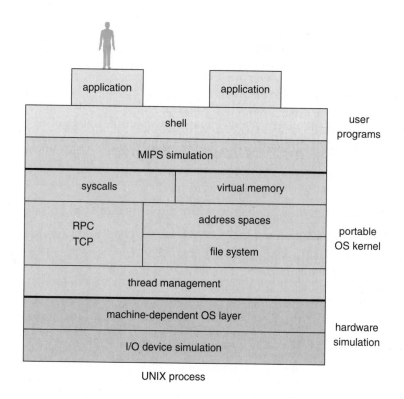

Figure A.1 How the major pieces in Nachos fit together.

own physical machine to test new versions of the kernel. Now that personal computers are commonplace, is there still a reason to develop an operating system on a simulator, rather than on physical hardware?

We believe that the answer is yes, because using a simulator makes debugging easier. On real hardware, operating-system behavior is nondeterministic; depending on the precise timing of interrupts, the operating system may take one path through its code or another. Synchronization can help to make operating-system behavior more predictable, but what if we have a bug in our synchronization code such that two threads can access the same data structure at the same time? The kernel may behave correctly most of the time, yet crash occasionally. Without being able to repeat the behavior that led to the crash, however, it would be difficult to find the root cause of the problem. Running on a simulator, rather than on real hardware, allows us to make system behavior repeatable. Of course, debugging nonrepeatable execution sequences is part of life for professional operating-system engineers, but it did not seem advisable for us to make this experience part of anyone's introduction to operating systems.

Running on simulated hardware has other advantages. During debugging, it is important to be able to make a change to the system quickly, to recompile, and to test the change to see whether it fixed the problem. Using a simulator reduces the time required for this edit−compile−debug cycle, because otherwise the entire system has to be rebooted to test a new version of the kernel. Moreover, normal debugging tools do not work on operating-system kernels, because, for example, if the kernel stops at a breakpoint, the debugger cannot use the kernel to print the prompt for the next debugging command. In practice, debugging an operating-system kernel on real hardware requires *two* machines: one to run the kernel under test, and the other to run the debugger. For these reasons, many commercial operating-system development projects now routinely use simulators to speed development.

One approach would be to simulate the entire workstation hardware, including fetching, decoding, and executing each kernel- or user-mode instruction in turn. Instead, we take a shortcut for performance. The Nachos kernel code executes in native mode as a normal (debuggable) UNIX process linked with the hardware simulator. The simulator surrounds the kernel code, making it appear as though it is running on real hardware. Whenever the kernel code accesses an I/O device — such as a clock chip, a disk, a network controller, or a console — the simulator is invoked to perform the I/O activity. For instance, the simulator implements disk I/O using UNIX file routines; it implements network packet transfer via UNIX sockets.

In addition, we simulate each instruction executed in user mode. Whenever the kernel gives up control to run application code, the simulator fetches each application instruction in turn, checks for page faults or other exceptions, and then simulates its execution. When an application page fault or hardware interrupt occurs, the simulator passes control back to the kernel for processing, as the hardware would in a real system.

Thus, in Nachos, user applications, the operating-system kernel, and the hardware simulator run together in a normal UNIX process. The UNIX process thus represents a single workstation running Nachos. The Nachos kernel, however, is written as though it were running on real hardware. In fact, we could port the Nachos kernel to a physical machine simply by replacing the hardware simulation with real hardware and a few machine-dependent device-driver routines.

Nachos is different from earlier systems in several significant ways:

1. We can run normal compiled C programs on the Nachos kernel, because we simulate a standard, well-documented, instruction set (MIPS R2/3000 integer instructions) for user-mode programs. In the past, operating-system projects typically simulated their own ad hoc instruction set, requiring user programs to be written in a special-purpose assembly language. However, because the R2/3000 is a RISC, it is straightforward to simulate its instruction set. In all, the MIPS simulation code is only about 10 pages long.

2. We simulate accurately the behavior of a network of workstations, each running a copy of Nachos. We connect Nachos "machines," each running as a UNIX process, via UNIX sockets, simulating a local-area network. A thread on one "machine" can then send a packet to a thread running on a different "machine"; of course, both are simulated on the same physical hardware.

3. The simulation is deterministic, and kernel behavior is reproducible. Instead of using UNIX signals to simulate asynchronous devices such as the disk and the timer, Nachos maintains a simulated time that is incremented whenever a user program executes an instruction and whenever a call is made to certain low-level kernel routines. Interrupt handlers are then invoked when the simulated time reaches the appropriate point. At present, the precise timing of network packet delivery is not reproducible, although this limitation may be fixed in later versions of Nachos.

4. The simulation is randomizable to add unpredictable, but repeatable, behavior to the kernel thread scheduler. Our goal was to make it easy to test kernel behavior given different interleavings of the execution of concurrent threads. Simulated time is incremented whenever interrupts are enabled within the kernel (in other words, whenever any low-level synchronization routine, such as semaphore P or V, is called); after a random interval of simulated time, the scheduler will

cause the current thread to be time sliced. As another example, the network simulation randomly chooses which packets to drop. Provided that the initial seed to the random number generator is the same, however, the behavior of the system is repeatable.

5. We hide the hardware simulation from the rest of Nachos via a machine-dependent interface layer. For example, we define an abstract disk that accepts requests to read and write disk sectors and provides an interrupt handler to be called on request completion. The details of the disk simulator are hidden behind this abstraction, in much the same way that disk-device−specific details are isolated in a normal operating system. One advantage to using a machine-dependent interface layer is to make clear which portions of Nachos can be modified (the kernel and the applications) and which portions are off-limits (the hardware simulation — at least until you take a computer-architecture course).

A.3 ■ Sample Assignments

Nachos contains five major components, each the focus of one assignment given during the semester: thread management and synchronization, the file system, user-level multiprogramming support, the virtual-memory system, and networking. Each assignment is designed to build on previous ones; for instance, every part of Nachos uses thread primitives for managing concurrency. This design reflects part of the charm of developing operating systems: You get to use what you build. It is easy, however, to change the assignments or to do them in a different order.

In Sections A.3.1 through A.3.5, we discuss each of the five assignments in turn, describing what hardware-simulation facilities and operating-system structures we provide, and what we ask you to implement. Of course, because Nachos is continuing to evolve, what is described here is a snapshot of what is available at the time of printing. Section A.4 explains how to obtain more up-to-date information.

The assignments are intended to be of roughly equal size, each taking approximately 3 weeks of a 15-week (semester) course, assuming that two people work together on each. The file-system assignment is the most difficult of the five; the multiprogramming assignment is the least difficult. Faculty who have used Nachos say that they find it useful to spend 1/2 to 1 hour per week discussing the assignments. We have found it useful for faculty to conduct a design review with each pair of students the week before each assignment is due.

Nachos is intended to encourage a quantitative approach to operating-system design. Frequently, the choice of how to implement an operating-system function reduces to a tradeoff between simplicity and performance.

Making informed decisions about tradeoffs is one of the key tasks to learn in an undergraduate operating-system course. The Nachos hardware simulation reflects current hardware performance characteristics (except that kernel execution time is estimated, rather than being measured directly). The assignments exploit this feature by asking that you explain and optimize the performance of your implementations on simple benchmarks.

The Nachos kernel and simulator are implemented in a subset of C++. Object-oriented programming is becoming more popular, and it is a natural idiom for stressing the importance of modularity and clean interfaces in building systems. Unfortunately, C++ is a complicated language; thus, to simplify matters, we omitted certain aspects from standard C++: derived classes, operator and function overloading, C++ streams, and generics. We also kept inlines to a minimum. The Nachos distribution includes a short primer to help people who know C to learn our subset of C++; we have found that our students pick up this subset quickly.

A.3.1 Thread Management

The first assignment introduces the concepts of threads and concurrency. The baseline Nachos kernel provides a basic working thread system and an implementation of semaphores; the assignment is to implement Mesa-style locks and condition variables using semaphores, and then to implement solutions to a number of concurrency problems using these synchronization primitives.

In much the same way as understanding pointers can be difficult for beginning programmers, understanding concurrency requires a conceptual leap. We believe that a good way to learn about concurrency is to take a hands-on approach. Nachos helps to teach concurrency in two ways. First, thread management in Nachos is *explicit*: it is possible to trace, literally statement by statement, what happens during a context switch from one thread to another, from the perspectives of an outside observer and of the threads involved. We believe that this experience is crucial to demystifying concurrency. Precisely because C and C++ allow nothing to be swept under the carpet, concurrency may be easier to understand (although more difficult to use) in these programming languages than in those explicitly designed for concurrency, such as Ada or Modula-3.

Second, a working thread system, like that in Nachos, provides a chance to practice writing, and testing, concurrent programs. Even experienced programmers find it difficult to think concurrently. When we first used Nachos, we omitted many of the practice problems that we now include in the assignment, thinking that students would see enough concurrency in the rest of the project. Later, we realized that many students were still making concurrency errors even in the final phase of the project.

Our primary goal in building the baseline thread system was simplicity, to reduce the effort required to trace through the thread system's behavior. The implementation takes a total of about 10 pages of C++ and one page of MIPS assembly code. For simplicity, thread scheduling is normally nonpreemptive, but to emphasize the importance of critical sections and synchronization, we have a command-line option that causes threads to be time sliced at "random," but repeatable, points in the program. Concurrent programs are correct only if they work when a context switch can happen at any time.

A.3.2 File Systems

Real file systems can be complex artifacts. The UNIX file system, for example, has at least three levels of indirection — the per-process file-descriptor table, the system wide open-file table, and the in-core inode table — before you even get to disk blocks. As a result, to build a file system that is simple enough to read and understand in a couple of weeks, we were forced to make some difficult choices about where to sacrifice realism.

We provide a basic working file system, stripped of as much functionality as possible. Although the file system has an interface similar to that of UNIX (cast in terms of C++ objects), it also has many significant limitations with respect to commercial file systems: there is no synchronization (only one thread at a time can access the file system), files have a very small maximum size, files have a fixed size once created, there is no caching or buffering of file data, the file name space is completely flat (there is no hierarchical directory structure), and there is no attempt to provide robustness across machine and disk crashes. As a result, the basic file system takes only about 15 pages of code.

The assignment is (1) to correct some of these limitations, and (2) to improve the performance of the resulting file system. We list a few possible optimizations, such as caching and disk scheduling, but part of the exercise is to decide which solutions are the most cost effective.

At the hardware level, we provide a disk simulator, which accepts read sector and write sector requests and signals the completion of an operation via an interrupt. The disk data are stored in a UNIX file; read and write sector operations are performed using normal UNIX file reads and writes. After the UNIX file is updated, we calculate how long the simulated disk operation should have taken (from the track and sector of the request), and set an interrupt to occur that far in the future. Read and write sector requests (emulating hardware) return immediately; higher-level software is responsible for waiting until the interrupt occurs.

We made several mistakes in developing the Nachos file system. In our first attempt, the file system was much more realistic than the current one, but it also took more than four times as much code. We were forced to rewrite it to cut it down to code that could be read and understood quickly. When we handed out this simpler file system, we did not provide sufficient code for it to be working completely; we left out file read and file write to be written as part of the assignment. Although these functions are fairly straightforward to implement, the fact that the code did not work meant that students had difficulty understanding how each of the pieces of the file system fit with the others.

We also initially gave students the option of which limitation to fix; we found that students learned the most from fixing the first four listed. In particular, the students who chose to implement a hierarchical directory structure found that, although it was conceptually simple, the implementation required a relatively large amount of code.

Finally, many modern file systems include some form of write-ahead logging or log structure, simplifying crash recovery. The assignment now completely ignores this issue, but we are currently looking at ways to do crash recovery by adding simple write-ahead logging code to the baseline Nachos file system. As it stands, the choice of whether or not to address crash recovery is simply a tradeoff. In the limited amount of time available, we ask students to focus on how basic file systems work, how the file abstraction allows disk data layout to be changed radically without changing the file-system interface, and how caching can be used to improve I/O performance.

A.3.3 Multiprogramming

In the third assignment, we provide code to create a user address space, to load a Nachos file containing an executable image into user memory, and then to run the program. The initial code is restricted to running only a single user program at a time. The assignment is to expand this base to support multiprogramming, to implement a variety of system calls (such as UNIX **fork** and **exec**) as well as a user-level shell, and to optimize the performance of the resulting system on a mixed workload of I/O- and CPU-bound jobs.

Although we supply little Nachos kernel code as part of this assignment, the hardware simulation does require a fair amount of code. We simulate the entire MIPS R2/3000 integer instruction set and a simple single-level page-table translation scheme. (For this assignment, a program's entire virtual address space must be mapped into physical memory; true virtual memory is left for assignment 4.) In addition, we provide an abstraction that hides most of the details of the MIPS object-code format.

This assignment requires few conceptual leaps, but it does tie together the work of the previous two assignments, resulting in a usable — albeit limited — operating system. Because the simulator can run C programs, it is easy to write utility programs (such as the shell or UNIX **cat**) to exercise the system. (One overly ambitious student attempted unsuccessfully to port emacs.) The assignment illustrates that there is little difference between writing user code and writing operating-system kernel code, except that user code runs in its own address space, isolating the kernel from user errors.

One important topic that we chose to leave out (again, as a tradeoff against time constraints) is the trend toward a small-kernel operating-system structure, where pieces of the operating system are split off into user-level servers. Because of Nachos' modular design, it would be straightforward to move Nachos toward a small-kernel structure, except that (1) we have no symbolic debugging support for user programs, and (2) we would need a stub compiler to make it easy to make remote procedure calls across address spaces. One reason for adopting a micro-kernel design is that it is easier to develop and debug operating-system code as a user-level server than if the code is part of the kernel. Because Nachos runs as a UNIX process, the reverse is true: It is easier to develop and debug Nachos kernel code than application code running on top of Nachos.

A.3.4 Virtual Memory

Assignment 4 is to replace the simple memory-management system from the previous assignment with a true virtual-memory system — that is, one that presents to each user program the abstraction of an (almost) unlimited virtual-memory size by using main memory as a cache for the disk. We provide no new hardware or operating-system components for this assignment.

The assignment has three parts. The first part is to implement the mechanism for page-fault handling — the kernel must catch the page fault, find the needed page on disk, find a page frame in memory to hold the needed page (writing the old contents of the page frame to disk if the page frame is dirty), read the new page from disk into memory, adjust the page-table entry, and then resume the execution of the program. This mechanism can take advantage of the code written for the previous assignments: The backing store for an address space can be represented simply as a Nachos file, and synchronization is needed when multiple page faults occur concurrently.

The second part of the assignment is to devise a policy for managing the memory as a cache — for deciding which page to toss out when a new page frame is needed, in what circumstances (if any) to do read-ahead, when to write unused dirty pages back to disk, and how many pages to bring in before starting to run a program.

These policy questions can have a large effect on overall system performance, in part because of the large and increasing gap between CPU speed and disk latency — this gap has widened by two orders of magnitude in only the past decade. Unfortunately, the simplest policies often have unacceptable performance. So that realistic policies are encouraged, the third part of the assignment is to measure the performance of the paging system on a matrix multiply program where the matrices do not fit in memory. This workload is not meant to be representative of real-life paging behavior, but it is simple enough to illustrate the influence of policy changes on application performance. Further, the application illustrates several of the problems with caching: Small changes in the implementation can have a large effect on performance.

A.3.5 Networking

Although distributed systems have become increasingly important commercially, most instructional operating systems do not have a networking component. To address this omission, we chose the capstone of the project to be to write a significant and interesting distributed application.

At the hardware level, each UNIX process running Nachos represents a uniprocessor workstation. We simulate the behavior of a network of workstations by running multiple copies of Nachos, each in its own UNIX process, and by using UNIX sockets to pass network packets from one Nachos "machine" to another. The Nachos operating system can communicate with other systems by sending packets into the simulated network; the transmission is accomplished by socket send and receive. The Nachos network provides unreliable transmission of limited-sized packets from machine to machine. The likelihood that any packet will be dropped can be set as a command-line option, as can the seed used to determine which packets are "randomly" chosen to be dropped. Packets are dropped but are never corrupted, so that checksums are not required.

To show how to use the network and, at the same time, to illustrate the benefits of layering, the Nachos kernel comes with a simple post-office protocol layered on top of the network. The post-office layer provides a set of mailboxes that route incoming packets to the appropriate waiting thread. Messages sent through the post office also contain a return address to be used for acknowledgments.

The assignment is first to provide reliable transmission of arbitrary-sized packets, and then to build a distributed application on top of that service. Supporting arbitrary-sized packets is straightforward — you need merely to split any large packet into fixed-sized pieces, to add fragment serial numbers, and to send the pieces one by one. Ensuring reliability is more interesting, requiring a careful analysis and design. To reduce the time required to do the assignment, we do not ask you to implement congestion control or window management, although of course these are important issues in protocol design.

The choice of how to complete the project is left open. We do make a few suggestions: multiuser UNIX talk, a distributed file system with caching, a process-migration facility, distributed virtual memory, a gateway protocol that is robust to machine crashes. Perhaps the most interesting application that a student built (that we know of) was a distributed version of the "battleship" game, with each player on a different machine. This application illustrated the role of distributed state, since each machine kept only its local view of the gameboard; it also exposed several performance problems in the hardware simulation, which we have since fixed.

Perhaps the biggest limitation of the current implementation is that we do not model network performance correctly, because we do not keep the timers on each of the Nachos machines synchronized with one another. We are currently working on fixing this problem, using distributed simulation techniques for efficiency. These techniques will allow us to make performance comparisons between alternate implementations of network protocols; they will also enable us to use the Nachos network as a simulation of a message-passing multiprocessor.

A.4 ■ Information on Obtaining a Copy of Nachos

You can obtain Nachos by anonymous ftp from the machine ftp.cs.berkeley.edu by following these steps:

1. Use UNIX ftp to access ftp.cs.berkeley.edu:

   ftp ftp.cs.berkeley.edu

2. You will get a login prompt. Type the word anonymous, and then use your e-mail address as the password.

   Name: anonymous
   Password: tea@cs.berkeley.edu (for example)

3. You are now in ftp. Move to the Nachos subdirectory.

   ftp> cd ucb/nachos

4. You must remember to turn on "binary" mode in ftp; unfortunately, if you forget to do so, when you fetch the Nachos file, it will be garbled without any kind of warning message. This error is one of the most common that people make in obtaining software using anonymous ftp.

   ftp> binary

5. You can now copy the compressed UNIX tar file containing the Nachos distribution to your machine. The software will automatically enroll you in a mailing list for announcements of new releases of Nachos; you can remove yourself from this list by sending e-mail to nachos@cs.berkeley.edu.

ftp> get nachos.tar.Z

6. Exit the ftp program:

ftp> quit

7. Decompress and detar to obtain the Nachos distribution. (If the decompress step fails, you probably forgot to set binary mode in ftp in step 4. You will need to start over.)

uncompress nachos.tar.Z
tar -xf nachos.tar

8. The preceding steps will produce several files, including the code for the baseline Nachos kernel, the hardware simulator, documentation on the sample assignments, and the C++ primer. There will also be a README file to get you started: It explains how to build the baseline system, how to print out documentation, and which machine architectures are currently supported.

cat README

Mendel Rosenblum at Stanford has ported the Nachos kernel to run on Sun SPARC workstations, although user programs running on top of Nachos must still be compiled for the MIPS R2/3000 RISC processor. Ports to machines other than Digital Equipment Corporation MIPS UNIX workstations and Sun SPARC workstations are in progress. Up-to-date information on machine availability is included in the README file in the distribution. The machine dependence comes in two parts. First, the Nachos kernel runs just like normal application code on a UNIX workstation, but a small amount of assembly code is needed in the Nachos kernel to implement thread context switching. Second, Nachos simulates the instruction-by-instruction execution of user programs, to catch page faults and other exceptions. This simulation assumes the MIPS R2/3000 instruction set. To port Nachos to a new machine, we replace the kernel thread-switch code with machine-specific code, and rely on a C cross-compiler to generate MIPS object code for each user program. (A cross-compiler is a compiler that generates object code for one machine type while running on a different machine type.) Because we rely on a cross-compiler, we do not have to rewrite the instruction-set simulator for each port to a new machine. The SPARC version of Nachos, for instance, comes with instructions on how to cross-compile to MIPS on the SPARC.

Questions about Nachos and bug reports should be directed via e-mail to nachos@cs.berkeley.edu. Questions can also be posted to the alt.os.nachos newsgroup.

A.5 ■ Conclusions

Nachos is an instructional operating system designed to reflect recent advances in hardware and software technology, to illustrate modern operating-system concepts, and, more broadly, to help teach the design of complex computer systems. The Nachos kernel and sample assignments illustrate principles of computer-system design needed to understand the computer systems of today and of the future: concurrency and synchronization, caching and locality, the tradeoff between simplicity and performance, building reliability from unreliable components, dynamic scheduling, object-oriented programming, the power of a level of translation, protocol layering, and distributed computing. Familiarity with these concepts is valuable, we believe, even for those people who do not end up working in operating-system development.

■ Bibliographic Notes

Wayne Christopher, Steve Procter, and Thomas Anderson (the author of this appendix) did the initial implementation of Nachos in January 1992. The first version was used for one term as the project for the undergraduate operating-systems course at The University of California at Berkeley. We then revised both the code and the assignments, releasing Nachos, Version 2 for public distribution in August 1992; Mendel Rosenblum ported Nachos to the Sun SPARC workstation. The second version is currently in use at several universities including Carnegie Mellon, Colorado State, Duke, Harvard, Stanford, State University of New York at Albany, University of Washington, and, of course, Berkeley; we have benefited tremendously from the suggestions and criticisms of our early users.

In designing the Nachos project, we have borrowed liberally from ideas found in other systems, including the TOY operating system project, originally developed by Ken Thompson while he was at Berkeley, and modified extensively by a collection of people since then; Tunis, developed by Rick Holt [Holt 1983]; and Minix, developed by Andy Tanenbaum

[Tanenbaum 1987]. Lions [1977] was one of the first people to realize that the core of an operating system could be expressed in a few lines of code, and then used to teach people about operating systems. The instruction-set simulator used in Nachos is largely based on a MIPS simulator written by John Ousterhout.

We credit Lance Berc with inventing the acronym "Nachos" Not Another Completely Heuristic Operating System.

BIBLIOGRAPHY

[**Abbot 1984**] C. Abbot, "Intervention Schedules for Real-Time Programming," *IEEE Transactions on Software Engineering,* Volume SE-10, Number 3 (May 1984), pages 268–274.

[**Accetta et al. 1986**] M. Accetta, R. Baron, W. Bolosky, D. B. Golub, R. Rashid, A. Tevanian, and M. Young, "Mach: A New Kernel Foundation for Unix Development," *Proceedings of the Summer 1986 USENIX Conference* (June 1986), pages 93–112.

[**Agrawal et al. 1986**] D. P. Agrawal, V. K. Janakiram, and G. C. Pathak, "Evaluating the Performance of Multicomputer Configurations," *Communications of the ACM,* Volume 29, Number 5 (May 1986), pages 23–37.

[**Agrawal and El Abbadi 1991**] D. P. Agrawal and A. El Abbadi, "An Efficient and Fault-Tolerant Solution of Distributed Mutual Exclusion," *ACM Transactions on Computer Systems,* Volume 9, Number 1 (February 1991), pages 1–20.

[**Ahituv et al. 1987**] N. Ahituv, Y. Lapid and S. Neumann, "Processing Encrypted Data," *Communications of the ACM,* Volume 30, Number 9 (September 1987), pages 777–780.

[**Akl 1983**] S. G. Akl, "Digital Signatures: A Tutorial Survey," *Computer,* Volume 16, Number 2 (February 1983), pages 15–24.

[**Ammon et al. 1985**] G. J. Ammon, J. A. Calabria, and D. T. Thomas, "A High-Speed, Large-Capacity, 'Jukebox' Optical Disk System," *Computer,* Volume 18, Number 7 (July 1985), pages 36–48.

[Anderson et al. 1989] T. E. Anderson, E. D. Lazowska, and H. M. Levy, "The Performance Implications of Thread Management Alternatives for Shared-Memory Multiprocessors," *IEEE Transactions on Computers,* Volume 38, Number 12 (December 1989), pages 1631–1644.

[Anderson et al. 1991] T. E. Anderson, B. N. Bershad, E. D. Lazowska, and H. M. Levy, "Scheduler Activations: Effective Kernel Support for the User-Level Management of Parallelism," *Proceedings of the Thirteenth ACM Symposium on Operating Systems Principles* (October 1991), pages 95–109.

[Anyanwu and Marshall 1986] J. A. Anyanwu and L. F. Marshall, "A Crash Resistant UNIX File System," *Software—Practice and Experience,* Volume 16 (February 1986), pages 107–118.

[Apple 1987] Apple Computer Inc., *Apple Technical Introduction to the Macintosh Family,* Addison-Wesley, Reading, MA (1987).

[Apple 1991] Apple Computer Inc., *Inside Macintosh, Volume VI,* Addison-Wesley, Reading, MA (1991).

[Artsy 1989a] Y. Artsy, Ed., Special Issue on Process Migration. *Newsletter of the IEEE Computer Society Technical Committee on Operating Systems* (Winter 1989).

[Artsy 1989b] Y. Artsy, "Designing a Process Migration Facility: The Charlotte Experience," *Computer,* Volume 22, Number 9 (September 1989), pages 47–56.

[AT&T 1986] AT&T, Steven V. Earhart, Ed., *UNIX Programmer's Manual,* Holt, Rinehart, and Winston, New York, NY (1986).

[Babaoglu and Joy 1981] O. Babaoglu and W. Joy, "Converting a Swap-Based System to Do Paging in an Architecture Lacking Page-Referenced Bits," *Proceedings of the Eighth ACM Symposium on Operating System Principles* (December 1969), pages 78–86.

[Bach 1987] M. J. Bach, *The Design of the UNIX Operating System,* Prentice-Hall, Englewood Cliffs, NJ (1987).

[Baer 1980] J. L. Baer, *Computer System Architecture,* Computer Science Press, Rockville, MD (1980).

[Balkovich et al. 1985] E. Balkovich, S. R. Lerman, and R. P. Parmelee, "Computing in Higher Education: The Athena Experience," *Communications of the ACM,* Volume 28, Number 11 (November 1985), pages 1214–1224.

[Barak and Kornatzky 1987] A. Barak and Y. Kornatzky, "Design Principles of Operating Systems for Large Scale Multicomputers," *Experience with Distributed Systems, Lecture Notes in Computer Science,* Volume 309, Springer-Verlag (September 1987), pages 104–123.

[Bayer et al. 1978] R. Bayer, R. M. Graham, and G. Seegmuller, Eds., *Operating Systems — An Advanced Course*, Springer-Verlag, Berlin (1978).

[Bays 1977] C. Bays, "A Comparison of Next-Fit, First-Fit, and Best-Fit," *Communications of the ACM*, Volume 20, Number 3 (March 1977), pages 191–192.

[Belady 1966] L. A. Belady, "A Study of Replacement Algorithms for a Virtual-Storage Computer," *IBM Systems Journal*, Volume 5, Number 2 (1966), pages 78–101.

[Belady et al. 1969] L. A. Belady, R. A. Nelson, and G. S. Shedler, "An Anomaly in Space-Time Characteristics of Certain Programs Running in a Paging Machine," *Communications of the ACM*, Volume 12, Number 6 (June 1969), pages 349–353.

[Ben-Ari 1990] M. Ben-Ari, *Principles of Concurrent and Distributed Programming*, Prentice-Hall, Englewood Cliffs, NJ (1990).

[Bernstein and Goodman 1980] P. A. Bernstein and N. Goodman, "Timestamp-based Algorithms for Concurrency Control in Distributed Database Systems," *Proceedings of the International Conference on Very Large Data Bases* (1980), pages 285–300.

[Bernstein and Siegel 1975] A. J. Bernstein and P. Siegel, "A Computer Architecture for Level Structured Operating Systems," *IEEE Transactions on Computers*, Volume C-24, Number 8 (August 1975), pages 785–793.

[Bernstein et al. 1987] A. Bernstein, V. Hadzilacos, and N. Goodman, *Concurrency Control and Recovery in Database Systems*, Addison-Wesley, Reading, MA (1987).

[Bershad and Pinkerton 1988] B. N. Bershad and C. B. Pinkerton, "Watchdogs: Extending the Unix File System," *Proceedings of the Winter 1988 USENIX Conference* (February 1988).

[Bershad et al. 1990] B. N. Bershad, T. E. Anderson, E. D. Lazowska, and H. M. Levy, "Lightweight Remote Procedure Call," *ACM Transactions on Computer Systems*, Volume 8, Number 1 (February 1990), pages 37–55.

[Bhuyan et al. 1989] L. N. Bhuyan, Q. Yang, and D. P. Agrawal, "Performance of Multiprocessor Interconnection Networks," *Computer*, Volume 22, Number 2 (February 1989), pages 25–37.

[Bic and Shaw 1988] L. Bic and A. C. Shaw, *The Logical Design of Operating Systems*, Second Edition, Prentice-Hall, Englewood Cliffs, NJ (1988).

[Birman and Joseph 1987] K. Birman and T. Joseph, "Reliable Communication in the Presence of Failures," *ACM Transactions on Computer Systems*, Volume 5, Number 1 (February 1987).

[Birrell 1989] A. D. Birrell, "An Introduction to Programming with Threads," Technical Report 35, DEC-SRC, Palo Alto, CA (January 1989).

[Birrell and Nelson 1984] A. D. Birrell and B. J. Nelson, "Implementing Remote Procedure Calls," *ACM Transactions on Computer Systems,* Volume 2, Number 1 (February 1984), pages 39−59.

[Black 1990] D. L. Black, "Scheduling Support for Concurrency and Parallelism in the Mach Operating System," *IEEE Computer* (May 1990), pages 35−43.

[Black et al. 1988] D. L. Black, D. B. Golub, R. F. Rashid, A. Tevanian Jr., and M. Young, "The Mach Exception Handling Facility," Technical Report, Carnegie-Mellon University (April 1988).

[Black et al. 1992] D. L. Black, D. B. Golub, D. P. Julin, R. F. Rashid, R. P. Draves, R. W. Dean, A. Forin, J. Barrera, H. Tokadu, G. Malan, and D. Bohman, "Microkernel Operating System Architecture and Mach," *Proceedings of the USENIX Workshop on Micro-Kernels and Other Kernel Architectures* (April 1992), pages 11−30.

[Blair et al. 1985] G. S. Blair, J. R. Malone, and J. A. Mariani, "A Critique of UNIX," *Software—Practice and Experience,* Volume 15, Number 6 (December 1985), pages 1125−1139.

[Bobrow et al. 1972] D. G. Bobrow, J. D. Burchfiel, D. L. Murphy, and R. S. Tomlinson, "TENEX, a Paged Time Sharing System for the PDP-10," *Communications of the ACM,* Volume 15, Number 3 (March 1972).

[Boorstyn and Frank 1977] R. R. Boorstyn and H. Frank, "Large-Scale Network Topological Optimization," *IEEE Transactions on Communications,* Volume COM-25, Number 1 (January 1977), pages 29−47.

[Bourne 1978] S. R. Bourne, "The UNIX Shell," *Bell System Technical Journal,* Volume 57, Number 6 (July-August 1978), pages 1971−1990.

[Bourne 1983] S. R. Bourne, *The UNIX System,* Addison-Wesley, Reading, MA (1983).

[Boykin et al. 1993] J. Boykin, D. Kirschen, A. Langerman, and S. LoVerso, *Programming under Mach,* Addison-Wesley, Reading, MA (1993).

[Boykin and Langerman 1990] J. Boykin and A. B. Langerman, "Mach/4.3BSD: A Conservative Approach to Parallelization," *Computing Systems,* Volume 3, Number 1 (Winter 1990).

[Brent 1989] R. Brent, "Efficient Implementation of the First-Fit Strategy for Dynamic Storage Allocation," *ACM Transactions on Programming Languages and Systems* (July 1989).

[Brereton 1986] O. P. Brereton, "Management of Replicated Files in a UNIX Environment," *Software—Practice and Experience,* Volume 16 (August 1986), pages 771−780.

[Brinch Hansen 1970] P. Brinch Hansen, "The Nucleus of a Multiprogramming System," *Communications of the ACM*, Volume 13, Number 4 (April 1970), pages 238−241 and 250.

[Brinch Hansen 1972] P. Brinch Hansen, "Structured Multiprogramming," *Communications of the ACM*, Volume 15, Number 7 (July 1972), pages 574−578.

[Brinch Hansen 1973] P. Brinch Hansen, *Operating System Principles*, Prentice-Hall, Englewood Cliffs, NJ (1973).

[Brownbridge et al. 1982] D. R. Brownbridge, L. F. Marshall, and B. Randell, "The Newcastle Connection or UNIXes of the World Unite!" *Software—Practice and Experience*, Volume 12, Number 12 (December 1982), pages 1147−1162.

[Brumfield 1986] J. A. Brumfield, "A Guide to Operating Systems Literature," *Operating Systems Review*, Volume 20, Number 2 (April 1986), pages 38−42.

[Brunt and Tuffs 1976] R. F. Brunt and D. E. Tuffs, "A User-Oriented Approach to Control Languages," *Software—Practice and Experience*, Volume 6, Number 1 (January-March 1976), pages 93−108.

[BSTJ 1978] "UNIX Time-Sharing System," *The Bell System Technical Journal*, Volume 57, Number 6, Part 2 (July-August 1978).

[BSTJ 1984] "The UNIX System," *The Bell System Technical Journal*, Volume 63, Number 8, Part 2 (October 1984).

[Burns 1978] J. E. Burns, "Mutual Exclusion with Linear Waiting Using Binary Shared Variables," *SIGACT News*, Volume 10, Number 2 (Summer 1978), pages 42−47.

[Carvalho and Roucairol 1983] O. S. Carvalho and G. Roucairol, "On Mutual Exclusion in Computer Networks," *Communications of the ACM*, Volume 26, Number 2 (February 1983), pages 146−147.

[Carr and Hennessy 1981] W. R. Carr and J. L. Hennessy, "WSClock — A Simple and Effective Algorithm for Virtual Memory Management," *Proceedings of the Eighth Symposium on Operating System Principles* (December 1981), pages 87−95.

[Caswell and Black 1989] D. Caswell and D. Black, "Implementing a Mach Debugger for Multithreaded Applications," Technical Report, Carnegie-Mellon University, PA (November 1989).

[Caswell and Black 1990] D. Caswell and D. Black, "Implementing a Mach Debugger for Multithreaded Applications," *Proceedings of the Winter 1990 USENIX Conference* (January 1990), pages 25−40.

[Cerf and Cain 1983] V. G. Cerf and E. Cain, "The DoD Internet Architecture Model," *Computer Networks*, Volume 7, Number 5 (October 1983), pages 307−318.

[Chang 1980] E. Chang, "N-Philosophers: An Exercise in Distributed Control," *Computer Networks*, Volume 4, Number 2 (April 1980), pages 71–76.

[Chang and Mergen 1988] A. Chang and M. F. Mergen, "801 Storage: Architecture and Programming," *ACM Transactions on Computer Systems*, Volume 6, Number 1 (February 1988), pages 28–50.

[Chen and Patterson 1990] P. Chen and D. Patterson, "Maximizing Performance in a Striped Disk Array," *Proceedings of the Seventeenth Annual International Symposium on Computer Architecture* (May 1990).

[Cheriton and Zwaenepoel 1983] D. R. Cheriton and W. Z. Zwaenepoel, "The Distributed V Kernel and Its Performance for Diskless Workstations," *Proceedings of the Ninth Symposium on Operating Systems Principles* (October 1983), pages 129–140.

[Cheriton et al. 1979] D. R. Cheriton, M. A. Malcolm, L. S. Melen, and G. R. Sager, "Thoth, a Portable Real-Time Operating System," *Communications of the ACM*, Volume 22, Number 2 (February 1979), pages 105–115.

[Chi 1982] C. S. Chi, "Advances in Computer Mass Storage Technology," *Computer*, Volume 15, Number 5 (May 1982), pages 60–74.

[Chow and Abraham 1982] T. C. K. Chow and J. A. Abraham, "Load Balancing in Distributed Systems," *IEEE Transactions on Software Engineering*, Volume SE-8, Number 4 (July 1982), pages 401–412.

[Chu and Opderbeck 1976] W. W. Chu and H. Opderbeck, "Program Behavior and the Page-Fault-Frequency Replacement Algorithm," *Computer*, Volume 9, Number 11 (November 1976), pages 29–38.

[Coffman and Kleinrock 1968] E. G. Coffman and L. Kleinrock, "Feedback Queuing Models for Time-Shared Systems," *Journal of the ACM*, Volume 15, Number 4 (October 1968), pages 549–576.

[Coffman and Denning 1973] E. G. Coffman and P. J. Denning, *Operating Systems Theory*, Prentice-Hall, Englewood Cliffs, NJ (1973).

[Coffman et al. 1971] E. G. Coffman, M. J. Elphick, and A. Shoshani, "System Deadlocks," *Computing Surveys*, Volume 3, Number 2 (June 1971), pages 67–78.

[Cohen and Jefferson 1975] E. S. Cohen and D. Jefferson, "Protection in the Hydra Operating System," *Proceedings of the Fifth Symposium on Operating System Principles* (November 1975), pages 141–160.

[Comer 1984] D. Comer, *Operating System Design: the Xinu Approach*, Prentice-Hall, Englewood Cliffs, NJ (1984).

[Comer 1987] D. Comer, *Operating System Design — Volume II: Internetworking with Xinu*, Prentice-Hall, Englewood Cliffs, NJ (1987).

[Comer 1991] D. Comer, *Internetworking with TCP/IP, Volume I*, Second Edition, Prentice-Hall, Englewood Cliffs, NJ (1991).

[Comer and Stevens 1991] D. Comer and D. L. Stevens, *Internetworking with TCP/IP, Volume II*, Prentice-Hall, Englewood Cliffs, NJ (1991).

[Comer and Stevens 1993] D. Comer and D. L. Stevens, *Internetworking with TCP/IP Principles, Volume III*, Prentice-Hall, Englewood Cliffs, NJ (1993).

[Cooper and Draves 1987] E. C. Cooper and R. P. Draves, "C Threads," Technical Report, Carnegie-Mellon University, PA (July 1987).

[Corbato and Vyssotsky 1965] F. J. Corbato and V. A. Vyssotsky, "Introduction and Overview of the MULTICS System," *Proceedings of the AFIPS Fall Joint Computer Conference* (1965), pages 185–196.

[Corbato et al. 1962] F. J. Corbato, M. Merwin-Daggett, and R. C. Daley, "An Experimental Time-Sharing System," *Proceedings of the AFIPS Fall Joint Computer Conference* (1962), pages 335–344.

[Courtois et al. 1971] P. J. Courtois, F. Heymans, and D. L. Parnas, "Concurrent Control with 'Readers' and 'Writers'," *Communications of the ACM*, Volume 14, Number 10 (October 1971), pages 667–668.

[Creasy 1981] R. J. Creasy, "The Origin of the VM/370 Time-Sharing System," *IBM Journal of Research and Development*, Volume 25, Number 5 (September 1981), pages 483–490.

[CSRG 1986] Computer Systems Research Group — University of California at Berkeley, *BSD UNIX Reference Manuals*, six volumes, USENIX Association (1986).

[Custer 1993] H. Custer, *Inside Windows/NT*, Microsoft Press, Redmond, WA (1993).

[Davcev and Burkhard 1985] D. Davcev and W. A. Burkhard, "Consistency and Recovery Control for Replicated Files," *Proceedings of the Tenth Symposium on Operating Systems Principles*, Volume 19, Number 5 (December 1985), pages 87–96.

[Davies 1983] D. W. Davies, "Applying the RSA Digital Signature to Electronic Mail," *Computer*, Volume 16, Number 2 (February 1983), pages 55–62.

[Day and Zimmerman 1983] J. D. Day and H. Zimmerman, "The OSI Reference Model," *Proceedings of the IEEE*, Volume 71 (December 1983), pages 1334–1340.

[deBruijn 1967] N. G. deBruijn, "Additional Comments on a Problem in Concurrent Programming and Control," *Communications of the ACM*, Volume 10, Number 3 (March 1967), pages 137–138.

[Deitel 1990] H. M. Deitel, *An Introduction to Operating Systems*, Second Edition, Addison-Wesley, Reading, MA (1990).

[Deitel and Kogan 1992] H. M. Deitel and M. S. Kogan, *The Design of OS/2*, Addison-Wesley, Reading, MA (1992).

[Denning 1968] P. J. Denning, "The Working Set Model for Program Behavior," *Communications of the ACM*, Volume 11, Number 5 (May 1968), pages 323−333.

[Denning 1971] P. J. Denning, "Third Generation Computer System," *Computing Surveys*, Volume 3, Number 34 (December 1971), pages 175−216.

[Denning 1980] P. J. Denning, "Working Sets Past and Present," *IEEE Transactions on Software Engineering*, Volume SE-6, Number 1 (January 1980), pages 64−84.

[Denning 1982] D. E. Denning, *Cryptography and Data Security*, Addison-Wesley, Reading, MA (1982).

[Denning 1983] D. E. Denning, "Protecting Public Keys and Signature Keys," *IEEE Computer*, Volume 16, Number 2 (February 1983), pages 27−35.

[Denning 1984] D. E. Denning, "Digital Signatures with RSA and Other Public-Key Cryptosystems," *Communications of the ACM*, Volume 27, Number 4 (April 1984), pages 388−392.

[Dennis 1965] J. B. Dennis, "Segmentation and the Design of Multiprogrammed Computer Systems," *Journal of the ACM*, Volume 12, Number 4 (October 1965), pages 589−602.

[Dennis and Van Horn 1966] J. B. Dennis and E. C. Van Horn, "Programming Semantics for Multiprogrammed Computations," *Communications of the ACM*, Volume 9, Number 3 (March 1966), pages 143−155.

[Diffie and Hellman 1976] W. Diffie and M. E. Hellman, "New Directions in Cryptography," *IEEE Transactions on Information Theory*, Volume 22, Number 6 (November 1976), pages 644−654.

[Diffie and Hellman 1979] W. Diffie and M. E. Hellman, "Privacy and Authentication," *Proceedings of the IEEE*, Volume 67, Number 3 (March 1979), pages 397−427.

[Digital 1981] Digital Equipment Corporation, *VAX Architecture Handbook*, Digital Equipment Corporation, Maynard, MA (1981).

[Dijkstra 1965a] E. W. Dijkstra, "Cooperating Sequential Processes," Technical Report EWD-123, Technological University, Eindhoven, the Netherlands (1965); reprinted in [Genuys 1968], pages 43−112.

[Dijkstra 1965b] E. W. Dijkstra, "Solution of a Problem in Concurrent Programming Control," *Communications of the ACM*, Volume 8, Number 9 (September 1965), Page 569.

[Dijkstra 1968] E. W. Dijkstra, "The Structure of the THE Multiprogramming System," *Communications of the ACM,* Volume 11, Number 5 (May 1968), pages 341−346.

[Dijkstra 1971] E. W. Dijkstra, "Hierarchical Ordering of Sequential Processes," *Acta Informatica,* Volume 1, Number 2 (1971), pages 115−138; reprinted in [Hoare and Perrott 1972], pages 72−93.

[Doeppner 1987] T. W. Doeppner, "Threads: A System for the Support of Concurrent Programming," Technical Report CS-87-11, Department of Computer Science, Brown University (June 1987).

[Donnelley 1979] J. E. Donnelley, "Components of a Network-Operating System," *Computer Networks,* Volume 3, Number 6 (December 1979), pages 389−399.

[Douglis and Ousterhout 1987] F. Douglis and J. Ousterhout, "Process Migration in the Sprite Operating System," *Proceedings of the Seventh IEEE International Conference on Distributed Computing Systems* (1987), pages 18−25.

[Douglis and Ousterhout 1989] F. Douglis and J. Ousterhout, "Process Migration in Sprite: A Status Report," *Newsletter of the IEEE Computer Society Technical Committee on Operating Systems* (Winter 1989).

[Douglis et al. 1991] F. Douglis, M. F. Kaashoek, and A. S. Tanenbaum, "A Comparison of Two Distributed Systems: Amoeba and Sprite," *Computing Systems,* Volume 4 (Fall 1991).

[Draves et al. 1989] R. P. Draves, M. B. Jones, and M. R. Thompson, "MIG — The MACH Interface Generator," Technical Report, Carnegie-Mellon University, PA (November 1989).

[Draves et al. 1991] R. P. Draves, B. N. Bershad, R. F. Rashid, and R. W. Dean, "Using Continuations to Implement Thread Management and Communication in Operating Systems," *Proceedings of the Thirteenth ACM Symposium on Operating Systems Principles* (October 1991), pages 122−136.

[Duncan 1990] R. Duncan, "A Survey of Parallel Computer Architectures," *IEEE Computer,* Volume 23, Number 2 (February 1990), pages 5−16.

[Eager et al. 1986] D. Eager, E. Lazowska, and J. Zahorjan, "Adaptive Load Sharing in Homogeneous Distributed Systems," *IEEE Transactions on Software Engineering,* Volume SE-12, Number 5 (May 1986), pages 662−675.

[Eisenberg and McGuire 1972] M. A. Eisenberg and M. R. McGuire, "Further Comments on Dijkstra's Concurrent Programming Control Problem," *Communications of the ACM,* Volume 15, Number 11 (November 1972), page 999.

[Ekanadham and Bernstein 1979] K. Ekanadham and A. J. Bernstein, "Conditional Capabilities," *IEEE Transactions on Software Engineering,* Volume SE-5, Number 5 (September 1979), pages 458−464.

[English and Stepanov 1992] R. M. English and A. A. Stepanov, "Loge: A Self-Organizing Disk Controller," *Proceedings of the Winter 1992 USENIX Conference*, San Francisco, CA (January 1992), pages 238−252.

[Eskicioglu 1990] M. Eskicioglu, "Design Issues of Process Migration Facilities in Distributed Systems," *Newsletter of the IEEE Computer Society Technical Committee on Operating Systems* (Summer 1990).

[Eswaran et al. 1976] K. P. Eswaran, J. N. Gray, R. A. Lorie, and I. L. Traiger, "The Notions of Consistency and Predicate Locks in a Database System," *Communications of the ACM*, Volume 19, Number 11 (November 1976), pages 624−633.

[Eykholt et al. 1992] J. R. Eykholt, S. R. Kleiman, S. Barton, S. Faulkner, A. Shivalingiah, M. Smith, D. Stein, J. Voll, M. Weeks, and D. Williams, "Beyond Multiprocessing: Multithreading the SunOS Kernel," *Proceedings of the Summer 1992 USENIX Conference* (June 1992), pages 11−18.

[Farrow 1986a] R. Farrow, "Security Issues and Strategies for Users," *UNIX World* (April 1986), pages 65−71.

[Farrow 1986b] R. Farrow, "Security for Superusers, or How to Break the UNIX System," *UNIX World* (May 1986), pages 65−70.

[Feitelson and Rudolph 1990] D. Feitelson and L. Rudolph, "Mapping and Scheduling in a Shared Parallel Environment Using Distributed Hierarchical Control," *Proceedings of the 1990 International Conference on Parallel Processing* (August 1990).

[Ferguson et al. 1988] D. Ferguson, Y. Yemini, and C. Nikolaou, "Microeconomic Algorithms for Load Balancing in Distributed Computer Systems," *Proceedings of the Eighth IEEE International Conference on Distributed Computing Systems* (1988), pages 491−499.

[Feng 1981] T. Feng, "A Survey of Interconnection Networks," *Computer*, Volume 14, Number 12 (1981), pages 12−27.

[Filipski and Hanko 1986] A. Filipski and J. Hanko, "Making UNIX Secure," *Byte* (April 1986), pages 113−128.

[Finkel 1988] R. A. Finkel, *Operating Systems Vade Mecum*, Second Edition, Prentice-Hall, Englewood Cliffs, NJ (1988).

[Folk and Zoellick 1987] M. J. Folk and B. Zoellick, *File Structures*, Addison-Wesley, Reading, MA (1987).

[Forsdick et al. 1978] H. C. Forsdick, R. E. Schantz, and R. H. Thomas, "Operating Systems for Computer Networks," *Computer*, Volume 11, Number 1 (January 1978), pages 48−57.

[Fortier 1989] P. J. Fortier, *Handbook of LAN Technology*, McGraw Hill, New York, NY (1989).

[Frank 1976] G. R. Frank, "Job Control in the MU5 Operating System," *Computer Journal*, Volume 19, Number 2 (May 1976), pages 139–143.

[Freedman 1983] D. H. Freedman, "Searching for Denser Disks," *Infosystems* (September 1983), page 56.

[Fujitani 1984] L. Fujitani, "Laser Optical Disk: The Coming Revolution in On-Line Storage," *Communications of the ACM*, Volume 27, Number 6 (June 1984), pages 546–554.

[Gait 1988] J. Gait, "The Optical File Cabinet: A Random-Access File System for Write-On Optical Disks," *Computer*, Volume 21, Number 6 (June 1988).

[Garcia-Molina 1982] H. Garcia-Molina, "Elections in Distributed Computing Systems," *IEEE Transactions on Computers*, Volume C-31, Number 1 (January 1982).

[Garfinkel and Spafford 1991] S. Garfinkel and G. Spafford, *Practical UNIX Security*, O'Reilly & Associates, Inc., Sebastopol, CA (1991).

[Geist and Daniel 1987] R. Geist and S. Daniel, "A Continuum of Disk Scheduling Algorithms," *ACM Transactions on Computer Systems*, Volume 5, Number 1 (February 1987), pages 77–92.

[Genuys 1968] F. Genuys (Editor), *Programming Languages*, Academic Press, London, England (1968).

[Gerla and Kleinrock 1977] M. Gerla and L. Kleinrock, "Topological Design of Distributed Computer Networks," *IEEE Transactions on Communications*, Volume COM-25, Number 1 (January 1977), pages 48–60.

[Gifford 1982] D. K. Gifford, "Cryptographic Sealing for Information Secrecy and Authentication," *Communications of the ACM*, Volume 25, Number 4 (April 1982), pages 274–286.

[Golden and Pechura 1986] D. Golden and M. Pechura, "The Structure of Microcomputer File Systems," *Communications of the ACM*, Volume 29, Number 3 (March 1986), pages 222–230.

[Goldman 1989] P. Goldman, " Mac VM Revealed," *Byte* (September 1989).

[Grampp and Morris 1984] F. T. Grampp and R. H. Morris, "UNIX Operating-System Security," *AT&T Bell Laboratories Technical Journal*, Volume 63 (October 1984), pages 1649–1672.

[Gray 1978] J. N. Gray, "Notes on Data Base Operating Systems," in [Bayer et al. 1978], pages 393–481.

[Gray 1981] J. N. Gray, "The Transaction Concept: Virtues and Limitations," *Proceedings of the International Conference on Very Large Data Bases* (1981), pages 144–154.

[Gray et al. 1981] J. N. Gray, P. R. McJones, and M. Blasgen, "The Recovery Manager of the System R Database Manager," *ACM Computing Surveys*, Volume 13, Number 2 (June 1981), pages 223–242.

[Grosshans 1986] D. Grosshans, *File Systems Design and Implementation*, Prentice-Hall, Englewood Cliffs, NJ (1986).

[Gupta and Franklin 1978] R. K. Gupta and M. A. Franklin, "Working Set and Page Fault Frequency Replacement Algorithms: A Performance Comparison," *IEEE Transactions on Computers*, Volume C-27, Number 8 (August 1978), pages 706–712.

[Habermann 1969] A. N. Habermann, "Prevention of System Deadlocks," *Communications of the ACM*, Volume 12, Number 7 (July 1969), pages 373–377 and 385.

[Hagmann 1989] R. Hagmann, "Comments on Workstation Operating Systems and Virtual Memory," *Proceedings of the Second Workshop on Workstation Operating Systems* (September 1989).

[Haldar and Subramanian 1991] S. Haldar and D. Subramanian, "Fairness in Processor Scheduling in Time Sharing Systems," *Operating Systems Review* (January 1991).

[Hall et al. 1980] D. E. Hall, D. K. Scherrer, and J. S. Sventek, "A Virtual Operating System," *Communications of the ACM*, Volume 23, Number 9 (September 1980), pages 495–502.

[Halsall 1992] F. Halsall, *Data Communications, Computer Networks, and Open Systems*, Addison-Wesley, Reading, MA (1992).

[Harker et al. 1981] J. M. Harker, D. W. Brede, R. E. Pattison, G. R. Santana, and L. G. Taft, "A Quarter Century of Disk File Innovation," *IBM Journal of Research and Development*, Volume 25, Number 5 (September 1981), pages 677–689.

[Harrison et al. 1976] M. A. Harrison, W. L. Ruzzo, and J. D. Ullman, "Protection in Operating Systems," *Communications of the ACM*, Volume 19, Number 8 (August 1976), pages 461–471.

[Havender 1968] J. W. Havender, "Avoiding Deadlock in Multitasking Systems," *IBM Systems Journal*, Volume 7, Number 2 (1968), pages 74–84.

[Hecht et al. 1988] M. S. Hecht, A. Johri, R. Aditham, and T. J. Wei, "Experience Adding C2 Security Features to UNIX," *Proceedings of the Summer 1988 USENIX Conference* (June 1988), pages 133–146.

[Hendricks and Hartmann 1979] E. C. Hendricks and T. C. Hartmann, "Evolution of a Virtual Machine Subsystem," *IBM Systems Journal*, Volume 18, Number 1 (1979), pages 111–142.

[Hennessy and Patterson 1990] J. L. Hennessy and D. A. Patterson, *Computer Architecture: a Quantitative Approach*, Morgan Kaufmann Publishers, Palo Alto, CA (1990).

[Henry 1984] G. Henry, "The Fair Share Scheduler," *AT&T Bell Laboratories Technical Journal* (October 1984).

[Hoagland 1985] A. S. Hoagland, "Information Storage Technology — A Look at the Future," *Computer*, Volume 18, Number 7 (July 1985), pages 60−68.

[Hoare 1972] C. A. R. Hoare, "Towards a Theory of Parallel Programming," in [Hoare and Perrott 1972], pages 61−71.

[Hoare 1974] C. A. R. Hoare, "Monitors: An Operating System Structuring Concept," *Communications of the ACM*, Volume 17, Number 10 (October 1974), pages 549−557; Erratum in *Communications of the ACM*, Volume 18, Number 2 (February 1975), page 95.

[Hoare and Perrott 1972] C. A. R. Hoare and R. H. Perrott, Eds., *Operating Systems Techniques*, Academic Press, London (1972).

[Hofri 1980] M. Hofri, "Disk Scheduling: FCFS Versus SSTF Revisited," *Communications of the ACM*, Volume 23, Number 11 (November 1980), pages 645−653.

[Holley et al. 1979] L. H. Holley, R. P. Parmelee, C. A. Salisbury, and D. N. Saul, "VM/370 Asymmetric Multiprocessing," *IBM Systems Journal*, Volume 18, Number 1 (1979), pages 47−70.

[Holt 1971] R. C. Holt, "Comments on Prevention of System Deadlocks," *Communications of the ACM*, Volume 14, Number 1 (January 1971), pages 36−38.

[Holt 1972] R. C. Holt, "Some Deadlock Properties of Computer Systems," *Computing Surveys*, Volume 4, Number 3 (September 1972), pages 179−196.

[Holt 1983] R. C. Holt, *Concurrent Euclid, the Unix System, and Tunis*, Addison-Wesley, Reading, MA (1983).

[Hong et al. 1989] J. Hong, X. Tan, and D. Towsley, "A Performance Analysis of Minimum Laxity and Earliest Deadline Scheduling in a Real-Time System," *IEEE Transactions on Computers*, Volume 38, Number 12 (December 1989) pages 1736−1744.

[Howard 1973] J. H. Howard, "Mixed Solutions for the Deadlock Problem," *Communications of the ACM*, Volume 16, Number 7 (July 1973), pages 427−430.

[Howard et al. 1988] J. H. Howard, M. L. Kazar, S. G. Menees, D. A. Nichols, M. Satyanarayanan, and R. N. Sidebotham, "Scale and Performance in a Distributed File System," *ACM Transactions on Computer Systems*, Volume 6, Number 1 (February 1988), pages 55−81.

[Howarth et al. 1961] D. J. Howarth, R. B. Payne, and F. H. Sumner, "The Manchester University Atlas Operating System, Part II: User's Description," *Computer Journal*, Volume 4, Number 3 (October 1961), pages 226–229.

[Hsiao et al. 1979] D. K. Hsiao, D. S. Kerr, and S. E. Madnick, *Computer Security*, Academic Press, New York, NY (1979).

[Hyman 1985] D. Hyman, *The Columbus Chicken Statute, and More Bonehead Legislation*, S. Greene Press, Lexington, MA (1985).

[Iacobucci 1988] E. Iacobucci, *OS/2 Programmer's Guide*, Osborne McGraw-Hill, Berkeley, CA (1988).

[Iliffe and Jodeit 1962] J. K. Iliffe and J. G. Jodeit, "A Dynamic Storage Allocation System," *Computer Journal*, Volume 5, Number 3 (October 1962), pages 200–209.

[Intel 1985a] Intel Corporation, *iAPX 86/88, 186/188 User's Manual Programmer's Reference*, Intel Corp., Santa Clara, CA (1985).

[Intel 1985b] Intel Corporation, *iAPX 286 Programmer's Reference Manual*, Intel Corp., Santa Clara, CA (1985).

[Intel 1986] Intel Corporation, *iAPX 386 Programmer's Reference Manual*, Intel Corp., Santa Clara, CA (1986).

[Intel 1989] Intel Corporation, *i486 Microprocessor*, Intel Corp., Santa Clara, CA (1989).

[Intel 1990] Intel Corporation, *i486 Microprocessor Programmer's Reference Manual*, Intel Corp., Santa Clara, CA (1990).

[Isloor and Marsland 1980] S. S. Isloor and T. A. Marsland, "The Deadlock Problem: An Overview," *Computer*, Volume 13, Number 9 (September 1980), pages 58–78.

[ISO 1981] "ISO Open Systems Interconnection—Basic Reference Model," ISO/TC 97/SC 16 N 719, *International Organization for Standardization* (August 1981).

[Jensen et al. 1985] E. D. Jensen, C. D. Locke, and H. Tokuda, "A Time-Driven Scheduling Model for Real-Time Operating Systems," *Proceedings of the IEEE Real-Time Systems Symposium* (December 1985), pages 112–122.

[Jones 1978] A. K. Jones, "Protection Mechanisms and the Enforcement of Security Policies," in [Bayer et al. 1978], pages 228–250.

[Jones 1991] M. Jones, "Bringing the C Libraries With Us Into A Multi-Threaded Future," *Proceedings of the Winter 1991 USENIX Conference* (January 1991), pages 81–92.

[Jones and Liskov 1978] A. K. Jones and B. H. Liskov, "A Language Extension for Expressing Constraints on Data Access," *Communications of the ACM*, Volume 21, Number 5 (May 1978), pages 358–367.

[Jones and Schwarz 1980] A. K. Jones and P. Schwarz, "Experience Using Multiprocessor Systems — A Status Report," *Computing Surveys*, Volume 12, Number 2 (June 1980), pages 121–165.

[Jul et al. 1988] E. Jul, H. Levy, N. Hutchinson, and A. Black, "Fine-Grained Mobility in the Emerald System," *ACM Transactions on Computer Systems*, Volume 6, Number 1 (February 1988), pages 109–133.

[Katz et al. 1989] R.H. Katz, G.A. Gibson, and D.A. Patterson, "Disk System Architectures for High Performance Computing," *Proceedings of the IEEE*, Volume 77, Number 12 (December 1989).

[Kay and Lauder 1988] J. Kay and P. Lauder, "A Fair Share Scheduler," *Communications of the ACM*, Volume 31, Number 1 (January 1988), pages 44–55.

[Kenah el al. 1988] L. J. Kenah, R. E. Goldenberg, and S. F. Bate, *VAX/VMS Internals and Data Structures*, Digital Press, Bedford, MA (1988).

[Kenville 1982] R. F. Kenville, "Optical Disk Data Storage," *Computer*, Volume 15, Number 7 (July 1982), pages 21–26.

[Kernighan and Pike 1984] B. W. Kernighan and R. Pike, *The UNIX Programming Environment*, Prentice-Hall, Englewood Cliffs, NJ (1984).

[Kernighan and Ritchie 1988] B. W. Kernighan and D. M. Ritchie, *The C Programming Language*, Second Edition, Prentice-Hall, Englewood Cliffs, NJ (1988).

[Kessels 1977] J. L. W. Kessels, "An Alternative to Event Queues for Synchronization in Monitors," *Communications of the ACM*, Volume 20, Number 7 (July 1977), pages 500–503.

[Khanna et al. 1992] S. Khanna, M. Sebree, and J. Zolnowsky, "Realtime Scheduling in SunOS 5.0," *Proceedings of the Winter 1992 USENIX Conference*, San Francisco, CA (January 1992), pages 375–390.

[Kieburtz and Silberschatz 1978] R. B. Kieburtz and A. Silberschatz, "Capability Managers," *IEEE Transactions on Software Engineering*, Volume SE-4, Number 6 (November 1978), pages 467–477.

[Kieburtz and Silberschatz 1983] R. B. Kieburtz and A. Silberschatz, "Access Right Expressions," *ACM Transactions on Programming Languages and Systems*, Volume 5, Number 1 (January 1983), pages 78–96.

[Kilburn et al. 1961] T. Kilburn, D. J. Howarth, R. B. Payne, and F. H. Sumner, "The Manchester University Atlas Operating System, Part I: Internal Organization," *Computer Journal*, Volume 4, Number 3 (October 1961), pages 222–225.

[Kleinrock 1975] L. Kleinrock, *Queueing Systems, Volume II: Computer Applications*, Wiley-Interscience, New York, NY (1975).

[Knapp 1987] E. Knapp, "Deadlock Detection in Distributed Databases," *Computing Surveys*, Volume 19, Number 4 (December 1987), pages 303–328.

[Knuth 1966] D. E. Knuth, "Additional Comments on a Problem in Concurrent Programming Control," *Communications of the ACM*, Volume 9, Number 5 (May 1966), pages 321–322.

[Knuth 1973] D. E. Knuth, *The Art of Computer Programming, Volume 1: Fundamental Algorithms*, Second Edition, Addison-Wesley, Reading, MA (1973).

[Koch 1987] P. D. L. Koch, "Disk File Allocation Based on the Buddy System," *ACM Transactions on Computer Systems*, Volume 5, Number 4 (November 1987), pages 352–370.

[Kogan and Rawson 1988] M. S. Kogan and F. L. Rawson, "The Design of Operating System/2," *IBM Systems Journal*, Volume 27, Number 2 (1988), pages 90–104.

[Korn 1983] D. Korn, "KSH, A Shell Programming Language," *Proceedings of the Summer 1983 USENIX Conference* (July 1983), pages 191–202.

[Korth and Silberschatz 1991] H. F. Korth and A. Silberschatz, *Database System Concepts*, Second Edition, McGraw Hill, New York, NY (1991).

[Kosaraju 1973] S. Kosaraju, "Limitations of Dijkstra's Semaphore Primitives and Petri Nets," *Operating Systems Review*, Volume 7, Number 4 (October 1973), pages 122–126.

[Krakowiak 1988] S. Krakowiak, *Principles of Operating Systems*, MIT Press, Cambridge, MA (1988).

[Kramer 1988] S. M. Kramer, "Retaining SUID Programs in a Secure UNIX," *Proceedings of the 1988 Summer USENIX Conference* (June 1988), pages 107–118.

[Lamport 1974] L. Lamport, "A New Solution of Dijkstra's Concurrent Programming Problem," *Communications of the ACM*, Volume 17, Number 8 (August 1974), pages 453–455.

[Lamport 1976] L. Lamport, "Synchronization of Independent Processes," *Acta Informatica*, Volume 7, Number 1 (1976), pages 15–34.

[Lamport 1977] L. Lamport, "Concurrent Reading and Writing," *Communications of the ACM*, Volume 20, Number 11 (November 1977), pages 806–811.

[Lamport 1978a] L. Lamport, "Time, Clocks, and the Ordering of Events in a Distributed System," *Communications of the ACM*, Volume 21, Number 7 (July 1978), pages 558–565.

[Lamport 1978b] L. Lamport, "The Implementation of Reliable Distributed Multiprocess Systems," *Computer Networks*, Volume 2, Number 2 (April 1978), pages 95–114.

[Lamport 1981] L. Lamport, "Password Authentication with Insecure Communications," *Communications of the ACM*, Volume 24, Number 11 (November 1981), pages 770–772.

[Lamport 1986] L. Lamport, "The Mutual Exclusion Problem," *Journal of the ACM*, Volume 33, Number 2 (1986), pages 313–348.

[Lamport 1991] L. Lamport, "The Mutual Exclusion Problem Has Been Solved," *Communications of the ACM*, Volume 34, Number 1 (January 1991), page 110.

[Lamport et al. 1982] L. Lamport, R. Shostak, and M. Pease, "The Byzantine Generals Problem," *ACM Transactions on Programming Languages and Systems*, Volume 4, Number 3 (July 1982), pages 382–401.

[Lampson 1968] B. W. Lampson, "A Scheduling Philosophy for Multiprocessing Systems," *Communications of the ACM*, Volume 11, Number 5 (May 1968), pages 347–360.

[Lampson 1969] B. W. Lampson, "Dynamic Protection Structures," *Proceedings of the AFIPS Fall Joint Computer Conference* (1969), pages 27–38.

[Lampson 1971] B. W. Lampson, "Protection," *Proceedings of the Fifth Annual Princeton Conference on Information Science Systems* (1971), pages 437–443; reprinted in *Operating System Review*, Volume 8, Number 1 (January 1974), pages 18–24.

[Lampson 1973] B. W. Lampson, "A Note on the Confinement Problem," *Communications of the ACM*, Volume 10, Number 16 (October 1973), pages 613–615.

[Lampson and Sturgis 1976] B. Lampson and H. Sturgis, "Crash Recovery in a Distributed Data Storage System," Technical Report, Computer Science Laboratory, Xerox, Palo Alto Research Center, Palo Alto, CA (1976).

[Landwehr 1981] C. E. Landwehr, "Formal Models of Computer Security," *Computing Surveys*, Volume 13, Number 3 (September 1981), pages 247–278.

[Larson and Kajla 1984] P. Larson and A. Kajla, "File Organization: Implementation of a Method Guaranteeing Retrieval in One Access," *Communications of the ACM*, Volume 27, Number 7 (July 1984), pages 670–677.

[Lazowska et al. 1984] E. D. Lazowska, J. Zahorjan, G. S. Graham, and K. C. Sevcik, *Quantitative System Performance*, Prentice-Hall, Englewood Cliffs, NJ (1984).

[Leach et al. 1982] P. J. Leach, B. L. Stump, J. A. Hamilton, and P. H. Levine, "UID's as Internal Names in a Distributed File System," *Proceedings of the First Symposium on Principles of Distributed Computing* (August 1982), pages 34–41.

[Leffler et al. 1978] S. J. Leffler, R. S. Fabry, and W. N. Joy, "A 4.2BSD Inter-process Communication Primer," *Unix Programmer's Manual*, Volume 2C, University of California at Berkeley, CA (1978).

[Leffler et al. 1983] S. J. Leffler, W. N. Joy, and R. S. Fabry, "4.2BSD Net-working Implementation Notes," *Unix Programmer's Manual*, Volume 2C, University of California at Berkeley, CA (1983).

[Leffler et al. 1989] S. J. Leffler, M. K. McKusick, M. J. Karels, and J. S. Quarterman, *The Design and Implementation of the 4.3BSD UNIX Operating System*, Addison-Wesley, Reading, MA (1989).

[Lehmann 1987] F. Lehmann, "Computer Break-Ins," *Communications of the ACM*, Volume 30, Number 7 (July 1987), pages 584–585.

[Le Lann 1977] G. Le Lann, "Distributed Systems — Toward a Formal Approach," *Proceedings of the IFIP Congress 77* (1977), pages 155–160.

[Lempel 1979] A. Lempel, "Cryptology in Transition," *Computing Surveys*, Volume 11, Number 4 (December 1979), pages 286–303.

[Lett and Konigsford 1968] A. L. Lett and W. L. Konigsford, "TSS/360: A Time-Shared Operating System," *Proceedings of the AFIPS Fall Joint Computer Conference* (1968), pages 15–28.

[Leutenegger and Vernon 1990] S. Leutenegger and M. Vernon, "The Performance of Multiprogrammed Multiprocessor Scheduling Policies," *Proceedings of the Conference on Measurement and Modeling of Computer Systems* (May 1990).

[Letwin 1988] G. Letwin, *Inside OS/2*, Microsoft Press, Redmond, WA (1988).

[Levin et al. 1975] R. Levin, E. S. Cohen, W. M. Corwin, F. J. Pollack, and W. A. Wulf, "Policy/Mechanism Separation in Hydra," *Proceedings of the Fifth ACM Symposium on Operating System Principles* (1975), pages 132–140.

[Levy and Lipman 1982] H. M. Levy and P. H. Lipman, "Virtual Memory Management in the VAX/VMS Operating System," *Computer*, Volume 15, Number 3 (March 1982), pages 35–41.

[Levy and Silberschatz 1990] E. Levy and A. Silberschatz, "Distributed File Systems: Concepts and Examples," *Computing Surveys*, Volume 22, Number 4 (December 1990), pages 321–374.

[Lichtenberger and Pirtle 1965] W. W. Lichtenberger and M. W. Pirtle, "A Facility for Experimentation in Man-Machine Interaction," *Proceedings of the AFIPS Fall Joint Computer Conference* (1965), pages 589–598.

[Lions 1977] J. Lions, "A Commentary on the UNIX Operating System," Technical Report, Carnegie-Mellon University (April 1988).

[Lipner 1975] S. Lipner, "A Comment on the Confinement Problem," *Operating System Review*, Volume 9, Number 5 (November 1975), pages 192–196.

[Lipton 1974] R. Lipton, "On Synchronization Primitive Systems," PhD. Thesis, Carnegie-Mellon University (1974).

[Liskov 1972] B. H. Liskov, "The Design of the Venus Operating System," *Communications of the ACM,* Volume 15, Number 3 (March 1972), pages 144–149.

[Litzkow et al. 1988] M. J. Litzkow, M. Livny, and M. W. Mutka, "Condor—A Hunter of Idle Workstations," *Proceedings of the Eighth IEEE International Conference on Distributed Computing Systems* (1988), pages 104–111.

[Liu and Layland 1973] C. L. Liu and J. W. Layland, "Scheduling Algorithms for Multiprogramming in a Hard Real-Time Environment," *Journal of the ACM,* Volume 20, Number 1 (January 1973), pages 46–61.

[Lobel 1986] J. Lobel, *Foiling the System Breakers: Computer Security and Access Control,* McGraw-Hill, New York, NY (1986).

[Loepere 1992] K. Loepere, "Mach 3 Kernel Principles," Technical Report, Open Software Foundation, MA (January 1992).

[Loucks and Sauer 1987] L. K. Loucks and C. H. Sauer, "Advanced Interactive Executive (AIX) Operating System Overview," *IBM Systems Journal,* Volume 26, Number 4 (1987), pages 326–345.

[Lynch 1972] W. C. Lynch, "An Operating System Design for the Computer Utility Environment," in [Hoare and Perrott 1972], pages 341–350.

[MacKinnon 1979] R. A. MacKinnon, "The Changing Virtual Machine Environment: Interfaces to Real Hardware, Virtual Hardware, and Other Virtual Machines," *IBM Systems Journal,* Volume 18, Number 1 (1979), pages 18–46.

[Maekawa 1985] M. Maekawa, "A Square Root Algorithm for Mutual Exclusion in Decentralized Systems," *ACM Transactions on Computer Systems,* Volume 3, Number 2 (May 1985), pages 145–159.

[Maekawa et al. 1987] M. Maekawa, A. E. Oldehoeft, and R. R. Oldehoeft, *Operating Systems: Advanced Concepts,* Benjamin/Cummings, Menlo Park, CA (1987).

[Maples 1985] C. Maples, "Analyzing Software Performance in a Multiprocessor Environment," *IEEE Software,* Volume 2, Number 4 (July 1985).

[Marsh et al. 1991] B. D. Marsh, M. L. Scott, T. J. LeBlanc, and E. P. Markatos, "First-Class User-Level Threads," *Proceedings of the Thirteenth ACM Symposium on Operating Systems Principals* (October 1991), pages 110–121.

[Massalin and Pu 1989] H. Massalin and C. Pu, "Threads and Input/Output in the Synthesis Kernel," *Proceedings of the 12th Symposium on Operating Systems Principles* (December 1989), pages 191–200.

[Mattson et al. 1970] R. L. Mattson, J. Gecsei, D. R. Slutz, and I. L. Traiger, "Evaluation Techniques for Storage Hierarchies," *IBM Systems Journal,* Volume 9, Number 2 (1970), pages 78–117.

[McGraw and Andrews 1979] J. R. McGraw and G. R. Andrews, "Access Control in Parallel Programs," *IEEE Transactions on Software Engineering,* Volume SE-5, Number 1 (January 1979), pages 1–9.

[McKeag and Wilson 1976] R. M. McKeag and R. Wilson, *Studies in Operating Systems,* Academic Press, London (1976).

[McKeon 1985] B. McKeon, "An Algorithm for Disk Caching with Limited Memory," *Byte,* Volume 10, Number 9 (September 1985), pages 129–138.

[McKusick and Karels 1988] M. K. McKusick and K. J. Karels, "Design of a General Purpose Memory Allocator for the 4.3BSD UNIX Kernel," *Proceedings of the Summer 1988 USENIX Conference* (June 1988), pages 295–304.

[McKusick et al. 1984] M. K. McKusick, W. N. Joy, S. J. Leffler, and R. S. Fabry. "A Fast File System for UNIX," *ACM Transactions on Computer Systems,* Volume 2, Number 3 (August 1984), pages 181–197.

[McNamee and Armstrong 1990] D. McNamee and K. Armstrong, "Extending the Mach External Pager Interface to Accommodate User-Level Page-Replacement Policies," *Proceedings of the USENIX MACH Workshop,* Burlington, VT (October 1990).

[McVoy and Kleiman 1991] L. W. McVoy and S. R. Kleiman, "Extent-like Performance from a UNIX File System," *Proceedings of the Winter 1991 USENIX Conference* (January 1991), pages 33–44.

[Mealy et al. 1966] G. H. Mealy, B. I. Witt, and W. A. Clark, "The Functional Structure of OS/360," *IBM Systems Journal,* Volume 5, Number 1 (1966).

[Menasce and Muntz 1979] D. Menasce and R. R. Muntz, "Locking and Deadlock Detection in Distributed Data Bases," *IEEE Transactions on Software Engineering,* Volume SE-5, Number 3 (May 1979), pages 195–202.

[Metzner 1982] J. R. Metzner, "Structuring Operating Systems Literature for the Graduate Course," *Operating Systems Review,* Volume 16, Number 4 (October 1982), pages 10–25.

[Meyer and Seawright 1970] R. A. Meyer and L. H. Seawright, "A Virtual Machine Time-Sharing System," *IBM Systems Journal,* Volume 9, Number 3 (1970), pages 199–218.

[Microsoft 1986] Microsoft Corporation, *Microsoft MS-DOS User's Reference* and *Microsoft MS-DOS Programmer's Reference,* Microsoft Press, Redmond, WA (1986).

[Microsoft 1989] Microsoft Corporation, *Microsoft Operating System/2 Programmer's Reference,* 3 Volumes, Microsoft Press, Redmond, WA (1989).

[Microsoft 1991] Microsoft Corporation, *Microsoft MS-DOS User's Guide and Reference*, Microsoft Press, Redmond, WA (1991).

[Milenkovic 1987] M. Milenkovic, *Operating Systems: Concepts and Design*, McGraw-Hill, New York, NY (1987).

[Mohan and Lindsay 1983] C. Mohan and B. Lindsay, "Efficient Commit Protocols for the Tree of Processes Model of Distributed Transactions," *Proceedings of the Second ACM SIGACT-SIGOPS Symposium on the Principles of Distributed Computing* (1983).

[Morris 1973] J. H. Morris, "Protection in Programming Languages," *Communications of the ACM*, Volume 16, Number 1 (January 1973), pages 15−21.

[Morris et al. 1986] J. H. Morris, M. Satyanarayanan, M. H. Conner, J. H. Howard, D. S. H. Rosenthal, and F. D. Smith, "Andrew: A Distributed Personal Computing Environment," *Communications of the ACM*, Volume 29, Number 3 (March 1986), pages 184−201.

[Morris and Thompson 1979] R. Morris and K. Thompson, "Password Security: A Case History," *Communications of the ACM*, Volume 22, Number 11 (November 1979), pages 594−597.

[Morshedian 1986] D. Morshedian, "How to Fight Password Pirates," *Computer*, Volume 19, Number 1 (January 1986).

[Motorola 1989a] Motorola Inc., *MC68000 Family Reference*, Second Edition, Prentice-Hall, Englewood Cliffs, NJ (1989).

[Motorola 1989b] Motorola Inc., *MC68030 Enhanced 32-Bit Microprocessor User's Manual*, Second Edition, Prentice-Hall, Englewood Cliffs, NJ (1989).

[Mullender and Tanenbaum 1985] S. J. Mullender and A. S. Tanenbaum, "A Distributed File Service Based on Optimistic Concurrency Control," *Proceedings of the Tenth Symposium on Operating Systems Principles* (December 1985), pages 51−62.

[Mullender et al. 1990] S. J. Mullender, G. Van Rossum, A. S. Tanenbaum, R. Van Renesse, and H. Van Staveren, "Amoeba: A Distributed-Operating System for the 1990s," *IEEE Computer*, Volume 23, Number 5 (May 1990), pages 44−53.

[Mutka and Livny 1987] M. W. Mutka and M. Livny, "Scheduling Remote Processor Capacity in a Workstation-Processor Bank Network," *Proceedings of the Seventh IEEE International Conference on Distributed Computing Systems* (1987).

[Needham and Walker 1977] R. M. Needham and R. D. H. Walker, "The Cambridge CAP Computer and its Protection System," *Proceedings of the Sixth Symposium on Operating System Principles* (November 1977), pages 1−10.

[Nelson and Cheng 1992] B. Nelson and Y. Cheng, "How and Why SCSI is better than IPI for NFS," *Proceedings of the Winter 1992 USENIX Conference,* San Francisco, CA, (January 1992), pages 253–270.

[Nelson et al. 1988] M. Nelson, B. Welch, and J. K. Ousterhout, "Caching in the Sprite Network File System," *ACM Transactions on Computer Systems,* Volume 6, Number 1 (February 1988), pages 134–154.

[Newton 1979] G. Newton, "Deadlock Prevention, Detection, and Resolution: An Annotated Bibliography," *Operating Systems Review,* Volume 13, Number 2 (April 1979), pages 33–44.

[Nichols 1987] D. A. Nichols, "Using Idle Workstations in a Shared Computing Environment," *Proceedings of the Eleventh ACM Symposium on Operating Systems Principals* (October 1987), pages 5–12.

[Norton 1986] P. Norton, *Inside the IBM PC,* Revised and Enlarged, Brady Books, New York, NY (1986).

[Norton and Wilton 1988] P. Norton and R. Wilton, *The New Peter Norton Programmer's Guide to the IBM PC & PS/2,* Microsoft Press, Redmond, WA (1988).

[O'Leary and Kitts 1985] B. T. O'Leary and D. L. Kitts, "Optical Device for a Mass Storage System," *Computer,* Volume 18, Number 7 (July 1985).

[Obermarck 1982] R. Obermarck, "Distributed Deadlock Detection Algorithm," *ACM Transactions on Database Systems,* Volume 7, Number 2 (June 1982), pages 187–208.

[Oldehoeft and Allan 1985] R. R. Oldehoeft and S. J. Allan, "Adaptive Exact-Fit Storage Management," *Communications of the ACM,* Volume 28, Number 5 (May 1985), pages 506–511.

[Olsen and Kenley 1989] R. P. Olsen and G. Kenley, "Virtual Optical Disks Solve the On-Line Storage Crunch," *Computer Design,* Volume 28, Number 1 (January 1989), pages 93–96.

[Organick 1972] E. I. Organick, *The Multics System: An Examination of its Structure,* MIT Press, Cambridge, MA (1972).

[OSF 1989] Open Software Foundation, *Mach Technology: A series of Ten Lectures,* OSF Foundation, Cambridge MA (Fall 1989).

[Ousterhout et al. 1988] J. K. Ousterhout, A. R. Cherenson, F. Douglis, M. N. Nelson, and B. B. Welch, "The Sprite Network-Operating System," *IEEE Computer,* Volume 21, Number 2 (February 1988), pages 23–36.

[Parmelee et al. 1972] R. P. Parmelee, T. I. Peterson, C. C. Tillman, and D. Hatfield, "Virtual Storage and Virtual Machine Concepts," *IBM Systems Journal,* Volume 11, Number 2 (1972), pages 99–130.

[Parnas 1975] D. L. Parnas, "On a Solution to the Cigarette Smokers' Problem Without Conditional Statements," *Communications of the ACM,* Volume 18, Number 3 (March 1975), pages 181–183.

[Parnas and Habermann 1972] D. L. Parnas and A. N. Habermann, "Comment on Deadlock Prevention Method," *Communications of the ACM,* Volume 15, Number 9 (September 1972), pages 840–841.

[Patil 1971] S. Patil, "Limitations and Capabilities of Dijkstra's Semaphore Primitives for Coordination Among Processes," Technical Report, MIT (1971).

[Patterson et al. 1988] D. A. Patterson, G. Gibson, and R. H. Katz, "A Case for Redundant Arrays of Inexpensive Disks (RAID)," *Proceedings of the ACM SIGMOD International Conference on the Management of Data* (1988).

[Peacock 1992] J. K. Peacock, "File System Multithreading in System V Release 4 MP," *Proceedings of the Summer 1992 USENIX Conference* (June 1992), pages 19–29.

[Pease et al. 1980] M. Pease, R. Shostak, and L. Lamport, "Reaching Agreement in the Presence of Faults," *Journal of the ACM,* Volume 27, Number 2 (April 1980), pages 228–234.

[Pechura and Schoeffler 1983] M. A. Pechura and J. D. Schoeffler, "Estimating File Access Time of Floppy Disks," *Communications of the ACM,* Volume 26, Number 10 (October 1983), pages 754–763.

[Peterson 1981] G. L. Peterson, "Myths About the Mutual Exclusion Problem," *Information Processing Letters,* Volume 12, Number 3 (June 1981).

[Pfleeger 1989] C. Pfleeger, *Security in Computing,* Prentice-Hall, Englewood Cliffs, NJ (1989).

[Pinkert and Wear 1989] J. Pinkert and L. Wear, *Operating Systems: Concepts, Policies, and Mechanisms,* Prentice-Hall, Englewood Cliffs, NJ (1989).

[Popek 1974] G. J. Popek, "Protection Structures," *Computer,* Volume 7, Number 6 (June 1974), pages 22–33.

[Popek and Walker 1985] G. Popek and B. Walker, Eds., *The LOCUS Distributed System Architecture,* MIT Press, Cambridge, MA (1985).

[Powell et al. 1991] M. L. Powell, S. R. Kleiman, S. Barton, D. Shaw, D. Stein, and M. Weeks, "SunOS Multi-threaded Architecture," *Proceedings of the Winter 1991 USENIX Conference* (January 1991), pages 65–80.

[Prieve and Fabry 1976] B. G. Prieve and R. S. Fabry, "VMIN — An Optimal Variable Space Page-Replacement Algorithm," *Communications of the ACM,* Volume 19, Number 5 (May 1976), pages 295–297.

[Purdin et al. 1987] T. D. M. Purdin, R. D. Schlichting, and G. R. Andrews, "A File Replication Facility for Berkeley UNIX," *Software—Practice and Experience,* Volume 17 (December 1987), pages 923–940.

[Quarterman 1990] J. S. Quarterman, *The Matrix Computer Networks and Conferencing Systems Worldwide,* Digital Press, Bedford, MA (1990).

[Quarterman et al. 1985] J. S. Quarterman, A. Silberschatz, and J. L. Peterson, "4.2BSD and 4.3BSD as Examples of the UNIX Systems," *Computing Surveys,* Volume 17, Number 4 (December 1985), pages 379–418.

[Quarterman and Hoskins 1986] J. S. Quarterman and H. C. Hoskins, "Notable Computer Networks," *Communications of the ACM,* Volume 29, Number 10 (October 1986), pages 932–971.

[Rashid 1986] R. F. Rashid, "From RIG to Accent to Mach: The Evolution of a Network-Operating System," *Proceedings of the ACM/IEEE Computer Society, Fall Joint Computer Conference* (1986).

[Rashid and Robertson 1981] R. Rashid and G. Robertson, "Accent: A Communication Oriented Network-Operating System Kernel," *Proceedings of the Eighth Symposium on Operating System Principles* (December 1981).

[Raynal 1986] M. Raynal, *Algorithms for Mutual Exclusion,* MIT Press, Cambridge, MA (1986).

[Raynal 1991] M. Raynal, "A Simple Taxonomy for Distributed Mutual Exclusion Algorithms," *Operating Systems Review,* Volume 25 (April 1991), pages 47–50.

[Redell and Fabry 1974] D. D. Redell and R. S. Fabry, "Selective Revocation of Capabilities," *Proceedings of the IRIA International Workshop on Protection in Operating Systems* (1974), pages 197–210.

[Reed 1983] D. P. Reed, "Implementing Atomic Actions on Decentralized Data," *ACM Transactions on Computer Systems,* Volume 1 (February 1983), pages 3–23.

[Reed and Kanodia 1979] D. P. Reed and R. K. Kanodia, "Synchronization with Eventcounts and Sequences," *Communications of the ACM,* Volume 22, Number 2 (February 1979), pages 115–123.

[Reid 1987] B. Reid, "Reflections on Some Recent Widespread Computer Break-Ins," *Communications of the ACM,* Volume 30, Number 2 (February 1987), pages 103–105.

[Ricart and Agrawala 1981] G. Ricart and A. K. Agrawala, "An Optimal Algorithm for Mutual Exclusion in Computer Networks," *Communications of the ACM,* Volume 24, Number 1 (January 1981), pages 9–17.

[Ritchie 1979] D. Ritchie, "The Evolution of the UNIX Time-Sharing System," *Language Design and Programming Methodology, Lecture Notes on Computer Science,* Volume 79, Springer-Verlag, Berlin (1979).

[Ritchie and Thompson 1974] D. M. Ritchie and K. Thompson, "The UNIX Time-Sharing System," *Communications of the ACM*, Volume 17, Number 7 (July 1974), pages 365−375; a later version appeared in *Bell System Technical Journal*, Volume 57, Number 6 (July-August 1978), pages 1905−1929.

[Rivest et al. 1978] R. L. Rivest, A. Shamir, and L. Adleman, "On Digital Signatures and Public Key Cryptosystems," *Communications of the ACM*, Volume 21, Number 2 (February 1978), pages 120−126.

[Rosen 1969] S. Rosen, "Electronic Computers: A Historical Survey," *Computing Surveys*, Volume 1, Number 1 (March 1969), pages 7−36.

[Rosenblum and Ousterhout 1991] M. Rosenblum and J. K. Ousterhout, "The Design and Implementation of a Log-Structured File System," *Proceedings of the 13th ACM Symposium on Operating Systems Principles* (October 1991), pages 1−15.

[Rosenkrantz et al. 1978] D. J. Rosenkrantz, R. E. Stearns, and P. M. Lewis, II, "System Level Concurrency Control for Distributed Database Systems," *ACM Transactions on Database Systems*, Volume 3, Number 2 (June 1978), pages 178−198.

[Ruschitzka and Fabry 1977] M. Ruschizka and R. S. Fabry, "A Unifying Approach to Scheduling," *Communications of the ACM*, Volume 20, Number 7 (July 1977), pages 469−477.

[Rushby 1981] J. M. Rushby, "Design and Verification of Secure Systems," *Proceedings of the Eighth Symposium on Operating System Principles* (December 1981), pages 12−21.

[Rushby and Randell 1983] J. Rushby and B. Randell, "A Distributed Secure System," *Computer*, Volume 16, Number 7 (July 1983), pages 55−67.

[Russell and Gangemi 1991] D. Russell and G. T. Gangemi, Sr., *Computer Security Basics*, O'Reilly & Associates, Inc., Sebastopol, CA (1991).

[Saltzer and Schroeder 1975] J. H. Saltzer and M. D. Schroeder, "The Protection of Information in Computer Systems," *Proceedings of the IEEE*, Volume 63, Number 9 (September 1975), pages 1278−1308.

[Samson 1990] S. Samson, *MVS Performance Management*, McGraw-Hill, New York, NY (1990).

[Sandberg 1987] R. Sandberg, *The Sun Network File System: Design, Implementation, and Experience*, Sun Microsystems, Inc., Mountain View, CA (1987).

[Sandberg et al. 1985] R. Sandberg, D. Goldberg, S. Kleiman, D. Walsh, and B. Lyon, "Design and Implementation of the Sun Network Filesystem," *Proceedings of the 1985 USENIX Summer Conference* (June 1985), pages 119−130.

[Sanguinetti 1986] J. Sanguinetti, "Performance of a Message-Based Multiprocessor," *Computer*, Volume 19, Number 9 (September 1986), pages 47–56.

[Sarisky 1983] L. Sarisky, "Will Removable Hard Disks Replace the Floppy?" *Byte* (March 1983), pages 110–117.

[Satyanarayanan 1980] M. Satyanarayanan, *Multiprocessors: A Comparative Study*, Prentice-Hall, Englewood Cliffs, NJ (1980).

[Satyanarayanan 1989] M. Satyanarayanan, "Integrating Security in a Large Distributed System," *ACM Transactions on Computer Systems*, Volume 7 (August 1989), pages 247–280.

[Satyanarayanan 1990] M. Satyanarayanan, "Scalable, Secure, and Highly Available Distributed File Access," *Computer*, Volume 23, Number 5 (May 1990), pages 9–21.

[Sauer and Chandy 1981] C. H. Sauer and K. M. Chandy, *Computer Systems Performance Modeling*, Prentice-Hall, Englewood Cliffs, NJ (1981).

[Schell 1983] R. R. Schell, "A Security Kernel for a Multiprocessor Microcomputer," *Computer*, Volume 16, Number 7 (July 1983), pages 47–53.

[Schlichting and Schneider 1982] R. D. Schlichting and F. B. Schneider, "Understanding and Using Asynchronous Message Passing Primitives," *Proceedings of the Symposium on Principles of Distributed Computing* (August 1982), pages 141–147.

[Schneider 1982] F. B. Schneider, "Synchronization in Distributed Programs," *ACM Transactions on Programming Languages and Systems*, Volume 4, Number 2 (April 1982), pages 125–148.

[Schrage 1967] L. E. Schrage, "The Queue M/G/I with Feedback to Lower Priority Queues," *Management Science*, Volume 13 (1967), pages 466–474.

[Schroeder et al. 1985] M. D. Schroeder, D. K. Gifford, and R. M. Needham, "A Caching File System for a Programmer's Workstation," *Proceedings of the Tenth Symposium on Operating Systems Principles* (December 1985), pages 25–32.

[Schultz 1988] B. Schultz, "VM: The Crossroads of Operating Systems," *Datamation*, Volume 34, Number 14 (July 1988), pages 79–84.

[Schwartz and Weissman 1967] J. I. Schwartz and C. Weissman, "The SDC Time-Sharing System Revisited," *Proceedings of the ACM National Meeting* (August 1967), pages 263–271.

[Schwartz et al. 1964] J. I. Schwartz, E. G. Coffman, and C. Weissman, "A General Purpose Time-Sharing System," *Proceedings of the AFIPS Spring Joint Computer Conference* (1964), pages 397–411.

[Seawright and MacKinnon 1979] L. H. Seawright and R. A. MacKinnon, "VM/370 — A Study of Multiplicity and Usefulness," *IBM Systems Journal*, Volume 18, Number 1 (1979), pages 4–17.

[Seely 1989] D. Seely, "Password Cracking: A Game of Wits," *Communications of the ACM,* Volume 32, Number 6 (June 1989), pages 700–704.

[Shore 1975] J. E. Shore, "On the External Storage Fragmentation Produced by First-Fit and Best-Fit Allocation Strategies," *Communications of the ACM,* Volume 18, Number 8 (August 1975), pages 433–440.

[Shrivastava and Panzieri 1982] S. K. Shrivastava and F. Panzieri, "The Design of a Reliable Remote Procedure Call Mechanism," *IEEE Transactions on Computers,* Volume C-31, Number 7 (July 1982), pages 692–697.

[Silverman 1983] J. M. Silverman, "Reflections on the Verification of the Security of an Operating System Kernel," *Proceedings of the Ninth Symposium on Operating Systems Principles,* Volume 17, Number 5 (October 1983), pages 143–154.

[Simmons 1979] G. J. Simmons, "Symmetric and Asymmetric Encryption," *Computing Surveys,* Volume 11, Number 4 (December 1979), pages 304–330.

[Singhal 1989] M. Singhal, "Deadlock Detection in Distributed Systems," *IEEE Computer,* Volume 22, Number 11 (November 1989), pages 37–48.

[Smith 1982] A. J. Smith, "Cache Memories," *ACM Computing Surveys,* Volume 14, Number 3 (September 1982), pages 473–530.

[Smith 1985] A. J. Smith, "Disk Cache-Miss Ratio Analysis and Design Considerations," *ACM Transactions on Computer Systems,* Volume 3, Number 3 (August 1985), pages 161–203.

[Smith 1988] A. J. Smith, "A Survey of Process Migration Mechanisms," *Operating Systems Review* (July 1988).

[Spafford 1989] E. H. Spafford, "The Internet Worm: Crisis and Aftermath," *Communications of the ACM,* Volume 32, Number 6 (June 1989), pages 678–687.

[Spector and Schwarz 1983] A. Z. Spector and P. M. Schwarz, "Transactions: A Construct for Reliable Distributed Computing," *ACM SIGOPS Operating Systems Review,* Volume 17, Number 2 (1983), pages 18–35.

[Stallings 1984] W. Stallings, "Local Networks," *Computing Surveys,* Volume 16, Number 1 (March 1984), pages 1–41.

[Stallings 1992] W. Stallings, *Operating Systems,* Macmillan, New York (1992).

[Stankovic 1982] J. S. Stankovic, "Software Communication Mechanisms: Procedure Calls Versus Messages," *Computer,* Volume 15, Number 4 (April 1982).

[Stankovic and Ramamrithan 1989] J. S. Stankovic and K. Ramamrithan, "The Spring Kernel: A New Paradigm for Real-Time Operating Systems," *Operating Systems Review* (July 1989).

[Staunstrup 1982] J. Staunstrup, "Message Passing Communication versus Procedure Call Communication," *Software—Practice and Experience,* Volume 12, Number 3 (March 1982), pages 223–234.

[Stein and Shaw 1992] D. Stein and D. Shaw, "Implementing Lightweight Threads," *Proceedings of the Summer 1992 USENIX Conference* (June 1992), pages 1–9.

[Stephenson 1983] C. J. Stephenson, "Fast Fits: A New Method for Dynamic Storage Allocation," *Proceedings of the Ninth Symposium on Operating Systems Principles* (December 1983), pages 30–32.

[Stevens 1990] W. R. Stevens, *UNIX Network Programming,* Prentice-Hall, Englewood Cliffs, NJ (1990).

[Stevens 1992] W. R. Stevens, *Advanced Programming in the UNIX Environment,* Addison-Wesley, Reading, MA (1992).

[Strachey 1959] C. Strachey, "Time Sharing in Large Fast Computers," *Proceedings of the International Conference on Information Processing* (June 1959), pages 336–341.

[Sun Microsystems 1990] Sun Microsystems, *Network Programming Guide,* Sun Microsystems, Inc., Mountain View, CA (1990), pages 168–186.

[Svobodova 1976] L. Svobodova, *Computer Performance Measurement and Evaluation,* Elsevier North-Holland, New York, NY (1976).

[Svobodova 1984] L. Svobodova, "File Servers for Network-Based Distributed Systems," *ACM Computing Surveys,* Volume 16, Number 4 (December 1984), pages 353–398.

[Tabak 1990] D. Tabak, *Multiprocessors,* Prentice-Hall, Englewood Cliffs, NJ (1990).

[Tanenbaum 1987] A. S. Tanenbaum, *Operating System Design and Implementation,* Prentice-Hall, Englewood Cliffs, NJ (1987).

[Tanenbaum 1988] A. S. Tanenbaum, *Computer Networks,* Second Edition, Prentice-Hall, Englewood Cliffs, NJ (1988).

[Tanenbaum 1990] A. S. Tanenbaum, *Structured Computer Organization,* Third Edition, Prentice-Hall, Englewood Cliffs, NJ (1990).

[Tanenbaum 1992] A. S. Tanenbaum, *Modern Operating Systems,* Prentice-Hall, Englewood Cliffs, NJ (1992).

[Tanenbaum and Van Renesse 1985] A. S. Tanenbaum and R. Van Renesse, "Distributed-Operating Systems," *ACM Computing Surveys,* Volume 17, Number 4 (December 1985), pages 419–470.

[Tanenbaum et al. 1990] A. S. Tanenbaum, R. Van Renesse, H. Van Staveren, G. J. Sharp, S. J. Mullender, J. Jansen, G. Van Rossum, "Experiences with the Amoeba Distributed-Operating System," *Communications of the ACM,* Volume 33, Number 12 (December 1990), pages 46–63.

[Tay and Ananda 1990] B. H. Tay and A. L. Ananda, "A Survey of Remote Procedure Calls," *Operating Systems Review*, Volume 24, Number 3 (July 1990), pages 68−79.

[Teorey and Pinkerton 1972] T. J. Teorey and T. B. Pinkerton, "A Comparative Analysis of Disk Scheduling Policies," *Communications of the ACM*, Volume 15, Number 3 (March 1972), pages 177−184.

[Tevanian et al. 1987a] A. Tevanian, Jr., R. F. Rashid, D. B. Golub, D. L. Black, E. Cooper, and M. W. Young, "Mach Threads and the Unix Kernel: The Battle for Control," *Proceedings of the Summer 1987 USENIX Conference* (July 1987).

[Tevanian et al. 1987b] A. Tevanian, Jr., R. F. Rashid, M. W. Young, D. B. Golub, M. R. Thompson, W. Bolosky, and R. Sanzi, "A UNIX Interface for Shared Memory and Memory Mapped Files Under Mach," Technical Report, Carnegie-Mellon University, Pittsburgh, PA (July 1987).

[Tevanian and Smith 1989] A. Tevanian and B. Smith, "Mach: The Model for Future Unix," *Byte* (November 1989).

[Thompson 1978] K. Thompson, "UNIX Implementation," *The Bell System Technical Journal*, Volume 57, Number 6, Part 2 (July-August 1978), pages 1931−1946.

[Thurber and Freeman 1980] K. J. Thurber and H. A. Freeman, "Updated Bibliography on Local Computer Networks," *Computer Architecture News*, Volume 8 (April 1980), pages 20−28.

[Traiger et al. 1982] I. L. Traiger, J. N. Gray, C. A. Galtieri, and B. G. Lindsay, "Transactions and Consistency in Distributed Database Management Systems," *ACM Transactions on Database Systems*, Volume 7, Number 3 (September 1982), pages 323−342.

[Tucker and Gupta 1989] A. Tucker and A. Gupta, "Process Control and Scheduling Issues for Multiprogrammed Shared-Memory Multiprocessors," *Proceedings of the Twelfth ACM Symposium on Operating System Principles* (December 1989).

[USENIX 1990] USENIX Association, *Proceedings of the Mach Workshop*, Burlington, VT (October 1990).

[USENIX 1991] USENIX Association, *Proceedings of the USENIX Mach Symposium*, Monterey, CA (November 1991).

[USENIX 1992a] USENIX Association, *Proceedings of the File Systems Workshop*, Ann Arbor, MI (May 1992).

[USENIX 1992b] USENIX Association, *Proceedings of the USENIX Workshop on Micro-kernels and Other Kernel Architectures*, Seattle, WA (April 1992).

[Vuillemin 1978] A. Vuillemin, "A Data Structure for Manipulating Priority Queues," *Communications of the ACM,* Volume 21, Number 4 (April 1978), pages 309–315.

[Wah 1984] B. W. Wah, "File Placement on Distributed Computer Systems," *Computer,* Volume 17, Number 1 (January 1984), pages 23–32.

[Walmer and Thompson 1989] L. R. Walmer and M. R. Thompson, "A Programmer's Guide to the Mach System Calls," Technical Report, Carnegie-Mellon University, Pittsburgh, PA (December 1989).

[Weizer 1981] N. Weizer, "A History of Operating Systems," *Datamation* (January 1981), pages 119–126.

[Wilhelm 1976] N. C. Wilhelm, "An Anomaly in Disk Scheduling: A Comparison of FCFS and SSTF Seek Scheduling Using an Empirical Model for Disk Accesses," *Communications of the ACM,* Volume 19, Number 1 (January 1976), pages 13–17.

[Wood and Kochan 1985] P. Wood and S. Kochan, *UNIX System Security,* Hayden, Hasbrouck Heights, NJ (1985).

[Woodside 1986] C. Woodside, "Controllability of Computer Performance Trade-offs Obtained Using Controlled-Share Queue Schedulers," *IEEE Transactions on Software Engineering,* Volume SE-12, Number 10 (October 1986), pages 1041–1048.

[Wulf 1969] W. A. Wulf, "Performance Monitors for Multiprogramming Systems," *Proceedings of the Second ACM Symposium on Operating System Principles* (October 1969), pages 175–181.

[Wulf et al. 1981] W. A. Wulf, R. Levin, and S. P. Harbison, *Hydra/C. mmp: An Experimental Computer System,* McGraw-Hill, New York, NY (1981).

[Zahorjan and McCann 1990] J. Zahorjan and C. McCann, "Processor Scheduling in Shared Memory Multiprocessors," *Proceedings of the Conference on Measurement and Modeling of Computer Systems* (May 1990).

[Zayas 1987] E. R. Zayas, "Attacking the Process Migration Bottleneck," *Proceedings of the Eleventh ACM Symposium on Operating Systems Principles* (October 1987), pages 13–24.

[Zhao 1989] W. Zhao, Ed., Special Issue on Real-Time Operating Systems, *Operating System Review* (July 1989).

[Zobel 1983] D. Zobel, "The Deadlock Problem: A Classifying Bibliography," *Operating Systems Review,* Volume 17, Number 4 (October 1983), pages 6–16.

CREDITS

Fig. 3.11 from Iaccobucci, *OS/2 Programmer's Guide*, © 1988, McGraw-Hill, Inc., New York, New York. Fig. 1.7, p. 20. Reprinted with permission of the publisher.

Fig. 5.8 from Khanna/Sebree/Zolnowsky, "Realtime Scheduling in SunOS 5.0," Proceedings of Winter USENIX, January 1992, San Francisco, California. Derived with permission of the authors.

Fig. 8.28 from "_80386 Programmer's Reference Manual," Fig. 5-12, p.5-12. Reprinted by permission of Intel Corporation, Copyright/Intel Corporation 1986.

Fig. 9.15 reprinted with permission from *IBM Systems Journal*, Vol. 10, No. 3, © 1971, International Business Machines Corporation.

Fig. 11.7 from Leffler/McKusick/Karels/Quarterman, *The Design and Implementation of the 4.3BSD UNIX Operating System*, © 1989 by Addison-Wesley Publishing Co., Inc., Reading, Massachusetts. Fig. 7.6, p. 196. Reprinted with permission of the publisher.

Figs. 15.10, 15.11, and 15.13 from Halsall, *Data Communications, Computer Networks, and Open Systems, Third Edition*, © 1992, Addison-Wesley Publishing Co., Inc., Reading, Massachusetts. Fig.1.9, p. 14, fig. 1.10, p. 15, and fig. 1.11, p. 18. Reprinted with permission of the publisher.

Fig. 18.2 from Silberschatz/Korth, *Database System Concepts, Second Edition*, © 1991, McGraw-Hill, Inc., New York, New York. Fig. 15.8, p. 506. Reprinted with permission of the publisher.

Fig. 19.1 from Quarterman/Wilhelm, *UNIX, POSIX and Open Systems: The Open Standards Puzzle,* © 1993, by Addison-Wesley Publishing Co., Inc., Reading, Massachusetts. Fig. 2.1, p. 31. Reprinted with permission of the publisher.

Figs. 20.1, 20.6, and 20.8 reproduced with permission from Open Software Foundation, Inc. Excerpted from Mach Lecture Series, OSF, October 1989, Cambridge, Massachusetts.

Figs. 20.1 and 20.8 presented by R. Rashid of Carnegie Mellon University and Fig. 20.7 presented by D. Julin of Carnegie Mellon University.

Fig. 20.6 from Accetta/Baron/Bolosky/Golub/Rashid/ Tevanian/Young, "Mach: a new kernel foundation for UNIX development," Proceedings of Summer USENIX, June 1986, Atlanta, Georgia. Reprinted with permission of the authors.

Sections of chapter 6 and 18 from Silberschatz/Korth, *Database System Concepts, Second Edition,* © 1991, McGraw-Hill, Inc., New York, New York. Section 10.1.1, p. 314, 10.3.1, p. 323-324, 10.3.2, p. 329, 10.6, p. 333-334, 11.1.2, p. 352-353, 11.3.1, p. 365, 11.3.2, p. 369, 11.4.2, p. 375-376, 15.7, p. 498-500, 15.8, p. 502-506. Reprinted with permission of the publisher.

Appendix on Nachos is derived from Christopher/Procter/Anderson, "The Nachos Instructional Operating System," Proceedings of Winter USENIX, January 1993. Reprinted with permission of the authors.

Timeline information for the back end papers was assembled from a variety of sources which include "The History of Electronic Computing," compiled and edited by Marc Rettig, Association for Computing Machinery, Inc. (ACM), New York, New York, and Shedroff/Hutto/Fromm, *Understanding Computers,* © 1992, Vivid Publishing, distributed by SYBEX, San Francisco, California.

Timeline information for the front end paper was assembled by the designer of the cover, Howard S. Friedman.

INDEX

2PC, 578-579
  defined, 578
  failure handling, 579-581
  phase 1, 578
  phase 2, 578-579

Abbot, C., 162
Abort operation, 199, 200
Abraham, J.A., 523
Accent operating system, 129, 688
Access-control problem, 197
Access lists, 374-376
  comparison of, 445
  defined, 374
  length of, 375
  for objects, 443
  revocation, 446
  in VMS, 375-376
  see also Access rights
Access matrix, 438-442, 455, 457
  access list, 443
  capability lists, 443-444
  control rights, 442
  with copy rights, 440
  defined, 438
  with domains as objects, 439

global table, 443
  illustrated, 438
  implementation, 443-446
  lock-key mechanism, 445
  modified, 442
  with owner rights, 441
  policies, 439
  processes/domains, 439
  see also Access rights
Access rights, 433
  amplification, 448
  auxiliary, 448
  copying, 440
  default set of, 443
  revocation of, 446-448
  see also Access lists; Access matrix
Accetta, M., 93, 129, 688
Accounting, 64-65,100
Acyclic-graph directories, 369-371, 379-380
  advantage, 372
  complexity, 370-371
  deletion, 371
  disadvantage, 372
  illustrated, 370
  see also Directory structure; Links

Adaptive mutexes, 198
Address
  binding, 250-251
  linear, 293
  logical, 255-256
  physical, 255-256
  relocatable, 250
  translation
      Intel 80386, 295
      in MULTICS, 292
      for two-level paging, 279
  virtual, 255
Addressing modes, 308-309
  autodecrement, 308-309
  autoincrement, 308-309
Address Resolution Protocol (ARP),
  502
Aging, 143
Agrawala, A.K., 602
Agrawal, D.P., 55, 603
Ahituv, N., 475
AIX operating system, 78
Akl, S.G., 475
Algorithms
  bakery, 171-172
  banker's, 230-234, 242
  bully, 595-597
Allan, S.J., 299
Allocation, disk space
  contiguous, 387-390
  indexed, 392-395
  linked, 390-392
  performance, 395-397
  see also Disk space
Allocation, frame
  algorithms, 327-328, 342, 343
  equal, 328
  global vs. local, 329
  proportional, 328
  see also Frames
Allocation, memory
  contiguous, 259-267
  multiple-partition, 261-264
  single-partition, 260-261
  in some multiple of bytes, 265

Ammon, G.J., 427
Amoeba operating system, 523
Analytic evaluation, 153-154
Ananda, A.L., 129
Anderson, T., 713
Anderson, T.E., 129, 162
Andrew File System (AFS), 528,
  550-555, 569
  caching, 552-554
  callback mechanism, 553-554
  client machines, 550
  client mobility in, 551
  consistency semantics, 552-554
  fid, 552
  file operation, 552-554
  heterogeneity, 551
  implementation, 554-555
  overview, 550-551
  protection, 551
  security, 551
  server machines, 550
  session semantics, 553
  shared name space, 552
  volumes, 552
Andrews, G.R., 457
Anyanwu, J.A., 657
Apollo Domain system, 569
Append operation, 374
Apple Macintosh operating system.
  see Macintosh Operating System
Architecture
  general system, 51-52
  I/O, 32-37
  storage, 37-42
Argument stack, 515
Armstrong, K., 689
Arpanet, 489
ARPANET Reference Model (ARM),
  452, 657
  host-host layer, 653
  network hardware layer, 653
  network interface layer, 653
  process/application layer, 653
  protocol layers, 653
Artsy, Y., 523

Assignment edge, 221
Associative registers, 273
  hit ratio, 274, 275
  with page tables, 273-275
Asymmetric multiprocessing, 21-22, 150
Asynchronous I/O, 33
  advantages, 35
  I/O priority, 36
Atlas operating system, 691-692
  extra codes, 691
  memory management, 692
  spooling, 692
Atomicity, 577-581, 600
Atomic transactions, 199-208
  checkpoints, 202-203
  concurrent, 203-208
  log-based recovery, 201-202
  system model, 199-201
  see also Transactions
Audit log, 469-470
Authentication, 461-463
  see also Passwords
Automatic job sequencing, 8

Babaoglu, O., 657
Bach, M.J., 162, 657
Backing store, 256
  defined, 258
  demand paging, 311-312
Backup, 409, 425
Baer, J.L., 55
Bakery algorithm, 170-172
Balkovich, E., 523
Banker's algorithm, 230-234, 242
  data structures required for, 231
  defined, 230
  illustrative example, 233-234
  safety algorithm, 232
Barak, A., 523
Batch systems, 7-13
Bays, C., 299
BCPL language, 65
Belady, L.A., 348
Belady's anomaly, 318

Berc, L., 714
Berkeley Software Distributions, 609
Bernstein, A., 92, 457, 603
Bernstein, P.A., 215
Bershad, B.N., 129, 474
Bhuyan, L.N., 55
Biased protocol, 584
Birman, K., 506, 523
Birrell, A.D., 129
Bit vector, 397-398
Black, D.L., 129, 162, 688-689
Blair, B.S., 657
Bliss language, 65
Block synchronization operation, 177
Blocks, 383, 410
  boot, 418
  clusters of, 391
  disk, 410, 425
  bad, 418-419
  flush, 534
  free contiguous, 399
  free disk
    grouping, 398
    linking, 398
  index, 393
  reading, 425
  replacement, 402-403
Block transfer, 424-425
Bobrow, D.G., 698
Boorstyn, R.R., 506
Boot disk, 418
Booting, 90
Bootstrap program, 30, 90, 417
  on disk, 418
  in ROM, 418
Bounded-buffer problem, 109, 181, 214
Bourne shell, 624
Bourne, S.R., 92, 657
Boykin, J., 689
Brent, R., 299
Brereton, O.P., 569
Brinch Hansen, P., 92, 129, 195, 214, 694
Broadcast, 558

Brownbridge, D.R., 569
Brunt, R.F., 92
BSD UNIX file system, 386, 408
  combined scheme indexing, 394
  drawbacks, 662
  see also UNIX operating system
Buffering, 121-123
Bully algorithm, 595-597
Burkhard, W.A., 569
Burns, J.E., 214
Busy waiting, 176
Byzantine generals problem, 598

Cache, 44
  block buffer, 646-647
  coherency, 45
  location, 532-533
  management, 44
  update policy, 533-534
    delayed-write, 533
    write-on-close, 534
    write-through, 533
    see also Caching
Cache-consistency problem, 532,
  536, 568
Caching, 43-44, 531
Cain, E., 657
Callback, 535, 553-554
Cambridge CAP system, 450-451
  data capability, 450
  software capability, 450
Cambridge Digital Communications
  Ring, 497
Capability, 444, 457
  lists, 443-444
  possession, 444
  revocation, 446-447
  software, 450, 453-454
Capability-based systems, 448-451
  Cambridge CAP, 450-451
  Hydra, 448-450
Card readers, 11
Carr, W.R., 348
Carrier sense with multiple access
  (CSMA), 496-497

Carvalho, O.S., 603
Cascading termination, 108
Caswell, D., 129, 688
Central processing unit. see CPU
Cerf, V.G., 657
Chandy, K.M., 161
Chang, A., 299
Chang, E., 603
Checkpoints, 202
Chen, P., 427
Cheng, Y., 427
Cheriton, D.R., 523
Chi, C.S., 55, 408
Chow, T.C.K., 523
Christopher, W., 713
Chu, W.W., 348
Cigarette-smokers problem, 212, 214
Circuit switching, 495
Circular wait, 219
Claim edge, 229-230
Client, 513
  diskless, 529
  interface, 526
  with local disks, 529
  see also Servers
C-lists, 648
C-LOOK scheduling, 416
Close file operation, 353, 378
Clustering, 521
Clusters, 391
CMS operating system, 84
Code
  absolute, 250
  reentrant, 281-282
  relocatable, 250
  sharing, 281-283
    in paging environment, 283
    in segmentation environment,
      287-289
    transient operating system, 261
Codewords, 457
Coffman, E.G., 161, 246
Cohen, E.S., 457
Collision detection, 496-497
Comer, D., 505, 657, 658

Command-interpreter, 62, 75
system, 62-63
in UNIX, 62, 71, 75-76
Commit operation, 199, 200
Commit protocol, 578-579
Communication
direct, 118-119
indirect, 120-121
message-based, 512
as operating system service, 64
system calls, 73
system programs, 75
unreliable, 598-599
Communication network, 62, 491-497, 504
connection strategies, 491, 495-496
contention, 491, 496-497
design considerations, 491
name resolution, 491-493
routing strategies, 491, 493-495
Compaction, 265-267
algorithm, 266
swapping combined with, 267
Compatible Time-Sharing System (CTSS), 27-28
Computer operator, 7
Computer system
components, 3
distributed, 22-23, 26
operation, 29-32
parallel, 20-22, 26
resource sharing, 45
structures, 29-53
Concurrency control, 203, 209, 215, 581-586, 601
locking protocols, 205-206, 582-584
timestamping, 206-208, 585-586
serializability, 203-205
Concurrent transactions, 203-208
Conditional critical regions
see Critical regions
Conditional-wait construct, 196
Confinement problem, 442
Conflicting operations, 204

Connection strategies, 495-496
circuit switching, 495
message switching, 495
packet switching, 496
Consistency semantics, 378-379
Andrew file system, 378-379
immutable-shared-files, 379
UNIX, 378
Context switch, 50, 105
Contiguous allocation, disk, 387-390, 405
indexed allocation with, 396
new files, 388
on floppy disks, 389
problems, 389
Contiguous allocation, memory, 259-267
external fragmentation, 264-267
internal fragmentation, 264-267
multiple-partition, 261-264
single-partition, 260-261
Control-card interpreter, 9, 63
Control cards, 9-10
Controlled access, 374
Control operation, 440
Control program, 5
Control statements, 63
Cooper, E.C., 688
Copy operation, 440
Corbato, F.J., 28, 161, 696
Counting algorithms, 324-325
Courtois, P.J., 214
CP/67 operating system, 92
CP/M operating system, 698
C programming language, 608, 614
CPU, 3, 29
burst, 132-133
protection, 49-50
registers, 99
utilization, 135
CPU scheduling, 15, 131-159
basic concepts of, 131-135
criteria, 135-137
CPU utilization, 135
response time, 136

throughput, 136
turnaround time, 136
waiting time, 136
dispatcher, 135
multilevel feedback queue, 147-149, 158
multilevel queue, 145-147, 158
multiple-processor, 149-150
nonpreemptive, 134, 138, 140-141, 142
MVS policies, 162
OS/2 policies, 162
preemptive, 134-135, 140-141, 142, 144
priority, 141-143
real-time, 150-152
round-robin, 143-145, 158
shortest-job-first, 138-141, 158
shortest-remaining-time-first, 141
UNIX, 162, 630-632
Creasy, R.J., 92
Critical regions, 186-190, 209, 214
Critical-section problem, 165-172
multiple-process solutions, 170-172
solution requirements, 166
two-process solutions, 167-170
CRT, 15
C-SCAN disk scheduling, 414-415
CSMA/CD, 496-497
C threads package, 667-670
general synchronization routines, 668
mutual exclusion routines, 668
thread-control routines, 667-668
CTSS (Compatible Time-Sharing System), 695-696
Cylinders, 409-410

Daemons, 73
FTP, 509
RPC, 513
telnet, 509
Daniel, S., 428
DARPA Internet protocols, 652
Data Encryption Standard, 471

Datagram, 500
Data transfer, 52
Davcev, D., 569
Davies, D.W., 475
Day, J.D., 506
DCE, 515
condition-variable calls, 526
kill-thread calls, 516, 517
mutexes, 516
scheduling calls, 516, 517
synchronization calls, 515
thread-management calls, 515
Deadlock avoidance, 227-234, 241-242
banker's algorithm, 230-234
resource-allocation graph algorithm, 229-230
safe state, 228-229
Deadlock-detection, 235-237, 242
in centralized system, 235-236
in distributed system, 588-595
Deadlock prevention, 224-227, 241
circular wait, 226-227
in distributed system, 587-588
wait-die scheme, 587
wound-wait scheme, 588
hold and wait, 225
mutual exclusion, 224
no presumption, 225-226
Deadlocks, 179-180, 217-242, 591
characterization, 219-222
detection of, 234-238, 242
infinite blocking, 180
methods for handling, 223-224
necessary conditions for, 219-220
recovery, 238-240
resource-allocation graph, 220-223
starvation, 180
deBruijn, N.G., 214
Debuggers, 67
DEC-20, 698
DEC PDP-11, 273
Deitel, H.M., 408
Dekker's algorithm, 210, 214
Dekker, T., 214

Demand paging, 303-309, 342, 348
  hardware, 307
  performance, 309-312
  swap space, 311-312
  UNIX, 634
  valid-invalid bit, 304-305
  see also Page faults; Page replacement; Paging
Demand segmentation, 303, 341-342, 348
Denning, D.E., 474, 475
Denning, P.J., 27, 161, 348
Dennis, J.B., 299, 457
Deterministic modeling, 153-154
Device controllers, 29, 32-33
Device drivers, 6, 36, 384-385
Device management, 72
Device queues, 101
Device-status table, 34
DFS, 521-522, 525-568
  caching, 531-536, 568
  clients, 526, 567
  example systems, 539-567
    Andrew, 550-555
    Locus, 560-567
    NFS, 542-550
    Sprite, 555-560
    UNIX United, 539-542
  file replication, 538-539
  naming scheme, 529-530, 568
  naming structures, 527-531
  performance, 526-527
  remote file access, 531-536
  stateful service, 536-538
  stateless service, 536-538
  transparent, 527-531, 567
Diffie, W., 474
Dijkstra, E.W., 92, 214, 245, 246, 693
Dining-philosophers problem, 183-186, 214
  deadlock remedies, 185
  monitor solution, 194
  structure, 185
Direct access method, 359-360

Direct communication message system, 118-119
Directories, 362, 379-380
  current, 367
  device, 362
  master file (MFD), 364
  operations performed on, 363
  path names, 365, 368
  protection, 377
  root, 366
  search path, 366
  UNIX, 616, 638-639
  User File Directory (UFD), 364
  see also Directory structure; Files; Subdirectories
Directory implementation, 399-400, 406
  hash table, 400, 406
  linear, 399-400
  see also Directories
Directory structure, 349, 361-373
  acyclic-graph, 369-371, 379-380
  general graph, 372-373, 380
  single-level, 364
  tree-structured, 366-369, 379
  two-level, 364-366, 379
  see also Directories
Disk cache, 402, 408
  see also Cache; Caching
Disk controller, 41, 402
Disk I/O, 411
Disk queue, 411
Disks
  addresses, 387
  backup, 404-405
  blocks, 410, 425
  booting from, 418
  consistency checking, 404
  cylinders, 409-410
  formatting, 417
  free-space management, 397-399
  latency time, 410
  magnetic, 39-41, 44
  management of, 417-419
  moving-head, mechanism, 39

multipart address, 409
optical, 41-42, 44, 427
RAM, 403
reliability of, 422-424
restoring, 404-405
sectors, 410
seek, 410
speed of, 410-411
structure of, 409-410
tracks, 409-410
transfer time, 411
virtual, 403
see also Floppy disks; Hard disks; Magnetic disks; Secondary storage
Disk scheduling, 410-416, 425, 427
C-LOOK, 416
C-SCAN, 414-415
FCFS, 411-412
LOOK, 415
performance, 415
SCAN, 413-414
SSTF, 412-413
Disk space
allocation, 387-397
efficiency, 401-402
free, management of, 397-399
performance, 402-403
Disk striping, 422
Dispatcher, 135
Dispatch latency, 135
Distributed Computing Environment. see DCE
Distributed coordination, 571-601
atomicity, 577-581
concurrency control, 581-586
deadlock handling, 586-595
election algorithms, 595-597
event ordering, 571-574
mutual exclusion, 574-577
reaching agreement, 598-600
Distributed file system. see DFS
Distributed operating system, 480, 509-511, 523
Distributed system(s), 22-23, 26, 479, 504

advantages, 482
communication, 23, 482
computation speedup, 23, 481
deadlock handling, 586-595
defined, 479
design issues, 519-521
distributed operating system, 509-511
failure detection, 517-518
failure recovery, 518-519
fault tolerance, 519
network operating system, 507-509
reliability, 23, 481-482
robustness, 517-519
scalability, 519-520
structures, 507-522
transaction manager, 581
transparency, 519
see also Distributed coordination
DMA (direct memory access), 36
controller, 36
illustrated, 36
structure, 35-37
Doeppner, T.W., 129
Domain bit, 435
Domain name service (DNS), 492-493
Donnelley, J.E., 28, 523
Douglis, F., 523
Draves, R.P., 688
Dual-mode operation, 46-47
Dynamic linking, 252-253
Dynamic loading, 252
Dynamic storage-allocation problem, 264, 388

Eager, D., 523
Edges
assignment, 221
claim, 229-230
request, 220-221
Eisenberg and McGuire's algorithm, 211, 214
Ekanadham, K., 457
El Abbadi, A., 603

Election algorithms, 595-597
  bully, 595-597
  ring, 597
Elevator algorithm. *see* SCAN disk
  scheduling
Encryption, 471-472, 473
English, R.M., 428
Enhanced-second-chance algorithm,
  323-324
Error correcting code (ECC), 417
Error detection, 46, 64
Eskicioglu, M., 523
Eswaran, K.P., 215
Ethernet devices, 502
Ethernet packet, 503
Ethernet protocol, 497
Event ordering, 571-574
  global ordering, 573
  happened-before relation, 572-573
  implementation, 573-574
  total ordering, 574
Exception handling, Mach, 671-673
External Data Representative (XDR),
  544
External fragmentation, 264-265
  first-fit/best-fit, 388
  linked allocation, 391
  segmentation, 289-290
  solutions to, 265-266, 267-268
  see also Fragmentation
Eykholt, J.R., 129, 162, 215

Fabry, R.S., 161, 348, 457
Fail-soft, 20
Farrow, R., 474
Fault tolerance, 519-520
FCFS CPU scheduling, 137-138,
  153-154, 158
FCFS disk scheduling, 411
FCFS ordering, 195-196
Feitelson, D., 162
Feng, T., 506
Ferguson, D., 523
Fids, 552
FIFO algorithm, 317-318, 348

illustrated, 317
page-fault curve for, 318
performance, 317-318
problems, 318
File access methods, 358-361
  direct access, 359-360
  file index, 360-361
  ISAM, 361
  sequential access, 359
  see also Files; Remote file access
File-allocation table (FAT), 391-392
  allocation scheme, 392
  illustrated, 392
File attributes, 350-351
  location, 350
  name, 350
  protection, 351
  size, 350
  time, date, user identification, 351
  type, 350
  see also Files
File descriptor, 385
  UNIX, 617
File handle, 545
File migration, 528
File modification, 74
File mounting, 543
  illustrated, 543
  in NFS, 544
  static, 545
  UNIX, 640-641
  see also Files
File operations, 526
File-organization module, 385
File protection, 18, 349
Files, 61, 349, 379-380
  access, 374-377, 380
  appending, 352
  archive, 355
  backing, 556
  batch, 355
  closing, 72
  copying, 352
  creating, 72, 351, 363
  deleting, 72, 352, 363

encrypted, 357
executable, 350, 355
extension, 355-356
index, 360-361
library, 355
Locus, 563-566
memory-mapped, 349,353
opening, 72, 352
organization, 379
protection, 373-377
    access lists/groups, 374-376
    controlled access, 374
    types of, 373-374
reading, 351
renaming, 352, 363
replication of, 527, 538-539, 568
repositioning within, 352
searching for, 363
shared, 369
    immutable, 379
    implementation, 369-370
source, 350, 355
text, 350, 355
truncating, 352
types of, 354-356
UNIX, 616
user classifications of, 375
Vice, 552
writing, 351
see also Directories; File attributes;
    File mounting; File structures;
    File system
File session, 378
File structures, 350, 356-358
File system, 349-380
    Andrew, 378-379
    basic, 385
    BSD UNIX, 386
    concept, 349-358
    consistency semantics, 378-379
    design problems, 384
    directory implementation, 399-401
    disk-based, 379
    implementation, 383-406
    interfaces, 382

I/O control, 384-385
    layered, 384
    layers, 380
    levels, 384
    logical, 385
    manipulation, 64
    mounting, 386-387
    NFS, 382
    organization, 363, 384-386
    protection, 373-377
    recovery, 403-405
    structure, 383-387
    tape-based, 379
    traversing, 363
    UNIX, 636-645
        allocation policies, 642-645
        implementations, 642
        layout, 642-645
    VMS, 357
    see also Files; File structures
File Transfer Program (FTP), 508-
    509
Filipski, A., 474
First-come, first-served scheduling.
    see FCFS CPU scheduling; FCFS
    disk scheduling; FCFS ordering
Floppy disks, 41, 389, 427
Folk, M.J., 408
Format command, 418
Formatting, disk, 417
    logical, 417
    physical, 417
    see also Disks
Forsdick, H.C., 523
Fortier, , P.J., 505
FORTRAN
    compiler, 6-7
    operating systems in, 88
    system calls, 65
Fragmentation, 264-267
    external, 264-265
        first-fit/best-fit, 388
        linked allocation, 391
        segmentation, 289-290
        solutions to, 265-266, 267-268

internal, 265, 358, 389
in memory management strategy, 295-296
Frame-allocation, 315, 327-328
Frames, 268
  allocation, 271-272, 326-329, 342, 343
  free, 271-272
  minimum number of, 326-327
  splitting, 327-328
  used in I/O, 339
Frame table, 271
Frank, G.R., 92
Frank, H., 506
Franklin, M.A., 348
Free-behind, 403
Freedman, D.H., 55, 427
Freeman, H.A., 506
Free-space list, 397
Free-space management, 397, 406
  bit vectors, 397-398
  counting, 398-399
  grouping, 398
  linked list, 398
FTP, 508-509
Fujitani, L., 55, 427
Fully connected networks, 483
Fully distributed algorithm, 575-577
  for deadlock-detection, 592-595
  for mutual exclusion, 575-577

Gait, J., 55, 427
Gangemi, G.T., 474
Gantt chart, 137-144
Garbage collection, 373
Garcia-Molina, H., 603
Garfinkel, S., 474
Gateways, LAN, 488-489
Geist, R., 428
General graph directory, 372-373, 380
Gerla, M., 506
Gifford, D.K., 475
Global descriptor table (GDT), 293
Global page replacement, 329

Golden, D., 381
Goldman, P., 348
Goodman, N., 215
Graceful degradation, 20
Grampp, F.T., 474, 657
Graphical user interface (GUI), 698
Gray, J.N., 215, 603
Grosshans, D., 381
Gupta, R.K., 162, 348

Habermann, A.N., 246
Hagmann, R., 348
Haldar, S., 161
Hall, D.E., 92
Halsall, F., 505
Halt instruction, 51
Handshaking procedure, 517
Hanko, J., 474
Hard disks, 40
Hardware, protection, 45-50
Harker, J.M., 55, 427
Harrison, M.A., 457
Hartmann, T.C., 93
Hash table, 400, 406
  collisions, 400
  lookups, 400
Havender, J.W., 246
Head-disk assemblies, 40
Hecht, M.S., 474
Hellman, M.E., 474
Hendricks, E.C., 93
Hennessy, J.L., 55, 299, 348
Henry, G., 162
Hierarchical networks, 484-485
Hit ratio, 274-275
Hoagland, A.S., 55, 408
Hoare, C.A.R., 193, 195, 214
Hofri, M., 428
Hold and wait, 219
  deadlock prevention, 225
Holes, memory, 263-264
  best-fit, 264, 388
  first-fit, 264, 388
  worst-fit, 264
  see also Memory

Holley, L.H., 92
Holt, R.C., 245, 246, 658, 713
Hong, X. Tan, 162
Hoskins, H.C., 505
Host name, 73
Hosts, 479-480
  naming structure, 492
Howard, J.H., 246, 569
Howarth, D.J., 299, 691
Hsiao, D.K., 474
Hydra, 448-450, 457
  auxiliary rights, 448
  operations, 448
  mutually suspicious subsystems,
    449
  procedure call mechanism, 449
  rights amplification, 448
  subsystem, 449-450
  trustworthy procedures, 448
Hyman, H., 246

Iacobucci, E., 93, 162, 348, 408
Iliffe, J.K., 457
Index block, 393
  combined scheme, 394
  direct, 394
  double indirect, 394
  indirect, 394
  linked scheme, 394
  multilevel index, 394
  single indirect, 394
  triple indirect, 394
  see also Blocks
Indexed allocation, 392-395, 405
  contiguous allocation, 396
  illustrated, 393
  performance, 396
  wasted space, 393
Indirect communication, 120-121
Infinite blocking, 142
Inodes, UNIX, 395, 637
  mapping file descriptor to, 639-640
  number, 642
  structure, 640
  see also UNIX

Input/output (I/O) devices, 3
  list of, 100
  operation of, 11
  see also I/O system
Input queue, 250, 263
Instruction registers, 37
Instructions, 249
  binding, 250-251
  executing, 308
  execution cycle of, 249
  restarting, after page faults, 308
Intel 80386, 293
  address translation, 295
  logical address, 294
  paging hardware, 348
  physical address, 293
  two-level paging, 294
Interactive jobs, 16
Interactive systems, 15-17
Internal fragmentation, 265
International Standards Organization.
    see ISO
Internet network, 465, 505
  FTP, 508-509
  naming on, 492-493
  telnet facility, 507, 509
  worm, 465-468
Interprocess communication, 116-126
  see also IPC facility
Interrupts, 30-32
  disabled, 32
  enabled, 32
  functions of, 31
  I/O, 33-35
  lost, 32
  masked, 32
  service routines, 31, 35
  triggering, 30
  UNIX, 135
Interrupt vector, 31
Inverted page table, 279-281
  defined, 280
  example, 280-281
  shared memory, 283
  systems using, 280

I/O bandwidth, 423
I/O burst cycle, 132-133
I/O control, 384
I/O devices, 32-37
I/O instructions, 38
I/O interlock, 338-340
I/O methods, 36
I/O operations, 63
  asynchronous, 33, 35, 36
  synchronous, 33
  system calls for, 52
I/O redirection, 626
I/O system, 60
  interrupts, 33-35
  management, 60
  protection, 47
  structure, 32-37
  UNIX, 625-626, 645-648
IPC facility, 117, 129
Indexed Sequential Access Method
  (ISAM), 361
Isloor, S.S., 246
ISO, 498
  network message, 501
  network model, 498
  protocol stack, 499

Jefferson, D., 457
Jensen, E.D., 162
Job control, 67-71
Job Control Language (JCL), 9
Job queues, 101
Jobs, 97, 622
  background, 622
  batched, 7
  foreground, 622
  interactive, 15
  pools of, 13
  see also Process(es)
Job scheduling, 13-14
Jodeit, J.G., 457
Jones, A.K., 55, 92, 162, 457
Joseph, T., 506, 523
Joy, W., 657
Jul, E., 523

Kajla, A., 408
Kanodia, R.K., 603
Karels, K.J., 657
Kay, J., 162
Kenah, L.J., 382
Kenly, G., 55, 427
Kenville, R.F., 55, 427
Kernel, 5
  Nachos, 701
  RC 4000, 694
  security, 474
  threads, 116
Kernighan, B.W., 657
Kessels, J.L.W., 214
Key-distribution problem, 471
Keys, 445, 447
Khanna, S., 162, 215
Kieburtz, R.B., 457
Kilburn, T., 27, 299, 348, 691
Kitts, D.L., 55, 427
Kleiman, S.R., 408
Kleinrock, L., 161, 162, 506
Knapp, E., 603
Knuth, D.E., 214, 299
Kochan, S., 474, 657
Kock, P.D.L., 408
Kogan, M.S., 129
Konigsford, W.L., 28
Korn, D., 657
Kornatzky, Y., 523
Korth, H.F., 381
Kosaraju, S., 214
Kramer, S.M., 474

Lamport, L., 214, 474, 602, 603
Lampson, B., 161, 457, 603
Landwehr, C.E., 474
Langerman, A.B., 689
Language-based protection, 451-455
  advantages, 452
  software capability, 453-454
  techniques for, 452
  see also Protection
Larson, P., 408
Lauder, P., 162

Layer structures, 79-81
  advantages of, 79
  debugging, 79
  disadvantages of, 80-81
  illustrated, 79
  implementation of, 80
  overhead of, 81
  MS-DOS, 77
  OS/2, 82
  THE, 80
  UNIX, 78
  Venus, 81
Layland, J.W., 162
Lazowska, E.D., 161
Lazy swapper, 304
Leach, P.J., 569
Least recently used algorithm. *see*
    LRU algorithm
Leffler, S.J., 408, 657
Lehmann, F., 474
Le Lann, G., 602, 603
Lempel, A., 475
Lett, A.L., 28
Letwin, 28
Leutenegger, S., 162
Levin, R., 457
Levy, H.M., 348
Libraries
  shared, 253
  system, 252
Lichtenberger, W.W., 28, 692
Lightweight process (LWP). *see* Threads
Lindsay, B., 603
Line printers, 11
Linked allocation, 390-392, 405
  direct access, 395-396
  directory entries, 390
  disadvantages, 391
  external fragmentation, 391
  FAT, 391-392
  illustrated, 390
  reliability, 391
Linking
  dynamic, 252-253
  static, 252

Links, 370
  hard, 371
  resolving, 370
  symbolic, 370
  UNIX, 616
  see also Acyclic-graph directories
Lions, J., 714
Lipman, P.H., 348
Lipner, S., 457
Lipton, R., 214
Liskov, B.H., 92, 457
LISP, 338
List operation, 374
Little's formula, 155
Litzkow, M.J., 523
Liu, C.L., 162
Livny, M., 523
Load balancing, 523
Loader, 9
Loading, dynamic, 252
Load sharing, 23, 523
Load time, 250
  address-binding schemes, 255
Lobel, J., 474
Local-area network (LAN), 18, 488-
    489, 504
  communication speed, 488
  configurations, 488
  gateways, 488-489
  illustrated, 489
  links, 488
Local descriptor table (LDT), 293
Locality, 331
  in memory reference pattern, 332
  model, 331
  of reference, 307
  stack, 338
Local page replacement, 329-330
Location independence, 527
Location-independent file identifiers,
    530
Location transparency, 527-528
Lock bit, 338-340
Locking protocols, 205-206, 209,
    582-584

biased protocol, 584
lock modes, 205
lock/unlock requests, 206
majority protocol, 583-584
multiple-coordinator approach, 583
nonreplicated scheme, 582
primary copy, 584
single-coordinator approach, 582-583
timestamp-based, 206-208
two-phase locking, 206, 215
Lock-key scheme, 445
comparison of, 445
revocation, 447-448
Locks, 198-199, 445
defined, 445
Solaris 2, 209, 215
see also Locking protocols
Locus system, 523, 560-567, 569
abort system call, 564
commit count, 566
commit system call, 564
file-access semantics, 561
file operations, 563-565
file replication, 561
mount/unmount system calls, 562
name structure, 561-562
operation in faulty environment, 566-567
overview, 560-561
packs, 561-562, 566-567
primary copy policy, 564
server processes, 561
synchronized file access, 565-566
Loepere, K., 689
Log-based recovery, 201-202
Loge project, 428
Logical address, 255-256
Intel 80386, 294
in MULTICS, 292
space, 255, 256, 283
see also Address
Logical file system, 385
Logical records, 358, 359
Log record, 202

Long-term scheduler, 103
LOOK disk scheduling, 415
Lookup operation, Sprite, 557
Loosely coupled systems. see Distributed systems
Loucks, L.R., 93
LRU algorithm, 319-322, 325
illustrated, 320
implementation, 320-321
page-fault rate for, 320
LRU approximation algorithms, 322-324
additional-reference-bits, 322-323
enhanced second-chance, 323-324
second-chance, 323
Lynch, W.C., 27

McCann, C., 162
McGraw, J.R., 457
Mach operating system, 125-126, 659-687
components, 662-666
CPU scheduler, 670-671
C threads package, 667-670
design goals, 687
design principles, 661-662
emulation library, 685-686
exception handling, 671-673
history, 659-661
IPC, 673-679
Mach 3 structure, 660
memory management, 464, 679-685
memory object, 664, 679
messages, 664, 675-676
NetMsgServer, 677-679
NORMA IPC subsystem, 678-679, 686
pageout policy, 682
ports, 663-664, 674
process management, 666-673
programmer interface, 685-686
Release 2, 660
Release 3, 660
RPC messages, 671

shared memory, 684-685
synchronization, 679
task, 663
threads, 663, 666
user-level memory managers, 681-684
virtual copy, 665
virtual memory, 676
Macintosh Operating System, 18, 356, 382, 698
bit vector, 397
disk space management, 408
file protection, 376
files, 356
file structure in, 357
file system mounting in, 387
page locking, 340
McKeag, R.M., 693, 698
McKeon, B., 408
MacKinnon, R.A., 92, 93
McKusick, M.K., 657
McNamee, D., 689
McVoy, L.W., 408
Maekawa, M., 602
Magnetic disks, 39-41, 53
drum, 41
fixed-head, 40
floppy, 41
head crashes in, 41
moving-head, 40
platter, 39, 40
removable, 40
sectors, 39
storage, 44
tracks, 39
see also Disks; Hard disks
Magnetic tape, 11, 42, 53, 409
Mailboxes, 120, 125
full, 126
owners and users of, 121
Main memory, 37, 38-39, 53
cache, 43-44
limitations, 37
management, 59
memory-mapped I/O, 38

Majority protocol, 583-584
Maples, C., 55
Marsh, B.D., 129
Marshall, L.F., 657
Massalin, H., 129
Master Control Program (MCP), 88
Master file directory (MFD), 364
Mattson, R.L., 348
MCP operating system, 698
Mealy, G.H., 697
Medium-term scheduling, 104-105
Memory, 3
logical, 268
logical vs. physical address space, 255-256
main, 37, 38-39, 43-44, 53
manager, 257
mapping, 353
over-allocating, 312
physical, 268
protection, 48-49, 275-277
read-only (ROM), 24
release, 258
request, 258
shared, 64, 283
inverted page tables, 283
Mach, 684-685
UNIX, 649
user's view of, 283
see also Allocation, memory; Memory management; RAM disk; Virtual memory
Memory controller, 29
Memory management, 249-296
algorithms, 294
contiguous allocation, 259
fragmentation, 295-296
hardware support, 294
Mach, 464, 679-685
OS/360, 697
paging, 267-283
partitions, 260-261
fixed-sized, 261
illustrated, 260
performance, 294-295

protection, 296
relocation, 296
segmentation, 283-290
sharing, 296
strategies, 294-296
swapping, 256-259, 296
UNIX, 632-636
see also Memory
Memory-management unit (MMU), 255
Memory managers, 681-684
default, 682
external, 682-683
responsibilities, 682
user-level, 681-684
see also Memory management
Memory-mapped I/O, 38
Menasce, D., 603
Mergen, M.F., 299
Message passing, 64
Message queues, 121-122
Messages, 125
lost, 124
Mach, 664, 675-676
scrambled, 124
see also Message systems
Message slots, 497
Message switching, 495
Message systems, 117, 127
bounded capacity, 122
direct communication, 118-119
exception conditions, 123-124
lost messages, 124
process terminates, 123-124
scrambled messages, 124
implementation questions, 117
indirect communication, 120-121
link implementation, 118
types of, 118
unbounded capacity, 122
zero capacity, 121
see also Messages
Meyer, R.A., 92
MFT, 261
MFU algorithm, 325

Microkernel-based operating systems, 78
Microsoft Windows operating system. see Windows operating system
Migration
computation, 510-511
data, 509-510
file, 528
process, 511
Minidisks, 84, 376
Minix operating system, 613
Mode bit, 46
Modems, 491
Modularity, 79
Mohan, C., 603
Monitor calls. see System calls
Monitor mode, 46-47
Monitors, 190-197, 209, 214
automatic signaling, 214
condition variables, 192
resource-allocation, 197
semaphores implementation, 194-195
solution to dining-philosopher problem, 194
syntax, 190
Morris, J.H., 457, 569
Morris, R.H., 474, 657
Morris, Robert Tappan Jr., 465
Morshedian, D., 474
Motorola 68030, 348
Mounting. see File mounting
Mount protocol, 545
Mount table, 640
MS-DOS, 18, 382, 698
command-interpreter in, 62
disk layout, 418
execution, 70
file protection, 376
file structure, 357
layer structure, 77
relocation registers, 255
version 3.1, 93
Mullender, S.J., 569
Multiaccess bus networks, 486-487

MULTICS operating system, 19,
348, 696
address translation, 292
CPU scheduling, 696
logical address in, 292
multilevel directory structure, 381
paged segmentation in, 290-292
protection domains, 436-438
ring protection structure, 436-438
virtual address, 696
Multilevel feedback queue scheduling,
147-149, 158
Multilevel queue-scheduling, 145-
147, 158
Multiple-processor scheduling, 149-
150
asymmetric multiprocessing, 150
heterogeneous system, 149
homogeneous system, 149
load sharing, 149
Multiprocessing, 20
asymmetric, 21-22
symmetric, 21-22
Multiprogramming, 13, 25
Multitasking, 15, 18
Muntz, R.R., 603
Mutex, in DCE, 516
Mutex variable, 186, 194, 203
Mutka, M.W., 523
Mutual exclusion, 166
Peterson's algorithm, 170
bakery algorithm, 172
deadlocks, 219, 224
in distributed environment, 574-
577, 600
with semaphores, 177
with Swap instruction, 174
with Test-and-Set instruction, 173
token-passing approach, 577
MVS operating system, 162
MVT, 261

Nachos operating system, 699-714
components, 705-711
defined, 699

design of, 700-701
file systems, 707-708
kernel, 701, 704
multiprogramming, 708-709
networking, 710-711
obtaining copy of, 711-713
overview, 700-702
questions about, 713
sample assignments, 705-711
simulated hardware, 702-703
software structure, 702-705
thread management, 706-707
virtual memory, 709-710
Naming, 527-531
defined, 527
implementation of, 530-531
schemes, 529-530
structures, 527-529
Needham, R.M., 457
Nelson, B., 129, 427
Nelson, M., 408, 569
NetMsgServer, 677-679
IPC forwarding by, 678
kernel, 677
operation example, 678
Network File System (NFS), 382,
510, 542-550, 569
architecture, 547-548
layers of, 547
schematic view of, 547
automount feature, 530
cascading mounts, 544, 548
consistency semantics, 550
lookups, 548
mount protocol, 545
naming scheme approach, 529-530
overview, 543-545
path-name translation, 548-549
protocol, 545-546
remote operations, 549-550
RPC, 549
servers, 546
Network operating system, 480,
507-509
remote file transfer, 508-509

remote login, 507-508
see also Distributed system(s)
Network layers, 498-499
  application, 499
  data-link, 499
  network, 499
  physical, 498
  presentation, 499
  session, 499
  transport, 499
Network structures, 479-504
  background, 479-480
  communication, 491-497
  design strategies, 498-501
  example, 501-504
  local-area (LAN), 488-489, 504
  network types, 488-491
  reasons for building, 481-482
  topology, 482-487
  system naming in, 491-493
  types of, 488-491
  wide-area (WAN), 489-491, 504
Network topology
  fully connected, 483
  hierarchical, 484-485
  multiaccess bus, 486-487
  partially connected, 483-484
  ring, 486
  star, 485-486
  tree-structured, 485
Newcastle Connection, 541-542
Newton, G., 246
Nichols, D.A., 523
Nodes, 22
No-op instruction, 110
Norton, P., 28, 382

Obermarck, R., 603
Objects, 432-433, 455
Off-line processing, 11-12, 25, 27
Oldehoeft, R.R., 299
O'Leary, B.T., 55, 427
Olsen, R.P., 55, 427
ONC+, 529, 542
On-line file system, 16, 17

Opderbeck, H., 348
Open-file table, 352, 385
  illustrated, 386
  multiple levels, 386
  open count, 353
  system wide, 386
Open file operation, 352, 378
Operating systems
  batch, 7-15
  as control program, 5
  database-system techniques in, 199
  defined, 3
  goals of, 5
  history of, 6-7
  interrupt-driven, 32
  microkernel, 78, 87
  multiprogrammed, 131
  for PCs, 18-20
  real-time, 23-25, 26
  as resource allocator, 4-5
  structures of, 57-91, 523
  time-sharing, 15-17
  see also System components;
    System design; System genera-
    tion; System programs
Operating-system services, 63-65
  accounting, 64-65
  communications, 64
  error detection, 64
  file system manipulation, 64
  I/O operations, 63
  program execution, 63
  protection, 65
  resource allocation, 64
  see also Operating systems
Operating systems, list of
  Accent, 129, 688
  AIX, 78
  Atlas, 691-692
  CMS, 84
  CP/67, 92
  CP/M, 698
  Mach, 125-126, 659-687
  Macintosh, 18, 340, 356-357, 376,
    382, 387, 397, 408, 698

MCP, 698
Minix, 613
MS-DOS, 18
MULTICS, 19, 290-292, 348, 381, 436-438, 696
MVS, 162
OS/2, 18, 28, 81, 82, 88, 293-294
OS/360, 17, 27, 696-698
Plan 9, 382
Primos, 88
RC 4000, 694-695
RSK, 698
SCOPE, 698
Sprite, 523, 533, 555-560, 569
THE, 80, 693-694
Thoth, 122
TOPS-20, 356
Tunis, 613, 658
UNIX, 19, 77-78, 88, 134-135, 356, 376-377, 465-468, 607-655
Venus, 80, 81, 554, 555, 694
VM, 83
VMS, 107, 357, 375-376, 698
VMS/CMS, 387
Windows, 19, 259, 698
Windows/NT, 88, 259, 515
XDS-940, 692-693
Xinu, 613, 658
Optical disks, 41-42, 44, 427
Orange Book, 474
Organick, E.I., 299, 348, 381, 457, 696
Orphan detection and elimination, 537
OS/2 operating system, 18, 88, 293-294
    32-bit architecture, 293-294
    layer structure, 81, 82
    scheduling policies, 162
OS/360 operating system, 17, 27, 696-698
OS/MVT, 697
Ousterhout, J.K., 428, 523, 569, 714
Overlays, 253-255
    defined, 253

for two-pass assembler, 253-254
usage, 255

Packet switching, 496
Packing, 358
Page buffering algorithm, 325
Page-fault frequency algorithm (PFF), 334-335
Page-fault rate, 315
    demand paging, 311
    for LRU algorithm, 320
    monitoring scheme, 348
    optimal algorithm, 318-319
    thrashing, 334
Page faults, 280-281, 305
    performance cost of, 337
    process for handling, 306
    restarting instructions after, 308
    sequence resulting from, 310
    service time components, 310
    steps in handling, 307
    see also Demand paging; Page-fault rate; Paging
Pager, 304
Page replacement, 312-315, 343
    functioning of, 313
    illustrated, 314
    modify (dirty) bit, 314
    need for, 313
    page-fault service routine for, 313-314
    see also Demand paging
Page-replacement algorithms, 315-325, 343
    counting, 324-325
    FIFO, 317-318, 348
    global replacement, 329
    local replacement, 329
    LRU, 319
    LRU approximation, 322-324
    optimal, 318-319, 348
    page buffering, 325
Pages, 268
    invalid, 305
    locked, 338, 339

memory resident, 305
reference bit for, 322
shared, 281-283
size of, 269, 335-337
see also Page faults; Page table; Paging; Segments
Page table, 272
associative registers, 273-275
hardware implementation, 273-275
inverted, 279-281
in MULTICS, 291-292
outer, 278-279
with pages not in memory, 305
partitioning, 277
protection, 275-277
structure, 272-277
UNIX, 628
valid/invalid bit in, 275-276
see also Page Faults; Pages
Page-table base register (PTBR), 273
Page-table length register (PTLR), 277
Paging, 267-283
defined, 268
demand, 303-309, 337-338, 342, 348
dynamic relocation, 270
four-level, 279
hardware, 268
method of, 268-272
multilevel, 277-279
prepaging, 334-335
segmentation with, 290-294
shared pages, 281-283
three-level, 279
two-level, 277-279
UNIX, 633-636
XDS-940, 693
see also Page Faults; Pages; Page table; Segmentation
Panzieri, F., 129
Parallel systems, 20-22, 26
Parnas, D.L., 214, 246
Partially connected networks, 483-484

Partitions, 349, 362
Passwords, 376, 461
account sharing, 462
changing, 463
cracking, 474
disadvantages of, 376
encrypted, 463
guessing, 461-462
keeping secret, 463
paired, 463
system-generated, 462
UNIX, 463
usage, 461
user-selected, 462
see also Encryption
Path names, 365
absolute, 368, 616
relative, 368, 616
translation, 548-549
see also Directories
Patil, S., 214
Patterson, D.A., 55, 299, 427
PC, 17-20, 25
CPUs for, 18
defined, 17
file protection, 18-19
operating systems for, 18-20
PDP-10, 698
PDP-11, 698
shared memory, 649
size constraints, 614
UNIX development, 608
Peacock, J.K., 129
Pease, M., 603
Pechura, M., 55, 381, 427
Personal-computer systems. *see* PCs
Personal workstation, 20
Peterson, G.L., 214
Physical address, 255-256
space, 255, 256
see also Address
Physical blocks, 358
Pickup operation, 193
Pike, R., 657
Pinkerton, C.B., 474

Pinkerton, T.B., 427
Pirtle, M.W., 28, 692
Pl/360 language, 65
Plan 9 operating system, 382
Polling, 32
Popek, G., 457, 523, 569
Port, 120, 125, 512
  addresses, 513
  defined, 512
  Mach, 663, 674
  sets, 664, 674
Powell, M.L., 215
Preemption points, 151
Prepaging, 334-335
Prieve, B.G., 348
Primary copy, 584
Primary storage, 59-60
Primos operating system, 88
Priority inheritance protocol, 151-152
Priority inversion, 151
Priority scheduling, 141-143
  aging, 143
  infinite blocking, 142
  preemptive/nonpreemptive, 142
Process control block (PCB), 99-100,
    127
  illustrated, 100
  UNIX, 627-630
Process(es), 16, 58
  address space, 107
  children of, 106
  communication, 116-126
  concept, 97-100
  control, 67-71
  cooperation, 108-111, 127
  CPU-bound, 104
  creation, 106-107
  deadlocked, 179-180, 218-219
  defined, 98-99, 126, 619
  faulty, 599-600
  foreground, 145
  heavyweight, 111
  identifier, 107, 619
  I/O-bound, 104
  lightweight. see Threads

  management, 58-59
    Mach, 666-673
    UNIX, 627-632
  migration, 511
  operation, 105-108
  parent, 106
  real-time, 340-341
  resource use, 58, 218, 433
  rollback, 240
  scheduling, 100-105
  starvation, 225, 240
  states, 99, 126-127
  swapped, 256-257
  termination, 107-108
  thrashing, 330-331
  tree, 106
  UNIX, 619
  see also Jobs; Process control
    block; Process synchronization
Processor sharing, 144
Process synchronization, 163-209
  critical regions, 186-190
  critical-section problem, 165-172
  monitors, 190-197
  problems, 181-186
    bounded-buffer, 181
    dining-philosophers, 183-186
    readers and writers, 181-183
    cigarette-smokers, 212, 214
    sleeping-barber, 212, 214
  semaphores, 175-181
  in Solaris 2, 198-199
  see also Process(es)
Proctor, S., 713
Program counter, 58, 98, 99
Programmer interface, 78
  Mach, 685-686
  UNIX 4.3BSD, 615-623
  see also User interface
Programs
  application, 75
  execution, 63
  loading and execution programs,
    75
  time-profiles of, 70

Program threats, 464-465
Project Athena, 523
Protection, 431-455
  access matrix, 438-442
  Andrew file system, 551
  capability-based, 444
  defined, 431
  directory, 377
  file, 349, 373-377
    access lists/groups, 374-376
    controlled access, 374
  goals, 431-432
  language-based, 451-455
  reasons for, 432
  role of, 432
  see also Security
Protection domain(s), 432-438
  access matrix, 439-440
  capability lists for, 443-444
  changing, 435
  defined, 433
  examples, 435-438
    MULTICS, 436-438
    UNIX, 435-436
  methods of realization, 434
  processes, 433-434
  structure, 433-434
  see also Protection
Protection system, 61-62
Public key-encryption scheme, 472
Pu, C., 93, 129
Purdin, T.D.M., 569

Quarterman, J.S., 505, 657
Queueing diagram, 102
Queueing-network analysis, 155
Queues
  background, 146
  common-ready, 149-150
  device, 101-102
  disk, 411
  feedback, 161
  FIFO, 317
  foreground, 146
  input, 250, 263

I/O request, 127
  job, 101
  message, 121-122
  priority, 161
  ready, 101-102, 258
  scheduling between, 146
  time slice between, 147
  see also Multilevel feedback queue
    scheduling; Multilevel queue-
    scheduling algorithm
Queueing models, 155-156

Race condition, 165
RAM disk, 403
Randell, B., 474, 569
Random-access devices, 12
Rashid, R., 129, 688
Raw device interfaces, 647-648
Rawson, F.L., 129
Raynal, M., 214, 603
RC 4000 operating system, 694-695
  CPU scheduler, 694
  I/O devices, 695
  kernel, 694
  message queues, 694
  primitives, 695
Reaching agreement, 598-600
  faulty processes, 599-600
  unreliable communications, 598-
    599
Readers and writers problem, 181-
  183, 214
Read-only memory (ROM), 24, 417-
  418
Ready queues, 101, 258
Real-time systems, 23-26, 150-152,
  162
  hard, 24, 150
  soft, 24, 150-151
  time constraints, 24
Receive IPC operation, 117
  in direct communication, 118-119
  implementing, 118
  in indirect communication, 120
Redell, D.D., 457

Redo operations, 201-202, 203, 209
Redundant Arrays of Inexpensive Disk
    (RAID), 423, 427
  block interleaved parity, 423
  fault tolerance, 519
  mirroring, 423
  use of, 423-424
Reed, D.P., 215, 603
Reference bit, 322
Reference string, 315
Registers
  associative, 273-275
  base, 48
  index, 43
  limit, 48
  in page-table implementation, 273
  programmable, 43-44
  relocation, 255
Reid, B., 474
Relative access method. *see* Direct
    access method
Relocation registers, 255-256
  hardware support for, 261
  illustrated, 256
  MS-DOS, 255
  see also Registers
Remote file access, 531-536
  cache location, 532-533
  cache update policy, 533-534
  caching scheme, 532
  consistency, 534-535
  remote service/caching comparison,
    535-536
  see also File access methods
Remote file transfer, 508-509
Remote job entry (RJE), 21
Remote login, 75, 507-508
Remote procedure call (RPC), 123,
    129, 510, 512-514, 522, 531
  daemons, 513
  execution, 514
  semantics, 513
  server/client communication, 513
  usage, 513
  see also DCE

Remote service, 512, 531
Rendezvous synchronization, 121
Request edge, 220
Resident monitor, 7-10
  defined, 8
  functioning of, 9
  memory layout for, 8
  parts of, 9-10
Resource
  allocation, 64
  preemption, 239-240
  release, 218
  request, 218
  reservation, 150
  sharable, 224
  use policies, 432
  utilization, 218, 225
Resource-allocation graph, 220-223
  algorithm, 229-230
  with cycle but no deadlock, 223
  with deadlock, 222
  for deadlock avoidance, 230
  defined, 220
  illustrated, 220
  unsafe state in, 231
  see also Wait-for graph
Resource-allocation state, 227
  deadlock, 228
  safe, 228-229
  unsafe, 228
Response time, 16, 136
  predictable, 136
  variance in, 136
Revocation, 446-448, 457
  in access-list scheme, 446
  capabilities, 446-447
  lock-key scheme, 447-448
Ricart, G., 602
Richie, D.M., 657
Rights. *see* Access rights
Ring networks, 486
Ritchie, D.M., 382, 607-608
Rivest, R.L., 475
Robertson, G., 129, 688
Rollback, 240

Rosenblum, M., 428
Rosenkrantz, O.J., 603
Rosen, S., 27
Roucairol, G., 603
Round-Robin (RR) scheduling, 143-
    145, 158
  average waiting time, 143
  deterministic modeling of, 154
  performance, 144
  preemptive, 144
  processor sharing, 144
  schedule, 144
  time quantum, 143
  turnaround time, 145
Routers, 490, 495
Routing, 493-495
  dynamic, 494
  fixed, 494
  protocol, 495
  strategies, 493-495
  table, 494
  virtual, 494
RSX operating system, 698
Rudolph, L., 162
Ruschitzka, M., 161
Rushby, J.M., 474
Russell, D., 474

Safety algorithm, 232
Saltzer, J.H., 457
Samson, S., 162
Sandberg, R., 382, 569
Sanguinetti, J., 55
Sarisky, L., 55, 427
Satyanarayanan, M., 55, 506, 569
Sauer, C.H., 93, 161
Scalability, 519-520
SCAN disk scheduling, 413-414
Schedulers, 103-105
  CPU, 103
  job, 103
  long-term, 103, 104
  medium-term, 104
  short-term, 103
  see also Scheduling

Schedules, concurrency control, 204
  conflict serializable, 205
  serial, 204
Scheduling, 127
  CPU. see CPU scheduling
  disk, 410-416
  job, 13-14
  threads, 521
Schell, R.R., 474
Schlichting, R.D., 129
Schneider, F.B., 129, 603
Schoeffler, J.D., 55, 427
Schrage, L.F., 161
Schroeder, M.D., 382, 457
Schultz, B., 93
Schwartz, J.I, 28
Schwarz, P., 55, 162, 603
SCOPE operating system, 698
SCSI disk/controller, 419, 427
SDC Q-32 system, 28
Seal operation, 454, 457
Seawright, L.H., 92
Secondary storage, 60
  efficiency, 401-402
  file system, 383, 405
  management, 59-60
  performance, 402-403
  structure, 409-426
  see also Disks; Storage
Second-chance algorithm, 323-324
Sectors, 410, 419
  forwarding, 419
  slipping, 419
  see also Disks
Security, 65, 459-473
  Andrew file system, 551
  authentication, 461-463
  defined, 431
  encryption, 471-472
  kernel, 474
  levels, 460-461
  password, 462
  problem, 459-461
  program threats, 464-465
  system threats, 465-469

threat monitoring, 469-470
UNIX, 474
violations, 460
see also Protection; Protection system; Threats
Seely, D., 474
Segmentation, 283-290
advantages, 287
defined, 283-284
demand, 303, 341-342, 348
example, 286
external fragmentation, 289-290
hardware, 285-286
method of, 283-284
paged, 290-294
in 386, 293-294
in MULTICS, 290-292
protection, 287-289
sharing, 287-289
see also Paging
Segment descriptors, 341
Segments, 283-284
base, 285
code, 289
data, 421
elements within, 283
name and length of, 284
paging, 290
read-only data, 289
sharing, 288
text, 421
see also Pages; Segmentation; Segment tables
Segment-table base register (STBR), 287
Segment-table length register (STLR), 287
Segment tables, 285
entries in, 285
implementation of, 286-287
paging, 292
placement of, 286-287
use of, 285
see also Segmentation; Segments
Semaphores, 175-181, 208

atomic execution of, 178
binary, 180-181
counting, 180
deadlocks and starvation, 179-180
defined, 175
implementation, 176-179
monitor implementation using, 194-195
mutual exclusion implementation with, 177
spinlock, 177
usage, 176
Send() operation, 117
in direct communication, 118-119
implementing, 118
in indirect communication, 120
Sequential-access devices, 12
Sequential access method, 359
on direct-access file, 361
optimizing, 403
Serializability, 203-205, 209, 215
defined, 203
insuring, 205, 208, 209
Servers, 513
defined, 526
NFS, 546
process structure of, 521
single-process, 521
stateless file, 536-538
see also Client
Set-uid bit, 435
Shah, D., 129
Shared memory, 127
Mach, 684-685
UNIX, 649
see also Memory
Shared-memory model, 73
Shell, 63, 71
Shore, J.E., 299
Shortest-job-first scheduling. see SJF algorithm
Shortest-seek-time-first. see SSTF disk scheduling
Short-term scheduler. see Schedulers
Shrivastava, S.K., 129

Siegel, P., 92
Signal synchronization operation, 175, 203
  definition, 176
  example using, 178
  execution, 178
  monitors, 193
  on counting semaphores, 181
  usage, 176
Signals, UNIX, 621-622
  ignoring, 621
  interrupt, 621
  kill, 621
  lost, 621-622
  quit, 621
  SIGWINCH, 622
Silberschatz, A., 381, 457
Silverman, J.M., 474
Simmons, G.J., 475
Simulations, 156, 158-159
  CPU scheduler evaluation by, 157
  distribution-driven, 156
  generating data for, 156
Singhal, M., 603
Single-coordinator approach, 582-583
Single-level directory, 364
Sites, 22
SJF algorithm, 138-141, 158
  deterministic modeling of, 154
  difficulty in, 139
  exponential average, 140
  optimal, 139
  preemptive/nonpreemptive, 140-141
Sleeping-barber problem, 212, 214
Smith, A.J., 55, 299, 408, 523
Smith, B., 688
Sockets, 649-652
  addresses of, 649
  client-server model, 651
  communication domain, 649
  datagram, 650
  descriptor, 650-651
  protocols, 653
  raw, 650

  reliably delivered message, 650
  sequenced packet, 650
  single, 649
  stream, 650
  system call, 650, 651
  types of, 650
Software
  capability, 450, 453-454
  engineering, 87
Solaris 1, 422
Solaris 2, 114-116
  adaptive mutexes, 198
  kernel structures, 402
  locks, 209, 215
  real-time computing, 341
  swap space, 421
  synchronization in, 198-199
  thread structure, 129
Spafford, E.H., 474
Spafford, G., 474
SPARC architecture, 279
Spawner process, 542
Spector, A.Z., 603
Spinlocks, 177, 198-199
Spooling, 12-13, 25
  defined, 12
  first use of, 27
  illustrated, 13
  performance, 13
  uses, 12
Sprite network operating system, 523, 555-560, 569
  backing files, 556
  broadcast, 558
  caching, 533
  delayed-write, 559
  interface, 555-556
  lookup operation, 557
  overview, 555-556
  prefix tables, 556-559
  read-only replication, 559
  version-number scheme, 559-560
  virtual-memory system, 556
SSTF disk scheduling, 412-413
Stable storage, 200, 426

Stack algorithms, 321-322
Stallings, W., 506
Stankovic, J.S., 28, 129
Star networks, 485-486
Starvation, 225, 240, 412
Stateful file service, 536
Stateless file service, 536-538
Staunstrup, J.A., 129
Stein, D., 129
Stepanov, A.A., 428
Stephenson, C.J., 299
Stevens, D.L., 657
Stevens, W.R., 505, 657
Storage
  hierarchy, 42-45
  nonvolatile, 53, 200, 349
  secondary, 37-38, 53, 383
  speed and cost of, 42
  stable, 200, 426
  structure, 37-42
  volatile, 42, 53, 200
  see also Magnetic disks; Main
    memory
Strachey, C., 27
Stub, 252
Sturgis, H., 603
Subdirectories, 367
  shared, 369
  see also Directories; Directory
    structure
Subramanian, S., 161
Sun Microsystems, 382
  NFS, 382, 510, 542-550, 569
SunOS, 408
Svobodova, L., 161, 569
Swap instruction, 173-174
  definition, 173
  mutual-exclusion implementation
    with, 174
Swap maps, 421
  data segment, 421
  text segment, 422
Swappable space, 241
Swapper, 304
  lazy, 304

UNIX, 633
  see also Pager
Swapping, 104, 256-259
  compaction combined with, 267
  constraints, 258-259
  illustrated, 257
  in memory management, 296
  roll out/roll in, 257
  UNIX, 259, 421, 632-633
  Windows, 259
Swap space, 311-312, 425
  in 4.3BSD, 421
  demand-paging, 311-312
  in disk partition, 420-421
  estimating, 420
  in file system, 420
  location, 420-421
  management, 419-422
  Solaris 2, 421
  UNIX, 420
  use, 420
  see also Swapping
Switching
  circuit, 495
  message, 495
  packet, 496
Symmetric multiprocessing, 21-22
Synchronization. see Process synchronization
Synchronous I/O, 33
Syscall instruction, 51
SYSGEN program, 89
System calls, 65-73, 90-91
  abort, 561
  accept connection, 73
  categories of, 67
  in changing current directory, 367
  close, 73
  close connection, 73
  commit, 561
  communications, 73
  in debugging, 69-70
  defined, 33
  device manipulation, 72
  exec, 71
  executing, 51

exit, 71
file manipulation, 71-72
fork, 71
function of, 65
get hostid, 73
get processid, 73
information maintenance, 72-73
invoking, 51
map memory, 73
occurrences of, 66-67
open, 73, 352, 353
open connection, 73
for performing I/O, 52
preemptible, 151
process control, 67-71
types of, 68
UNIX, 616
wait for connection, 73
System components, 57-63
command-interpreter system, 62-63
file management, 60-61
I/O system management, 60
main-memory management, 59
networking, 62
process management, 58-59
protection system, 61-62
secondary-storage management, 59-60
see also Operating systems
System design, 86-87, 91
mechanisms and policies, 87
system goals, 86
user goals, 86
see also Operating systems
System-development time, 85
System disk, 418
System generation, 89-90
approaches, 90
defined, 89
see also SYSGEN program
System implementation, 87-89, 91
System programs, 74-76
applications programs, 75
categories of, 74-76
communications, 75

file manipulation, 74
file modification, 74
program loading and execution, 75
programming language support, 74-75
status information, 74
System scan, 470
System structure, 76-82, 91
layered, 78-82
simple, 76-78
see also Operating systems
System threats, 465-469
viruses, 468-469
worms, 465-468

Tabak, 28
Tanenbaum, A.S., 28, 55, 299, 505, 523, 569, 658, 689, 713
Tasks, 97, 127
Tay, B.H., 129
TCP/IP, 500
hosts, 501
protocol layer summary, 502
Telenet system, 489
Tenex system, 698
Teorey, T.J., 427
Test-and-Set instruction, 172-175
definition, 173
mutual-exclusion implementation with, 173-175
Tevanian, A., 129, 688
Text pages, 421
Text section, 98
THE operating system, 80, 693-694
cooperating processes, 693
deadlock control, 694
layer structure, 80
memory management, 694
Thompson, K., 382, 474, 607-608, 657, 713
Thompson, M.R., 688
Thoth operating system, 122
Thrashing, 329-334, 348
cause of, 330-332
defined, 330

illustrated, 332
page-fault frequency, 334
page-fault rate, 334
preventing, 331
working-set model, 332-334
Threads, 111-116, 127, 514-517
in distributed systems, 514-517
encountering locks, 198
functionality of, 111-112
implicit receive, 515
kernel, 116
Mach, 663, 664
Nachos, 706-707
performance issues, 129
pop-up, 515
processes, 112
scheduling, 521
sleeping, 198
Solaris 2, 114-116
structure, 111-114
switching among, 113-114
user-level, 111, 114-116
Threats
monitoring, 469-470
program, 464-465
system, 465-469
see also Protection; Security
Throughput, 20, 136
Thurber, K.J., 506
Tightly coupled systems, 20
Timeouts, 124
Time-out scheme, 517, 598
Time quantum, 143
Timers, 49-50
Time-Sharing Option (TSO), 17
Time-sharing systems, 15-17, 25
development of, 16
first use of, 27-28
history of, 17
I/O interrupts in, 35
on-line file systems, 17
see also Multitasking
Time-slice, 50
Timestamp-based protocols, 206-208,
209, 215

Timestamping, 585-586
Timestamps, 585, 601
generation of, 585-586
global, 601
ordering scheme, 586
Timing errors, 209
TLB, 273
flushed, 274
Motorola 68030 processor, 275
paging hardware with, 274
see also Associative registers
Token passing, 497, 577
TOPS-20 operating system, 356, 698
Trace tapes, 156
Tracks, 409-410
Traiger, I.L., 603
Transaction coordinator, 578
Transaction manager, 581
Transactions, 199, 209
lock/unlock requests, 206
rolled back, 200
terminated, 200
see also Atomic transactions
Translation look-aside buffer.
see TLB
Transmission Control Protocol/Internet
Protocol. see TCP/IP
Transparency, 527
location, 527
naming, 527-531
Trap door, 464-465
Trap instruction, 51
Traps, 32
see also Interrupts
Tree of processes, 106
Tree-structured directories, 366-369,
379
directory deletion, 368
illustrated, 367
other user files, 368
paths, 369
Trojan horse, 464
TSS/360, 698
Tucker, A., 162
Tuffs, D.E., 92

Tunis operating system, 613, 658
Turnaround time, 10, 136, 146
Two-level directory, 364-366, 379
Two-phase commit protocol. *see* 2PC

UDP/IP, 500-501, 543
Undo operation, 201-202, 203, 209
UNIX operating system, 19, 356
  4.3BSD, 613
    cylinder group, 643
    kernel I/O structure, 645
    layer structure, 615
    network implementation, 652
  4.4BSD, 610
  Berkeley software, 609-610
  block buffer cache, 646-647
  block devices, 645, 646
  blocks, 636-637
    direct, 637
    indirect, 637
  Bourne shell, 624
  character devices, 645, 646
  C-lists, 648
  command-interpreter in, 62, 71,
    75-76
  controlled access in, 376
  CPU scheduling, 630-632
  C shell, 625
  cylinder group, 643-644
    header information, 644
    superblock, 643
  DARPA Internet protocols, 652
  data blocks, 636
  DCE, 515
  design principles, 613-616
  device driver, 646
  device number, 646
  directories, 616, 638-639
  directory name cache, 639
  directory protection in, 377
  directory structure, 618
  disk-allocation routines, 644
  disk structures, 640-641
    boot block, 641
    superblock, 641

  Fast File System, 644
  Fat Fast File System, 644
  file descriptor, 617
  file manipulation, 616-619
  files, 356, 616
  file structure, 357-358
  file system, 636-645
    allocation policies, 642-645
    control blocks, 639
    implementations, 642
    layout, 642-645
    mounting, 386, 640
  finger program, 466-467
  fragments, 636-637
  group identifier, 621
  hard links, 616
  history of, 607-613
  information manipulation, 623
  inodes, 395, 637
  Internet worm, 465-468
  interrupts, 135
  I/O redirection, 626
  I/O system, 645-648
  IPC, 649-654
  kernel, 77
  library routines, 623
  magic number, 356
  make program, 614
  memory management, 632-636
  mount table, 640
  multiple processes, 613
  network programming, 505
  network reference models and layering,
    654
  network support, 652-654
  page-replacement algorithm, 634
  page tables, 628
  paging, 633-636
  panic, 614
  password encryption, 620
  passwords, 463
  path names, 616
    absolute, 616
    relative, 616
  pipe, 620, 649

pipelines, filters, shell scripts, 626-627
preemptive scheduling, 134-135
process
    communication, 620
    control, 619-621
    control blocks, 627-630
    creation, 619
    defunt, 620
    finding parts of, 629
    getty, 620
    groups, 622
    init, 620
    kernel stack for, 629
    login, 620
    management, 627-632
    pagedaemon, 634-635
    scheduler, 633, 634-635
    scheduling priority, 630
    sleep, 631
    structure, 627-628
    termination, 108, 619
    wakeup, 631
    zombie, 620
programmer interface, 615-623
protection domains, 435-436
raw device interfaces, 647-648
raw mode, 648
scheduling policies, 162
security, 474
sendmail program, 466-467
shared memory, 649
sharing files/subdirectories, 369-370
shell programming, 627
shells and commands, 624-625
shell script, 627
signals, 621-622
socket interface, 645
sockets, 649-652
soft links, 616
Software Organization (USO), 611
Source Code Control System (SCCS), 614
standard I/O, 625-626

standardization, 611
standard user interface, 613
structure, 77-78
Support Group (USG), 608
swapper, 633
swapping in, 259, 421, 632-633
swap space, 420, 632
symbolic links, 616
System III, 608
System V, 608-609
system calls, 616
    directory, 619
    execve, 619, 630
    file information, 619
    fork, 619-620, 629
    socket, 650, 651
    vfork, 629-630
system mode, 629
system programs, 77, 623-624
text structure, 628
timeout mechanism, 631
tree of processes on, 106
user identifiers, 621
user interface, 615, 623-627
user mode, 628
user structure, 628
uses, 614
UUCP network facilities, 652
VAX 4.3BSD, 613
Version 7, 608
version history illustrated, 612
virtual address space, 628
UNIX Programmer's Manual (UPM), 615, 657
UNIX United, 539-542, 569
    architecture, 541
    component systems, 539
    component units, 539-540
    directory structure, 539-540
    file systems, 542
    illustrated, 540
    Newcastle layer, 541
    overview, 539-541
    root directories, 540
Unseal operation, 454, 457

USENET News, 689
User Datagram Protocol/Internet Protocol, 500-501
User file directory (UFD), 364
User interface, 78
    UNIX 4.3BSD, 615, 623-627
        pipelines, filters, shell scripts, 626-627
        shells and commands, 624-625
        standard I/O, 625-626
    see also Programmer interface
User mode, 46-47
User programs, 97

Van Horn, E.C., 457
Van Renesse, R., 28, 523
VAX
    architecture, 278
    multilevel paging, 277, 278
    UNIX, 609
VAX/VMS system, 325
Venus operating system, 80, 694
    caching, 554, 555
    layer structure, 81
    path-name translation, 554
Vernon, M., 162
Virtual disk, 403
Virtual File System (VFS), 547-548
Virtual machines, 82-86
    advantages, 85
    model, 83
    system-development time, 85
    virtual I/O, 85
    virtual monitor mode, 84
    virtual user mode, 84
Virtual memory, 17, 24, 301-343
    defined, 301, 302
    demand paging, 303-312
    demand segmentation, 303
    frame allocation, 326-329
    implementation of, 303
    Nachos, 709-710
    page replacement, 312-325
    physical memory, 303
    thrashing, 329-334

Viruses, 18-19, 468-469
    defined, 468
    examples, 468-469
    functioning of, 468
    protection against, 469
    see also Worms
V kernel, 523
VM operating system, 83
VMS/CMS operating system, 387
VMS operating system, 107, 698
    access control lists, 375-376
    file system, 357
Volume-location database, 552
Volumes, 552
    see also Partitions
Volume table, 362
Vuillemin, A., 161
Vyssotsky, V.A., 28

Wah, B.W., 569
Wait-for graph, 234
    construction options, 590
    in distributed system, 588-589
    global, 590
    illustrated, 235
    local and global, 591
    maintaining, 235
    see also Resource-allocation graph
Waiting time, 136
Wait synchronization operation, 33, 175, 203
    definition, 176
    example using, 178
    execution, 178
    on counting semaphores, 180
    usage, 176
Wakeup synchronization operation, 177
Walker, B., 523, 569
Walker, R.D.H., 457
Walmer, L.R., 688
Weizer, N., 27
Wide-area network (WAN), 489-491, 504
    communication processors in, 490

Internet, 490
links, 489-490
routers, 490
see also Local-area network
Wilhelm, N.C., 428
Wilson, R., 693, 698
Wilton, R., 382, 408
Windows/NT operating system, 88
 DCE, 515
 swapping, 259
Windows operating system, 19, 698
 swapping, 259
Wood, P., 474, 657
Woodside, C., 162
Working set model, 332-334
Workstations, 523, 700
Worms, 465-468
 composition of, 466
 defined, 465
 Internet, 465-468
 see also Viruses
Write-ahead logging, 201, 209, 215,
 424, 425
Wulf, W.A., 348, 457

XDS-940 operating system, 692-693
 paging, 693
 system calls, 693
Xinu operating system, 613, 658

Zahorjan, J., 162
Zayas, E.R., 523
Zhao, W., 162
Zimmerman, H., 506
Zobel, D., 246
Zoellick, B., 408
Zwaenepoel, W.Z., 523